"A little gem."
—*Newsday*

"A personalized approach with attention to detail that has had a major impact on the entire guidebook industry."
—National Trust for Historic Preservation

". . . captures the flavor of the B&B and its proprietors."
—Associated Press

"[Chesler is] the bed and breakfast guru."
—*Travel Agent* magazine

"The quintessential B&B book. They don't make a better one."
—WELI, New Haven, Conn.

"For all the answers—the book to get."
—WBZ-TV, Boston

"The bible to the industry."
—*The Cape Codder*

"Absolutely wonderful . . . and enormous fun to dip into."
—Estelle Bond Guralnick, regional editor, *Country Home,*
Traditional Home, Better Homes & Gardens

"Guests who come from your book read. . . . They're literate . . . and interesting!"
—Marianne Vandenburgh, House on the Hill, Waterbury, Conn.

"Bought several B&B guides . . . [this is] by far the most useful and informative."
—Liz Daish, Cayman Islands

". . . excellent guide . . . very helpful and reliable . . . gave factual information and a fair picture of the spirit of each place."
—J. B. Cook, East Sussex, England

"All accommodations of an excellent standard . . . superb breakfasts . . . a taste of true New England hospitality . . . book enabled us to have a memorable and perfect honeymoon."
—Kirsten and Richard Evans, West Yorkshire, England

"According to guests from Germany, this is the very best B&B book. They should know—having traveled to the U.S. eight times in the last ten years."
—Carolyn and Arnold Westwood, Windfields Farm, Cummington, Mass.

"Through some alchemy of enthusiasm, love of travel, and good writing, Bernice Chesler combines scads of detail and practical information into engaging summaries of special places. . . . I sometimes skim her guide when I have no intention of going anywhere—just to inspire myself!"
—Lynda Morgenroth, contributor, *Boston Globe*

The only B&B book recommended by the *Michelin Guide to New England.*

Number 4 on the *Boston Globe* best-seller list.

🐦 Also by BERNICE CHESLER

AUTHOR:

In and Out of Boston with (or without) Children
Mainstreaming through the Media
Bed &Breakfast in the Northeast
Bed & Breakfast Coast to Coast
Bed & Breakfast in the Mid-Atlantic States

COAUTHOR:

The Family Guide to Cape Cod

EDITOR AND COORDINATOR:

The ZOOM Catalog
Do a ZOOMdo
People You'd Like to Know

Selections from *Bernice Chesler's Bed & Breakfast in New England* are accessible in searchable electronic format on the Internet at www.obs-us.com/chesler/ or www.bernicechesler.com

For information write to obs@obs-us.com or call (978) 546-7346.

BERNICE CHESLER'S

Bed & Breakfast in New England

Connecticut, Maine, Massachusetts,
New Hampshire, Rhode Island, Vermont

SEVENTH EDITION

CHRONICLE BOOKS

SAN FRANCISCO

🖋 *To David*

Printed in the United States of America.

ISBN: 0-8118-2389-X

Library of Congress Cataloging-in-Publication Data available.

Book design and composition: Jaime Robles
Cover design: David Valentine
Cover illustration: William Low

Distributed in Canada by Raincoast Books
8680 Cambie Street, Vancouver, B.C. V6P 6M9
10   9   8   7   6   5   4   3   2   1

Chronicle Books
85 Second Street
San Francisco, CA 94105
www.chroniclebooks.com

Contents

INTRODUCTION

WELCOME! That's what bed and breakfast and this book are all about—still, more than twenty years since a Vermont host, a farmer, offered me cow salve to soothe leg muscles that ached from pedaling over the hilly terrain.

Who would have guessed then that bed and breakfast was to become *the* trend in American travel? Or even a household phrase? Or a concept that has been adopted by and adapted to facilities with more than a hundred rooms?!

The acceptance of B&Bs on this side of the ocean came just as my husband and I were discovering the joys of bicycling from B&B to B&B, from one interesting experience to another, in what is now a total of fourteen states and seven countries. Fourteen B&B books and thousands of interviews later, this latest edition reflects the wide spectrum of possibilities—everything from a home away from home to a picture-perfect restoration—with hosts who range from twentysomething to "almost eighty now." Although some B&Bs have expanded (and been grandfathered into this book), generally the places selected fit into my original interpretation of bed and breakfast: a maximum of about ten guest rooms; common room provided; breakfast included in the rate, but no public restaurant or bar on the premises; owner/innkeeper as host. Among the "exclusives"— very small B&Bs you will find in no other book—are some pioneers who were in my very first B&B book, *Bed and Breakfast in the Northeast,* published in the early 1980s, when there weren't enough B&Bs in New England to fill a book!

Each description aims to save travelers' time by anticipating questions: Located on a main road? Off the beaten path? What time is breakfast? Sample menu? Size of bed? What floors are rooms on? Bath with shower and tub? Is smoking allowed? Any pets in residence? How do the $80, $95, and $150 rooms differ? . . . And the hallmark: What about the innkeepers? (B&B travelers are a curious lot.) For many owners—people who have restored everything from churches to schoolhouses, from beach cottages to mansions— B&B has become a second or third career. The hosts do such a good job that one out of five guests leaves with the dream of opening a B&B.

International travelers, too, appreciate American B&Bs for the personalized style, for hosts who help to give a sense of place. Now many B&B hosts have plotted back-road routes for guests. Now bed and breakfasts are everywhere: in cities and suburbs and in rural areas too.

So what's changed? Lots! Right under my computer keys. New owners—who tend to 'upscale' the property—are often in residence. New places continue to open. Most have private baths. In many locations, whirlpool tubs are definitely in demand. So are fireplaces, TV, an in-room phone, access to a fax and a modem too. We have B&Bs that provide tables for two or breakfast baskets outside your door. (But there are still many "never-ending" breakfasts around a big dining room table.) Beyond the luxuries expected by many guests, new layers of regulations have added to costs and rates. Some innkeepers find themselves adding a few rooms to keep their B&B economically viable. Some move across the street or next door. While choosing America's most envied profession, they have learned to hire an inn-sitter now and then.

To distinguish private homes from inns, this book has a symbol (☛) for private homes that have one, two, or three guest rooms. B&B inns are likely to be larger, with, perhaps, one or more hired staffers. Other symbols will lead you (quickly) to a romantic place; to one on the waterfront or off the beaten path; to a spot that is great for kids; or to a B&B where your group, family, or colleagues might book the entire place. See the key to symbols that appears on the back cover and at intervals throughout the book.

By popular demand, there is one new symbol in this edition. ❤ is for weddings. For a given B&B, this could stand for small affairs by the fire. Or tented events on the grounds. Could be for a maximum of one wedding scheduled per month. Or just during certain months. Innkeepers, especially those romantics who can't get through a ceremony without shedding tears, have learned that weddings require much time and effort, hand-holding, referring, organizing, and preparation. And a wedding can be hard on the property. Hence, there are charges—and a contract—to cover all the variables.

What about you, the traveler? The art of correspondence is alive! Excerpts from some of the thousands of enthusiastic letters, cards and e-mails written to me are included in this book. Many people write about being "converted" by their first B&B experience. Others, B&B fans who describe "the best B&B in all my travels," refer to hosts (always) and places that are quite varied. This is one of the reasons I hesitate to recommend "the best" B&B in an area. There really is a letter of the day, usually one that reinforces the concept of a people-to-people program—and makes you feel good all over.

Every detail was confirmed just before press time. But please keep in mind that successful hosts sometimes make *changes in rooms, beds, menu, or decor—and, yes, in rates too.*

My thanks go to unflappable Robert Carson, who annually handles tens of thousands of pieces of paper. He deciphers floor plans, decodes hieroglyphics, and, with great patience, leads the manuscript and its author through the electronic world. It is a joy to work with Jay Howland, my copy editor, who remembers everything and everyone. Additional support and encouragement have come from Christine Carswell and Steve Mockus of Chronicle Books. And from the staff at Open Book Systems (OBS) (obs-us.com), whose 1994 interactive site made this book the very first travel guide on the Internet. Among the millions of site visits have come an offer from Germany to buy an inn and, from Hong Kong, a booking for a tea at a Victorian B&B!

And once again David, my husband, has planned all our trips by plane, car, and bicycle. He listens, offers judgment when I solicit objectivity, and acts as my computer expert in residence.

Suggestions and comments about people and places are most welcome. Please address them to bbchesler@juno.com or write to me at Chronicle Books, 85 Second Street, San Francisco, CA 94105.

Bernice Chesler

Answers to Frequently Asked Questions

WHAT IS BED AND BREAKFAST?

Basic question, but—ta-dah!—no longer asked so frequently, now that B&Bs are everywhere, in a gazillion variations. The essential concept, much embellished by many newer B&Bs in the United States, is a package arrangement that includes overnight accommodations and breakfast. B&Bs described in this book are generally small, owner-occupied places. Even with all the amenities that many offer, the keynote is hospitality.

ARE BATHS SHARED?

Today, a few are—usually with just one other room. But depending on the number of guests, a shared bath could be private for you. American B&Bs have followed the trend to all private baths (of various sizes), sometimes with a shower but no tub, sometimes with a two-person whirlpool tub too.

HOW MUCH DO B&BS COST?

Rates for two people include breakfast—sometimes a brunch—and range from about $60 to well over $150 (with much in between). The season, location, amenities, food, length of ownership, maintenance costs, taxes—all affect the rate. Remember: Nothing is standardized at B&Bs. In this book, check under "Rates" to see what *credit cards* are accepted at a particular B&B. Small places may prefer cash or travelers' checks. *And it's a good idea to check on deposit requirements; refund policies differ.* Required local and/or state taxes vary from place to place and are seldom in the listed rates.

TO TIP OR NOT?

In a private home, tipping is not a usual practice, but it does happen occasionally. And in a private home where B&B is rather constant, owners realize that paid help helps. Those B&B owners also know that some remembrance is appreciated by the part-time folks who contribute to your memorable stay. In a B&B inn, treat staff as you would in a hotel. *Some inns, particularly those in resort areas, add gratuities to the tab.* Some others who don't like that practice may leave an envelope-for-tip in your room. Another approach: When paying, guests might ask the innkeeper for a "suggested amount."

An interesting phenomenon: An amazing number of travelers write heartfelt thank-you notes to surprised and delighted hosts.

HOW DOES B&B DIFFER FROM A HOTEL?

At all the places described in this book, you will be greeted by the owner or a family member or assistant, or occasionally by a note. *Every room is different in size, layout, and decor.* A B&B may not provide the privacy—or the loneliness—of a hotel; yet some luxurious suites or separate buildings are very private indeed. Because business travelers have discovered B&Bs, there may be a phone and TV in the room. And a modem too.

Reminder: There is no desk clerk. Please call the B&B during reasonable hours—preferably between 10 A.M. and 9 P.M. And if you must have things exactly as they are in the hotel you usually go to, go to the hotel!

IS B&B FOR EVERYONE?

Many B&Bs are perfect for unwinding and a change of pace, for romantics, for pampering, or for a home-away-from-home environment. If you seek anonymity, look for a B&B that has a private cottage, perhaps one where breakfast is brought to you in a basket.

Tastes and interpretations differ. Take charm, for example. "Tell me," said the older guest, "what's so charming about a tub on legs? I was so glad when built-ins finally became the fashion." Recommendation: Tell the host if this is your first time at a B&B. When making the reservation, if privacy is a real concern, say that too. Hosts' listening skills are usually well tuned.

HOW DO B&BS ON THIS SIDE OF THE ATLANTIC DIFFER FROM THOSE IN THE BRITISH ISLES OR OTHER COUNTRIES?

The style of B&B-and-away-you-go is not necessarily the norm in North America. Although there are B&Bs with just one room and many where you are expected to leave for the day, guests are often invited to spend more time after breakfast "at home"—by the pool or fireplace, on the hiking trails, or on borrowed bicycles. Even hosts are amazed at what they do when they get involved in others' lives! They worry about late arrivals. They have been known to drive someone to a job appointment or to do laundry for a business traveler whose schedule changed or to prevail upon the local auto mechanic when the garage was closed.

CAN I BOOK THROUGH TRAVEL AGENTS?

Many travel agents have caught on to the popularity of B&Bs. In this book B&Bs with the ❖ in the "Rates" section pay commissions to travel agents. And some agents will make arrangements for you, whether or not they receive a commission from the B&B.

DO B&BS WELCOME CHILDREN?

In this book B&Bs with the symbol 🕴 are always happy to host children. Some B&Bs without the symbol also welcome children, though not necessarily by the houseful! Although there are B&Bs that provide everything from the sandbox to the high chair—and a babysitter too—some B&B hosts have been known to say (tactfully), "Children find us tiresome." Check the "Plus" section in the descriptions in this book. Consider the facilities, the room and bath arrangements, and the decor. Are your kids enticed by candlelit breakfasts? Are they used to being around "don't touch" antiques? Are rooms limited to two persons? Is a crib provided? Are there lots of animals on the farm? Is there a built-in playmate, perhaps an innkeeper's child? Remember what you looked for B.C. (before children). If you do bring the kids and still wish for some private time at the B&B, please arrange for a sitter. Be fair to yourself and your children, to other guests, and to the host/chef/gardener/interior designer/historian—who really does love children.

WHAT ABOUT FACILITIES FOR PHYSICALLY HANDICAPPED PERSONS?

Rooms that are handicapped accessible are noted in the detailed "Bed and Bath" section of each B&B description in this book. In addition, each write-up mentions the floor locations of guest rooms.

ARE THERE B&BS THAT PROHIBIT SMOKING?

Many do. (Note the ⚱ symbol in this book.) In addition, some hosts note that they are concerned even about smokers who are willing to refrain indoors; their clothing can leave a room with an unwanted trace. Among the B&Bs that do allow smoking, many limit it to certain areas or rooms.

WHAT DO YOU RECOMMEND TO THOSE WHO DREAM ABOUT OPENING A B&B?

For starters, attend one of the workshops or seminars given by adult education centers, extension services, colleges, trade associations, realtors, libraries, innkeepers, or B&B reservation services. Apprentice, even for a weekend; or give yourself a practical test by signing up with a reservation service and hosting in your own home.

Every host in this book enjoys what they call "the great emotional rewards of a stimulating occupation." Some remind couples who wish to make B&B a vocation that it helps to have a strong marriage. One who encourages prospective innkeepers to "Just do it!" adds, "but be aware that you have to be more gregarious than private. You have to learn to carve time out for yourself. Hosting requires a broad range of talents (knowledge of plumbing helps), a lot of flexibility, an incredible amount of stamina, and perseverance. And did I mention you might need some capital?"

CAN A HOST OR RESERVATION SERVICE PAY TO BE IN THIS BOOK?

No. All selections are made by the author. There are no application fees. And all descriptions are written by the author; no host or service proprietor can write his or her own description. A processing fee is paid after each selected B&B and reservation service reviews its write-up. The fee offsets the extensive research that results in highly detailed write-ups reflecting the individual spirit of each B&B. The author pays for all her personal stays.

WHAT ARE SOME OF YOUR FAVORITE B&BS?

Even when you stay in hundreds, you tend to remember the hosts of each B&B more than the place. We have arrived on bicycles and been greeted with the offer of a car to go to dinner. There's the horticulturist, a septuagenarian, whom we could hardly keep up with as she toured us through her spectacular gardens. There's the couple who built their own solar house. Multifaceted retirees—some who have restored several houses. The history buffs who filled us in on the area and recommended back roads. The literary buffs who suggested good books. Hosts in a lovely residential section just minutes off the high-way. Hosts we have laughed with. Yes, even some we have cried with too. Great chefs. People who are involved in their communities and trying to make this a better world. People whose home has been a labor of love and who love sharing it with others. We have enjoyed rather luxurious settings and some casual places too. It is true that each B&B is special in its own way. That's why the place to stay has become the reason to go. It's wonderful.

HOLIDAYS INCLUDED IN "OPEN" (SEASON) AND "RATES":

January 1   *New Year's Day*
February 14   *Valentine's Day*
February (third Monday)   *Presidents' Day*
May (last Monday)   *Memorial Day*
July 4   *Independence Day*
September (first Monday)   *Labor Day*
October (second Monday)   *Columbus Day*
November (fourth Thursday)   *Thanksgiving*
December 25   *Christmas Day*

B & B Reservation Services

A reservation service is in the business of matching screened hosts and guests. Although it can be a seasonal operation, in some areas the service is a full-time job for an individual, a couple, partners, or a small group. For hosts, it's a private way of going public, because the host remains anonymous until the service (agency) matches host and guest. This unique system allows hosts in private homes to have an off-and-on hosting schedule.

Listings may be in major cities or in communities where there are no overnight lodging facilities, or they may provide an alternative to hotels or motels. Although most services feature private homes, others include B&B inns with six to fourteen guest rooms and unhosted accommodations too. The possibilities are detailed with each reservation service description in this book.

Each service determines its own area and conducts its own inspections and interviews. A service may cover just one community, or a metropolitan area, or an entire region.

Advance notice is preferred and even, with many services, required. Length-of-stay requirements vary. Some services stipulate a one-night surcharge; some require a minimum of two nights.

Rates are usually much lower than at area hotels. The range may cover everything from "budget" to "luxury." Deposits are usually required. Refund policies, detailed with each reservation service description in this book, differ.

Fee arrangements vary. Many services include their commission in the quoted nightly rate. For a public inn the service's quoted rate may be the same as what the inn charges, or it could be a total of the inn's rate plus a booking fee (about $5–$18).

Before contacting the service for possibilities, think about details such as bed and bath arrangements, parking, smoking, pets, children, air conditioning, phones or TV in the room—whatever is important to you.

A reservation service acts as a clearinghouse. In high season especially it can save everyone time and money. Frequently a reservation service provides an opportunity to stay at a B&B that would not be available any other way.

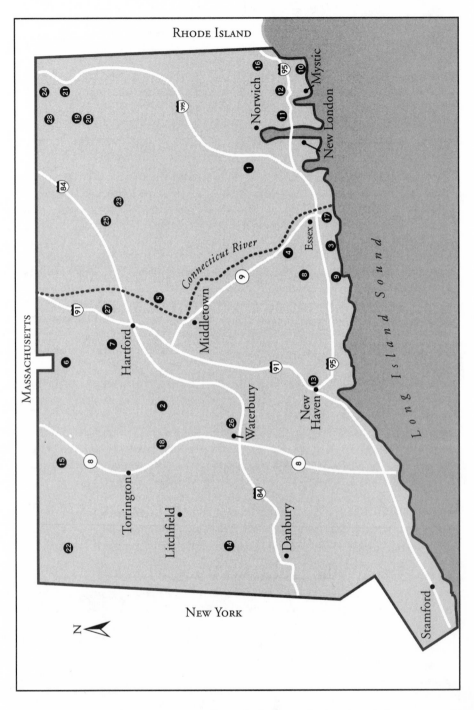

RHODE ISLAND

24 21

28 19 20

395

16

95 10

Norwich

12

Mystic

11

New London

84

1

23

25

17

Connecticut River

4 Essex 3

9

8 9

Long Island Sound

5

Middletown

91 27

7

Hartford

91

95

6

13

2

New Haven

26

Waterbury

18

8

15 8

84

Torrington

Litchfield

Danbury

22

14

Stamford

MASSACHUSETTS

NEW YORK

N

The numbers on this map indicate the locations of B&Bs described in detail in this chapter.

CONNECTICUT

Can't find the community you wish to visit? Check with a reservation service described at the beginning of this chapter.

ᡐ Bed and Breakfast, Ltd.

P.O. Box 216, New Haven, CT 06513

PHONE: 203/469-3260, during the academic year (Jack teaches full time), 5–9:30 P.M. weekdays; anytime weekends or summer months.

URL: www.bedandbreakfastltd.com

LISTINGS: More than 125. "From elegantly simple to simply elegant." Located throughout Connecticut. Some listings in Massachusetts and Rhode Island; new listings constantly added. Mostly private residences. A few inns and unhosted private residences.

RESERVATIONS: For one day or up to three months. Same-day service usually available. "A quick phone call encouraged to discuss availability and appropriate placement." Thereafter, guests have direct advance contact with host.

RATES: $65–$95 singles, $75–$185 doubles. Suites and deluxe accommodations slightly higher.

JACK ARGENIO emphasizes variety—in types of homes as well as in price range. Many are historic residences filled with antiques. He selects knowledgeable and congenial hosts and tries to personalize matches to suit guests' needs and budget.

PLUS: In-ground pools, Jacuzzis, gourmet dinners, hiking trails. Some hosts meet guests at airports or train stations.

ᡐ Covered Bridge

69 Maple Avenue, Norfolk, CT 06058-0447

PHONE: 860/542-5944, 9 A.M.–6 P.M. daily; other times, answering machine.

FAX: 860/542-5690

E-MAIL: tremblay@essfink.com

LISTINGS: Seventy. Most are hosted private residences in Connecticut's Litchfield County and shoreline communities, in the Berkshires of Massachusetts, and in Rhode Island and New York towns bordering Connecticut. A few are unhosted and some are inns. A free sample list is available. Directory (booklet), $3.

RESERVATIONS: One to two weeks' advance notice preferred. Two-day minimum for weekends, three for holidays. Available through travel agents.

RATES: $75–$185. Some family, senior citizen, and weekly rates available. Prepayment in full is required. Cancellations received at least ten days before expected arrival date will be refunded less a $15 handling charge. With less than ten days' notice, entire prepayment may be forfeited unless room is rebooked. ❖

HANK AND DIANE Tremblay, former corporate executives, are nationally recognized innkeepers (Manor House, page 24) who work with travelers on an individual basis to try to accommodate their needs. Most of their selected hosts live in antiques-furnished historic homes that are sometimes featured in major national publications. Many are in idyllic settings. Hearty breakfasts are a feature.

ᕯ *Nutmeg Bed & Breakfast Agency*

P.O. Box 271117, West Hartford, CT 06127-1117

PHONE: 860/236-6698 or 800/727-7592, Monday–Friday, 9:30–5, year round; machine at other times.

FAX: 860/232-7680

E-MAIL: Nutmegbnb@home.com

URL: www.BnB-Link.com

LISTINGS: Located throughout Connecticut—near all major cities and towns and along the shore—and in bordering Rhode Island towns and New York. Hosted private residences and some inns. No charge for brief descriptions of all places in each area of the state.

RESERVATIONS: One week's advance notice preferred. Two-night minimum on holidays and graduation weekends and at other times at some locations.

RATES: $55–$125 single; $65–$210 double; average $75–$95. Family and weekly rates available. $3 booking fee. Amex, MC, Visa to hold reservations. $15 charge for confirmed cancellation. One night's lodging charged if notice received less than seven days before expected arrival; fourteen days for holidays and special events.

MICHELLE SOUZA, a B&B convert who has traveled extensively, offers quality accommodations for tourists and business travelers. Her well-established service specializes in "selecting just the right getaway spot" and finding temporary and permanent housing for relocating executives. She also works with colleges, private schools, and hospitals to provide lodging for visiting faculty, parents, and patients in private homes.

⫷ *Blueberry Inn*

40 Bashon Hill Road,
P.O. Box 186, Bozrah, CT 06334

860/889-3618
888/357-4305
FAX 860/892-0046

HOSTS: Ray and Jacqueline Dows
LOCATION: Peaceful. On 17 acres, surrounded by 3 acres of lawn and gardens. Within half hour of Mystic (to the southeast) and Putnam antiques shops (to the north.)
OPEN: Year round. Two-night minimum on weekends, June until mid-November.
RATES: $125–$135 queen. $110 double bed. MC, Visa. ♥ ☕ ⊞❖ ⚄ ⚲ ♨

AFTER RAY BUILT what he and Jackie dub their "dream house," a variation on *Southern Living* Cape-style plans, Jackie put a "Blueberry Inn" sign on the back because, as Ray tells it, she liked the idea of living in the atmosphere of a B&B—without guests!" We-e-ll, when the town ruled in 1993 that B&Bs were "okay," the Dowses decided to try it. Ever since, guests have commented on the peace and quiet, the breakfasts, and the ever popular dogs. Eclectic furnishings include reproductions.

Ray, retired from the real estate business, is active in the town and in the area B&B association. Jackie, a decorative artist who teaches weekly classes right here, paints on wood "for fun and pleasure."

IN RESIDENCE: "Our schnauzers, Sadie and Gracie."
BED AND BATH: Three second-floor rooms, all private baths. Two with queen beds (one with shower bath, other with tub/shower bath). Room with double bed, shower bath.
BREAKFAST: At 9. "Plentiful real country fare." Pancakes, sausage, scrambled eggs, homemade biscuits. Orange juice. Hot beverages. In sunroom or in dining room.
PLUS: Central air conditioning. Wood-burning fireplaces in living room and great room. Cookies and milk upon arrival.

*T*HE TRADITION *of paying to stay in a private home—with breakfast included in the overnight lodging rate—was revived in time to save wonderful old houses, schools, churches, and barns all over the country from the wrecking ball or commercial development.*

⌂ *Chimney Crest Manor*   860/582-4219

5 Founders Drive, Bristol, CT 06010   FAX 860/584-5903

HOSTS: Dan and Cynthia Cimadamore
LOCATION: On a hilltop overlooking Farmington Valley. In historic Federal Hill area, one-quarter mile from Bristol Clock Museum, 1 mile from New England Carousel Museum; 14 miles from Litchfield Hills. Twenty minutes west of Hartford, fifteen east of Waterbury.
OPEN: Year round. Two-night minimum stay on holiday weekends and in foliage season.
RATES: September–April double $105, $115, $125, $145, $165. Singles $15 less. Children seven and older $15. Weekly and monthly rates available. Corporate, senior citizen, and Lovers Weekend (two-night stay) discounts (holidays excepted). Amex, MC, Visa. ♥ ⊞❖ ⚔ ⅄ ❂

TENT WEDDINGS ARE now booked on the grounds of this sprawling National Register thirty-two-room Tudor mansion with tile roof, arches, gardens, and multiflue chimneys. British royalty, honeymooners, and many business travelers have walked along the 40-foot-long arcade. There's a cherry-paneled library, a Spanish-tiled sunroom, six hand-crafted fireplaces, and ornate plaster ceilings. Furnishings are traditional.

The estate was built in 1930 by the Barnes family, known locally for specialty steels and springs. The residence for three generations became a B&B after the second Cimadamore child was born; Cynthia was ready for "something else to do at home." (Dan is an environmental engineer.) It's a B&B offering privacy and warm hospitality, large full guest suites, meeting rooms, and space for receptions.

IN RESIDENCE: Diana, during college vacations. Dante is fifteen. Cheri is the family's bichon frise.
BED AND BATH: Four suites and two rooms. Large, very private garden suite (great for families or meeting leaders) with fireplaced living room, queen-bedded (canopied) room, wet bar. Three second-floor suites with king or queen bed, full bath, sitting room. One suite with wood-burning fireplace, one with Jacuzzi, two with full kitchens. First-level apartment has private entrance, parking.
BREAKFAST: Full. Continental after 10. Fruit salad and homemade breads plus yogurt pancakes, French toast, or eggs. Sugar-free and low-fat diets accommodated. Presented with linen, china, and crystal in fireplaced dining room.
PLUS: Bedroom air conditioning. Fan, clock radio, television with cable, telephone and VCR in each suite. Garden. Large patio.

⌂ From Canada: *"Magnificent home with warm atmosphere. . . . Comfortably furnished. . . . Immaculately clean. . . . Sumptuous breakfast. . . . Terrific hostess. . . . Attention to detail. Highly recommended."* From Washington: *"A hidden treasure. Warm welcome. Impeccable decor."*

⚞ *Captain Dibbell House*   860/669-1646

21 Commerce Street,   FAX 860/669-2300
Clinton, CT 06413-2054   **www.clintonct.com/dibbell**

HOSTS: Helen and Ellis Adams
LOCATION: Two blocks from harbor, on a historic residential street. One mile south of
I-95, just off Route 1. Two miles to Hammonasset State Beach; 10 to Essex;
40 to Mystic; 23 to Yale University; 3 to Salt Meadow National Wildlife
Refuge; 1 to Clinton Crossing (outlet shopping).
OPEN: April 1–December 31. Two-night minimum stay on holidays and for special
events.
RATES: $109 for two. Singles $89. Off-season, multiple-night-stay, and corporate
rates available. Amex, MC, Visa. ♥ ❖ ⚲ ✂

⚞ From Georgia, California, Holland, New York: *"Nice surroundings. . . .*
Breakfasts are hearty, delicious, plentiful. . . . Ellis prides himself on always having fresh cook-
ies, brownies, or cakes for the taking. . . . Adorable bears artfully arranged on bed [for turn-
down]. . . . Tandem bicycle . . . guests' restaurant reviews . . . in a quiet town with antiques
shops and period museums plus Hammonasset State Park just a bike ride away . . . a couple of
the nicest and most hospitable people we've had the pleasure of staying with."

THE RESTORED 1866 Victorian, "not the ornate kind," is furnished with family pieces and
auction finds and without clutter. Classical music is almost always playing.

"Poughkeepsie, New York, seems very far away now that we have been innkeeping
since 1986." Elllis, a former health inspector, and Helen, a former caseworker, selected this
coastal town after spending several summers in the area on their sailboat.

IN RESIDENCE: Two Abyssinian cats—Ramses, "Mr. Personality," and "shy Desdemona."
BED AND BATH: Four second-floor rooms, all private baths. Three with queen bed; two
with shower bath, one tub/shower bath. One room with king/twins option, shower bath.
BREAKFAST: 8:30–10. An egg dish. Freshly baked muffins, scones (most requested recipe),
or coffee cake. Juice, fruit, teas, freshly ground coffee. For honeymooners or anniversary
celebrants, served (by request) in gazebo.
PLUS: Bedroom ceiling fans and air conditioners. Puzzles, games, cards. Borrowables—bicycles, beach chairs with umbrella, cooler.

I<small>F YOU HAVE MET ONE</small> B&B <small>HOST, YOU HAVEN'T MET THEM ALL.</small>

🪶 *Riverwind*

860/526-2014

209 Main Street,
Deep River, CT 06417-1704

FAX 860/526-0875
www.innformation.com/ct/riverwind

HOSTS: Barbara Barlow and Bob Bucknall
LOCATION: Adjacent to the town green, in a small Connecticut River Valley village between Essex and Chester. Minutes to Goodspeed Opera House, Gillette Castle, Hammonasset Beach, fine dining, antiquing; half hour to Mystic Seaport.
OPEN: Year round. Two-night minimum, Saturday inclusive, April 15–January 2.
RATES: Per room. $95 (the one with unattached bath) to $175 ("Champagne and Roses"). Additional occupant, 50 percent of room rate. MC, Visa.
♥ ⊞✗ ❤◡

PERFECT FOR FEATURES in several magazines, including *Country Living* and *Country Inns*. Recipient of a "ten best country inns" award. The site of more than a hundred small weddings. (Barbara is a justice of the peace.) Romance also plays a part in this inn's history.

Barbara, a Virginia junior high school learning-disabilities teacher who had experience restoring three other houses, came north for a week and found and bought the abandoned 1850 house. She uncovered fireplaces, hand sanded floors, wired, tiled, and stenciled. In 1984 she drove a truck up from Smithfield, Virginia, filled with family and other country antiques. Now, *everywhere* you look—up, down, and around—there's an incredible collection of folk art showing Barbara's sense of display, imagination, whimsy, and joie de vivre.

When it was time to expand, Barbara planned an authentically styled eighteenth-century keeping room along with four more new-but-look-old guest rooms, some quite luxurious. She hired Bob Bucknall, a local contractor and Deep River native. In fairytale fashion, they fell in love; they married (in Virginia); and Bob became full-time co-innkeeper.

BED AND BATH: Eight air-conditioned rooms (some with ceiling fan) on first and second floors. All private baths; six tub/shower, one hall bath with shower, no tub; one with Victorian claw-foot tub and hand-held shower. Each room quite different. Queen or double beds. Some are canopied; some, four-posters. "Champagne and Roses" features queen canopied bed, bath with Japanese steeping tub, separate shower, private balcony, complimentary champagne.
BREAKFAST: Usually 9–10. (Coffee and tea for early risers.) A Southern buffet in two dining rooms. Hot entrée (baked French toast), Smithfield ham, pig-shaped biscuits, fruit compote, coffee cake, juices, coffee, tea.
PLUS: Plenty of common space including game room and library for privacy, sitting by the fire, reading. One of four fireplaces is a 12-foot stone cooking hearth. Welcoming drink. Guitar. Mints. Flowers. Piano; old sheet music. Plant- and wicker-filled wraparound (glassed-in) porch with ceiling fans. Directions to "best-kept secret" nature preserve.

🪶 Guests wrote: *"Charming . . . relaxing . . . warm hospitality."*

➢ *Butternut Farm*   860/633-7197

1654 Main Street, Glastonbury, CT 06033-2962   FAX 860/659-1758

HOST: Don Reid
LOCATION: On 2 wooded and landscaped acres. "Within ninety minutes of most of Connecticut." Ten minutes from Hartford by expressway; 1.6 miles south of Glastonbury Center to Whapley Road. Enter by first hole in the bushes on left. "Don't run over the chickens, please."
OPEN: Year round.
RATES: $79 room. $89 suite. $99 apartment. Amex. ♥ ♦♦ ⊞ ⚏ ⚒

➢ From Michigan: *"Everything about this amazing place, from the lovingly restored old house and farm buildings to the antique furnishings and exotic animals, from the homemade breakfast jam to the bedtime sherry, conspires to make a couple of nights and breakfasts quite unforgettable."*

OTHER FAMILY MEMBERS attending our nephew's wedding agreed with the mother of the bride from Michigan.

Don restored this 1720 center entrance architectural gem with its eight wide fireplaces, pumpkin pine floors, and paneled walls while he was a banker. (Then he was a schoolteacher for seven years.) Along the way, in the 1970s, he was asked to accommodate a neighbor's guests.

Everywhere you look, there's an eighteenth-century treasure—a cherry highboy, a gateleg table, banister-back chairs, English delft—in addition to hand-hammered hinges, exposed beams, and twelve-over-twelve windows. Outside, there are flower and herb gardens, and Adirondack chairs on a stone patio. And those animals. All contribute to the experience appreciated by first-time as well as repeat guests.

IN RESIDENCE: "The neighborhood petting zoo—Abyssinian cats Chester, Rupert, and Millie crave attention." Fifteen goats with names, fifty pigeons without names, fifty chickens with eggs! And Harry, the goose; six ducks; "one gorgeous golden pheasant and two miniature pigs"; and Mark, the llama.
FOREIGN LANGUAGES SPOKEN: French, some German and Italian.
BED AND BATH: Two rooms, two suites, one apartment—all modern private baths. One room with two twin "hired man's" beds and one with a canopied double bed, each with full bath. One suite with a four-poster double, private full bath; one with double sofa bed, shower bath, private entrance. Barn apartment has canopied double bed, full bath, kitchen, private garden.
BREAKFAST: Usually 8:30; flexible for business travelers. Juice and fruit. Fresh-from-the-barn eggs and milk. Toast. Homemade jam. Don's honey. Cheeses. Goat's milk, coffee, tea. Served in intimate breakfast room or in early eighteenth-century dining room.
PLUS: Air conditioning. Individual thermostats. Private phone, TV, and VCR in some rooms. Beverages. Guest refrigerators. Several common rooms.

ᔓ *Nutmeg Bed & Breakfast Agency Host #416*

Granby, CT

LOCATION: In historic residential area. On 6 acres with garden, grape arbor, and big yard backed by woods. About eight-minute drive from Bradley Airport, five to International (ice) Skating Center in Simsbury. Near several private schools.

RESERVATIONS: Year round through Nutmeg Bed & Breakfast (page 3), 860/236-6698 or 800/727-7592. E-mail nutmegbnb@home.com

RATES: $105; $95 smaller room. ⊞ ❖ ⊗ ⅊

WHAT A MATCH! The most recent occupant of this 1812 Colonial summer house—now all winterized—was a landscaper, a member of the family that had owned the house since the 1800s. Since the hostess, a floral designer (and piano teacher), bought the house in 1999, she has been working on restoring the gardens. Inside, too, there's been a lot going on—rebuilding, installation of central air conditioning, and redecorating (by the hostess) with a Victorian flair. "All just ten minutes from where I had been living. And to think I learned about the property from a brochure I picked up at the grocery store just as I was on my way to Vermont to look at a place that had the potential of fulfilling my fifteen-year dream!" In spring the lilacs bloom. The wisteria drapes over a picture window. A big side porch overlooks a garden. The townspeople are happy. Guests say, "It's heavenly."

BED AND BATH: Four second-floor rooms with private large (and new) shower baths, TV/VCR. One with king bed, working fireplace, bath just outside door. Two with queen bed; one has working fireplace. One room with two twin beds.

BREAKFAST: Memorable. Main dish is different every day. Could be baked pancake, citrus puffs, or pineapple soufflé. Juices, fresh fruit, muffins, hot beverages. Served in dining room.

Aᴌᴌ ᴛʜᴇ B&Bs with this ☕ symbol want you to know that they are a private home set up for paying guests (rather than an inn). Although definitions vary, these private home B&Bs tend to have one to three guest rooms. For the owners—people who enjoy meeting people—B&B is usually a part-time occupation.

⟿ *Homespun Farm Bed and Breakfast*   860/376-5178

306 Preston Road,
Griswold, CT 06351

FAX 860/376-5587
E-MAIL innkeeper@homespunfarm.com
www.homespunfarm.com

HOSTS: Kate and Ron Bauer
LOCATION: Country setting. With panoramic sunset views. Less than 1 mile from I-395. Across from new (1999) golf course. Ten minutes to casinos. Within thirty minutes of Mystic attractions.
OPEN: Year round. Two-night minimum on all holiday weekends.
RATES: $85 double, $110 suite. Less November through March. Discover, MC, Visa.
♥ ᵗᵗ ⬛ ⸼

"I FEEL AS IF we are just the caretakers of this 1740 house. It was part of a family dairy and orchard business for more than two centuries. While we moved a lot—Ron is in the U.S. Navy—I always dreamed of living in an old house. This one needed *everything.* Together we did everything. Ron knows how! He helped build the B&B my parents had in Hawaii. Now we've applied for National Register status for this house with its exposed beams, wide-board pine and oak floors, and original latch hooks. We've brought back the orchard of apples, pears, and peaches. I have become a Master Gardener through Connecticut State College. And the property is a Certified National Wildlife Federation Backyard."

IN RESIDENCE: Whimsey, a Yorkshire terrier/Chihuahua mix. A canary. Two teenaged sons.
BED AND BATH: One room and one suite (with more to come soon). First-floor room—double bed, TV, full bath (robes provided) shared with innkeepers. Second-floor suite with slanted ceilings—queen bed (made by Ron from wood of dismantled barn across the road) in one room, single bed in other, TV, private full bath with claw-foot tub, large shower. Air conditioners in summer.
BREAKFAST: 8–10. French toast or other hot entrée. Juice. Fresh fruit. Blueberry muffins, cinnamon rolls, apple morning cake (a sweet cornbread with eggs and scallions), or French toast. Served in the candlelit keeping room or by koi pond.
PLUS: Woodstove in kitchen. TV/VCR in living room. Hammock under grape arbor. Pick-your-own orchard. Children welcome; with advance arrangements, pets are too. Gift shop on premises offers handmade candles; crafts; homespun fashions such as ladies' dresses, skirts, aprons.

     ⟿ From Washington: *"Warm, welcoming old farmhouse in prime shape. . . . Personal care surpassed the superb service received at area resort."* From New Jersey: *"Woke up to tantalizing smell of muffins . . . great spread of breakfast foods. . . . Our teenaged son, who had wanted to stay in a motel, played video games with Kate's son and loved every minute."* From Maryland: *"Fresh garden flowers . . . even in my melon! . . . wonderfully decorated . . . no detail left undone."*

⇗ *Acorn Bed and Breakfast* 860/663-2214

628 Route 148,
Killingworth, CT 06419-1145

(TOLL-FREE) 877/978-7842
FAX 860/663-2214
E-MAIL richard@acornbedandbreakfast.com
www.acornbedandbreakfast.com

HOSTS: Carole and Richard Pleines
LOCATION: A quiet, wooded, residential area on a scenic road. Near fine restaurants. Three miles from Route 79, 4 from Route 81. Twenty minutes to Gillette Castle, Goodspeed Opera House, Chester-to-Haddam ferry, state parks, beaches, outlets, antiquing. Forty-five minutes to Hartford, New Haven, New London, casinos.
OPEN: Year round. (Best to call in evenings.)
RATES: $125 May–October, $110 November–April. $95 corporate rate. Amex, Discover, MC, Visa. ☛ ⚋ ⚋

THE CENTRALLY air-conditioned Cape Cod with gambrel addition was built by Carole and Dick 25 years ago. Now their children are grown and gone. Still, the fine antiques change "as we find pieces we like even better." Amenities include everything from turn-down service to a year-round outdoor hot tub.

Dick, a former science teacher, is chamber of commerce president. Carole, a retired social worker, is a guardian ad litem and paints oils on canvas. They are antiques dealers and Old Hickory furniture reps. They make their own wine and design the labels. They love to travel. And, as guests note, they love to share their home and their knowledge of this area.

IN RESIDENCE: Three cats: Buddy is the official greeter; Molly and Sam are shy. In backyard, the almost-famous turkey and guinea hen.
BED AND BATH: Two second-floor (slanted-ceilinged) rooms. Each has queen bed (with headboard fashioned from old Maine church rail), private walk-in shower bath, individual heat control.
BREAKFAST: 8–9 (earlier by arrangement). Bread pudding with warm raspberry sauce, poached pears, baked apples, homemade sticky buns. Fresh fruit—with sherbet in summer. Garnished with edible flowers or fresh herbs. Presented with sterling silver, fine crystal, different table settings including Depression glass and 1940s Franciscan Apple Ware. Special diets accommodated.
PLUS: Landscaped yard with in-ground pool in summer. Fireplaced living room. Guest refrigerator with complimentary beverages. Line-dried, ironed antique linens. Porch swing.

⇗ From Connecticut, Vermont (innkeepers), New York, New Jersey, Virginia: *"Incredible food . . . enjoyable conversation . . . home oozes charm . . . home filled with lovely antiques . . . perfect place for visiting our children who live nearby . . . super room and bed. . . . Mr. Tom Turkey [a pet often photographed] was a delight to watch. . . . Not just a place to stay. It was part of our vacation."*

⚞ Tidewater Inn   203/245-8457

949 Boston Post Road, Madison, CT 06443   FAX 203/318-0265

HOSTS: Jean Foy and (husband) Rich Evans
LOCATION: Wooded residential area. On 2 landscaped acres with tidal wetlands visible in front and back. Minutes' walk to village. In area known for antiques shops, boutiques, restaurants. One and a half miles to several Long Island beaches. Ten minutes to two outlet malls. Twenty minutes east of Yale University.
OPEN: Year round. Two-night weekend minimum Memorial Day–Labor Day and holidays. (Check-in time 2–8 P.M.; later with advance arrangements.)
RATES: Memorial Day–Columbus Day weekends $110 double, $140 queen or twins, $170 king; midweek about 10 percent less. Rest of year weekends $110 double fireplace, $90 double, $110 queen or twins, $140 king; midweek—10 percent less. January–April, two-night stay includes dinner gift certificate. Year round, midweek single business rate. Amex, MC, Visa. ♥ ⊞ ⚘ ✂

⚞ From California, Connecticut, New York, New Jersey, Massachusetts: *An aura of elegant comfort . . . our room was of average size but lavishly appointed . . . chocolate by the bed, fireplace stocked, chamber music . . . made to feel special . . . relaxed atmosphere . . . Hosts are attentive but unobtrusive (a perfect combination) . . . knowledgeable about area and restaurants . . . Breakfast—plentiful . . . sensations for the palate. . . . A unique find!"*

"JUST TWO HOURS from New York (two and a half from Boston) but in a different world," say many guests, including artists, theater producers, newlyweds, and Yale University conference attendees. From the outside the 1800s stagecoach stop looks like a French stucco farmhouse. Furnishings are a mixture of 1800s antiques and estate pieces from the 1930s and '40s. The grounds include a lovely English garden, a shaded yard with benches, umbrella tables and chairs, and land that slopes to a creek.

Jean, a former IBM systems engineer and project manager, and Rich, a corporate CFO, enjoyed B&B visits for fifteen years before they bought their own in 1996.

IN RESIDENCE: Two cats—not allowed in inn.
FOREIGN LANGUAGE SPOKEN: "A little French."
BED AND BATH: Nine air-conditioned corner rooms, each with private bath, TV, outgoing phone. Two first-floor rooms, each with double bed, wood-burning fireplace, shower bath. Six second-floor rooms. One with king four-poster, shower bath. Others with shower bath—queen canopied, queen four-poster, double canopied or two twin beds. Cottage suite has king bed, Jacuzzi for two, extra-large shower, sitting room.
BREAKFAST: 8:30–9:30. Sunday–Thursday, 7:15 continental for business travelers. Favorite entrées include lemon cream or pear almond waffles, egg puff, Western oven omelet or coconut French toast. Juice, fruit or yogurt, baked goods, cereals. Served in fireplaced sitting room with bay window at one table for eight, one for four, and one for two.
PLUS: Beamed living room with fresh flowers and wood-burning fireplace. Cold drinks

always available. Complimentary wine and tea, coffee, hot chocolate on weekend evenings. Special occasions acknowledged with engraved wine bottles or wine gift basket from local winery. Beach passes and chairs provided.

☞ *Brigadoon B&B*   860/536-3033

180 Cow Hill Road,   FAX 860/536-1628
Mystic, CT 06355   E-MAIL innkeepers@brigadoonofmystic.com

HOSTS: Kay and Ted Lucas
LOCATION: On 1½ acres, surrounded by stone walls and fruit trees. Half mile off I-95, along the street that leads into Mystic. Five-minute drive to Mystic Seaport; ten to Ocean Beach in New London, twenty to Rocky Neck Beach in East Lyme.
OPEN: Year round. Two-day weekend minimum May–October and holidays.
RATES: First floor rooms $140; $150 with deck. Second-floor rooms $130. (Monday Thursday $110–$130). Third adult or child over ten $20. Under age ten free. Amex, MC, Visa. ♥ ⊞❖ ⚄ ⅃

OUTSIDE THERE'S a Scottish flag, sign of the hospitality offered inside by Scottish-born Kay, a freelance writer/doting grandmother/tourism committeewoman, and Ted, a Connecticut-born mechanical engineer/sailor/gardener who will gladly pose in chef's hat for photographers.

During one of their many trips to Mystic, after having lived all over the country, the Lucases chanced, in 1987, upon a FOR SALE sign in front of this comfortable, rambling fifteen-room Victorian (with attached barn and outbuildings). Since opening with four guest rooms, they have enlarged rooms, redecorated, added baths and gas fireplaces—and, in the main hall, kept the framed 1800s house deed with Charles Hancock's signature. Was he a relative of John Hancock? Such research is ongoing. As are events: Victorian teas, seminars, and family reunions too.

IN RESIDENCE: Two cats in hosts' quarters.
FOREIGN LANGUAGE SPOKEN: "A little high school French."
BED AND BATH: Eight air-conditioned bedrooms (small, medium-sized, or large; some with wide floorboards) All private baths. First floor—queen four-poster with wood-burning fireplace; queen with wood-burning fireplace; honeymoon suite with king bed, cable TV, cathedral ceilings, French door, deck, private exterior entrance. Second floor—beds (some canopied) are king, queen, or king/twins; four rooms have gas fireplace.
BREAKFAST: Usually 8:30–10. Continental after 10 or 10:30. Daily special—maybe Belgian waffles, strawberry walnut pancakes, crepes, French toast, strata. Fruit compote. Eggs, bacon, sausage. French toast and scones. Muffins or nut breads. Bagels and cream cheese. Served in large, many-windowed dining room or in garden.
PLUS: Air-conditioned common rooms. Afternoon tea. Beverages. Candy. Garden flowers. TV/VCR room, books, games.

～ *House of 1833*   860/536-6325

72 North Stonington Road,   800/367-1833
Mystic, CT 06355-0341   www.visitmystic.com/1833

HOSTS: Carol and Matt Nolan
LOCATION: Quiet country setting. On 3 landscaped acres with tall maples and stone
walls. Across from steam-powered cider mill. Five-minute drive to Mystic
Seaport.
OPEN: Year round. Two-night weekend minimum.
RATES: May–October—weekends $155, $175; $215 canopied bed, clawfoot tub in
front of fireplace, private porch; $225 with whirlpool tub; weekdays $115-
$165. November–April—weekends $115–$165; weekdays $95–$135. MC,
Visa. ♥ ⊞❖ ⚲ ⚗

GRAND OUTSIDE. Gracious within. From the columned porch of this 1833 Greek Revival
mansion you enter a tiled foyer that features a dramatic circular staircase and mural.
When the Nolans bought the property in 1993, they commissioned the same muralist, an
octogenarian, to do more. The chandeliered music room has a baby grand piano and a
pump organ. Antiques and fine traditional furnishings are throughout. Baths feature a
hand-painted ceramic sink set in an antique bureau, a period washstand with brass sink,
or whirlpool tubs. Some guest rooms have yards of moiré or paisley fabric draped from
four-posters or the ceiling. A decorative fence surrounds the lap pool. A Har-Tru tennis
court is in place, and eighteen-speed bicycles are available for touring the countryside.

Matt, the breakfast pianist, was a teacher in California. Carol was a former Manhattan
investment counselor. "When we married, we decided to work together." Their place to
stay has become the reason to go.

IN RESIDENCE: Son Alex, age four, "assistant innkeeper."
BED AND BATH: Five very large rooms, all with queen bed (some canopied), private full
bath (one with slipper tub in bedroom), working fireplace. First-floor room has oversized
shower, double whirlpool tub, private porch. Third-floor room has woodstove, double
whirlpool, separate shower, stairway to private cupola sitting room.
BREAKFAST: Presented at 9. (Breakfast basket option for honeymooners.) Fruit plate,
muffins, Peet's Coffee. Puffed pancakes with apple-cinnamon sauce, spinach Florentine
in puff pastry, tomato/broccoli or San Geronimo quiche. In formal dining room at one
large table.
PLUS: Central air conditioning. Eight fireplaces. Freshly baked cookies and fudge brownies. Candles in rooms. No TV. Guest refrigerator. Porch rockers. Special occasions
acknowledged.

ᴫ *Pequot Hotel Bed & Breakfast*   860/572-0390

711 Cow Hill Road,   FAX 860/536-3380
Mystic, CT 06355   E-MAIL pequothtl@aol.com
    www.visitmystic.com/pequothotel

HOSTS: Nancy and Jim Mitchell
LOCATION: On 23 acres with trailed woods, open fields, ponds, gardens. In interesting historic district. At intersection of Cow Hill (leads to I-95) and Packer Roads. Two and a half miles to downtown Mystic and Mystic Seaport. Ten miles to casinos.
OPEN: Year round. Two-night minimum on some holidays and weekends.
RATES: Double with fireplace $135. Queen with fireplace, whirlpool $155. Suite $110. Extra person $20. MC, Visa. ♥ ♦♦ ⊞❖ ⊅ ⊁

ᴫ From Massachusetts, New York, New Jersey, Connecticut: *"On route between New York and Boston, provided us with a comfortable, warm, delicious experience. . . . Knowledge of area saved us a lot of time. . . . Felt at home. . . . Inviting décor. . . . Catered to our wishes. . . . This place is what dreams are all about."*

FEATURED IN the National Trust's 1998 Historic America calendar, this intimate B&B—just three guest rooms—is a big wonderful 1840 Greek Revival stagecoach stop brought back to life by Connecticut natives. The Mitchells' labor of love began in 1976. "My father said, 'Don't do it' when he saw the condition of the place," recalls Nancy, a recently retired flight attendant who, together with Jim, a mechanical engineer, restored everything except the kitchen and the now luxurious baths. "In 1991, when we had completed enough to wonder what we would do with it, Jim had the great idea of B&B." Many antiques are family pieces. There's a rare book library. Rumford fireplaces. Carved moldings. Old-song lyrics—plastic mounted and a big hit—in showers. The Mitchells' chickens supply farm-fresh breakfast eggs. Berries and herbs come from the garden. As one Texan, in New England for the first time, said, "The hosts are just like us—s-o-o nice!"

IN RESIDENCE: "Popular and photogenic Mason—"barkless, no shedding" —is a male basenji, not allowed on guest floor. Two cats: Molly, shy (or aloof), warms up with a loud purr. Felicity is a friendly Maine Coon cat."
FOREIGN LANGUAGES SPOKEN: "A bit of German and Spanish."
BED AND BATH: Three air-conditioned second-floor rooms (one is a suite), all with individual thermostat, ceiling fan, private bath. Ballroom was divided (soundproof wall) into two large rooms with 12-foot ceilings. One has antique double four-poster, shower bath. Other has canopied queen bed, whirlpool tub with double shower heads. Suite has two bedrooms with hall doorways—room with double bed and room with two single beds, connecting shower bath.
BREAKFAST: Flexible. Usually 8:30 in summer, 9–9:30 in winter. Juice. Fresh fruit cup, baked apple or broiled fruit. Garnished French toast, waffles, pancakes, or egg dish. "Jim

continued . . .

is the omelet king." Ham, sausage, or bacon. Potatoes Pequot with fresh thyme. Cereals. In light-filled room with woodstove.

PLUS: Wicker-furnished screened porch. TV and VCR in rear parlor. Patio. Picnic table with umbrella. Gas grill. Badminton. Croquet. Horseshoes. Homemade cookies.

🐦 *Applewood Farms Inn*   860/535-2022

528 Colonel Ledyard,   800/717-4262
Ledyard, CT 06339-1649   FAX 860/536-6015
                                        E-MAIL applewoodfarms@yahoo.com
                                                      www.obs-us.com

   HOSTS: Frankie and Tom Betz
LOCATION: On 33 acres. A Colonial farm surrounded by stone walls and lawn. Five
             miles north of Mystic. Six miles south of casinos.
    OPEN: Year round. Two-night minimum stay on weekends.
   RATES: May–October $125–$290. November–April $105–$250. Third person $25.
             Off-season rates exclude holidays. Amex, Discover, MC, Visa. ♥ ⊞❖

To THINK this property with its 1826 house was considered for condominiums in the 1980s! When the Betzes bought it in 1985, they restored everything. Most walls are simulated whitewash. There's stenciling and handhewn chestnut floorboards. And antiques, primitives, a grandfather clock, and a large pewter collection. On the grounds are a "chipping fairway," a USGA-designed putting green (a few clubs available), a gazebo, and a pond with fish to feed. The latest addition is a hot tub built into a former (roofed) corn crib, complete with lighting and a radio.

Tom's farming days started at age eleven, long before he had a marine electronics business (and a home in Mystic with a greenhouse). Here, he wears a cowboy hat, rides a tractor, and grows roses. Tom and Frankie, known for her award-winning jams, have linked their interests in horticulture, birding, and travel.

IN RESIDENCE: Two basset hounds—Millie and Annie. One cat. Granddaughter's horse.
BED AND BATH: Five air-conditioned rooms (may be combined into suites). Four with working fireplace. All with private bath. Rooms are on first and second floors and have king, queen, or double bed.
BREAKFAST: 8:30–9:45. Juice. Tropical fruit dish with sherbet. Eggs with bacon and toast.
PLUS: Two common rooms. Fruit, mints, seasonal wildflowers. Hiking trails here and on adjoining Nature Conservancy land. "Polite pets welcomed; kennel and stable provided." Note: Smoking allowed.

☞ *Stonecroft*

515 Pumpkin Hill Road,
Ledyard, CT 06339

860/572-0771
800/772-0774
FAX 860/572-9161
E-MAIL stoncrft@concentric.net
www.stonecroft.com

HOSTS: Joan and Lynn Egy

LOCATION: Very private and rural—ten minutes to the water—with acres of lawns, gardens and meadows. Next to 350 acres of wooded nature conservancy with trails, and five-minute walk to equestrian center (trail riding). Five miles north of Mystic Seaport—"our reason for locating here, after a lifetime of sailing for pleasure on Long Island Sound." Five miles south of casinos.

OPEN: Year round. Two-night weekend and holiday minimum.

RATES: May–October—weekends $130–$250; weekdays $125–$195. November–April—weekends $130–$250; weekdays $125–$195. Four- or five-day stays, 10 percent less. Amex, Discover, MC, Visa. ♥ ⊞ ❖ ⚔ ⚰ ❤❍

AN INCREDIBLE success story: What started in 1994 as a four-room B&B particularly suited to couples who want to spend time alone is all of that and then some. The main house, on the National Register, features twelve-over-twelve windows, a 9-foot-wide Rumford fireplace, and murals done by the same artist who did some of the walls at the Inn at National Hall in Westport. In 1999 the Egys completed (from a shell) The Grange, which immediately was discovered; its spacious and luxurious rooms host many corporate meetings and small weddings. The Grange's ground-level granite-and-glass-walled dining room—"Best New (2000) Restaurant in Connecticut" according to *Connecticut* magazine's readers' poll—has become known for its food and presentation. It is under the direction of Drew Egy, executive chef (and son), who brings culinary experience from leading hotels and restaurants in the United States and Europe. Joan, a certified psychosynthesist, organizes many annual events, including one for the Spinal Cord Injury Foundation. Lynn had a career as a systems manager for a major international bank.

IN RESIDENCE: Two friendly cats and a Sheltie.

BED AND BATH: Ten air-conditioned rooms (one is handicapped accessible); all private full baths. King or queen beds; some canopied. Each of six Grange rooms (vaulted ceilings on upper floor) has corner fireplace, TV, huge bathroom with two-person whirlpool tub, bidet, his-and-hers vanities, heated towel bars, access to public deck.

BREAKFAST: 8–10. Continental with entrée options from the menu. (Care packages provided for very early travelers.) Lemon waffles with homegrown blackberries, smoked salmon and chive omelet with whole wheat biscuits and orange butter, or blueberry buttermilk pancakes. At tables for 2, 4, or 6.

PLUS: Wood-burning fireplaces and air conditioning in sitting rooms. Terry slippers provided (low-heeled shoes requested) in main house. Boules court. Croquet. Horseshoes. Hammock. Water garden. Grapevine-shaded pergola.

continued . . .

☞ From Connecticut, New York, Florida: *"Absolutely unbelievable . . . marvelous accommodations . . . charming . . . spotless . . . a treat to sit on patio and watch the moon come up . . . 'neat' hosts. . . . Romantic . . . room was beautiful . . . food fantastic. . . . Our first B&B experience. Can't wait to go back."*

☞ The Old Mystic Inn

860/572-9422

52 Main Street, P.O. Box 733,
Old Mystic, CT 06372-0733

FAX 860/572-9954
www.visitmystic.com/oldmysticinn/

HOST: Michael Cardillo, Jr.
LOCATION: On a two-lane main street (Route 27) in the village. Five minutes north of Mystic Seaport.
OPEN: Year round. Two-night minimum on weekends.
RATES: May–October $165 weekends, $135 weekdays. November–April $145–$155 weekends, $105–$110 weekdays. $30 rollaway. Amex, MC, Visa.
♥ ♟♦ ⊞ ❖ ⚔ ⚓ ♥♡

PEOPLE AS WELL as the place have made this a landmark. The oft-photographed painted sign recalls the years that the 1784 house was a bookstore. Through the 1990s the innkeepers—one was dubbed the mayor of Old Mystic—added a gazebo, fireplaces, whirlpool tubs, and extensive gardens. Ta-dah! At the turn of the century, Michael—age twenty-nine—fulfilled his dream when he bought the inn. He began his lifelong interest in the culinary arts "as the son of an Italian couple who were always by the stove." A Culinary Institute of America graduate, he also has a degree in hotel/restaurant management as well as experience in catering and as a (loved) private chef. Here in the inn, which is decorated in Colonial colors and with antiques and reproductions, the Connecticut native shares his many talents—and his enthusiasm—with travelers from all over the world.

BED AND BATH: Eight air-conditioned rooms (five with working fireplaces); all queen beds (five are canopied), all private tub/shower baths. In inn—one first-floor room, three (one with porch) on second floor. In carriage house—four ground-floor rooms, two with (single) whirlpool tub and a fireplace.
BREAKFAST: Usually 8:30–9:30. Repertoire includes banana stuffed French toast with warm maple walnut syrup, poached eggs Florentine on polenta diamonds with hollandaise sauce, quiche, waffles, pancakes. Fresh fruit. Homemade muffins, breads, coffee cake. Presented at candlelit tables set for four in bay-windowed dining room with wood-burning fireplace.
PLUS: Fireplaced living room. Afternoon refreshments. Bottomless cookie jar (Old Mystic Inn tradition). Chocolate kisses. Saturday evening wine and cheese—on porch in summer. Bicycles. Train station pickup service.

⋙ Nutmeg Bed & Breakfast Agency Host #211

New Haven, CT

LOCATION: In Oyster Point, a National Historic District. On corner lot in urban neighborhood of Victorian houses. Faces a small park with Civil War memorial and shade trees. Two blocks to waterfront with marina, seafood restaurant, day spa. Five-minute drive to Yale campus. One mile to Long Wharf.

RESERVATIONS: Year round (closed week between Christmas and New Year's) through Nutmeg Bed & Breakfast (page 3), 860/236-6698 or 800/727-7592. E-mail nutmegbnb@home.com. Two-night minimum for Yale graduation and parents' weekends.

RATES: $125; $135 room with fireplace. ⊞ ❖ ⚔ ✑

JOY. SOME LUXURY. And conviviality. Appreciated by corporate as well as academic travelers. It's all here in this redone Queen Anne Victorian. Outside, the house is painted traditional New England creamy yellow-with-white with blue-gray trim. Inside, guest rooms reflect southern France, Italy, and New England—regions that evoke the shore community feel the hosts were seeking when they searched for property. One host worked in public health, the classical music field, and real estate management. He notes that since opening here in 1999, and thanks to the Swan Cove innkeepers (page 20) he has been introduced to a part of town that he missed when he was a Yale psychology student in the 1970s. (Many harbor proposals highlight the Oyster Point area, which is about to focus, once again, on the sea.) The other co-innkeeper, also a native New Yorker, is dovetailing hosting with his Manhattan position as a social securities administrator.

BED AND BATH: Five rooms (some can be combined as suites). Second floor: One room with queen bed, separate study/dressing room, Roman-styled shower with two pairs of body jets plus overhead shower. One with queen bed, two-person Jacuzzi, separate oversized shower stall, small sitting porch. Largest suite has room with queen bed, separate sitting room with sleep sofa, gas fireplace, Jacuzzi tub with shower. Third floor: two queen-bedded rooms share a tub/shower bath, dining room, kitchen.

BREAKFAST: 8–9. Pancakes, omelets, French toast, or feather-bed eggs. Fruit cup, whole-grain cereal with fruit topping, fresh yogurt. Juice and hot beverages.

PLUS: Central air conditioning. Evening sherry. In summer, fresh lemonade and homemade cookies.

*U*NLESS OTHERWISE STATED, *rates in this book are for two and include breakfast in addition to all the amenities in "Plus."*

⤚ Swan Cove Bed & Breakfast Inn

203-776-3240

115 Sea Street,
New Haven, CT 06519

877/499-8165
FAX 203/776-8649
E-MAIL raquel@javanet.com
www.travelassist.com/reg/ct806.html

HOSTS: Raquel and Warren Seacord
LOCATION: On a Long Island Sound cove where swans feed in the wetlands. On a daytime-busy street in a historic district, an oyster-fishing village at the turn of the century. Five-minute drive to Yale University, theaters, museums. Minutes' walk to Long Wharf theater, Chart House restaurant, walk along marina.
OPEN: Year round. Three-night weekend minimum for Yale special events.
RATES: $99 single, $150 double. $185–$285 suite; varies according to season and number of guests. ♥ ❖ ⌀ ⅄ ⚘

PLENTY OF PRIVACY. With a warm welcome. And a convenient location. In an 1890s Queen Anne house that has had the magic touch of the owners. All those bay windows were planned by the host, an architectural and landscape designer who commutes to Manhattan. His wife, a Californian who worked for a Park Avenue interior design firm, furnished eclectically—with drapes and lace and Mediterranean, equestrian, and safari themes. Some Long Wharf actors stay for months. Theatergoers and Yale visitors love this place. Corporate guests come for overnight or for small conferences. Membership clubs send their overflow here. And sometimes there are art receptions in this gracious home.

IN RESIDENCE: One cat, Kismet.
BED AND BATH: Three suites, each with dining area, living room, private bath. Garden level—bedroom with double bed, tile shower, living room with daybed, gas fireplace. First floor—one room with queen bed, ceiling fan, bay window; another with double bed; tub/shower bath; living room with beamed ceiling and wood-burning stove; full kitchen that seats four. Third (treetop) floor—room with two twin beds, another with queen bed, open bar kitchen, TV/living room with window seat overlooking water.
BREAKFAST: Weekdays 8:30, earlier for business guests. Weekends 9:30. Served for up to three people on second floor in French kitchen with window seat, draperies, wood-burning fireplace. Option of eating in your own suite at table set with fruit bowl by hostess. Juice, yogurt, and milk in refrigerator. Coffee all set for pushbutton operation. Basket of scones and muffins brought to each suite in morning.
PLUS: Afternoon tea. Small garden with seating area, maple tree shade.

⤚ Guests wrote: *"So much private space! We loved it. . . . Had planned on going out to dinner, but did take-out so that we could spend more time in those marvelous rooms."*

✍ The Barton House

860/354-3535

34 East Street, New Milford, CT 06776

E-MAIL Barton Hou@aol.com

HOSTS: Ray and Rachel Barton
LOCATION: On 3 acres in a quiet parklike setting on Route 202. One block from village green, shops, restaurants. Ninety minutes from New York City.
OPEN: Year round. Two-night minimum, May–October weekends.
RATES: $95. Third person $18. Amex, MC, Visa. ♥ ☛ ⚥ ⚔

THIS FAMILY HOME, an 1850 Colonial where Ray and the children of Ray and Rachel were raised, became a B&B in 1997. For a sense of history, take a tour and hear about "Miss Barton's School," a well-known private kindergarten run here in the 1940s and '50s by Ray's aunts. Ray's grandfather and his local department store (founded in 1896 and closed in 1990) appear in some of the turn-of-the-century family photographs. Today the old W. G. BARTON & SON sign hangs over the barn door.

Rachel first came to New Milford to audition for a show. That's when she met Ray, who was in the show. "I'll sing if you play the piano or violin," says Rachel. A music major and registered pharmacist, she now dovetails B&B with acting, teaching dramatics to children, and managing her in-town clothing shop. Ray dovetails hosting here with his job as manager of a large New Milford inn.

FOREIGN LANGUAGES SPOKEN: "A little French and Spanish."
BED AND BATH: Two first-floor air-conditioned rooms (on opposite sides of house). One with queen brass bed, private shower bath. Other has two twin four-poster beds, private tub/shower bath.
BREAKFAST: 7:30–10. Blueberry pancakes, Bailey's Irish Cream French toast, pecan waffles, or frittatas. Fresh fruit. Homemade breads. Yogurt. Served on terrace overlooking grounds or with candlelight in large (earlier families were big) dining room.
PLUS: Wood-burning fireplace and upright piano in living room. Front porch rockers. Solar porch. Badminton. Croquet. Hammock between trees by brook. Barton-designed area driving tour. On-site massage arranged.

✍ From New York, Washington, Illinois, Ohio, New Jersey, Connecticut, Maryland, Florida: *"A charming, gorgeous home . . . delightful hosts . . . beautiful, scrupulously clean, comfortable room . . . breakfast was a feast—gourmet style . . . after riding our bikes, enjoyed the stream on the Barton grounds and lunch at a small café in town . . . a refuge from the angst of the day when my son was rushed to New Milford Hospital . . . spent most of the morning in huge backyard . . . good restaurants within walking distance."*

⤙ The Homestead Inn   860/354-4080

5 Elm Street,   FAX 860/354-7046
New Milford, CT 06776   www.HomesteadCt.com

HOSTS: Rolf and Peggy Hammer
LOCATION: In the village center, near village green, shops, restaurants, movie
theater.
OPEN: Year round. Two-night minimum holiday and May–October weekends.
RATES: In the inn, $82–$97 single, $92–$107 double. In Treadwell House, $72–$82
single, $82–$92 double. Amex, Diners, Discover, MC, Visa. ♥ ♦♦ ❖ ⚔ ✄

UNIQUE! THIS INN, discovered by business travelers as well as vacationers, is really two
buildings: an 1850 Victorian, an inn since 1928, and the neighboring Treadwell House, a
former motel with inn decor.

The Hammers, experienced restorers and gardeners, refurbished this property in 1985.
They have decorated with antiques, reproductions, wallpaper, traditional fabrics, and
works by local artists. Rolf was in corporate sales and marketing before becoming an
innkeeper; he is active in state and New England tourism. Peggy, a physical and massage
therapist, collects children's books. Both hosts are experts on hiking trails, scenic drives,
wineries, historic sites—"so much in these beautiful Litchfield Hills!"

IN RESIDENCE: Solitaire, a golden retriever, is not allowed in guest rooms.
BED AND BATH: All private baths; most are tub and shower. Eight inn rooms (one with
tin ceiling, two with bay windows) on two floors. Rooms have one or two double beds, a
queen bed, a queen and one twin, or king/twins option. The six Treadwell House rooms
have queen or two doubles. Rollaway and crib available.
BREAKFAST: Buffet 8–10 weekends; 6:30–9 weekdays. Fresh fruit, juice, English muffins,
cereals, dark bread, coffee cake, yogurts, cheese. In beamed and fireplaced living room.
PLUS: Air conditioners, telephones, TV in bedrooms. Wicker-furnished front porch. Soft
drinks and ice in guest refrigerator.

⤙ From Massachusetts: *"In all our travels, one of the best for cleanliness, atmosphere, and service . . . warm, friendly hosts!"*

C AN'T FIND A LISTING *for the community you are going to? Check
with a reservation service described at the beginning of this chapter.
Through the service you may be placed (matched) with a welcoming B&B that is near
your destination.*

ᔆ Angel Hill Bed and Breakfast

860/542-5920

54 Greenwoods Road East,
P.O. Box 504, Norfolk, CT 06058-0504

www.angelhill.com

HOSTS:	Donna and Del Gritman
LOCATION:	On 8 acres (3 are lawn) with gardens, gazebo, woodlands, brook. In neighborhood of historic homes. Five-minute walk to village green, restaurants, antiques, shops, library, Norfolk Chamber Music Festival.
OPEN:	Year round. Two-night minimum with Saturday stays, three nights on holiday weekends.
RATES:	$150–$190 weekends. Weekly rate for carriage house, $600. Extra person $20. Twenty percent midweek discount for two or more nights. ♥ ⊞❖ ⚉ ⚒

THE GRITMANS' FANS, including many romantics, followed them from The Breezes B&B (now a private home), where they hosted for seven years, to this 1880 Victorian. Angel Hill features a periwinkle front door, English country interior ambiance, and a carriage house. There are traditional furnishings, heirlooms, a collection of auction treasures, and works by local artisans. Yards and yards of fabrics have been sewn by Donna into window, bed, and table treatments. Rooms have robes, candles, glasses and wine buckets, stereo/tape players—and lots of touches that allow Donna to use her experience as a floral and interior designer. Del, an experienced painter and paperhanger, is about to retire from the U.S. Postal Service.

BED AND BATH: Two rooms, two suites, and one carriage house. All private tub/shower baths. First floor—two large rooms, each with individual thermostat, canopied queen bed, and fireplace. Second floor—suite with canopied queen bed, sitting room, large bath with double whirlpool; air-conditioned suite with king/twin option, seven windows, reading/dressing room, whirlpool tub. Queen canopied bed in air-conditioned second-floor treetop apartment in very private carriage house.

BREAKFAST: Usually 9–10:30. Juice. Fresh fruit with edible flowers and herbs. Homemade lemon or strawberry bread or muffins, or scones. Heart-shaped oven-baked French toast, eggs Benedict, crepe puff with fresh fruit, or vegetable frittatas. Fruit/yogurt parfaits. In dining room or large enclosed sunporch, or in suites or rooms.

PLUS: Fireplaced living room. Second-floor library. Some VCRs and "hidden TVs." Guests' refrigerator and butler's pantry. Tea, coffee, snacks. Croquet. Picnic baskets to borrow. Arrangements made for carriage rides, canoe use, massage therapy, gift baskets, flowers.

ᔆ From Canada: *"Wonderful . . . surprises in every corner of this charming B&B."*

➷ Manor House

69 Maple Avenue,
Norfolk, CT 06058-0447

860/542-5690

FAX 860/542-5690
E-MAIL tremblay@esslink.com
www.manorhouse-norfolk.com

HOSTS: Diane and Hank Tremblay
LOCATION: On 5 beautifully landscaped acres, within walking distance of quiet village, historical society, antiquing, Yale chamber music concerts. On a side street off Route 44. Twenty miles to Tanglewood. Two and a half hours from Boston and New York.
OPEN: Year round. Two-day weekend minimum, three days on holiday weekends.
RATES: $95–$225. $135–$195 with balcony. $135–$185 two-room suite. $150–$185 with two-person soaking tub. $150–$225 with Jacuzzi. $150–$225 with fireplace. $20 additional person. Less in March, April, and midweek. Amex, MC, Visa. ♥ ⊞❖ ⚗ ⚖ ❤○

QUITE GRAND, according to *Gourmet* magazine. A perfect getaway, according to romantics. And great for business meetings too. With hosts who know how to "spoil their guests with unflappable affability" (*Philadelphia Inquirer*). Their very large antiques-furnished English Tudor, built in 1898 by Charles Spofford, designer of London's underground system, has the original cherry paneling, Tiffany stained glass windows—and, for one room, a private elevator. In another baronial-sized guest room there's a king-sized lace-canopied bed, a sitting area, a working fireplace, and a balcony. Manor House may be the only B&B in the world that offers free accommodations with the purchase of a harpsichord (from nearby builder's studio).

Beekeeper/gardener/chef Hank is also known for great cooking demonstrations in Bloomingdale's and Macy's, where thousands of copies of his orange waffle recipe have been distributed. Until 1985 both hosts were executives with a large Connecticut-based insurance company. Their commitment to personalized quality B&Bs (see "Plus" below) carries over to their reservation service (page 2) for other B&Bs in the area.

IN RESIDENCE: "Mineau is our friendly and affectionate cat."
FOREIGN LANGUAGE SPOKEN: French.
BED AND BATH: Nine rooms—four with fireplace—on second and third floors. Some with private balcony. All with private bath; most have shower without tub; one has two-person soaking tub; two have two-person Jacuzzi. King, queen, double, or two twin beds; some rooms with daybed too.
BREAKFAST: Usually 8:30–10. Blueberry pancakes, those almost-famous orange waffles, stuffed French toast, or poached eggs with lemon chive sauce. Homemade muffins and Hank's yeast breads; Tremblays' honey; local maple syrup; homegrown vegetables, herbs, and berries; special teas and coffee brewed with spring water. Special diets accommodated. Served in dining room, on porch—or in bed!

PLUS: Massage appointments made (here or there) with neighboring licensed therapist. Bedroom ceiling fans. Enormous fireplace with grand piano, 78-rpm record collection, and CDs (most were produced by Grammy award–winning guest). Library. Flannel sheets. Down comforters. Huge bath towels. Garden flowers. Guest refrigerator. Town lake passes. Christmas sleigh rides. Horse-drawn historic tours.

› From Connecticut: *"Five stars! . . . simply sublime . . . a retreat from hustle and bustle of daily living. . . . Romantic decor . . . fantastic hosts . . . great breakfasts. . . . Perfect."*

› Antiques & Accommodations

860/535-1736

32 Main Street,   800/554-7829
North Stonington, CT 06359   FAX 860/535-2613
                                     www.visitmystic.com/antiques

HOSTS: Ann and Tom Gray
LOCATION: In a village center with eighteenth- and nineteenth-century homes and a meandering stream (where children fish). Fifteen minutes to Mystic, Stonington, and Watch Hill (Rhode Island) beaches. Five miles to casino.
OPEN: Year round. Two-night minimum on May–December weekends.
RATES: Victorian midweek $99, $129, $149 with fireplace; weekends $169, $189, $199 fireplace. Cottage midweek $129–$169; weekends $169–$199. Suite midweek $149–$229; weekend $229 one couple, $269 two couples. Package rates for wine-tasting or festival weekends. ♥ ⊞ ❖ ⚔ ✸

"THIS DINING ROOM is even more beautiful than it looked in the *Country Inns* cover feature," said the stockbroker who immediately scheduled two seminars here. (Three days after those pictures were taken for a spring feature, *Woman's Day* arrived for a Christmas photography session!) It's an 1861 Victorian filled—from thirty trips to England—with eighteenth- and nineteenth-century antiques, including furniture, sterling silver accessories, Oriental rugs, and lamps—some for sale. The Grays opened the B&B in 1988, just about the time Tom had considered attending culinary school; later they made the neighboring 1820 center chimney Colonial their "garden cottage" with beautifully stenciled furnishings and floor-length curtains. (Ann says, "At the Waverly fabric store, they know my telephone voice.") Separating the two houses are brick-lined gravel paths and mature English gardens with flowers including edible varieties. Contented (and pampered) guests include international travelers, honeymooners, and families who appreciate the cottage accommodations.

IN RESIDENCE: Martha, an outdoor cat. Britt, a black Labrador.
FOREIGN LANGUAGE SPOKEN: Elementary German.
BED AND BATH: Five rooms and one suite. In Victorian, private baths (one full, one shower only) for two air-conditioned second-floor rooms, each with a canopied double

continued . . .

bed. First-floor room has queen four-poster, working fireplace, private en-suite full bath. Cottage accommodations on ground level—two queen-bedded rooms, each with large full bath, share a fireplaced keeping room/library. Three-bedroom suite with kitchen, living room, full bath, covered patio.

BREAKFAST: 8:30–9:30. Full. Ever-changing menu. Eggs fresh from the chickens next door. Fresh fruits; in season, berries picked that very morning. Quiches, omelets, French toast with pecans—often garnished with pansies. Juice. Homemade muffins and jams. By candlelight. With classical music. Special diets accommodated with day-before notice.

PLUS: Complimentary sherry. Plant-filled porch. Courier service for touring shops. Fresh flowers (wild ones in season); often, cuttings shared. In cottage, crib, high chairs, toys. Sometimes, babysitting.

⟿ Guests wrote: *"Savored every moment and antique. . . . A memorable fortieth anniversary. . . . A wonderful first anniversary. . . . Beautiful things to look at everywhere. . . . Divine breakfast."*

⟿ High Acres Bed and Breakfast   860/887-4355

222 Northwest Corner Road,   **E-MAIL** Hacre@aol.com
North Stonington, CT 06359

HOSTS:	Peter and Liz Agnew
LOCATION:	High on a quiet country road. Panoramic views "with mountains 30 miles distant." Ten miles to Mystic Seaport and Aquarium, 6 to Foxwoods Resort Casino.
OPEN:	Year round. Two-night weekend minimum, May–October.
RATES:	Weekends mid-April–Thanksgiving $125–$160, fourth night free. Weekdays and Thanksgiving–mid-April $100–$125, third night free. (Trail rides, $30 per person.) MC, Visa. ♥ ⁂⁂⁂

BE FOREWARNED: You may come with an agenda and be lulled into just enjoying this 150-acre country estate, the library fireplace, the 40-foot-long porch with hammock and ceiling fans, the meadows and trails, and the 10,000-Christmas-tree plantation. Some guests sleep later than they planned or even take a midday nap. The decor in this lovely 1740 Colonial with 1840 and 1940 add-ons is enhanced by family heirlooms and comfortable pieces. Peter, "an ardent sailor and devoted skier," was a schoolteacher in New York and Colorado. Here he has cleared miles of walking and riding trails. Liz breeds and boards horses. The Agnews will gladly tour you through their six-stall barn; and, if you'd like, they'll lead you on leisurely horseback rides right here.

IN RESIDENCE: Two Jack Russells who accompany guests on walks. "Maggie is a ball chaser extraordinaire. Petey is in perpetual motion."

BED AND BATH: Four air-conditioned rooms; all with cross-ventilation, feather beds, private en-suite tub/shower baths. First floor—king bed. Second floor—two queen-bedded rooms and a two-bedroom suite with queen beds, shared bath.

BREAKFAST: 8:30–9:30. A variety of pancakes with Vermont maple syrup or waffles made with whipped egg whites. Ham. Scones, fresh fruit, gourmet coffee, juice. In fireplaced dining room. Very leisurely.

PLUS: TV in living room. Tea anytime. Fresh flowers. "Loaner" maps. Fine dining suggestions.

⚞ The Deacon Timothy Pratt House

860/395-1229

325 Main Street, Old Saybrook, CT 06475

FAX 860/395-4748

E-MAIL shelley.nobile@snet.net

www.topwebsite.com/pratthouse

HOST: Shelley Nobile

LOCATION: In historic district on wide gaslit main street. Next door to old-fashioned ice cream parlor/art gallery. Across from old house museum and pillared white church. Minutes' walk to shops, restaurants, coffeehouses with entertainment. One mile to two beaches on Long Island Sound and to Fort Saybrook Monument Park (both along marvelous bicycle route). One mile to Amtrak station. Ten minutes to outlet stores, Essex steam train and riverboat. Near lighthouses, playhouses, wineries, and antiquing; half hour to Mystic and casinos.

OPEN: Year round. Two-night minimum, weekends; three on holidays.

RATES: $100–$150 weekdays, $150–$190 weekends. Suite $125–$200. Discount for four nights or more. Third person $20. Singles $10 less.

♥ 👫 💺 ⊞❖ ⚔ ⚒ ❥

PASSION! Shelley has it—for old houses, architecture, period furnishings, decorative arts, gardening, history, perfection, sunsets, and entertaining (and horseback riding and ice skating too). From 1994 to 1999, with the help of family and friends, she restored this 1746 center chimney Colonial. Now it has refinished wide-board floors, wainscoting, a corner cupboard, a beehive oven, hand-hewn beams, and six working fireplaces. The dream fulfilled includes "the set stage" with stenciling, classic wallcoverings, and lovely antiques as well as a strong sense of history about the house and area. On the grounds there's a handsome century-old maple tree, swing, hammock, patio, and gardens. Shelley, an area native, was an electrical engineer for the navy for eight years before becoming a full-time innkeeper.

FOREIGN LANGUAGE SPOKEN: "A little Spanish."

BED AND BATH: Three air-conditioned corner rooms with private baths (one with whirlpool tub/shower, two shower only), phone/modem lines, and cable TV. First-floor room has queen bed, wood-burning fireplace, sitting area, library. On second floor, two-room suite with queen four-poster, wood-burning fireplace, French doors to sitting room with single daybed. Room with canopied queen bed, wood-burning fireplace, and whirlpool tub.

continued . . .

BREAKFAST: One sitting, between 8 and 10, at time chosen/agreed upon by guests. Heart-shaped blueberry or chocolate chip pancakes, Belgian waffles, thick French toast or eggs Benedict. Fresh fruit. Muffins or breads.

PLUS: Wood-burning fireplace in living and dining rooms. Beverages. Snacks. Guest refrigerator. A before-and-after album. Transportation provided to/from bus station or Amtrak train station. Discount coupons for some local restaurants. Massage therapy arranged on premises—by your fire, if you'd like.

⤳ Guests wrote: *"Lovingly restored . . . immaculate . . . charming, attentive innkeeper . . . knowledgeable about area. . . . I grew up in that house. Very impressed. . . . Room was elegant. . . . Peaceful environment. . . . Full house and we never heard anyone else. . . . Fresh flowers. . . . Was on a business trip. My first B&B. Have now recommended it to many others."*

⤳ *Nutmeg Bed & Breakfast Agency Host #407*

Plymouth, CT

LOCATION: On 3 acres of grounds with perennial gardens and fountain. Near hiking, antiquing, fine restaurants. Five minutes to Thomaston Opera House and railroad museum (and rides). Ten minutes from I-84; 25 miles southwest of Hartford; 12 miles south of Litchfield and White Flower Farm.

RESERVATIONS: Year round through Nutmeg Bed & Breakfast (page 3), 860/236-6698 or 800/727-7592. E-mail nutmegbnb@home.com

RATES: Private bath $90. Shared bath $80, queen bed; $70 twins or double bed. $10 one-night weekend surcharge, July–October. ⊞ ❖ ⚔ ⚐

OLD-HOUSE LOVERS appreciate this imposing 1825 Greek Revival house with its columns and balcony in front, wainscoting in the dining room, refinished wide chestnut board floors, and antique and reproduction furnishings. And they love the hosts, who love the area. In 1994, after looking all over the Northeast, the hosts, a utility company safety director and a legal assistant who were living a half hour away, saw a FOR SALE sign.

Now the house, owned by a famous carriage maker in the 1800s, is in a National Historic District, part of a village that has two town greens. In 1995 this B&B was on the town's Bicentennial House and Garden Tour.

BED AND BATH: Four second-floor rooms share two baths (private bath arranged for most dates). Queen (with air conditioner), double, or twin beds.

BREAKFAST: French toast, omelets, or Finnish pancakes. Juice, fresh fruit, homemade muffins, cereals. Host is primary chef. Hostess is the baker. Served in large dining room.

PLUS: Fireplaced guest parlor with cable TV, guests' refrigerator.

⁂ *Chickadee Cottage Bed & Breakfast*   860/963-0587

70 Averill Road,   FAX 860/963-0594
Pomfret, CT 06259   E-MAIL sspackman@compsol.net
           www.webtravels.com/chickadeecottage

HOSTS: Tom and Sandy Spackman

LOCATION: Peaceful. On 4 rural acres, bordered by Audubon nature preserve (hiking trail along former railroad bed) on one side, open space on other. Within ten minutes of winery, fine dining, country stores, Putnam's antiques shops, National Scenic Byway.

OPEN: Year round. Two-night minimum in October.

RATES: $95/night. $10 third person. Cottage $125; weekly and monthly rates available. Valentine's and other package rates. Amex, MC, Visa. ♥ ❖ ⚲ ⚴ 🏃

PERHAPS YOU'VE seen Chickadee Cottage getaway features in the *New York Times,* the *Boston Globe,* or the *Hartford Courant*—or on TV. In 1999 Sandy and Tom moved here and brought their B&B name 2 miles down the road to this updated 1940s Cape-style house—with private cottage—which they bought from a couple who had booked their wedding guests with the Spackmans! This B&B is furnished with traditional pieces, family antiques, and an art collection primarily from Chester County, Pennsylvania (where Tom has a real estate business). It was Sandy's former corporate marketing and PR position that brought the Spackmans to Connecticut. Now she dovetails consultant work with innkeeping.

IN RESIDENCE: "Katy and Lucy, two lovable, declawed indoor cats."

FOREIGN LANGUAGE SPOKEN: Some French.

BED AND BATH: Two rooms with private baths. Private cottage has very large second-floor air-conditioned room with double four-poster canopied bed, single sleep sofa, ceiling fan, sitting area, gas fireplace, dining area, full kitchen, shower bath, deck overlooking woods. In centrally air-conditioned main house, second-floor low-ceilinged room has queen bed, private hall tub/shower bath.

BREAKFAST: 9 on weekends, earlier as needed on weekdays. Fresh fruit, yogurt, granola, homemade muffins, and coffee cake. Freshly brewed teas, coffee with chickory, juices. Served in dining room with linens, crystal, silver flatware; cottage guests have option of breakfast on private deck.

PLUS: TV in living room and guest rooms. April open house.

     ⁂ From Connecticut, New York, Massachusetts: *"Visited many B&Bs. Chickadee Cottage stands out. . . . Beautifully decorated. . . . Charming and helpful hostess. . . . Very private. . . . Wonderful place. . . . Wish we could have stayed . . . . Very relaxing."*

ᔛ *Clark Cottage at Wintergreen* 860/928-5741

354 Pomfret Street,
Pomfret Center, CT 06259

FAX 860/963-2611
E-MAIL gurg@neca.com

HOSTS: Doris and Stan Geary
LOCATION: Quiet. On parklike grounds in this semirural New England town. Set way
back from Routes 44 and 169. Next to Pomfret School; a half mile south of
Rectory School; 1½ miles to Hyde School; 3 miles to The Learning Center.
Thirty minutes to Sturbridge Village, Worcester, Providence; forty-five to
Hartford, New London, and Mystic Seaport. Two minutes to The Harvest,
"great restaurant"; six minutes to Golden Lamb Restaurant; necessary ad-
vance reservations (months, sometimes) made by Gearys.
OPEN: Year round.
RATES: Private bath $80, with fireplace $90. Shared bath $65. MC, Visa.
ᔛ⬛⊞❖🙌🍴🧑

ᔛ Guests wrote: *"I would go out of my way to stay in this place . . . very private
setting . . . wonderful breakfasts . . . lovingly restored . . . immaculately maintained . . . ami-
cable hosts . . . good directions to Brimfield . . . wonderful porch greetings . . . evening chats
around the kitchen table . . . difficult goodbyes!"*

FOUR ACRES of rolling lawns and extensive oft-photographed gardens surround the
eighteen-room house, once part of the 1,000-acre Clark estate. The 1885 Victorian has six
fireplaces and five porches. Furnishings include eighteenth- and early nineteenth-century
antiques. Although many guests come for the area private schools, the Gearys introduce
other travelers, including antiques dealers and those looking for a getaway, to an unspoiled area—a place with marvelous old homes, lots of open space, and wonderful valley
views. Stan, an Oyster Bay, Long Island, native and sailor (now a financial consultant),
had an earlier business career in New York before he and Doris, grandparents of eight,
moved here in 1984.

BED AND BATH: Four large second-floor rooms; private phone in all, three with TV. One
with Italian antique queen bed, working fireplace, private adjoining shower bath. One
with queen bed, private shower bath can be a suite with adjoining room that has two
twin beds. When booked alone, that twin-bedded room shares a tub/shower hall bath
with another room that has two twin beds and a working fireplace.
BREAKFAST: Upon request. Fresh fruit, freshly baked bread or muffins. Pancakes, stuffed
French toast, omelets, or bacon and eggs. In breakfast room or dining room.
PLUS: Three bedrooms are air conditioned. Ceiling fan in some. Beverages. Down comforters. Flannel sheets. Robes. Fresh fruit. Garden flowers. Adirondack chairs. Spectacular
sunsets.

⋙ *Nutmeg Bed & Breakfast Agency Host #413*

Putnam, CT

LOCATION: Quiet country road. On 5 acres; large lawn and big old maple trees in front. Across from church (lighted steeple at night) with fields in back. Four-mile drive to Putnam's antiques shops (450 dealers); close to area private schools, restaurants. About forty-five minutes to Sturbridge Village or Caprilands.

RESERVATIONS: Year round through Nutmeg Bed & Breakfast (page 3), 860/236-6698 or 800/727-7592. E-mail nutmegbnb@home.com.

RATES: $95 queen with private bath; $120 as suite. $85 double with private bath; $100 as suite. 田 ❖ ⚔ ⚔

"OUR GUESTS come for peace and quiet—and find it! In addition to getaway guests, we meet many who visit the private schools in the area. And yes, they ask how we started doing B&B. When we lived in Massachusetts, I was a teacher. We lived in several houses that my husband, now a retired building contractor, and I remodeled and redecorated. We had been looking for a place with horses when, in 1997, we bought this too-big-for-the-two-of-us fourteen-room 1850s Greek Revival." It has numerous porches. The first floor has refinished floors with area rugs. Traditional furnishings are throughout.

BED AND BATH: Two second-floor carpeted suites, each with shower bath, porch, view of fields and woods. One with queen bed in one room, two twin beds in other, adjoining sitting room. Other has double bed, connecting hall to room with twin bed.

BREAKFAST: Juice, fruit, cereals, coffee cake, cinnamon rolls, hot beverages.

⋙ *Thurber House* 860/928-6776

78 Liberty Way, Putnam, CT 06260-3113

HOSTS: Betty and George Zimmermann

LOCATION: Rural and quiet. On a hill overlooking the village common and white-spired church. Good cycling and hiking area. Within ten minutes of Putnam antique shops and Pomfret; thirty minutes to Worcester, forty-five to Sturbridge.

OPEN: Year round.

RATES: $70 per room. ♥ ⅙⅙ ■ ⚔ ⚔

SOME EXTRAORDINARY sunsets are enjoyed from the back porch of this handsome Federal Colonial house but the Zimmermanns haven't forgotten the guests who tarried so long watching the celestial fireworks that they were late for the wedding that brought them to town. Many other guests come for area private schools, or to enjoy the countryside, Sturbridge Village, and antiquing.

continued . . .

Originally a summer house built in the early 1800s for artist T. J. Thurber's family, this became a year-round residence around 1870. In 1967 the hosts bought the house—in need of complete restoration. Throughout there are fine antiques, Oriental rugs, drapes and swags on the windows, and many Thurber paintings. And then there's that porch, the one that overlooks gardens, long vistas, and many a long-remembered sunset.

IN RESIDENCE: Elsie, the cat.
BED AND BATH: Two second-floor rooms with working fireplaces. Larger room with double antique spool bed. One room with double four-poster. Baths are private or, sometimes, shared.
BREAKFAST: 7–9. Fresh fruit, juice, "and a hearty main dish and home-baked goods." In semiformal dining room; sometimes on porch.
PLUS: Piano. Bicycles for guests' use. Window fans. Usually, tea and evening snacks.

‭ From Kentucky: *"I have stayed in many B&Bs, visited others, and even worked for a time in one, and can honestly say that I enjoyed the tranquil country setting and Zimmermann hospitality . . . big dining room . . . lovely china . . . terraced backyard . . . as much as any I've known."* From New Jersey: *"Great attention to every immaculate detail. . . . Picture-perfect gardens."* From New York: *"Charming . . . beautifully furnished with antiques . . . comfortable . . . unusually fine breakfast."* From Canada: *"The Zimmermanns are our cup of tea!"*

‭ *The Earl Grey Bed and Breakfast*   860/435-1007

Chittenden House, P.O. Box 177,   FAX 860/435-1007*51
Salisbury, CT 06068-0177   E-MAIL rboyle@discovernet.net

HOSTS: Richard and Patricia Boyle
LOCATION: On a quiet, private hill (with barn) in and overlooking Salisbury village center. Minutes to Hotchkiss School. Three-minute drive to lake. Ten minutes to Norfolk (Yale's summer Music Festival); forty to Jacob's Pillow and Tanglewood. Near theater, museums, antiquing.
OPEN: Year round. Usually, two-night weekend minimum June–October.
RATES: $135–$160. ♥ ✗ ✂

THE BOYLES WERE worth waiting for. They were my memorable hosts in a Philadelphia townhouse when I gave a B&B presentation at a National Trust for Historic Preservation conference. They subsequently sold the Philadelphia property; spent two years in Tokyo (where Richard was professor of art history at Temple University's Japan campus); and then, in 1995, revitalized this 1850s Italianate house. Everywhere there are fascinating collections—books, art, and antiques ranging from eighteenth-century to Art Deco to contemporary. Currently Richard is working on a guidebook to Tokyo museums as well as a guide to American art in United States museums. Patricia, who has done all the interior design (lots of ideas to inspire guests) and planned the gardens, presents breakfasts to delighted travelers—including several romantics who have proposed here.

IN RESIDENCE: "One elegant, friendly cat named 'Earl Grey II.'"
FOREIGN LANGUAGES SPOKEN: "French, German, some Dutch, a little Japanese."
BED AND BATH: Two large rooms. First floor—antique canopied queen bed, woodburning fireplace, tub/shower bath, French doors to private terrace and garden entrance. Second-floor room has an 1850 queen sleigh bed, tub/shower bath.
BREAKFAST: Flexible hours. "Intentionally sensational" menus, often garnished with edible flowers, include French toast with slivered almonds and apricot sauce or apple pancakes. Fresh fruit, homemade muffins and breads. Served on 6-foot-long antique marble table in fireplaced dining room, or on porch.
PLUS: Afternoon beverages. Turndown service. Fresh fruit and flowers. Robes. No TV.

⪼ *Storrs Farmhouse*   860/429-1400

418 Gurleyville Road, Storrs, CT 06268

HOST: Elaine Kollet
LOCATION: Rural. Five minutes to University of Connecticut campus, 7 miles to Caprilands Herb Farm, 20 to Sturbridge Village. Five-minute walk to antiques shop or to Fenton River for fishing (stocked trout) and hiking trail along river. Half hour to Hartford, casinos, or Logee's Greenhouse (rare plants). Ninety minutes to Boston; three hours to New York City or Maine.
OPEN: Year round. Advance reservations required.
RATES: $45 single. $65 double. $15 rollaway. ♛ ⊘ ⤚

GUESTS SPEAK OF "warmth and care in this 'real' English-style B&B," a center chimney Cape farmhouse that Elaine and her husband built in the 1970s. (As a youngster Elaine learned from her father about carpentry, bricklaying, and tiling.) Furnishings include antiques, a grandmother clock, and Oriental rugs. One room has huge tropical plants hanging from a half-glassed roof and many windows that look out onto pastures and flower gardens—and, in the spring, bluebirds.

IN RESIDENCE: Benjamin, a golden retriever "loved by all." Chickens.
BED AND BATH: Four large air-conditioned rooms. All private en-suite shower baths; one has tub also. First floor—one room with queen bed, one with double. Second floor—one double bed. Very large room has queen and a twin bed, refrigerator, microwave.
BREAKFAST: 7–9. Homemade muffins, popovers, or sweet breads. Fresh eggs in made-from-scratch waffles, French toast, or pancakes. Fresh fruit. Juice and hot beverages. High chair available.
PLUS: Refrigerators and microwave for guests' use. Wool mattress pads. Exercise equipment in greenhouse.

᪥ *Captain Parker's Inn*   860/935-5219

32 Walker Road, Quinebaug, CT 06262-0183   800/707-7303

HOSTS: David and Bozena Parker

LOCATION: Quiet rural neighborhood of older homes. On 1.5 acres, surrounded by lawn. Three houses off Route 197. Twenty minutes to Old Sturbridge Village. Ten minutes to antiques shops in Putnam; 8 miles to Bigelow Hollow State Park ("crystal clear water for swimming"); 6 miles to Thompson Dam, "huge and gorgeous, without a house in sight." Near restaurant in 1700s building.

OPEN: Year round. Two-night minimum on weekends.

RATES: Weekends $85; $95 larger rooms. Midweek $65 one night, $125 two nights, $175 three nights, $210 four nights. Packages include Old Sturbridge Village admission, theater tickets, horseback riding, midweek golf. ♥ ☞ ⚹ ⑂

᪥ From Virginia: *"We were thrilled to get off the highway and meander through Connecticut to this pleasant surprise . . . spacious rooms, large luxury private baths, and QUIET! . . . Spotless. . . . Floors are especially beautiful. . . . Room had a lovely stained glass window overlooking a quiet street. . . . Delicious breakfast with generous portions. . . . We are world travelers who seldom rave about 'finds.'"* From England: *"Helpful, kind, and informative."* From Pennsylvania: *"A lot of conversation and laughing at breakfast. . . . really impressed with the house."*

"IN THE 1980s I restored houses and sold them. Then I ran a charter business in Newport, Rhode Island, and I met many B&B owners whose guests were passengers on my sunset sails. At one B&B holiday party I met Bozena—from Poland—who was traveling with relatives. When I bought this Connecticut property, I intended to replace the roof (only). After taking most of the house down, I spent about six years rebuilding. I designed it to be a B&B and used different woods—ash, cherry, birch, maple, red and white oak—in each room. *[To maintain the floors, no shoes are worn in the house.]* The entire first floor is common area. A woodstove is in the library. The entertainment room has stereo, TV/VCR, and 180 movies. A grand piano is in the foyer. The outdoor hot tub is in, and we have a big deck. Now I am a courier who has a renewed appreciation of this trafficless, gorgeous area. Bozena operates a beauty salon/spa (massage, waxing, pedicures, manicures, facials) in one room of the house. I am known for being 'brutally honest,' known for telling people what I think! . . . It is heavenly living around here."

FOREIGN LANGUAGE SPOKEN: Polish.

BED AND BATH: Six rooms (some with fireplace) on second and third floors. All private baths: some tub/shower, others shower only, one with tub—and fireplace—in bedroom. Beds are king, extra-long twins, or queen.

BREAKFAST: Usually 8–10. Cheese blintzes, spinach quiche, potato or banana walnut pancakes, apple/blue cheese omelets. Homemade hash, "real" kielbasa, ham, boneless pork and cumin on the grill. Fresh fruit. Tea and flavored coffees.

PLUS: Screened porch. Picnic baskets, $20; no additional charge for three-day stay. Bicycles and maps for those quiet and oh-so-beautiful roads.

🐦 *The Tolland Inn*   860/872-0800

P.O. Box 717,   FAX 860/870-7958
63 Tolland Green,   E-MAIL tollinn@ntplx.net
Tolland, CT 06084-0717   www.tollandinn.com

HOSTS: Susan and Stephen Beeching
LOCATION: In historic district, facing the village green. Steps from country store and genealogical library. Three minutes from I-84. Seven miles to University of Connecticut, 20 to Hartford and Old Sturbridge Village, 6 to Caprilands Herb Farm.
OPEN: Year round. Two-day minimum on May and October weekends.
RATES: Double bed $80 or $85. King/twins $90. Canopied queen $95; with fireplace and sitting area $120, with spa and fireplace $140; with hot tub, sitting area, fridge, and microwave $140. Amex, Diners, Discover, MC, Visa.
❖ 🐾 ⊱

"I WAS TOTALLY enchanted," wrote one guest after visiting with the Beechings. (I was too.) Beyond rave reviews for the hospitality and food, everyone comments on Steve's craftsmanship and ingenuity. In addition to making marvelous one-of-kind fine furnishings, he has made the most creative use of limited space. The enlarged sunporch has hand-planed raised panels, a coffered ceiling, a (new) Rumford fireplace, and Steve's pierced tin sconces. There are nooks and crannies with interesting collections and/or a window seat. The Nantucket Suite, which has art of and by islanders from Susan's hometown, features a mahogany canopied bed and wall-mounted end tables that could be another Beeching signature item.

Susan, who teaches second grade, is a third-generation innkeeper. In 1985, she and Stephen bought the white-clapboarded former inn (1880s until 1959), which had become a private home, and began creating their much-appreciated peaceful ambiance.

BED AND BATH: Seven air-conditioned rooms on first and second floors; all have private baths and phones. Features vary and include private exterior entrance and strobe fire alarm for hearing impaired; canopied queen beds; working fireplace; sunken hot tub with view of lawn. Two two-room suites; one with hot tub in a very lovely and interesting room built with interior windowed wall, shower bath; the other with antique tub and shower stall. Upstairs, low-ceilinged rooms with chestnut beams. Two double-bedded rooms; one with full hall bath, one with en-suite shower bath. King/twins option, en-suite shower bath. Tall handmade double bed, en-suite shower bath.
BREAKFAST: 8–9:30. Juices, fresh fruit or baked apples. Belgian waffles, cinnamon/raisin French toast, or feather-bed eggs. Muffins, coffee cakes, cobblers, breads. Their own

continued . . .

granola and flavored butters. At trestle dining room table or on wicker-furnished sun-porch.

PLUS: Wraparound porch overlooking rear garden. Books everywhere "for readers of any sort." Beverages. Classical music. And a look at Steve's shop with projects in progress.

🏃 *House on the Hill*   203/757-9901

92 Woodlawn Terrace,   EMAIL wrcvb@aol.com
Waterbury, CT 06710-1929   www.travelhero.com/prophome.cfm?id=5275

HOST: Marianne Vandenburgh
LOCATION: High on a hill in historic residential district. One mile from I-84 and Route 8. Within ten minutes' drive of University of Connecticut branch; Teikyo Post University; Westover and Taft Schools; Cheshire Academy; minor-league baseball; old-fashioned duck-pin bowling. Twenty miles to Litchfield; 90 from New York airports.
OPEN: January 15–December 15; two-night minimum on weekends.
RATES: $130–$160. By arrangement only, romantic dinner ($150 for two) with custom-designed menu presented by fire or on a silver tray in your room. Weekend cooking classes, symphony and theater packages.
♥ ▣ ⊞ ❖ ⅍ 𐐘 ❤❍

A READY-MADE SET for the White Flower Farm Christmas Catalog, for *Victoria* and *Fine Gardening* magazines, and for a New Zealand *House and Garden* feature. Painted in six colors (the neighbors sent thank-you notes), the twenty-room Victorian *rus in urbe* ("our Latin motto: country in the city") place is surrounded by glorious perennial gardens. Arched wraparound porches lead to an eclectically furnished interior where there's original mahogany, cherry, and oak woodwork, recently restored brass chandeliers, and a re-done kitchen with a twenty-one-drawer mahogany chest from a 1920s department store.

This award-winning B&B, built in 1888 by a brass manufacturer and inventor, is today the creation of Marianne, a Renaissance woman—a home economist/former SoHo antiques shop owner and elderly services administrator turned house restorer/freelance decorator/garden designer/community activist/wedding coordinator/Bloomingdale's guest chef/caterer extraordinaire. She travels to New York City for culinary classes—and to England for tea and family visits (with grandchildren).

BED AND BATH: Four suites, three with ceiling fan; all with phone, cable TV, Russell Hobbs (English) kettle. One with canopied double bed, en-suite tub/shower bath with option of second room that has brass-and-iron double bed. One room with queen bed, sitting area, private porch, hall bath with tub. Turret has queen bed, pocket doors leading to sitting room, and a twin bed "in wall." Third floor—air-conditioned room with double bed, en-suite tub/shower bath, complete kitchen.
BREAKFAST: Flexible timing. Pancakes (made with cornmeal ground by hand by

Marianne's family on their Ohio farm) or thick fresh lemon French toast, smoked sausages, homemade "four-berry/barb" (rhubarb) sauce, orange juice, coffee (freshly ground beans from Zabar's) or "properly made tea." Served in fireplaced dining room. PLUS: Welcoming refreshments. In-room coffee, tea, hot chocolate; corkscrews and wine glasses. Turndown service. Weddings (catered by Marianne), small corporate seminars, and Victorian-style teas. Inquire about weekend cooking classes, winter concerts, and special symphony and theater weekends.

⋙ From Florida (symphony artistic director): *"The combination of a beautifully restored Queen Anne–style mansion, wonderfully landscaped grounds, delicious food, and a warm and friendly atmosphere is a real winner."* From Connecticut (bank officer): *"Best-kept secret in Waterbury . . . [with] Marianne's hospitality . . . a perfect informal setting for informational meetings."*

⋙ Charles R. Hart House

860/688-5555

1046 Windsor Avenue,
Windsor, CT 06095-3460

FAX 860/687-1992
E-MAIL harthous@ntplx.net
www.ntplx.net/~harthous

HOSTS: Dorothy and Bob McAllister
LOCATION: Residential area of main street. Eight miles southeast of Bradley International Airport; 6 miles north of Hartford; 1.5 miles from Amtrak station; 1 mile to Loomis Chaffee School.
OPEN: Year round. Two-night minimum on holiday and special weekends.
RATES: $90. Singles $70. ♥ ☕ ⊞ 𝕩 ✄

FEATURED IN *America's Painted Ladies,* this turreted Queen Anne house is painted in shades of blue and tan and furnished with many Victorian antiques. Original (1890) hall wallpaper, and reproduction patterns on the ceiling too. There's a collection of clocks, a disc music box, a hammock on the lawn, rocking chairs and wicker on the porch. The showstopper gardens—with perennials, fruits, and vegetables—are tended by Dorothy, a former registered nurse, and Bob, a municipal bond salesman. For about twenty years, while they lived around the corner, they admired this house, the turn-of-the-century country home of Charles Hart, a Hartford merchant of floor and wallcoverings. Shortly after the McAllisters bought it, already restored, in 1991, they hosted a groom who arranged for a photographer to be present while the bride was carried over the threshold. Now, many couples arrange for wedding photography shoots here. And there's a warm story to be told about the winter junk-art sculpture on the front lawn.

BED AND BATH: Four air-conditioned rooms, all private shower baths. Second-floor rooms have queen bed, extra-long double bed with wood-burning fireplace, or two twin beds. Turret (third-floor) room has twin beds.

continued . . .

BREAKFAST: 7–9. Baked apple with raisins and walnuts topped with heavy cream, Swiss-style shirred eggs with toasted six-grain bread, or French toast with cream cheese filling. Hot lemon poppy-seed muffins, homemade strawberry or grape jelly, tea or coffee. In fireplaced dining room.
PLUS: Central air conditioning. Welcoming beverage. Grand piano.

⤳ *Elias Child House*

50 Perrin Road, Woodstock, CT 06281

860/974-9836
877/974-9836
E-MAIL tfelice@compuserve.com
www.eliaschildhouse.com

HOSTS:	MaryBeth Gorke-Felice and Tony Felice
LOCATION:	Rural. On 47 acres with stone walls, flowering trees, perennial gardens, and newly cut trails for hiking and maybe cross-country skiing too. Ten miles from I-84 or I-395. Twenty minutes to University of Connecticut.
OPEN:	Year round. Two-night minimum on graduation and parents' weekends at area schools/universities.
RATES:	$95 double, $120 suite. $10 extra person. Package rates for Valentine's Day, summer barbecues, Halloween Happenings, hearth cooking demos. Discover, MC, Visa. ♥ ♨ ⊞ ❖ ⤫ 𝍄 ♥♡

HERE THEY ARE—just 18 miles from Maple Hill Farm (now a private home), their popular B&B for thirteen years in Coventry. "As soon as we saw this 1700s central hall Colonial with its twelve-over-twelve windows, taller-than-Maple-Hill ceilings, original floors and wainscoting, and fireplaces everywhere, we bought it instantly!" Guests enjoy the 18-by-36-foot pool. They feed carrots to the horses in the pasture, photograph the Amish wedding buggy. They find several very unusual antiques that are great conversation pieces. They come for hearth cooking demos. And they come for MaryBeth and Tony who, too, "are having a great time." MaryBeth, a semiretired nurse practitioner, teaches, runs a well-child clinic, and is a hospice volunteer. Tony, an industrial salesman, is headquartered in that building overlooking the pool.

IN RESIDENCE: Murphy O'Brien, "our tennis-playing miniature poodle."
BED AND BATH: Two rooms and one suite; all with working fireplaces and private baths. First floor—one double and one three-quarter bed, shower bath. Second floor—double bed, shower bath; suite has one queen and one single bed, sitting room, tub and shower bath. Rollaway available.
BREAKFAST: 7:30–9 (or by arrangement). Fresh fruit dish, homemade breads and granola, eggs to order, Tony's "special" French toast. Served by the hearth with classical music.
PLUS: Library. Screened porch. Patio. Massage by appointment. Loan of bicycles.

⤳ From New York: *"From the hearth cooking to the champagne and chocolates, MaryBeth and Tony made our weekend relaxing and romantic. A delightful spot with gor-*

geous scenery, fireplaces in every room, impressive antiques, and an extremely friendly dog. . . . Fabulous. . . . Peace and warmth embrace you the moment you enter. . . . A homey feeling . . . Murphy, a big hit. . . . A 'must visit' for B&B lovers."

☞ *Taylor's Corner B&B*

860/974-0490

880 Route 171,
Woodstock, CT 06281-2930

888/503-9057
FAX 860/974-0498
E-MAIL taylors@neca.com
www.neguide.com/taylors

HOSTS: Peggy and Doug Tracy
LOCATION: Pastoral setting on a winding country (state) road. With pastures, gardens, big old trees. Within fifteen minutes of restaurants, antiques shops, private schools. Twenty minutes to University of Connecticut and Old Sturbridge Village.
OPEN: Year round.
RATES: $70–$80 weekdays. $105–$110 weekends. $15 rollaway. $325 two-night theme weekends including winter hearthside cooking demos (and dinner). Other packages for in-room candlelit breakfast, celebrations, Valentine's Day. ♥ ⊞ ⚲ ⚞ 牪

A TREASURE! In 1996 when the Tracys found this 1795 Colonial—"all restored and with the perfect layout for B&B"—their two-year search ended. Windows are nine-over-nine (or six). Walls are plaster. Decor is country style, with crafts, century-old furnishings, and reproductions. One conversation piece is a framed letter (found by the house restorers), dated May 22, 1795. And by the fire there's a comfortable couch and love seat, "the kind that guests fall asleep on." Hidden in back are wonderful English-style gardens developed by the previous owner who had an herbary here. Still, the major attraction is Jessie-Brown, a friendly longhorned Scotch Highland cow, a gift from a nearby farmer. (It's a great story that includes the addition of Jessie-Brown's calf, Earlene, born here during the summer of 1999.)

Before becoming innkeeper, Peggy had a typing business. Doug, who has degrees in engineering and business management, commuted two hours to south of Boston until 1999, when he began his own industrial supply business right here—in the newly built eighteenth-century–style barn.

BED AND BATH: Three second-floor rooms—queen bed or king/twins option—with cross-ventilation, floor fans, and air conditioners. Each has working (Duraflame log) fireplace, private shower bath, private phone, individual thermostat.
BREAKFAST: 7–9. Weekends: Fruit—fresh or baked dish. Aebleskivers (Danish pancake balls), vegetarian or sausage oven omelet, or French toast casserole with pecans and pure

continued . . .

maple syrup. Homemade biscuits, scones, muffins or cinnamon rolls. Juice and hot beverages. Weekdays: Juice, fruit, cereals. Muffins, scones, bagels, homemade jams, hot beverages. Special diets accommodated.

PLUS: Wood-burning fireplaces in keeping room (with beehive oven), parlor, and dining
room. TV/VCR in parlor. Beverages. Stone patio with Adirondack chairs overlooking
backyard "hidden" gardens and pasture. Winter hearth cooking demos with participatory
possibilities.

From New York and Connecticut: *"A great romantic getaway . . . very afford-
able . . . interesting history . . . very clean . . . all amenities to make you comfortable . . . perfect hosts who are knowledgeable about the area . . . area vineyards are fun to visit . . . highly
recommended . . . Proposed on our first visit. Returned for our first anniversary. Look forward
to our next stay."*

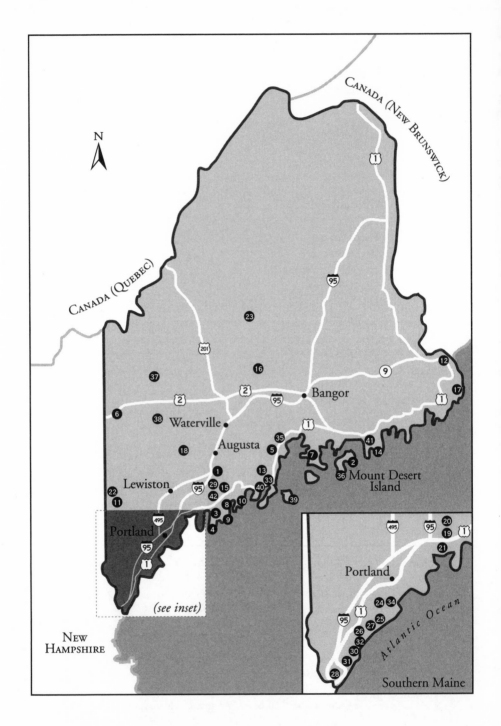

The numbers on this map indicate the locations of B&Bs described in detail
in this chapter.

MAINE

♨ *Maple Hill Farm B&B Inn*

Outlet Road,
RR 1, Box 1145,
Hallowell, ME 04347

207/622-2708
800/622-2708
FAX 207/622-0655
E-MAIL stay@MapleBB.com
www.MapleBB.com

HOSTS: Scott Cowger and Vincent Hannan
LOCATION: Serene. Set far back from road on 130 acres with fields, woods, swimming hole. Adjacent to 550-acre wildlife management area. Five minutes to Augusta, Maine Turnpike, Hallowell center ("great dining and antiquing"), Cobbossee Lake; ten to golf.
OPEN: Year round. Two-day minimum on some summer and fall weekends.
RATES: $65–$95 double bed. $75–$100 two doubles or queen and double sofa bed. $80–$100 queen or king, $95–$125 queen with whirlpool. Singles $10 less. Extra person $15. Crib $5. Weekly rates. Government rates and off-season discounts. Amex, CB, Diners, Discover, MC, Visa. ♥ ♦♦ ⊞ ❖ ⚲ 猫 ❥

THIS VICTORIAN farmhouse, restored and enlarged as a B&B in the 1980s, was acquired in 1992 by Scott Cowger, a civil engineer and native Mainer with an interest in ecology, gardening, music, theater, photography, people—and politics. (Results of a 1997 *Maine Times* survey: Maple Hill voted "best [Maine] B&B hands down" and Scott "best state representative.") Vince is a former electronics technician who loves the farm and is a great cook. They meet business, wedding, and conference (many held here) guests as well as cyclists, vacationers from around the world, and families.

IN RESIDENCE: "Maxine, our elegant cat, will follow you to your room." In barn (guided tours on request): one pony, two llamas, two cows, goats, chickens, sheep—all with names.
FOREIGN LANGUAGE SPOKEN: Some French.
BED AND BATH: Seven air-conditioned rooms, all with private baths, phones, color TV. First-floor handicapped-accessible double-bedded room has full bath with hand-held shower, deck, and optional exterior entrance. Second-floor rooms—double bed, hall full bath; two double beds, en-suite full bath with whirlpool; queen bed, en-suite full bath with whirlpool. In newer wing—one room with double bed, hall shower bath; two queen-bedded rooms, each with en-suite shower bath, one with separate whirlpool (for two) room. Cots and crib available.
BREAKFAST: 7–9. (Earlier upon request; continental after 9.) Fresh fruit cup. Orange juice. Homemade muffins. Cooked-to-order entrées—Eggs Benedict Arnold, plain or

continued . . .

blueberry pancakes, French toast with warm Maine maple syrup, "our own farm-fresh eggs," hot oatmeal. Farm fries, sausage, and oven-baked bacon. Cold cereals and low-fat milk available. Teas. Freshly ground coffee. Served in fireplaced dining room or art gallery.

PLUS: Beverages and snacks. Garden or field flowers. Cast iron furniture and hanging plants on covered porch with sun-brewed iced tea served in summer. Croquet. Horseshoes. Renovated carriage house accommodates fifty for wedding receptions (200 for tent events) and conferences. Art gallery featuring local artists. Full liquor service.

From Massachusetts, Rhode Island, North Carolina, Florida, California, New Jersey: *"Wonderful place. On top of a hill surrounded by big fragrant hay fields, wooded trails behind them. . . . Friendly easygoing host. . . . My six-year-old son said, 'It's a good place to catch frogs, all the rooms are nice and pretty, and they have beds.'. . . Celebrated our tenth anniversary there. . . . Immaculate, unpretentious. Excellent food, nearby theater and restaurants. Classical music. Ah. . . . Beautiful farm . . . extremely clean . . . our room had four large windows with views . . . always had freshly baked cookies . . . fires in living and dining rooms. . . . Perfect getaway. . . . Hosts are a lot of fun to be with. Also treated our eleven-month-old daughter as a little queen . . . unusual animals . . . beautiful landscape. . . . Whole place is totally inviting."*

Bar Harbor Tides   207/288-4968

119 West Street, Bar Harbor, ME 04609-1430   FAX 207/288-2997
                                             E-MAIL info@barharbortides.com
                                                 www.barharbortides.com

HOSTS: Joe and Judy Losquadro
LOCATION: Overlooking Frenchman's Bay. On 1.5 acres of landscaped grounds. Ten-minute walk to town shops and restaurants.
OPEN: Year round. Two-night minimum June 16–October 31.
RATES: June 16–October 31 $175; suites $275, $295, $325. November 1–June 15 $125; suites $175, $195, $225. Discover, MC, Visa. ♥ ⚥ ⚰ ⚘

IT IS BOTH grand and comfortable. This National Register property is a pillared 1887 Greek Revival estate—a Bar Harbor "cottage" with a beautiful setting and a magnificent ocean view. With just four accommodations. And with fireplaces—in the upstairs and downstairs living rooms, in the dining room, in the suites, *and* on the rear veranda.

In Washington, D.C., Judy, a registered nurse who is an accomplished needleworker, worked with an executive search firm. Joe, a retired naval officer, was a computer marketing executive. Bar Harbor innkeepers since 1992, they fell in love with the community, Acadia National Park, and the idea of a waterfront location. The recently restored Tides became their home and inn in 1996.

BED AND BATH: Three suites plus one room; all have remote control cable TV. Master Suite has king bed, fireplaced bedroom, water views, private parlor, bath with claw-foot tub and separate modern tile shower. Ocean Suite has water views from every room, including the bedroom, living room, and bath. King bed, fireplaced bedroom, private balcony, bath with large tiled shower. Captain's Suite (commanding water views)—king bed, living room, bath with claw-foot tub, separate large tiled shower. Mate's Room has queen bed, bath with shower.

BREAKFAST: 8–9. (Coffee ready at 7:30.) Juice. Garnished fruit. Homemade muffins. French Acadian buckwheat blueberry pancakes; quiche; thick-cut cinammon French toast; baked sausage/egg/cheese strata or "Tides Benedict." Served on veranda overlooking lawn that borders Frenchman's Bay with view of ferry to/from Nova Scotia. Or in candlelit dining room with curved wall of windows for The View.

PLUS: Veranda photo opportunity at captain's wheel. Adirondack chairs by the water. Piano in living room. Coffee and tea always available. Recommendations—for restaurants, simple to elegant; for hiking and cycling trails; for whale-watching trips. Reservations made for "the most wonderful gardens you can imagine—open (free) on Thursdays only."

⇗ *Black Friar Inn*   207/288-5091

10 Summer Street,   **FAX** 207/288-4197
Bar Harbor, ME 04609-1424   **E-MAIL** blackfriar@blackfriar.com
        www.blackfriar.com

HOSTS: Perry and Sharon Risley (and Falke)
LOCATION: On a quiet in-town street next to municipal parking lot, 1 mile from Acadia National Park. Walk to shops and restaurants.
OPEN: May through November. Two-night minimum mid-June through mid-October.
RATES: Mid-June through October, second floor $105–$120, third floor $90–$100, suite $145. Off-season, second floor $75–$85, third floor $55–$65, suite $115.
♥ ♦♦ ⊞ ⚔ ⅙ ♥♡

"I KNEW THIS area from childhood summers, but in a funny way, our love of skiing brought us here. When we thought about post-Air Force life, we thought about our own inn stays worldwide, a small-town atmosphere, and a chance for skiing vacations. When this unusual inn with its beautiful woodwork and outstanding craftsmanship became available, we jumped at the opportunity."

Architectural features from old Bar Harbor mansions were used when this Victorian house was completely rebuilt in the early 1970s. There's a mantel used as a headboard; the sunroom has cypress and tin walls that came from a Maine church; the Pub Room, a common room complete with fireplace, was a private library.

continued ...

IN RESIDENCE: "Falke is our orange and white 'freckled' Brittany with a 2-inch tail that wags constantly. He loves to run and hunt with Perry."

BED AND BATH: Seven rooms (sizes vary) with air conditioning; most have ceiling fan also. First-floor suite: one large room (22 by 12 feet) has king bed, queen sofa bed, gas fireplace, en-suite shower bath. Second- and third-floor rooms have queen bed, individual thermostat, private bath; three that have hall bath (robes provided) have sink in room.

BREAKFAST: 8–9:30. "Grandmother's baked eggs" or waffles or crepes. Homemade breads and muffins. Served in sunroom.

PLUS: Afternoon refreshments. Down comforters. Robes. Small third-floor rear deck. Inquire about sea kayak school and fly-fishing programs. Off-street parking.

From California, Pennsylvania, Delaware, Connecticut, New York, Massachusetts, Alabama: *"Welcomed us like old friends . . . knowledgeable about Bar Harbor and Acadia National Park . . . wonderful restaurant suggestions . . . immaculate . . . well decorated . . . good food . . . especially liked gingerbread waffles . . . helped us plan our days. . . . Our first B&B experience and it was great . . . fabulous hosts . . . especially liked afternoon fire in pub room with conversation and refreshments."*

Castlemaine Inn

207/288-4563

39 Holland Avenue,
Bar Harbor, ME 04609

800/338-4563
FAX 207/288-4525
www.castlemaineinn.com

HOSTS: Norah O'Brien and Terry O'Connell
LOCATION: On a quiet street, 2 blocks from waterfront. Five-minute walk to shops and restaurants. One mile from Acadia National Park and Bluenose ferry terminal.
OPEN: May 15–October 25. Two-night minimum July and August and on holiday weekends.
RATES: $98–$118 queen, $135 with fireplace or balcony. $148–$185 large rooms and suites. $25 third person. Less May, June, September, and October. MC, Visa. ♥ ✕ ⅄

From Maryland, Massachusetts, New York, Delaware, New Jersey, Colorado, California, Illinois: *"A treat to stay there . . . Norah goes beyond immaculate [everyone concurs]. . . . I suffer from allergies and found the inn dust free and pet fur free. . . . Norah knows about walking and hiking trails. . . . By mail, we still exchange information on new or newly discovered mystery writers. . . . Beautiful restoration with Victorian atmosphere. . . . As a single traveler, felt secure. . . . Lovely furnishings . . . starched Irish table linens . . . homey, warm feeling. . . . The nicest and most reasonably priced of all the places we stayed on our two-week trip. . . . I'm a picky lady with great taste! . . . unlimited amounts of all sorts of breads, scrumptious scones, bagels, muffins . . . nooks and crannies everywhere . . . the inn was our deciding factor to stay in Bar Harbor for a few extra days . . . fresh flowers throughout . . . warm and sincere hosts. . . . It's magical!"*

THE WALK is canopied. The baths and fireplaces and wallcoverings have been redone. And designer comforters are on the beds of this rambling circa 1886 Victorian, which the hosts converted to a B&B in 1981. They knew the area from vacations. When they lived in Ohio, Norah was a teacher. Terry was a project manager for a Chicago construction company.

BED AND BATH: Ten air-conditioned rooms—vary in size—on three floors. "Sorry, no elevator!" King or queen (many are canopied) beds. All with cable TV, VCR, private en-suite bath (most have both tub and shower). Some have two-person whirlpool, Duraflame fireplace, a private balcony. One first-floor honeymoon suite has private exterior entrance, king four-poster in large fireplaced room, mini refrigerator, whirlpool bath, 4-foot-square shower, private deck. More changes every year—but they "finally named one elaborate room 'Suite Finis!'"

BREAKFAST: 7:30–9:30. Continental-plus buffet style. Muffins, coffee cake, scones, cereal, homemade bread, fresh fruit bowl, bagels with cream cheese, preserves, cheese, juices, imported teas, gourmet coffee. In breakfast room, in fireplaced parlor, or on veranda.

PLUS: Video library. Books, including paperback lending library. Wicker-furnished front porch.

ᔑᔑ *Coach Stop Inn*   207/288-9886

P.O. Box 266,   FAX 207/288-4241
Bar Harbor, ME 04609   E-MAIL info@coachstopinn.com
www.coachstopinn.com

HOST: Kathy Combs
LOCATION: On 3 acres with arbors, gardens, wildflower field, apple trees, and fences. Along Route 3, 2 miles north of Acadia National Park's main entrance. Five miles to downtown Bar Harbor.
OPEN: May–October. Two-night minimum on holiday weekends.
RATES: May–June 30 $49–$59; $75–$85 suite. July 1–Labor Day: $69–$99; $109–$129 suite. Labor Day–October 20 $69–$90; $92–$110 suite. Amex, MC, Visa. ♥ ♦ ♦ ⋇ ⊁

HISTORY: a former coach stop/tavern, circa 1804. Architecture: Cape Cod–added-on-to Colonial. Good food: "I love to cook." Great knowledge of area: Kathy was chamber of commerce president and Ted, her husband, is a national park ranger. Moderate rates. Family cooperation. And hospitality. It's all here in Kathy's third "and final!" restoration project, the oldest surviving lodging establishment in the Bar Harbor/Acadia National Park area. Exposed beams and original wide-plank pine floors form a backdrop for rooms decorated with quilts, designer fabrics and wallcoverings, country antiques, and coach-stop

continued . . .

prints. "My husband was a professor of microbiology when we lived in Connecticut. In the mid-1980s, after years of extending our Acadia vacations, we finally figured out a way to stay here permanently." As college students, the Combses' children helped during summers with a large Victorian B&B they formerly owned. The Coach Stop Inn, most recently a private residence, was unoccupied for three years before the Kathy and Ted restored it and opened in 1996.

BED AND BATH: Three rooms and two two-room suites, each with queen bed (some with extra twin bed or room for rollaway), ceiling fan, en-suite private shower bath (one suite has queen sofa bed and tub/shower bath). Some rooms have individual thermostat, sitting room, working fireplace, private entrance with patio or porch. Second-floor two-room suite has slanted ceiling and air conditioning.
BREAKFAST: 8–9:30 (coffee and tea from 7:30). Cranberry-apple brown betty with crème fraîche, cheese blintzes with warm blueberry sauce, stuffed French toast with sautéed apples, or griddle cakes with bacon or sausage. Cereal bar (on mid-nineteenth-century Queen Atlantic wood cookstove). Award-winning baked goods. For early departures— juice, baked goods, hard-boiled eggs, fruit, cheese, cereal bar, hot beverages.
PLUS: Afternoon refreshments with freshly baked goodies. Guest refrigerator. Wood-burning fireplace and TV in common room. Parking.

➹ *Graycote Inn*   207/288-3044

40 Holland Avenue, Bar Harbor, ME 04609-1432   FAX 207/288-2719
                                                E-MAIL innkeepers@graycoteinn.com
                                                        www.graycoteinn.com

HOSTS: Roger and Pat Samuel
LOCATION: On a quiet 1-acre side street lot with large lawn, gardens, shade trees. Five-minute walk to restaurants, shops, waterfront. Five-minute drive to Acadia National Park.
OPEN: Year round. Two-day minimum June 16–October 15 plus Memorial Day weekend.
RATES: June 16–October 15 $95–$159, suites $200 for four guests. Off season $65–$100, suites $135. Discover, MC, Visa. ♥ ⊞ ⚔ ✂

➹ From Virginia, Florida, Massachusetts, Maryland, Connecticut, New Jersey, Pennsylvania, Ohio: *"A perfect place to spend our first two nights in Maine. It was everything we dreamed about for a warm and romantic getaway. . . . Pat and Roger seem to have the ability to be elegant and informal at the same time . . . personable, knowledgable hosts . . . inn allows for private space as well as homey space for interacting with fellow guests . . . trip tapes and personal explanations greatly appreciated. . . . One of the most organized and well-thought-out B&Bs we have ever stayed at: maps to borrow, daily weather reports, early-morning coffee, lovely rooms. . . . Breakfast is a special event. . . . We loved the cats too. . . . Afternoon home-made cookies and tea . . . perfect location. . . . I travel extensively. Graycote exceeded all our ex-pectations."*

YEAR ROUND the Samuels get rave reviews for their "next" career, which began when they bought this restored inn in 1996. Since, *Country Inns* magazine pictured it in a Bar Harbor feature. Built in 1881, the inn has pastel backgrounds that give a light and airy feel to rooms furnished with traditional and Victorian pieces. Roger was a civil engineer for Boeing be-fore he became research manager at MIT's Sloan School of Management. Pat, who com-pleted her PhD in chemistry in Seattle, was on the faculty at Boston University. Their own B&B stays inspired the career change "to work together in a personalized business."

IN RESIDENCE: Phoebe and Chloe, Maine coon cats that are "very much part of the fam-ily; not allowed in guests' rooms."

FOREIGN LANGUAGES SPOKEN: "Some French and German."

BED AND BATH: In main house—ten rooms (one with skylight) on three floors. Some with wood-burning fireplace, balcony, or private sunroom; some with air conditioner or fan (ceiling or window). Plus two suites in carriage house. All private baths; some are full, others shower only. Beds are king or queen; most are canopied. Carriage-house suites, each with private living room, have a king bed in one room, queen in other, shower bath.

BREAKFAST: 8–9. (Early coffee and tea placed outside rooms.) Pancakes (blueberry butter-milk, orange-pecan, ranch house), vegetable frittata, raised waffles, brunch eggs, fruit-and-ricotta-stuffed French toast, Western bread/cheese casserole, breakfast burrito. Juice, fresh fruit, homemade muffins or bread. Cereal. Hot beverages. Special diets accommo-dated. Served on enclosed porch at tables for two or four or in dining room.

PLUS: Fireplaces in living and dining rooms. Grand piano. Plenty of books. Guest refrig-erator. Wicker-furnished veranda. Croquet. Hammocks on lawn.

*M*ANY B&Bs *that allow smoking restrict it to certain rooms and/or public areas. Although some of those B&Bs that have the* ⚡ *symbol allow smoking on the porch and/or patio, others do not allow smoking any-where on the property.*

🦜 *Hatfield Bed & Breakfast*   207/288-9655

20 Roberts Avenue,   FAX 207/288-0360
Bar Harbor, ME 04609-1820   E-MAIL hatfield@hatfieldinn.com
                                                    www.hatfieldinn.com

HOSTS: Sandy and Jeff Miller
LOCATION: Quiet side street. Two blocks to town center. Five-minute drive to Acadia
National Park or to ferry to Nova Scotia.
OPEN: Year round. Two-night minimum, July 4 through Columbus Day.
RATES: June 14–October 15 shared bath $75 and $85; private bath $95, $115. October
16–May 19 shared bath $50, $55; private bath $60, $65. May 20–June 13 shared
bath $60–$70; private $75–$95. Discover, MC, Visa. ♥ ⊞ ⚮ ✁

THIS IS A love story of sorts. After Jeff graduated from college in 1981, he discovered Bar
Harbor, returned home to Pennsylvania, and shared his enthusiasm. Soon his sister and
brother-in-law came for their vacations and became Hearthside (facing page) innkeepers.
Meanwhile Jeff met Sandy. They came in all seasons and were determined to find a way to
stay here. "Sandy loved the mountains. I loved the water. We both love a small town. Our
roots are in small rural town in Pennsylvania"—Hatfield. There Jeff worked at a consulting firm in the environmental science field. Sandy was employed by a computer software
company. In 1996, when their son was in college, the Millers bought this B&B, an 1895
Victorian, and furnished it with a mix of antiques and new country furnishings. "It's not
the fanciest place in town, but we offer comfort and hospitality that is unsurpassed!"
Guests (see below) concur.

IN RESIDENCE: "One spoiled conure, Ozzie, who has a vocabularly of two words. Haley is
our 'inn puppy,' a mixed breed of sorts."
BED AND BATH: Six rooms, four with private bath. First floor (just off dining room)—
queen bed, shower bath. Second floor—queen four-poster, full bath. Smaller room with
high-back double bed shares (robes provided) shower bath with room that has antique
iron queen bed. Third floor—one room with antique queen bed, private (detached)
shower bath. "Sandra's Favorite" has antique iron queen bed, shower bath. Rollaway
available.
BREAKFAST: 8–9. Apple cinnamon French toast, potato-and-egg casserole, or blueberry
pancakes. Juices. Fresh fruit. Homemade muffins and breads. Cereals. Special diets
accommodated.
PLUS: Living room with fireplace. Third-floor sundeck, front porch (outdoor smoking
area). Tea and cake at 4 p.m. Transportation available to/from Bangor bus or airport.
"Sorry, even smokers who are willing to abstain are discouraged."

🦜 From Pennsylvania, Oregon, Florida: *"Serve a hearty breakfast . . . more food
than you can eat . . . lots of charm, no squeaking floors, many interesting collections, plus
nooks and crannies to explore . . . wonderful knowledge of area . . . awesome innkeepers inter-
acted with all ages . . . made my parents (in their eighties) feel 'at home' . . . guests get to know*

each other. . . . Charming atmosphere. . . . Made suggestions that made a dreary day quite delightful. . . . Made us feel that their home was ours and that we have friends in Bar Harbor."

☙ *Hearthside B&B*

7 High Street,
Bar Harbor, ME 04609-1816

207/288-4533

FAX 207/288-9818
E-MAIL BCHESB@hearthsideinn.com
www.hearthsideinn.com

HOSTS: Barry and Susan Schwartz
LOCATION: On a quiet side street. Two blocks from the waterfront. Five-minute drive to Acadia National Park.
OPEN: Year round. Two-night minimum July and August and on holiday weekends.
RATES: Per room. First floor—queen bed, fireplace, whirlpool tub/shower, porch $140. Upper floors—$95 (detached private full bath, private porch), $100, $105, $130, $140 depending on room size, amenities. Less in winter and spring. Discover, MC, Visa. ♥ ⊞ ⚋ ⚌

☙ From Connecticut: *"Far better than the description in your book. Barry and Susan put their hearts in everything, from pancakes to the impeccable restoration."* From New Mexico: *"A wondrous tapestry combining clean, delightfully appointed rooms with touches of Victoriana . . . vivacious conversation, good suggestions."* From Pennsylvania: *"A sanctuary. . . . Like home, yet you feel pampered."* From Connecticut: *"Fantastic. Felt at home but still had our space. We'll go back."* From California: *"Far exceeded our highest hopes and expectations. Highlight of our two-week trip to the east coast."*

ALL THOSE guests' letters confirm that the couple who, in 1987, just "upped and moved with our two school-aged kids," made a good decision. The Schwartzes—"We can't imagine ourselves doing anything else"—left New Jersey, where Barry was a corporate executive and Susan a teacher.

Winston Churchill, Romeo and Juliet, Queen Victoria, and Emily Dickinson are some of the names of the guest rooms in the restored 1907 house, originally built as a doctor's home. The carpeted inn is furnished with Victorian and country antiques. The list of suggestions includes kayaking; rock climbing; snowshoeing; and, for honeymooners, a quiet beautiful spot.

BED AND BATH: Eight air-conditioned rooms (all with ceiling fan) on three floors. King-sized bed in seven; one room with queen. Some with wood-burning fireplace and/or private porch. All private baths—some full, some shower only, three with whirlpool tub.
BREAKFAST: 8–9:30. Buffet style. Hot dish may be pancakes, French toast, or eggs. If meat served, it's on the side. Fruit salad, strawberry or other homemade breads, maybe poppy-seed cake, muffins, bagels, homemade granola, hot/cold cereal, juice, tea, coffee.
PLUS: Afternoon tea.

⁂ The Inn at Bay Ledge

207/288-4204

1385 Sand Point Road,
Bar Harbor, ME 04609

FAX 207/288-5573
E-MAIL bayledge@downeast.net
www.maineguide.com/barharbor/bayledge

HOSTS: Jack and Jeani Ochtera

LOCATION: Dramatic and peaceful. Overlooking Frenchman's Bay. At top of 80-foot cliff with seventy-nine steps (and some benches along the way) leading to private (Maine-stone) beach. On 2 acres of tall pine trees. Five miles to town center, 2 to Acadia National Park main entrance.

OPEN: May–October. Two-night minimum, July–October 15.

RATES: May–June 15, first floor $85, larger room $110; second floor $150 queen, $200 king with Jacuzzi bath; cottage $85, $125 king with working fireplace. June 16–October $160, $175, $250, $300; cottage $140, $170. MC, Visa.
♥ 田 ✄ ⊁ ♨ ♙ ♡

⁂ From Indiana, Texas, Tennessee, Pennsylvania, Florida, Arizona, Maine, Georgia: *"An all-time favorite . . . memorable inn and innkeeper . . . wonderful breakfast each morning . . . cheery fire every evening . . . country charm and hospitality second to none . . . . Spectacular view. Absolutely beautiful room. Service was homey, friendly, and warm. . . . Charm, character, view, ambiance. . . . Superb . . . special and unique place."*

THE SUPERLATIVES go on and on. Every main-house room has an ocean view. There is an in-ground pool; a redwood sauna; a steam room; and, between birches, a suspended hammock. Eagles fly by. You see migrating waterfowl. From the deck you watch seals eating their breakfast. The "added-to a million times" early 1900s house has welcoming fireplaces (one in common room has a cedar mantel), Oriental rugs, and rooms with feather beds, antiques, designer linens, and down comforters. It's a wedding site, recommended by *Brides* magazine—one-year advance booking required.

When the Ochteras, energetic grandparents who work at the Sunday River ski area in winter, purchased and renovated this property in 1994, Jack left his position with McDonald's to become full-time innkeeper/groundskeeper.

IN RESIDENCE: Maggie, a wheaten terrier.

BED AND BATH: Ten rooms (sizes vary) on first (with direct view of ocean) and second (with private decks and ocean view) floors, some with skylight and private entrance. All with private bath (three with Jacuzzi). King, canopied queen, or antique double four-poster. Across the street in huge pine grove—three connected cottages, each with private shower bath, wicker-furnished porch. One has king bed, fieldstone fireplace. Two have queen bed, single daybed also.

BREAKFAST: 8–9. Entrée possibilities include blueberry strata, peaches-and-cream French toast, and cheese puffs with fresh tomato salsa. Homemade muffins and breads. Fresh fruit. Juice. Hot beverages. Served by fireplace in cathedral-ceilinged pine dining room or in fireplaced sunporch with that ocean view.

PLUS: Fireplace in living room and sunroom. Second-floor library with TV and VCR. Afternoon tea. Beach towels.

➳ *The Inn at Canoe Point*   207-288-9511

P.O. Box 216,   FAX 207/288-2870
Bar Harbor, ME 04609-0216   E-MAIL canoe.point@juno.com
                                                www.innatcanoepoint.com

HOSTS: Tom and Nancy Cervelli
LOCATION: Secluded. Fabulous entrance along 2 acres of pine forest on the rocky coast of Frenchman's Bay. Quarter mile from Acadia National Park entrance. One mile to Nova Scotia ferry. Two miles to Bar Harbor.
OPEN: Year round.
RATES: Memorial Day–October 31 $160–$265. Off-season $80–$160. Discover, MC, Visa. ♥ ⚄ ⚹ ☘ ♞

➳ From Indiana: *"We have never felt so relaxed at an inn. In twelve years of inngoing, we rate Canoe Point as one of the best."*

EXTRAORDINARY. An unforgettable setting. With privacy. At the edge of the ocean, with an enormous wraparound deck that juts out above the water. With intentionally simple interior design featuring neutral colors "to allow the large windows to create a feeling of being surrounded by natural beauty." (You are.) There's a floor-to-ceiling granite fireplace in the Ocean Room with those mesmerizing views of the bay and the mountains beyond. It's all in a stucco Tudor summer cottage, built as a private home in 1889 and converted to this intimate inn in 1986.

For about a dozen years the Cervellis had vacationed here on Mount Desert Island. "We ate lobster, hiked, biked, played golf, and took boat excursions." (They still do.) In 1990 they left their computer jobs on Long Island (New York) and became innkeepers in nearby Southwest Harbor. One day in 1995 guests who were looking to buy an inn asked the Cervellis if they would be interested in selling! They did sell. And then, while looking for another inn, found this magnificently sited B&B.

BED AND BATH: Three queen-bedded rooms and two suites; all private baths with tub/shower or shower only. Smallest and most popular room overlooks the water and has windows on three sides, private exterior entrance, and whirlpool tub for one. Two suites: one with king bed and air conditioning occupies entire third floor; one with queen bed has gas fireplace in sitting area with French doors and deck.
BREAKFAST: Usually 8–9 (coffee and tea available at 7). Eggs Benedict and home fries; bacon or sausage served with lemon French toast or blueberry or apple-cinnamon pancakes; quiches; or waffles. Muffins, coffee cake or breads. Fresh fruit, fruit cobbler or apple crisp. Served by fieldstone fireplace in Ocean Room (pictured in *Country Inns* magazine feature) or on outside deck.

continued . . .

PLUS: Grand piano. Hot tea or mulled cider by the fire. Iced tea or lemonade on the deck. Cookies; cheese and crackers. Guest refrigerator.

⤳ *The Maples Inn*   207/288-3443

16 Roberts Avenue,   FAX 207/288-0356
Bar Harbor, ME 04609   E-MAIL maplesinn@acadia.net
                                                                                  www.maplesinn.com

HOST: Tom and Sue Palumbo
LOCATION: On a quiet, tree-lined residential street. One and a half blocks to ocean; three- to ten-minute walk to restaurants and shops; 2 miles to Acadia National Park.
OPEN: Year round. Two-night minimum on holiday weekends.
RATES: June 15–October 15, $90, $100, $110, $115, $120; suite $150. Rest of year $60–$95. Extra person $15. Package rates for Christmas Tree Trimming and (April) Women's Pampering Weekends. Discover, MC, Visa. ♥ ⊞ ⚉ ⚄

BY DESIGN. The Palumbos first of eight stays here—it was love at first sight—was for an innkeeping course given in 1993 by the popular then-owner. An apprenticeship took place in 1997. And in 1998, Tom, a Hewlett-Packard business planner (for twenty years), and Sue, a software installation company staffer, moved from New Jersey to become the new innkeepers. "Because we have vacationed in the area since 1981, we're familiar with everything from restaurants to rainy-day activities. Now most of our hiking is done in the winter months. It's wonderful." Sue is an avid photographer. Her pictures are in guest rooms, and her collection of antique cameras and photographs are in the library. Tom plays ten instruments, and he composes and records original music. A flood of guests' comments attest to the continuing legacy at this comfortably furnished "painted lady" Victorian house.

FOREIGN LANGUAGE SPOKEN: Some Spanish.
BED AND BATH: Six queen-bedded rooms (one is a suite), all with private shower baths. Second floor—two-room suite with modified-canopy bed, fireplaced living room with queen hide-a-bed, private shower bath; one room with separate sitting room and twin hide-a-bed; one with bay window, detached bath (robes provided). Third floor (individual thermostats)—one air-conditioned room under eaves, en-suite shower bath; room with four-poster bed, mountain view, en-suite shower bath; another room with en-suite shower bath is three steps away from private deck with lounge, table and chairs, mountain and village view.
BREAKFAST: 8:30–9. (Requests filled for coffee outside your door at 7:30.) Fruit repertoire includes blueberry crisp, bananas with rum cream, fresh fruit with peach melba sauce, poached pears in wine sauce. Among entrées—pineapple upside-down French toast, baked eggs with red pepper pesto, blueberry stuffed French toast, glazed ham and leek quiche. Special diets accommodated. Served in candlelit dining room.

PLUS: Afternoon tea and cookies by fire or on rocker-filled porch. Down comforters. Guest refrigerator; complimentary sodas. Beach towels. Trail, biking, kayaking, and climbing books for borrowing. Special occasions acknowledged. Games, cards, puzzles, audiocassettes, give-and-take books.

🐎 From Australia, France, Maine, Connecticut, Massachusetts, Florida, New Jersey, Maryland, Oregon, Pennsylvania, California, Indiana: *"A perfect B&B.... Attention to detail—even an 'I forgot' basket—makes it above the ordinary.... Totally delightful... cozy, welcoming, gourmet breakfast artistically presented... afternoon tea... spotlessly clean.... Five stars!... Top-quality amenities.... A lovely respite from the rest of the world... blissfully tranquil... breakfasts to die for.... Like staying at Grandma's house—caring atmosphere and wonderful hospitality....Gracious hosts even opened a bottle of champagne for our birthday celebration.... Arrived in a blizzard after eight hours of driving. A very warm welcome, beautiful interior design, names on our door and homemade cookies. We stayed an extra day before our journey to Boston and our flight back to England. Highly recommended.... Everything one could hope for."*

🐎 *Nannau-Seaside B&B*   207/288-5575

396 Main Street, P.O. Box 710,   FAX 207/288-5421
Bar Harbor, ME 04609-0710   www.nannau.com

HOSTS: Ron and Vikki Evers
LOCATION: Shorefront setting. A mile from town center, down a long private driveway in a quiet wooded area adjoining Acadia National Park.
OPEN: May–October. Two-night minimum Memorial Day–October.
RATES: With fireplace—$165 bath en suite, $135 private nonadjoining bath. Third floor $135 for one room; two-bedroom suite $145 for two, $165 for three, $185 for four. MC, Visa. ♥ ⚂ ⚃ ⚅ ⚇

IF YOU HAVE ever wanted to stay in one of the area's famed summer cottages, here is your chance. From the grand front hall your eyes focus ahead to the enormous full-length window with ocean views. To the left is the living room seen on the cover of the premiere issue of *Old House Interiors* magazine—with a wonderful coral-colored hand-printed William Morris paper. Listed on the National Register, the 1904 house with "the most beautiful interior of any of the island's hostelries" (*New England Travel Guide*) is furnished with many period pieces, large comfortable sofas and chairs, and Japanese and twentieth-century Maine woodblock prints.

With prompting, Ron and Vikki, the first year-round residents of the house, will share their unlikely experience of taking a hike in 1984, seeing an empty house without a FOR SALE sign, and finally buying the place, which was "much too big for the two of us." The art history major turned researcher/fine wallpaperer/cook/gardener together with her husband, a talented carpenter and baker, have done most of the restoration work themselves.

continued...

Now the grounds, too, are "coming together," complete with perennial gardens, organic vegetable gardens, fruit trees, and berry bushes. Guests come for the beauty of the island and, as many returnees say, "to feel refreshed and relaxed in 'the Nannau Time Zone.'"

IN RESIDENCE: Chomper, a large orange-and-white cat.
BED AND BATH: Four queen-bedded rooms with ocean views, private baths. Second floor—bay-windowed room, working fireplace, claw-foot tub and hand-held shower. Room with working fireplace, nonadjoining bath with claw-foot tub and hand-held shower. Third floor—room with new tiled full bath; two-bedroom suite with queen bed, two twins, large full bath with hand-held shower.
BREAKFAST: 8–9. (Coffee by 7.) Maybe omelets and homemade croissants, almond-filled French toast with maple syrup, eggs Florentine with English muffin, or Belgian waffles with whipped cream, fresh berries.
PLUS: Private beach. Screened porch. Ocean-facing terrace with teak tables and chairs.

⟿ Benjamin F. Packard House   207/443-6069

45 Pearl Street,   800/516-4578
Bath, ME 04530   E-MAIL packardhouse@clinic.net
                             www.mainecoast.com/packardhouse/

      HOSTS: Debby and Bill Hayden
   LOCATION: In historic district, 1 block from the Kennebec River. Within walking distance of shops and restaurants. One and a half miles from the Maine Maritime Museum; fifteen minutes from Bowdoin College, twenty from L.L. Bean, forty from Portland.
       OPEN: Year round. Two-night weekend minimum, May through October.
      RATES: $75 queen or king. $80 twin. $85 suite. $5 less off-season. $15 third person in suite sitting room. Amex, Diners, Discover, MC, Visa. ♥ ⊄ ⊁

THE RESTORED 1800s Georgian house, purchased by the Haydens in the summer of 1995, is furnished with antiques and reproductions and, thanks to descendants of shipbuilder Benjamin F. Packard, Packard family memorabilia.

    As Debby says, "I have wanted to do this since, as a teenager, I worked with my maternal grandmother in Scarborough, Maine. She had fourteen cabins in addition to four guest rooms in her house. During the twenty-one years that I worked for American Airlines, I was the one who tried to make it all better when the bag was lost or mutilated. Bill, who served in the navy, has a lively interest in maritime history and genealogy—his or anyone else's. [Author's note: Guests from as far away as Australia have appreciated Bill's help in tracing family history.] As soon as he retired from his thirty years with American Airlines, we looked for a B&B in the Bath area. Here he's an active Rotarian [Debby, too, is active in the community]. And he has been elected to the City Council. We are happily sharing this lovely place with travelers from all over the world."

FOREIGN LANGUAGE SPOKEN: Some French.

BED AND BATH: Three second-floor rooms with private baths. One large room with queen four-poster with shower bath. One with king/twins option, shower bath. Suite has queen cannonball bed, adjoining private shower bath, sitting room with pull-out sofa.

BREAKFAST: Arranged with guests. Maybe Debby's Norwegian *pannekake* recipe with lingonberry topping, French toast, waffles, or egg dishes made with homegrown herbs. Almost-famous lemon bread. Served in formal dining room.

PLUS: English garden in enclosed courtyard. Window fans. Dinners—if guests are snowed in!

🐦 Fairhaven Inn

118 North Bath Road,
Bath, ME 04530-9304

207/443-4391
888/443-4391
FAX 207/443-6412
E-MAIL fairhvn@gwi.net
www.mainecoast.com/fairhaveninn

HOSTS: Susie and Dave Reed

LOCATION: Quiet. On 17 acres of trees, meadows, lawns, bordered by the tidal Kennebec River. Birding, snowshoeing, and cross-country skiing right here. Five-minute drive to town center and Maine Maritime Museum, twenty minutes to Freeport. Twelve miles to Popham Beach, 8 to Bowdoin College. Five minutes to Hyde School.

OPEN: Year round. Two-night minimum on some weekends and holidays.

RATES: May–October single $60–$70; double shared bath $70; private bath $80, $85, $90, $100, $110, $120; third person $15. November–April single $50 $60; double $60–$95; third person $10. Discover, MC, Visa.

♥ ☞ ⊞ ❖ ⚸ ⚷ ♨ 🐾

TRADITION! The previous owners, who have built a house across the street, had also been guests who immediately fell in love with this "magical inn" and its quiet country setting—with birds and wildflowers and nearby beaches that have sand, dunes, and tidal pools. It's a 1790s shingled Georgian Colonial furnished with antiques and country pieces, and without clutter. In Washington, D.C., Susie studied with the White House pastry chef before she and Dave, bread baker at the Washington Hilton, owned a cookie business. Then they established a wholesale/retail pastry shop, now owned by the Reeds' former employees, whose scones the *Washington Post* declared "the best in Washington." The Reeds were active with a nationwide network of chefs who raise money to feed hungry people, with cooking classes for low-income moms, with a food bank, and in preparing meals for the homeless. Here, they win first prize in holiday gingerbread house contests. They work at L.L. Bean and with Rotary, the Red Cross, the Forestry Committee, and the chamber. Want a sense of place? Take their suggestion for a gorgeous on-site 1-mile woodland walk to the river. We loved it.

continued . . .

IN RESIDENCE: Two cats—Annie and Alice, in owners' quarters (only) and outdoors.

BED AND BATH: Eight rooms with king, queen, or twin beds. First-floor queen-bedded room has private full bath. Seven second-floor rooms; baths (five are private, two rooms share a bath) are full or with shower only.

BREAKFAST: 8–9. (Coffee available at 7.) Homemade fat-free granola. Custard-filled corn bread. Baked eggs in crepe cups, curried fruit or fruit crisps, blintzes with bananas and strawberries. Served in informal fireplaced dining room with river view. Special diets accommodated.

PLUS: Inquire about cooking classes, some for Christmas cookies and gingerbread houses.

       ⤙ From Massachusetts: *"A charming, wonderful place for a special weekend."* From North Carolina: *"Feel like we have new friends."*

⤙ *Galen C. Moses House*   207/442-8771

1009 Washington Street,   888/442-8771
Bath, ME 04530   FAX 207/443-6861
                        E-MAIL galenmoses@clinic.net
                        www.galenmoses.com

      HOSTS: Jim Haught and Larry Kieft
  LOCATION: In historic district on main street. Five-minute walk to center and antiques shops.
       OPEN: Year round. Two-night minimum weekends, May–October.
     RATES: $99–$129 queen bed, $89–$119 double, $79–$109 twins. Summer only— $79 shared bath. MC, Visa. ♥ ☛ ⊞ ⚵ ⚶

Now THIS 1874 Italianate Victorian mansion, on the National Register, is known for its impeccable restoration, incredible breakfasts, and personable hosts. And it is also known for its plum-colored exterior with teal and pink accents—a color scheme "accepted by 85 percent of New Englanders and most Mainers!"

In Buffalo, New York, Larry was a florist; Jim, a high school principal. Their next career, in the early 1990s, was as antiques dealers who restored a smaller Victorian house. In 1994 they found this then-unoccupied Bath treasure "with marvelous huge stained glass windows; significant woodwork; and, on the third floor, a movie theater complete with stage and projection booth." As this book was going to press, restoration of the iron fencing around the property—around the widow's walk too—was on the to-do list, but the kitchen was on its way to becoming a showplace.

IN RESIDENCE: Emma, an adopted (rescued) greyhound.

FOREIGN LANGUAGES SPOKEN: A little French and German.

BED AND BATH: Four second-floor rooms, all private baths. Queen bed, tub/shower bath. Queen bed, shower bath. Room with twin beds, tub/shower bath. One with double bed, shower bath. In summer, room in attached carriage house shares a bath.

BREAKFAST: 8 and 9 (continental at 7). Juices, fresh fruit, cereals, hot rolls, coffee. Entrée may be quiche, baked French toast, frittatas, or casserole. Served in formal dining room that has built-in oak buffet.

PLUS: Wood-burning fireplace in library. Grand piano in living room. TV/VCR in study. Down comforters. Porch rockers. Gardens. "More spirits than just those served with tea at 4."

⁂ The Inn at Bath   207/443-4294

969 Washington Street,   FAX 207/443-4295
Bath, ME 04530   E-MAIL innkeeper@innatbath.com
                                                       www.innatbath.com

HOST: Nick Bayard
LOCATION: In historic district on main street with lovely old well-kept homes. Ten-minute walk to town shops and restaurants; longer to Maine Maritime Museum. Fifteen minutes to Bowdoin College. Within twenty-five minutes of two ocean beaches; twenty minutes to L.L. Bean in Freeport.
OPEN: Year round. Two-night minimum on weekends.
RATES: Memorial Day weekend–October 31 $85–$185; suites $165–$350. Off-season $75–$185; suites $150–$350. Midweek, multiple-night, and corporate discounts except for national holidays. Amex, Discover, MC, Visa.
♥ ♦♦ ⊞ ❖ ⅟

THE YEAR WAS 1990. Bath innkeepers, longtime friends of Nick, drove by this for-sale 1810 Greek Revival and mentioned that it would make a wonderful B&B. And that's how Nick, a Wall Street investment banker for twenty-seven years (who also worked at the World Bank on Third World industrial development projects), became an innkeeper. Many renovations and additions later, Nick offers luxurious accommodations furnished with many fine antiques. In 1999 he celebrated his tenth anniversary in innkeeping with his own getaway to Spain, China, and New Zealand.

IN RESIDENCE: Inspector Clouseau, a male Shih Tzu.
BED AND BATH: Nine spacious air-conditioned rooms. All with private full bath, telephone, cable TV, clock radio, VCR; several have a desk and a sofa. First floor—one handicapped-accessible room (can be a suite) with private exterior entrance, beamed ceiling, king/twins option, wood-burning fireplace, desk, sofa/extra-long twin daybed. Two ground-level rooms—one with queen four-poster, the other with king/twins option—can be connected to form a suite; each has private shower bath and, in bedroom, a wood-burning fireplace and two-person Jacuzzi. Second floor—canopied queen with oversized bath; canopied double with sofa in bay window; suite with king/twins and smaller room (not booked alone) with double bed; renovated hayloft with hand-hewn ceiling beams, fireplace, queen bed, sofa. Daybed, cot, and portacrib available.

continued . . .

BREAKFAST: 8–9:30. Earlier for business guests and fishing parties; continental "until 12 or so." Fresh fruit, juice, homemade bran muffins, eggs from nearby farm with cut-to-order bacon, homemade granola, hot cereal. Or banana French toast or blueberry pancakes. Locally made jams. In main dining room or in smaller room (for couples or for meetings) that has wide pine floorboards and hand-stained silk pattern on walls.
PLUS: Fireplaced parlors. Beverages at 6 p.m. Guest refrigerator. Beach towels. Off-street parking.

➮ From New Jersey: *"Much more than a place to sleep . . . newly appointed bath with fine-quality soaps and towels . . . immaculate . . . wonderful breakfast in elegant dining room."* From Germany: *"Felt so very welcome."*

➮ The Kennebec Inn

207/443-5202

1024 Washington Street,
Bath, ME 04530-2718

800/822-9393
FAX 207/443-1411
E-MAIL kennebecinn@clinic.net
www.kennebecinn.com

HOSTS: Blanche and Ron Lutz
LOCATION: In a mansion-lined historic district. Five-minute walk—through park overlooking river—to shops, galleries, and restaurants.
OPEN: Year round. Two-night minimum on summer weekends and during holidays.
RATES: June–October $100–$165. Less November–May. Corporate rates available. Amex, Discover, MC, Visa. ♥ ⊞ ❖ ⚥ ⚔

RON, A COLONEL, was in the army for twenty-three years. Most recently he was chief of anesthesiology at Walter Reed Army Medical Hospital in Washington, D.C. Blanche, a retired lawyer, is an accomplished fiber artist who is now interested in basket weaving. For their "next step," the Lutzes chose Maine—and stayed, as they had in many countries, in B&Bs. In 1997 they purchased this 1860 brick Italianate, which has been featured in *Colonial Homes* magazine. They redecorated, added baths, and furnished with their collections of antiques from all over the world. Guests enter through 12-foot-high double doors that have leaded and stained glass panes. In the double living room is an electronic player piano—as well as an 1860 gold-leaf chandelier with tiers of crystals, and over the marble fireplace mantel, an ornate gold-leaf-framed mirror. The formal dining room features the original Scalamandré tapestry wallcoverings and mahogany wainscoting. Travelers comment on the food ("the best waffles in the world") and on the elegant property, the hospitable hosts, and the attention to detail.

BED AND BATH: Seven air-conditioned, tall-ceilinged second-floor rooms; one has a fireplace. Each room has king or queen four-poster, hair dryer, 20-inch color cable TV, pri-

vate phone, data port. All private baths—three with Jacuzzi, one with original Scottish (wraparound beehive) shower.
BREAKFAST: 7–9. Earlier by arrangement. Repertoire includes homemade pumpkin waffles, cheese scrambled eggs, upside-down French toast, and sausage egg casserole. Homemade Anadama bread. Chocolate zucchini cake. Served buffet style in formal candlelit dining room by the fire at table made by Maine craftsman; classical music plays.
PLUS: Fireplace and games in living room. Special occasions acknowledged. Recipes shared. Setups provided. Beach chairs and towels. English-style garden.

Coveside B&B

462 North End Road, HC 33, Box 462,
Georgetown, ME 04548

207/371-2807
800/232-5490
FAX 207/371-2923
E-MAIL innkeeper@covesidebandb.com
www.covesidebandb.com

HOSTS: Tom and Carolyn Church
LOCATION: A secluded rocky cove with Sheepscot Bay beyond. On 5 acres; lawn slopes to private dock. Short walk or canoe paddle to village of Five Islands with lobster wharf (picnic-table dining). Five-minute drive to Reid State Park (miles of sandy beaches and rocky headlands). One hour north of Portland; 13 miles from Route 1 and Bath.
OPEN: May–October. Two-night minimum on weekends.
RATES: $110–$145. Special rates for stays of four days or longer in May, June, September, October. ♥ ⊞ ❖ ⚘ ⚡ ≋ ⛹

From Massachusetts, Wisconsin, Indiana, Texas, Minnesota, Iowa, New York, Connecticut, Pennsylvania, Germany: *An unforgettable treat. . . . Relaxed and beautifully prepared breakfast. Different every day . . . crab cakes! . . . fresh fruit and whipped cream in a wine goblet! . . . Serenity of surroundings complements the exceptional cuisine and friendliness of Carolyn and Tom. . . . Share directions to the best restaurants, antique haunts, beaches, and bike trails. . . . Peace and quiet. . . . Rooms have character and style just like their owners. . . . We loved it. . . . Quintessential Maine coastline. . . . A treasure."*

AND IT'S ALL because the Churches couldn't find a place to stay in Brunswick when their daughter graduated from Bowdoin College in 1997. They stayed here, fell in love with the setting "in unspoiled Georgetown," responded to the FOR SALE sign, hosted in 1998, and reopened in 1999 with a completely rebuilt shingled turn-of-the-century seaside cottage. Furnishings include Stickley, wicker, Arts and Crafts, and painted—"nothing fussy."

Carolyn, a former pastry chef and caterer in San Francisco and Albany, New York, has experience in the travel industry. Tom, cohost at this "summerlong house party," teaches political science at the State University of New York at Albany.

continued . . .

IN RESIDENCE: Max, "a standard poodle who welcomes guests and chases airplanes."
FOREIGN LANGUAGE SPOKEN: "Some French."
BED AND BATH: *Main house:* Four waterview rooms, all with private tile baths. First floor—queen bed, semiprivate porch, tub/shower bath. Second floor—three rooms with cathedral ceilings and ceiling fans. One room with queen bed, gas fireplace, Jacuzzi, separate shower. One with queen bed, tub/shower bath. One with king/twins option, shower bath. *Carriage house:* Two housekeeping apartments with queen bed in bedroom, queen sofa bed in living room, full kitchen with dishwasher, small deck.
BREAKFAST: 8–9. Maine berries and cream, fresh fruit parfaits, or fruit crisp. Repertoire includes Maine crab cakes, lobster fricassee on corn cakes, pecan/cranberry waffles, scrambled eggs with smoked salmon in cheese-puff shells, homemade sausage. Blueberry/orange muffins. Served in dining area or on deck overlooking the cove and lobster boats.
PLUS: Canoe and bicycles for guests. Beach towels. Fireplaced living room. Coffee, tea, and cookies in afternoon or evening. Guest refrigerator with drinks. Phone jacks for computer modems in all rooms. Terrace facing water.

☞ *The Alden House B&B*   207/338-2151

63 Church Street,   E-MAIL alden@agate.net
Belfast, ME 04915   www.bbonline.com/me/alden

HOSTS: Jessica Jo Jahnke and Marla A. Stickle
LOCATION: Residential. On 1 acre in historic district. Minutes' walk to downtown restaurants and waterfront. In a town now known for its antiques shops, art galleries, live theater, sea kayaking, bookstores, art deco movie theatre and nearby hiking. Thirty miles to Camden; 50 to Bar Harbor.
OPEN: Year round.
RATES: Private bath $85 double bed, $95 queen with detached bath, $110 queen with en-suite bath. Shared bath $75. Amex, MC, Visa. ♥ ⊞ ❖ ⚲ ⚷

UNPRECEDENTED! Within days of the 1997 grand opening of this B&B, the innkeepers were interviewed and filmed for the *Oprah Winfrey* show. The producers, in town for a feature on Belfast as one of the most culturally interesting small towns in the country, were enthralled with the career change of two academicians who had experience restoring their previous residences in Ohio and Maine. During a two-year search (150 properties), Jessica (former dean of education) and Marla (counselor) made their first visit to Belfast. After purchasing the 1840 Greek Revival house, they began a nine-month metamorphosis. They gutted and rebuilt the entire building, restored the cherry stair rail and tin parlor ceilings, designed a scalloped fence for the property, and installed exterior shutters and awnings. At their open house, one neighbor dubbed the decor "uncluttered Victorian." Antique furnishings are carved and tufted. A grand player piano—with 150 rolls available—graces one parlor. Period wallcoverings are throughout. Guests write to me about "impeccable attention to detail . . . a must-stay place . . . simple beauty and elegance . . . ribbon-wrapped towels . . . manicured grounds . . . everyone feels special."

IN RESIDENCE: In hosts' quarters—two dogs.

BED AND BATH: Seven rooms with queen (one has a wood-burning fireplace), double, or twin beds. First-floor room has double bed, en-suite shower bath. Up circular staircase to six second-floor rooms (four with private shower bath). Room with double bed shares (robes provided) shower bath with room that has two twin beds.

BREAKFAST: 8:30–9:30. Menu varies. Sample: house blend of fruit juice (made in blender properly assembled!), raspberry streusel muffins, fresh fruit, smoked turkey-and-asparagus crepes. Served in candlelit dining room at tables for two.

PLUS: Wood-burning fireplace in two parlors and in library. VCRs (500-plus films available) brought to rooms by request. Room window fans available.

ᔛ The Jeweled Turret Inn

207/338-2304

40 Pearl Street,　　　　　　　　　　　　　　　　　　800/696-2304
Belfast, ME 04915-1907　　　　　www.bbonline.com/me/jeweledturret/
　　　　　　　　　　　　　　www.maineguide.com/belfast/jeweledturret/

HOSTS: Carl and Cathy Heffentrager
LOCATION: Residential. Two blocks from Victorian downtown. Half mile from "super park overlooking ocean"; 17 miles north of Camden; within 20 miles of four state parks. Fifty-five miles south of Bar Harbor and Acadia National Park
OPEN: Year round. Two-night minimum during holiday weekends.
RATES: June 15–October $85–$130. November–June 14 $75–$90. Honeymoon rooms $110–$130. Singles $5 less. Third person $15. ♥ ⊞ ❖ ⚅ ⅍

"A BED AND breakfast vacation in beautiful historic Maine" is the answer to "What brought you from Anchorage, Alaska, where you were born and raised?" Several trips and years later, in the mid-1980s, the Heffentragers, still in their twenties, found Belfast, a "stepping-back-in-time town," and this house with its stone verandas and gables and turrets. Now on the National Register of Historic Places, the house has been restored—all the woodwork too—by Carl, who grew up doing carpentry and construction, and Cathy, a piano teacher. They have filled the house with Victorian antiques, lots of lace, and their knickknack collections. Some guests describe it as "a magnificent grand old Victorian lady." Others wrote: *"Memorable breakfasts . . . spotless . . . cordial hosts. . . . I'll always remember the sun streaming through, throwing prism colors on the wall."*

IN RESIDENCE: Daughter Megan, age nineteen. Crumpet, a cairn terrier, and Murphy, a Yorkshire terrier.

continued . . .

BED AND BATH: Seven rooms on first and second floors, all private baths. (Ceiling fans in three rooms.) Queen-bedded and double-bedded rooms with full bath. One room with queen bed has fireplace. One with two twin beds has shower bath. Rollaway available.
BREAKFAST: At 8 and 9. Poached cinnamon pears, fruit cup, or baked apples. German pancakes, sourdough gingerbread waffles, Belgian waffles, quiche, or French toast. Scones are house specialty. Teas and freshly ground gourmet coffee.
PLUS: Afternoon hot tea or chocolate; iced tea and lemonade on veranda. Garden.

☞ The Thomas Pitcher House B&B

207/338-6454

19 Franklin Street,
Belfast, ME 04915

888/338-6454
E-MAIL tpitcher@acadia.net
www.thomaspitcherhouse.com

> **HOSTS:** Fran and Ron Kresge
> **LOCATION:** Residential. One block from Main Street. Few minutes' walk to harbor, restaurants, galleries, shops. Twenty minutes north of Camden; seventy minutes to Bar Harbor and Acadia National Park.
> **OPEN:** Year round.
> **RATES:** $75–$85 double bed (or double and twin), $85–$95 queen. MC, Visa. ❌ ✂

WHILE RON was teaching secondary-school German (for twenty-seven years) in Northampton, Pennsylvania, he took a course in hotel and restaurant management. Fran worked as a senior systems analyst in the computer department of a local company. "Ron did most of the cooking at home. We loved our B&B stays and we loved our Maine vacations. Belfast, with its residential and architectural characteristics—but not overly touristy or crowded—is a town where we can walk to just about everyplace. It is a great base for day trips. And Ron is our chef!"

In 1991 they bought this 1873 Victorian with original woodwork, a marble fireplace, and large bay windows. Before the Kresges moved here and opened in 1994, they made many changes. They added baths. And a new furnace and water system—"plenty of hot water!" Wallcoverings include stripes and florals. Furnishings are antiques and reproductions. Music, available throughout the house, has individual controls in all guest rooms. Now many returnees are among their guests.

IN RESIDENCE: Winston, half pug, half cocker spaniel.
FOREIGN LANGUAGES SPOKEN: German and some French
BED AND BATH: Four second-floor rooms; all private baths. Queen four-poster, en-suite bath with shower and claw-foot tub. Queen brass bed, reading bay, hall shower bath. Room with antique oak double bed has rocking chairs, tub/shower bath. Room with one double and one twin bed has shower bath.
BREAKFAST: 8:30. Freshly squeezed orange juice. Homemade scones, muffins, or cakes. French toast puff with Maine maple syrup, ham-and-cheese soufflé, Maine blueberry

buttermilk pancakes with sausage, or *apfelpfannkuchen* (German apple pancake). Served in the dining room on Maine-made pottery and antique crystal.

PLUS: TV/VCR and videos in library. Porch rockers. Deck with wicker furniture and picnic table. Protected storage for bicycles. Cookies and chocolates. Beach towels.

⇗ From North Carolina: *"Beautiful room . . . tasteful furnishings . . . brand-new modern bath! . . . The warm ambiance was dwarfed by the hospitality. Ron and Fran are a delight. . . . Each breakfast an adventure in good eating that really began the evening before with the marvelous aromas."* From Pennsylvania: *"From floor to ceiling and everything in between, you can see the care, detail, and personality—colorful, historic, comfortable, and quiet."*

⇗ Chapman Inn

On the Commons,
P.O. Box 1067,
Bethel, ME 04217-1067

207/824-2657
877/359-1498
FAX 207/824-7152
E-MAIL chapman@nxi.com
www.chapmaninn.com

HOSTS: Fred Nolte and Sandra Frye
LOCATION: Facing the town green in historic district. Across from cross-country trails, eighteen-hole championship golf course, historical society. Ten minutes to Sunday River and Mount Abram ski areas. Walk to shops, restaurants, theater.
OPEN: Year round. Two-night minimum on winter weekends and holidays.
RATES: Winter $105 suite, $95 private bath, $85 shared bath, $25 extra adult, $10 extra child. Fall $16 less. Spring and summer $26 less ($15 extra adult, $5 extra child). Singles $10 less. Breakfast for "others" $7.50 per person. Amex, Discover, MC, Visa. ♙♙ ⊞ ❖ ⅍ ♥♡

BREAKFAST IS SO popular here that word of mouth (only—there's no sign) brings other-than-overnight guests to the table. The big Federal-style house, built by a sea captain in 1860, has been a B&B since 1984. Fred, a former food service manager who trained at Chicago's Drake Hotel, and Sandra, who had experience in retail management, bought the property in 1997. They exposed and refinished the first-floor hardwood floors, painted and papered, and kept the casual homey ambiance.

IN RESIDENCE: Mike is "the consummate inn dog—smiles, wags his tail, and offers a friendly no-bark greeting."
BED AND BATH: Ten rooms; most are air conditioned. First-floor suite with queen and two twin beds, full kitchen, dining/sitting area with TV/VCR, private shower bath. Second-floor rooms with private bath have one or two double beds; some with one or two twin beds also. Two third-floor rooms, each with double bed, share a shower bath. Dorm area for groups.

continued . . .

BREAKFAST: 7–9. Fresh fruit, juice, yogurt, homemade granola, cereal. Homemade muffins, pastries, and breads. Eggs to order; ham, bacon, sausage. Entrée possibilities include three-mushroom omelet, (portobello, crimini, and oyster) served with home fries made with caramelized sweet onions; French toast waffles with Maine maple syrup. PLUS: Wood-burning fireplace in living room. TV/VCR. Game room. Fitness room. Two saunas in converted barn. Laundry facilities. Picnic baskets ($7.50–$20 per person).

⇜ *Eggemoggin Reach Bed & Breakfast*   207/359-5073

92 Winneganek Way (off Herrick Road),   FAX 207/359-5074
Brooksville, ME 04617   E-MAIL mmcanon@ctel.net
                                                      www.eggreachbb.com

HOSTS: Susie and Michael Canon
LOCATION: Secluded. On a bluff with a quarter mile of rocky shorefront and spectacular
           Penobscot Bay views. Down a long drive surrounded by hundreds of
           wooded acres (hiking to scenic outlooks and picnic spots). One hour south
           of Bar Harbor; one hour from Bangor Airport; fifteen minutes to Blue Hill.
           Five minutes to Deer Isle.
OPEN: May 15–October 15. Two-night (Friday/Saturday) minimum on weekends.
RATES: $160–$185. Additional person $50. MC, Visa. ♥ ❖ ⚲ ⅄ ≛ 𐐚

SOME FARMHOUSE. What the Canons built in 1988—a post-and-beam family retreat in traditional Maine farmhouse style—became an I-could-stay-here-forever kind of B&B in
1993. A large old-brick fireplace, flanked by bookshelves, is in the open first floor. More
recently built structures, too, combine a rustic ambiance with pure comfort. Guests who
arrive by land or sea feel as if they've made a discovery. (Upon departure, many make next-
year reservations.) Other innkeepers rave about this "incredibly beautiful place." *USA
Today* did too. There are soaring wood ceilings and wood-burning or gas-fired stoves.
Pickled pine paneling is on the walls. Some cedar baths. Large private porches provide a
mesmerizing view of everything—lighthouse, islands, and, in the distance, Camden Hills.
And Mike, a mergers and acquisitions specialist, and Susie share a (contagious) zest for life.

BED AND BATH: Nine waterview rooms (some are suites or studios) in three buildings. All
private baths. Most rooms have king bed (one room has two twins); all have a sofa bed
and a refrigerator. *Cottage* has two studios. *Carriage house* has full kitchen. Six rooms in
barn-design *Bay Lodge;* some with a woodstove, all with kitchen, living room area,
screened porch.
BREAKFAST: 7–9:30. Baked French toast or an egg casserole. Fresh fruit, fresh juice.
Cereals. Yogurt. Homemade breads. Served buffet style on the wraparound deck overlooking the water, or in the dining room.
PLUS: Den with woodstove. Ice machine. Dock—steps from the house—with picnic
table. Deep-water mooring. Canoe and rowboat for guests' use. Adirondack chairs in

secluded spots along shoreline. Arrangements made for excursions, kayaking, whale watching, or golf, and for catered dinner delivered here.

    ➳ From Maryland: *"It's all wonderful, warm, and inviting . . . with paneling, fabrics, country antiques, Oriental rugs, family silver . . . decorated with flair without the feeling of newness . . . homey, not cutesy . . . woke up to loons, ospreys . . . saw windjammers sail by . . . . saw an eagle . . . cocktails on the porch at sunset . . . very quiet . . . unique . . . romantic . . . best part is Susie and Mike; made us feel as if we had visited our best friends."*

➳ Oakland House's Shore Oaks Seaside Inn　　207/359-8521

435 Herrick Road,　　　　　　　　　　　　　　　　800/359-7352
Brooksville, ME 04617-9714　　　　　　　　E-MAIL jim@oaklandhouse.com
　　　　　　　　　　　　　　　　　　　　　www.oaklandhouse.com

HOSTS: Jim and Sally Littlefield
LOCATION: Definitely off the beaten path. Along a half mile of oceanfront with sandy ocean (and lake) beaches, dock, and moorings. Facing Eggemoggin Reach, Penobscot Bay, Pumpkin Island Lighthouse, and distant Camden Hills. On 50 acres with hiking trails to wondrous outlooks. On a narrow road "25 miles from nearest stoplight." Fifty miles from Bangor International Airport or Trailways/Concord bus terminal.
OPEN: April through October. Two-day weekend minimum.
RATES: (Include dinner; $10 less for B&B, which includes Sunday brunch in high season.) Mid-June through Labor Day $155–$209 private bath, $129–$159 shared bath; singles $109–$119 private bath, $89–$99 shared bath; extra person on sofa bed $49. Off-season $135–$169 private bath, $109 shared bath; $85–$129 in May. MC, Visa. ♥ ⊞ ❖ ⚲ ⅄ ☂ ⚄ ❤○

A LEGEND! Part of an old-fashioned colony. Rustic and unspoiled, but updated after Sally, a trained designer with historical society and art museum experience, married Jim, a fourth-generation innkeeper and raconteur in true Down East dialect—in 1994. A degreed engineer, Jim follows his family tradition on this idyllic property originally granted to his many-times-great-grandfather by King George III of England. The 1907 half-stone, half-shingled three-storied cottage known as Shore Oaks has been completely renovated, fulfilling what Sally saw as its "campy but with potential" promise. Now, in addition to the original Arts and Crafts furnishings, there are other period pieces, some upholstered wicker, and oak too. A large stone fireplace is in the common room. Old maps and prints are in the library. Perched on a rock in Eggemoggin Reach is a gazebo, site of many intimate weddings. The original hotel, Oakland House, is now a restaurant (seats ninety). The whole spread-out complex includes fifteen cottages—some in the woods, but most on the water.

continued . . .

Returnees include three generations. A few guests come for one night, then wish they could stay longer to reflect, to unwind, to write, to hike; to find tidal pools, listen to the loons, and watch the sunset. As one guest from Maryland wrote, *"Shore Oaks is what I've been searching for. . . . My soul was soothed."* Another from Wisconsin penned, *"Surpassed our dreams of a first-time visit to Maine."*

FOREIGN LANGUAGES SPOKEN: Varies according to (personable—they are!) staff.
BED AND BATH: On three floors—ten rooms, six with individual thermostat, intentionally without TV and phones. Seven rooms on first and second floors have private baths (some with soaking tub, some with tub and shower). Two rooms with wood-burning fireplace. Rooms have one double bed, one queen (one with a double sofa bed too), two twins, or one single bed. Three third-floor rooms share one modernized (but made to look original) full bath. Queen suite with twin sofa bed; one with single bed only; one room with double bed.
BREAKFAST: 8–9:30. (Often, first cup of coffee is on the rocker-filled wraparound porch.) Fresh fruit. Juices. Muffins. Eggs Benedict, lobster and broccoli frittata, French toast made with homemade bread, wild blueberry pancakes with Maine maple syrup. Served in oceanfront dining room. (Sunday brunch and all dinners are served in the main Oakland House restaurant.)
PLUS: Recreation barn with upright piano, TV/VCR, movies, Ping-Pong. Guests' refrigerator. Lawn for croquet, volleyball, soccer. Rowboats for guests' use. Extensive perennial gardens. Arrangements made for schooner and powerboat excursions. A highlight: Jim's Thursday-night lobster picnics on the beach. In summer, box lunches may be purchased. A single phone for guests' use plus a guests' office with phone jacks, electrical outlets, big desk.

ACCORDING TO GUESTS (many are preservationists and/or house restorers), there ought to be a medal for the meticulous work— everything from research to labor—done by B&B owners. Indeed, many hosts have won preservation awards.

⇝ *Hodgdon Island Inn*

207/633-7474

P.O. Box 492, Barter's Island Road,
Boothbay, ME 04571

FAX 207/633-0571
E-MAIL info@hodgdonislandinn.com
www.hodgdonislandinn.com

HOSTS: Peter Wilson and Peter Moran
LOCATION: Rural and residential. On an island overlooking Sheepscot Cove. Walk to lobster and seafood market (across street), working lobster pound, botanical gardens. Five-minute drive to downtown Boothbay Harbor.
OPEN: Year round. Two-night minimum on holiday weekends.
RATES: $95–$115 queen, $125–$130 king. ♥ 田 ⚸ ⤢ ⚘ ⚘

THE HALLMARK here is friendliness—friendly hosts and guests from all over the world. By the water. With a heated pool. With a homey feeling. All in an old c. 1810 sea captain's house that was raised in 1873 when a new first floor was "inserted." In the early 1990s the property was completely rejuvenated as a bed and breakfast.

As the two Peters say, "We looked at it one Sunday morning. Made an offer that night. And within a few weeks this Victorian in pristine condition—in the Maine we love—was ours! We opened in June 1999 with wicker, oak, and pine furnishings—and plans to change (over time) to more mahogany and cherry." Throughout, the Peters have hung their extensive collection of more than 150 works by well-known contemporary New England artists. Peter Moran works in Portland (Maine) as a nurse case manager. Peter Wilson—"I like to cook, to keep a nice house, and to entertain"—is primary innkeeper, having sold the Massachusetts beauty salon that he owned for twenty-seven years.

BED AND BATH: Six waterview rooms, all with private bath and ceiling fan. First floor—king/twins option, shower bath. Second floor (two rooms share a covered porch overlooking cove)—king/twins option, full bath; queen- or king-bedded rooms, each with shower bath.
BREAKFAST: 8–9:30 (Early coffee by 7.) Fresh fruit. Hot muffins. Juices. Homemade granola and other cereals. One hot entrée such as waffles, French toast, blueberry pancakes, baked eggs, strata with sausage and bacon. Freshly brewed coffee and decaf. Herbal and regular teas. Special diets accommodated with advance notice.
PLUS: In summer, chlorine-free heated outdoor pool. Beverages on covered porch. Tea in cooler weather. Adirondack chairs by the water. Gas fireplace in library.

B ED AND BREAKFAST IS THE HOTTEST TREND IN AMERICAN TRAVEL.

☞ *Kenniston Hill Inn* 207/633-2159

Route 27, P.O. Box 125,
Boothbay, ME 04537-0125

800/992-2915
FAX 207/633-2159
E-MAIL innkeeper@maine.com
www.maine.com/innkeeper/

HOSTS: Susan and David Straight
LOCATION: Two miles north of bustling Boothbay Harbor, set back from the road on a hill, surrounded by maple and oak trees. Next door to eighteen-hole golf course.
OPEN: Year round.
RATES: $69–$79 double beds, $89 and $110 twin beds. Queen or king $89; with fireplace $99–$110. Less off-season. Discover, MC, Visa. ♥ ⊞ ❖ ⚄ ⚿ 🖤

"How OLD IS this house?" is the usual question asked by guests as they enter the beamed living room, which has a huge hearth with two bake-ovens and a David-reproduced mantel. Period wallpapers, stenciling, wainscoting, country primitives, and David's decorative moldings are in some rooms. The handsome 1786 center chimney Georgian Colonial has seen several remodelings. Yes, its history is complete with a ghost story.

Susan, who was working in banking, and David, a creative cabinetmaker (reproducing early country pieces) and a craftsman (of Nantucket Lightship baskets), purchased the established inn in 1990. Many of their guests linger to enjoy the house and grounds. Others go antiquing, seal watching, or sightseeing.

IN RESIDENCE: Jack, a Yorkshire terrier, "a good napper."
BED AND BATH: Ten rooms; all with private attached bath. Six rooms with individual heat control and/or ceiling fan; three with private exterior entrance. Arrangements include rooms with Duraflame fireplaces and full baths (other baths are shower, no tub). Beds (many four-posters) include king, queen, double, or two twins. Two rooms—one in main house, other in carriage house—have a queen and a twin.
BREAKFAST: Usually 8–9. Flexible for early risers and boat trippers. Intentionally special. Perhaps bacon-and-three-cheese pie, ham and Swiss wrapped in puff pastry, eggs Benedict, peaches-and-cream French toast. Herb garnishes. (Special diets accommodated.) Fruit. Home-baked goods. Family style on fine china with starched and pressed napkins at table surrounded by handcrafted Windsor chairs.
PLUS: Special occasions acknowledged. Seasonal afternoon refreshments. Perennial and Colonial-style herb gardens.

I F YOU'VE BEEN TO ONE B&B, YOU HAVEN'T BEEN TO THEM ALL.

⋙ Five Gables Inn

207/633-4551

P.O. Box 335, Murray Hill Road,
East Boothbay, ME 04544-0335

800/451-5048
E-MAIL info@fivegablesinn.com
www.fivegablesinn.com

HOSTS: Mike and De Kennedy
LOCATION: On a hill overlooking lobster boats in the bay. Ten-minute walk to center of shipbuilding village. Five-minute walk through woods to summer community of Bayville. Three miles from Boothbay Harbor. Ninety minutes north of Portland.
OPEN: Mid-May–October.
RATES: Without fireplace—$110, $115, $145. With fireplace—$115, $145; $175 for extra-large room with king bed. MC, Visa. ♥ ⊞ ❖ ⚄ ⚒ ♨

IT'S VICTORIAN—and all done over. It's a bit of quintessential Maine on the water. With innkeepers whose various experiences include a hint of fantasy. In the 1990s they worked on a yacht in Tahiti before traveling around the world for two years "for our midlife break." Mike, a graduate of the Culinary Institute of America, has been a chef "from Cape Cod to Hong Kong." For many years, starting in the 1980s, he had a renovation business (Victorians) in Atlanta; there he met and married De, an artist/teacher who "as daughter of an old Southern family, organized many house parties at their summer antebellum estate." Mike's other careers: merchant seaman, Montana logger, member of an American theater group in Paris, actor in TV commercials, and leader of historic tours in Atlanta. In 1996 all these experiences led to the world of innkeeping here in the region's only remaining Victorian (1890s) hotel; which had been saved and transformed in the late 1980s by the previous innkeepers. Every room now has a water view and, yes, a private bath. Some have fireplaces. Throughout, there are reproduction and traditional furnishings and some of De's family pieces. Once again the wide veranda with hammock and lots of wicker is filled with guests enjoying the view and serenity. For those who come by sea, the inn has one mooring.

IN RESIDENCE: Puddy, "lap cat extraordinaire."
BED AND BATH: Fifteen carpeted rooms (five with fireplace) have queen bed, king, or king/twins option; all with bay view. All private baths, some shower only, some tub/shower.
BREAKFAST: 8–9:30. Fresh fruit. Tomato-basil frittata, apples baked in puff pastry or blueberry stuffed French toast, roasted herb potatoes. Freshly baked bread, homemade muffins or scones. Jams and flavored butters. Homemade granola and muesli. Cereals. Juices. Buffet style; eat in common room or on the veranda.
PLUS: Wood-burning fireplace in common room. Afternoon tea or lemonade with baked goods. Fresh fruit. Maps for off-beaten-path tours. Swimming—in typical (cold) Maine water—from dock across the street.

⋙ From Massachusetts: *"What a fantastic place!"*

ᕵ *Anchor Watch*   207/633-7565

9 Eames Road,   E-MAIL diane@lincoln.midcoast.com
Boothbay Harbor, ME 04538-1005   www.maineguide.com/boothbay/anchorwatch

HOSTS: Diane Campbell and daughter Kathy Reed
LOCATION: Shorefront. Off main thoroughfare, on a dead-end street, a five-minute walk
to town's shops, restaurants, and boat trips. Near 500 acres of Land Trust
scenic hiking acres.
OPEN: Year round. Two-night minimum holiday weekends.
RATES: Vary according to view of ocean. Summer $130–$145. Winter $90–$105;
packages include (restaurant) Ebb Tide's chowder and boat trip. $20 third
person. MC, Visa. ♥ ⊞ ⚥ ⅄ ⚒ ⚒

ᕵ Rave reviews keep coming from guests who remember *"the pink light of morn-
ing reflected off the ocean . . . fresh flowers, spotless everything, hot breakfast breads . . . outstanding breakfasts . . . presentation of meals superb . . . make-yourself-at-home atmosphere . . .
everything you hope a B&B will be. . . . Of all B&Bs we (honeymooners from England) stayed
in, this was our favorite. . . . A treasure tucked right outside of town."* Letters come from
guests who have slept in every room and guests who have returned with in-laws and babes-
in-arms.

IN 1985 Diane Campbell and her husband left their jobs as English teacher and design engineer to return to the town where they grew up. To accommodate their ferry passengers
(to Monhegan—with its hiking trails—and Squirrel Islands), they bought the house next
door, decorated in country cottage style, and became innkeepers. Now there's a pier and
float for fishing and swimming. Now daughter Kathy—and her nine-year-old daughter
Kimberly—assist. Son Bill operates the fleet of three boats for Monhegan trips, conducts
harbor tours, and offers sailboat rides (on a Friendship sloop). Always, there's the view:
two lighthouses, six islands, yachts and sometimes cruise ships. When harvest time is
right, lobstermen are close enough to chat with guests.

IN RESIDENCE: Smokey, an outside cat.
BED AND BATH: Five Monhegan Island theme rooms on first (with private entrance and
water view), second (with ceiling fans), and third (with air conditioning) floors. All private baths; two full, three with shower and no tub. Third-floor rooms have ocean views
and shared deck. Views of ocean or garden from second-floor rooms (one has French
door leading to balcony). Three queen-bedded rooms. One with both a queen and a twin
bed. One with a king.
BREAKFAST: 8–9. (Continental after 9.) "A morning party." Could be apple pancakes and
blueberry muffins; orange/pineapple or blueberry blintzes and bran muffins;
banana/strawberry popovers with warm applesauce and rhubarb muffins; or baked orange French toast. Most special diets accommodated. Served in seaside room (by fire in
winter) with seven windows facing the water; in summer, tray tables for porch or deck.
PLUS: Afternoon tea table. In season, discount coupons for harbor tour. Microwave popcorn. Laundry facilities. Fishing lines available. In evening, kitchen facilities available.

1830 Admiral's Quarters Inn

207/633-2474

71 Commercial Street,
Boothbay Harbor, ME 04538

FAX 207/633-5904
E-MAIL loon@admiralsquartersinn.com
www.admiralsquartersinn.com

HOSTS: Les and Deb Hallstrom
LOCATION: At head of harbor. Downtown. With lawn on harbor side; minutes to shops and restaurants.
OPEN: Mid-February through November.
RATES: June 15–October 15 $125 twin beds, $135 queen, $155 queen suite. Off-season $75–$105. Third person $20. Discover, MC, Visa ♥ ⊞ ⅍ ⚱

🛏 From Scotland, Florida, Vermont, New York, New Jersey: *"This was by far the best B&B throughout our trip . . . sincere welcome . . . felt we were staying with friends. . . . Our favorite place in Maine. . . . Beautiful landscaping, solarium for watching harbor come alive and the sunset. . . . Perfect! . . . Hated to leave. . . . From the spotless rooms to the wonderful breakfast to the family atmosphere, it deserves five stars."*

"AFTER BOOTHBAY Harbor, there's only heaven," says Les. When he and Deb, avid B&B travelers, found they were spending more weekends here than in the Boston area, they purchased this white clapboard B&B, originally built by a sea captain in 1830. They made extensive renovations inside and out, painted all the walls white, and furnished with family heirlooms, lots of wicker, loon artifacts, and a teddy bear collection. Since opening in 1996—"with a coming-home ambiance"—they offer front-row seats for the 180-degree harbor view, including the July 4 Windjammer Cup. For chilly times there's a woodstove in the popular solarium. For "what to do," the hosts custom design day trips that may include hiking, sea kayaking, or coves and rockbound outlets "for picnics, reading, destressing." And, if you'd like, Les will take you on a driving tour of the coast. In the 1960s he managed Boston's Parker House hotel. More recently he was a realtor.

BED AND BATH: Six carpeted harborview rooms; four are two-room suites. Each has private exterior entrance and deck, private bath, ceiling fan, direct-dial phone, cable TV. Lower level—queen bed, shower bath, private patio. First floor—twin beds, sitting room, shower bath. Second floor—two suites, each with queen bed plus a daybed in sitting room, shower bath. Loft suite has queen bed on lower level, extra-long king on upper (with slanted ceilings), tub/shower bath. One room with queen bed, tub/shower bath.
BREAKFAST: 8–9:30. Banana pancakes, blueberry French toast, creamed eggs, or breakfast pizza. Homemade doughnuts, breads, muffins, coffee cake, biscuits. Juice, fresh fruit, yogurt, cereal. Always, dessert—bread pudding with ice cream, fruit crisp, or Grape-Nut pudding. (Optional menu for guests making early departures.) Buffet style. Eat in dining room or solarium, on porch, or on your own private deck.
PLUS: Afternoon tea, coffee, fruited iced tea, or mulled cider with cookies. Guest refrigerator. Lantern-lit wooden glider with awning. Rocking chairs on deck. Laundry facilities available.

🐦 The Noble House

207/647-3733

37 Highland Road, P.O. Box 180,
Bridgton, ME 04009-0180

FAX 207/647-3733

HOST: Jane Starets
LOCATION: Set back on a hill overlooking (across street from) scenic Highland Lake. Minutes' walk to antiques and crafts shops. "Near romantic restaurants" and Sabbathday Shaker Village. Five miles to Shawnee Peak at Pleasant Mountain ski area; 30 to North Conway (New Hampshire) outlet shopping; seventy-five minutes to L.L. Bean. Near swimming, hiking, skiing, golf, tennis.
OPEN: June through October; two-night minimum on weekends in July through October. Rest of year by advance reservation only.
RATES: $85 shared bath, $105–$135 private bath. Third person $15 child, $25 adult. No charge for portacrib; rollaway and bassinet also available.
♥ ♦♦ ⊞ ❖ ⚆ ♨

GUESTS PAINT the sunset. They fall asleep in the lakeside hammock. They write to me about the family that came from California in 1984 to the house built for a senator in 1903: "Enjoyed the hospitality, the location, the accommodations, and all the great food!" The Starets family bought the big well-maintained Queen Anne–style house from Dr. Noble, the town dentist for forty years. They converted the carriage house and decorated with wicker and antiques, comforters, and color-coordinated linens. As guests say, "It couldn't be a better choice for a summer retreat."

BED AND BATH: Nine rooms. Queen four-poster or double bed in three second-floor rooms that share a large full bath and porch. Huge third-floor suite with two twin beds and a double bed, private shower bath. In converted carriage house, two adjoining ground-level rooms, one with queen bed and private Jacuzzi bath; other with two twins and private shower bath. Both of these rooms open onto a large screened porch with lake view. Two other rooms with queen beds, one with Jacuzzi bath. Lakeview honeymoon suite has queen brass bed, whirlpool bath.
BREAKFAST: 8–9. Freshly squeezed orange juice, fruit, eggs, homemade bread. Cheese strata, blueberry or whole wheat pancakes, or rum raisin French toast. By fireplace in Victorian dining room.
PLUS: Grand piano. Antique organ in fireplaced parlor. Porch rockers. Special attention for honeymooners. Use of pedal boat and canoe. Hammock and barbecue at lakeside.

G UESTS ARRIVE AS STRANGERS, LEAVE AS FRIENDS.

⋙ *Kingsbrae Arms Relais & Châteaux*   506/529-1897

219 King Street, St. Andrews,
New Brunswick E5B 1Y1, Canada
Mailing address: P.O. Box 992,
Calais, ME 04619

FAX 506/529-1197
E-MAIL Kingsbrae@nbnet.nb.ca
www.kingsbrae.com

HOSTS: Harry Chancey and David Oxford
LOCATION: Twenty miles beyond the Calais border crossing. On a hill along a spacious avenue in estate district of St. Andrews. With views of Passamaquoddy Bay, islands, and countryside. Adjacent to Kingsbrae Horticultural Gardens; paths lead to a rose garden, a butterfly garden, a maze, an orchard, a wooded area, and much more. Minutes to eighteen-hole golf course. Two hours from Bangor, Maine, airport; one hour from airport in Saint John.
OPEN: Year round. Three-night weekend minimum May–October. Two-nights minimum all other times.
RATES: (In U.S. dollars. Include breakfast and dinner.) $350 double rooms. $450 double suites. MC, Visa. ♥ ⊞ ⛵ 𝅘𝅥 ♥○

⋙ From Massachusetts: *"Beautifully appointed residence. Most impressive. In the style of—maybe even better than!—the French Relais et Châteaux we have visited.* And *a delightful host."*

EXCEPTIONAL in every way. And to think the 1897 estate was about to be demolished in 1995, the year that Harry, a former PBS executive (WNET, New York), and David, a retired lawyer—they're both still youngish—"discovered" St. Andrews, a fashionable summer resort since the turn of the century. Undaunted—and encouraged by the fact that the neighboring 27 acres opened in 1998 as the must-see Kingsbrae Horticultural Gardens—the two visionaries purchased and revitalized (rebuilt) the historic structure. They had already restored seven other homes, including Centennial House, their upscale antiques-filled East Hampton, Long Island, B&B. Here "in one of the most beautiful spots on earth," inn guests are surrounded by elegance and comfort—gorgeous chandeliers; fabric-lined dining room walls; a paneled and beamed library; art and artifacts; a parlor with grand piano on raised platform (once again, musicales take place here); mahogany armoires and bedsteads crafted by skilled local residents; and fine antiques—many with stories shared by the innkeepers, longtime devotees of estate sales and auctions. Now Harry is chef. The grounds are manicured. The outdoor (16-by-32-foot) pool is heated. Glorious weddings are held here. Steps from the main house there's a fully equipped business and conference center with its own kitchen and executive lodging accommodations. Indeed, Canada's first five-star inn and the only Relais & Château in the Canadian Maritime Provinces is a vision.

IN RESIDENCE: Two dogs—Lady Edwinna, a Llasa apso, and Max, a Shih Tzu.
FOREIGN LANGUAGE SPOKEN: Some French.

continued . . .

BED AND BATH: On second and third (with view of Minister's Island) floors—five guest rooms and three suites, most with canopied king bed (some have drapes that can be drawn); one has two queen beds; suites also have a sofa bed in sitting area. All have marble full bath (some with original deep claw-foot tub or two-person whirlpool and separate glass-enclosed shower); fireplace; individual climate control; cable TV; radio; phones with voice mail; fax and computer access; plus, "for fun and a sense of history," the original servants' bell.

BREAKFAST: 8:30-10. Entrée possibilities include buttermilk pancakes, strawberry French toast, eggs and grits, jumbo croissants. Served in fireplaced dining room or on dining porch.

PLUS: Central air conditioning. Living room with two fireplaces. Full-service bar in library. Extensive wine list. An attentive staff. Vegetable and herb gardens—with St. John's Wort for tea. Dogs allowed with advance permission.

⇒ *The Camden Bed and Breakfast Association*

P.O. Box 553, Camden, ME 04843   (**BROCHURE REQUESTS ONLY**) 800/813-5015
                                                          www.camdeninns.com

LISTINGS: Fourteen owner-occupied inns, all within walking distance of village and all in 1800s houses that include Federals, Capes, Victorians, farmhouses, mansions, and restored carriage houses. Number of guest rooms: four to eleven. Although most are B&Bs serving breakfast only, many serve afternoon tea. Two serve dinner also; one has a famous restaurant.

RESERVATIONS: Travelers make their own reservations directly with each inn. From May through October, association members act as a clearinghouse, providing a referral system for available openings.

RATES: $75–$205. All inns accept credit cards. Cancellation policies differ from inn to inn. Inquire about package rates that include dinners at "your" or another inn, theater tickets, lighthouse cruises, and stitchery weekends.

MEMBERS OF this association are hospitable innkeepers, originally from many parts of the country, who have all fallen in love with this coastal village, a destination known for its harbor, shipyards (in continuous business for more than 200 years), windjammers, view from Mount Battie, art festivals, galleries, antiques shops, boutiques, and cultural and historic attractions. The hosts' interests include historic homes, music, gardening, antiques, lighthouses, Camden—and travelers! Before-innkeeping job descriptions include airline pilot, retailer, sculptor, decorative designer, chef, army and navy officers, teacher, engineer, advertising director, luxury hotel restaurant managers, foreign currency trader, marketer, registered nurse, librarian, customer service manager, and team member on the *Saturn V* launch vehicle project.

❧ *Hawthorn Inn*

9 High Street, Camden, ME 04843

207/236-8842

FAX 207/236-6181
E-MAIL hawthorn@midcoast.com
www.camdeninn.com

HOSTS: Patty and Nick Wharton
LOCATION: On an acre and a half, with lovely harbor views. Two-minute walk to village center. Ninety minutes to Acadia National Park and Portland.
OPEN: Year round.
RATES: June–October $120, $140, $160 main house; $175 or $205 carriage house (two-night weekend minimum stay). November–May $80–$160 main house, $175 carriage house. $35 third person. Amex, MC, Visa. ♥ ❖ ✗ ⊁ ♨

❧ From Connecticut: *"A great discovery. We do a considerable amount of traveling . . . gorgeous Victorian . . . impeccably maintained . . . our initial impression was one of charming elegance that continued through the cheerfully appointed interior . . . consummate hosts . . . sumptuous breakfast (be sure to try the 'secret sauce') rivaled only by incredible vista from dining room."*

FROM THE OUTSIDE it's a grand Queen Anne Victorian with turret. Inside there's the feeling of light and space, thanks to all those windows *and* the spacious entry hall; it has modern lighting and a staircase that is open to the third floor (done by previous owner, an architect). Also converted was the 1894 carriage house—into four guest rooms, each with sliding glass doors that lead to a private deck overlooking the expansive lawn and harbor beyond. Throughout the main house there are antiques, hardwood floors, and, everywhere, those tall windows. The carriage house is furnished similarly. In Texas, Patty was a corporate secretary and bank officer. In Texas, Chicago, and London, Nick managed a foreign currency trading operation. In 1995 they made their career change "to work together in a small beautiful place near good sailing waters." And what of the charming elegance? "The day an English couple came to breakfast in pajamas and robes was a compliment to our relaxed atmosphere!"

BED AND BATH: Ten rooms; some with fireplace, double Jacuzzi, private deck, harbor view, TV, VCR. All private baths. *Main house*—six rooms on second and garden levels (one with fireplace, two with soaking tub). In adjacent *carriage house*—four rooms with TV/VCR and private deck or patio. Two with harbor view have Jacuzzi and fireplace. Two garden-view rooms; one with Jacuzzi, other with fireplace. Most rooms have a queen bed. One main-house room has two twins. One carriage-house room has one queen and one twin bed.
BREAKFAST: 8–9. Entrée might be Lexlee's Exotic Eggs or crème caramel French toast. Fresh fruit; homemade granola; home-baked coffee cakes, scones, muffins, and breads. In fireplaced dining room or on deck overlooking grounds and harbor.
PLUS: Wood-burning fireplaces in living and dining rooms. That great deck overlooking gardens and harbor.

～ *A Little Dream*   207/236-8742

60 High Street, Camden, ME 04843   FAX 207/236-8742
                                                         E-MAIL dreamers@mint.net

HOSTS: Joanne Ball and (husband) William Fontana
LOCATION: In historic district on Route 1. Across the road from Norumbega, a castlelike manor house. With winter views of bay and islands. Ten-minute walk to harbor and restaurants.
OPEN: Year round. Two-night minimum in July and August and on holiday weekends.
RATES: May 15–October 30 $95, $129, $139, $159 queen; $159 king; $169–$225 suites. Off-season $95 queen, $120 king, $120–$185 suites. Amex, MC, Visa.
♥ ⚥ ⅙

～ From New Jersey: "*Everything is a treat to the eyes. . . . Joanne leaves books in your room on your interests . . . informs you about antiques shows or auctions . . . ready with restaurant recommendations and reservations . . . teddy bears dressed in Victorian clothing . . . breakfasts so artfully arranged. . . . Classical music plays . . . attention to detail is amazing.*"

AND MORE: bay windows, antique dolls, quilts, plants, high-button shoes, lace, florals, ribbons and flowers, wicker-furnished porch, and plenty of comfort. It's elegant and whimsical. It's English country. Joanne calls it "a romantic fantasy . . . serendipity really. In 1989 we drove by this Victorian cottage with big wraparound porch, bought it that day, and thought, Now what? How about a B&B? A little dream. . . . Bill is a sculptor who does commissions. I do decorative art for stores; some can be seen on Newbury Street in Boston. When we lived in New York we owned (upscale) toy stores and children's shops. Here we meet guests from all over the world, people with interesting viewpoints on life, many honeymooners, actors, musicians, film producers, sailors. . . . It's wonderful." *Country Inns* and *Glamour* magazines concur.

FOREIGN LANGUAGES SPOKEN: Italian, plus some French and German. (Joanne lived in Switzerland as a child.)
BED AND BATH: Seven rooms; six are air-conditioned. Room sizes vary. All with phones, antique beds, en-suite private baths. In main house on first floor—two rooms with queen bed, full bath; one is turreted room with air conditioning, gas fireplace, small bath, TV. Second floor—canopied king, air conditioning, shower bath, TV, private deck; queen, shower bath, private deck. In carriage house (water view)—air-conditioned suite with queen bed, skylights, sitting room, TV, wet bar, shower bath, French doors leading to private deck with telescope; very large air-conditioned suite with king bed, water view, gas fireplace, TV, full bath, and private covered porch; second floor has large air-conditioned room with queen bed, TV, cathedral ceiling, full bath.
BREAKFAST: At 8, 8:30, 9, or 9:30; choose the night before. Off-season, "whenever." Lemon-ricotta soufflé pancakes with raspberry sauce, fresh fruit crepes, omelets including smoked salmon or apple brie, banana-pecan waffles, poached pears. Kentucky butter cake

or strawberry almond muffins. Edible flower garnish. At candlelit dining room table with linen, silver, and china, or on glassed-in porch at small tables for two.

PLUS: Gas-fireplaced living room. Afternoon refreshments. Wicker-furnished glassed-in porch and plant-filled tiled sunroom. Turndown service.

ᗷ Maine Stay Inn   207/236-9636

22 High Street,   FAX 207/236-0621
Camden, ME 04843-1735   E-MAIL innkeeper@mainestay.com
                                                         www.mainestay.com

HOSTS: Peter and Donny Smith and Diana Robson
LOCATION: On 2 acres along Route 1, among homes on National Register of Historic Places. Five-minute walk to harbor.
OPEN: Year round.
RATES: June through late October $100, $150. ($40 for third person). Lower rates off-season. Amex, MC, Visa. ♥ ⊞ ❖ ⚉ ⊬

AN AWARD WINNER. Popular year round. The home of nationally known Stitch-Inn (needlework) weekends. There s an antique coal stove in the country kitchen. A glassed-in porch that looks out onto a lovely garden. Period furnishings, Oriental rugs, and wide-board floors are here too.

What to do? Printed suggestions galore. Activities measured in blocks and miles from the door. Places you've heard a lot about. Places you've never heard a word about. A walking tour. Gardens. A woodland path. Hints: "Don't sit next to the foghorn." Bicycle tours. Driving tours. Maps. Small business meeting arrangements. Recipes at the touch of a computer key. Sometimes, a song or two with guests in the kitchen. (Peter sang with barbershop quartets. His wife, Donny, a registered nurse, and her twin sister, Diana, a music major and librarian, have competed in Sweet Adelines groups.) It all happens in a house that began in 1802 and continues to see changes to this day. As Peter says, "After thirty-six years in the navy, we wanted to drop anchor in a nice spot and let the world come to us." Guests—and press features galore—have summed it up: "Delightful."

BED AND BATH: Eight rooms (four with fireplace); all with private bath, individual thermostat, ceiling fan. On ground floor, very private 16-by-19-foot room has queen bed, woodstove, views of woods, private patio. Other rooms on second and third floors include two huge rooms, one with cathedral ceiling; one two-room suite and one three-room suite.

BREAKFAST: Usually 8:30, but as early as 7. (Coffee at 6.) Fresh fruit, egg dish, waffles, French toast, or whole wheat pancakes. Breads, muffins, or scones. Served on English china with sterling silver and crystal.

PLUS: Afternoon tea. Freshly baked cookies. Flannel sheets. Two fireplaced parlors. TV room with VCR. Behind the barn—reached by stone bridge over brook—a holly grove with secluded bench. Transportation to/from airport or windjammers.

⚓ The Black Duck on Corea Harbor   207/963-2689

Crowley Island Road,   FAX 207/963-7495
P.O. Box 39,   E-MAIL bduck@acadia.net OR blackduck@blackduck.com
Corea, ME 04624-0039   www.blackduck.com

HOSTS: Barry Canner and Robert Travers
LOCATION: In a small fishing village. Overlooks harbor, lobster cooperative, outer islands. On 12 acres with rock outcrops and berry bushes. Minutes' walk to
sand beach; 800 feet to salt pond and marsh. Five miles to Schoodic section
of Acadia National Park. Ten-minute drive to restaurants.
OPEN: Year round. Three-night minimum stay on holiday weekends.
RATES: Per room. Ocean view $90–$110 with shared or private bath. Forest view
$75, shared bath. Suite $155. Studio cottage $100. Third person $15.
Discover, MC, Visa. ♥ 🎴 ✣ ⚸ ⚹ ⚘ ⚶ 🐾

⚓ From dozens of guests who have written long lyrical letters and e-mails to
me: *"Though I had imagined getting away from it all, I discovered that we got to it all —
peace, well-being, good company—and surroundings that opened eyes and soul. . . . Hosts had
eaten in nearly every restaurant around and had been to many more spots on and off the
beaten path than could fit into any guidebook. . . . The house is comfortable, beautifully furnished without being decorated. . . . Food was excellent, absolutely fresh, imaginatively served,
different every day. . . . This is the place to taste your first nasturtium. . . . This is the place if
you dream of coming home to a kinder, gentler (de-flowered) Grandma Moses. . . . Corea
Harbor is one of Maine's treasures. . . . I was not prepared to have my fantasies exceeded. . . .
Took hundreds of photographs just because we slowed down enough to appreciate the nuances
of what we were seeing. . . . A short walk away one can cross a sandbar at low tide to a wonderful island with views of others nearby. . . . Gave our daughter and her friend ideas for blueberry picking, marsh finding, animal care . . . people sit on the porch and talk or read and
doze. Cottage is a writer's dream by the sea. . . . Gorgeous setting. . . . Hosts are hospitable and
humorous . . . a special place."*

DEFINITELY off the beaten path. A rambling 1800s fisherman's house that is freshly decorated and furnished with the hosts' antiques, Oriental rugs, contemporary art, oil lamps,
and tin toy collection. Guests find the area so calming that many who arrive for one or
two nights stay longer when space is available. In Massachusetts, Barry was a city planner
in Newton and Brockton; now he consults in several Maine communities and rents local
shorefront homes for neighbors. Bob, who sold security systems, now sells real estate.
Both vacationed in the area for five years before opening here in 1991. Travelers from all
over—from Dubai to Camden, Maine—have applauded these contented innkeepers.

IN RESIDENCE: Two dogs, Pepper and Max. Cats—Ralph (female) and Alley, her mother.
Dolly Bacon, a potbellied pig.
FOREIGN LANGUAGES SPOKEN: Danish and limited French.

BED AND BATH: Four rooms; two with ocean view. First floor—room with one queen and one twin bed, private en-suite shower bath, private entrance and deck. Second floor— one room with queen bed and water view, and one with forest view and two antique brass twin beds (can be a suite), share a full bath. Waterview room with metal queen sleigh bed, private full bath, sitting room. Rollaway available. Plus two harborfront studio cottages May–October.
BREAKFAST: Usually at 8. By advance request, continental after 9. Blueberry pancakes, "Eggs Black Duck" (low fat and cholesterol), orange-glazed French toast, or baked Victorian French toast. Homemade breads and muffins. Fresh fruit. Cereal. Juice, coffee, teas. (Special diets accommodated with advance notice.) Can last for two hours on foggy or rainy days.
PLUS: Fireplaced living room. Woodstove in TV/sitting area. Library. Outdoor lounge chairs. Guest refrigerator.

⤞ Brannon-Bunker Inn

207/563-5941

349 State Route 129,
Walpole, ME 04573

800/563-9225
E-MAIL brbnkinn@lincoln.midcoast.com

HOSTS: Jeanne and Joe Hovance
LOCATION: Rural, with spectacular sunsets, "in a town that is seldom on a Maine map!" Five-mile drive from Route 1 on the road to Christmas Cove. Ten minutes to Damariscotta, fifteen to Pemaquid Point, forty-five to Camden or Boothbay.
OPEN: April–December. Advance reservations preferred.
RATES: $65 shared bath, $75 private. Suite $85 for two, $105 for three, $125 for four. Singles $5 less. Third person $10 adult, $5 child. Amex, Discover, Diners, MC, Visa. ♥ ♦♦ ⊞ ❖ ⚄ ✂

THE LAYOUT of the barn-turned-inn is fascinating. It is attached to a Cape-style house and has a wide interior staircase and a low ceiling on the first floor, creating a wonderful gathering area in the Publyck Room with its huge fieldstone fireplace. Actually, the first conversion of the barn was into a 1920s dance hall called "La Hacienda."

Jeanne, an experienced house restorer, has decorated each "deliberately old-fashioned" room with a different era of antiques and with stenciling, print wallpapers, homemade quilts, and country crafts. Joe, a collector of World War I memorabilia, was director of an environmental center and historic sites in New Jersey. After the family moved here in 1984, he combined innkeeping with an antiques shop and chair caning. Recently he returned to public education as a special education teacher in the local high school. "We welcome children because we know what it is like to travel with them. Our suggestions include everything from restaurants to a gem of a canoeing place."

continued . . .

IN RESIDENCE: One teenaged son, Jim.

BED AND BATH: Seven rooms; five with private bath. Queen, double bed, or twin beds. Two handicapped-accessible rooms—one has twin beds; the other has queen bed, shower bath, kitchenette. In second-floor suite, one double-bedded room, one with twin beds, living room area, kitchen. Cot and crib available.

BREAKFAST: 8–9:30. Early-bird special available. Juices, fresh fruit, homemade muffins, toast, cereal; coffee, tea, or milk.

PLUS: TV, games, books. Picnic table. Outdoor seating. Kitchen facilities. Babysitting.

⋙ Brewster Inn   207/924-3130

37 Zion's Hill Road, Dexter, ME 04930   E-MAIL brewster@nconline.net

HOSTS: Ivy and Michael Brooks

LOCATION: On 2 acres in a quiet residential neighborhood. Adjacent to playground with wooden equipment and picnic pavilion. Five-minute walk to downtown (antiques shops) and to Dexter Shoe factory and outlet. Ten-minute walk to 3-mile-long Lake Wasookeag (sandy beach and use of hosts' canoe and rowboat). About fifteen minutes to restaurants located between Dexter and Dover-Foxcroft. Forty miles northwest of Bangor. An hour to coastal Belfast and to Moosehead Lake. Ninety minutes to Bar Harbor and Baxter State Park. Fifteen miles off Route 1-95.

OPEN: Year round.

RATES: $59. $69 handicapped-accessible room with a double and a twin bed, and for large room with queen and daybed. $79 suite or huge room. $89 with Jacuzzi bath. Singles $49–$79. $10 per additional adult. Ten percent less for seniors or AAA members. MC, Visa. 🛉🛉 ⊞ ❖ ⌀ ⌖ ❤

⋙ From Florida, Massachusetts, Oklahoma, New York, New Hampshire, Maine: *"Ivy and Michael are super folks . . . friendly atmosphere. . . . Rooms are charming. . . . Enjoyed different entrée each morning. . . . Gardens are beautiful . . . romantic honeymoon suite."*

WHEN PRESIDENT Truman stayed here, he, too, entered through the porte cochere that leads to the front door of this classic 1930s Colonial Revival house. Built for Governor (later, Senator) Ralph Owen Brewster, it has the original lighting fixtures and tile baths. There are two covered porches; a wicker-furnished sunroom; and, in the living room, wing chairs by the fire.

In Philadelphia, Ivy was a graphic designer and college professor. Michael, a skilled carpenter who enjoys sailing, was a computer instructor, guitar teacher (he also plays the banjo and piano), and ham radio operator. After many inn stays inspired a lifestyle change, an ad in the National Trust's *Preservation* magazine led them to this established (1988) B&B in "a small town away from the crowds but just an hour's drive to major attractions." The National Register property has more than an acre of blossoms in the mature rose and perennial gardens with their arched trellises and a pergola. Warm hospitality is offered to business and wedding guests, to skiers (Eaton and Harmon mountains are within twenty minutes), and to day-trippers who explore the coast.

IN RESIDENCE: In hosts' quarters, one friendly cat.
FOREIGN LANGUAGE SPOKEN: Spanish.
BED AND BATH: Seven air-conditioned rooms; all with TV, phone, and private bath. First floor— handicapped-accessible room has one double bed and one extra-long twin; paneled suite with queen canopy bed and double whirlpool bath and fireplace. Wide stairs to second floor—queen brass bed, woodstove, sitting room with sofa bed; corner room with brass queen bed plus daybed with trundle, shower bath; brass queen bed plus twin bed, tub/shower bath; queen bed, tub/shower bath; huge paneled room with king brass bed and a three-quarter bed, woodstove, shower bath.
BREAKFAST: 7–10 (earlier by request). Buffet of fruits, juice, homemade baked goods, cereal. Entrée possibilities—gingerbread pancakes, Swiss and broccoli quiche, French toast, sausage and apples, or strata. Eat at individual tables in dining room or on benches in the garden.
PLUS: Wood-burning fireplace and an organ, "a treasure brought from Philadelphia," in living room. Coffee and tea always available. Guest refrigerator. Picnic baskets (extra charge). Clay tennis court.

⪢ *Todd House*   207/853-2328

1 Capen Avenue, Eastport, ME 04631-1001

HOST: Ruth McInnis
LOCATION: At Todd's Head on Passamaquoddy Bay in this coastal fishing village.
OPEN: Year round; minimum-stay required Fourth of July weekend.
RATES: $45 twins, $55 double or twins with fireplace, $70 or $80 queen with private bath, furnished kitchenette. $10 additional person. $5 less, six or more days.
♥ ♦♦ ⊞ ❖ ⅍ ⚘

⪢ Guests wrote: *"A haven. . . . Like an imagined visit with one's favorite relative. . . . I enjoyed meeting the assorted cast of nice characters who wandered in and out of the place . . . blueberry muffins a high point . . . (uncluttered) rooms are exquisite—"all the modern conveniences in a 200-year-old setting. . . . A little piece of heaven."*

EVERYONE REMEMBERS their visit with Ruth, who, until 1980, when she returned to Eastport to teach in her hometown, had taught in Portland. B&B is her way of sharing her love of old houses, history, and Eastport.

With advice from the Maine Historic Preservation Commission, Ruth became a restoration expert. When the chimney was rebuilt, she learned that this house was a cabin

continued . . .

in 1775 before becoming a Cape. You can almost follow the history of the house through
the Indian Room and the Cornerstone Room and into a 1990 addition. As the house is on
the National Register, the street side of the addition looks almost as it did years ago; but
the water side is all glass. Also taking advantage of the view in the spacious simple yard:
chairs by garden and fish pond, an 8-foot-tall fieldstone barbecue, and a deck.

IN RESIDENCE: Kitty, the cat, "a hit with many guests." Two birds—Polly and Hawkeye,
cockatiels. (Guests' well-behaved pets are welcome; the "most unusual" award goes to a
large parrot.)

BED AND BATH: Six rooms on two floors. First-floor queen-bedded room with private
bath. One second-floor room with a queen and a twin bed, private bath. The four rooms
that share two baths have a double or two twin beds. Some have working fireplaces, cable
TV, sitting areas, view of water. Some on first floor are handicapped accessible. Two trundle beds.

BREAKFAST: 7:30–9. Juices, coffee, tea, milk, cereals, granolas, homemade muffins and
breads, fruit. Served at antique table by huge fireplace with bake-oven and views of the
ocean.

PLUS: Tours of the house and area. Books on local history. Will meet guests at the airport
or bus. Kitchen privileges.

🦅 *Weston House Bed & Breakfast*   207/853-2907

26 Boynton Street,   800/853-2907
Eastport, ME 04631-1305   FAX 207/853-0981
                              www.virtualcities.com/me/westonhouse.htm

        HOSTS: Jett and John Peterson
     LOCATION: On a hill overlooking Passamaquoddy Bay and Campobello Island. In east-
                ernmost U.S. city, 7 miles southeast of Route 1.
         OPEN: Year round.
        RATES: Per room. $50 single, $60 double bed, $65–$70 queen, $75 king. $15 extra
                bed. ▉ ⊞ ⚲ ⚲ ☙ ⚹ ♥♡

ACCLAIMED VERMONT innkeepers wrote: "Worth traveling to the end of the earth for."
That's just what the Petersons thought in 1985 when they came from northern California
to this well-maintained 1810 Federal house—with picket fence and arbor entrance—listed
on the National Register of Historic Places. They learned its history and furnished it with
a mixture of antiques and family treasures, with antique clocks and Oriental rugs. They
experimented with orchids. And watched a lemon tree flourish—dozens harvested—in
the living room.

    John was with the U.S. Forest Service. Jett, a former junior high school teacher, super-
vised legal caseworkers in the district attorney's office. Moving to the East Coast has
meant more time to work with foods (a hit at a Fisherman's Forum) and needlepoint; to

do woodworking and gardening; to offer (by reservation) high tea in December or candle-light dinners for special occasions; and "to meet great people who come here for business or pleasure."

IN RESIDENCE: Duncan is a Scottish terrier; Aggie, a brindle Scottish terrier.
BED AND BATH: Five large second-floor rooms share (robes provided) one tub/ shower and one shower bath. King-bedded room has working fireplace, color cable TV, bay view. Two rooms each with a queen bed. One double-bedded room. One room with single brass bed. Rollaway available.
BREAKFAST: "A holiday every day." Accompanied by classical music. Could be fish-shaped puff pastry filled with smoked salmon and topped with dill, poached egg, hollandaise sauce. Hallmark dish—pancakes with brandied apricot sauce and bacon curls. Cinnamon bread pudding with fresh berries and "a fabulous raspberry sauce." Wild blueberry or cranberry walnut muffins. Special dietary needs accommodated. Served in dining room or on porch.
PLUS: Afternoon tea or sherry. Mints. Fresh flowers. Kitchen woodstove. Fireplaced living and dining rooms. Croquet. Lawn chairs. A list of sixteen reasons to come to Eastport.

     From Scotland: *"Best breakfast I've had in my entire life."* From Ottawa: *"Truly the best B&B we've stayed in."* From Rhode Island: *"All parts of ourselves were nourished."* From Connecticut: *"Great food, conversation, and dogs!"*

Home-Nest Farm   207/897-4125

Baldwin Hill Road, Fayette, ME
Mailing address: RR 3, Box 2350, Kents Hill, ME 04349

       HOSTS: Arn and Leda Sturtevant and daughter Laura
    LOCATION: A 200-acre farm in hill and lake country with 65-mile panoramic view to White Mountains; 18 miles west of Augusta, 1½ miles from Route 17, "beyond a small stretch of gravel, a small annoyance that blesses us with relative isolation."
        OPEN: Year round. Reservations required. Two-night minimum stay July 1– October 15.
        RATES: Main house $60 per room. The Red Schoolhouse $120. Lilac Cottage $120. East wing $100 one floor, $120 two floors. Weekly—five times daily rate.
         ♥ ♦♦ ☒ ⅍ ⚘

MORE THAN an experience, Home-Nest gives the feeling of discovery—all because of Mainers who share their love of history and one of the prettiest spots on planet Earth with new friends. Arn is a sixth-generation resident; the family homestead restorer; a retired bank president; a farmer; and a cofounder of Norlands, a nearby living history museum where you can churn butter, cut ice, milk cows. He and Leda can direct you to waterfalls,

continued . . .

to abandoned orchards in woods, or to private local swimming holes. If you'd like, they'll show you slides of all the possibilities and help plan day trips. You are invited to picnic in the meadow, pick berries, fish, ski from the door, enjoy their sheep, peruse the published 500-page Sturtevant family history. It's no wonder that guests speak of "an oasis" and "down-home hosts."

IN RESIDENCE: Winters, daughter Laura is host. One Shetland pony; twenty-two sheep (each has a name); two horses; one donkey.

BED AND BATH: Eight rooms in three antiques-furnished historic buildings, each with kitchen and oil heat. In hosts' residence (1817 Greek Revival)—on second floor, canopied queen bed, private tub bath. East wing (1784 saltbox)—first floor, canopied queen, private bath, fireplaced parlor with TV, living/dining room with old cooking fireplace, kitchen; two bedrooms and bath on second floor. Lilac Cottage (1800 Cape)—three bedrooms on two floors (one king, two doubles); two baths, woodstove. Red Schoolhouse (1830 Greek Revival)—two large bedrooms, one with king bed and air conditioning, one with double bed; a twin sleeper couch in living room; bath with shower; woodstove. Rollaway available.

BREAKFAST: Prepared by guests in own well-appointed kitchen with well-stocked larder of fresh fruit, homemade bread/muffins, fresh eggs, cereals, juices, coffee, jams and jellies.

PLUS: Window fans. Laundry facilities. Canoes (no charge) at nearby lakes. Beach privileges. Boat rentals available at several beaches.

    From Pennsylvania: *"Watched falling stars . . . found the Milky Way . . . heard hoot-owl . . . listened to loons . . . picked blueberries."* From England: *"A place everyone should holiday in, at least once in a lifetime . . . spacious east wing, canopied and comfortable bed, antiques here and there. . . . Laura sent us on a walk where we watched moose grazing in a glade—a magical sight."* Excerpt from poem by Bostonians: *"That sense of home. The way the light falls. The way the fog settles in. Those things that touch the soul."*

B ED AND BREAKFAST GIVES A SENSE OF PLACE.

⤳ *Brewster House Bed & Breakfast*   207/865-4121

180 Main Street,   800/865-0822
Freeport, ME 04032-1419   FAX 207/865-4221

HOSTS: Amy and Matthew Cartmell
LOCATION: Five-minute walk to L.L. Bean and outlets.
OPEN: Year round. Minimum stay required some holidays and weekends.
RATES: Mid-May–October 31 and weekends through December 31, $110–$130; suites $150–$190. November–mid-May $85–$100; suites $110–$160. Extra person $20. Discover, Amex, MC, Visa. ♥ ♦♦ ⊞ ✗ ✄

NOW THE ONCE familiar all-white Queen Anne house has a gray-green exterior with white gingerbread trim. The interior, completely done over when the Cartmells opened as a B&B in 1994, has traditional decor and Laura Ashley fabrics. (Several rooms have been re-done since.) Earlier, Amy and Matthew were private school teachers (at Kents Hill in Maine) who had lived in a dormitory with fifty teenaged girls. They also have experience in catering and hospitality fields.

IN RESIDENCE: In separate hosts' residence—Matthew, age eight, and Nicholas, age five, sometimes assist with breakfast setups. Lindsay is two. Sarah is one. Two black Labs and a cat are not allowed in guest areas.
FOREIGN LANGUAGE SPOKEN: Limited Spanish.
BED AND BATH: Seven air-conditioned and soundproofed rooms, each with individual thermostat and private attached bath. First floor—twin beds, shower bath. Second floor—four queen-bedded rooms (two with bay window), all with tub/shower bath and ceiling fan. Two air-conditioned third-floor suites—one with king bed; one with queen; both with ceiling fan, private tub/shower bath, and attached room with full bed.
BREAKFAST: Usually 7:30–9. Fresh fruit, homemade bread, muffins, coffee cake. Omelet with choice of ham, bacon, cheese, vegetables; eggs any style; waffles; pancakes; French toast; "healthy options." Served at separate tables in the tin-ceilinged dining room.
PLUS: Gas fireplace and upright piano in living room. Off-street parking.

⤳ From Kentucky, Massachusetts, Pennsylvania: *"Great!... Friendly hospitality... scrumptious coffeecake... a winner... bright and cheerful dining room... a beautiful place."*

B&Bs OFFER THE OPPORTUNITY TO GET AWAY WITHOUT GOING AWAY.

♒ *Captain Briggs House B&B*   207/865-1868

8 Maple Avenue,   800/217-2477
Freeport, ME 04032   FAX 207/865-1868

HOSTS: The Frank family
LOCATION: On a tree-lined side street. "Steps to Main Street, Harraseeket Inn, and other restaurants. Minutes' walk to L.L. Bean and other shops."
OPEN: Year round. Two-night minimum on holidays.
RATES: Summer and fall $87 doublebed, $97–$115 queen or king. Winter and spring $62–$67 double, $77–$97 queen or king. $15 extra person. MC, Visa. ♥ ᴉᴉ ᴉ ⊞ ⚔ ⚒

"THE SUNDAY *New York Times* article (August 1999) on the area was a complete surprise to me! The writer, Daisann McLane, used such marvelous words—'spotless . . . cheery . . . beautifully restored . . . gorgeous original hardwood floors . . . all for $75 including a full breakfast.' The phone hasn't stopped ringing with bookings! I never thought such a thing would happen. I moved here from Connecticut, where I had been in teaching and banking. Our family always vacationed in Maine. I bought this sea captain's house, which had become a day care center. A crew of twenty-eight people—it seemed like half of Freeport!—worked here for four months. Everyone comments on the refinished hardwood floors, especially in the dining room, where there are alternating maple and walnut boards. Lace and sheer curtains cover the windows. The walls have light colors and small-print wallcoverings. Some furnishings are antiques; most are new. It's intentionally homey. Most of my guests shop till they drop. And they ask about good lobster restaurants and what they shouldn't miss on their way to Bar Harbor, the White Mountains, or Canada." On busy weekends Mara is assisted by her grown children, Lars and Heide.

BED AND BATH: Six rooms; five are air conditioned, three have private phone. All private en-suite shower baths (room with king bed has tub/shower bath). First floor—queen bed, tall bay window; two smaller rooms, each with a double and a single bed. Second-floor rooms (with slanted ceilings on two walls)—one room with king bed, large bath; one with a queen and a double; one with a queen and cable TV.
BREAKFAST: 8–9. French toast or pancakes. Muffins and bread. Fresh fruit. Served buffet style.
PLUS: Mobile phone available to all. Seating in front yard. Living/dining room has upright piano, cable TV, VCR, books, games. Turndown service. Guest refrigerator. Off-street parking.

O NE OUT OF FIVE GUESTS LEAVES WITH THE DREAM OF OPENING A B&B.

ॐ *White Cedar Inn*

207/865-9099

178 Main Street (U.S. Route 1),
Freeport, ME 04032-1320

800/853-1269
E-MAIL capandphil@aol.com
http://members.aol.com/bedandbrk/cedar

HOSTS: Carla and Phil Kerber
LOCATION: Two blocks north of L.L. Bean.
OPEN: Year round.
RATES: Memorial Day weekend–November 1, $100–$130. Off-season, $85–$100.
Third person in room $15 year round. Amex, Discover, MC, Visa. ♥ ⊘ ⅄

As PHIL TELLS IT, "We always wanted to run an inn, so in 1986 I sold my restaurant in Berkeley Springs, West Virginia, and bought this century-old house, which had belonged to Arctic explorer Donald MacMillan when he accompanied Robert Peary to the North Pole. Carla is a nurse (part time) at the Maine Medical Center. Innkeeping is enhanced by the friendly guests, people who make us feel as if we have one of the world's largest extended families." As Carla tells it, "Phil is the reason guests return!"

To Maine the enthusiastic couple brought interests in skiing, hiking, fishing, and snowshoeing, and added carpentry, wallpapering—and parenting. Many guests wrote to me about "impeccably clean, cozy, and comfortable rooms; excellent hosts; and fantastic food."

BED AND BATH: Seven air-conditioned rooms—three on first floor, four on second. All with private bath, antique white-painted iron beds. Queen or queen and twin bed with shower bath. One first-floor room has private entrance, two queen beds, sitting area with TV, private shower bath. One second-floor room with a double and a twin bed has private hall tub/shower bath.

BREAKFAST: 7:30–9:30. Juices, homemade muffins and jams, fresh fruit, wild Maine blueberry pancakes, French toast, scrambled eggs, egg/cheese casserole, bacon or sausage or ham, waffles, coffee cake, coffee. Served in sunporch with floor-to-ceiling windows facing landscaped grounds and spired church or in dining area at top of spiral stairway.

PLUS: Common room with woodstove and TV. Picnic table. Outdoor grill.

*I*N THIS BOOK *a "full bath" includes a shower and a tub. "Shower bath"
indicates a bath that has all the essentials except a tub.*

⟿ *The Bagley House*   207/865-6566

1290 Royalsborough Road,   800/765-1772
Durham, ME 04222   FAX 207/353-5878
                                                  E-MAIL bglyhse@aol.com
                                    http://members.aol.com/bedandbrk/bagley

HOSTS: Susan Backhouse and Suzanne O'Connor
LOCATION: Six miles from downtown Freeport. On Route 136 (an old stagecoach
          route). On 6 acres with large maple trees, flowers, peace and quiet. Forty
          minutes to Popham Beach State Park and Bailey's Island ("our favorite
          spot"). Within thirty minutes of Bates and Bowdoin Colleges, art galleries,
          fairs, festivals.
OPEN: Year round.
RATES: January–May $90; $115 with wood-burning fireplace; $135 family suite with
       gas fireplace. June–December $105–$110; $125 with fireplace; $145 family
       suite. Third person $15. Singles $15 less. Amex, Discover, MC, Visa.
       ♥ ⫟⫨ ⊞ ❖ ⚆ ⅙

⟿ From New York, Florida, New Jersey, Massachusetts, Rhode Island: *"A gift to
be away from the bustle of cities, tours, and busy harbors. . . . The green fields, profusion of
wild blossoms, bird songs, and wide vistas soothe the soul. . . . Our early morning walk along
country roads was a perfect start to the day. . . . So, so clean. . . . When you think about running from home, this is the place to come . . . peace and quiet, firm mattress, great food, cozy
company."*

"HOME" HERE means hot water bottles to warm beds in cold weather. Lots of laughter.
One hostess (English-born Sue B.) wears a different hat from her collection every morning. The other (Boston-born Sue O.) "rides her John Deere mower around the estate." In
Boston the two Sues had been nurses for twenty years before becoming a computer programmer and a pre–hospital stay reviewer. In 1993 the two, who "both came from families
who were always having overnight guests," bought this well-established B&B, a restored
1772 Greek Revival house that is now on the National Register. In 1998 they built a separate addition, a post-and-beam barn with large rooms and marvelous views of field and
woods. Family reunions have been held here. Honeymooners from across the country
have called to say they arrived home safely. Itinerary planning—especially for those who
have limited time and want to see "everything"—is a feature. For a sunset cycle, the Sues
directed us to a wondrous (flat!) rural route. One family has memories of a great first-time
lobster dinner orchestrated by the Sues. This is home.

IN RESIDENCE: Orphan Andy is an outdoor cat. Lady Emma, a regal greyhound, really
loves people.
BED AND BATH: *Main house*—five rooms, each quite different. On first floor, queen
Shaker bed, adjoining full bath. On second floor, three queen-bedded rooms: one with
wood-burning fireplace, en-suite shower bath; one with en-suite shower bath; one with

tub/shower hall bath. Room under eaves has double bed and a three-quarter bed, stuffed animals and toys, hall shower bath. *New barn*—handicapped-accessible room with king or two twins, gas fireplace, shower bath. On second floor, large room with queen bed, shower bath, gas fireplace, sitting area. Suite with a queen and a trundle bed, shower bath, gas fireplace. Extra cot and portacrib available.

BREAKFAST: At 8 or 9. (Time arranged night before; earlier for business travelers. Continental for early departures; breakfast-to-go arranged. Coffee always available at 7:15.) Fresh fruit. Poached peaches or pears, strawberries. Muesli, yogurt, homemade granola, bread, muffins, sweet breads, scones. Huge entrée repertoire includes sourdough Belgian waffles, egg-and-cheese strata, pancakes, French toast, soufflés, frittata. Their own honey. Special diets accommodated. Served at long table in kitchen with beehive oven and large fireplace.

PLUS: Afternoon refreshments. Guest refrigerator. Beach towels. Window fans. Down comforters. Outside gas grill, picnic table, chairs, croquet, *boccie.* In new barn—large living room (available for small conferences or private parties) with wood-burning stove.

⋙ *Atlantic Seal B&B*   207/865-6112

25 Main Street, P.O. Box 146,   (TOLL-FREE) 877-ATL SEAL
South Freeport, ME 04078-0146

HOST: Captain Thomas Ring
LOCATION: On the water, in a quiet neighborhood overlooking Freeport harbor. Minutes' walk to famous open-air/indoor lobster restaurant. Three miles to L.L. Bean and outlets.
OPEN: Year round. Two-day minimum on holiday weekends.
RATES: $125, $135 with fireplace, $175 with Jacuzzi. Off-season $95. Third person $15. ♥ ♦♦ ☞ ⊞ ❖ ♨ ⅍ ☙ 椒

A GREAT B&B. That's what many people, including some interested in Tom's spring-through-summer excursion boat (for island visits, seal watching, and lobstering demonstrations), suggested for this 1850s Cape Cod-style house, the house that Tom grew up in. Now one guest room features a Jacuzzi; another, a wood-burning fireplace. The guest parlor is furnished with family pieces—nautical memorabilia, Victorian sofa, oil paintings, and spinning wheel. Always, there's the view. And guests are welcome to use the private dock—featured in *Yankee* magazine—for swimming or launching their own canoes or kayaks. Rowboats and two mountain bikes are available for guests.

Tom, a Maine Maritime Academy graduate who steers some tugboats coming into Portland harbor, knows the area—and the water! He will show your kids how to hold a sextant and look through a telescope "the way Admiral Peary found his location on the North Pole." Beyond shopping, he suggests the theater (Bowdoin College is 8 miles away), historic houses, lighthouses and museums.

continued . . .

IN RESIDENCE: Mittens, "a very friendly cat."
BED AND BATH: Four air-conditioned rooms; all private baths. First floor—queen bed, wood-burning fireplace, private bath with shower seat, washer/dryer. Second-floor rooms, each with water view: room with one queen and a double, Jacuzzi for two, shower, refrigerator, cable TV/VCR, and balcony. One with king bed, Rumford wood-burning fireplace, window seat, slanted ceilings, private shower bath, cable TV. One with queen bed, hall full bath. Rollaway available.
BREAKFAST: Usually 8:30. (Earlier for L.L. Bean Fishing School and plane departures.) Lobster omelet is seasonal house specialty. Fresh fruit, sausages, homemade muffins, orange juice, fresh-brewed coffee, teas. In dining room on antique china.
PLUS: Wood-burning fireplace in living room. Snacks. Beach towels. Picnic tables. Stone terrace. Stone steps (twenty-one) to shore. Reservations made for Tom's half-day excursions.

☺ From Michigan, Massachusetts, Texas, Florida, California: *"Picture-perfect views, great comfortable rooms, hearty breakfast. The cruise was wonderful. What a vacation! . . . Sunrise was wonderful. . . . The delicious apple pancake breakfast surpassed only by the beauty of the home, the view of the harbor, and the hospitality. . . . Have stayed in more than 251 B&Bs. This is #1 so far."*

☺ Acres of Austria

Route 5, Firelane 48,
Fryeburg, ME 04037

207/925-6547
800/988-4391
FAX 207/925-6547
E-MAIL info@acresofaustria.com
www.acresofaustria.com

HOSTS: Candice and Franz Redl and (young) son Nick
LOCATION: Secluded. At end of a half-mile-long drive. On 65 acres of woods with paths (groomed trails in winter) throughout and along the Old Saco River. With mountain views. Seven miles to Fryeburg Fairgrounds; 4 to Lovell Restaurant; 10 miles east of outlets in North Conway, New Hampshire. Five miles to Shawnee Peak ski area. Near horse-drawn sleigh rides.
OPEN: Year round.
RATES: May 15–October 31 and holidays $89 queen, $109 queen suite, $109 queen and sofa, $135 king and twin, $165 king and twin with Jacuzzi. November 1–May 14 $10–$15 less. Monday–Thursday $59 single (host-selected room). Additional adult $19; child (three to eleven years) $12. $30 less for third consecutive night. Package rates for Murder Mysteries, July Fourth Lobster Feast, Austrian Candlelit Christmas, Thanksgiving, New Year's Eve, Valentine's. MC, Visa. ♥ 𝍐 ⊞ ✄ ⛱ 𝍖

"EVERYONE WONDERS if there *is* something at the end of the dirt drive. Then they come to the pavement and the gate to this peaceful and private surprise, a contemporary lodge we were fortunate enough to find when we decided to move from Austria. We lived in Franz's native Vienna, where he owned the family business, a bus company. But, as he told me on our very first meeting, he really wanted to be a professional chef, and he dreamed of coming to America. Often he would cook for his tennis club gatherings, and we entertained frequently. After college (in Michigan), not knowing what I wanted to do, I had traveled with two suitcases and a typewriter to Vienna. I taught English and swimming—and married Franz! In 1996 we bought this empty-for-three-years property, built in 1978 as a company retreat. That's why it has all this marvelous common area, with a 16-foot ceiling and a balcony reached by a stairway from either end. There are windows galore, window seats, and a large fireplace. Before we opened in June 1997, we did a lot of work with the help of Franz's visiting parents and the craftsmen in my family. We decorated with stenciling and various kinds of faux finishes. Antiques are here and there, including our 1920s Austrian billiard table. This area is so romantic! You can paddle our canoe for about 4 miles along the quiet Old Saco River to a covered bridge. We see blue heron and wood ducks and lots of wildlife."

IN RESIDENCE: Son Nicky, age six, and dog, Jessie, "are both very happy to find someone to play ball with."

FOREIGN LANGUAGE SPOKEN: German.

BED AND BATH: Six rooms. All have phone and attached private bath; some have mini-refrigerator. Two balcony rooms: one has a queen bed; the other is a suite with queen bed in one room, queen sofa bed in other; each has a shower bath, sliding glass doors to deck. Two handicapped-accessible rooms in wing; one has a king bed and one twin, bath with shower/oversized corner tub for two; other has queen bed and a queen sofa bed, tub/shower bath. Carriage house air-conditioned loft rooms have king bed, Jacuzzi bath, TV/VCR.

BREAKFAST: 7:30-9. (Continental, 6–7:30 and 9–10.) Juice, fresh fruit, and homemade pastries. Choice of sweet (apricot crepes, French toast made with homemade cinnamon raisin bread, or Belgian waffles) or savory (veggie omelet, burritos, scrambled eggs with homemade spicy beef sausage) entrée. Yogurt, granola, cereals.

PLUS: Dinner by advance arrangement—at least 24 hours. (Inquire about current dates.) Entrées $13–$25. Appetizers and desserts $4–$6. Some specialties include Wiener schnitzel or *kasknocken* (homemade pasta with blend of cheeses). Sacher torte.

From New York: *"Excellent . . . immaculate. . . . Franz is destined to be Chef of the Year!"* From Rhode Island: *"Picture-postcard setting reminiscent of Austria itself."* From Tennessee: *"European amenities and foods with Southern hospitality."* From Massachusetts: *"Everything—absolutely marvelous."*

≈ The Blair Hill Inn at Moosehead Lake   207/695-0224

Lily Bay Road, P.O. Box 1288,   FAX 207/695-4324
Greenville, ME 04441   E-MAIL blairhill@moosehead.net
                              www.blairhill.com

HOSTS: Dan and Ruth McLaughlin
LOCATION: Spectacular and majestic. Overlooking Moosehead Lake and its islands and surrounding mountains. On 15 acres of manicured lawns, wildflower meadows, gardens, woods, and a pond. Two minutes' drive from downtown Greenville. Close to all area activities.
OPEN: Year round. Two-night minimum on weekends.
RATES: Vary according to room and bed size, view, amenities. November through May $175, $200, $220, $250. June through October $175, $220, $230, $265. Additional person $20. Discover, MC, Visa. ♥ ⊞ ⚗ ⚒ ☘ ♨

CONSIDERED "WORLD CLASS" and even magical by many well-traveled guests, this 1891 Victorian—with just eight guest rooms—is both informal and luxurious. When ESPN filmed a fly-fishing special, the inn served as the set for discussions and as the camera location for panoramic lake and mountain views. In 1999, the inn's second year, the *New York Times* food critic, recognized by a guest, lauded the twenty-four-seat restaurant (which may be limited to overnight guests). Architecturally, a 20-foot-tall stone retaining wall perches the mansion at treetop level, providing guests a breathtaking view of the region. There's a porte cochere, walnut paneling, seven wood-burning fireplaces, pocket doors, and, yes, huge picture windows. For the pièce de résistance, there's a 90-foot-long veranda with wicker and rockers, hummingbirds at the feeders, calls of the loons, and sunsets.

How did the McLaughlins find this treasure? "The *Historic Preservation* magazine ad jumped off the page," says Ruth, who together with Dan had collected antiques for their "someday" inn. Both sold computer software systems for Chicago-based companies. They loved to entertain, won awards for their home landscaping, and had considerable old-house restoration experience. Here they rebuilt and added baths, installed a new kitchen with wood-burning grill, and embellished the gardens. They take canoe trips, explore trails, and in winter downhill ski at Squaw Mountain. They enjoy the community, "gorgeous views always," and grateful guests.

IN RESIDENCE: In hosts' quarters—daughter Lily is eight; son Jack is nine.
BED AND BATH: Eight rooms (four with wood-burning fireplace); one is a suite. All private baths (one is cedar); some tub/shower, some shower only, one with double tub. Second floor—five rooms with king four-poster or queen (one is canopied); suite with queen bed in one room, two twins in other. Third floor—queen or one or two double beds. One small room with twin-sized daybed ($75 or $100) available only with adjoining double-bedded room.
BREAKFAST: 8–9. Entrées made to order. Fresh fruit with Grand Marnier cream sauce; buttermilk waffles with bananas and toasted pecans; eggs Benedict with fresh Maine lobster; or eggs with salmon, lemon, and garden chives. Freshly blended strawberry/banana

smoothie. Broiled grapefruit with caramelized brown sugar. Juices and hot beverages. Served on windowed porch at tables set with white linen, silver, china, fresh flowers. PLUS: Cocktails available after 4 P.M. Baby grand piano in living room. Library with books, games, TV. VCR in armoire. Fine linens. Robes. Feather beds. Spring water. Chocolates. Croquet. Concierge service for everything including fly-fishing, moose safaris, kayaking, white-water rafting, seaplane rides, golf, dog sledding.

The Lodge at Moosehead Lake   207/695-4400

Box 1167,   FAX 207/695-2281

Upon Lily Bay Road,   E-MAIL innkeeper@lodgeatmooseheadlake.com

Greenville, ME 04441   www.lodgeatmooseheadlake.com

HOSTS: Roger and Jennifer Cauchi (Cow-key)

LOCATION: Quiet. "Wilderness!" Overlooking Moosehead Lake (huge) and Squaw Mountain (10 miles to skiing). Two and a half miles from village; ninety minutes from Bangor International Airport.

OPEN: Year round. Two-night minimum.

RATES: Lodge rooms $165–$295; retreat suites $250–$395. Extra person $50. Discover, MC, Visa. ♥ ⚅ ⚇ ⚉

From New Hampshire, Massachusetts, Germany, Florida: *"Guests are pampered by special people. . . . Delightful, interesting, and charming decor. . . . Helped arrange a hike on Mount Kineo requiring a boat ride. . . . Never found anything in the United States that compares . . . elegant, tasteful, warm, luxurious, comfortable, fun. . . . Breakfast, a feast . . . paradise . . . every conceivable comfort with impeccable service. . . . Extraordinary."*

EXTRAORDINARY BY DESIGN. What was a shingled Cape Cod Colonial summer house in 1917 now has everything from sound-insulated walls to four-poster beds hand carved with bear, totem poles, moose, trout, or loon—and, in the carriage house, three luxurious suites. (Jennifer is an interior design consultant for inns.) There are traditional furnishings, Oriental rugs on carpeting, rustic twig pieces, antlers for curtain rods, and folk art— all hailed by the media, including *Country Inns* and *Country Living* magazines and the Learning Channel's *Great Country Inns.* Awards include one for "the most outstanding North American Johansen Association member inn or hotel member."

Roger, who is Maltese and English—"everyone asks"—comes to Maine via England (where he was trained in hotel management), the French Riviera, the New York Hilton, and Pennsylvania—where he met, hired, and then married Jennifer. The granddaughter of a Maine woodsman, she had worked in the hospitality industry in Florida, Yellowstone National Park, and Germany. They opened here in 1994 after leaving their own international corporate meeting/planning business. Together they share magnificent sunsets with authors (at least two novels partially written here) and with other guests who extol everything.

continued . . .

IN RESIDENCE: Two English cocker spaniels, Bosley and Jesse.
FOREIGN LANGUAGE SPOKEN: *"Un petit peu de Français."*
BED AND BATH: Five air-conditioned rooms (two are handicapped accessible) plus three retreat 15-by-35-foot suites (two with suspended beds; one with additional fireplace in bath). All but one room have lake view and queen beds; one (forest view) with double bed. Amenities vary—private patio, private deck, sofa bed, separate living room. All with private Jacuzzi bath, hair dryer, gas fireplace, TV/VCR, sitting area, coffeemaker.
BREAKFAST: Usually 8–9. Appetizer might be fresh fruit with maple syrup and coconut. Apple and walnut pancakes, deviled eggs pizza, or toasted French bread with caramelized pears—all garnished with fresh fruit. Yogurts, cereal, breads, bagels, English muffins. At individual dining room tables or on deck; both with panoramic lake view.
PLUS: Four common rooms, two with (off-season) wood-burning fireplace. Full liquor license (no bar). Turndown service. Pool table. Croquet. Arrangements for trail bike, canoe, and ski rentals; and for dog sledding, moose safaris, and ski plane service for day trips to Sugarloaf. Sometimes, the distant sound of Montreal–Halifax train.

⤚ *The Alewife House*   207/985-2118

756 Alewive Road,   E-MAIL alewifehouse@mainecoast.net
Kennebunk, ME 04043-6021   www.virtualcities.com/ons/me/k/mek95020.htm

HOSTS: Maryellen and Tom Foley
LOCATION: On Route 35, which connects area beaches, villages, and exit 3 of Maine Turnpike. On 6 acres with gardens, orchards, woods, and a brook. Ten minutes to Dock Square.
OPEN: Year round.
RATES: $95–$99. Additional person in room $45. MC, Visa. ♥ ☛ ⊞ ❖ ⌀ ⌁

THIS LARGE 1756 house of post-and-beam construction, owned by the same family for 200 years, was purchased in 1986 by the well-traveled Foleys. Tom is a retired bank personnel director and army officer who has worked in the computer industry. In 1996 he was an International Executive Service Corps volunteer with a technical company in Egypt. Maryellen, a former curator for the Kennebunkport Historical Society, is a teacher and writer and has an antiques shop on the premises.

BED AND BATH: Two second-floor air-conditioned rooms. One is a suite with a queen bed and two working fireplaces, private stairway to first-floor sitting room and shower bath. Other has a double bed and private first-floor tub/hand-held shower bath, access to private fireplaced sitting room.
BREAKFAST: Usually 8–9. Fresh fruits, homemade muffins, vanilla yogurt with wild Maine blueberries, freshly brewed coffee, tea. Served in garden room that has wide-board pine floors (Tom's 1995 project) and huge windows overlooking gardens and forest.
PLUS: Large screened porch. Expansive rear lawns with croquet. Beach parking passes. Turndown service upon request. Three guest sitting rooms.

➵ Guests wrote: *"Antiques and artifacts are incredible. . . . Tom Foley is truly an ambassador for Maine. Could answer questions about local and state matters . . . hospitable innkeepers proud of the house's history . . . setting is so lovely. . . . Great people!"*

➵ *The Waldo Emerson Inn*   207/985-4250

108 Summer Street,
Kennebunk, ME 04043

FAX 207/985-6574
E-MAIL mainelyquilts@cybertours.com
www.bbhost.com/waldoemersoninn

HOSTS: Wayne and Maggie Carver
LOCATION: In historic district, on Route 35—on the way to Kennebunkport and beaches (2 miles farther). Next to the elaborate gingerbread Wedding Cake House, Maine's most famous private home. Surrounded by lawns, meadows, forest.
OPEN: May–December.
RATES: May and June $75 single, $85 double. July–December $90 single, $100 double. $10 use of fireplace. $15 extra person. Amex, Discover, MC, Visa.
♥ ♦♦ ❖ ⚡ ✂

➵ From Australia: *"It's New England through and through. The hosts are lovely. And, yes, the quilts are marvelous."*

IT IS "NEW ENGLAND"—together with a story that includes B&B stays while backpacking in Europe in the 1970s, search trips from Canada to Cape Cod, and Wayne spotting a FOR SALE sign being mounted here in 3 feet of snow in the winter of 1992. Now local residents, too, are delighted with Wayne's restoration of the beautifully preserved Dutch Colonial built in 1753 by shipbuilder Waldo Emerson, uncle of Ralph Waldo. Fireplaces have rare Wedgwood tiles. There are wide-board floors. All new private baths. Period antiques. Windowpanes etched with the initials of residents of the past two hundred years. And a hundred original exterior shutters, which were stored in the very tilted barn. "You straightened out the barn," say tourists when they see the 1995 replica, home of Maggie's dream shop; she sells handmade and antique quilts here and in a second location in Dock Square. In Sarasota, Florida, she was an emergency room medical technologist and learned quilting from the local Amish women. Wayne—"I have always loved cooking"—was in the construction equipment rental business. Guests and hosts agree: "This B&B is wonderful."

IN RESIDENCE: Son Jud, age eighteen. Three dogs—"Trickie-woo and Remi, two Shih Tzus, and their constant companion, Gus, a golden retriever."
BED AND BATH: Up grand staircase to four second-floor rooms, each with three large windows, private bath. Three rooms have queen beds—one has adjacent hall full bath; others have en-suite shower baths; all have wood-burning fireplaces. One room has two twin beds, en-suite shower bath.

continued . . .

BREAKFAST: 8–9:30. Coffee earlier. Fresh melons. Cinnamon swirl French toast with sausages. And baked cashew granola. Served in beamed kitchen that has woodstove and meadow view, or in handsome fireplaced dining room.

PLUS: Two parlors with fireplaces. Autumn afternoon refreshments—maybe popcorn and cider.

ᔰ *Arundel Meadows Inn*   207/985-3770

Route 1, Arundel, ME   E-MAIL docmy@aol.com
Mailing address: P.O. Box 1129,   www.gwi.net/arundel_meadows_inn
Kennebunk, ME 04043

HOSTS: Murray Yaeger and Mark Bachelder
LOCATION: On 3½ acres next to Kennebunk River with meadows and perennial gardens. Ten minutes to Kennebunk Beach and Kennebunkport. Eight miles to Ogunquit; 5 to Rachel Carson Reserve or to quiet paths, woods, and ocean at Laudholm Farm.
OPEN: Year round. Two-night weekend minimum, summer and holiday weekends.
RATES: $75–$110; with fireplace $95–$110. Suites $110–$135. Additional guest (up to two) $20. Less Columbus Day–Memorial Day, except for holiday weekends. Inquire about special packages. MC, Visa. ❖ ⚲ ⊁

ᔰ From Illinois: *"This inn is a must! . . . many services beyond the call."* From Massachusetts: *"Enhanced by antique furnishings and Murray's paintings . . . wonderful afternoon tea. . . . Charming place with attentive owners . . . big suite is a great deal and very quiet."* From Connecticut: *"Rooms are perfectly done . . . ambiance clearly sophisticated without any sense of hauteur."* From everyone (seemingly) about breakfast: *"Phenomenal . . . attractively presented . . . French toast not to be missed . . . homemade croissant . . . out of this world . . . sumptuous."*

BEFORE BECOMING an innkeeper, Mark studied with Madeleine Kamman and cooked for her as well as at other Boston area restaurants. He was also an administrator at Boston's Parker House and Copley Plaza hotels. Murray is a professor emeritus at Boston University's College of Communications. The 1830 farmhouse, just about rebuilt before its 1986 B&B opening, has seen additional changes, including a suite that can be converted to a conference room, rooms made larger here, sliding glass doors added there.

IN RESIDENCE: Emma, a schnauzer.
BED AND BATH: Seven air-conditioned rooms, three with working fireplaces. All private baths; five full, two shower (no tub). Two rooms with private entrances. Queen beds in most rooms. One suite with queen-bedded room and a room with two twin beds. One suite with king bed, sitting room. One room with two double beds.
BREAKFAST: At 8 and 9. Blueberry pancakes, quiche, fresh vegetable tart, seafood crepes,

or amaretto French toast. Juices, fruit compote (homegrown berries). Homemade muffins, coffee cakes, croissants. In dining room overlooking patio.
PLUS: Hot tub. French doors leading to patio. Cable TV in several bedrooms. Small seasonal pool. Antiques shop and art gallery in barn.

✈ *The Ocean View*   207/967-2750

171 Beach Avenue,   **FAX** 207/967-5418
Kennebunk Beach, ME 04043   **E-MAIL** arena@theoceanview.com
                                                   www.theoceanview.com

HOSTS: Bob and Carole Arena
LOCATION: Directly on Kennebunk Beach, 1 mile from center of Kennebunkport. On the ocean (with views of lobster boats) and in an area of stately summer homes.
OPEN: April–December.
RATES: Late June–late October and first December weekend $195–$275. April–late June and late October–December $125–$225. (Higher rates are for suites and/or weekends.) ♥ ⚔ ⅍ ☀

CAROLE HAD years of inn experience while managing the White Barn Inn in Kennebunkport, and Bob had a considerable background in human resources; so "opening our own place" seemed quite natural. "We bought a beach cottage, located around the corner from our home. It had become a white elephant, but with a wonderful history as a summer guest house dating back to the days when travelers arrived by train."

Since they opened in 1985, the Arenas have made *many* changes, decorating with a light, airy, whimsical feeling—with interesting and colorful fabrics and with touches of luxury. Now their "painted lady" has Oriental rugs on the original hardwood common-room floors. Now, enthusiastic guests (many returnees) say that this is "the closest you'll find to a bed on the beach." Some say the location gives them a feeling of being on a boat. One from Connecticut wrote: "The atmosphere is wonderful inside and out. An ocean lover's paradise."

FOREIGN LANGUAGE SPOKEN: French.
BED AND BATH: Nine oceanfront rooms. All with private bath, telephone, CD/clock-radio, minifridge, ceiling fan, hand-painted bed ensemble. Suites have color cable TV. In main house, five rooms with queen or twin beds and many hand-painted furniture pieces. One suite with two-person shower, TV/VCR, extraordinary view. Ocean View Too, a wing of the main house (where you have breakfast in bed), has four junior suites each with canopied queen bed, sitting area, and private terrace or balcony.
BREAKFAST: 8–9:30. (Coffee at 7.) Fresh fruit. Croissants. Granola. Yogurt. Menu possibilities include baked bosc pears with yogurt, honey, and almonds; then yogurt-based Belgian waffle with seasonal fruits and crème fraîche. Or baked pineapple with brown

continued . . .

sugar glaze and dried fruits, then a breakfast pizza or lobster wrap. Served in oceanfront breakfast room. (Suites have breakfast in bed or on balcony overlooking sea.)
PLUS: Fresh flowers throughout. Robes. Fireplaced living room. TV/VCR room. Oceanfront porch with rockers. Lending library. Refreshments at 4 p.m. Beach towels. Concierge service includes arrangement of day trips (great maps for back roads).

⋙ Bufflehead Cove

207/967-3879

P.O. Box 499,
Kennebunkport, ME 04046

FAX 207/967-3879
www.buffleheadcove.com

HOSTS: Harriet and Jim Gott and daughter Shannon
LOCATION: A gem. A surprise at the end of a long unpaved drive. On 6 acres of woods and orchard. Five-minute drive from town center. On the tidal Kennebunk River, with view of Kennebunkport.
OPEN: Mid-April through December. (Possibly longer; inquire!) Two-night minimum stay.
RATES: June–October $145–$295 (suite); with balcony $275; studio $155; Hideaway $295. Off-season $20–$40 less; Hideaway $210. ♥ 田 ⚸ ⅍ ☆ 𝍖

⋙ Ecstatic guests wrote: *"Bufflehead Cove is the serenity and beauty that one seeks to feel in Maine . . . a spot that you can place inside you and reclaim once you return to your own chaos . . . wonder and anticipation down the wooded private road [to a] sea captain's home with wraparound porch smack dab on the river. . . . Decorated with flair and attention to detail . . . the most amazing breakfast served with such style . . . freshly picked flowers in every corner. . . . Harriet and Jim are special people with superb intuition . . . [know] the best secret picnic spots, hidden coves, perfect beaches. . . . From the dock we paddled upstream as adventurous as Lewis and Clark. . . . Like being in a fairy tale."*

THIS HIDDEN treasure is known for its three p's—privacy, peace, and pampering. Long, lyrical guests' letters reminisce about the Gotts, Maine natives, and their style of sharing this house on the cove "where even the gulls find shelter during an ocean storm." L.L. Bean was here for a catalog location shoot. This B&B has been featured in *USA Today* and in *Country Inns* magazine and filmed for *Houses of the World* for Tokyo television.

Harriet, who grew up in the travel industry, has hiked in Costa Rica. Jim, a commercial fisherman, has searched for his roots in Ireland. Together they have spent several months in Mexico and New Zealand.

IN RESIDENCE: Female black Lab named Lilly.
FOREIGN LANGUAGE SPOKEN: "Nonfluent Spanish."
BED AND BATH: Five rooms. All private baths. River view from all but studio, which has a private entrance and courtyard, queen bed, sitting room, shower bath, view of apple orchard and woods. Queen-bedded room has small balcony, water view, and small shower

bath. King-bedded room has two-person whirlpool, gas fireplace, large glassed balcony with water view. Suite with queen bed and shower bath has sitting room with couch, gas fireplace, private balcony. Very private air-conditioned Hideaway has king bed, gas fireplace, whirlpool tub, vaulted ceilings, ceiling fan, many windows, sweeping water views. **BREAKFAST:** 8:30–9. A typical example: freshly squeezed orange juice, fruit plate, asparagus cheese strata, bread stuffed with sausage and spices, homemade cranberry muffins. Served in dining room or on the porch; for Hideaway and balcony rooms, served in the room if requested. **PLUS:** Some rooms have ceiling fans. Wine, tea, or mulled cider by fireside in spacious beamed living room. Bose radio. Private dock and rowboats right here.

The Captain Fairfield Inn

207/967-4454

Pleasant and Green Streets, P.O. Box 1308,
Kennebunkport, ME 04046

800/322-1928
FAX 207/967-8537
E-MAIL jrw@captainfairfield.com
www.captainfairfield.com

HOSTS: Janet and Rick Wolf
LOCATION: In historic district. Surrounded by elm trees, gardens, and other sea captains' homes. Across from Village Green. One block from river. Five-minute walk to Dock Square, restaurants, shops, galleries.
OPEN: Year round. Two-day minimum on weekends; three days on some holidays.
RATES: Mid-June–October $170–$190; library suite $250 with canopied queen bed, fireplace, double whirlpool, private porch. Late October–mid-June $110–$140 weekdays, $120–$165 weekends; library suite $200–$225. Winter and spring packages with discounts for two- and three-day midweek stays. Amex, Discover, Diners, MC, Visa. ♥ ⊞ ⚸ ⚹

Guests wrote: *"Highlight of our honeymoon. . . . Made our trip so special. . . . Lovely inn. Great breakfast, fabulous gardens, gracious hospitality—what more could you ask for?"*

RICK DOES ALL the cooking. Janet, a former fund-raiser, is the baker. Before becoming innkeepers here in 1999, they entertained extensively in their Connecticut home—when Rick was not traveling around the world. As a CEO involved in apparel sales and marketing, he made thirty trips to Japan, seventeen to Australia, and many more to other countries. Now, here "in a New England village environment near the water" they have become known for their hospitality, for their breakfasts, and for decor that is traditional with a touch of elegance. A black ebony baby grand piano is the focus of the music room. Some fine antiques, some whimsical items, watercolors, old prints, and even an old Cunard Line poster are among the furnishings in this 1813 Federal Colonial mansion. Full concierge service includes advance reservations for dinner, theater, golf, and sailing.

continued . . .

IN RESIDENCE: "JJ is our affectionate and oft-photographed Bernese mountain dog. And we have two lap-loving cats."

BED AND BATH: On first two floors—nine large air-conditioned rooms with queen beds; some are canopied or four-posters. Some rooms have additional twin daybed. All with individual thermostat, private full bath (library suite has whirlpool for two). Four rooms with gas fireplace.

BREAKFAST: 8:30–9:30 weekdays. 8:30-10 weekends. (Coffee and tea available at 7.) Choose from varying daily menu. Fresh fruit and juice. Omelets, crepes, apple or blueberry pancakes, eggs Benedict. Homemade granola, muffins, and bread. Yogurt. Gourmet coffee. Fine teas. Hot chocolate in winter. By huge gathering-room hearth, in breakfast room overlooking gardens, or on patio.

PLUS: Wood-burning fireplace in living room. Cable TV in armoire in music room. Afternoon and evening refreshments. Guest refrigerator stocked with ice, spring water, and iced tea. Beach passes and towels. Special occasions acknowledged. Off-street parking.

⟿ *The Captain Lord Mansion*   207/967-3141

Pleasant and Green Streets, P.O. Box 800,   **FAX** 207/967-3172
Kennebunkport, ME 04046-0800   **E-MAIL** captain@biddeford.com
                                                             www.captainlord.com

HOSTS:	Rick Litchfield and (wife) Bev Davis
LOCATION:	Set back from road with huge lawn in front. Across from Kennebunk River. Three blocks from shops and restaurants.
OPEN:	Year round. Two-night minimum on all weekends.
RATES:	June–October and weekends through December $189–$299. Captain's Suite $399. Less off-season. Third person $25. Package rates for special Romantic or Antiquing Weekends. Discover, MC, Visa. ♥ ❖ ⌀ ⅃

COUNTLESS "BEST" awards. Magazine picture perfect for many major publications. An elegant, welcoming 1812 Federal mansion, on the National Register, that has period wallpapers, fine antiques, and many personalized touches. All created by innkeepers, almost a legend in their own time, who personally did everything—sanding, plastering, and carpentering—from the first day of ownership in 1978 until 1983, "when we could afford to hire a painting crew!" Today they live just down the street from the inn and have a wonderful staff.

Bev, who had an earlier career as a McDonald's advertising manager, dovetails behind-the-scenes work—including window treatments and ongoing decorating decisions—with her horse farm. (The entire family rides.) Rick, a former advertising account manager, has a long list of community activities—and awards. Five days a week he greets many romantics, returnees, business travelers, and guests who dream of becoming an innkeeper. And he shares the history of this glorious mansion.

BED AND BATH: Sixteen air-conditioned rooms (fifteen with gas fireplaces); some with minibar. All private baths (some with double sinks); some tub and shower, some shower only. In each room, four-poster bed (many are canopied)—king, queen, or two double beds—plus a sitting area. Full-size twin bed for third person. First-floor Captain's Suite has fireplaced room with king canopied bed, and a fireplaced bath with double whirlpool (and mood lights), bidet, marble hydromassage shower, double sinks, TV/VCR, Nordic Track "health rider" and mini–stairstepper.

BREAKFAST: Announced with chimes. Served at 8:15 and 9:30. Coffee earlier. Blueberry or apple-cinnamon pancakes, French toast, ham quiche, or cheese strata. Fresh fruit, muffins, yogurt, muesli cereal, eggs. Family style in air-conditioned country kitchen.

PLUS: Beach towels, mats, umbrellas. Lawn chairs. Afternoon tea and sweets. Chocolates. Cookies. Hair dryers.

> From many guests: *"In a word, the ultimate!"*

Cove House Bed & Breakfast

207/967-3704

11 South Maine Street,
Kennebunkport, ME 04046

E-MAIL covehouse@hotmail.com
www.covehouse.com

HOST: Barry Jones
LOCATION: Residential street with houses from early 1700s to contemporaries. On a tidal cove. Ten-minute walk to Dock Square or beach.
OPEN: Year round. Two-night minimum on all weekends.
RATES: Memorial Day–Labor Day $92 per room. Off-season $85. Singles $10 less. No charge for portacrib. Cottage $650 per week. MC, Visa.

> Guests wrote: *"Charming spot, away from traffic but within walking distance of beach. . . . Large screened porch is great. . . . Homey, rather than like a museum."*

HOME IT IS. Barry's home since he was seven years old. And the Joneses' B&B for many years. In 1998 Barry's parents purchased a larger nearby inn; and in 1999 Barry, upon graduating from college (photography major), became the sole innkeeper in this antiques-furnished Colonial farmhouse. (The oldest part was built in 1793.) He continues the traditions of value and "no rushing and plenty of relaxing" while wearing several hats, including those of gardener, maintenance man, host who serves afternoon tea, and chef—utilizing his work experiences in area restaurants.

IN RESIDENCE: In hosts' quarters—Nutmeg, "a Heinz 57 variety dog."
BED AND BATH: Four second-floor rooms with private baths and individual thermostats. Two with queen bed, en-suite shower bath. Room with three twin beds has hall tub/shower bath. Room with double bed can be booked alone or with another room and shared bath arrangement. Housekeeping cottage (sleeps two or three) with screened porch and option of breakfast in the B&B.

continued . . .

BREAKFAST: 8:30-9:30. (Coffee available at 7.) Fresh fruit. Blueberry muffins. Cinnamon French toast or egg scrambles. Vegetarian menu available.
PLUS: Woodstove and TV in living room/library. Wood-burning fireplace in den. Window fans. Lawn chairs.

⚓ Crosstrees

207/967-2780

6 South Street, P.O. Box 1333,
Kennebunkport, ME 04046-1333

800/564-1527
FAX 207/967-2610
E-MAIL info@crosstrees.com
www.crosstrees.com

HOSTS: Dennis Rafferty and Keith Henley
LOCATION: In quiet historic district within walking distance of shops, galleries, restaurants, ocean. Twenty miles south of Portland.
OPEN: Year round. Two-night minimum on weekends.
RATES: July through October queen $150, $160; king $165; suite $215. November–June $100–$175. MC, Visa. ♥ ⊞ ⚋ ⚌

ECHOES OF CHEERS! *Everyone,* including Kennebunkport colleagues, raves about the midwesterners who came to this beautiful area and wonderful community in 1998. Dennis and Keith changed the B&B name (from Kylemere House) back to that given the house by artist Abbott Fuller Graves, who lived here in the early 1900s. Completely redone inside and out and now centrally air-conditioned, the 1818 Federal house is decorated with Waverly prints and fabrics, fine furnishings, and original art. There are thirty of Dennis's works (acrylics, watercolors, and/or oils) in the fireplaced suite.

In Kansas, Dennis taught art in the public schools and at the Kansas City Art Institute. (Here he holds small classes at the inn on Wednesday nights.) Oklahoma-born Keith, a former banker, was a lawyer and headed the Kansas Corporation Commission, which regulates utilities. Here he works with a Maine B&B real estate agency.

IN RESIDENCE: Nessie, "our West Highland terrier, who doesn't bark and loves people."
FOREIGN LANGUAGE SPOKEN: German.
BED AND BATH: Four rooms; all with private en-suite bath, sitting area, cross-ventilation. Suite in attached barn with hand-hewn exposed post-and-beam construction, skylights, king-bedded room with gas fireplace, two-person whirlpool, oversized shower, sitting room with TV/VCR, small refrigerator, private exterior entrance. First-floor room has queen four-poster, wood-burning fireplace, shower bath. Second floor—Victorian Room with king bed, gas fireplace, shower bath. Extra-large room with queen four-poster, queen sofa bed, five windows, tub/shower bath.
BREAKFAST: 8:30. (Coffee at 7:30 for early risers.) Freshly squeezed juice. Muffins, croissants, biscuits, or fruit breads. Honey pecan French toast, crab or lobster quiche, blueberry pancakes, or broccoli-and-artichoke frittata. Served in the formal dining room with china, silver, and crystal. Special diets accommodated.

PLUS: Grand piano in living room. Guest refrigerator stocked with soft drinks and bottled water. Deck overlooking gardens. "Sinfully delicious room treats" such as freshly made caramel brownies or chocolate chip–peanut butter mini muffins.

🐟 From Washington, Connecticut, New Jersey, Massachusetts, New Hampshire, Minnesota: *"Outstanding. Owners were as hospitable as a good friend and as helpful as a five-star hotel concierge. . . . With the incredible breakfast they serve, this should be a 'breakfast and bed.' . . . We're going back with three other couples—taking over the whole inn. . . . Good maps and suggestions. . . . We almost never go to same place twice; Crosstrees is worth returning to. . . . Impeccable. Details—fresh flowers, chocolates, baked goodies and wine . . . we're returning with the whole family during the holidays. . . . Best of all—hospitality and comfort offered by Dennis and Keith. Great food, interesting conversation, respect privacy of guests. . . . Keith and Dennis make it special. . . . Elegant, inviting, good location, perfect hosts."*

🐟 *The Inn at Harbor Head*   207/967-5564

41 Pier Road,   FAX 207/967-1294
Kennebunkport, ME 04046-6916   **www.harborhead.com**

HOSTS: Eve and Dick Roesler
LOCATION: Quiet. On Cape Porpoise. On the harbor, with private dock. Set back from a picturesque winding road, 2 miles from Kennebunkport.
OPEN: February–December. Two-night minimum, weekends and holidays.
RATES: February–mid-May and mid-October–December $130–$230. Mid-May–mid-October and Christmas prelude and holidays $190–$315. MC, Visa. ♥ ⊞ ⌖ ⌖ ⌖

THIS IS A PEACEFUL waterfront showplace with marvelous murals and trompe l'oeil effects. It's a destination on an intimate scale that has appeared in many national "best" lists. During a 1998 B&B stay in Bar Harbor, Eve and Dick heard the inn was for sale. On their way back to Massachusetts, they looked and declared it "perfect for the lifestyle we want." They resigned their jobs at Rockport, a division of Reebok. Dick, who had built his own home, was human resources vice-president. Eve, who loves to cook, was assistant to the president. Now here they are—newlyweds as of January 1999—greeting guests who comment on "hospitality, warmth, charm, beauty, food, gardens, lobster boats, relaxation." The gulls swoop. The bell buoy beckons.

BED AND BATH: Five imaginative antiques-furnished rooms. Each with private bath, ceiling fan, air conditioning. On first floor, waterview room with queen four-poster bed, shower bath, French doors, and private deck. Plus one room with king four-poster, large Jacuzzi bath with hand-painted tiles. Upstairs, one room has queen bed, shower bath. Three-room suite has canopied four-poster king bed, skylit shower bath with soaking

continued . . .

tub, tiled gas log fireplace in sitting room with French doors to waterview balcony. Another suite has king bed, sitting area, large bath with two-person Jacuzzi and bidet, corner gas fireplace, cathedral ceiling, skylight, "unparalleled" view from private balcony. **BREAKFAST:** At 9. (Coffee and tea at 8.) Freshly squeezed juice in stemmed glasses. Fruit (maybe fruit brulée or grapefruit and kiwi in champagne). Sweet or savory entrée—perhaps crabmeat-and-bacon quiche with broiled tomato and fresh baked rolls; eggs Florentine served over Canadian bacon and toast rounds with asparagus and Hollandaise; honey pecan French toast; or wild blueberry pancakes with warm maple syrup. (Special diets accommodated.) At table set with flowers, linen, and silver in Oriental-style dining room. **PLUS:** Music (often classical or jazz). Down pillows and comforters. Phone jacks. Special occasions acknowledged. Beverages, cheese and crackers. Afternoon tea in off-season. Hammocks. Library, games, puzzles. Beach passes and towels.

≈ The Inn on South Street

207/967-5151

P.O. Box 478A, South Street, Kennebunkport, ME 04046

800/963-5151
FAX 207/967-4385
E-MAIL edowns@cybertours.com
www.innonsouthst.com

HOSTS: Eva and Jacques Downs
LOCATION: On a quiet tree-lined street in the historic village area, within easy walking distance of shops, restaurants, and beaches.
OPEN: May-November. Minimum stay on weekends, holidays, and high season July–October.
RATES: June–October $145–$165; suite $205. Off-season $125; $175 with fireplace; suite $205–$225; some special packages. MC, Visa. ♥ ⊞ ❖ ⚡ ⚡

≈ Guests wrote: *"A gem . . . that special something you long to come back to . . . exquisite traditional furnishings . . . beautiful gardens . . . a charming, romantic getaway . . . breakfast is the best time . . . gracious hosts who are good storytellers and listeners."*

"GRACIOUS" ALSO applies to the nineteenth-century Greek Revival house, which became a beautifully decorated and impeccably maintained B&B when the Downs children were in college. There are wonderful window treatments made by Eva, an Oriental influence in the living room, attractive perennial gardens, and "presented" cuisine that inspires poets. Plus a room arrangement that provides much privacy.

Jack is a retired professor of American history; he is also an expert on the early American trade with China. Before becoming full-time innkeeper—"with just four rooms so that we can carry out our personal style"—Eva, a great source for all kinds of area information, was an occupational therapist and child-care administrator.

FOREIGN LANGUAGES SPOKEN: Spanish and German fluently; some Russian.

BED AND BATH: Three spacious rooms, one per floor, plus an apartment/suite; all with in-room phones. On first floor, canopied four-poster queen bed, a single daybed, shower bath with hand-painted tiles, fireplace (Duraflame logs), small refrigerator. On second, queen brass bed, full bath, small refrigerator. On third, queen bed, a twin sleigh bed, decorated floor, full bath. First-floor apartment/suite (perfect for honeymooners or a family) has private entrance, kitchen, room with four-poster queen bed, gas fireplace, living room with double sofa bed, full bath with Jacuzzi.

BREAKFAST: 8:30–9. Intentionally special. Soufflé-omelets with fruit sauces, filled German pancake, or blintzes. Juice. Fruit. Homemade jams. Served in country kitchen; or in garden, weather permitting.

PLUS: Coffee at 7:30. Afternoon beverage. Living room with gas fireplace, balcony. Fresh flowers. Terrace, goldfish pond, perennial garden. No TV.

➳ *Lake Brook Bed & Breakfast*   207/967-4069

P.O. Box 762, Lower Village,   **E-MAIL** carolyn@lakebrookbb.com
57 Western Avenue,   **www.lakebrookbb.com**
Kennebunkport, ME 04046

HOST: Carolyn A. McAdams

LOCATION: On a tree-lined main street. One mile from beach. "Across street from out-standing restaurant." Half mile from Kennebunkport's Dock Square. Facing salt marsh and a tidal brook that ebbs and flows. "Excellent birding. And quite an array of wildlife—sometimes moose, fox, or deer."

OPEN: Year round. Two-night weekend minimum; three nights on holidays.

RATES: Late June–October and Christmas season $95 double bed, $110 queen, $130 suite. Child $15; extra person $15. Less off-season. ♥ ♦♦♦ ☞ ⊞ ❖ ♨ ✂

    ➳ From Massachusetts: *"A peaceful B&B . . . a warm, caring hostess . . . our hide-away . . . a different creative menu each day."* From Canada: *"Carolyn manages with a deft touch . . . comfortable beds, delicious breakfasts, and good conversation in a dazzling natural setting—keeping everything unaffected."* From Vermont: *"The essence of Maine hospitality."*

SPECTACULAR GARDENS, too, are a feature at this turn-of-the-century farmhouse. Carolyn changed the floor plan, changed the baths (they're all private), and hung Maine seacoast watercolors. A former Peace Corps member, Carolyn returned to Costa Rica in 1988 and stayed with some of the same families she had lived with twenty years earlier. Since, she has had many other interesting travels. "In many ways, the Peace Corps (and B&B too) makes us realize we are all the same."

IN RESIDENCE: Cali, a "very friendly double-pawed calico cat."

FOREIGN LANGUAGE SPOKEN: Spanish.

continued . . .

BED AND BATH: Three rooms and one suite. Second-floor rooms each have ceiling fan and private exterior entrance. Double bed, shower bath. Art deco room with queen bed, shower bath. Queen bed (with garden bench headboard), large full bath. July and August—third-floor suite (three ocean-breeze windows) with double bed, full kitchen, single daybed in living room, shower bath.
BREAKFAST: 8–9. Fresh fruit, juice; tea and Carolyn's own special blend of coffee. Repertoire includes homemade English muffin bread; *boeuf à la Newburg* on toast; Finnish puff with fruit poached in sherry, sausage on side; ricotta/orange bake; Mexican torte; baked French toast; asparagus/cheese strata. In dining room or on wraparound porch overlooking tidal brook.
PLUS: Porch rockers. In summer, refreshing beverage. Ceiling fans in second-floor rooms. Down comforters. Free loan of beach parking passes.

⋙ Maine Stay Inn and Cottages

207/967-2117

34 Maine Street, P.O. Box 500a,
Kennebunkport, ME 04046-1800

800/950-2117
FAX 207/967-8757
E-MAIL innkeeper@mainestayinn.com
www.mainestayinn.com

HOSTS: Lindsay and Carol Copeland
LOCATION: On a main street in a residential historic district. On more than an acre of lawn. Five-minute walk to Dock Square and harbor.
OPEN: Year round. Two-night minimum on most weekends.
RATES: Inn rooms and one-bedroom cottages $160–$195. Suites, fireplace cottages, and two-bedroom cottage $185–$245. Mid-October–late June $105–$175, $135–$225. Off-season two-night package, November–May. Amex, MC, Visa. ♥ ♦♦ ❖ ✗ ✂

IT'S ROMANTIC. It's historic. And families are comfortable here too. It's all according to the plan that evolved when Lindsay, who was in bank marketing for seventeen years, and Carol, who was in strategic planning and product management, decided to make a living "in a hands-on way, in a small year-round town that has a diversity of culture." They moved from Seattle in 1989. For decor they chose a Victorian flavor, using period wallcoverings, wicker, and reproduction headboards. During breakfast and at tea, Lindsay and Carol are often asked about restaurants—including some that are kid-friendly—and about off-the-beaten-path suggestions such as apple picking, back roads, a low-tide walk to Goat Island Light, a lobster-boat cruise, cycling routes . . . "full concierge service!"

Built in square block Italianate style around 1860, the inn is on the National Register of Historic Places. The main house has had many additions—including bay windows, porches, a cupola, and a suspended flying staircase.

BED AND BATH: All private baths; tub and shower or shower only. And all rooms are air-conditioned. Six main-house rooms—four corner rooms with queen bed; one with private deck and gas fireplace, one with double whirlpool tub. First-floor suite has queen bed, fireplaced parlor with double sofa bed. Second-floor suite has carved mahogany four-poster king bed, gas fireplace in bedroom, parlor with double sofa bed. Ten cottage rooms, six with fireplace (three are wood-burning; three are gas); seven with kitchenettes and three with breakfast nooks and whirlpool tubs; one cottage is two-bedroom, rest have one bedroom. Plus cozy queen-bedded cottage suite without kitchenette but with sitting room, two-sided gas fireplace, and double whirlpool tub. In cottage rooms with kitchen, option of breakfast brought in a basket.

BREAKFAST: 8–9:30. Sumptuous. Varies daily. Entrée repertoire includes baked omelet, cheese blintzes, apple-spice pancakes, French toast. Fresh fruit. Muffins, breads, or scones. Homemade granola. Yogurt. In dining room set with lace cloths, china, and mugs—or on wraparound porch.

PLUS: Color cable TV (hidden in armoires in main inn) and hair dryer in each room. Setups. Afternoon tea, coffee, lemonade, or cider with homemade cookies or brownies. Swing set and climber. Beach passes.

Old Fort Inn

207/967-5353

P.O. Box M, Old Fort Avenue,
Kennebunkport, ME 04046-1688

800/828-3678
FAX 207/967-4547
E-MAIL ofi@ispchannel.com
www.oldfortinn.com

HOSTS: Sheila and David Aldrich

LOCATION: Secluded and quiet. On 15 acres in an area of large summer estates. One block from the ocean.

OPEN: Mid-April through mid-December. Two-day minimum on all weekends; also July–Labor Day and mid-September through mid-October. Three-day minimum on holiday weekends.

RATES: June–December: $135–$150 smaller room. $150–$210 two double beds and a daybed. $165–$210 larger rooms. $160–$225 large corner rooms with Jacuzzi. $225–$325 suite. $25 third person. November and spring midweek package rates. Amex, Discover, MC, Visa. ⊞ ❖ ⚥ ⚰

WHEN THE Aldriches created an intimate inn and miniresort—with 25-by-50-foot freshwater heated pool, tennis court, and shuffleboard—they converted an 1880s barn to a lodge with a massive brick fireplace, exposed beams, and weathered pine wall boards. A turn-of-the-century brick and stone carriage house now has antiques-furnished guest rooms, each with air conditioning, electric heat, wall-to-wall carpeting, color TV, a wet bar, and a direct dial phone.

continued . . .

This has been home to the Aldriches since 1980, when David left the oil industry and Sheila, a former flight attendant, brought antiques-shop experience. Her decor features country pieces, Laura Ashley papers and prints, and stenciling. David oversees construction and maintenance—and spends time in the antiques shop, where he's always ready to discuss tennis or skiing, or maybe the restoration of antique cars.

BED AND BATH: Sixteen large rooms, all with private bath (some with Jacuzzi and/or gas fireplace). All with canopied or four-poster bed—king, queen, two doubles. Suite has canopied king, sitting room, another room with sleep sofa.
BREAKFAST: 8:30–10. "Deluxe buffet." Juice, fresh fruit, quiche, waffles, cereals, yogurt, homemade granola, muffins, croissants, hot beverages.
PLUS: Entire inn is air conditioned. One hour of free tennis daily. Cookies. Candies. Laundry for guests' use.

    From Ohio: *"Staying at twelve different places made this inn stand out more by comparison. . . . We'll call well ahead before next summer to ensure we can stay for an extended time."*

The Inn at Portsmouth Harbor   207/439-4040

6 Water Street, Kittery, ME 03904-1641   FAX 207/438-9286
E-MAIL innph@cybertours.com
www.innatportsmouth.com

HOSTS: Kim and Terry O'Mahoney
LOCATION: On the town green and the banks of the Piscataqua River. Fantastic cycling country. Ten-minute walk across bridge to Portsmouth, New Hampshire (more than eighty restaurants, Strawbery Banke, arts festival, concerts, boat excursions, antiquing); fifteen-minute scenic drive to ocean beaches, twenty minutes to University of New Hampshire. Fifteen minutes from Exeter, N.H. (home of Philips Exeter Academy); two minutes from Kittery's 160-plus outlet stores.
OPEN: Year round. Two-night weekend minimum May–October and "some special periods."
RATES: May–October $135–$155. November–April $85–$155. Weekday discounts November–April. Amex, MC, Visa. ♥ ⊞ ❖ ⚄ ⌇

    From Connecticut: *"Stayed during UNH's parents weekend. Felt we had rediscovered old friends. Even the dog treated us like family! . . . Sunday morning first cup of coffee around the center island in well-equipped kitchen. . . . Then, seated across from dining room crackling fire, our taste buds were overwhelmed by the day's special of wild blueberries cascading over French toast."* From Pennsylvania: *"Immaculate. . . . Fine antique furnishings . . . helpful suggestions."* From Massachusetts: *"Everything was perfect! Although Portsmouth was our destination, the trek across the bridge to Kittery was well worth it. Terry's mellow manner complements Kim's enthusiasm to create a great comfortable atmosphere. Of note—corn pancakes with smoked salmon, crème fraîche, dill, and capers."*

As GUESTS can tell, the O'Mahoneys found (in 1998) their idea of the perfect place and lifestyle. The area reminds Terry of his native Portsmouth in Devonshire, England. "I love smelling the salt air in the morning and hearing the seagulls wail. And it's wonderful to be able to follow the activities of Chase (hockey) and Aine (lacrosse)—something I couldn't do in California, where I started a bank in the 1980s." (He traveled extensively.) Kim, a former nurse, loves to cook—incredible dishes—and has always been involved in community projects. Their 1889 brick Italianate Victorian, formerly known as the Gundalow Inn, is eclectically furnished with antiques and with watercolors of maritime scenes in England. How are they doing? One couple wrote to me: "Our favorite innkeepers during our stays at six bed and breakfasts in New England!"

IN RESIDENCE: Daughter, Aine, age sixteen; son, Chase, age thirteen. Murphy, a friendly golden retriever "not allowed in guest rooms."
FOREIGN LANGUAGES SPOKEN: French and some Spanish.
BED AND BATH: Five rooms, all with TV, air conditioning (in season), in-room voice mail, and private tub/shower baths. (Third floor has hand-held showers.) On second floor, two queen-bedded rooms, river views; one king with feather bed. On third, one with queen bed, one with two twins, skylit river views.
BREAKFAST: 8–9 (early coffee and newspapers at 7:30). Freshly squeezed juice. Seasonal fruit dish (cranberry applesauce, baked apple, poached winter fruit compote, spiced citrus compote). Entrée might be corn pancakes with smoked salmon, goat cheese soufflé with prosciutto, streusel French toast with wild blueberry sauce, gingerbread pancakes with sautéed apples. Special diets accommodated with advance notice. Served at individual tables in the beamed-ceilinged dining room with fireplace and river view.
PLUS: Completely sprinklered. Ceiling fans. Individual thermostats. Beach towels. Perennial and herb gardens. Rockers on porch overlooking river.

*I*NNKEEPING MAY BE *America's most envied profession. As one host mused, "Where else can you get a job where, every day, someone tells you how wonderful you are?"*

➳ Flying Cloud Bed & Breakfast   207/563-2484

P.O. Box 549, 45 River Road,   E-MAIL stay@theflyingcloud.com
Newcastle, ME 04553-0549   www.theflyingcloud.com

> **HOSTS:** Betty and Ron Howe
> **LOCATION:** In a neighborhood with some other 1800s ship captains' homes. Across from 250-year-old shipyard "still in same family, still building wooden sailing vessels." Half mile to Damariscotta downtown; 14 miles to Boothbay Harbor and Pemaquid Point, 30 to Camden, 33 to Freeport.
> **OPEN:** Year round.
> **RATES:** $80 twin beds, $95 queen, $105 king and suite. Additional person $20. Amex, MC, Visa. ♥ ♦♦ ⊞ ♨ ♥♡

METICULOUS AND comfortable, yes. With a flexible hostess, a native Mainer, who is loved, even by the guest who complained—really—about the bird that pooped on his car. (Her response: "That's part of the Maine experience.")

In 1998 the Howes sold their Lewiston home, an old farmhouse, and bought this well-established, recently renovated B&B, an 1840 Greek Revival that is added to a 1790 original Cape. Some floors are wide pumpkin pine. Furnishings are a blend of antiques, country, and traditional. Ron, who still commutes—41 miles—to his insurance business in Lewiston, is the official lawnkeeper, paperer, and painter. Betty, full-time innkeeper, had a career with AT&T (information systems) and as a manager with United States Cellular. Now, every day, she greets guests who delight in this area. They savor the scene of a moored lobster boat or worm diggers across the way. The sunsets over the water. And the informal at-home feeling. Many return.

BED AND BATH: Five rooms; four with river view. All private baths. First floor—corner room with queen bed, private shower bath, old beehive Dutch oven. Second floor—suite with queen bed in one room, two twins in the other; claw-foot tub with shower. Large corner room with floor-to-ceiling windows, high king four-poster, private hallway bath with bidet and double-wide shower. Third floor—two carpeted rooms (one with two twin beds, one with queen), each with three-way ventilation, skylight, shower bath.
BREAKFAST: Usually 8–8:30. Sourdough blueberry pancakes, Grand Marnier French toast, Belgian waffles, apple quiche, stratas. Muffins. Fresh fruit, yogurt, juice. Special diets accommodated. In dining room, on front deck overlooking river, or on rear screened porch.
PLUS: "Cookies and lemonade or hot beverages always waiting." Wood-burning fireplace in two common rooms. Spinet piano in living room. Large standing fans.

⤜ *The Harborview Inn at Newcastle*   207/563-2900

34 Main Street, Newcastle, ME 04553   **FAX** 207/563-2900
E-MAIL joe@theharborview.com
www.theharborview.com

HOST: Joe McEntee
LOCATION: On Route 1, across from church. High on a knoll with marvelous view of Damariscotta/Newcastle harbor. One-quarter mile (minutes' walk) to Damariscotta restaurants and shops. Twenty miles to Boothbay Harbor and Pemaquid Point.
OPEN: April through November.
RATES: $110–$150. Singles $90–$130. MC, Visa. ⚹ ⚹

TALK ABOUT career changes! Affable Joe has loved them all—his roles as financial manager and chief financial officer (Corning Glass Works and MasterCard); as naval officer; as company president (printing and color imaging businesses) and executive vice president (*Parade* magazine and premier Philadelphia restaurants); and, in the 1980s, as culinary school student and later chef and manager. Yes, he has kept a journal. (I asked.) After purchasing this 1841 Cape house in 1996, Joe restored it, furnished with antiques and original art, and became, as one guest said, "a warm, charming, thoughtful host." Dozens of others sent me long detailed notes that included the following raves.

     ⤜ Guests wrote: *"An extraordinary haven. . . . Accommodations equal the best of any Relais & Chateaux we've stayed at. . . . Waking up to breakfast at Joe's is like going home, if your home is a four-star restaurant. . . . Creative breakfast is a bouquet! We all took pictures. . . . Breakfast is an event. . . . Joe is a warm, charming, thoughtful host . . . the consummate innkeeper. . . . Good directions and information about sights and activities. . . . I'm a computer buff; took so many pictures, Bernice, that I'm sending you a slide show. . . . Superb harbor view. . . . Beautifully restored house. . . gorgeous flower arrangements. . . ideal location close to quaint shops, a wonderful bookstore and great crabcakes in Damariscotta . . . a special place . . . a bit of heaven . . . elegant and comfortable."*

IN RESIDENCE: Charlie, "an affectionate and well-trained golden retriever who makes a living room appearance by guest invitation only."
BED AND BATH: Three large rooms, each with private tiled bath, phone, ceiling fan, cable TV, individual thermostat. First floor—handicapped-accessible room with king/twins option, full bath. Second-floor carpeted rooms each have gas fireplace, private entrance, deck, water view. One room has queen four-poster, extra-large shower in bath; other (very) large room has wood-paneled beamed cathedral ceiling, king bed, full bath.
BREAKFAST: At 8. (Earlier by arrangement; coffee available at 6:30.) Freshly squeezed orange juice. Table settings and menus vary daily. Could be "A little French toast" with crème fraîche and applesauce or "a little pumpkin waffle." Stuffed corn husks, roasted thyme potatoes with bacon and tomato, poached egg atop potato latke, or grilled chicken

continued . . .

with parsley béchamel sauce. Nutmeg or orange sour cream coffee cake. Individual menus printed and personalized. Served by old brick fireplace in dining room or on spacious deck overlooking the river.

PLUS: Waterview deck has steps to gardens and lawn chairs. Second-floor reading room with hundreds of books, including recent releases. Upright piano and Celtic harp in beamed, light-filled (nine windows) living room.

ᗷ The Pine Hill Inn

207/361-1004

14 Pine Hill South, P.O. Box 2336,
Ogunquit, ME 03907

FAX 207/361-1815
E-MAIL pinehill@cybertours.com
www.pinehillinn.com

HOSTS: Frank and Lou-Ann Agnelli
LOCATION: Secluded, "with just the sound of birds." On a knoll overlooking gardens. Five-minute walk to Perkins Cove, restaurants, shops, beginning of Cliff Walk. Two-mile trolley ride to sandy beach; ten minutes to Kittery outlets. Sixty-eight miles from Logan Airport.
OPEN: February–December 15. Two-night minimum July, August, and September.
RATES: King $140. Queen $115–$130, $140 with private deck, $160 king. Additional person $25. Less off-season. Cottage $850/week, four guests. MC, Visa.
♥ ⊞ 林

ᗷ From Massachusetts, Colorado, Rhode Island, Connecticut, Pennsylvania: *"Fabulous hosts, breakfast, house, decor, location. . . . Near Perkins Cove. Away from the crowds. . . . Loved their new puppy and new orchid plants so much that I bought one of each at the same places! . . . Warm ambiance of old-fashioned hospitality and Victorian charm. . . . Beautifully appointed. . . . A place to melt away your stress and rejuvenate your batteries. . . . Elegant, comfortable, relaxing. A jewel of an inn."*

THE AGNELLIS had all these impressions the first time *they* were guests here in 1997. Perfect timing. The inn, a century-old Victorian, was for sale. Frank, a food company manager, and Lou-Ann, a former social worker who has interior design experience, had dreamed of owning an inn "when the kids grew up." The day came. Here, from the 50-foot-long porch you hear harbor sounds and birds. The living room features unusual original floor-to-ceiling tongue-and-groove pine walls and ceiling. There's a Victorian fireplace; Tiffany lamps; lace; a tufted antique sofa; an Oriental rug; and, for a coffee table, a put-your-feet-on old trunk. Even on the phone, you can tell that these innkeepers are in love with Maine, food, decor, and people. The enthusiasm is contagious.

IN RESIDENCE: "Our cocker spaniel, Mr. Max. is a beach bum. Often, he accompanies guests to Perkins Cove."
BED AND BATH: Five air-conditioned rooms with king or queen beds. Each with private bath, robes, individual heat control, ceiling fan. All beds have European linens and

feather beds. First-floor room has private deck and exterior entrance. Another room has private deck. Cottage has two bedrooms (sleeps four), air conditioning, TV/VCR, full kitchen, deck, gas grill.

BREAKFAST: Usually 8–9. Freshly squeezed orange juice, fruit cup, homemade granola, yogurt. House special: stuffed French toast with strawberry sauce. Crepes or pancakes. Homemade muffins, pastries (pear tart a favorite), breads, jams, jellies. Served in great room or on screened porch.

₰ *Woodland Gardens Bed & Breakfast*   207/361-1310

150 Josiah Norton Road,
Cape Neddick, ME 03902

E-MAIL woodland@cybertours.com
www.woodlandgardens.com

HOSTS: Paulette and Peter O'Connor

LOCATION: Secluded wooded country, no other house in view. On 4 acres with spectac-ular perennial and vegetable gardens. Two miles from Ogunquit's summer theater, restaurants, antiquing, gift shops, art galleries, and 3-mile-long white sand beach. Thirty-five minutes south of Portland, twenty from Kittery's factory outlets.

OPEN: Year round.

RATES: $120–$135 summer; less for midweek two- and five-night stays. Ten to 15 percent less in fall and winter. Dinner packages with two nearby restaurants. $25 additional person. ♥ ♦♦ ⊞ ⚶ ⚸

₰ Echoed on dozens of cards: *"A wonderful retreat with a friendly, relaxed at-mosphere in a luxurious setting. Magnificent breakfast. And wildlife. . . . Beautifully ap-pointed rooms. . . . Hospitality cannot be compared to anywhere else we have been. . . . A perfect mix of scenic beauty, outstanding gourmet cooking, and down-home country hospital-ity. . . . The best B&B we have ever been to! . . . Just wonderful. Five stars. . . . Paulette's cook-ing and eye for decorating blow Martha Stewart out of the water!"*

"YOU LOOK fifteen years younger!" exclaimed the Johnson & Johnson board member when Paulette—makeupless, in casual clothes, and with ponytail hairdo—greeted him here at the O'Connors' dream house, built in 1997 and furnished with traditional pieces. No more power suit—worn during her years as secretary to the J&J president. Plenty of outdoor activity—clearing the land and establishing the gardens. And plenty of home-making—jams, jellies, sewing, baking, embroidering, flower arranging, "all the things I loved when our five kids were growing up in the Boston area." Now, Peter, a corporate tax accountant, gives tractor rides on the property. He (proudly) wears red suspenders, a gift from a Mainer, as he escorts guests to the henhouse to gather eggs. (Photo opportunity.) And on many weekends, between 6 and 7 p.m., there's live piano music provided by Kim Karchenes, their daughter. A New England Conservatory of Music graduate, Kim is known for her playing in the Ogunquit Music Series, at Boston's Four Seasons and Ritz-

continued . . .

Carlton hotels, and in Austria too. Deer, moose, and wild turkey wander onto the grounds. The gardens enchant. The hosts share the Maine they love.

IN RESIDENCE: Misty, a gentle beagle.
BED AND BATH: Three carpeted rooms, all with air conditioning, private bath, cable TV, individual heat control, feather bed, garden views. *Main house*—room with canopied queen bed, shower bath just outside the door. Air-conditioned *carriage house* (connected to main house via breezeway)—two Williamsburg rooms, one with queen four-poster, other with two doubles; both with private exterior entrance, ceiling fan, 12-foot ceilings, two-person shower baths with seats.
BREAKFAST: 8–9. Omelets, pancakes, French toast, crepes, waffles, breakfast pies. (Secret ingredients: those freshly laid eggs and homegrown berries, melons and veggies.) Home-baked breads, muffins, or scones. Granola. Fruit crisps, apple fritters, or cobblers. Served in the kitchen or on patio by shade garden.
PLUS: Wood-burning fireplace, grand piano, and TV/VCR in 34-foot-long living room. Welcoming snacks. Turndown service. Moose-shaped gingerbread cookies. Three covered porches (one screened) with rockers, wicker furniture, ferns, and hanging plants. Hummingbirds. Nearby in winter, sleigh rides booked and cross-country skiing on 500-acre dairy farm with groomed trails and equipment rentals.

❧ *Holiday Guest House*   207/646-5582

U.S. Route 1, Wells, ME   800/891-1548
Mailing address: P.O. Box 2247,   **www.holidayguesthouse.com**
Ogunquit, ME 03907-2247

HOSTS: Rose and Lou LePage
LOCATION: On Route 1. Near Wells/Ogunquit town line. On landscaped grounds. Flanked by restaurant in old house on one side; motels on other. Across from Rachel Carson Wildlife Preserve woods. One mile to beach; 1.5 miles to Ogunquit village.
OPEN: Year round. Two-night minimum in July and August and on holiday weekends.
RATES: April, May, June $65–$85. Summer $75–$95. September–November $65–$85. Winter $65–$85. Amex, MC, Visa. ♥ ⊞ ❖ ⚡ ⚞

THE 1814 SHINGLED farmhouse was once an overnight stop for Eleanor Roosevelt on her way to Campobello and for Fala, the dog, too. Since 1987 it has been the LePages' B&B, furnished with family treasures and decorated in country style. A woodstove is in the large kitchen, which features a beamed ceiling and mounted red-handled kitchen utensils from the 1920s and 1930s. Summer guests visit on the large screened "piazza" with its wicker furnishings, rocking chairs, porcelain-topped table, and glider. Returnees come "home" to Lou, a former Connecticut insurance company tax accountant, and Rose, a nurse who has worked with hospice and head trauma patients.

BED AND BATH: Three air-conditioned second-floor rooms; each with private bath, brass bed(s), ceiling fan, small refrigerator. One with brass twin beds, en-suite shower bath. One with queen bed, detached tub/shower bath (robes provided), vaulted ceiling. Large room has canopied queen bed, TV/VCR, gas fireplace, en-suite bath with oversized shower for two.
BREAKFAST: 7:30-10. Orange juice. Fresh fruit. Cereals. Bagels, muffins, and coffee cake. Hot beverages. Buffet style in country kitchen or on screened porch.
PLUS: Grounds with lawn chairs and gardens. TV/VCR in living room with working Rumford fireplace. In-ground pool surrounded by chain-link fence and canopied area.

⚓ From Oregon, Maine, Massachusetts, Connecticut, Vermont, New Hampshire, Maryland, California: *"Delightful experience. . . . Especially enjoyed hearing about the history of the house. . . . Felt like we came HOME from a long trip!! . . . A-plus! . . . Made us feel as if we were part of the family. . . . Good directions and recommendations. . . . A place with character and quiet charm. . . trolley stop for Ogunquit just down the road. . . . Plentiful and diverse breakfast. . . . Stayed a few nights before taking a course in Haystack, Maine. Was so pleased I decided to go back after my class as well. . . . A real find: historic, beautiful, clean, comfy; warm and genuinely friendly owners."*

⚓ *Tatnic B&B*

207/676-2209

62 Tufts Road,
Wells, ME 04090-7427

FAX 207/676-5567
E-MAIL tjsmith@gwi.net

HOSTS: Tin and Jane Smith
LOCATION: Secluded. On 63 acres, across a footbridge, at the end of a 5-mile uphill road off of Route 1. Five miles to Ogunquit's beaches and Marginal Way walk, 15 to Kennebunkport.
OPEN: Year round.
RATES: $42 single, $60 double. $10 each daybed. Discover, MC, Visa. 👫 ▬ ❖ ✄

AN EXPERIENCE. A warm, inviting environment enhanced by two easy-to-be-with people who haven't changed their outlook since building their passive-solar, almost maintenance-free home "with the help of all our friends" from 1978 to 1980. It heats with about four cords of wood in the winter. Insulation and cross-ventilation keep it cool "like a cave" in summer.

Tin, an avid sea kayaker and organic farm inspector, is a talented builder-by-doing and gardener (130 fruit trees plus crops). He also works at the Laudholm/Wells Reserve, a fabulous place to walk. Since being featured in *Family Circle* for her ingenious patterns, Jane, a professional quilt maker and admired (loved!) teacher, travels nationwide to give workshops.

As in an expanded New England farmhouse, a solar addition was built in 1986 for Tin's mother, Marie-Louise Smith, who tends to the enormous (and gorgeous) flower and vegetable gardens. Tin's newest addition is a two-storied studio for Jane with a Gammill quilting machine (for comforters).

continued . . .

IN RESIDENCE: Kamik, a friendly dog. "Our workhorses—Chrissy and Sparky, Belgians—help farm, gather wood, and pull carts. Plus Duffy, Chrissy's "baby," born here in 1999. Guests are welcome to walk the quarter mile with Tin for morning feedings."
FOREIGN LANGUAGE SPOKEN: Marie-Louise speaks Danish.
BED AND BATH: Two "treetop" rooms—reached via open curved oak staircase from two-storied living room—share first-floor full bath. One room with extra-long queen bed and space for three cots; one with king/twins option.
BREAKFAST: Flexible hours. Fruit; corn pancakes with real maple syrup; homemade blueberry muffins or bread; granola or eggs. Cheerios for kids. Special diets accommodated. Served in dining area by fireplace and windowed walls that overlook beautiful gardens (and hummingbirds when we were there).
PLUS: Custom map according to your interests. Tree swing. Outdoor furniture (and maybe mosquitoes too). Ideas for a floor plan with well-designed built-ins. Kitchen facilities for dinner preparations. Wednesday quilt sessions, $12 for three hours. Inquire about spring quilt tours to Pennsylvania.

❰ From Canada, England, Connecticut, California: *"Charmant B&B est un oasis de paix. . . . A side of USA life we had never seen before. . . . Comfortable, interesting, and quite beautiful. . . . Makes us think of Anne of Green Gables. . . First visit was on our honeymoon. . . . Relaxing. . . . Special hosts in a special place."*

❰ Lakeshore Inn   207/594-4209

184 Lakeview Drive,   FAX 207/596-6407
Rockland, ME 04841   E-MAIL lakshore@midcoast.com
                                                www.midcoast.com/~lakshore

HOSTS: Joseph McCluskey and Paula Nicols
LOCATION: Facing Chickawaukie Lake (swimming, fishing, boating, parasailing). At the foot of Dodge Mountain. Surrounded by century-old trees, gardens, small orchard, and large front lawn. Set back from State Route 17, but within view of wildlife such as foxes on the property. Five-minute drive to center of Rockland and boat rentals; 7 miles south of Camden. Five minutes to Wyeth Family Center at Farnsworth Art Museum.
OPEN: Year round. Three-night minimum during lobster festival; two nights for Schooner Days and summer weekends.
RATES: Per room. $135 attached bath. $120 private across-hall bath. Ladies' Spa Weekend packages, October–June. Amex, MC, Visa. ♥ ⊞ ❖ ⚔ ⅍ ♨ 𝍖

A SKIP-LUNCH breakfast. Lake views. A deck. A patio. Enclosed outdoor Jacuzzi hot tub. Wood-burning fireplaces—one in a nine-windowed sunroom. Recently remodeled rooms and baths. Eclectic furnishings with some antiques and a touch of elegance. A huge kitchen, all done over. All in a house that was built in 1767! And found in 1993 with a FOR SALE sign when two Chicagoans were in Rockland for the Maine Lobster Festival.

Paula is the daughter of a restaurateur. She is a licensed hairdresser who has worked in accounting and retailing. Joe was executive vice president and general manager of a Colorado-based mining company. When their search for a New Hampshire B&B was unsuccessful, it was the lobster festival that brought them over the border. "And here we are!"

In the off-season Paula schedules well-received Ladies' Spa Weekends. "One seventy-five-year-old woman came with her four daughters." Programming has included yoga, facials, manicures, in-room massages, t'ai chi, and reflexology; candlelit dinners are prepared by a professional chef.

FOREIGN LANGUAGE SPOKEN: Greek.
BED AND BATH: Four air-conditioned second-floor lakeview rooms; all private baths with hand-held showers and telephones. Two rooms have a deck. Each has queen bed (one has a trundle under daybed). Rollaway available.
BREAKFAST: Usually 8:30. Plentiful buffet. Belgian waffles with apples and walnuts; peach pancakes with blueberry sauce; feta omelets with garden chives. Breakfast meats. Dried fruit compote. Fresh fruit. Juices. Breads.
PLUS: Wood-burning fireplace in living room. Sunroom with fireplace, TV/VCR, and videos. Guest refrigerator. Late-afternoon refreshments. Spa towels. Robes. Hair dryers. Special occasions acknowledged. Transportation provided to/from bus stop, Owl's Head airport, schooners.

　From Missouri: *"A perfect refuge in a perfect spot. . . . Made our first visit to Maine memorable."*

*U*NLESS OTHERWISE STATED, *rates in this book are per room for two and include breakfast in addition to all the amenities in "Plus." As for taxes and gratuities, please see page IX.*

ᵃ Crown 'n' Anchor Inn   207/282-3829

121 North Street,   800/561-8865
P.O. Box 228,   FAX 207/282-7495
Saco, ME 04072-0228   E-MAIL cna@gwi.net

HOSTS: John Barclay and Martha Forester
LOCATION: On 2 acres of landscaped lawns in historic district. One mile from I-95, exit
       5. Five-minute walk to museum, library, Thornton Academy. Four miles to
       Saco Beach, 12 to Kennebunkport, 10 to Portland, 5 to University of New
       England.
OPEN: Year round.
RATES: June 15–October 15 $70 (smallest) single or double. Other rooms $100,
       $110, $120. Rest of year $10 less. Singles $10 less. Third person $15. Amex,
       MC, Visa. ♥ ⊞ ❖ ⅍ ❤○

ADULT CHILDREN give their parents a gift weekend here. Honeymooners return for anniversaries. Weddings are held outdoors or in the formal antiques-appointed double parlor with its magnificent floor-to-ceiling marble-based gold-leaf mirror. Furnishings range
from Victorian rococo to primitives. More than four thousand volumes are in the second-
floor barn library, a wonderfully redone 30-foot-square area with exposed 1700s pegged
rafters, brass chandelier, and comfortable chairs and sofa. The grounds, too, are of particular interest, because the property, on the National Register, was once owned by Dr.
George Lincoln Goodale, the botany professor who was responsible for acquiring the
Harvard University glass flower exhibits made by the Blaschka family of Germany.
   The elegant Federal/Greek Revival house had been vacant for four years before John, a
book jobber and retired banker, worked on the restoration in 1991 with Martha's husband,
Jim, a retired Louisiana professor who didn't live to see his dream. Since Martha and John
(the official chef and flower arranger) opened in 1992, the inn has been discovered by business
travelers, historians, wedding planners, house tour goers, and HGTV's *If Walls Could Talk*.

BED AND BATH: Six rooms (five with private phone); all private baths. Main house second
floor—two high Victorian rooms (one with whirlpool bath) with double bed, fireplace,
Indian shutters. In early (1760) wing of house—three (smaller) rooms with twin beds,
king/twin option, or queen bed; all in casual country decor. In converted barn—one very
large room with double bed, whirlpool bath, private deck overlooking rear garden.
BREAKFAST: At 7, 8:30, and 10. Elaborate. Freshly squeezed orange juice, almost-famous
fruit/ice-cream dish, home-baked bread, meat and egg dishes, tea, Louisiana dark roast
coffees. In candlelit dining room or on deck.
PLUS: "Books that have followed us home." Fresh flowers throughout. Wicker-furnished
front porch. Corporate meeting facilities. Summer and foliage season—high tea from 3 to
5. TV. VCR. Beverages. Special occasions acknowledged. Guest refrigerator. Dinner by
advance reservation only. Small pets welcomed by prior arrangement only.

   ᵃ Guests wrote: "*Beautiful . . . luxurious . . . cozy . . . warm hospitality . . .
romantic setting . . . good recommendations for restaurants and touring . . . great food . . .
breakfast was an experience . . . outstanding.*"

🪶 *Brass Lantern Inn*   207/548-0150

81 West Main Street,   800/691-0150
Searsport, ME 04974   FAX (CALL FIRST) 207/548-0304
                    E-MAIL stay@BrassLanternMaine.com
                    www.BrassLanternMaine.com

HOSTS: Dick and Maggie Zieg
LOCATION: "In antiques capital of Maine." Overlooking Penobscot Bay, 1.5 miles north of Moose Point State Park. Within walking distance of waterfront, Penobscot Marine Museum, restaurants, and shops. Less than an hour to Acadia National Park and Bar Harbor, Camden, Rockland, Bangor, and Augusta.
OPEN: Year round.
RATES: May 15 through October $85–$100. Third person $20. Off-season specials include soup and homemade bread the first night of two-night reservations with afternoon tea on second day. MC, Visa. ♥ ❖ ⚥ 🍴

🪶 From Illinois, Ohio, Massachusetts, Maine, New Hampshire, Florida, New Mexico: "*This B&B is absolutely wonderful! The hosts are excellent. The breakfast is a splendid event. We slept like sleeping beauties. Highly recommended! . . . Everything about the Brass Lantern is exquisite, from the tasteful furnishings to the unique architectural details to the gracious hospitality. . . . Well worth the visit. . . . A++. . . . Delightful and sensitive innkeepers . . . printout of lighthouses with directions . . . Maine atlas to use. . . . Even a hug when we left! . . . Secret Garden Room is fairy tale–like . . . quilts, flowers, modern bath, clean! . . . The place is elegance itself.*"

How MANY more superlatives could describe any one B&B that has also appeared in *Down East, Country Living,* the *New York Times,* and *AAA Today?* Several rooms in the National Register 1850 Victorian have wide-plank floors. All have interior shutters. The dining room has an intricate tin ceiling. Furnishings include antiques, reproductions, and collectibles from Maggie's native England and her two-year stay in Ethiopia. Evenings, candles are lit throughout the house.

In Washington, D.C., Dick was operations manager for a landscaping company. (He has a similar position here in Maine. "I now know great back-road routes!") Maggie worked with a large association in the human relations field. They bought this B&B, "a long-held dream," in 1997 and moved in March during the season's first memorable-in-every-way snowstorm. Often, guests share their day-trip experiences at breakfast and during "impromptu parties in the kitchen at night over cookies or brownies and decaf."

FOREIGN LANGUAGE SPOKEN: "Maggie spoke fluent German at one time; it comes back when used more frequently."
BED AND BATH: Five rooms. All private baths (four are shower only, one is tub/shower bath). First floor—double four-poster bed, private adjacent full bath. Second floor—one room with queen bed; three rooms with double bed; two rooms have additional twin bed.

continued . . .

BREAKFAST: Usually at 8:30. (Hot beverages available at 7:30.) Fresh fruit. Juices. Homemade popovers, muffins, breads, and/or coffee cakes. Homemade jams. Entrée repertoire includes blueberry French toast; cheese-and-potato quiche; puff pastries filled with cheeses, herbs, sautéed onions. (Fresh eggs from chickens here.)

PLUS: One parlor with chaise longue and piano; TV/VCR, games, books, and coal stove in another. Afternoon refreshments. Guest refrigerator. Fresh flowers. Free pass for Penobscot Marine Museum, 1 mile north. Locked barn for bicycles. Special occasions acknowledged. Loan of maps, guidebooks, binoculars for day trips.

≈ Watchtide B&B by the Sea   207/548-6575

190 West Main Street (Route 1),   **RESERVATIONS** 800/698-6575
Searsport, ME 04974   **E-MAIL** stay@watchtide.com
                                                   www.watchtide.com

HOSTS: Nancy-Linn Nellis and husband, H. P. (Jack) Elliott
LOCATION: On ocean side of Route 1, with panoramic views of meadow and ocean and hills across the bay. Bordered on both sides by gardens and woods. Across from two houses—one a residence, the other a real estate agency. One mile south of Searsport village; half a mile to Moose Point State Park and swimming. Forty-five miles to Acadia National Park.
OPEN: Year round.
RATES: Bayview rooms $115 first night, $110 subsequent nights; With whirlpool (two-night minimum) $150 first night, then $145. Front rooms $90/$95. Less off-season. Additional person $20. Discover/Novus, MC, Visa.
♥ ⊞ ❖ ⚸ ⚄ ♨ 🐾 🐾

PATIENCE, dear traveler. This writer missed telling you about Nancy-Linn when she had a B&B in Pennsylvania in the 1980s. "I've had many careers, but innkeeping is what I love the most!" A guest at that B&B, a cousin of Jack's, reunited Nancy-Linn and Jack who had first met in the 1940s. "We're really from all over." They married in 1992 and opened here—"the view sold us"—in 1994. Now nominated for the National Register, the 200-year-old sea captain's house, known for many years as the College Club Inn, is furnished with antiques. The 60-foot-long sunporch has a periwinkle-blue floor "that leads your eye right out to the sea."

IN RESIDENCE: "Flossie Fox, known to sleep in phlox bed, and Woodye Woodchuck are frequent visitors, along with Raquel and Rachel Raccoon."
FOREIGN LANGUAGES SPOKEN: "A little French. And we 'manage' in German and Italian."
BED AND BATH: Four second-floor rooms with 6-foot, 5-inch-high ceilings. All with private en-suite baths. Two very quiet waterview rooms—one with king/twins option, two-person Jacuzzi, skylight, and shower; other with one double bed, shower bath with skylight. Front rooms—two king-bedded rooms, one with shower bath; other with tub/shower bath.

BREAKFAST: 8:30 in summer. 9 in winter. Entrée possibilities (thirty-eight in repertoire) include blintzes with strawberry Grand Marnier sauce, Belgian waffles, harvest cinnamon apple crepe, fiddlehead or crabmeat omelets, smoked salmon *clafouti.* Juices with sparkling seltzer. Maine apple cake, popovers, breads. Sweet Italian sausage, marinated turkey fillets, thick bacon. Herbal teas, freshly ground coffees. Tables set with sterling silver, crystal, and fine china. On flower-bedecked sunporch (with gas fireplace in winter), overlooking bird sanctuary and Penobscot Bay.

PLUS: Living room with gas fireplace and century-old German upright piano. TV and books in library. Afternoon/evening refreshments. Sheep-wool bed coverings. Turndown service. Beach towels. Croquet. Horseshoes. Bicycles for guests' use. Transportation to/from Concord bus stop. "Angels and Antiques Shop" in barn here.

> ⤳ Guests wrote, in long enthusiastic e-mails: *"Absolutely outstanding. Each room beautifully and comfortably appointed. . . . Breakfasts surpass anything one can image. . . . Without ever prying, they provide you with a wealth of information about day trips and area resources. . . . Gorgeous high quality antiques. . . . I'll always remember awakening to the sun over Penobscot Bay. . . . Food and presentation challenges four-star restaurants. . . . Birds of every description at the feeders. . . . Terrific hosts who spoil their guests. . . . Wildlife in backyard surprised us. . . . A delight for all your senses."*

⤳ *The Inn at Southwest*   207/244-3835

371 Main Street, P.O. Box 593,
Southwest Harbor, ME 04679

FAX 207/244-9879
E-MAIL innatsw@acadia.net
www.innatsouthwest.com

HOST: Jill Lewis
LOCATION: On Main Street, with harbor view. Across from bicycle shop (rentals available). Minutes' walk to restaurants, shops, marina, lobster wharves. Five minutes' drive to Acadia National Park; twenty to park visitor center.
OPEN: May 1–October 31. Two-night minimum on holiday weekends.
RATES: Mid-June to mid-October $95, $110, $120, $145. Off-season $65–$105. Additional person $20. Discover, MC, Visa. ♥ ⊞ ⚥ ⚼ ♨

> ⤳ From Connecticut, Massachusetts, Michigan, Maryland: *"Have never been at an inn where the atmosphere was so conducive to becoming so friendly and comfortable with the other guests, the innkeeper. . . a charming old house . . . wraparound porch is perfect for reading or just watching the world go by. . . . Had dietary restrictions. Jill prepared a delicious breakfast for me. . . . Jill makes you feel like a long-lost cousin. . . . Glowing fire greeted us on a damp New England day . . . furnished with antiques. . . . Stayed with a group. Jill worked to book appropriate rooms for our needs . . . served us breakfast earlier than usual for a trip . . . made us feel at home. . . . A week at the inn is definite proof that Maine truly is life as it should be."*

continued . . .

WHEN JILL decided to leave her position with a computer company in Ann Arbor, Michigan, she came to Maine with memories of a summer job in the hospitality business. Almost presto—in time for the 1995 season, she bought this established B&B, an 1884 mansard-roofed Victorian that has tall ceilings, wide halls, and third-floor chapel windows. Since 1995 Jill has been dovetailing innkeeping "and the fun of helping guests plan their day" with off-season computer work in Michigan and with plenty of golfing and some travel too. (One year, Florida; another, Australia.) In both 1996 and 1997 this inn was an "Editors' Pick" in *Yankee* magazine's *Travel Guide to New England.*

BED AND BATH: Nine carpeted rooms, all with ceiling fan, on second and third floors. King/twins or queen bed. All private baths; some full, some shower without tub. **BREAKFAST:** 8–9. Specialties include poached pears in wine sauce, blueberry cornbread, crab potato bake (house specialty). Broiled grapefruit, blueberry stuffed French toast (guests' favorite), sausage links. Watermelon topped with blueberry yogurt sauce, eggs Florentine, raspberry coffee cake. Or blueberry apple crisp; vanilla Belgian waffles topped with raspberry sauce, bacon. Fresh fruit, cold cereals, oatmeal, toast. Special diets accommodated. In dining room at tables for two or four. **PLUS:** Wraparound porch with antique wicker furnishings (including chaise longue). Upright piano and wood-burning fireplace in living room. Afternoon tea and homemade cookies. Guest refrigerator stocked with sodas. Robes for rooms with detached baths. Designer linens; white down comforters. Daily newspaper. Games and puzzles. Suggestion for little-known cove with dam, view of sound and mountains. Jill's own cookbook for sale.

🐦 *The Island House*

207/244-5180

Box 1006, Clark Point Road, Southwest Harbor, ME 04679-1006

E-MAIL islandab@acadia.net
www.acadia.net/island_house/

HOSTS: Ann and Charlie Bradford
LOCATION: Across street from harbor. Ten-minute walk to village center; five minutes to lobster docks, Oceanarium, and Coast Guard station. Five-minute drive to Acadia National Park and ocean.
OPEN: Year round. Two-night minimum in August.
RATES: November–March $65 double, $60 single. April–May $75 double, $70 single. June–October $85 double, $80 single. $25 third person in room. Carriage-house loft apartment $110 for two; $130 for three; $145 for four.
♥ 🏃 🖥 🎴 🛇 ✄

CHARLIE IS not only an island native. A former fisherman, he now works at a local boat-yard and gives guests a sense of place. He and Ann live in a freshly decorated house that was once part of Mount Desert Island's first summer hotel. Today it has much of the original pine woodwork, old photos, and a page from an old register. Furnishings reflect Ann's childhood years in Southeast Asia. Many small-world stories emerge from breakfast conversations. And you can count on suggestions from these experienced hosts. Among grateful guests: one who arrived just in time to get directions to the mountaintop—for his marriage proposal at sunset.

BED AND BATH: Four rooms with twin beds, a double, a queen, or a king/twins option. All private baths—one is tub and shower; others have shower, no tub. Second-floor rooms could be two two-room suites. Cot available. Plus loft efficiency apartment that sleeps up to four (who eat breakfast in main house).
BREAKFAST: Usually 7:30–9. (Coffee and tea at 7.) Fresh fruit or juices. Home-baked bread, muffins, Danish, or coffee cake. Eggs Florentine, a vegetable omelet, blueberry pancakes, oven French toast with caramel-nut topping, or fresh fruit crepes with home-made blueberry sauce. Granola and dried cereals. Served in dining room or on veranda.
PLUS: Piano, books and music, TV with VCR. Porch glider, large garden with picnic table.

 From two Massachusetts guests: *"Like staying at your loving auntie's house. . . . Loft was sunny and romantic."* From Tennessee: *"Iced tea on arrival, spotlessly clean baths, a newspaper, exquisite breakfasts."* From Pennsylvania: *"A delight. In good old Maine tradition, their Island House is warm, relaxed, and homey."*

Island Watch B&B   207/244-7229

73 Freeman Ridge Road, Southwest Harbor, ME 04679

HOST: Maxine M. Clark
LOCATION: Quiet. (Follow state road signs on Route 102.) High atop Freeman Ridge, with view of Cadillac Mountain and Somes Fiord and overlooking Southwest Harbor and Mount Desert Harbor. Five-minute walk by graveled road through woods to the village, fifteen-minute walk by paved town road. Within walking distance of Seal Cove's narrow graveled Acadia National Park Road with scenic winding trails.
OPEN: June–October. Two-night minimum.
RATES: $85. Single $50 in one double-bedded room. Third person in room $20.
♥ ⬛ ⊞ 𝄃 𝄃 ⚶ 𝆺 ❤

YOU FEEL AS if you're living above the treetops. (The songbirds love the area too.) All this with a treat of a sunrise (I loved it) and the mesmerizing view of yacht-filled harbors and mountain backdrop. This is a family-built (1967) house with floor-to-ceiling windows, white walls, and clear, uncluttered space—all using the great outdoors as its primary decor.

Maxine, grandmother of four (ranging from age twenty-four to thirty-three), likes to hike, snowmobile, sail, sew, and cook. A professional Realtor, she spent her early years on an island in a house that was later sold to the Nature Conservancy of Maine. (Maxine was the broker!) As a teenager, when her father was a lighthouse keeper, she lived in Bass Harbor Lighthouse. If you ask, you may hear tales of bootleggers during Prohibition, rain as the water supply, coal for fuel, sheepshearing, and gulls' eggs.

continued . . .

IN RESIDENCE: Two poodles, seldom seen by guests.

BED AND BATH: Six rooms (two have ceiling fans). All private baths (one with tub, rest with showers). Two handicapped-accessible rooms (suites), each with a double and a single bed. King or queen beds plus cot available.

BREAKFAST: 7–8:30. French toast, pancakes, waffles, or bacon and eggs. (Special diets accommodated.) Homemade breads. Coffee, juice, and cereal. Maxine cooks in a marvelous arrangement that allows her simultaneously to work in the kitchen, socialize with guests in the dining area, and point out the Canadian ferry rounding the tip of the island. One table is on outside deck; the others are in glassed-in flower room.

PLUS: Those decks—for sun, shade, harbor views, and stargazing. Barbecue. Storage space for bikes, camping equipment.

🐦 Guests wrote: *"Surrounded by forest with an amazing view of the water. . . . A beautiful home. A special treasure. . . . Felt like we were leaving a good friend rather than someone we had just met."*

🐦 *Kingsleigh Inn 1904*   207/244-5302

P. O. Box 1426, 373 Main Street,   FAX 207/244-7691
Southwest Harbor, ME 04679-1426   E-MAIL info@kingsleighinn.com
                                                     www.KingsleighInn.com

HOSTS: Ken and Cyd Champagne Collins

LOCATION: At edge of village, 100 yards from harbor. Walk to restaurants, shops, museums, art galleries. Minutes to Acadia National Park.

OPEN: Year round. Two-day minimum October 1–16 and on holiday weekends.

RATES: January–May 15 $60–$70, $115 turret suite. May 16–June 15 $75–$95, $135 turret suite. June 16–October 15 $95–$125, $190 turret suite. October 16–December 31 $60–$70, $115, except last two weeks of October $135 turret suite, $95 rooms with private balcony. $20 additional person. MC, Visa.
♥ ⚄ ⊁

ONE NIGHT'S stay in 1996 did it! In Boston, Ken sold high-tech electronics for twenty years. Cyd, a registered dietitian for cardiac care and diabetes clinics, worked at Massachusetts General Hospital. They had vacationed in the Mount Desert area since 1980—at first as campers. When they decided to become innkeepers, they stayed at this then-not-for-sale inn. Next morning they made an offer. And here they are, in a freshly painted 1904 Colonial Revival with refinished hardwood floors, period furnishings, and wicker too. It's a comfortable home—enter through the kitchen—with original art and collections of antique working decoys and carved shorebirds. Plants and overflowing window boxes abound. Upon departure, many guests book for "next year."

IN RESIDENCE: Benjamin, "our lovable golden retriever."

BED AND BATH: Eight rooms, all with private baths and all with ceiling fans. Two first-floor rooms and five second-floor rooms (three are air-conditioned, two have a balcony overlooking harbor) have queen beds (one has daybed also), shower baths. Air-conditioned turret suite with harbor view has room with king four-poster and working fireplace; living room with color TV; and, in turret, telescope (view islands and Hinckley boatyard) and large tub and shower bath.

BREAKFAST: 8–9:30. (Continental for early departures.) Entrée repertoire includes mascarpone-filled French toast with warm berry sauce, individual egg soufflés with homemade sweet roasted red pepper sauce, Belgian waffles with fresh fruit and homemade whipped cream, omelets, eggs Benedict with "out-of-this-world lemon sauce," lemon French toast with warm blueberry sauce. Fresh fruit cobblers. Homemade coffee cakes and lemon/ginger pear muffins. Homemade granola. Special diets accommodated. In candlelit dining room with music or on wraparound porch overlooking harbor.

PLUS: Fireplaced living room. Library/sitting room. Hot beverages. Home-baked treats at 4 p.m. in high season. Guest refrigerator.

     From Pennsylvania: *"It's worth the drive from Pennsylvania! . . . elegant but comfortable accommodations. Terrific food. Warm, helpful innkeepers. Never felt more at home at a B&B in this country or abroad."* From North Carolina: *"Very clean and comfortable. Impressed with the meals, snacks, rooms, fresh-cut flowers, and especially the hospitality."* From California: *"Exceptional attention to detail. . . . Fabulous breakfasts."* From Massachusetts: *"Marvelous inn and innkeepers."*

Putt's Place Bed & Breakfast

207/246-4181

P.O. Box 126, 8 Main Street,
Stratton, ME 04092

800/862-6720 CODE #77

HOSTS: Elaine and Jim Poitras
LOCATION: Along the main road in a quiet rural area. With view of mountains and lake. Snowmobile and cross-country ski trail through the yard. Seven miles to Sugarloaf U.S.A.
OPEN: January–May.
RATES: $50. ♥ ♦♦ ♣ ⊞ ✗ ⌖ ❤

     From Canada, England, Massachusetts, New Hampshire, Maine, New Jersey: *"Felt like part of the family. . . . Entertaining hosts. . . . Feather beds a welcome treat. . . . Woke up to smell of muffins baking. . . . After skiing, loved coming 'home' to room heated by a woodstove. . . . If only the world were full of people like this, what a life we would have. . . . Gracious and comfortable family room. . . . Awesome! . . . Very clean. . . . Our stay surpassed the writeup in your book. . . . Great restaurant recommendations. . . . Only downside—no bath upstairs. . . . Bathroom is a piece of artwork and graffiti (encouraged). . . . different breakfast each day . . .*

continued . . .

bountiful, with everything homemade. . . . Hand in hand with Sugarloaf, the best Eastern ski vacation."

JIM, WHO OWNS a carpet business (even some walls here have carpets on them), built this modified A-frame in 1972 as a ski vacation home for the family. Elaine, who does counted cross-stitching "almost every night," has experience as a summer guide and as a phone representative for L.L. Bean. Since opening as a B&B—"the greatest job of all"—in 1987, the ardent snowmobilers have been having just as much fun as their guests in this "take-off-your-shoes-and-talk" kind of place.

BED AND BATH: Four second-floor rooms (and the hosts) share two first-floor baths. Two rooms with double beds; one with two twin beds and futon sofa; one with two twins; all with feather beds.

BREAKFAST: 7:30. Juices. Fruit cup. Dessert breads (recipes shared). Homemade muffins. French toast with homemade cinnamon raisin bread; blueberry pancakes; Belgian waffles; ham baked with pineapple, bacon, sausage. Served by woodstove at 6-foot oak table made by Jim.

PLUS: Fireplaced living room with cable TV. Individual thermostats. Hot chocolate and tea always available. Down comforters. Flannel sheets. Guest refrigerator. Fresh fruit. Sometimes "moose or a small deer herd out back."

⇗ *Morrill Farm B&B*   207/388-2059

85 Morrill Farm Road, Sumner, ME 04292

    HOSTS: Larry and Pat Perron
LOCATION: A 217-acre working farm with nature (hiking) trails and 3 miles of groomed cross-country ski trails. With panoramic mountain views. On a secluded road, 1 mile from state road 219. Twenty minutes to Mount Abram, forty-five to Sunday River. Fishing and swimming in nearby ponds. Half hour to Norlands Living History Museum; ninety minutes from Portland and Freeport (L.L. Bean).
    OPEN: Year round.
    RATES: $45 single, $55 double. $65 extra-large room. $10 additional person. Special packages available. MC, Visa. ♦♦ ♦ ⊞ ♢ ⅙ ♦♦

    ⇗ From Massachusetts: *"If the experience of a real working farm, friendly people, a beautiful and peaceful setting near lakes, mountains, rivers, and woods is what you'd like, this place is a spot of paradise for you. . . . Have created a retreat from our hectic world in their welcoming, comfortable farmhouse. . . . Personal warmth and knowledge of Maine further enhances a stay . . . interesting, thoughtful 'real' people . . . Everything is spotless, nicely appointed with a charm all its own. Having stayed at B&Bs in England, Scotland and this country, I am confident I know a special one when I see it—and this one is very special. . . .*

One of best values anywhere. . . . Feel restored when I visit this part of Maine, in large part because of the Perrons and their delicious hospitality." From Rhode Island: *"Delightful to be back in the cradle of a lifestyle ne'er forgotten. . . . an honor to be their guest."* From South Africa: *"We loved our stay in Maine inns along the coast— all good, but Morrill Farm was our happiest stay. Food was great, water piping hot, but it was the hosts who made the visit so outstanding . . . embraced us as friends . . . tranquil, peaceful, unforgettable."*

"WE HAD A dairy farm and sold it in 1989 to come out farther into the country for a slower pace of life. We started the B&B in 1993. Larry raises animals for other people. We have a commitment to a philosophy of self-sufficiency and simplicity of living—sharing our skills and resources with neighbors and friends, finding ways to make home and family the center of our lives, making time for fun and leisure. Artists enjoy painting the distant church-in-the-mountains scene. The spinning wheel is used to spin wool from our sheep, and a loom usually has a piece in progress. A blacksmith shop is occasionally operated by our son. (Items can be made to order.) In summer we make butter weekly. In the evening we light a kerosene lamp and join guests on the screened porch, where we can hear coyotes."

IN RESIDENCE: One dog. Three barn cats. A horse named Princess, eight goats, a milking cow, several head of cattle.

FOREIGN LANGUAGES SPOKEN: *"Nous parlons français."*

BED AND BATH: Three spacious second-floor rooms share a shower bath—plus a second bath in main part of house. Largest room has two double beds and room for a rollaway; other two have one queen bed in each.

BREAKFAST: 8 (or by arrangement). Homegrown bacon and sausage. Farm-fresh organic eggs with home fries and fresh-baked bread with home-churned butter. Pancakes or French toast with Maine maple syrup. Served family style in kitchen that has wood cookstove—and "for decor" an old slate sink with water pump, a coffee grinder, lanterns and an icebox.

PLUS: Upright piano in living room. Homestyle dinner (by reservation) at a neighboring farmhouse; drive over, or walk via a half-mile trail through the woods. "Flannel sheets and soapstones to warm your bed."

HOSPITALITY IS THE KEYNOTE OF B&B.

🐟 Fox Island Inn   207/863-2122

P.O. Box 451, Vinalhaven, ME 04863   E-MAIL gailrei@juno.com

HOST: Gail Reinertsen
LOCATION: In an island fishing village, a seventy-five-minute ferry ride from Rockland. Twelve-minute walk from ferry landing. Within 2 blocks of restaurants and summer activities. A little more than a mile to swimming quarries.
OPEN: June–September. Two-day minimum stay required, by advance reservation.
RATES: $45–$50 single, $60 twins, $55–$60 double, $75 queen with single. $15 extra person. "All major credit cards accepted." 🏠 ✗ ⚟ 🐾

"EVERYONE TELLS ME that they come to get away, and that's just what they do on an island like this. It's a fishing village with about 1,200 year-round residents. The summer population is close to 5,000—with all of thirty-two rooms available for paying overnight guests. (Nantucket, we're not!) There are art shows, concerts, and charming restaurants. Guests enjoy the outdoors—nature preserves, quiet woodland walks, the rocky shoreline, the spring-fed warm-water quarries for swimming, church suppers, flea markets, the lack of shops, and 39 miles of paved roads (good for cycling) plus many that are unpaved (used by mountain cyclists). This comfortable place with shared baths fits right into the simple style here."

Gail is a Tallahassee, Florida, resident who is married to a law professor. A former law librarian, she was a guest at many B&Bs while traveling as a law book publisher's representative. Those B&B stays inspired her to become a bed and breakfast manager, first on Cape Cod and then in Florida, before she bought this B&B in 1991. Now she owns another B&B in Tallahassee.

IN RESIDENCE: Yankee, a golden retriever, "in guests' area only by popular demand."
BED AND BATH: Six rooms; all shared baths. First floor: One large shower bath and one half bath shared by small single room with three-quarter bed, two small double-bedded rooms (one reserved for single travelers), and a large room with two twin beds. Second floor (can be a suite): One small double-bedded room and a large room with a queen and one twin bed share a large shower bath.
BREAKFAST: At 8. Left on tray outside each room—fresh fruit, juice, homemade granola, homemade breads, muffins, scones, gourmet coffee. Rooms have chairs and table. Option—eat in common room or take tray outside.
PLUS: Upright piano in living room. No TV. Beach towels. Guest kitchen for preparing picnics/light meals. Fresh flowers and robes in rooms. Several bikes loaned; rentals available on island.

⋙ *Broad Bay Inn and Gallery*   207/832-6668

P.O. Box 607,   800/736-6769
1014 Main Street,   E-MAIL brdbayin@midcoast.com
Waldoboro, ME 04572   www.broadbayinn/midcoast.com

HOST: Libby Hopkins
LOCATION: In residential midcoast Maine village, a half mile off U.S. Route 1. Short
drive to Monhegan Island, Islesboro, and Vinalhaven ferries. Close to
Audubon wildlife sanctuary, Damariscotta Lake, Medomak River, Camden.
OPEN: Year round. Two-night minimum on August weekends.
RATES: Per room. May–October, $70 Victorian double, $75 Canopy Room, $70
and $60 second- and third-floor rooms. Other months 20 percent less.
Thanksgiving and Christmas packages. MC, Visa. 🚶‍♀️ 🛏 ⊞ ⊀ ⟊ 🐾 ❤🐾

WALDOBORO REMINDS Libby of North Carolina summer stock days, when she ran art
shows at the theater and met one Jim Hopkins, a designer/actor/puppeteer/singer. Three
decades later, having been artists with Princeton University, the Educational Testing
Service, and the *Wall Street Journal,* the Hopkinses settled here. They opened an art gallery;
established summer workshops (still ongoing) with renowned instructors; and became professional caterers as well as community leaders—with the reopened Waldo Theatre, the library and schools, the Woman's Club, and much more. Guests remember sleigh rides, a
wedding in the garden, the decor, the food (one recipe published in *House Beautiful,* another on a two-page spread in a *Better Homes and Gardens* cookbook), and the host.

FOREIGN LANGUAGE SPOKEN: Some French.
BED AND BATH: Five rooms, three shared (robes provided) full baths. First-floor double-
bedded room shares hosts' bath. Two second-floor baths are shared by second-floor
double-bedded room, one room with canopied four-poster double (floor-to-ceiling
windows overlooking garden), one with two twin beds, and third-floor room (reached by
steep stairs) that has two twin beds.
BREAKFAST: 8–9. (Continental after 9.) Host's whim. Maybe blueberry muffins, homemade breads; frittata, Parmesan baked eggs, meats, pancakes, crepes, cereals (by request),
fresh fruit ambrosia. (Special diets accommodated with advance notice.) Served on
English china on starched hand-embroidered white tablecloths, in dining room or by
kitchen woodstove.
PLUS: Sundeck overlooking garden. Screened porch. Hammock. Evening tea or sherry.
Fresh flowers and fruit. VCR; musical film tapes. Art and theater library. Fans. TV,
games, piano. In January, the possibility of attending Libby's slide talks on her annual visits to Monet's garden in France. Watercolor classes by well-known artists held right here.
Dinner by advance reservation.

⋙ Guests send accolades: *"Breakfasts are hearty, subtle, delicious—served with
such flair! . . . Never felt so welcomed and cared for by an innkeeper. . . . One feels both comfortable and a sense of occasion."*

⤞ Le Va•Tout

218 Route 32 South, Kalers Corner,
Waldoboro, ME 04572

207/832-4969

FAX 207/832-4969

HOSTS: Eliza Sweet
LOCATION: Residential neighborhood along Route 32 South, a scenic route with water views all the way (20 miles) to Pemaquid Light. Five-minute walk to shops and restaurants. Ten miles to Damariscotta; 15 to Camden harbor; half mile from Route 1.
OPEN: Year round. November–June reservations preferred.
RATES: June–October shared bath $75 double or twin beds; private bath $85 queen or double. Off-season $55, $65. Singles $10 less. Third person $10. Cribs, no charge. (Special rates for bicyclists. Inquire.) MC, Visa. 👫 🛏 🏢 ⚄

⤞ From Maine, Massachusetts, New Jersey: *"So informal and so friendly. A woman of great wit, humor, energy . . . and she has a true interest in other people . . . a very good cook . . . restores rugs that need a great deal of delicate reconstruction. . . . Accommodations simply appointed in classic New England style . . . long leisurely breakfasts were healthy and fresh with seasonal berries. A real treat! . . . gardens with lovely views of historic Waldoboro . . . magnificent vegetable gardens and beehives. . . . For her gallery, Eliza, an artist herself, selected participating artists for variety, style, and medium. . . . sumptuously planted garden, brimming with flowers and replete with lawn sculptures in both stone and metal . . . helpful information and maps . . . impeccable room . . . blueberry pancakes were perfection."*

SINCE ELIZA bought this 1830s extended Cape house, a B&B known for its award-winning absolutely spectacular gardens, she has added a wood-fired sauna and hot tub in the former garden shed. Every room has original art and eclectic furnishings. The textile conservatory is a home studio. Eliza, an avid bicyclist, has a degree in art history and experience in running a wilderness fishing camp in Labrador.

IN RESIDENCE: Daughter Cecily is thirteen; son Spencer is eleven. Two long-haired cats.
FOREIGN LANGUAGE SPOKEN: French. (Sometimes used on the phone for guests of other B&Bs.)
BED AND BATH: Five rooms. First floor—antique brass double bed, private tub/shower bath. Second floor (under eaves)—room with a queen and a twin bed, shower bath, private garden entrance. Three rooms—one with a queen and a twin, one with a double four-poster, and one with two twin beds—share a shower bath.
BREAKFAST: 7:30–9 (earlier by arrangement). Fresh fruit salad garnished with garden mint. Omelets with freshly picked asparagus, blueberry pancakes with real maple syrup, homemade honey and jams, popovers, bacon or ham, freshly baked coffee cakes and rhubarb muffins. Served family style in large eat-in kitchen.
PLUS: Lawn chairs and deck. Cable TV in living room. Tea, coffee, or cold drinks. Guest refrigerator. Recommendations for "the best bike rides and special lakes for swimming." Bag lunches (extra charge). Saturday night lobster bakes, "a big hit" (about $25 per person); served in garden.

⤜ *The Sunset House*

Route 186, HCR 60, Box 62,
West Gouldsboro, ME 04607

207/963-7156
800/233-7156
FAX 207/963-5859
E-MAIL lodging@sunsethousebnb.com
www.sunsethousebnb.com

HOSTS: Carl and Kathy Johnson
LOCATION: On Schoodic Peninsula near Flander's Bay. Bordered by 2½ -mile-long Jones Pond. Forty minutes "down east" of Bar Harbor. Five miles to Bartlett Winery (tastings).
OPEN: Year round. Two-night minimum August weekends.
RATES: May–October $99 private bath, $79 shared bath. Extra person $10. Off-season rates less. MC, Visa. ♥ ⊞ ⚄ ⚁ ♨

MESMERIZING SUNSETS. Moonlit nights on the pond. There's swimming warmer than local salt water, fishing, canoeing, cross-country skiing, ice skating, and ice fishing. A mill stream with babbling water running to the bay. Kathy's dream of a small farm. And Carl, an executive chef at a large seasonal hotel, who uses locally grown products.

The Johnsons, active community members, came from Cape Cod in 1989 to this aptly named Victorian B&B, which "has been modernized only by heat, electricity, and running water." The country decor changes with ongoing projects. In 1999 Carl was named Maine Chef of the Year. Kathy raises purebred Alpine goats and produces her own special goat cheese.

IN RESIDENCE: Maggie, "official greeter," an apricot toy poodle. Slash, a cat. Dairy goats in pasture.
FOREIGN LANGUAGE SPOKEN: Some German.
BED AND BATH: Seven rooms—one overlooks pond with king, queen, or double bed. Four with queen beds have ocean view. Second-floor rooms have private shower baths. Three third-floor rooms (all have access to a full kitchen) share (robes provided) a shower bath.
BREAKFAST: 7–9. Specialties include sour cream cinnamon-raisin French toast, yeast-raised sourdough waffles, omelets with herbed goat cheese and smoked salmon. Special diets accommodated.
PLUS: Tea or coffee with homemade goat cheeses, pastries, or breads. Parlor woodstove. Beach towels. Window quilts. In winter, dinners (extra charge). "Guests are welcome to watch the daily milking of goats."

    ⤜ From Australia: *"We enjoyed it very much. And still talk about the beautiful cheesecake and waffles."* From Massachusetts: *"The view was breathtaking, the sea air invigorating, Carl's feast memorable. . . . Highly recommended for a place to get away and renew yourself."*

⁓ The Squire Tarbox Inn   207/882-7693

Box 1181, Westport Island,   FAX 207/882-7107
Wiscasset, ME 04578   E-MAIL squiretarbox@ime.net
                                                        www.squiretarboxinn.com

HOSTS: Karen and Bill Mitman
LOCATION: "Down a country road to nowhere." Surrounded by fields, stone walls, and
woods on Westport Island, a small rural area. Eight and a half miles south of
Wiscasset and Route 1. Within thirty-minute drive of beaches, antiquing,
museums, lobster shacks, harbors, L.L. Bean.
OPEN: Mid-May through October.
RATES: $90–$112 double bed, $112–$134 small queen room, $132–$154 queen,
$152–$179 king/twins option. Amex, Discover, MC, Visa. ♥ ❖ ⚗ ⚘ 繳

ONE OF A KIND. Featured in many publications, including *US News & World Report,
GBH, USA Today, Downeast, Yankee, The Washington Post,* and *Cheese Primer* by Steve
Jenkins. The very style of country living envisioned by the Mitmans—"with no 'remote
control' amenities"—when they were administrators (Copley Plaza Hotel marketing and
hospital personnel) in Boston. Their classic old New England rambling farmhouse—the
oldest part was built in 1763—has original beams, moldings, fireplaces, and carvings.
There are antiques, rocking chairs, candles, quilts, books—and good reading lights. A
pine-needled path leads to a screened house by the saltwater marsh. And the immaculate
barn, moved here and restored in 1990, is a story in itself.

Karen, a quilter, and Bill, a private pilot, are cheese makers who produce a ton a year
from the milk of their award-winning, scene-stealing, "wonderfully responsive" Nubian
goats. Since buying the inn in 1983, the hosts have continued to share their lifestyle "surrounded by nature" with many grateful guests. We loved it all.

IN RESIDENCE: Fourteen goats, two donkeys, one horse, five chickens, two barn cats.
BED AND BATH: Eleven rooms on first and second floors with double, queen, or
king/twins option; all private shower baths. Four are large, more formal main-house
rooms with working fireplaces. Seven are more informal carriage barn (connected to
house) rooms with exposed beams; three have private entrance.
BREAKFAST: 8–9:30. Fresh fruit. Juice. Granola. Oatmeal. Home-baked breads and cakes.
Yogurt. Quiche. Hot beverages. Buffet style. Eat in dining room or on sundeck.
PLUS: All those fireplaces. Player piano in music room. Woodstove in barn sitting room.
Window fans; air conditioners in some rooms. Individual thermostats. Full liquor license. Beach towels. Rowboat, bikes, and swings. Beverages and cookies available all day.
By reservation, marvelous dinner, $31 per overnight guest, presented at 6 (sometimes with
performing harpist); includes goat cheese hors d'oeuvres, creative entrées, homegrown
vegetables and herbs, homemade pastas, rolls made with goat's milk whey.

✻ Guests wrote: *"Left with images of the caring for the animals; the magic created in the dining room; the harp music; happy people; and our wonderful row on the pond with the last bit of light left in the sky. A pervasive sense of stillness, peace, and centeredness—an unexpected gift."*

THE PLACE TO STAY HAS BECOME THE REASON TO GO.

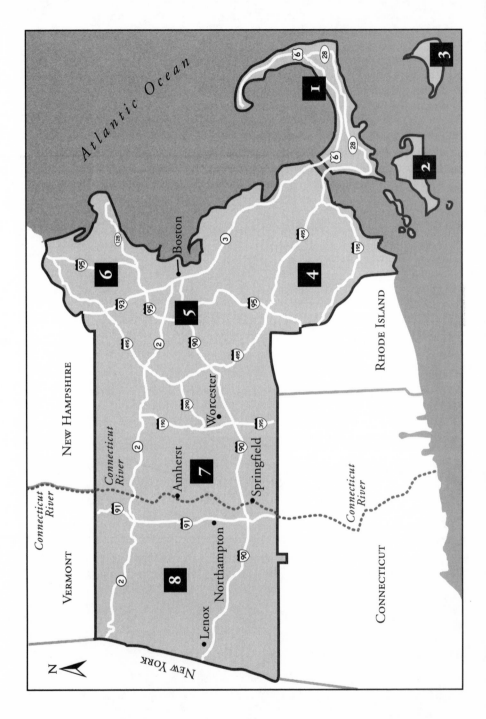

The numbers on this map indicate the regions described in detail
in this chapter.

MASSACHUSETTS

Can't find the community you wish to visit? Check with a reservation service described at the beginning of this chapter.

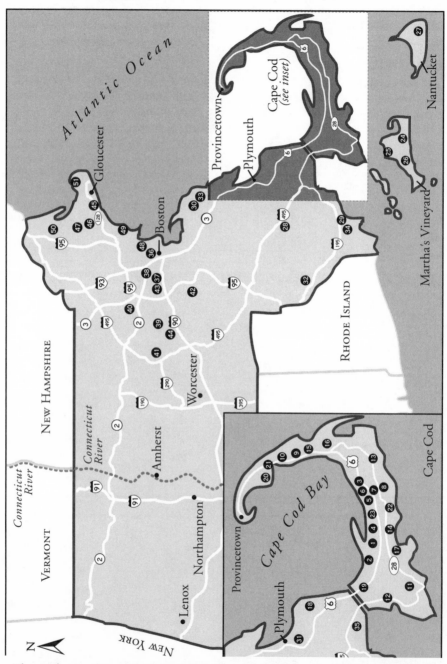

The numbers on this map indicate the locations of eastern Massachusetts B&Bs described in detail in this chapter. The map for B&Bs in Central Massachusetts, Pioneer Valley, and Berkshires is on page 274.

CAPE COD, MARTHA'S VINEYARD, AND NANTUCKET; SOUTHEASTERN MASSACHUSETTS; BOSTON AREA; JUST A LITTLE WEST; NORTH OF BOSTON

In this book, areas of Massachusetts are arranged roughly from east to west. Please see page 275 for Central Massachusetts, Pioneer Valley, and Berkshires.

---

*Can't find the community you wish to visit? Check with one of the reservation services
described throughout this chapter.*

♔ Bed and Breakfast Cape Cod

P.O. Box 1312, Orleans, MA 02653

PHONE: 508/255-3824 or 800/541-6226, 8 a.m.–9 p.m. daily, late May through mid-October. Off-season Monday–Friday, 9–5.
FAX: 508/240-0599
E-MAIL: info@BedandBreakfastCapeCod.com
URL: www.BedandBreakfastCapeCod.com
LISTINGS: One hundred thirty-five B&Bs and small inns. "We represent every town on the Cape with the exception of Provincetown. We also represent places on Martha's Vineyard and Nantucket. Almost all have accommodations with private baths. Most are air conditioned. Some have swimming pools. We list historic house tour homes, contemporaries, properties with water views, some on freshwater ponds, some within walking distance of beaches, and some in the woods. A (very) few accept pets in the summer." A free directory describes each place. Web site has pictures for all.
RESERVATIONS: Advance reservations preferred. Last-minute, if available, accommodated. Two-night minimum, three nights on holidays.
RATES: $65–$300. $10 booking fee waived for repeat guests. Deposit of 25 percent of the total reservation cost is required. (Deposit for the islands varies according to individual policies of inns.) If cancellation is received at least ten days before expected arrival date, refund less $20 processing fee is made. Amex, Discover, MC, Visa.

SUSANNE AND GILLES Thibault are world travelers, fluent in both French and German, and they know all about bed and breakfast—inside and out! Before they bought this well-established reservation service in 1996, they hosted for eight years. They inspect their listings annually. As Cape Cod residents for a quarter century, they—a child therapist/hockey player (Gilles) and a trompe l'oeil artist and teacher (Susanne)—now share their appreciation for the area through this attention-to-detail service and the distribution of much printed information about Cape Cod.

PLUS: Entire wedding parties accommodated. (How nice; the Thibaults take care of all the organizing and booking, then present the bride and groom with a master list of who is where, when. Great service.)

OTHER RESERVATION SERVICES WITH SOME B&Bs ON CAPE COD:

CAPE COD B&Bs

Many Cape Cod hosts report that guests come to see all of Cape Cod in a weekend. "Please remind them in your book that Cape Cod is 90 miles long." The following B&Bs are in alphabetical order according to the towns and villages where they are located. B&Bs on the islands of Martha's Vineyard and Nantucket are on pages 195–216.

✏ Ashley Manor

P.O. Box 856, 3660 Old King's Highway (Route 6A),
Barnstable, MA 02630

508/362-8044
888/535-2246
FAX 508/362-9927
E-MAIL ashleymn@capecod.net
www.capecod.net/ashleymn

HOST: Donald Bain

LOCATION: On 2 acres of parklike grounds, set back from Route 6A, up a sweeping driveway behind huge privet and boxwood hedges. Within walking distance of harbor, beach, village, whale-watch excursions.

OPEN: Year round. Reservations recommended. Two-night minimum on weekends, more on some holidays.

RATES: Queen-bedded room $135; $145 with working fireplace. Suites with working fireplace and whirlpool $185. Hideaway $195. Discover, MC, Visa.
♥ ⊞ ❖ ⚕ ⚘

✏ Guests wrote: *"Enchanting . . . romantic . . . sophisticated . . . historic . . . charming . . . a gem. . . . Gourmet breakfast kept us going into the afternoon . . . special coffee . . . constant supply of logs . . . daily fresh flowers and chocolate in one's room . . . cookies every night . . . fireplace, books, brandy, magazines, good conversation (should you desire it). . . . Even breakfast butter served on ice in a crystal dish. A sanctuary, thanks in no small measure to the personality and wit of Mr. Donald Bain."*

UNTIL 1986 Donald was a lawyer in Manhattan. Here he is surrounded by antiques, Oriental rugs, and comfortable sofas. The property, built in 1699, has seven fireplaces, wide floorboards, the original steep stairway, and Cape Cod blown glass windows. The secret passageway that now connects two suites was probably used as a hiding place for Tories during the Revolutionary War. Restored in 1964, the house has been an inn since 1985. Outside there's a gazebo and a 44-foot brick terrace facing 2 acres of manicured lawns, a tennis court, a fountain garden, and age-old plantings including cherry and apple trees.

FOREIGN LANGUAGE SPOKEN: French.

BED AND BATH: Six spacious air-conditioned rooms, all private baths. Five with wood-burning fireplace. Downstairs suite with canopied queen bed. Three second-floor suites; one with canopied king bed, two canopied queens. Two queen-bedded rooms. The Hideaway, a separate wing, has queen bed, sitting area, fireplace, bath, terrace.
BREAKFAST: 8:30–9:30. Freshly squeezed orange juice, coffee, teas, homemade breads and muffins, cereals including homemade granola. French toast with bacon, quiche, omelets, Swedish pancakes. Served on terrace or by candlelight in fireplaced formal dining room.
PLUS: Complimentary wines. Fresh fruit. Candies. Flowers. Coffee and tea in rooms. Fine linens. Free loan of bicycles. Croquet.

🌿 Beechwood

2839 Main Street, Route 6A,
Barnstable, MA 02630

508/362-6618

800/609–6618
FAX 508/362-0298
E-MAIL info@beechwoodinn.com
www.beechwoodinn.com

HOSTS: Debbie and Ken Traugot
LOCATION: Behind tall hedges in historic district. Flanked by two huge beech trees. Half mile to village, harbor, small beach, whale-watching boats.
OPEN: Year round. Two-night weekend minimum, May–October and some holiday weekends. Two-night minimum all of August.
RATES: First floor $150; $175 canopied. Second floor $140, except room with king and single $175. Third floor $140. Third person $25. Less November–April. Off-season packages. Amex, Discover, MC, Visa. ♥ ⊞ ❖ ⚡ ✂ ☲

ROMANTICS AND entire wedding parties love this impeccably restored and authentically furnished Queen Anne Victorian, bought in mint condition by the Traugots one 1994 weekend. The Traugots enthusiasm is contagious—for the inn, the Cape, food, and people. Ken, who grew up on Long Island in a "restaurant family," traveled all over the world while he was a Los Angeles–based financial executive. Twenty years before that, he was an engineer in Ohio. In California, Debbie, the acclaimed chef whose father taught his four daughters to be "handy," worked as a bank human resources professional. Here, they are active in the community. Joy reigns.

IN RESIDENCE: Morgan, six-year-old daughter. Hobbes, Libby, and Gem, golden retrievers.
FOREIGN LANGUAGE SPOKEN: Some French.
BED AND BATH: Six rooms. All private baths; some full, some shower only. Two first-floor rooms, each air-conditioned with working fireplace—one with brass queen, one with canopied queen bed. Up steep curving staircase to second floor—one air-conditioned room with queen bed, hand-painted cottage furniture, stained glass windows; one (air conditioned) with one queen and one double, (seasonal) view of harbor and bay; one (air

continued . . .

conditioned) with fireplace, king bed, and single bed. Third-floor air-conditioned sloped-ceiling room with panoramic bay view—queen brass bed, double sinks in bath.

BREAKFAST: 8:30–9:30 (flexible for early ferry). Repertoire includes Hawaiian French toast, apple-filled pancakes, eggs in puff pastry with cheese sauce, crepes, waffles. Baked pear or grapefruit, apricot peach crisp; giant banana—chocolate chip muffins, raspberry bread. Homemade jams. Served in tin-ceilinged dining room by fireplace at tables for two with flowers and small oil lamps.

PLUS: In summer, iced teas and lemonade on wraparound veranda—"some guests spend all day here"—furnished with wicker, rocking chairs; in other seasons, tea and sweets. Bedroom fans. Beech-shaded lawn chairs.

⚞ *Honeysuckle Hill B&B*

591 Old King's Highway, Route 6A,
West Barnstable, MA 02668-1128

508/362-8418
800/441-8418
FAX 508/362-8386
E-MAIL stay@honeysucklehill.com
www.honeysucklehill.com

HOSTS: Bill and Mary Kilburn
LOCATION: Surrounded by almost 2 acres of lawn and gardens. In historic district, along scenic road with gift and antiques shops and weaving studio. Five-minute drive to 6-mile-long Sandy Neck Beach.
OPEN: Year round. Two-night minimum on weekends; three nights on some holidays.
RATES: May–October $120, $140, $150. Suite $200 for two, three, or four guests. November–April $100, $120, $130; suite $180. Amex, Discover, MC, Visa.
♥ 🛋 ⚉

FRESH FLOWERS in the rooms. An intimate inn near the ocean. An 1810 National Register property that is so typically Cape Cod that photographers often stop to take pictures. The shingled, stone-foundation cottage surrounded by mature plantings is "just right" for the Kilburns, most recently of Trail's End (Vermont inn) fame. In 1997, after twelve years in the mountains with three times the number of guest rooms, they "scaled down in size but increased personalized service. And we're closer to grandkids!" Furnishings include antiques, family pieces, and lots of wicker. Colors are light and summery. If you'd like, Mary and Bill are happy to show you their own marvelous great room overlooking the extensive lawn and gardens. Guests from all over the world also find Honeysuckle "just right." One couple from New Zealand wrote, "Everything was perfect! Everything *very* clean. Felt very much at home."

IN RESIDENCE: "Madison, our black Lab, welcomes guests at the door."
BED AND BATH: Three rooms and one suite, each with private oversized marble shower bath, air conditioning, feather bed. First floor—queen four-poster bed. Second-floor

slanted-ceiling rooms—two with queen bed (one with private entrance and stairway) and one two-room suite with a double bed in each room.

BREAKFAST: At 8:30. (Coffee available earlier.) Sample menu—juice, bananas in cream with brown sugar, Grand Marnier French toast, sausage, raisin scones, hot beverage. Served in candlelit dining room at table with painted ladderback chairs.

PLUS: Wood-burning fireplace in living room. Sherry, port, chocolates, apples, nuts. Large wicker-furnished screened porch with guest refrigerator (complimentary soft drinks and bottled water). Umbrella table on patio. Rain umbrellas. Beach chairs and umbrellas. Adirondack lawn chairs. Today's *Boston Globe*.

The Candleberry Inn on Cape Cod

508/896-3300

1882 Main Street (Route 6A),
Brewster, MA 02631

FAX 508/896-4016
E-MAIL candle@cape.com
www.candleberryinn.com

HOSTS: Gini and David Donnelly

LOCATION: On 2 landscaped acres in historic district along scenic Route 6A. In a neighborhood of former sea captains' homes and old churches. Walk to restaurants, town (bay) beach, antiques shops, galleries.

OPEN: Year round. Two-night weekend minimum June through September.

RATES: June–September $95 double bed, $135 queen bed; suite $155 second floor, $195 carriage house. Off-season $80, $110 ($135 with fireplace), $140, $165. Amex, Discover, MC, Visa. ♥ ⊞ ⊄ ⊁

THE GRACIOUS Georgian, surrounded by beautiful gardens, was "all ready to go"—according to David—when the Donnellys bought the property in 1997. Even so, Gini, an artist/interior designer who had a photography studio and experience in children's theater, redecorated with wonderful colors and fabrics, with antiques, family heirlooms, Oriental rugs, quilts, and—everywhere—art books. Some wide-board floors are refinished; others are painted. And now added rooms, including a luxury suite, are in the carriage house.

David ("I'm sous-chef") took early retirement from the Mobil Corporation. Chef Gini creates memorable breakfasts. Returnees abound.

IN RESIDENCE: In hosts' quarters only—two small dogs and one cat.

BED AND BATH: Nine air-conditioned rooms (two suites); all private baths. Main house (on first and second floors) has six (five are very large) rooms and one suite, three with gas fireplace. King, queen (one is canopied), double, and twin beds. Carriage house rooms have TV; one has king bed, bath with two-person Jacuzzi, separate shower, double vanity, sliding glass doors leading to private terrace. On carriage-house second floor, one room with queen bed, other with two double beds share a deck overlooking rear gardens.

BREAKFAST: 8:30–9:30. Fresh fruit. Homemade muffins and breads—sweet potato/cranberry, rhubarb, banana/chocolate chip. Feta, spinach, and sun-dried tomato scramble;

continued . . .

orange/spice French toast; poppy-seed pancakes with hard cider syrup. Served in dining room (oldest room in the house) or on covered brick terrace (furnished with wicker and wrought iron).

PLUS: Woodstove in common room and dining room. TV. Sherry and cookies or cheese at 5 p.m. Guest refrigerator with soft drinks. Hair dryers. Robes.

⤜ From California: *"The location great. The accommodations beautiful. The food delicious, creative, attractively presented, and served with good cheer. The whole experience was a pure delight."*

⤜ The Captain Freeman Inn

508/896-7481

15 Breakwater Road,
Brewster, MA 02631

800/843-4664
FAX 508/896-5618
E-MAIL visitus@capecod.net
www.captainfreemaninn.com

HOSTS: Carol and Tom Edmondson
LOCATION: On a quiet road that leads to a bay beach. Faces historic town square and c. 1700 church. Walk to galleries, antiques shops, restaurants.
OPEN: Year round. Two-night minimum, June–October and special event weekends.
RATES: June–October $150–$175; $200–$225 with fireplace, whirlpool tub, TV/VCR, phone. Off-season $110, luxury room $190. Third person $30. Amex, MC, Visa. ♥ ▦ ❖ ✗ ⅄

IT'S ROMANTIC: The Edmondsons were married here. It's historic: a sea captain's house, with a big wraparound porch. It's all restored by the Edmondsons, who had computer industry careers in Boston. They furnished with canopied beds, antiques, and some of Tom's stained glass pieces. Here he's a real estate broker in addition to being gardener for the herb and perennial gardens surrounding the pool; he grows orchids too. And then there's the food, all created by Carol, a "magician" of a demonstrator (biscotti) who held a Barnes & Noble audience spellbound. Since becoming a innkeeper in 1991, she has written a cookbook and established a cooking school in the inn kitchen, which becomes a TV studio for her own local cable TV cooking show. Year round, pampering is the order of the day.

IN RESIDENCE: Captain, a female Airedale.
BED AND BATH: Twelve rooms (two are handicapped accessible); each with canopied queen bed and private bath. On three floors. Large luxury rooms have air conditioning, wood-burning fireplace, large sitting area, balcony with whirlpool bath, TV/VCR, refrigerator, private phone.
BREAKFAST: 8:30–10. All low-fat specialties. Granola pancakes, cinnamon French toast, seafood omelets. Muffins, banana bread, or coffee cake. Freshly squeezed orange juice. Served on screened porch overlooking pool and gardens or by dining room fireplace.

PLUS: Afternoon tea/lemonade/mulled cider with cookies or cake. Croquet. Loan of bicycles. Transportation to/from Hyannis. How-to B&B seminars, May and November.

The Ruddy Turnstone Bed & Breakfast   508/385-9871

463 Main Street, Route 6A,   800/654-1995
Brewster, MA 02631   FAX 508/385-5696
                        www.sunsol.com/ruddyturnstone/

HOSTS: Gordon and Sally Swanson
LOCATION: Tranquil. On 3 acres set back from the road—with huge lawn in front. Extensive back yard with "real Cape" view of marsh and birds, and ocean beyond. Across from Sydenstriker Glass shop and studio. Two miles to Brewster center with country store.
OPEN: March through November. Two-night minimum weekends and in-season months.
RATES: Mid-June through Columbus Day $165 suite, $135 carriage house, $110 room. Off-season $135 suite, $110 carriage house, $90 room.♥ ■ ❖ ⚄ ⅋ ☙

THE CHOICE of a *New York Times* reporter on assignment, the *National Geographic Traveler* in a Cape Cod article, and a *Victoria* magazine highlight, this 1998 and 1999 "Best B&B on the Lower Cape" (*Cape Cod Life* magazine) is a renovated antique Cape. "We've come home," say the Swansons. They met and married on Cape Cod, and owned and operated two restaurants here over a twenty-five-year period before moving to New Hampshire, where they also had a restaurant. Since buying this property in 1993, they have shared their home, their joie de vivre, and their spectacular Cape Cod Bay view with delighted travelers from all over the world.

BED AND BATH: Five air-conditioned rooms, some with feather beds. All private full baths. On first floor, queen bed, attached bath. Good-morning staircase to two rooms— one with a queen, bath across hall (wallpapered with *New Yorker* covers); suite with queen bed, wood-burning fireplace, six large windows overlooking marsh and bay, en-suite bath. In recently restored carriage house, sitting room with marsh view; two large rooms with refinished barnboard walls, canopied queen bed, en-suite baths.
BREAKFAST: 8–9; earlier for those catching ferries to Nantucket or the Vineyard. Fruit-filled crepes with créme fraîche; seasoned scrambled eggs in puff pastry with bacon or sausage; or homemade Belgian waffles with strawberries. Homemade muffins and breads. Homegrown fresh fruit. Special diets accommodated. Served on porch overlooking yard and ocean or by dining room fire. Hosts join guests for coffee.
PLUS: Fireplace in downstairs common room. Binoculars and view from upstairs common room. Library. Mints on the pillow. Patio. Hammock under trees. Adirondack chairs. Setups for afternoon cocktails. Suggestions and directions provided for sunsets, lookouts, beaches, restaurants . . . "just about anything you want to do."

continued . . .

> ≈ From Germany, Minnesota, California, Massachusetts: *"Two unforgettable days in their lovely home. . . . Felt like [visiting] old friends. . . . Our last stop on a 1300-mile trip and by far the most memorable. . . . Creative breakfasts. . . . Suite is heaven on Cape Cod. . . . Friendliest people—and fun!"*

≈ The Acworth Inn   508/362-3330

4352 Old King's Highway,   800/362-6363
P.O. Box 256,   FAX 508/375-0304
Cummaquid, MA 02637   www.acworthinn.com

HOSTS: Cheryl and Jack Ferrell
LOCATION: Residential. Fronted by a hedge along historic Route 6A, just beyond Barnstable. Across from Kelly's Farm, "where Jean Iverson has grown vegetables and fruit organically for more than fifty years." Ten-minute walk to Cape Cod Bay, five to galleries and antiques shops.
OPEN: Year round. Two-night minimum on weekends and holidays.
RATES: Mid-May–October $120–$135; $150 with TV and Jacuzzi; $185 suite with Jacuzzi. November–mid-May $95–$105; $125 with fireplace; $135 with air, TV, and Jacuzzi; $185 suite with fireplace and Jacuzzi. Amex, Discover, MC, Visa. ♥ ❖ ⚄ ✄

Bon Appétit—via a reader's request for a breakfast recipe—is the latest to acknowledge one of the specialties of this B&B. Although it looks like a farmhouse from the outside, the interior is striking. It is awash with light and white-painted everything—even the floors and vintage furniture—with artistic touches. In 1994, after the Ferrells' nephew completed the renovation, Aunt Cheryl and Uncle Jack visited from Nebraska and bought the inn that very weekend. Since, *many* guests have written ecstatic notes to me. (Some excerpts are below.) Borders shoppers, too, fell in love with the Ferrells when they gave a cooking demo. In Nebraska Cheryl was a Marriott food service manager who oversaw the preparation of 6,000 meals a day. Genial cohost Jack, who backpacked across Chile with two sons in 1999 (we followed the amazing trip on the Internet), was a corporate vice president after his air force career.

FOREIGN LANGUAGE SPOKEN: Jack has a PhD in German.
BED AND BATH: Five air-conditioned rooms, each with queen bed, large area rug, private bath. On first floor, large room with queen bed, full bath, wood-burning fireplace. One attached carriage house luxury suite with two-person whirlpool, shower bath, gas fireplace, TV/ VCR, refrigerator. Up steep staircase to rooms with queen bed, shower bath; one room has TV and a Jacuzzi/shower bath.
BREAKFAST: 8–9:30 (continental for early ferry passengers and for late risers until 10:30). "Use of a lot of local products." Homemade low-fat granola, yogurt, cranberry nut sweet

bread, cream cheese chocolate muffins, bread baked daily with freshly ground grain (orange cinnamon swirl for French toast), waffles and pancakes. Juice, cereal, tea, coffee. In breakfast/dining area (with fireplace) or on back deck overlooking flower and herb gardens. PLUS: Guest refrigerator. Fresh flowers. Robes. Complimentary bicycles. A interesting and fun-to-read semiannual newsletter with recipes. A sample: "The following recipe— Chocolate Mint Sticks—comes from Mrs. Marconi in Colorado Springs, CO, our children's music teacher 20 years ago. She served these mint sticks at recitals. Our kids dreaded the recitals, but loved the mint sticks. They are now an evening favorite here at the inn."

➣ From Canada, Massachusetts, Illinois, Indiana, Virginia, New York, Texas, Vermont, Philippines, England: *"A real treasure . . . the best B&B ever. . . . All the details were perfect. . . . The most personable, helpful, and kind host and hostess. . . . Incredible breakfasts with heart-shaped cinnamon buns and waffles. . . . Beautifully served. . . . Bed very comfortable and well appointed. (Triple sheeting!) . . . Everything to spoil you. Not one stone unturned . . . spotless . . . charming, cheerful rooms . . . elegance of the inn matched the wonderful food and great innkeepers . . . worth coming all the way from Toronto for . . . soft classical music . . . relaxing . . . peaceful . . . attentive. . . . From the cranberry spritzers on arrival to the chocolates on pillow at night . . . hospitality that never ended! . . . Have been all over the world. Magic of the beautiful inn lies in the hosts. . . . Out of five B&Bs we stayed in New England, Acworth Inn was our favorite."*

➣ Isaiah Hall B&B Inn

508/385-9928

152 Whig Street, P.O. Box 1007,
Dennis, MA 02638

800/736-0160
FAX 508/385-5879
E-MAIL info@isaiahhallinn.com

HOSTS: Marie and Dick Brophy
LOCATION: In a quiet year-round residential area on the historic bay side. A half mile from the beach and one-third mile from the village and Route 6A. About fifteen minutes from Hyannis.
OPEN: End of April–mid-October. Two- or three-day minimum from mid-June to Labor Day and on weekends and holidays.
RATES: Vary according to room or bed size, balcony, fireplace. Mid-June– Labor Day $97, $112, $122, $128, $134; single $10 less. Suite $164. Spring $8–$15 less. Fall $5–$8 less. Extra person $20. Amex, MC, Visa. ♥ ♦♦ ⊞ ❖ ✗ ✁

INSIDE AND OUT, "the real Cape" was all there one weekend in May, when we took a short prebreakfast bicycle ride to the accompaniment of bird songs—to the endless beach where quahogs were being harvested; past sand dunes; and back to the 1857 Greek Revival farmhouse (and attached/renovated carriage house).

continued . . .

Since the Brophys came here in 1983, they have made major changes but retained the ambiance of another era, with beams and antique rockers, white curtains, and wicker. In the kitchen and dining room there is some artwork done by former owner Dorothy Gripp, whose work can be seen in museums all over the country. *Cape Cod Life* has published an Isaiah Hall feature. And *Yankee* selected Isaiah Hall for an "Editor's Pick."

Marie, a B&B consultant who likes to say that the inn is "more L.L. Bean than Armani," was a school counselor and then a high-tech compensation analyst. Dick hosts when he is at home from his consulting work.

BED AND BATH: Ten air-conditioned rooms on first or second floors, all with private bath, TV/VCR, and telephone. Five rooms in main house (steeper stairs), five in carriage house. Queen, double, or a queen (or double) and a single bed. One suite with TV/VCR and refrigerator, one with working fireplace; four in carriage house with balconies. Extra bed available.

BREAKFAST: 8:30–10. At 8 or "to go" put in guest refrigerator by request. (Coffee ready at 7.) Cereals. Fruit, English muffins, homemade breads and muffins, jams, jellies, raisins, yogurt. Juice, coffees, teas. On a nineteenth-century buffet in antiques-filled air-conditioned dining room made for camaraderie.

PLUS: Guests' parlor with air conditioning and Victorian coal stove. Air-conditioned great room in converted carriage house. Table games. TV. Porch rockers. Terry robes. Forgotten items. Clock radios. Bedroom fans. Ironing boards. Large yard with gardens, lawn chairs, badminton, volleyball, croquet. Use of refrigerator. Beach towels. A good brochure with guest-chosen photographs.

＞ From a flood of letters from both sides of the Atlantic: *"The general ambiance was delightful, the service exceptional. Marie made us feel so welcome . . . full of local knowledge. . . . The location and area are superb. Breakfast time is a hoot. . . . Roomy, light, comfortable, wonderful garden, good common area . . . peaceful. . . . Everything clean and fresh . . . homey . . . spotless . . . plenty of hot water. . . . Best of all inns we stayed in. . . . Like returning home to the opening arms of a favorite aunt. . . . Charming all around."*

*I*NNKEEPING MAY BE *America's most envied profession. As one host mused, "Where else can you get a job where, every day, someone tells you how wonderful you are?"*

⋙ Bed and Breakfast Cape Cod Host #DEN-04

East Dennis, MA

LOCATION: Residential. Across from stone wall fronting property with new homes. Ten-minute walk to bay beach (warm water), Dennis Playhouse, museum, fine restaurants, and town gazebo (summer Monday night band concerts).

RESERVATIONS: Year round through Bed and Breakfast Cape Cod (page 144), 508/255-3824 or 800/541-6226. Two-night minimum, three on holidays.

RATES: Late May–mid-October $95 room, $105 suite. Off-season $80 room, $85 suite. Suite weekly rates available. 🏃 ♨ 🚭 🍴

⋙ From Scotland: *"Happy memories . . . husband did rollerblading . . . warm and friendly house for visitors . . . wonderful couple . . . lovely home."*

"LOVELY" AND TRADITIONAL—just the way the hosts planned it when they built this centrally air-conditioned Cape Cod–style house in 1994. An Oriental rug is in the parlor, a needlepoint rug in the dining room. There are Hitchcock chairs, some Victorian pieces, an antique desk, Williamsburg colors, and four-poster beds. The recently retired hosts—a dental consultant and a dental assistant—"always had a second home on the Cape" while they lived a little west of Boston.

IN RESIDENCE: "Our schnauzer mixes with guests only if they choose to visit him in his own fenced area."

BED AND BATH: Two large air-conditioned, built-for-B&B second-floor rooms, each with en-suite shower that has built-in seat. One room has high queen four-poster. Antique king/twins option in other. Also suite with king/twins option (posted beds), large tub/shower bath, kitchenette with microwave, refrigerator, coffeepot.

BREAKFAST: Usually 8–9. (Bag breakfast for early departures.) Juices. Fresh fruit. Yogurt with vanilla. Cold cereals. Muffins or pastry. Hot beverages. Served in dining room. Option of taking tray to your room or to umbrella tables on deck that overlooks yard.

IF YOU HAVE MET ONE B&B HOST, YOU HAVEN'T MET THEM ALL. IF YOU'VE BEEN TO ONE B&B, YOU HAVEN'T BEEN TO THEM ALL.

≈ Captain Nickerson Inn

508/398-5966

333 Main Street,
South Dennis, MA 02660-3643

800/282-1619
FAX 508/398-5966
E-MAIL Captnick@capecod.net
www.bbonline.com/ma/captnick/

HOSTS: Pat and Dave York
LOCATION: Residential. In historic district. Ten-minute walk to conservation land along Bass River. Half mile to Cape Cod Rail Trail or to church with oldest working pipe organ in the country. Ten miles east of Hyannis.
OPEN: March 1 through December 7. Two-night minimum late May until mid-October; three nights on Fourth of July.
RATES: $85–$107. $140 for four. $15 third person. $10 portacrib fee. Off-season $75–$85. Singles $70–$80. One-night surcharge $5. Discover, MC, Visa.
🛉🛉 ▦ ❖ ⚫ ⅄ ≋

THIS QUEEN ANNE, built by a sea captain, retained its features—parquet and pumpkin pine floors, wrought-iron fireplace inset, stained glass windows, wainscoting, and woodwork—even though the house has seen many uses through the years. In 1994 the Yorks were living north of Boston when Pat, a government compliance officer, and Dave, who has a trucking and warehouse business, decided to find a home-based business. The house is completely refurbished—with reproductions throughout, deep-colored wallcoverings, lace curtains, added baths, and extra-firm mattresses. Pat is full-time innkeeper, and "informality reigns." Dave hosts evenings and weekends.

IN RESIDENCE: In hosts' quarters, Sarah, age nine, and David, age eleven. Two dogs—Brewster, a Brittany spaniel, travels with Dave during the week. Ginger, a miniature black poodle, "loves everyone."
BED AND BATH: Five second-floor air-conditioned rooms with clock radios, painted wideboard floors. Four with queen bed (two are four-posters), ceiling fan, private bath (three are en suite, all have shower, one has tub also). When coupled with a double-bedded room, one room becomes a suite with hall shower bath.
BREAKFAST: 8:30–9:30. Continental 7-11. Hazelnut/amaretto French toast, eggs any style with toast or grilled English muffin and bacon, pancakes with blueberries. Sunday special—berry crepe. Sometimes, surprises such as fresh tomatoes from a neighbor's garden. In fireplaced dining room at table for six or at smaller tables for two or three.
PLUS: TV/VCR in living room. Sodas and teas always available. Guest refrigerator. Fresh fruit. Beach towels. Bicycles for guests' use. Recommendations for "pleasant walks from the inn"; restaurants, including "lobster just down the street"; theater; short or long whale-watching trips; beaches; Cape Cod National Seashore programs.

≈ From Connecticut: *"We wanted peace and quiet, good food, and total relaxation. Pat and Dave provided a perfect match. Breakfast was delicious, dinner recommenda-*

tions on the money. We wanted to take Ginger, their dog, home with us. . . . Drove 500 miles for all of a forty-hour visit, but it was well worth it. Felt very much at home. Give them as many forks and stars as you allow. No, I'm not a relative!"

The Rose Petal B&B

508/398-8470

P.O. Box 974, 152 Sea Street,
Dennis Port, MA 02639–2405

E-MAIL info@rosepetalofdennis.com
www.rosepetalofdennis.com

HOSTS: Dan and Gayle Kelly
LOCATION: On a residential (through) street that ends (half mile away) at a sandy Nantucket Sound beach. Several restaurants within walking distance. Midway (ten minutes) between Hyannis and Chatham.
OPEN: Year round. Two- or three-night minimum for holiday weekends. Please make advance arrangements for young children.
RATES: Mid-June through mid-September $70 shared bath, $103–$109 private. Less off-season. Extra person $15. Amex, MC, Visa ♥ 👫 ⊞ ❖ ⚥ ✁

From Belgium: *"Enjoyed our eight-day stay enormously. . . . Rooms were well-appointed and comfortable. . . . Breakfasts delicious and, by European standards, copious . . . particularly appreciated their laundering our beach towels and giving us useful tips on restaurants and what to do and see."* From Massachusetts: *"Immaculate rooms, wonderful service, scrumptious food, and two innkeepers with personality plus."* From New York: *"Sunshine was here, even with wind, fog, and rain outside. Splendid hosts."*

DAN'S DAILY BAKING results in wonderful aromas. Sometimes you have an opportunity to see him decorate a three-tiered or other special occasion cake. Trained at the Culinary Institute of America, he now bakes for a local bakery/restaurant as well as for the B&B. Both Dan and Gayle, a substitute teacher in winter, have experience in university (Princeton and Rutgers) food service administration. Their impeccably kept house, built for early Dennis Port seafaring families, was a restaurant/guest house in the mid-1900s. When the Kellys purchased it from a religious order that had a boys' home here, they expanded their talents to include plastering, stenciling, and landscaping. (Passersby stop to photograph the yard roses.) Furnishings include antiques, brass beds, hand-stitched quilts, and lace curtains.

IN RESIDENCE: Patrick, age ten.
FOREIGN LANGUAGE SPOKEN: Gayle speaks "rusty" French.
BED AND BATH: Three second-floor rooms with private en-suite baths, air conditioning, individual heat control, wall-mounted hair dryer. Queen bed with shower bath. Queen and a twin daybed with tub/shower bath. The Captain's Room has queen and a twin daybed, shower bath, private staircase from kitchen, and private entrance from second-floor deck; shares first-floor footed-tub/shower bath with hosts.

continued . . .

BREAKFAST: Usually 8–9:30 (coffee by 7). Homemade muffins, croissants, strudels, coffee cake, Danish. Eggs Benedict (signature dish with croissant), Florentine eggs, omelets, or stuffed French toast with berry toppings. "We've done kosher-style, vegetarian, gluten-free, low-cholesterol . . . let us know, please." Juice, fruit, cereal, granola, cranberry butter, freshly ground coffee, specialty teas. Buffet style in dining room.

PLUS: Guest refrigerator with complimentary beverages. Complimentary homemade pastries "to go" for excursions. Guest living room with TV, piano, area publications. Beach towels. "And yes, we do welcome children!"

℀ Bed and Breakfast Cape Cod Host #EAS-20

Eastham, MA

> **LOCATION:** Quiet and lovely area. On a private road with older houses on lake side facing newer houses across the street. Walk to small freshwater town beach at one end of road; bicycle path is at other end. One mile to bay beaches; 1½ miles to National Seashore beach.
>
> **RESERVATIONS:** Year round through Bed and Breakfast Cape Cod (page 144), 508/255-3824 or 800/541-6226. Two-night minimum, three on holidays.
>
> **RATES:** $90–$110. ♥ ☕ ⚄ ⚄ ⚄

THIS MODIFIED Cape house, built by a merchant seaman during his land months, was completed in 1997. Now the old-fashioned farmer's porch has an old-fashioned porch swing made by the host, a former programmer turned craftsman. In his workshop here he makes custom furniture and stained glass works, and he repairs antiques. He and his wife, who retired from her retailing position in the Boston area, bought this "perfect-for-B&B house so close to everything" in 1998. They meet many guests who comment on the soaking tub, the suite, the breakfast served on bone china with silver, and the peace and beauty of Eastham.

BED AND BATH: On second floor—one room and one suite, both air conditioned and furnished eclectically. Queen-bedded room with sitting area, hall tub/shower bath. Suite with queen bed, sitting area, bath with large shower and separate soaking tub, dressing room, private balcony.

BREAKFAST: Usually 7–9. (Earlier for some ferry passengers; later if you were on a late whale watch.) Juice, fresh fruit, homemade muffins, hot beverages. Served in dining room or at umbrella table on rear deck.

> ℀ Guests wrote: *"Off the beaten path and so-o-o quiet. Most inviting . . . bubbles for the bath and a great breakfast."*

⋙ *The Overlook Inn*   508/255-1886

3085 County Road (Route 6),   FAX 508/240-0345
Eastham, MA 02642   E-MAIL stay@overlookinn.com
                                               www.overlookinn.com

HOSTS: Nan and Ian Aitchison
LOCATION: Way back from road, across from entrance to main Cape Cod National
Seashore visitors' area. Bike paths (and bicycle rental shop) right here; 3
miles to Orleans and fine restaurants.
OPEN: Year round. Reservations required.
RATES: Per room. Summer $130 private hall bath, $145 private en-suite bath, $175
family-size room. Spring and fall $115–$130. Winter $95. All major credit
cards accepted. ♥ ♦♦♦ ⊞ ❖ ♥⊃

⋙ From Michigan: *"A few of my favorite things: Tea at 4:00, a daily newspaper to
read, Winnie the dog, the pool table, looking at the wedding photo album, reading Mark's
bedside stories; all the interesting Scottish memorabilia and books made even a rainy day enjoyable."* From New York: *"Felt like I was in Scotland."* From Massachusetts: *"Our second
visit topped the first. Can't wait for the third."*

FIRST-TIME GUESTS think they've discovered Overlook. Named "Best Inn on the Outer
Cape" by *Cape Cod Life*, it has also been recommended by the *Sunday Times* (London)
and *Outside* magazine. "Our guests love 'the real Cape.' Many bicycle. They walk. And
bird-watch. And enjoy the beach year round. We host library garden parties and business
seminars. And many weddings—on the porch or by the parlor fire. We love this little
town, which reminds me of my own childhood days in a Scottish village. . . . When our
sons were in college, they spent two years restoring this long-established lodging establishment, a Queen Anne Victorian. We furnished with comfortable Victorian antiques,
wicker, lace, and fine artworks. Now son Mark and his wife, Tania, run a lodge on the
Amazon. Son Clive, a painter whose works are in many rooms, has studios on Cape Cod
and in Toronto. He and his wife, Marisa, help us here. Now that Ian, a chartered surveyor,
has retired, he has more time for enjoying our guests—and playing his bagpipes!"

IN RESIDENCE: Winnie, basset hound, and Cecil, a beagle.
BED AND BATH: On second and third floors, ten air-conditioned rooms with ceiling fans.
All private baths (some with shower, no tub); most are en suite (terry robes for hall bath).
Queen, double (one with working fireplace), or twin beds. Family room has a queen and
two twin beds and a butler's pantry with sink, microwave, and refrigerator. Cottage (dogs
allowed here) with full kitchen and bath.
BREAKFAST: 8–10. Hallmark Scottish fare. Maybe *kedgeree—finnan haddie,* rice, onions,
chopped eggs, raisins sautéed in butter, plus dab of mango chutney. Or cinnamon toast
with fresh strawberries and sour cream.
PLUS: Bagpipe serenades by the fire or, in summer in the garden during afternoon tea
(with hot scones). Five common rooms, including Winston Churchill library with books

continued . . .

and Victorian card table. Hemingway billiard room. Five fireplaces. Expansive lawn. Porches. New Year's celebration that has become an inn tradition.

➤ From England, New Jersey, Massachusetts: *"This is one popular inn, and for good reason . . . an elegant Victorian world . . . lovely tranquil retreat. . . . Meals are a treat to the palate, appealingly presented. . . . Interesting family. . . . Recommendations for fun beaches, historic sites, good places to eat . . . everything arranged for guests' comfort . . . a great experience."*

➤ The Whalewalk Inn

508/255-0617

220 Bridge Road,
Eastham, MA 02642-3215

FAX 508/240-0017
E-MAIL whalewak@capecod.net
www.whalewalkinn.com

HOSTS: Dick and Carolyn Smith
LOCATION: Residential back street. Three acres of lawn, gardens, meadows. Ten-minute walk to beaches; 100 yards to bike path. Ten-minute drive to National Seashore; five to galleries, shops, restaurants.
OPEN: February 15–December 15. Two-night minimum mid-May–mid-October and weekends; three nights on holiday weekends.
RATES: $160 queen, $225 king with fireplace and sitting area. $200 carriage house queen rooms with fireplace, $225 with fireplace and whirlpool tub, $275 carriage house king with fireplace and whirlpool tub. $235 guest house, barn suites, cottage queen. Off-season, $25–$50 less (depending on room). Amex, MC, Visa. ♥ ❖ ⚹ ✂

➤ From Massachusetts: *"Perfect . . . absolutely gorgeous . . . simply elegant. . . . I even asked for a recipe . . . gracious, friendly hosts."*

DEVOTEES ABOUND. *The New York Times, Yankee,* and *Glamour* have raved about the inn that *Cape Cod Life* readers six times have named "Best Inn on the Outer Cape." Intentionally, it is "simply elegant" (request brochure with photos)—with casual, happy innkeepers, former Boston advertising executives who initiated a fund-raising drive for the Nauset Light Preservation Society. Now Dick is an acclaimed cook. Carolyn's interior design talents were recognized as one of the top ten in a Waverly Country-Room-of-the-Year contest.

The main house, a Greek Revival built for a whaling captain, became a farm before being converted to an inn in 1953. Major renovations were done in the 1990s. And on the Fourth of July, 1997, the Smiths completed a six-room carriage house addition. Throughout there are country antiques—and some reproductions. Rooms are light and airy with soft colors: peach, rose, or blue. "And to think we're here just because, upon departure as guests, we told the innkeepers that we were thinking of doing this someday!"

BED AND BATH: Sixteen (total) air-conditioned rooms (some are suites), each with private bath. Beds (some are four-posters) in king, queen, or twin sizes. Baths are every possible configuration—with shower only; with soaking tub (and fireplace in view) and separate shower bath; with tub/shower; with two-person whirlpool; handicapped accessible roll-in shower. Kitchen/living room in some suites. Other amenities, depending on room: wet bar, gas or wood-burning fireplace, large sitting area, deck, individual thermostat, ceiling fan, full kitchen, private exterior entrance. Cottage has queen bed, full bath, kitchen/dining area, wood-burning fireplace, private patio.

BREAKFAST: Usually 8:30–9:30. Grand Marnier French toast, blueberry pancakes, baked omelet, apple walnut raisin crepes with ice cream, homemade breads, fresh fruits. Special diets accommodated. Served on garden patio under awning or in sunporch breakfast room.

PLUS: Hors d'oeuvres by the fire during BYOB cocktail hours. Down comforters. Guest refrigerator. Beach towels. Complimentary bikes.

⇗ *Penny House Inn*

508/255-6632

4885 County Road (Route 6), Eastham, MA
Mailing address: P.O. Box 238,
North Eastham, MA 02651-0238

800/554-1751
FAX 508/255-4893
E-MAIL pennyhouse@aol.com
www.pennyhouseinn.com

HOSTS: Margaret and (daughter) Rebecca Keith
LOCATION: Hidden behind a high wooden fence and tall privet hedge. On 1½ acres of lawn. In Cape Cod National Seashore area, midway between Hyannis and Provincetown. Minutes to bike trails and Massachusetts Audubon Society sanctuary.
OPEN: Year round. Three-night minimum on holiday weekends.
RATES: June–September $135 (first-floor rooms) to $195 (suite with working fireplace). Off-season $115–$175. Amex, Discover, MC, Visa.
♥ ♦♦♦ ⊞ ✦ ⚁ ⚄ ❤

A TWO-TIME winner of *Cape Cod Life*'s "Best Inn on the Outer Cape" designation, the late 1600s captain's house with bow roof and wide-planked floors reflects the shipbuilding techniques of the year it was built. Newer rooms added in the 1980s are also furnished with country antiques and collectibles; paintings from Australia, Margaret's homeland; and porcelain and some Chinese artworks. And now there's a new fireplaced public room as well as a sunroom with wet bar.

In 1987 the Keiths, world travelers—to destinations including Antarctica, Indonesia, New Zealand, and Japan—found this "right place," as Margaret calls it. (Rebecca's world travels began when she obtained her first passport at the age of five months. Six of her early

continued . . .

education years were in Australia.) Now Margaret and Rebecca, a biochemist married (here at the inn) to a biochemist, are co-innkeepers.

BED AND BATH: Eleven air-conditioned rooms on two floors. King or queen beds. All private baths (some tub/shower; others shower only, some with seats); robes provided for one in hall. Amenities vary and include private entrance and balcony, wood-burning fireplace, cathedral ceiling, skylight, bow roof ceiling, private phone, TV.
BREAKFAST: 8–10. French toast croissant, eggs Benedict, pecan waffles with bacon or sausage. Fresh fruit. Juice. Cereals. Yogurt. Homemade muffins. Served at tables for two in 1690 dining room that has Oriental rugs and 300-year-old beams.
PLUS: Afternoon tea. Oversized bath towels. Rear brick patio and garden with tables and chairs and English benches. Many books about Australia.

> ⤛ From Massachusetts: *"Classy, but not stuffy . . . delicious breakfasts . . . friendly conversation."* From New York: *"Cozy, very clean, and tastefully decorated rooms . . . appreciated extras such as beach towels and restaurant menus."*

⤛ Grafton Inn   508/540-8688

261 Grand Avenue South,   800/642-4069
Falmouth, MA 02540-3784   FAX 508/540-1861

HOSTS: Liz and Rudy Cvitan
LOCATION: Facing the ocean. Across the street from miles of sandy beach with great swimming. Less than a mile to village center. One block to two restaurants. Eight-minute walk to island ferry. Short drive to golf course and shops.
OPEN: Mid-February–mid-December. Two-night minimum on weekends, three on holidays.
RATES: Mid-May–mid-October $139, $169, $179, $189. Mid-October–mid-December and mid-February–mid-May $95–$159. Extra person in room $35. Amex, MC, Visa. ♥ ⚬ ⤙ ⚘

"IN A MOMENT of wild abandon" may be Liz's retort as to how a couple from upper New York State happened to become Cape innkeepers in 1984. In truth, Liz, the art gallery owner who represented 300 artists, and Rudy, an electronics manufacturer's representative, had long thought about having an inn on the ocean. Since buying this 1850 turreted shingled house, known in 1910 as The Grafton Hotel, they have done "just about everything—from triple-pane windows to redecorating several times over."

The inn has been cited for "civic beautification." This is home—filled with antiques, family treasures, and figurine lamps. Food is a feature here. How warm is the ocean? Guests watch Rudy as he takes the water temperature before swimming from jetty to jetty. They unwind on the porch or in the living room. As one wrote, "Peace at last!"

BED AND BATH: Ten air-conditioned rooms (five have direct ocean view, others a side view) on three floors. All have private shower bath, cable color TV, ceiling fan, lap desk, hair dryer, white-noise machine. First floor—one turret room with king bed and four large windows; one room with side ocean view has queen bed. Second floor—two rooms with queen bed, two with king bed. Third floor—one room with brass queen bed plus a twin, five windows; two with canopied queen bed; one with double bed under the eaves, sitting area.

BREAKFAST: 8–9. Quite a spread. Entrées include "Hawaiian toast"—Portuguese sweet bread with sliced banana and whipped cream; apple-stuffed pancakes; pecan/banana Belgian waffles (homemade blueberry, cranberry sauces); fresh broccoli/sharp cheddar omelet. Served at tables for two on enclosed porch overlooking beach.

PLUS: Wine and cheese hour, 5-6 p.m. Guest refrigerator, ice maker, and telephone. Chocolates. Sand chairs, beach umbrellas and towels. Off-street parking. Directions to a spectacular privately owned garden open to public. Transportation provided to/from Falmouth bus stop.

⚓ From Connecticut: *"I am very particular. . . . Cleanliness is beyond expectation. . . . Food is absolutely delicious. . . . Liz and Rudy are very warm and friendly people. . . . We love to relax on the beach, so the location is perfect. . . . My favorite part is the wine and cheese hour . . . good restaurant recommendations and Cape Cod stories. . . . Can't wait to go back."*

⚓ *Hewins House Bed and Breakfast*   508/457-4363

20 Hewins Street, Falmouth, MA 02540   (TOLL-FREE) 877/4-HEWINS

HOST: Virginia Price
LOCATION: On historic village green. One block to Falmouth center. Less than a mile to Surf Drive Beach. Three and a half blocks to shuttle for island ferries.
OPEN: May–October. Two-night minimum; three-night minimum on holiday weekends.
RATES: $110. Singles $10 less. Ten percent discount for stays of four or more nights. Amex, Diners, Discover, MC, Visa. ♥ ♦♦♦ ■ ⊞ ❖ ⚔ ✂

THE TRADITIONAL decor with antiques and Oriental rugs prompts many guests to ask, "Have you always lived here?" Often they enter with "We're home!"

The Prices, parents of four grown children, bought the Federal Colonial house in 1989 so that Albert, a periodontist, could have a professional office. Then it occurred to Virginia—a good cook and an avid horticulturist (she grows orchids)—that their home would also make a perfect B&B. Now guests look at the collection of before-and-after photographs—"our *This Old House* book"—to see what was done to enhance the beautiful structure, which has been featured on a house and garden tour. They rave about the breakfast, all made from scratch with "real ingredients—butter, cream, and maple syrup." Some play the grand piano. And they enjoy the formal gardens.

IN RESIDENCE: Husband Albert and son Andrew, age fifteen. "Harold, the cat, and his friend, Kathleen Kitty." Bear, a Samoyed.

continued . . .

BED AND BATH: Three air-conditioned second-floor rooms with private en-suite baths. Two with canopied queen bed, one with tub/shower bath and one with shower bath. One room with a double and a twin bed, tub/shower bath.
BREAKFAST: 8–9. Waffles with fruit, whipped cream, and maple syrup; gingerbread pancakes and sausage; blueberry muffins with bacon and eggs; corn bread with eggs Florentine. Fruit, juice, hot beverages. Served in formal Federal dining room.
PLUS: Wood-burning fireplace in living room. Off-street parking. Guest refrigerator. Columned porch off living room overlooking garden.

﹌ The Inn at One Main Street

508/540-7469

One Main Street,   888/281-6246
Falmouth, MA 02540-2652   FAX 603/462-5680
                                                   E-MAIL innat1main@aol.com
                                                   www.bbonline/ma/onemain

HOSTS: Ilona Cleveland and Jeanne (pronounced Jeannie) Dahl
LOCATION: Can't miss it! With tall white fence, in historic district, "on the bend" where the main road to Woods Hole begins. Very close to village green. Walk to ferry shuttle, beaches, dining, shopping, bike path.
OPEN: Year round. Three-night minimum on holiday weekends.
RATES: Vary according to room size. Late May–November 1 $105–$150. Extra person $25. Off-season $85–$100. Amex, Discover, MC, Visa. ♥ ☛ ⊞ ❖ ⚄ ⌇

"A PERFECT B&B" was the impression from the moment the two sisters saw this 1892 house, a well-established B&B that has spacious, light-filled guest rooms; a soft mauve-colored living room (with plenty of comfortable seating); a large yard; and a shaded porch. In nearby Plymouth, Ilona was an accountant. In faraway Arizona, Jeanne was director of quality management for a blood bank management system and was "ready for a career change." Since becoming innkeepers in 1998, they have created a family atmosphere—"romantics, too, join in, especially at breakfast time"—the kind of place where guests feel they are visiting a favorite relative. Trip planning is a specialty.

BED AND BATH: Six air-conditioned rooms (three with ceiling fan), all private shower baths, on first and second floors. Queen, twins, or queen and twin beds.
BREAKFAST: 8–9. Entrée possibilities include orange pecan French toast, pancakes with fruit topping, cheese strata, Southwestern egg dish. Juices, fresh fruit, sweet breads or muffins, hot beverages. Served in candlelit dining room. "Usually a lively and leisurely meal!"
PLUS: Living room with wood-burning fireplace and TV/VCR. Homemade cookies and coffee and tea. Fresh flowers. Special occasions acknowledged.

﹌ From Connecticut: *"Hosts have a perfect formula for making folks feel special. Truly enjoyed our stay."* From Scotland: *"Our room was gorgeous. Breakfasts were delicious. Hospitality exceptional. It was most relaxing."*

ᘐ Mostly Hall Bed & Breakfast Inn

27 Main Street, Falmouth, MA 02540-2652

508/548-3786
800/682-0565
FAX 508/457-1572
www.mostlyhall.com

HOSTS: Caroline and Jim Lloyd
LOCATION: Parklike. In quiet seclusion. Set back from the road on more than an acre of lawn, trees, and shrubs. In historic district, across from the village green. One mile to town beaches. Around corner from 4-mile bike path to Woods Hole and Martha's Vineyard ferry. Two blocks from bus station.
OPEN: Year round except for January and first two weeks of February. Two- or three-night minimum preferred May–October and weekends.
RATES: May–October $125–$150. Off-season $105–$120. Honeymoon and other packages. Amex, Discover, MC, Visa. ♥ ⚹ ✄

UNMISTAKABLY GRAND and gracious, even romantic, with 13-foot ceilings, Oriental rugs, antiques, dramatic floral wallpaper, a cupola "travel room" (with videotapes)—and, on the lovely grounds cited for civic beautification, a gazebo with swing and Adirondack chairs. A B&B since 1980, the four-storied residence was originally built in 1849 by a sea captain for his New Orleans bride. It was named decades ago by an owner's youngster when he first saw the inside of the new family home. In 1995 the inn became a set for a Discovery Channel film. It has also been featured in Swiss and Dutch magazines and in the calendar of the National Trust for Historic Preservation.

The Lloyds are avid travelers who have bicycled, hiked, and cruised on their own off-season getaways all over—Mexico, Costa Rica, Chile, Argentina, Egypt, Kenya, New Zealand, Vietnam, the Far East, India, Nepal, South Africa, China. . . . Before changing careers in 1986, Caroline was in retail merchandise management in Washington, D.C., Philadelphia, and Boston. Jim, an ardent cyclist and gardener, was a corporate computer executive.

FOREIGN LANGUAGE SPOKEN: Some German.
BED AND BATH: Six spacious corner rooms, each with private en-suite shower bath and canopied queen four-poster bed. All are air conditioned; most have ceiling fan.
BREAKFAST: Full at 9, or "breakfast to go" bags for early travelers. Juice, fresh fruit, home-made sweet breads or muffins. Entrée might be Mexicali eggs, stuffed French toast, or cheese blintzes with warm blueberry sauce. Special diets accommodated—with advance notice, please. Served in living room or on the covered porch that wraps around all four sides.
PLUS: Central air conditioning. Living room gas fireplace. Sherry and afternoon refreshments. Library/game area. Piano. Complimentary six-speed bicycles. Cookbook available.

ᘐ From British Columbia: *"Our ideal prototype of a charming New England B&B experience. We cannot rave about it enough!"*

⋙ The Palmer House Inn
508/548-1230

81 Palmer Avenue,
Falmouth, MA 02540-2857

800/472-2632

FAX 508/540-1878

E-MAIL innkeepers@palmerhouseinn.com

www.palmerhouseinn.com

HOSTS: Ken and Joanne Baker

LOCATION: In residential historic district, adjacent to village green. Two blocks to shops and restaurants, one block to bike path to Woods Hole. Close to bus station and ferry shuttles. One mile to town beaches.

OPEN: Year round. Two-night weekend minimum May through October; three nights on holiday weekends and special events.

RATES: Mid-June–mid-October $115 double bed, $135–$175 queen, $175–$199 king, $225 suite; $30 third person. May–mid-June and mid- to late-October $10 less ($105–$215); $25 third person. November–April $25–$35 less ($80–$190); $20 third person. AARP and AAA discounts. CB, Diners, Discover, MC, Visa. ♥ ⊞ ❖ ⚰ ⅄

FROM GRANDMA's house to elegance! When I first saw this Queen Anne Victorian, it had eight guest rooms. In 1994 the guest house, a 1910 carriage house, was restored, as was the 1915 beach cottage—"Suite Seclusion." In 1999 the Bakers built the spacious hardly-can-tell addition to the main inn. Decor includes lace curtains, Oriental rugs, silk wallcoverings, stained glass windows, and lots of Victoriana. Elaborate breakfasts, intentionally "an event," feature menus that are never repeated as long as you are a guest.

The Bakers came here from Pennsylvania in 1990 as grandparents and newlyweds who wanted to work together. Since then they have met guests from all over the world who confirm that these hosts made the right decision. Ken, the waiter and former truck driver, is pianist/gardener/cyclist/carpenter. Joanne, the chef, was in private practice as a certified public accountant for thirteen years.

IN RESIDENCE: Victoria, a Yorkshire terrier, "enjoys playing Frisbee and will pose for photographs." Two parrots, Jaime (who sings to Strauss and Vivaldi) and Gabby (who likes to give hugs and kisses).

BED AND BATH: Seventeen air-conditioned rooms, each with ceiling fan, in-room phone, TV, private bath; some main inn baths have shower without tub. *Main inn* rooms (some with refrigerator, two-person whirlpool tub): six on second floor, two staircases to six rooms on third. King, queen, double, or double and a twin bed. ("The Penthouse" has canopied king bed, fireplace, whirlpool tub—in bedroom—under skylit cathedral ceiling, bath with two-headed shower.) *Guest house:* four spacious first-floor corner rooms (one is handicapped accessible) with king, queen, or queen and twin bed; all have refrigerator, full bath (two with whirlpool tub and fireplace). Separate "Suite Seclusion" three-room cottage has king bed, whirlpool tub in bedroom alcove, separate tub/shower bath, living room with ceiling fan, small kitchen, deck, garden.

BREAKFAST: 8–9:30 Freshly blended juices (recipe printed in *Gourmet* and *Bon Appétit*). Maybe poached pears in raspberry sauce, creamed eggs with fresh chives, pineapple spice scones, a special coffee blend, imported teas. Low-fat options available. Served on fine china and crystal in candlelit dining room with classical music.
PLUS: Fireplaced living room with upright piano; library and game room. Porch rockers. Beach towels. Complimentary bikes. Directions to a spectacular (especially in spring) private garden. Snacks and beverages, 3–9.

› From Connecticut: *"If you love being pampered and being alone at the same time, this place is ideal! . . . Perfectly located for both shopping and beaches."* From Massachusetts: *"Wonderful hosts. . . . Fastidious . . . delicious breakfast. . . . Everything was perfect."*

› *Village Green Inn*

508/548-5621
800/237-1119
FAX 508/457-5051
E-MAIL vgi40@aol.com
www.villagegreeninn.com

40 Main Street,
Falmouth, MA 02540-2678

HOSTS:	Diane and Don Crosby
LOCATION:	On the village green, surrounded by homes and churches dating to early 1700s. Minutes' walk to shops and restaurants, bus station, ferry shuttle; bicycle path to beaches and Woods Hole.
OPEN:	Year round. Two-night minimum, June through October; three nights on weekends and holidays year round.
RATES:	Memorial Day–Columbus Day $140, $165 suite. Mid-October–late May $90–$125, $140 suite. $25 third person. Some off-season discounts. Amex, MC, Visa. ♥ ▇ ⊞ ❖ ⚝ ⚓

BEFORE THE Crosbys bought this B&B, an 1804 Federal house that was made into a Victorian, they stayed as overnight guests in every room. Since moving in 1995 from the west suburban area of Boston, where Diane was a nurse and Don a junior high school social studies teacher, they have met guests who comment on everything—the welcoming homey atmosphere; the attention to detail; the candlelit breakfast table; the chocolates, flowers, fluffy towels, and silken bed linens; the careful directions and Cape and Boston sightseeing suggestions; and, yes, the cheerful hosts.

BED AND BATH: Four large air-conditioned queen-bedded rooms (two on first floor) plus an L-shaped suite with a queen and a twin daybed. All with private bath (three with shower, two with tub and shower) and phone. Two rooms with working fireplace.
BREAKFAST: 8:30. (Boat bags for those catching the early ferry to Martha's Vineyard.) Chili cheese egg puffs, cranberry orange scones, fresh peach-raspberry medley,

continued . . .

caramelized French toast, honey pecan butter. Served in the dining room at one large table set with silver and china.

PLUS: Color cable TV in each room. Afternoon refreshments. Piano. Beach towels and chairs. Loan of bicycles. Martha's Vineyard ferry tickets sold here to guests.

❦ From Washington: *"Actual experience exceeded our high expectations. Nice extras you'd expect from an expensive hotel were there, but with added personal attention."* From Illinois: *"Have stayed in B&Bs in U.S., France, and Italy, and would rank Don and Diane as 'world class.'"* From Georgia: *"Exceptional—from charming ambiance to its scrumptious breakfasts. Diane and Don made the difference between a 'good' vacation and a 'great' one."* From Pennsylvania: *"Delighted with the beautiful appointments . . . creative and tasty breakfasts."* From Michigan: *"Perfect hosts—finding the balance between being helpful and friendly and providing a private atmosphere."* From New Jersey: *"Room was gorgeous . . . cozy fireplace, sparkling wood floors, antique stained glass window. A definite must for any B&B lover."*

❦ The Wildflower Inn

508/548-9524
800/294-5459
FAX 508/548-9524
E-MAIL WLDFLR167@aol.com
www.wildflower-inn.com

167 Palmer Avenue,
Falmouth, MA 02540

HOSTS: Donna and Phil Stone
LOCATION: In historic district. Ten-minute walk to village center, five to island ferry shuttle service. Five beaches within two miles.
OPEN: Year round. Two-night minimum May through October.
RATES: May–October $175 queen and twin with whirlpool; $175 queen with whirlpool; $160 tub/shower; $155 shower bath; $130 hall shower bath. Cottage $195. November–April $95–$125, cottage $150. Additional person $25. Amex, MC, Visa. ♥ ❖ ✂ ✄

KNOWN AS THE home of the edible flower breakfast. And for a TV cooking feature on PBS. Winner of a blue ribbon in a *Yankee* magazine recipe contest. Rooms reproduced as part of the set for a Tom Cruise film made in England. The lodging choice (at least twice) for the Boston Pops conductor and his wife. And a hearty recommendation in *Honeymoon* magazine.

The former two-family house, before being gutted and rebuilt, "looked like a Stephen King novel," according to Phil, a recently retired (and well loved) local barber. Quilts hint at the shop Donna, a former social worker, had in Falmouth. One honors her first husband, who died in his thirties; they had four children and several handicapped foster children. Phil, who also lost his spouse at an early age, has four children. "B&B is an extension of everything we've ever done," say the Stones, who married in 1984 when seven children were at the table. Now Donna and Phil are grandparents of twelve. The answer to the oft-asked question: "There was plenty of cooking, but plates were not garnished!" Since their opening in 1995, this homey, attention-to-detail B&B—and the innkeepers— have been one big hit.

BED AND BATH: Five rooms plus a cottage; all with queen bed, private bath, air condition- ing, and ceiling fan. Room with painted iron bed, shuttered windows, large bath with original claw-foot tub, separate shower stall. Canopied bed, private hall shower bath. Draped iron four-poster, shower bath. Third floor—one room with skylight over bed, large whirlpool tub, 5-foot-wide shower with two shower heads. Large room with skylight over rattan sleigh bed, window seat/ twin bed, double whirlpool, separate shower with two heads. Cottage has loft bedroom, tub/shower bath, living room, full kitchen.

BREAKFAST: At 8:30 (option of picnic breakfast delivered to your room after 8:30) with Flower Power theme; new recipes and flower jellies "all the time." Repertoire includes fresh fruit smoothie with yogurt and honey; calendula corn muffins with cilantro mint butter or pansy butter; homemade granola; ten-fruit compote with coconut yogurt sauce and roasted almonds, sprinkled with chopped marigolds; lemon pancakes stuffed with fresh flowers, served with fresh fruit sauce and flower butter. Freshly ground coffee, teas, cocoa, cappuccino. Special diets accommodated. (No secrets withheld: Donna tells you about all the ingredients.) Eat at two tables made with sewing machine bases.

PLUS: Central air conditioning on first and third floors; units on second. Complimentary beverages and snacks. Guest refrigerator. TV, VCR, and games in third-floor common area. Rockers on wraparound porch.

     From Massachusetts: *"You definitely know you are on vacation."* From Georgia: *"My stay was filled with delicious breakfasts, good conversation, and one of the most unique rooms I've ever had the pleasure of calling my own (at least for three nights). Delightful and relaxing."* From New York: *"Charmingly managed ... meticulously executed. ... Interior appointments with country flavor ... dining room presentation along with fabulous five-course breakfasts encourage conversation, companionship, and a hearty appetite."*

O NE RADIO INTERVIEWER COMMENTED, "BREAKFAST AT A B&B SOUNDS LIKE A DINNER PARTY EVERY MORNING!" TRUE.

◤ Woods Hole Passage

186 Woods Hole Road,
Falmouth, MA 02540

508/548-9575

800/790-8976
FAX 508/540-4771
E-MAIL inn@woodsholepassage.com
www.woodsholepassage.com

HOST: Deb Pruitt
LOCATION: Peaceful. On 2 acres of lawn, gardens, berry bushes, trees. Midway (2 miles) between Woods Hole (ferry landing) and Falmouth. Near ocean and bay beaches (quiet one reached by foot through woods), biking, dining, shopping. Walk to harbor sunsets over Buzzards Bay.
OPEN: Year round. "Two-day minimum preferred in season."
RATES: May–October $125–$145. November-April (packages available for theme weekends—wine tasting, architectural tour, antiquing, birthing classes) $85–$105. Additional person $20. Singles $5 less. Amex, Diners, Discover, MC, Visa. ♔ ⊞ ⊗ ⚕

THE SETTING. The property. The breakfasts. And the hospitality. All are remembered by guests who stay at this converted carriage house and renovated barn. Deb, a former social worker and administrator, gave herself a year's sabbatical, then bought the inn in 1997. She has added an outdoor after-beach shower and acquired bicycles and helmets for guests' use. She has also painted outside (a barn red) and in. The great room features a bold raspberry color, a large wood-burning fireplace, and, at the far end, a huge multipaned window overlooking the gardens. Curtains are lace. Rooms are uncluttered. Furnishings are traditional and eclectic.

IN RESIDENCE: "Divot, an affable and affectionate retriever, can remain unnoticed if necessary. Romeo, a cat, is a bit of a recluse."
BED AND BATH: Five large air-conditioned rooms. All private shower baths with seats. In main house, room with queen bed. In renovated barn, two rooms on first floor, two on second (with cathedral ceilings), queen beds. One room has a twin bed also.
BREAKFAST: Usually 8:30–9:30. (Coffee ready earlier.) Fruit dish, bread dish, and a hot entrée. Repertoire includes banana bread pudding, pear raspberry crumble, apple crepes, orange-cranberry scones, zucchini frittata, apricot-pecan French toast. Served in dining room at individual tables or outside on the terrace. "Breakfast to go" for early departures.
PLUS: Tea, cider, or lemonade with cookies or tea breads. Lawn chairs. Hammock. Croquet. Horseshoes. Map showing woodland route to little-known private residence with spectacular gardens open to the public. Library with "takeaway" books.

   ◤ From New Zealand: *"Delicious breakfast. Comfortable and attractive bedroom. Wonderful service. Wish we could have stayed for days!"* From Maine: *"Beautiful little retreat, calm and serene with a sense of style and country charm."* From Rhode Island: *"Wonderful rooms, exceptional grounds, great location, excellent hostess!"*

⤜ *Sjöholm Inn Bed & Breakfast*

508/540-5706

800-498-5706

17 Chase Road, P.O. Box 430,
West Falmouth, MA 02574-0430

HOSTS: Barbara and Bob White
LOCATION: In a quiet country area. "Away from traffic." On 1.5 acres, 1.7 miles to Chapoquoit Beach. Four galleries and three antiques shops within 1 mile. Minutes to Falmouth and Woods Hole.
OPEN: Year round. Two-night minimum in July and August; "two-night stay preferred" mid-May–mid-October.
RATES: Mid-March–November 1: sail loft $70, carriage house $105 private bath; main house shared bath $85, private $105. Winter: shared bath $60, private $70. Extra person in room $20. No charge for seventh consecutive night's stay. 👫 ⊞ ⚅ ⚹ 🎿 ❤🗝

⤜ From California: *"Our family argued that it was too much trouble to find one [Cape Cod–like] place for twenty-five people coming for a wedding from all over the United States and Canada . . . [but] we found the perfect spot. Quaint, charming. . . . Our family was able to reconnect, relax, and enjoy. . . . Bob and Barbara—friendly, helpful—made a real effort to get to know our incredibly diverse family relationships. Everyone was thrilled with our weekend together."*

CAPE COD IT IS. A farmhouse built almost 150 years ago. Not fancy. "Never will be," says Barbara, who, together with Bob, explored 20,000 miles searching the eastern half of the country for a new location and then a new occupation. Since buying this well-established B&B in 1996, they have met many guests who are inspired to suggest weekend workshops—everything from rug hooking to folk music, from bird carving to "Walking in Footsteps of Thoreau," from environmental issues to antiquing. (They are happening. Inquire.)

It all fits in with the Whites' experiences: They are parents of two grown daughters. Bob, who grew up on a farm, was grant and contract officer at Cornell University. Barbara, a museum professional with a cultural history perspective, shares an appreciation for local culture, historical context, the Cape's natural beauty—and the Sjöholm, too, "where you go to sleep hearing peepers and wake up hearing the birds."

IN RESIDENCE: "Chester, our short-haired cat with tuxedo markings, owns the inn—and is always dressed for the job. Chauncey, the Corgi, keeps a watchful eye and attentive ear."
FOREIGN LANGUAGES SPOKEN: "Spanish and enough German to make guests feel more at home."
BED AND BATH: Fifteen rooms May through October; ten during the rest of the year. Beds vary from twin to queen size. Some rooms sleep three or four. Private baths for four ground-floor rooms of carriage house and three in the inn. Four upstairs rooms in the inn share two baths. Four unheated (portable heaters available) sail loft rooms plus one four-person room (off the sleeping porch) share two baths.

continued . . .

BREAKFAST: 8–9:30. Hearty. Quiche, French toast, or Sjöholm pancakes—made with fruit and baked. Or Bob's Breakfast Sundaes—cooked cereal with poached fruit topping and real whipped cream. Homemade muffins, quick breads, or Cape Cod cranberry/orange bagels with orange butter. "We set a boardinghouse table that accommodates thirteen on the eating porch."

PLUS: Intentionally, no clocks, TVs, or radios in rooms. Ceiling fans in all but sail loft rooms. Outdoor hot/cold shower, available to beachgoers late on checkout day. Big screened porch with library and games. Cable TV, VCR, books, magazines. Picnic tables. Lawn chairs. Bicycle rack. Large grassy area for spontaneous ball games. Croquet. Use of refrigerators, outdoor clotheslines. Beach permits ($5/day). Steamship tickets for Martha's Vineyard available here.

✈ *Dunscroft-By-The-Sea*

24 Pilgrim Road, Harwichport, MA 02646-2304

508/432-0810

800/432-4345

FAX 508/432-5134

E-MAIL alyce@capecod.net

www.dunscroftbtythesea.com

HOSTS: Alyce and Wally Cunningham

LOCATION: Almost on (a few steps to) a 1½-mile-long (Nantucket Sound) warm-water beach. (Water view from some inn rooms.) In the village; walk (along beach, if you'd like) 2 blocks to restaurants, shops, galleries. Close to National Seashore and whale-watch boat tours, boat rentals, fishing, golf, scuba diving, Kennedy Museum.

OPEN: Year round. Generally, three-night minimum, July–Labor Day. Two nights on weekends in April, May, June, September, and October and on holidays.

RATES: Vary according to location and amenities. Memorial Day–November $135–$285. December–Memorial Day $95–$235. Extra person $35. Amex, MC, Visa. ♥ ⊞ ❖ ⚘ ⚗ ⚓ ⚒ W

✈ From England: *"A peaceful quality leaves you feeling very rested."* From Michigan: *"Something about it that made us feel like we were falling in love again for the first time . . . decorated with hearts everywhere . . . great conversations . . . unforgettable experience."* From Connecticut: *"Delightful place, gracious service, lovely rooms, excellent location, beautiful beach. We are sending our daughter and son-in-law for their first anniversary."* From Massachusetts: *"Very romantic . . . outstanding hospitality . . . down-to-earth hostess."* From Wisconsin: *"Delightful retreat, far enough from the madding crowd, yet within walking distance of enough amenities in the event you tire of silence."* From Connecticut: *"Out-of-this-world breakfast . . . charming B&B. . . . Superb hosts."*

HONEYMOONERS, business guests, and vacationers (singles, too) come to this weathered-shingled Colonial, which has been an inn since 1950. True to plan, when Alyce and Wally bought the property in 1987, they were married here. Since, they have made major renovations and decorated with floral fabrics, heart-shaped accessories, and family treasures. In Connecticut Wally had considerable experience in management for public utilities, and Alyce was a high school teacher of English. As owners of a Cape motel, they were inspired to become innkeepers. Now, in winter and spring, Wally serves in the Merchant Marine. Alice is official seamstress, tiler, cook (rave reviews), and holiday decorator—people come from miles around to see her Christmas ornaments.

FOREIGN LANGUAGE SPOKEN: Some French.

BED AND BATH: Eight rooms plus one cottage suite, all with air conditioning, private bath, phone, hair dryer, robes, iron, ironing board, crystal wine glasses. *Main house* rooms with king or queen bed (some are canopied) are on first floor and on second (where all but one are corner rooms). Amenities vary—location, fireplace, TV/VCR, Jacuzzi. *Cottage suite* has king canopied bed, living room with wood-burning fireplace, cable color TV/VCR, Jacuzzi bath and shower, kitchen.

BREAKFAST: 8:30–10. Juice, fresh fruit, French toast, pancakes, custards, cottage pudding, fried apples, muffins, cheese molds, cereal. Egg dishes with breakfast meats. Special diets accommodated; please give advance notice. Buffet/family style in dining room.

PLUS: Complimentary sherry. (In winter, mulled cranberry cider and cookies.) Wicker-furnished sunporch. Brick terrace, shaded lawn and perennial gardens, wrought-iron garden tables and chairs. Guest refrigerator/wet bar. Sweetheart baskets $85–$185 (including French champagne).

≈ *Harbor Walk*   508/432-1675

6 Freeman Street, Harwichport, MA 02646-1902

HOST: Marilyn Barry

LOCATION: One house in from Route 28, right behind the house known for miles around for its roses. Five-minute walk to sandy beach, restaurants, and shops; fifteen-minute walk to Nantucket ferry dock.

OPEN: Year round. Two-night minimum June–September.

RATES: $55 shared bath, $75 private bath. $20 extra bed. ♥ ♥♥ ⊞ ⚋ ⚋

"BY NOW SOME guests are grown children of our first guests. B&B is still just as I imagined it would be when I was a physical therapist in Philadelphia. Then, every day I used to notice a wallpaper scene of Wychmere Harbor. Why not live near the real thing? My husband and I wanted to be closer to our kids. So when he retired as a school administrator in 1978, we opened here, just across the road from the harbor. Now our son helps with the lawn and our daughters assist during their visits. Although this is a Queen Anne house, it's a summer place, with floors painted navy blue. Some of the stenciled walls are coordinated with the bed quilts. Some pencil-post beds are lace-canopied. Breakfast is the time when everyone talks about their first-ever trip to an island, antiquing, shopping, the

continued . . .

homes of the rich and famous, restaurants plain and fancy, and whale watching—which, we found out, is like seeing magic. Or they visit our West Harwich open space treasure, acquired by the Harwich Conservation Trust—16 glorious wooded acres, great for bird-watching. What a site—overlooking the Herring River estuary and sunsets!"

BED AND BATH: Six rooms, each with at least three windows, on first and second floors. Four with private en-suite shower baths; three have canopied queen beds (one on first floor has private sitting area), one has two twin beds. Room with canopied queen bed and one with two twin beds share a full bath. Rollaway available.

BREAKFAST: 8–9:30. Two fruit juices, fresh fruit platter or compote, home-baked goods (many requests for kuchen recipe), homemade granola, strawberry yogurt, cheese platter. Wednesday specialty: "Eggs McBarry." On porch in summer, family style in dining room (with ceiling fan) rest of year.

PLUS: Flannel sheets. Beach towels. Fresh flowers. Guest refrigerator. Will meet bus from Boston in Barnstable (fifteen-minute drive).

     ➳ Guests wrote: *"Felt so at home. . . . Lovely stay in this home. . . . Am envious of [Marilyn's] lifestyle. I think I am a beachcomber or country gal at heart. . . . Warm hospitality."*

➳ *The Inn on Sea Street*

358 Sea Street, Hyannis, MA 02601-4586

508/775-8030

FAX 508/771-0878
E-MAIL innonsea@capecod.net
www.capecod.net/innonsea

HOSTS: Sylvia and Fred LaSelva
LOCATION: In a quiet residential neighborhood, ten minutes from Route 6. Walking distance to beach, Kennedy compound and memorial, island ferries, bike rentals, restaurants.
OPEN: May–November.
RATES: Shared bath $85. Private bath $100 double bed, $130 canopied queen. Cottage $150. Additional guest $15. Amex, Discover, MC, Visa.
    ♥ ☎ ⊞ ❖ ⚄ ❤

THE BEACH, just steps away, may be a big draw, but it's the decor, the food, and the innkeepers themselves that make this a favorite B&B. The main inn, a Greek Revival house, is decorated with flair, with antique Persian carpets, a crystal chandelier in the foyer, a huge photograph of Grandfather over the mantel—all intentionally "not stuffily elegant." Across the street, a French mansard-roofed house features canopied beds, TVs hidden in armoires, its own living room, and Adirondack chairs on the wraparound porch. Behind that house is a very popular dollhouse of a cottage.

Sylvia was a Boston hospital administrator when she and Fred, who owns business service centers, bought this B&B in 1998. Earlier they had a (combined) antiques/handmade donut shop on Cape Cod. Now they meet romantics, wedding guests, vacationers, and many high-profile travelers in what was, in the early 1980s, the first B&B in Hyannis.

BED AND BATH: Five main-house rooms. First-floor room has antique double bed, private bath, private porch. Two second-floor rooms (both have canopied beds) share a hall bath. Third second-floor room is separated from its private bath by a back stairway. Down flagstone path and around the barn is garden room with canopied queen bed, TV, private full bath. Across the street—four rooms with canopied queen beds, private baths, and TVs. In white wicker-furnished cottage—living room with TV, queen bed, shower bath, kitchen, ceiling fan, telephone.

BREAKFAST: 8–9:30. Fresh fruit. Homemade baked goods. Vegetarian menu by request. Served to all guests in main inn's dining room and sunporch at tables set with sterling silver, china, linen, and fresh flowers.

PLUS: Most rooms are air conditioned; two have ceiling fans. Goose down pillows. Beach chairs and towels. Clock radios. TV in main inn. Use of refrigerator. Complimentary package of inn recipes. Book with guests' reviews of restaurants. Will meet guests at Hyannis airport or bus or train station. Often, an invitation to join Fred at the driving range.

⟫ *Academy Place Bed & Breakfast*   508/255-3181

8 Academy Place, P.O. Box 1407,   **FAX** 508/247-9812
Orleans, MA 02653-1407   **E-MAIL** academyplace@mindspring.com
                            www.academyplace.com

HOSTS:	Sandy and Charles Terrell
LOCATION:	On the village green, at the edge of Orleans's shopping district. At Route 28 and Main Street. Ten minutes from the National Seashore; 3/8 to 1/3 mile to bike trail; 2½ miles to Skaket and Nauset Beaches and Rock Harbor (charter fishing boats).
OPEN:	Late May–mid-October. Two-night minimum on all holidays and July–mid-October weekends.
RATES:	$80 queen bed or twins, shared bath. $100 queen or $120 king bed, private bath. $20 extra bed in room. Five-night discount. Off-season (May and June) 10 percent less. MC, Visa. ♥ ⊞ ⌀ ✄

"CHARLES GREW UP in this authentic 1790s Cape Cod house when his parents ran it as a guest house (1955–75). We exposed beams, painted and papered with Colonial colors, and opened as a B&B in 1989." Period furnishings include spool beds, spinning wheels, and a fainting couch.

Charles retired in 1997 from his position as National Environmental Coordinator for the Natural Resources Conservation Service in Washington, D.C. When the Terrells were year-round Massachusetts residents, he was a college biology professor; Sandy, a registered

continued . . .

nurse. Their fascinating house history (a copy is in each room) is complete with sketches and notes about the size of Cape houses—"small, to minimize heat loss." For vacationers they have compiled a walking tour of downtown Orleans and an extensive list of local attractions, including lighthouses to visit, whale watching (discount tickets available), seal watching—and even a 1950s drive-in theater (which shows the latest movies).

BED AND BATH: Five air-conditioned rooms. Two first-floor queen-bedded rooms overlook the village green; each has nonworking fireplace, private shower bath. Up steep, narrow steps to second floor with beamed skylit guests' lounge, one large king-bedded room with private shower bath. One room with two twin beds shares a full bath with queen-bedded room. Rollaway available.

BREAKFAST: 7:30–9. Buttermilk bran muffins, chocolate and other homemade breads, or blueberry coffee cake. Freshly brewed coffee or tea. Fruits and juices. By candlelight in beamed dining room.

PLUS: Entire house is air conditioned. Porch rockers. Rear sunken garden with picnic table. Two-person hammock between 100-year-old trees. TV in upstairs lounge. Hot or iced tea. Guest refrigerator. Outside hot/cold shower. Hosts' own local guide to shops, restaurants and tour sites. Take-away souvenir card with history of your room.

⊳ From New York: *"For readers who are not looking to spend a lot on accommodations but would like a B&B, I recommend Academy Place in the center of Orleans. . . . Well kept. . . . Delightfully surprised at variety and service of the continental breakfast."* From Sweden: *"Equals the best of B&Bs in England, and that says a lot. House is a true living house from 1800, beautifully furnished but not like a museum. A place to relax and feel at home."* From New Jersey: *"Charles has compiled scrapbooks about Orleans, Cape Cod, the building, and his family. Great!"* From Illinois: *"The perfect blend of friendliness and privacy. Location is fabulous."* From Massachusetts: *"Just as you described it, and we loved it. . . . Very pretty back yard with wonderfully big hammock."* From Georgia: *"Comfortable . . . immaculate. . . . Sandy introduced us to beach plum jelly, which we loved."* From Germany: *"Such a nice historical house . . . everything is so clean . . . couldn't be better."* From Pennsylvania: *"One would have to travel far and wide to find a more charming, hospitable B&B."*

THINK OF BED AND BREAKFAST AS A PEOPLE-TO-PEOPLE CONCEPT.

≈ Bed and Breakfast Cape Cod Host #ORL-06

Orleans, MA

> **LOCATION:** On a knoll overlooking the dunes of Nauset Beach and the Atlantic Ocean.
>
> **RESERVATIONS:** Year round through Bed and Breakfast Cape Cod (page 144), 508/255-3824 or 800/541-6226. Two-night minimum; three on holidays.
>
> **RATES:** $140 late May–early September. $110 fall. $90 late October through May. ♥ ⚲ ⚬ ☰

FROM EVERY guest room there are spectacular views of the Atlantic Ocean, sailboats, fishing boats, surf casters, and the boardwalk to the Cape Cod National Seashore's Nauset Beach. In 1998 the hosts removed the top floor of the family homestead and built the guest rooms. Decor is nautical with many blues and greens, mirroring the outdoors.

The host, a professional painter and wallpaperer, often shares fishing and lobstering experiences with guests. "He can tell when the striped bass and bluefish are out there." The hostess, who has experience in public relations and marketing, and as a flight attendant, is delighted to be here "by 'my' ocean. We meet travelers who bicycle, hike, swim, read, or sit right here and watch seals and whales. . . . It's wonderful!" Guests concur.

BED AND BATH: Four second-floor oceanview rooms with king, queen, or twin beds. All with en-suite tub/shower bath, cable TV, ceiling fan, individually controlled heat, large picture window.

BREAKFAST: 9–10. Juice, homemade muffins, hot beverages. Eat in sitting room, your own room, or outside.

PLUS: Guest living room with refrigerator. Two private entrances to guests' quarters. Many books and much information about Cape Cod.

KEY TO SYMBOLS

♥   Lots of honeymooners come here.

⚶   Families with children are very welcome.

⚑   This B&B is a private home, not an inn.

⊞   Groups can reserve this entire B&B.

❖   Travel agents' commissions paid.

⚲   Sorry, no guests' pets allowed.

⚬   No smoking inside *or* no smoking at all.

☰   Waterfront location.

⚸   Off the beaten path.

❦   Weddings booked here. For details, please inquire.

---

continued . . .

✈ Morgan's Way Bed & Breakfast   508/255-0831

Nine Morgan's Way,   FAX 508/255-0831 (OR -6700)
Orleans, MA 02653-3522   E-MAIL morgnway@capecod.net
www.capecodaccess.com/morgansway/

HOSTS: Page McMahan and Will Joy
LOCATION: Rural and peaceful. On 5 acres of landscaped grounds, 1 mile from Orleans center. Ten minutes to National Seashore, five to ocean and bay beaches.
OPEN: Year round. Two-night minimum stay; three nights on holiday weekends.
RATES: $125 May–October. $95 November–April. $25 additional person. Cottage $900 per week, $700 November through April. ♥ ☛ ⊞ ❖ ⚄ ⅍ 鮏

THIS ARCHITECT-DESIGNED Cape contemporary has cathedral ceilings; plenty of windows (many arched and half-circled); and a spacious downstairs living room with comfortable seating, porcelains, and original Cape art. An oak spiral staircase leads to an upstairs living room with piano, TV/VCR, wood-burning stove, library, small refrigerator, and a large window seat that overlooks a multilevel flower-filled deck and a 20-by-40-foot heated swimming pool. Beyond the extensive gardens—perennials, annuals, a kitchen garden, and a cut flower garden—are acres of woods and wetlands, a bird-watcher's paradise.

Page, the gardener, who is Will's partner in his engineering and surveying firm, sings with several groups and has strong interests in nutrition, fitness, health and human services, and the arts. Will, an outdoorsman, is president of his firm and is active in the community. They love sharing their property and Cape Cod.

IN RESIDENCE: Kitty-man is "an entertaining Himalayan."
BED AND BATH: Two air-conditioned rooms plus a cottage. *Main house:* On first floor, room with queen bed and private shower bath connects to pool and deck area. On second floor, very large queen-bedded room with adjacent private tub/shower bath overlooks pool and gardens. Self-catering *cottage* sleeps three.
BREAKFAST: 7:30–9. Varies. Fruit dish could be simmered plums with cream or honey walnut baked apples. Pancakes with maple syrup and sausages or Grand Marnier French toast with maple syrup and bacon. Carrot/pineapple bread or apple oat-bran muffins. Hot beverages. Yogurt, fruit, cereals, Egg Beaters always available. Garnished with fresh fruit, herbs, edible flowers.
PLUS: Bedroom floor fans. Guest refrigerator. Mints on pillow. Map of back roads to Provincetown. Complimentary champagne for special occasions. Fresh flowers.

     ✈ From New Jersey, Washington, Wisconsin, Virginia, Massachusetts, Bermuda, Switzerland: *"A gem . . . gorgeous home, grounds, room . . . remarkable hosts . . . made our thirtieth anniversary memorable . . . suggestions for every possible activity . . . relaxing . . . glorious breakfasts . . . in a word, superb."*

☙ Bed and Breakfast Cape Cod Host #ORL-03

East Orleans, MA

LOCATION: On Main Street, 1½ miles to Nauset Beach in one direction, 1½ miles to Orleans center in other. Walk to village with bakery, espresso, newspaper stand, restaurant.

RESERVATIONS: Spring through fall through Bed and Breakfast Cape Cod (page 144), 508/255-3824 or 800/541-6226. Two-night minimum; three nights on holidays.

RATES: Shared bath $70. Apartment $120, third person $20. ♟ ■ ⚄ ⚒

BREAKFAST IS an event at this B&B, a spacious and attractive country house that has an extensive (display) collection of antiques from the China trade. Guests from all over the world also enjoy the comfortably furnished living room; the large deck; the yard with a child's delight—a turtle/frog/shiners pond; and yes, the hosts!

In New York the host, an artist, was vice president in charge of sales and promotion for a department store. The German-born hostess was an administrative secretary. Their carved oak dining room table—"not very Cape Cod–like, but it's ours"—traveled south when the host held a position in Florida. With fond memories of family vacations, they chose Cape Cod for retirement and found this "too-big-for-two" house in a community that they love—and love to share.

IN RESIDENCE: One dog "loved by all of all ages."

FOREIGN LANGUAGES SPOKEN: A little Italian, French, and German.

BED AND BATH: Three air-conditioned second-floor rooms—one with queen bed, one with double, and one with a single twin—share one full bath. Garden apartment—great for families—has air-conditioned room with queen bed, living room with queen sofa bed, kitchen, living room, dining room, full bath.

BREAKFAST: Begins at 8:30. (Earlier for guests who fish.) Entrée possibilities include walnut pancakes, apple puff pancake, Belgian waffles, or Eggs Flaherty—"named after a friend who gave me the recipe." Juice, melon or compote, muffins, homemade breads and cakes, "bottomless cup of coffee." Served on fine china in dining room.

☙ Guests wrote: *"Treated royally. . . . Delicious breakfast. . . . Hospitality and thoughtfulness were wonderful."*

⋙ *The Nauset House Inn*   508/255-2195

143 Beach Road, P.O. Box 774,   FAX 508/240-6276
East Orleans, MA 02643-0774   E-MAIL info@nausethouseinn.com
          www.nausethouseinn.com

HOSTS: Diane and Al Johnson; Cindy and John Vessella
LOCATION: Residential. On 2 acres, a half-mile walk to Nauset Beach. Three-minute drive to town center. Close to bike trail, antiquing, shopping.
OPEN: April–October. Two-night minimum on weekends.
RATES: Shared bath $55 single, $75–$85 for two. Private bath $100 double bed or $110 twins, $135 king, queen, cottage, honeymoon suite. Discover, MC, Visa. ♥ ⅘ ⅙

⋙ From Pennsylvania: *"More important than the serenity and beauty of the greenhouse, the perfect attention to detail . . . the ideal location within walking distance of the beach and away from town, are the innkeepers—who have an uncanny ability to know which guests will like what and also to know when guests want solitude and when they want conversation."*

THIS INN is the answer for those who want a home-away-from-home ambiance—with a hint of fantasy (the conservatory)—yet not a very small B&B. It is owned and operated by two generations who garden (flowers arranged in every room); go whale watching; explore the area (great hand-drawn annotated map provided); go to auctions and hand-paint furniture; make dinner and theater reservations; cook (whimsical sketches in cookbook); and, everywhere, display arts and crafts including their own stained glass, quilts, pottery, and stenciling. Camellias and a weeping cherry tree grow in the 1907 conservatory (from Connecticut) that was added to the 1810 Cape-style dormered farmhouse. The family's ten-year dream was discovered by *Country Living* in 1983, shortly after Al left his executive position at Beechcraft Airplanes, just after Cindy graduated college.

BED AND BATH: Fourteen rooms. Eight with private baths; three with tub and shower, others with shower only. Three first-floor rooms share one bath; three upstairs rooms share one bath. Queen bed, double bed, and one single bed available. Also a cottage with queen bed, skylit sitting area. And a honeymoon suite (accessed by separate staircase) with queen bed, private balcony.
BREAKFAST: 8–9:30. Varies daily. Always muffins and omelet-of-the-day. French toast and sticky buns are specialties. Ginger pancakes (selected for *Yankee Magazine/Gold Medal B&B Recipe Sampler*). Family style in fireplaced, brick-floored publike beamed room that opens onto a terrace. Special diets accommodated when requests made before arrival.
PLUS: Wine and cranberry juice with hors d'oeuvres at 5:30. Fireplaced common room. Bedroom table fans. Guest refrigerator. Beach towels. Herb and perennial gardens. Picnic table.

⫘ *The Parsonage Inn*

202 Main Street, P.O. Box 1501,
East Orleans, MA 02643-1501

508/255-8217
888/422-8217
FAX 508/255-8216
E-MAIL innkeeper@parsonageinn.com
www.parsonageinn.com

HOSTS: Ian and Elizabeth Browne
LOCATION: In the village, on the road (1.5 miles) to Nauset Beach on the Atlantic Ocean. Within walking distance of fine restaurants and shops. Two miles from Route 6.
OPEN: Year round. Two-night minimum on June–October weekends. Three-night minimum Memorial Day, Labor Day, July 4, and Columbus Day weekends.
RATES: June–September $105, $115, $125, $135. October and November $85, $95, $105, $125. December–March $85–$95. April and May $80, $85, $95, $105. Additional person $20. Amex, MC, Visa. ♥ ⊞ ⌀ ⅍

SIT BY THE FIRE or on the patio and listen to Chopin, Mozart, or Liszt played by Elizabeth, a piano teacher who grew up in Kenya and lived in England—all before going to Chicago, where she taught forty students and met Ian, an English-born accountant and medical group executive director. When they decided to purchase an inn, they remembered their first inn experience right here in Orleans.

In 1991 they bought this B&B, a c. 1770s full Cape house that was a parsonage in the 1880s. Despite all the remodeling over the years, the house retains the feeling of history, of old Cape Cod. Today its uncluttered, fresh, crisp look is embellished with country antiques and some art from Africa, England, and California.

IN RESIDENCE: One outdoor cat, Pepper, a friendly tabby.
FOREIGN LANGUAGE SPOKEN: "A little French."
BED AND BATH: Eight (most are large, two are smaller) queen-bedded rooms, each with air conditioning, individual heat control, private en-suite bath (three with tub and shower, five with shower only); six have TV. Cedar Room has canopied bed and TV. Willow Room has private entrance, kitchen, TV/VCR, queen bed and sofa bed. Spacious Barn Room has vaulted ceiling, sitting area, sofa bed, TV, and refrigerator.
BREAKFAST: 8–9:30. Hearty and healthy—with a repertoire that includes low-fat recipes. Waffles, pancakes, French toast, crepes, or quiche. Scones with Devonshire-type cream, fruit breads, muffins, yogurt and granola, juices, Colombian coffee, teas. Served in dining room, on patio at umbrella tables, or in your room.
PLUS: Hors d'oeuvres 6–7 P.M. Fresh flowers. Guest refrigerator.

⫘ From Pennsylvania, New York, Massachusetts, New Jersey, California: *"Fantastic! . . . Nicely appointed. Pretty bed linens, fresh flowers, fluffy towels—the best of everything. Breakfasts are outstanding, served with class. . . . Great ideas for activities and sites. . . . Spent six nights here. Excellent accommodations. . . . I intend to return. . . . Exceptional innkeepers. Give much of their time and talents to make visit special. . . . As comfortable as being home, but ten times neater; well decorated and historic. . . . A special place."*

⇗ Bed and Breakfast Cape Cod Host #OST-02

Osterville, MA

LOCATION: Tranquil. Overlooking a cranberry bog. Surrounded by hundreds of acres of conservation land, woods, wildlife preserve.
RESERVATIONS: Year round through Bed and Breakfast Cape Cod (page 144), 508/255-3824 or 800/541-6226. Two-night minimum; three nights on holidays.
RATES: $115 for two. $20 extra person. ♥ ♦♦ ■ ⊗ ✁

HOME TO a renowned sculptor, who not only designed this post-and-beam residence to look like a barn: In 1984 "I put every nail into it." The very private guest area has pine floors, an Oriental rug in the master bedroom, a living room with wainscoting and a 9-foot-wide sliding door that leads onto a huge deck. It's perfect for romantics, for a family, or for two couples traveling together.

The Ohio-born hostess, a recently retired learning disabilities teacher, met her husband during a 1960s Cape vacation when he was a Craigville Beach lifeguard. The affable host, whose family "goes back to the boat that followed the Mayflower," was a plumber in the 1970s, when he started carving wood. "It evolved into clay with castings in bronze. Commissions came along." Yes, guests are invited into his studio to see works in progress.

BED AND BATH: On lower level, spacious suite/apartment with two air-conditioned rooms, each with an antique queen bed; living room with "the view," full kitchen, tub/shower bath. Private driveway and entrance.
BREAKFAST: Tray brought to you with pitcher of juice, carafe of coffee, fruit dish. Croissants, muffins, or coffee cakes. Cereals. Weather permitting, on the deck.
PLUS: Make-your-own coffee or tea anytime.

⇗ Sea Cliff   508/888-0609

2 Indian Trail, Box One, Sagamore Beach, MA 02562-0001

HOSTS: Jean and Joe Kennedy
LOCATION: Residential. On a cliff overlooking Cape Cod Bay. With view (to the south) of ships emerging from Cape Cod Canal, and view (to the north) of Plymouth. To the east, on a clear day, you can see Provincetown monument. Path beside house leads to stairs and beach below.
OPEN: Year round "except during our short winter vacation." Two-night minimum May 15–October 15.
RATES: May 15–October 15 king $150, queen $95. Off-season king $125, queen $75. ♥ ♦♦ ■ ❖ ✁ ♨ ⚭ ♥○

⇗ From New York: *"We are Belgians, living in New York. . . . Thanks to your guide, we discovered the incredible Sea Cliff, a part of paradise: the site, two wonderfully nice and* <u>clean</u> *rooms, with warm hospitality on top of all that. Your description is enthusiastic, but may be too low-key. This is perfection. This is indeed a secret to cherish!" From Massachusetts: "Romantic . . . near everything but not in middle of Cape hustle and bustle. . . . The only place without spectacular ocean views was the shower! . . . quiet and secluded beach." From Virginia: "Beautiful rooms . . . charming hospitality . . . great breakfast . . . fantastic place for a honeymoon."*

JEAN IS A retired Sagamore Beach postmaster. Joe retired from the box business. The Kennedys lived next door for ten years before building this three-storied shingled house in 1989. Most furnishings are antiques. The view is endless.

IN RESIDENCE: Emily and Betsy, well-trained lovable black Labradors. One cat named Sam.

BED AND BATH: Two carpeted second-floor rooms, each with individual thermostat, private phone, TV, and small refrigerator. Large air-conditioned "honeymoon suite" has king bed, ceiling fan, balcony, bath with shower and Jacuzzi for two. Queen-bedded room has a double shower.

BREAKFAST: Usually at 9. Pancakes with sausage; French toast with raspberry butter, syrup, and fruit; home fries with eggs and bacon. Homemade muffins or coffee cake. Fresh fruit. In dining room, in solarium, or on deck.

PLUS: Beamed living room with stone fireplace. Welcoming beverage. Beach towels, chairs, and umbrellas.

Captain Ezra Nye House

508/888-6142
800/388-2278
FAX 508/833-2897
E-MAIL captnye@aol.com
www.captainezranyehouse.com

152 Main Street,
Sandwich, MA 02563-2283

HOSTS: Harry and Elaine Dickson
LOCATION: In village center. Walk to Sandwich Glass, Heritage Plantation, Thornton Burgess, and Yesteryear's Doll museums and to fine dining. Less than a mile to beach.
OPEN: Year round. Two-night minimum on weekends and holidays.
RATES: June–October $110 canopied queen; $120 suite, queen four-poster with fireplace, or king. November–May $10 less. ♥ ⊞ ❖ ⌀ ⅟

From South Africa: *"Charming inn. . . . Breakfasts a delight. . . . When we wanted to know any information, we would, in chorus, say 'Just ask Harry.'"* From New Jersey: *"Elegant but homey . . . attention to detail . . . knowledgeable about the town and antiquing opportunities."* From Massachusetts: *"Six breakfasts and menu never repeated."* From Connecticut: *"In addition to charm and traditional appeal . . . meticulously maintained . . . friendly innkeepers . . . a delightful and memorable experience."*

continued . . .

HARRY AND ELAINE, world travelers, came to Sandwich on their honeymoon when Harry retired from ten years as an engineer with GTE (preceded by twenty-five in the air force). "This 1829 sea captain's house on a main street in a small town, near the ocean and surrounded by greenery, gives the feeling of a private home. It is just what we were looking for as a B&B in 1986. We had planned on a year to find the perfect place. It took a week! There's so much to do right here that you can leave your car for a few days and just walk."

They furnished with fine antiques, including some of Harry's family pieces and a collection of Chinese export china, and art and artifacts from the years they spent in New Mexico. Elaine's paintings have found a home here too. Praise has appeared in *Glamour* and *Innsider* magazines, and for five years Captain Ezra Nye House has been named in *Cape Cod Life* as "Best Upper Cape B&B."

BED AND BATH: Five rooms and one suite. All private baths. First-floor air-conditioned suite—queen bed, shower bath, sitting room with love seat, cable TV, outside entrance. Second floor—most rooms have shower bath; one has antique claw-foot tub/shower. Queen four-poster and wood-burning fireplace (most popular room), canopied queen bed, or king bed.
BREAKFAST: Sittings at 8 and 9, earlier by arrangement. Sample menu: orange juice, melon, puffed pancakes with blueberry sauce, bacon, scones and jam, ginger muffins, coffee and tea. Served in dining room at table for six to eight guests.
PLUS: Fireplaced living room. Den with books, TV, VCR. Large deck. Beach towels. Will meet guests at Sagamore bus stop.

⪼ *The Summer House*   508/888-4991

181 Main Street,   800/241-3609
Sandwich, MA 02563-2232   FAX 508/888-4991
                                                E-MAIL sumhouse@capecod.net
                                                www.capecod.net/summerhouse

HOSTS:	Phyllis Burg and Erik Suby
LOCATION:	In historic district of village, on the July 4 parade route. Walk to restaurants, museums, shops, pond, and gristmill. One mile to Heritage Plantation and beach.
OPEN:	Year round. Two-night minimum on weekends, late May through October.
RATES:	Late May–October 31 $85 (hall private bath), $95, $100, $110. Off season $65, $75, $85, $90. Amex, Discover, MC, Visa. ♥ ⊞ ❖ ⚄ ⅄ ❤○

"OUR SEARCH ended in 1998 when we found this established B&B in this great village. We have hung lace curtains while keeping the summer theme with floral prints, plants, and fresh flowers. By the time your book is published, we ll have repainted the almost-famous breakfast room checkerboard floor, the one seen in *Country Living,* The gardens, my love, are filled with perennials—antique roses, black-eyed Susans, and spider lilies."

The 1835 Greek Revival house features original wavy handmade window glass, detailed moldings, latch hardware, and seven fireplaces. Phyllis, the gardener, has experience as a jeweler, pearl buyer, and manager of a bridal shop in the Boston area. Here she dovetails innkeeping with work in the local hardware store. Erik, a former high school English teacher, coach, and farmer, works at a business that restores antique car radios.

BED AND BATH: Five rooms, all private baths. First-floor room has a queen four-poster, wood-burning fireplace, en-suite shower bath. On second floor, one room has king/twins option, en-suite shower bath. Wood-burning fireplaces in three rooms—one with canopied queen bed, en-suite shower bath; antique four-poster king/twins option with en-suite shower bath; queen-bedded room with tub/shower bath down the hall.
BREAKFAST: 8–9:30. Bountiful. (Continental or to-go prepared for early ferry passengers; coffee and tea ready at 7:30). Fresh fruit cup. Rhubarb pecan bread, or cranberry nut bread, or blueberry cake. Homemade muffins. French toast made with homemade bread, red pepper and broccoli frittata, bacon and Swiss cheese or vegetable quiche, cream cheese and chive omelet, or raspberry and banana pancakes. Served at linen-covered tables set for two or four or on sunporch.
PLUS: Wood-burning fireplace in breakfast room and living room. Late-afternoon or evening tea, lemonade, or cider with homemade cookies and cakes. Croquet. Hammocks. Special occasions acknowledged. "Lots to do here—including a terrific guided walking tour."

      From New Jersey: *"Nice touch: Finding a lit fire upon our return after a day's outing."* From Pennsylvania: *"Friendly atmosphere . . . outstanding breakfasts."*

☞ *The Village Inn at Sandwich*   508/833-0363

4 Jayvees Street,   800/922-9989
Sandwich, MA 02563-0951   FAX 508/833-2063
                          E-MAIL capecodinn@aol.com
                               www.capecodinn.com

HOST: Susan Fehlinger
LOCATION: Residential. In historic district, just off Main Street. Walk to museums, galleries, antiques shops, restaurants, bay beach.
OPEN: Year round.
RATES: May–October $105–$115 queen bed, private bath. $170 connected twin rooms, shared bath. Off-season $10 less. Amex, Discover, MC, Visa.

     👫 ⊞ ❖ ⚔ ⚕ ♥

WHILE SUSAN, a producer of TV commercials, was on location at the top of a mountain in northern China in 26-below-zero weather, she decided to return to New York and begin the search for a new career at a New England B&B near the ocean. In 1997 she dis-

continued . . .

covered quintessential Cape Cod in Sandwich. This 1830s Federal-style inn had been renovated by a skilled craftsman, who built the fence and made all the beds and armoires. Susan's love of color is evident throughout. Every room has original works done by artists who come from all over the country to conduct off-season workshops here, in the skylit studio Susan created in the former woodworking shop. Europeans love this place. Big city folks unwind. And many guests (see below) write to me.

IN RESIDENCE: Son Nick, age thirteen, assistant innkeeper. Scuppy, "our wacky, wonderful dog," a mixed terrier, not allowed in guest parlors, loves to play outside.
BED AND BATH: Eight rooms, all private en-suite shower baths. First floor—two queen-bedded rooms. Second floor—four rooms with queen beds; two have wood-burning fireplace. Third floor—two rooms tucked under eaves; each with two extra-long twin beds, connecting shower bath.
BREAKFAST: 8–10. At 9 on weekends, hot entrée such as baked blueberry or apple French toast or fritatta with vegetables. Juices. Fresh fruit. Homemade scones with strawberry butter, brown bread with cream cheese, orange yogurt muffins, banana nut bread. Buffet style in dining room that has hand-painted floor, French lace café curtains, tables set with Fiesta ware.
PLUS: Two guest parlors; each has ceiling fan and wood-burning fireplace. Fresh fruit. Beverages. Cookies. Guest wet bar. Rockers on wraparound porch. Perennial gardens.

⌖ From Pennsylvania: *"Susan not only helped with our wedding plans, but all of my friends and family found her charm to be absolutely delightful. Grounds are excellent."* From New York: *"Delighted with the rooms, breakfast, and warm hospitality of Susan."* From New Jersey: *"We loved the warmth and unpretentious atmosphere . . . simple elegance . . . accommodated our every need . . . relaxed, refreshing stay."* From Ohio: *"Exquisite decor . . . superb workshop with talented capable instructor."* From Massachusetts: *"Picturesque and comfortable. The real joy is Susan . . . makes each guest feel very welcome."* From Georgia: *"Beautiful setting . . . Susan's dog is beautiful. . . . Ears hang down until you approach, then they stick straight up, exposing very unusual beautiful eyes."*

*I*N THIS BOOK *a "full bath" includes a shower and a tub. "Shower bath" indicates a bath that has all the essentials except a tub.*

⋙ *Bed & Breakfast in Truro*   508/349–6610

Castle Road, Box 431, Truro, MA 02666-0431

HOST: Tonie Strauss
LOCATION: On a winding picturesque Cape road. Between ocean and bay, next door to the Truro Castle Hill Center for the Arts, in a quiet, rather sparsely settled residential area.
OPEN: May–October. Two-night minimum stay. Reservations required.
RATES: $85–$95. ♥ ☛ ⚲

TONIE'S FLAIR means that the house is comfortable and she welcomes you graciously, but there's nothing formal about the 200-year-old captain's house set among lilac bushes, apple trees, and rolling lawns. Tonie is an abstract colorist who paints in oil. She is happy to show you her studio as well as tell you the history of the house. "Most guests are seeking a quiet time. They come here because Truro leaves the hectic pace and fast-food concessions behind. Many leave by ten, enjoy the Cape, come back to get ready for dinner, and retire early."

IN RESIDENCE: Two miniature long-haired dachshunds.
FOREIGN LANGUAGES SPOKEN: French and German.
BED AND BATH: Two rooms, one guest bath (bath is private if just one room booked). Private guest entrance and up a captain's staircase to one room with double bed and air conditioning and another with twin beds. Furnished eclectically with antiques and "Cape decor." (No food in rooms, please.)
BREAKFAST: No real schedule—by popular demand. Help-yourself refrigerator with fresh juice, homemade jams, yogurts, cheese, coffee and tea. Basket of freshly baked rolls, muffins, and coffee cakes (and, by request, oatmeal) served 8–10 on covered porch or indoors at wonderful big table.
PLUS: Use of porch and refrigerator. Bedroom fans. Comforters. Duvets. Flowers. "Mints, of course." Landscaped grounds.

⋙ From Massachusetts: *"After our week at Tonie Strauss's, we were refreshed and energized. We savor many memories. Bountiful breakfasts, which looked like works of art, were served on her covered porch . . . quiet and private setting—restorative . . . amidst gardens and birdsong. . . . Our accommodations were tasteful, clean, and roomy. . . . European-style hospitality . . . a lovely introduction to Cape Cod."*

I F YOU'VE BEEN TO ONE B&B, YOU HAVEN'T BEEN TO THEM ALL.

⇒ *Parker House*   508/349–3358

P.O. Box 1111, Truro, MA 02666-1111

HOST: Stephen Williams
LOCATION: In the center of this tiny beautiful town. Two miles from Cape Cod
National Seashore ocean or bay beaches. Ten minutes' drive to
Provincetown (north) or Wellfleet (south). Between the Cobb Memorial
Library and the Blacksmith Shop restaurant. Near sailing, tennis, golf,
Audubon sanctuary, whale watches, art galleries, restaurants.
OPEN: Year round. Two-night minimum in July and August.
RATES: $50 single, $55 double ($5 surcharge for second bed), $65 triple. $5 sur-
charge for single nights. ☛ ⊞ ⊗ ⊬

THE CLASSIC full Cape house is filled with history, ancestors' portraits, books, period furniture, and wide painted floors.

"My great-grandmother bought this place for $4,500 in 1920. I have been restoring it
over many years, and now it's there! For the last ten years I have been carrying on the
B&B tradition established in the 1980s by my mother, Jane Parker, a world traveler and
writer."

Stephen, official B&B host/baker, is the town's building commissioner and agent to
the board of health. "Guests enjoy a secluded walk, the clean beaches, and the history of
the area. Some find that the house offers the perfect opportunity just to think or to curl
up and read."

BED AND BATH: Two second-floor rooms, each with (new) sink, share a full bath with
claw-foot tub under a skylight and a shower. A four-poster double and a day couch/single
bed in each room.
BREAKFAST: 7:30–10:30, "to the soft chimes of a ship's clock." Homemade muffins and
coffee cakes. Breads for toast. Jams. Cereals. Juice. Fresh fruit. Coffee or tea. By dining
room bay window or on screened porch. Can last for hours.
PLUS: Private off-street parking. Recipe for orange coffee cake.

⇒ Guests wrote: *"Superb accommodations, particularly in the registers of music,
atmosphere, directional and transportation resources, and engaging conversation."*

I F YOU HAVE MET ONE B&B HOST, YOU HAVEN'T MET THEM ALL.

ᨒ *Bed and Breakfast Cape Cod Host #WEL-01*

Wellfleet, MA

> **LOCATION:** With "a peek" of back side of Wellfleet harbor. Just off Route 6, on a quiet short street with newer homes. To cove beach—250 yards. To bay beach—1.5 miles. Within 2 miles of four ocean beaches.
>
> **RESERVATIONS:** Year round through Bed and Breakfast Cape Cod (page 144), 508/255-3824 or 800/541-6226. Two-night minimum; three nights on holidays.
>
> **RATES:** $90–$100. Extra person $40. 👫 ◼ ✗ 👪

BOTH PET- and child-friendly. In a fantastic location. Just seven minutes' walk along the marsh and over the Uncle Tim's (pedestrian) Bridge to Wellfleet center. Enjoy evenings in the garden. And Wednesday square dances on the nearby town pier. This lovely home, traditionally furnished, was built in 1989 as three-quarter (or upside-down) Cape, with the guest areas on the lower two levels and the hosts' quarters up top. One host is an avid sailor and recreation director. The other, who works for the chamber of commerce, is a music educator and professional singer. Looking for something to do? "Beaches, galleries, restaurants, theater, concerts, and lectures—and lots for kids, including a great town playground. If we don't know the answer, we know where to get it!"

BED AND BATH: Entire first floor (all for you) with a queen bedroom, room with a double trundle bed, en-suite large full tile bath, sitting room, private phone. Also ground-level private studio with queen bed, shower bath, kitchenette with microwave, refrigerator, dishes and utensils, patio with grill.

BREAKFAST: 8–8:30. Earlier for ferry departures. Continental after 8:30. Fresh fruit. Juice. Waffles, pancakes, or French toast. Scones or muffins. In great room or on huge deck.

PLUS: Use of washer and dryer for guests who book for one week. Pets welcome!

> ᨒ Guests wrote: *"Delightful home. Friendly atmosphere . . . . Great breakfast . . . loved the unusual and beautiful design of the house."*

---

*U*NLESS OTHERWISE STATED, *rates in this book are for two and include breakfast in addition to all the amenities in "Plus."*

༃ *The Inn at Lewis Bay*

508/771-3433

57 Maine Avenue,
West Yarmouth, MA 02673

800/962-6679
FAX 508/790-1186
E-MAIL stay@innatlewisbay.com
www.innatlewisbay.com

HOSTS: Rick and Liz Latshaw
LOCATION: Quiet residential area. One block to bay beach. One mile from Route 28 with fine restaurants and miniature golf. Three miles from Hyannis.
OPEN: Year round.
RATES: Mid-May–October and holidays, double bed $108; queen $108, $118–$128 with bay views. November–mid-May $68–$98. Third person $20. Singles $10 less. Honeymoon/romantic getaway, birthday, and anniversary packages available. Amex, MC, Visa. ♥ ⊗ ⁄ ☀

༃ From Massachusetts: *"From the scrumptious breakfast to the most comfortable bed, Rick and Liz do a great job.* From Maryland: *"Friendly, peaceful, and comfortable. Accommodated my unique dietary needs. Food was delicious."* From New Jersey: *"Wonderful food and hospitality. Charming ambiance. . . . A great place to get away from it all."*

"BECAUSE WE are so close to the beach, in 1999 we renamed our 'place to get away from it all.'" Formerly known as The Manor House, this place is just what the Latshaws had in mind when they decided to work together as innkeepers "someday." Rick, who is passionate about cooking (and golfing and skiing), was a soda distributor sales manager. Liz, a former Hallmark store manager, is a gardener and cat fancier who likes the idea of reading a good book at the beach. The young couple—now parents of two—were vacationing on Cape Cod when they "stumbled on The Manor House, then in dire need of love and attention." Originally the 1920s Dutch Colonial was a summer rental cottage owned by the Hotel Englewood, a beach resort that burned in 1962. "We saw the potential, returned to New Jersey, sold our house, left our jobs, and bought the inn in December 1994, six months after we had first seen it." They decorated with a Cape feeling, without clutter—in light colors with floral prints; some wicker; some pine and maple furniture (dressers are from the Englewood); and, in the many-windowed dining room, an Oriental rug. Rooms are named by themes: The walls of "Bird Song" have a handpainted tree with birdhouses. "'Sea Grass' is beachy. We have a casual style and a home-away-from home atmosphere—offering lots of pampering—in this fabulous and quiet location."

IN RESIDENCE: Two sons: Luke is three; Erick was born in 1999. Two cats: "Hairball loves the guests; guests rarely see Whitesocks."
BED AND BATH: Six rooms (two have bay view, five are air conditioned). Located on first and second floors. Each has queen bed (one room has a queen and a twin) and private en-suite shower bath.
BREAKFAST: 8:30–10. (Early-morning coffee and tea to take to your room, if you'd like.)

Fresh juice and fruit. Homemade bread or muffins with honey butter. Quiche, French toast, potato pie, or frittata. Served in dining room at large oak table that seats eight, under the chandelier. Takeaway continental breakfast for early departures.

PLUS: Wood-burning fireplace in living room. Late-afternoon tea with freshly baked cookies, brownies, or cake. Outdoor shower. Boccie. Springwater, ice, and snacks. A before-and-after album. Suggestion for "a little lobster shack located in the middle of nowhere. No ambiance, but fabulous lobster!"

ᔧ *Liberty Hill Inn*

77 Main Street, Yarmouth Port, MA 02675-1709

508/362-3976
800/821-3977
FAX 508/362-6485
E-MAIL libertyh@capecod.net
www.capecod.net/libertyhillinn

HOSTS:	Beth and Jack Flanagan
LOCATION:	On Old King's Highway (Route 6A), set back on a little hill (site of Revolutionary War rallying point) with park-like gardens. Across from a conservation area. Walk to fine restaurants and antiques and crafts shops. Near beaches, whale watching, golf, Cape Playhouse. Ten-minute drive to Hyannis.
OPEN:	Year round. Two-night minimum on summer and major holiday weekends.
RATES:	Memorial Day–Columbus Day $135 queen bed with canopy, $100–$120 other queens, $150 king. Two-bedroom family suite $170 for four. Barn rooms $185 with whirlpool and fireplace; $155 with queen and fireplace; $145 with queen or two double beds, fireplace. Five-night honeymoon package $650–$895. Off-season $85–$150; two-night getaway package includes dinner for two at an area restaurant, $115–$130 per night. Extra person $20. Singles $80–$110. Amex, MC, Visa. ♥ ⸙ ❖ ⚥ ⚔

ᔧ From New Jersey: *"Gracious and informative hosts . . . decorated tastefully with English charm . . . Valentine's weekend with fresh roses, delightful chocolates . . . relaxing getaway."* From Pennsylvania: *"Have raved about this lovely inn and their service—to everyone!"* From Australia: *"So authentically American historically . . . hospitality too. . . . One of our fondest memories."* From Texas: *"Have experienced a wide assortment of B&Bs. . . . Liberty Hill ranks at the top of my list."*

ALTHOUGH BETH and Jack had had experience restoring three houses, when it came time for a "retirement occupation" in 1987, they bought an 1825 shipowner's Greek Revival house that had already become a B&B. On the National Register—and seen in a wonderful *Colonial Homes* spread—it features a columned veranda, floor-to-ceiling windows, fresh decor, refinished wide-plank floors, and Queen Anne antiques.

continued . . .

Jack had been an auditor and in real estate in the New York/New Jersey area. (He is now a Cape broker.) Beth was an actress and worked in international college admissions. Now the Flanagans conduct seminars for prospective and new innkeepers. And they give guests great suggestions that include an old-time soda fountain, historic houses, and nature trails.

BED AND BATH: Nine large rooms with private baths, individual climate control, cable TV. Main house—three second-floor rooms with sitting areas have queen beds, two with stall shower and one with full bath. In separate wing—suite with queen bed in one room, two twins in other, bath with deep soaking tub and shower. Third-floor hideaway has king bed, full bath. In historic beamed barn (converted in 1997)—four rooms, each with private bath, gas fireplace, sitting area. On first floor, handicapped-accessible room with queen bed, single sofa bed, shower bath; room with canopied queen bed, whirlpool for two, and separate shower. On second floor, one room with canopied queen bed, full bath; one with two double beds, full bath. Rollaway available.
BREAKFAST: Usually 8–10. (Continental before 8, coffee ready at 7.) Includes recipes tested for Beth's B&B book. Fruit, apple strudel, quiche, meat and cheese casseroles, baked eggs, omelets, French toast, home-baked breads. Cheese, cereals, fresh fruit, juice, coffee, tea, and decaf. At separate tables in garden-view dining room.
PLUS: Complimentary setups for cocktail hour. Afternoon tea/coffee. Veranda chairs. Croquet lawn. Terraced garden. Library includes area restaurant menus and maps. Music collection and memorabilia from Beth's mother's 1920s days as a radio singer.

❧ *One Centre Street Inn*   508/362-8910

1 Centre Street,   888/407-1653
Yarmouth Port, MA 02675-1342   FAX 508/362-0195
                                    www.sunsol.com/onecentrestreet/

HOST: Karen Iannello
LOCATION: In historic district with sea captains' homes. On corner of Route 6A. Across from antiques shop. Within a mile of botanical trails, craft shops, art galleries, fine restaurants, ice-cream parlor (in 1800s pharmacy—with apothecary drawers still there), Parnassus Bookstore (old and new titles), long boardwalk (over bay), and sunsets at Gray's Beach.
OPEN: Year round. Two-night minimum on July and August weekends.
RATES: May 15–October 15 semiprivate bath $105; private bath $105 double bed, $120 or $130 queen, $145 suite. October 16–May 14 $10 less. Third person $20. Discover, MC, Visa. ♥ ⊞ ❖ ⚄ ⚼

❧ From a huge stack of notes written to me by contented American, Canadian, and European travelers: *"Perfect for a twentieth wedding anniversary. . . . Stayed during a 'Girls Golfing' weekend. Breakfasts to die for. . . . And what a kitchen! . . . Went far* *beyond the usual and necessary. . . . Service she gave the seven of us plus my [local resident] mother was <u>superb</u>. . . . Decor makes you feel comfortable, cozy, and spoiled . . . white lace-edged cotton bed linens. . . . I loved it! . . . Fabulous breakfasts. She outdid herself every morn-ing. . . . From glass doorknobs and beautiful wooden floors to the walls hung with watercolors painted by local artists—exquisite. . . . Our stay was a real highlight in the U.S.A. . . . over-whelmed by the charm of the innkeeper, beautiful house, unforgettable and delicious break-fasts . . . evening on the terrace with candlelight. . . . The name should really be 'The Care Inn' and Karen's name should be spelled 'Kareinn.' I have traveled all over the United States, Canada, Europe, and Africa and never have found such an appropriate and sensitive interpre-tation of innkeeping. . . . First class, run by a first-class innkeeper."*

FOR SURE, a winner! Karen—"I was named 'Karina' by my Great-Aunt Anna"—was a nurse in critical care. Often, her friends encouraged her to run a restaurant. In 1994 she moved from Washington, D.C., to this 1824 Greek Revival house, a former parsonage that is on the National Register. She furnished with a blend of traditional and Colonial, and decorated with lace curtains and interior shutters, some stenciled walls and no clutter. Some rooms have Laura Ashley linens. Others have handmade quilts. Cape artists' origi-nal prints and watercolors—for sale—are on the walls.

IN RESIDENCE: Chelsea, "a friendly dalmatian in charge of welcoming guests to 'her' inn."
BED AND BATH: Six rooms (most are air conditioned); four with private bath. First floor—large room with queen brass bed, double sofa bed, TV, private en-suite shower bath. Suite has queen iron bed, separate sitting room with double sofa bed, wood-burning fireplace, private shower bath. Second floor—room with queen wicker bed, pri-vate en-suite shower bath. Up narrow staircase to cozy room tucked under eaves with double bed, private en-suite tub/shower bath. Room with antique pine double bed shares (robes provided) shower bath with room that has a double and a twin bed.
BREAKFAST: 8–9:30. Juice. Banana crumble, fresh pineapple, or fresh fruit parfait with vanilla-honey sauce. Homemade breads, muffins, scones. Entrée possibilities include orange French toast with strawberry Grand Marnier sauce, apple phyllo crepes, or cran-berry–toasted pecan pancakes. Freshly brewed coffees, teas. Buffet style in new country kitchen, in formally set dining room, or on screened porch at tables for two and four. Special diets accommodated—"with advance notice, please."
PLUS: Upright piano in parlor. Two old-fashioned (no-speed, balloon tires) bikes. Adirondack chairs on lawn. Chocolates. Fresh flowers.

BREAKFAST IS WHERE THE MAGIC HAPPENS.

ᾱ *The Wedgewood Inn*   508/362-5157

83 Main Street, Yarmouth Port, MA 02675   FAX 508/362-5851

HOSTS: Milt and Gerrie Graham
LOCATION: On Route 6A, in the historic district. On 2 landscaped acres with patios and gardens. An eight-minute drive to island ferries or whale-watch boats. Near nature trails and beaches.
OPEN: Year round. Advance reservations recommended.
RATES: Per room. $155 with working fireplace, $125 without. Suite $165; $185–$195 with fireplace and sitting room. Rollaway $15. November 1–June 1 except holidays, off-season rates available. Amex, Diners, MC, Visa. ♥ ⊞ ❖ ⚴ ⅛

"SEND ME THERE!" said the Boston television interviewer as I was commenting on slides of B&Bs being shown for Valentine's Day suggestions. The touch of elegance in the area's first architect-designed house built in 1812 has also been seen on a *Colonial Homes* cover, on a *Great American Homes* cable TV show, and in the British press. And the inn has received four "Best of Cape Cod" awards.

Milt, a former professional football player, was with the FBI for twenty years. Now he does some mountain climbing—most recently in the Andes. And a few years ago he went on a five-week trek in Nepal. When the Grahams lived in Connecticut, Gerrie taught school in Darien. In 1986 they saw this inn with working fireplaces, spacious rooms, and wide-board floors, and their "what next" decision was made. Every guest room has upholstered wing chairs, an antique or handmade bed (many are pencil post), and a handmade quilt—all enhanced by a late-afternoon tea tray and fresh fruit. Lovely gardens and a gazebo are on the grounds.

BED AND BATH: Nine large air-conditioned rooms; no two have adjoining walls. All private baths; one with shower only, others with tub/shower. First-floor suites have fishnet-canopied queen bed, private screened porch, sitting area, working fireplace, full bath. On second floor—two queen-bedded rooms with working fireplace; one room with a queen and a twin daybed. Entire third floor (suite) has private exterior entrance accessed by narrow staircase, queen bed, and, in the sitting room, a single bed. In recently (1996) converted barn—three suites, each with king bed, fireplace, private deck, sitting room with TV.

BREAKFAST: 8–10; earlier for ferry schedule and business guests. French toast, scrambled eggs on puff pastry, or maybe Belgian waffles. Homemade and English muffins. Cereal. Yogurt. Served at tables for two set with china and flowers in dining room with handcrafted Windsor chairs.

PLUS: Individual thermostats. Patio. Gazebo. Lawn seating.

ᾱ From Texas: *"Fabulous . . . breakfasts . . . views from screened private porch . . . gardens . . . hosts. . . . Truly a magical place!"*

MARTHA'S VINEYARD ISLAND
RESERVATION SERVICES

THE FOLLOWING RESERVATIONS SERVICES REPRESENT B&Bs ON MARTHA'S VINEYARD:
Bed and Breakfast Associates Bay Colony, Ltd., page 230
Bed and Breakfast Cape Cod, page 144
Bed & Breakfast Reservations North Shore/Greater Boston/Cape Cod, page 231

✍ *The Arbor* 508/627-8137

222 Upper Main Street, P.O. Box 1228, Edgartown, MA 02539   **www.mvy.com/arborinn**

HOST: Peggy Hall

LOCATION: Six-minute walk into town, ten minutes to harbor. On the bicycle path. Just down the street from a nursery (with fabulous displays) and a supermarket. Shuttle bus to Edgartown center—"with wave of hand, bus stops at door." Bus to other towns and beach leaves from town center.

OPEN: May–October. (Usually a) three-day minimum July, August, and holiday weekends; two-day minimum May–June and September–October.

RATES: June 15–September 30, single bed $125. Double, semiprivate bath $125 or $130. Queen $185. Off-season, $100–$145. MC, Visa. ♥ ❖ ⚫ ✄

Wow. A few steps into the entrance of this weather-shingled house brings you to a dramatic 22-foot-high living room with mantel, pillar, balcony library, and handmade atrium window. The house, built in 1880 and moved in 1910 from the adjoining island of Chappaquiddick, has had several additions through the years. Rooms are decorated with painted walls, stenciling, shutters, ball fringe curtains, vintage furniture, and, in the living room, chintz-covered sofas. One bathroom is "wallpapered" with Peggy's photographic collection of Vineyard scenes—"some are gone now"—that appeared in real estate appointment calendars.

Before taking over the B&B in 1979, Peggy trained real estate brokers. Here she shares her love for the island and its hideaways with big-city folks who unwind—and with young people, singles, couples, and international travelers too.

BED AND BATH: Ten air-conditioned rooms, eight with private baths (four shower only, four are full). Seven are queen-bedded rooms. One cozy single room. Two double-bedded rooms share a full bath. Plus a one-bedroom small house available by the week.

BREAKFAST: 8–10. Juice; homemade corn and other breads or muffins; tea or coffee. Buffet style with linens, cloth napkins, silver service. Eat in breakfast room that has hand-painted mural, in fireplaced dining room at big table "with great conversations," outside at umbrella tables, or in the courtyard.

PLUS: Enclosed outdoor hot/cold shower. Under trees, hammock for two. Guest refrigerator. Beverage, cookies, and setups (ice, glasses, mix) 5–7 P.M. Bicycle rack. Antiques shop in former garage.

✍ Guests wrote: *"Grounds are beautiful . . . breakfast breads delicious. . . . Caring hostess who knows her island! Joyful and restful visit . . . cozy. . . . Super place either for being alone or for finding people to be with."*

⇢ *The Shiverick Inn*   508/627-3797

P.O. Box 640, Pease's Point Way,   800/723-4292
Edgartown, MA 02539–0640   FAX 508/627-8441
                                            www.mvweb.com/shiv

        HOSTS: Martin P. and Denise M. Turmelle
    LOCATION: On a corner, with residences and one inn as immediate neighbors. One
               block from Main Street's dining, shopping, historic area. Three blocks from
               waterfront.
        OPEN: December 31–mid-December. Three-night minimum July–September and
               on holidays. Two-night minimum other weekends.
       RATES: June 16–October 12, $225 queen, $240 king, $275 private treetop terrace,
               $325 suite. October 13–June 15, $130, $150 with fireplace, $200 suite. Amex,
               Discover, MC, Visa. ♥ ⊞ ❖ ⚥ ⌇

INTENTIONALLY "elegant but not stuffy"—with crystal chandeliers, brocades, gilt mirrors,
Oriental rugs, and ancestral portraits—this nineteenth-century Victorian was built in
1840, during the height of the whaling era, by Dr. Clement Shiverick, the town's physician. An inn since 1981 and restored—exquisitely—in 1987, it is now popular as a romantic getaway, complete with a lighted cupola chandelier as an evening landmark. Some
guests book because of a *CEO Traveler* newsletter feature. And others come "because our
friends said that this is the place to be."

     The Turmelles, parents of three and grandparents of eight—"we were married at a
young age"—looked all over New England for "a special place for special people. And we
found it!" In New Hampshire Marty was a utility executive. Denny, the other pamperer,
was in real estate sales and development.

IN RESIDENCE: Two bichons frises, Tucker and Tyler.
FOREIGN LANGUAGE SPOKEN: A bit of French.
BED AND BATH: Ten air-conditioned rooms, all private baths. First floor—king, canopied
queen, queen four-poster with wood-burning fireplace. Second floor—queen four-
poster; canopied king; rooms with wood-burning fireplace have canopied or four-poster
queen (together can be a suite with adjoining sitting room). Third floor—queen or
canopied queen with private rooftop terrace.
BREAKFAST: 8:30–10. Entrée such as egg soufflé, pumpkin pancakes, ricotta blintzes with
puree of raspberries, eggs Florentine. Juices, fruit, two cereals (homemade granola),
homemade English toasting bread, homemade pastry, coffee, tea. Served in fireplaced
garden room overlooking formal courtyard.
PLUS: Fireplaced living room. No TV. Tea and sweets at 4:30. Guest refrigerator. Ironed
sheets. Robes in rooms. Second-floor library with books, TV, wraparound outdoor terrace. Beach towels. Sand chairs.

⟿ Summer House

508/627-4857

96 South Summer Street, Edgartown, MA 02539

HOST: Chloe Dandison Nolan
LOCATION: Residential historic area. One block from harbor, 3 to town. Two blocks from island's first steepled church and from the Vineyard Museum.
OPEN: Mid-May through mid-October.
RATES: $165; $190 suite. ♥ ☛ ⊞ ⚞ ✄

A REAL HOME away from home. With a layout that provides lots of privacy. In a very quiet residential area that is minutes from everything. With spacious lawn, huge trees, lovely porch, and fenced yard. It's warm, welcoming, and comfortable, with "touches" but hardly fussy; and, yes, very summery. Originally, around 1850, this was a barn/carriage house 10 miles away in Chilmark. It was moved to Edgartown in the late 1800s. A century later, after renovations and a new addition, it was a feature on the Edgartown House Tour. Chloe's summer home since 1970, it became her B&B in 1980 at the suggestion of local innkeepers.

It was perfect for me during an early fall visit. Neighbors' guests are among the many returnees who love this place. And they love Chloe, a recently retired (1999) Vineyard third-grade teacher who also taught in private schools outside of Philadelphia.

IN RESIDENCE: Panda, "an engaging, friendly Border Collie."
BED AND BATH: Two rooms with private baths. Suite has large room with king bed, alcove bedroom with single daybed, two comfortable chairs, TV, phone, shower bath with skylight. Smaller room has king bed, TV, phone, large tub/shower bath.
BREAKFAST: Usually 8:30–10. Juice, fresh fruit, muffins, scones, breads, hot beverages. Served at long teak table in country kitchen—with old brick walls and original beams—overlooking yard, or on brick terrace with view of lush ivied wall.
PLUS: Inviting porch rockers. Guest refrigerator. Parking.

⟿ Guests from California, New York, Massachusetts, and England wrote: *"So peaceful! . . . Complete relaxation . . . wonderful, private garden . . . a sanctuary for birds. . . . Glorious warmth, hospitality, and comfort. Chloe is lively, energetic, informative, helpful, friendly. . . . Accommodations and owner are both delightful . . . abundant breakfast . . . delicious breads. . . . Quiet location. . . . House is spacious, welcoming, serene."*

*T*HE TRADITION *of paying to stay in a private home—with breakfast included in the overnight lodging rate—was revived in time to save wonderful old houses, schools, churches, and barns all over the country from the wrecking ball or commercial development.*

⋙ *Greenwood House*

508/693-6150

40 Greenwood Avenue, P.O. Box 2734,
Vineyard Haven, MA 02568-2734

800/525-9466
FAX 508/696-8113
E-MAIL innkeeper@greenwoodhouse.com
www.greenwoodhouse.com

HOSTS: Larry Gomez and Kathy Stinson
LOCATION: Quiet residential area. Five minutes from village center, restaurants, beaches, tennis, golf.
OPEN: Year round. Three-night minimum mid-June–mid-September.
RATES: Mid-September–mid-June $119 double, $169 queen, $169 suite with twins, $219 suite with queen. Mid-June–mid-September $189 double, $199 queen, $199 twin suite, $269 queen suite. Amex, CB, Diners, MC, Visa.
♥ ■ ❖ ⚔ ✂

"SAW AD. Made offer. ('You've never seen it,' said seller. 'We know your style,' said buyers.) Quit job. All in six weeks. Did we move too fast? We love it! . . . We're constantly making changes and are well on our way to having all 1920s Arts and Crafts or Stickley-style furnishings in this cozy three-storied 1906 bungalow. . . . In California I was a purchasing agent for a San Francisco area defense contractor; Kathy, an elementary school teacher. We were such frequent guests at the neighboring Thorncroft Inn that the innkeepers said we ought to buy a house. We did—in 1986—and came to the island even more often, including the month of April, when I run the Boston Marathon. On New Year's Day 1993 we were on the ferry, reading the paper, when we saw this B&B, then part of Thorncroft, for sale. Now we share our 'secret places' and fun things to do with terrific guests. And Kathy walks to the local school where she is a kindergarten teacher. Here we are—happily—for the duration!"

FOREIGN LANGUAGES SPOKEN: Some French. Hungarian—Kathy, born in Hungary, is fluent; Larry is self-taught.
BED AND BATH: Two rooms, three suites; each with private bath, air conditioning, private modem-compatible phone, cable color TV, refrigerator, microwave oven. First-floor suite—twin beds, ceiling fan, wicker-furnished porch sitting room. Second floor—queen bed, wicker furniture, shower bath; room with pencil-post double bed, tub/shower bath; suite with queen four-poster, shower bath, separate formal living room. Entire third floor—queen bed in one room, a twin bed in another, a sitting room, tub/hand-held shower bath.
BREAKFAST: 8:30–9:30. Bagels, cereal, toast. Fresh fruit. Pancakes, waffles, French toast, crepes, or quiche. Served in formal dining room at table set for eight.
PLUS: Garden on grounds with Adirondack chairs, picnic table, croquet set.

    ⋙ Guests wrote: *"From the moment we stepped into the lovely living room, we felt as if we were with friends we met a long time ago . . . clean . . . well-kept . . . meeting other*

continued . . .

guests around the breakfast table (a new experience for us) made our stay even more enjoyable . . . every day a different breakfast—plentiful and delicious. . . . A nice match of old-world quaintness and modern convenience. . . . Privacy . . . companionship and conversation . . . delicious evening treats. . . . We loved every minute."

⚜ *Martha's Place B&B*   508/693-0253

114 Main Street, P.O. Box 1182,   FAX 508/693-1890
Vineyard Haven, MA 02568   E-MAIL info@marthasplace.com
                                              www.marthasplace.com

HOSTS: Richard Alcott and Martin Hicks
LOCATION: In historic district. Overlooking harbor. One block to ferry, village shops, restaurants, island shuttle service. Across from park and beach.
OPEN: Year round. Two-night minimum; three nights in August and on holidays.
RATES: June–September $175, $225, $300, $395. Off-season $125–$275. MC, Visa.
♥ ▦ ❖ ⚔ ⚕ ☙ ♥

PHOTO OPPORTUNITIES abound day and night in this gracious and beautifully decorated Greek Revival. Walkers stare at the doorway. After sundown the showstopper is the 1840s crystal chandelier in the plum-colored dining room with floor-to-ceiling windows. In the living room there's an extraordinary 1840s faux black marble mantel. The fabrics, colors, swags, jabots, half testers, refinished floors, Oriental carpets, and fine antiques are "all Martin's doing," according to Richard, a merchant marine officer who has been around the world "a few times." Martin had experience with the Ritz-Carlton in Houston and with a Cape Cod inn. After the hosts bought this property in 1996, "everything" was done over for romantic getaways. Extensive media coverage includes the French magazine, *Maisons Côté Ouest*. To boot, guests can tell that the two innkeepers love what they are doing.

BED AND BATH: Six air-conditioned rooms, each with AM/FM/CD player. All private baths. First floor—overlooking courtyard: double bed, wood-burning fireplace, shower bath. One harborview room with queen bed, bay window, shower bath. Second floor—harborview suite with queen bed, bay window, wood-burning fireplace in sitting room, tub/shower bath. Three queen-bedded rooms with varying amenities: harbor view, wood-burning fireplace, granite tiled bath with whirlpool tub, bath with whirlpool and fireplace.
BREAKFAST: 9–10. Juice, yogurt, fresh fruit plate, breakfast breads, pastries, muffins, croissants, bagels, cheese, ham. On china with silver service in formal dining room with harbor view; or, if you'd like, breakfast in bed!
PLUS: Sunroom, overlooking harbor, with TV/VCR. Wood-burning fireplaces in living and dining rooms. Turndown service. Robes. Bicycles. Box lunches available. Morning newspaper. Sailboat available for charters. Beach chairs, towels, and coolers. Free parking. Afternoon tea.

⤞ *Pier Side* 508/693-5562

P.O. Box 1951, South Farm Road,
Lake Tashmoo, Vineyard Haven, MA 02568

HOSTS: Phil and Ilse Fleischman

LOCATION: Two and a half miles from "the hustle-bustle" of Vineyard Haven center. On Lake Tashmoo, a beautiful 1½-mile-long saltwater lake open to Vineyard Sound. Surrounded by a 30-acre farm. Near conservation lands with walking trails.

OPEN: Year round. Advance reservations required.

RATES: Per room. June 16–September 15, $165. Off-season, $125. Third person $15.
♥ ❖ ⚁ ⤝ ≋ ⚇

⤞ From California: *"Magical. Through quiet woods to a clearing . . . flower-filled patios . . . a warm welcome usually reserved for old friends. . . . The house blends Ilse's European flair with Philip's down-to-earth practicality . . . charming room (more like a studio apartment) with all the comforts of home and a private balcony overlooking sparkling blue water. . . . A lovely romantic spot."*

"AUDIENCES EVERYWHERE sigh when they see my slides of this treasure. After seventeen years of living in the German country–style house they designed and built in Edgartown, the Fleischmans moved to this "forever" spot—where "the total traffic consists of ducks, geese, seagulls, hawks, swans, otters, and a new family of ospreys."

Phil, an architect who has been a yacht captain and boatbuilder, designed this traditional New England house with cedar shingles and trim, French doors, red brick paths, and European details. He built it with Ilse, a kindergarten teacher in her native Germany and also in Greece, and now a travel agent here. Their informal style of hosting provides for opportunities to visit on the porch or in the garden—and sometimes on the pier, where the Fleischmans' and friends' boats are frequently tied up.

IN RESIDENCE: "One big gray cat that sleeps a lot."

FOREIGN LANGUAGE SPOKEN: German.

BED AND BATH: Overlooking the lake, two large rooms, each with private entrance and shower bath. King bed in air-conditioned Balcony Room; queen in cathedral-ceilinged (with ceiling fan) Patio Room, which has additional open-air shower under the stars.

BREAKFAST: Full breakfast provided in refrigerator of guests' rooms. Help-yourself arrangement.

PLUS: Deep-water pier (guests' boats are welcome) used for swimming. Horseshoes. Croquet. Boccie. Use of grill. Ample parking.

➣ *Thorncroft Inn*

508/693-3333

P.O. Box 1022, 460 Main Street,
Vineyard Haven, MA 02568

800/332-1236
FAX 508/693-5419
E-MAIL innkeeper@thorncroft.com
www.thorncroft.com

HOSTS: Karl and Lynn Buder
LOCATION: On 3½ acres in a residential area, a half mile beyond the edge of the village. One mile from ferry landing.
OPEN: Year round. Memorial Day–November 1 two-night midweek minimum, three nights on weekends.
RATES: Mid-June–Labor Day $225–$475. Off-season $170–$425. Amex, DC, Discover, MC, Visa. ♥ ❖ ⚸ ⚸

"IT'S THE TYPE of place where we find ourselves falling in love all over again." Since that comment from a guest appeared in my first B&B book, the Buders have continued to embellish (and then some) the house, which was built in 1918 for the son of an industrialist. Some rooms have a private hot tub or Jacuzzi. Many have cable TV equipped with headphones "so you can nap while your spouse watches CNN." Fireplaces are wood-burning. Throughout—in the main inn, the carriage house, and the recently built private cottage—there are four-poster and high-back Victorian beds, turn-of-the-century lamps, and Colonial pieces. As guests often say, it's the perfect blend of nostalgia, comfort, and elegance. A stay at this made-for-pampering inn was the grand prize on TV's *Wheel of Fortune*. And it was featured on the Learning Channel's *Great Country Inns*.

In 1981 Karl, who has a master's degree in public administration, was a probation officer and marathon runner. He and his father restored "everything" while Lynn commuted on weekends from her executive position with a Connecticut insurance company. As the family grew—the two sons are teenagers now—the Buders moved to a nearby house. Today Karl, the breakfast chef, coaches local football and baseball teams. He and Lynn meet many romantic getaway guests who return with colleagues for meetings. And guests remember the hospitality of these friendly hosts, who feature service along with their knowledge (and love) of "this cosmopolitan/small-town storybook island."

FOREIGN LANGUAGES SPOKEN: French, Spanish, Portuguese.
BED AND BATH: Fourteen rooms with queen (many canopied), king, or double bed. Most with match-ready wood-burning fireplace and/or a balcony. All with private bath; some full, others shower only. Three have two-person Jacuzzi, two have a private 300-gallon hot tub. Handicapped-accessible cottage has king four-poster, Jacuzzi bath, attached garage for equipped van.
BREAKFAST: Announced by a breakfast bell when the French doors are opened at 8:15 and 9:30. (Or a substantial meal brought at 9 or 10 by two staffers to guests in bed.) Buttermilk pancakes and bacon, blueberry honey sauce, almond French toast, quiche, "mountains of fresh fruit," home-baked goods or granola. With classical music. (Continental breakfast available for early departures.)

PLUS: Central air conditioning. Afternoon tea and pastries. Turndown service. *Boston Globe* at your door. Wicker-furnished sunroom. Victorian reading parlor. Lawn furniture. Extra bath for postcheckout refresher.

⌁ *Twin Oaks Inn on Martha's Vineyard*   508/693-8633

20 Edgartown Road, P.O. Box 1767,   800/696-8633
Vineyard Haven, MA 02568-1767   FAX 508/693-5833
E-MAIL dclark@vineyard.net
www.twinoaksinn.net

HOST: Doris Clark

LOCATION: On main road. Seven-minute walk to ferry, town, shopping, restaurants, cinema, bookstore, bike path. Shuttle bus stops at door. Three miles from Oak Bluffs, 7 from Edgartown, 18 from Aquinnah (home of Gay Head Cliffs).

OPEN: Year round. Two-night minimum on weekends.

RATES: Mid-May–mid-September shared bath $95 and $100, queen bed $140, suite $155, apartment $225. Off-season $5–$15 less. Package rates for book clubs and spa weekends. Amex, Discover, MC, Visa. ♥ ⊞ ❖ ⚔ ⏚

JOY. CONTAGIOUS LAUGHTER. Good cheer. Best atmosphere (*Boston Best Guide* Crème de la Crème award). It was all here each time Doris arrived from Tokyo in the early 1990s, when she dovetailed her job as a flight attendant with innkeeping. It was here when she was introduced to a friend of friends (former guests) on her front porch. (A year later, in 1994, she married Jay.) And today you can hear that welcoming smile on the phone.

Doris's family island roots go back to the 1800s. In 1991 she bought this white 1906 Dutch Colonial and made it homey with antiques, wicker, and plants. She painted the exterior shutters pink. And recently installed private phones in all the rooms. Now that she has retired from her twenty-six years with United Airlines, Doris combines innkeeping with teaching Vineyard high school career preparation workshops and New York University hospitality courses. She is a sales rep for recipe management software programs. The highlight of the year 2000: speaking in South Africa at the meeting of an international exchange, the People to People Ambassador Program. Her B&B success story has been chronicled in many publications including the *New York Times, Detroit Free Press*, and *Los Angeles Sentinel*. Her guest list has included President Clinton's staffers, first-time B&B guests, and others who first met here and now return every year to relax and unwind.

FOREIGN LANGUAGE SPOKEN: Portuguese.

BED AND BATH: Two rooms, two suites, and one apartment. Three with air conditioning. All with queen bed (except one with two double beds), ceiling fan, cross-ventilation, private phone with answering machine, data port, desk, TV. First floor—apartment with

continued . . .

fireplaced living room, sunroom, full kitchen, tub/shower bath, private entrance. Second floor—one smaller room and one suite that has bedroom and separate sitting room share a large tub/shower bath. One room with en-suite shower bath. One suite with two double beds in one room, separate sitting room, shower bath.

BREAKFAST: 9–10. Juice, fresh fruit, yogurt, homemade granola (specialty of the house), homemade muffins, bagels, hot beverages. In dining room, on windowed/screened front porch, or at umbrella tables on brick patio (with gazebo).

PLUS: Color TV, 32 inches, with WebTV (surf Web or check your e-mail). TV/VCR in living room. In winter, hot cider, cookies, and pastries. Bicycle parking rack.

⋙ *The Bayberry*

508/693-1984

Old Courthouse Road, P.O. Box 654,
West Tisbury, MA 02575

800/693-9960
FAX 508/693-4505
www.vineyard.net/biz/bayberry

HOSTS: Rosalie and (son) Jim Powell
LOCATION: Down a country lane where there are birds, woods, meadows, horses. Ten minutes to beaches. Five miles from ferry landing.
OPEN: Year round (except maybe January or February). Two-day minimum on many weekends.
RATES: June–September $125 twin beds or canopied queen, semiprivate bath; $160 canopied double; $175 king, private bath. Off-season $85–$105; special rug-hooking workshop rates. Amex, MC, Visa. ♥ ⊞ ❖ ⚲ ⤢ 柀

⋙ From Massachusetts: *"Rosalie Powell, a native who is a descendant of Governor Thomas Mayhew, founder of the Vineyard and Nantucket, extends herself in every way possible—from the quaint rooms, to fresh flowers bursting everywhere, to passes to wonderful beaches and tennis courts, to providing sherry and mints, to a gourmet breakfast . . . but most importantly, you feel welcomed and appreciated!"* From England: *"Stayed an extra day because of Rosalie's 'sense of island' suggestions. Fabulous!"*

OTHERS CALL The Bayberry "the perfect honeymoon spot" and comment on the "warm and tranquil environment." The rambling, weathered-shingled Cape Cod–style house was built (surprise) in 1970 on land settled by Rosalie's family in 1642. Opened as a B&B in 1984 when the hostess took early retirement from the University of Massachusetts Extension Service, it is filled with family heirlooms and restored antiques. There's an open country kitchen (watch Danish *aebleskivers* being made); a beamed ceiling with hanging baskets; pottery; quilts; a puzzle-in-progress, and wonderful hooked rugs. (Try a little rug hooking yourself, or return in June for Rosalie's acclaimed Bayberry Hooked Rug School.) Rosalie's son, Jim, a polyglot who has many opportunities to speak various languages with guests, teaches high school. Here he cuts the firewood and tends the chickens and the organic gardens (melons, raspberries, potatoes, apples, and pears). The meadow is filled with daisies. Hollyhocks, sunflowers, and roses grow. The bobwhite calls. The hearth beckons. So does the hammock under the trees. Flexibility is a byword here. And joie de vivre.

BED AND BATH: Five rooms. On first floor, two rooms share a hall full bath; one has an arched canopied queen bed, the other has two pineapple-post twin beds. On second floor, two rooms with king beds (one wicker, one high Victorian), private shower baths; one canopied double bed, private full bath.

BREAKFAST: Usually 8:30. (Coffeepot on for early risers; light breakfast for early ferry departures.) Great variety, including "Dreamboats," named by a guest and almost always photographed before being eaten. (I, too, took a picture.) Or Belgian waffles with fresh blueberry sauce; bacon, sausage, or ham. Farm-fresh organic eggs. Fruit or juice. Homemade muffins and jams. Special diets accommodated. Served with linens and china at fireside tables overlooking gardens or on flower-filled patio.

PLUS: Outside hot/cold shower big enough for two. Depending on guests' plans, afternoon tea, wine, hors d'oeuvres. Grand piano. Library of books on antiques. Bedroom fans. Croquet. Champagne for honeymooners. For beach—towels, cooler, chairs, umbrella, and hints for beaches with shells and fossils. Aromas: "Heavenly today. I am making beach plum jelly from the plums I picked yesterday on the sand dunes at Lobsterville."

B &Bs OFFER THE ULTIMATE CONCIERGE SERVICE.

Nantucket Reservation Services

The following reservation services represent B&Bs on Nantucket:
Bed and Breakfast Associates Bay Colony Ltd., page 230
Bed and Breakfast Cape Cod, page 144

Nantucket B&Bs

Nantucket's unique characteristics have always been appreciated by its residents. Today the island is much loved by off-islanders as well. (Some fly in for the day. Others are responsible for "mansionizing" properties.) The cobblestoned shopping area, adjacent to the ferry dock, can be very busy in summer. Recommendations: Walk and discover your very own Nantucket. Or rent a bicycle for views of lanes, flowers, architecture, and the moors. Taxi and a shuttle bus service are available too.

Accommodations, often requiring at least two- and sometimes three- or four-night minimums during the summer, are expensive. Some years, "high season weekends" may mean April through October. Canopied beds and fireplaces abound, but whirlpool tubs are rare. B&B hosts are marvelous concierges for all sorts of arrangements, including dinner reservations for the island's many fine restaurants.

B&B guests are sometimes surprised to find that there's little need to bring a car. If your stay is to be extended and you insist, advance reservations for autos (carried by the Steamship Authority only) are essential and are often made months before the summer season. The 2½-hour ferry ride from Hyannis is provided by the Steamship Authority (phone 508/540-2022 or TTY/TDD 508/540-1394) and by Hy-Line Cruises (508/778-2600; advance sales and parking 508/778-2602). From Harwichport (1¾ hours, available seasonally) you can take Freedom Cruise Lines (508/432-8999). The Nantucket airport—fifteen minutes by air from Hyannis, about thirty from Boston, an hour and ten minutes from New York/LaGuardia—is open year round and serviced by several airlines.

🐎 Centre Street Inn — Know this one

78 Centre Street,
Nantucket, MA 02554

508/228-0199
800/298-0199
FAX 508/228-8676
E-MAIL inn@nantucket.net
www.centrestreetinn.com

HOSTS: Sheila and Fred Heap
LOCATION: On a quiet street in historic district. Five-minute walk to town, ten minutes from ferries and to north shore beaches. Next door to fine dining.
OPEN: Mid-April–mid-December. Mid-June until mid-September three-night minimum on weekends (two nights preferred midweek).
RATES: Mid-June–mid-September $75 single; $125–$135 double bed with shared bath; $165–$195 queen or twins with private bath; $245 (plus $30 extra adult, $20 extra child) queen and double sleep sofa, fireplace, and private bath. Mid-April–mid-June and mid-September–mid-December: $55; $75–$85; $115–$135; $145; $30 extra adult; $20 extra child. Special midweek packages in off-season. Amex, Discover, MC, Visa. ♥ 👫 ✤ 🛇 🍴

continued . . .

SUCH A LEGACY: This whale trader's house (in the mid-1700s) turned guest house (in the late 1800s) was purchased in 1943 by Frances Moriarty, an island native who named it for her favorite film, *Holiday Inn*—eight years before the national chain was established. Mrs. Moriarty was manager until she retired in 1993 at age eighty-two. Enter the Heaps in 1994. They had summered on Nantucket for many years. And in the 1970s they had experience working together at a children's specialty shop they owned on the south shore of Massachusetts. Fred, a professor of management at several New England colleges, is a handyman par excellence. Sheila, a former small-company human resources manager, has an eye and capable hand for interior design. They have decorated the inn with fresh floral and gingham fabrics, white Battenburg curtains, decorative wall paintings, and antiques and family treasures. ("The island is great for auctions.") Oriental, dhurrie, and rag rugs are on the random-width floors. Guests stay in rooms that retained the names of holidays. And they meet innkeepers who, in true Nantucket tradition, share their love of the island, the community, and their home.

IN RESIDENCE: Two dogs—an Australian terrier, Murphy Brown; Britta, a Brittany.
BED AND BATH: Thirteen rooms (on three floors) range from spacious ones with working fireplace to some tucked under eaves. Private baths (most are shower without tub) with queen bed (some canopied) and one room with twin beds. One large room (sleeps four) with queen bed and double sleep sofa. Six smaller rooms (three with double bed, three with single bed) share two tub/shower baths (robes and hair dryers provided).
BREAKFAST: 8:30–10 (coffee at 7:30). Freshly baked breads, coffee cakes (cranberry sour cream is a favorite) or muffins, cereal or granola, fruit juice, herbal teas and freshly brewed coffee. Eat in common room, on patio, or in guest rooms.
PLUS: Brick patio with Adirondack chairs, birdhouses and feeders, and garden. Afternoon tea. Hot tea, coffee, or cocoa all day. TV/VCR in common room. Room fans. Individual heat control for second-floor rooms. Guest pantry with refrigerator, ice maker, corkscrews, ice buckets. Beach towels. Bicycle storage.

⚞ *The Century House*

508/228-0530

P.O. Box 603, 10 Cliff Road,
Nantucket, MA 02554-0603

E-MAIL CenturyBnB@aol.com
www.centuryhouse.com

HOSTS: Jean Heron and (husband) Gerry Connick
LOCATION: In quiet residential section of historic district. Three blocks from town center; ten-minute walk from steamship landing. On corner at top of hill "at highest elevation on the island." Surrounded by sea captains' mansions. Ten minutes to beach.
OPEN: Spring through late fall. Three-night weekend minimum, late June–late September; shorter stays, depending on availability, accommodated close to date.

RATES: Depend on room size. Late June–late September and holidays $125–$225. Off-season $95–$155. Off-season weekday packages. Group rates available. MC, Visa. ♥ 👫 ⌇

↪ From Pennsylvania, New York, Florida, Massachusetts, Ohio: *"Hosts were friendly and fun. . . . Terrific combination of friendliness and service. . . . Outrageous breakfasts. . . . Originally booked for location . . . returned for innkeepers. . . . Our home away from home with added amenities . . . comfortable beds . . . charming decor . . . ocean breezes . . . advice about sailing, bike riding, terrific finds at hospital thrift shop. . . . Would return in a heartbeat. . . . Delighted with room with four-poster bed and antiques . . . but more important—warmth and energy exudes."*

EXUBERANCE FOR Nantucket, for the inn, for life! Two former high-tech executives, Gerry (who was trained as an architect) and Jean answered a "needs work" real estate ad in 1984. Through the years they have renovated and decorated several times over, with Laura Ashley wallcoverings, a skylight here, a window seat there, and family treasures. As Jean says, "We wanted an inn with special appeal for people with stressful careers. It works! Guests enjoy the tranquillity of the island, the fireplace in our homey living room, the *New York Times* in peace on a Sunday." Some have written poems about their stay here.

When guests return from town at night, the lighted old-fashioned sign acts as a beacon to this hospitable place, an inn since 1833. Throughout, there are paintings done by the annual artist-in-residence. Paramount TV filmed here for several *Wings* segments. Still, as returnees confirm, "It's the friendly helpful innkeepers who make this personalized B&B a treat."

FOREIGN LANGUAGES SPOKEN: Several, according to staffing.

BED AND BATH: Fourteen rooms, most with ceiling fans, on three floors. All with recently renovated private shower baths; many with tub also. King/twins, queen, or double beds; most are four-posters or canopied. Down pillows (foam option). Cot available.

BREAKFAST: 8:30–10. Bach music indicates it's time for Gerry's incredible spread—fresh fruit, juice, English muffins, coffee cakes, almost-famous bread pudding, fruit tarts, pies, granola and cereals, bagels with cream cheese, hot beverages. Eat in pine kitchen (decorated with Gerry's collection of 1945 auto plates) or on the wraparound veranda or patio.

PLUS: BYOB cocktail hour (setups and munchies provided). Midafternoon iced tea on patio. Coffee, tea, cappuccino, cookies "all day long." Beach towels. Guests' refrigerator. Books—extensive collection of best-sellers. Sometimes, a chance to wave at Gerry (or take a picture of him) in his recently restored (on Nantucket) 1945 pickup truck.

GUESTS ARRIVE AS STRANGERS, LEAVE AS FRIENDS.

≈ *Cliff Lodge*

508/228-9480

9 Cliff Road,
Nantucket, MA 02554-4025

FAX 508/228-6308
www.nantucket.net/lodging/clifflodge/

HOSTS: Debby and John Bennett
LOCATION: About a seven-minute walk from ferry; five minutes to town. Residential area with many large homes dating back to whaling era. On a hill overlooking town and harbor.
OPEN: Year round. Three-night minimum on holiday weekends and in summer.
RATES: Mid-June–Columbus Day weekend, Christmas Stroll, Memorial Day $145–$185; $105 single. Spring and fall plus Thanksgiving and Christmas $110–$155; $90 single. November–April 19 $75–$95; $70 single. Apartment suite $2,000 a week in season ($300 per night). MC, Visa. ♥ ✍ ✂

THE DECOR makes you feel as if it's summer in Nantucket all year long. Throughout this 1770s captain's house, a guest house for more than fifty years, there's a designer touch—spatter-painted floors, white-painted woodwork, pine and white-painted furniture, white eyelet bedding, Laura Ashley wallpaper, rag rugs and dhurries—all very fresh and inviting.

And for hospitality, guests meet a Nantucket native who "is part of island history." John, a third-generation island landscaper and Nantucket High School faculty member (chemistry and biology), taught in New Hampshire for fifteen years before returning the island in 1990. For a while he was radiology department manager at Nantucket Cottage Hospital. That's when he fell in love (this is a romantic island) with Debby, a laboratory manager who had dreamed of opening a B&B when she lived in Vermont. Since this personable, multifaceted couple bought this much-in-demand inn in 1995, John has transformed the grassy back hill "where, as kids, we slid down on cardboard boxes" to another patio with glorious gardens.

BED AND BATH: Eleven air-conditioned rooms (on three floors), each with adjoining private bath, cable color TV, phone. King, queen, double, or twin beds. Two third-floor rooms, tucked under the eaves, have view of town and harbor. Apartment (double occupancy preferred, often booked a year in advance) has full kitchen, working fireplace, private deck.
BREAKFAST: 8–9:30. Fresh fruit. Homemade bread, granola, coffee cakes, muffins, apple-cranberry cobbler. Buffet in fireplaced breakfast room with door leading to garden patio. Or on trays to take to your room.
PLUS: Widow's walk with panoramic view of harbor is accessible to guests. Outside shower. Beach towels. Four common rooms. Pantry with refrigerator and ice maker. Parking lot.

⁂ *Corner House* — didn't like person anymore . 508/228-1530

49 Center Street, P.O. Box 1828, **www.cornerhousenantucket.com**
Nantucket, MA 02554-1828

HOSTS: Sandy and John Knox-Johnston
LOCATION: Residential. In Old Historic District. Around corner from village center, on a quiet side street. Few minutes' walk from Steamboat Wharf.
OPEN: Early April through mid-December. (Closed mid-December–early April.) Mid-June through mid-September, four-night minimum including Saturday; three nights during the week. (Inquire about shorter periods, often available.) Other times, two-night minimum required. (Maximum group size is generally four or five people traveling together.)
RATES: Vary according to room size. Late June–late September and Christmas Stroll $130–$210; suite $250. Mid-May–mid-June, late September–late October, Thanksgiving weekend $75–$125 midweek, $95–$145 weekend. Off-season excluding Thanksgiving and Daffodil Weekend $65–$95 midweek, $85–$115 weekend. Singles $5 less. Third person $25. Amex, MC, Visa. ♥ ⌗ ⌿

Gourmet magazine and Swedish and German publications are among many that have raved about everything from the muffins to the decor and the hospitality at this B&B, which now has all private baths, skylights, two fireplaced sitting rooms, afternoon tea with home-baked goods, an English garden terrace—and an actor as host. Filled with family antiques, original art, botanical prints, Oriental rugs ("with an old look"), antique brass and pewter, and big bouquets of dried flowers, the house built in 1723 is as the hostess hoped it would be: "quintessential Nantucket, without the decorator effect." It features knowledgeable concierge service—"better than the Ritz," according to one well-traveled Irish business-man—for everything from dinner and theater reservations to historical walking tours.

It all started in 1980 when Sandy, a designer and restorer of eighteenth- and nineteenth-century buildings, was asked to "do up" a former five-room boardinghouse for selling. "I loved it so I kept it!" she says. British-born John, whom she met in Nantucket, brought country house and rose-growing (and Lloyd's of London) experience—plus acting talent that he didn't know he had. Since his early-1990s roles in Nantucket summer theater, he has appeared in Cole Porter's *Swell Party* at Long Wharf Theater in New Haven, Connecticut. The Corner House is "our home, lifestyle, and joy."

IN RESIDENCE: Summer staff is from England, Scotland, and/or New Zealand.
FOREIGN LANGUAGES SPOKEN: Some French and a little German.
BED AND BATH: Fifteen rooms with air-conditioner units (fan option). All private en-suite baths; some full, some shower without tub. In main house—eight rooms on three floors. Most with canopied or four-poster bed and TV. King, queen, double, and twin beds available. In reproduction house nearby—four rooms, each with canopied queen bed, refrigerator, small TV. In Rose Cottage—harborview suite and two rooms, each with canopied queen bed and TV.

continued . . .

BREAKFAST: 8:15–9:45. Fresh fruit. Homemade muffins, coffee cakes, granola. Bagels and cream cheese. Juices, coffee, cocoa, teas. Cold cereal. Special diets accommodated. Buffet style in keeping room.

PLUS: Two fireplaced sitting rooms. Screened porch with wicker and flowers, overlooking the garden terrace. Cable TV. Library with games, puzzles, books, current magazines. Down pillows and comforters. Beach towels. Bike racks. Afternoon tea (4–6 P.M.)

＊ The Pineapple Inn   508/228-9992

10 Hussey Street,   FAX 508/325-6051
Nantucket, MA 02554-3612   E-MAIL info@pineappleinn.com
                                                  www.pineappleinn.com

     HOSTS: Caroline and Bob Taylor
LOCATION: Residential. In historic area, "on a little one-way lane" just two minutes
              from shops, restaurants, historic places. Fifteen-minute walk to nearest
              beach. Four blocks from ferry.
     OPEN: May through October. Three-night minimum on holidays and
              July–September weekends.
     RATES: Vary according to room size. $160–$295 June–mid-September plus October
              weekends, Memorial Day weekend, and Christmas Stroll. Shoulder season
              $125–$210. Off-season $110–$180. Amex, MC, Visa. ♥ ⊞ ⚿ ⅙

ELEGANCE, COMFORT, pampering, and perfection were the Taylors' goals when they completely redid this Greek Revival, built for a whaling ship captain in 1838. Fine art, Oriental rugs, antiques, and Federal period reproductions compliment the architectural details. Within a year after the 1997 opening, this was *Travel & Leisure*'s "Inn of the Month." Food, too, is a feature—for good reason: For fifteen years the Taylors were Nantucket restaurateurs.

In California Bob was a Presbyterian minister; Caroline, a teacher who worked for an educational publishing company. After one vacation on Nantucket, they bought and operated the island's Quaker House restaurant and inn. After one vacation in New Zealand, they made that their off-season residence. Here, the Taylors, resident innkeepers, meet many guests who dream of being innkeepers. And at least one guest, a corporate executive who networked—with Caroline's encouragement—with another guest, is now with the fellow guest's corporation.

BED AND BATH: Twelve air-conditioned rooms on four levels. Each with handmade four-poster lace-canopied king or queen bed, private white marble bath (some shower only, others with tub and shower), individual thermostat, cable TV, phone with voice mail and computer access.
BREAKFAST: 8–10. Freshly squeezed orange juice. Fresh fruit plate. Cereals including Bircher Muesli (most requested recipe) and oatmeal with raisins. Their own "from

scratch" pastries—croissants, cinnamon rolls, ginger scones with a nutmeg cream, blue-berry crumb cake, nectarine and blueberry tarts, cheese and spinach tart with basil tomato salsa. Espresso drinks—cappuccinos, coffee lattes, double espresso. Served in formal dining room or at umbrella tables in garden patio with fountain.
PLUS: Gas fireplace in living room. Central air conditioning. Beach towels.

➳ Guests wrote: *"Felt welcomed and comfortable. Recommendations for eating, touring, and cruising allowed us to experience many of the island's treasures in a short period of time. . . . Breakfast was heavenly. . . . Perfect environment for relaxing."*

➳ *Seven Sea Street* 3 ——— 195 ③   508/228-3577

7 Sea Street,   FAX 508/228-3578
Nantucket, MA 02554-3545   E-MAIL seast7@nantucket.net
                 www.nantucket.net/lodging/seast7/

HOSTS: Matthew and Mary Parker
LOCATION: On a quiet, shady side street in historic district. Two-minute walk to Harbor Beach and Steamship Wharf, five to Main Street and Nantucket Whaling Museum.
OPEN: Year round. Two-night minimum on April–October weekends, three nights on holiday weekends.
RATES: January–mid-April $75–$95 room, $145–$175 suite. Late May–late June and early fall $125–$165, $215–$245 suite. Late June–Labor Day and Christmas Stroll weekend $165–$215, $265–$295 suite. Mid-October–December $95–$135, $125–$205 suite. Columbus Day–late June, discounts for week-long stays or Sunday–Thursday three-day stays. Rollaway or crib $15. Amex, Discover, MC, Visa. ♥ ⚸ ⚼ ♨

➳ From Connecticut: *"A cozy inn . . . saw to guests' every need . . . warm hospitality . . . now we'll think of the inn as our home away from home in Nantucket."*

As MATT SAYS, "In cool weather, guests walk on the beach, use our Jacuzzi, play cribbage, and read by the fire. This year-round inn with a widow's walk, canopied beds, braided rugs, and local art is the realization of my childhood dream." Built in 1987, the year the Parkers were married, it's an early American–style post-and-beam Colonial with Scandinavian features (lots of natural wood).

Matt grew up in Rhode Island, vacationed on Nantucket, earned a BS in management engineering, and then joined his father in developing Nantucket real estate and designing Seven Sea Street. He met Mary when she was selling advertising for a publication that has become a quarterly magazine, *Nantucket Magazine,* originally published by the Parkers—who are now parents of three. Seven Sea Street was Matt's project from groundbreaking to working with the crew to assembling all the reproduction furnishings. Now, as

continued . . .

co-innkeeper, he finds that guests enjoy cultural activities, art galleries, restaurants—and the suggestion of a secluded beach with moorland views.

IN RESIDENCE: One assistant innkeeper. "Puddy is our discreet, lovable tabby."
FOREIGN LANGUAGE SPOKEN: French.
BED AND BATH: Eleven air-conditioned rooms including two two-room suites (with gas fireplace); most with fishnet-canopied queen bed, cable TV (in armoires), sink, private phone, and desk. All private baths with tiled bath floors and two-seat shower stalls. Rollaway and cribs available.
BREAKFAST: 8–10. Home-baked muffins. Bagels and coffee cake. Granola. Fresh fruit salad. Juice, coffee, tea, milk. Buffet style in fireplaced breakfast room. Or served in bed, if you'd like.
PLUS: Panoramic harbor views from widow's walk. Two common rooms with woodstoves, without TV. Individual thermostats. Guest refrigerators. Terry-cloth robes for Jacuzzi spa. Beach towels. Wall-mounted hair dryers. Bottomless cookie jar. Leather-bound classics in library.

☞ *Stumble Inne*

        508/228-4482

109 Orange Street,
Nantucket, MA 02554

FAX 508/228-4752
E-MAIL romance@nantucket.net
www.stumbleinne.com

HOSTS: Jeanne and George Todor
LOCATION: Ten-minute walk to island's Main Street and historic downtown. Twenty minutes to/from ferry. Five-minute walk to several gourmet restaurants. Steps to shuttle.
OPEN: Year round. Mid-June–mid-September, Memorial Day and fall weekends, three-night minimum in inn, four nights in garden cottage.
RATES: Mid-June–mid-September, Memorial Day, and fall weekends $160–$250. Garden cottage $350. Mid-May–mid-June, mid-September–mid-October and special event weekends $100–$185, cottage $250. Off-season $75–$145, Cottage $190. Additional person $30. Amex, MC, Visa. ♥ ⊞ ⌀ ⌁

"THE PERFECT PLACE at the perfect time," say the Todors, who were first "enchanted by Nantucket" in 1990. Then Jeanne went to college—at the same time their son attended. Her Bucks County, Pennsylvania, career path involved real estate, banking, and academia. Most recently she was assistant manager of a Nantucket inn! Since acquiring this well-established B&B in 1999, the couple has carried on the tradition of "Nantucket's friendliest inn." George, who for several months continued his job as national sales manager for a textile company, is now a very happy full-time co-innkeeper.

The 1704 house, destroyed by fire and rebuilt in the early 1800s in Greek Revival style, features random-width pine floors, Colonial colors, antiques and reproductions, and the

Todor/Nantucket style of light and airy—with four-poster and canopied beds, wicker, and crisp linens.

BED AND BATH: *Main inn*—seven rooms. All with refrigerator and TV; most have VCR. Six with private bath (some tub and shower, others shower only). Air conditioning in all queen rooms, the suite, and cottage. On first floor, canopied queen bed, shower bath, TV/VCR, ceiling fan. Two-room suite with queen bed (and ceiling fan) in one, trundle bed in other, connecting bath. Up narrow winding staircase to second-floor rooms with queen beds. One with a double bed has bath at bottom of stairs or can be booked with a queen room. Plus—rear *garden cottage* with king bed in one room, two twin beds in another, one bath, living room with ceiling fan and deck, TV/VCR, phone, fully equipped kitchen.

BREAKFAST: At 9; coffee at 7:30. Off-season, at 8. Fresh fruit. Juices. Homemade muffins, breads, coffee cakes, granola. Cereals. Portuguese bread for toasting. Hot beverages. Buffet style in fireplaced dining room.

PLUS: Fireplaced living room. Beach towels. Fresh fruit. Coffee available all day. Fresh flowers.

Queen- 120

🕊 *Union Street Inn*

508/228-9222

7 Union Street,
Nantucket, MA 02554

800/225-5116
FAX 508/325-0848
E-MAIL unioninn@nantucket.net
www.union-street-inn.com

HOSTS: Ken and Debbie Withrow
LOCATION: In historic district with patio that overlooks "Stone Alley," a historic cobble-stoned walkway. Two blocks from harbor (and ferry). One block to Main Street. Walk to everything—restaurants, shops, galleries, museums, bicycle rental, beaches (¾ of a mile to Nantucket Sound, 3 miles to Atlantic Ocean).
OPEN: February–December.
RATES: Late May–October $275 suite; $250 king with fireplace; $210 queen or twins, $225 with fireplace; $145–$180 double bed. Late April–late May $50 less. November–late April $70–$75 less. Amex, MC, Visa. ♥ ⚫ ⚫

TRADITIONAL NANTUCKET C. 1770 architecture with twelve-over-twelve windows. With wood-burning fireplaces, some floor-to-ceiling pine and painted paneling, and refinished wide-board floors. With antiques and reproductions, fresh décor, and traditional fabrics. An inn since the early 1920s, it was completely restored (all new plumbing and wiring and then some) in the early 1990s. The commercial kitchen—most unusual for a Nantucket B&B—allows the Withrows to serve hot breakfast entrées.

This host family knows the art of hospitality. They arrived here in 1995 after Ken had worked in the hotel business for twenty years. He managed several properties, including

continued . . .

the United Nations Plaza Hotel in New York and the Sutton Place in Chicago. During transfers that occurred about every three years, Deb worked in retail display with Henri Bendel, Fiorucci, Wempe, and Crate & Barrel. "When Kevin was born, we thought about a lifestyle change. B&B was the perfect fit. Nantucket was the icing on the cake. Many guests seem to be fascinated with year-round island living—and the fact that we have an elementary, a middle, and a high school. And we're happy to share 'discoveries' that can be made on foot, by bicycle, on an antique-carriage ride, or maybe with a picnic at a secluded, rather magical place."

IN RESIDENCE: Son, Kevin, age eleven. "Sparky is our bull terrier."
BED AND BATH: Twelve air-conditioned rooms (six with working fireplace) on first and second floors; all with private shower baths (two are tub/shower combination) and cable TV. Beds—some are four-posters or canopied—are king, king/twins option, queen, or double. Connecting rooms available.
BREAKFAST: 8:30–10 June–October; 8:30–9:30 off-season. French toast made with challah bread topped with fresh berries, powdered sugar, Vermont maple syrup, and sausage links; scrambled eggs with fresh dill and chives, bacon, freshly baked croissants; or pancakes—blueberry or apple-cinnamon—with Vermont maple syrup and bacon. Plus buffet: granola, cereals, fresh fruit, yogurts, orange juice, coffee and teas. Served in dining area (with kitchen in view) furnished with antique Colonial tables and chairs, or in a spacious, shaded (tall trees), and oh-so-serene brick garden patio—the kind of place where you could spend all morning with the paper or a good book.
PLUS: Guest refrigerator. Fresh fruit and flowers.

   Guests wrote: "Beautiful inn and scrumptious breakfasts. . . . Inn is delightful. Innkeepers' personalities make it extraordinary."

BED AND BREAKFAST IS THE HOTTEST TREND IN AMERICAN TRAVEL.

SOUTHEASTERN MASSACHUSETTS
RESERVATION SERVICES

THE FOLLOWING RESERVATION SERVICES REPRESENT SOME B&BS IN SOUTHEASTERN MASSACHUSETTS:
Bed and Breakfast Associates Bay Colony, Ltd., page 230
Host Homes of Boston, page 232

🦅 Zachariah Eddy House Bed & Breakfast   508/946-0016

51 South Main Street,   FAX 508/947-2603
Middleborough, MA 02346   E-MAIL zacheddy@aol.com
                                       www.bbhost.com/zacheddyhouse

HOSTS: Bradford and Cheryl Leonard

LOCATION: In historic district that is listed on the National Register. Next door to town hall (1873). Across from Barrows Mansion (1880), several antiques shops, and historic churches. Two blocks to museums and shops. Near cranberry bog tours and working farms. About 35 miles from Boston or Providence, 15 to Plymouth, 18 to Cape Cod Canal; 1 mile from I-495.

OPEN: Year round. Two-night minimum on weekends July–October and on holidays.

RATES: June 1–October 31 $85–$135. November 1–May 31 $69–$95. Vary according to events and private or shared bath (based on availability). Off-season only, $65 single. Additional person $10. Amex, Discover, MC, Visa.

♥ 👫 ⊞ ❖ 🛇 ⚲ 🐾

OPPORTUNITY knocks here. Often, guests are invited to accompany the Leonards on their lobstering, clamming, or saltwater fishing expeditions (twenty minutes away). Whether or not you go, the catch of the day (or evening) is likely to be featured in the elaborate and substantial morning meal.

The Leonards raised four children in this Greek/Colonial Revival house. When they converted it to a bed and breakfast in 1995, they decorated with antiques and reproductions. Light and airy, it has parquet floors, nooks and crannies, alcoves, window seats, and a "chapel bath" with stained glass oriel window. During an open house more than 500 people came to see the transformation of the local landmark.

Know somebody in Middleborough? Invite them to join you for coffee and muffins. What to do? Consult the hosts' list of "101 Things to Do." If you're an early riser and eat at the local diner, you'll be fined! (Great story behind that one.) Well-known musicians and public figures stay here. So do many foreigners, who are delighted with the idea of staying with hosts who are very involved in their community. Before becoming a full-time innkeeper, Cheryl had a cake and pastry business. Brad, the gardener, works in Boston in the state's Department of Social Services.

FOREIGN LANGUAGE SPOKEN: Very minimal French.

BED AND BATH: Three second-floor rooms with air conditioning, cable TV, HBO and Showtime. Two baths (one tub/shower; one with shower only has chapel theme, parquet flooring) are shared or private based on availability. One room with queen brass bed, oversized windows, half-turret vaulted ceiling, window seat, ceiling fan; room with two four-poster twins (or king bed—additional charge), ceiling fan; quietest room, with Victorian double bed, can be converted into minisuite with private bath.

BREAKFAST: 8–10. (By request, coffee and muffins earlier.) Fresh fruit plate, melon with orange cream and granola, French breakfast puff with strawberries and kiwi. Lobster quiche or omelet, clam—"actually, it's quahog"—chowder, breakfast pizza, baked apple pancake, or bread pudding with amaretto sauce. Home-baked breads and muffins. Served in formal dining room on crystal and china, on porch, or on sundeck overlooking historic buildings.

PLUS: Wood-burning fireplace and VCR in living room. Robes. Spontaneous treats. Horseshoes. Stereoscope collection. Racquets for use at nearby tennis courts. Loan of bicycles. One mile to commuter rail service to Boston (transportation provided with prior arrangement). Antique gramophone (Victrola) collection.

> From Cyprus: *"Even now, months later, we still relive those special few days. I should mention that we are British, and not usually given to effusiveness! Cheryl e-mailed us at length with suggestions. Nothing was too much trouble. We were even able to plan a special birthday dinner (lobsters wall to wall!) for our daughter, months ahead of time. She met us at the railroad station, took us to collect our hire car . . . house is even more charming and interesting than we had anticipated. Care and attention to detail are outstanding, as is the quality of the delicious food . . . invited to join them to pull lobsters from their own pots . . . left with tears in our eyes and long to return."* From Texas: *"Set a high standard for future B&B experiences."* From Massachusetts: *"Enhanced our twenty-fifth anniversary."*

Edgewater/Harborview Bed & Breakfast   508/997-5512

2 Oxford Street,
Fairhaven, MA 02719–3310

FAX 508/997-5784
E-MAIL kprof@aol.com
www.rixsan.com/edgewater

HOST: Kathy Reed

LOCATION: On the water, with 250-foot-long seawall, facing New Bedford harbor. In a quiet residential neighborhood of Fairhaven, a town with architectural gems that include a high school with Tiffany windows and Italian marble floors. Ten minutes to the New Bedford National Park with its Whaling Museum and historic district. Five minutes from I-195; fifteen to Tabor Academy, UMass, Dartmouth, Martha's Vineyard and Cuttyhunk ferries, and outlets; seventy-five to Boston. Within forty-five minutes of Plymouth, Massachusetts; Newport, Rhode Island; and Cape Cod.

OPEN: Year round. Two-night minimum on some holidays.

continued . . .

RATES: $80 first-floor rooms (queen bed). $90 canopied bed. $115 or $125 suite. Singles $10 less. Each extra person $20. Amex, Discover, MC, Visa. ♥ ⊞ ❖ ⚔ ⅄ ⚓

↝ From Massachusetts: "*Out of a fairy tale . . . decorated to soothe rather than astonish . . . perfect setting. . . . Our daughters made us promise that we would visit in winter and enjoy the fireplace and the view of water edged by snow.*" From Texas: *"A tub with a view! . . . Restful."*

"ABOARD SHIP" is the feeling you have from the dining and living room river views. When the lights are twinkling over the harbor, it's romantic. For all of these reasons, Edgewater made a *Boston* magazine "best" list.

The idea of living in a historic home and having a B&B had always appealed to Kathy, a college professor. This one was built in the 1760s by Elnathan Eldridge as his store and home when he was involved in shipbuilding and the East Indies trade. Kathy's home— since 1983—combines a more formal Victorian part with a Colonial section. Guest rooms vary and include "a suite, often chosen by honeymooners, that would befit a sea captain." One room that is reminiscent of a seaside cottage is the "real New England" for many visitors.

IN RESIDENCE: "Sadie, an adorable black-and-white fluffy dog."
BED AND BATH: Three rooms plus two waterview suites, each with a story behind the name; all with private bath and cable color TV. First floor—queen bed, tub and hand-held shower. Queen bed, shower bath, private exterior entrance. Second floor—canopied double bed, claw-foot tub, hand-held shower. Two suites with working fireplace and bay window seat; one with king bed and full bath, other with queen bed, kitchenette, shower bath, private exterior entrance.
BREAKFAST: Usually 8–9:30. Homemade muffins, toasted Portuguese sweet bread, cereal. Fruit, juice, jams; butter shaped into daisies, swans, roses.
PLUS: Spacious lawns bordering water. Menus from all local restaurants.

TO TIP OR NOT? (PLEASE TURN TO PAGE IX.)

🐾 *1810 House Bed & Breakfast*

781/659–1810

147 Old Oaken Bucket Road,
Norwell, MA 02061

888/833-1810
E-MAIL tuttle1810@aol.com

HOSTS: Susanne and Harold Tuttle
LOCATION: Residential. Five-minute drive to ocean or to three excellent restaurants. Near antiques shops, Routes 3 and 3A; 20 miles south of Boston.
OPEN: Year round. Two-night minimum April–October weekends and holidays. Year round, $10 surcharge for single night.
RATES: $75–$95. ♥ ▣ ❖ ⚔ ⚒

🐾 From Oklahoma, California, Illinois, Pennsylvania: *"A wonderful historic home that they obviously enjoy sharing. . . . Gorgeous original floors . . . lovely room . . . conversation was as enjoyable a feast as the food . . . took us on a tour of the bay . . . gave us good advice (we are starting a B&B) . . . good sightseeing tips . . . a treasure . . . filled with antiques and personal touches. . . . I'm an inn owner myself. . . . A-plus in warmth and hospitality . . . beautifully decorated. . . . Home-away-from-home atmosphere. . . . Warm, hospitable, very helpful hosts . . . most comfortable bed I've slept in while traveling."*

WEDDING GUESTS are among the travelers who discover that this B&B is a great place from which to explore the south shore. The house, featured on holiday tours and in *Country* magazine, has Colonial decor, antiques (thirty-five years of collections), stenciling, hand-crocheted bedspreads, and Oriental rugs. Originally a full Cape, it was cut in half at the turn of the century. Additions were made in the 1970s.

Harold, who recently retired from industrial sales, is a woodworker and antique car buff. He and Susanne, a dental hygienist, have been hosting since 1986. "If time and weather permit, we take our guests in Harold's restored 1915 Model T depot hack along the nearby Cohasset and Hingham coast. A gorgeous route!" (It is.)

BED AND BATH: Three air-conditioned rooms. Second floor (with individual thermostats)—queen bed, private modern full bath; can be shared arrangement for same party that books other second-floor room with king/twins option. First floor—canopied queen, en-suite full bath, individual thermostat, ceiling fan.
BREAKFAST: 7:30–9. Omelets with local farm eggs, waffles, pancakes, quiche, homemade bread and muffins, fresh fruit, juice, coffee. Served in fireplaced kitchen or on screened porch.
PLUS: Large fireplaced family room with spinet piano, TV, VCR. Evening beverage. Down comforters. Fresh flowers.

≈ Plymouth Bay Manor Bed & Breakfast

508/830-0426

259 Court Street,
Plymouth, MA 02360

800/492-1828
FAX 508/747-3382
E-MAIL info@plymouthbaymanor.com
www.plymouthbaymanor.com

HOSTS: Larry and Cindi Hamlin

LOCATION: On an acre of lawns and gardens with panoramic views of bay and ocean. In a neighborhood of Victorian and Colonial homes. Five-minute walk via rear garden to quiet beach. One mile to town center with Plymouth Rock and *Mayflower II*.

OPEN: Year round.

RATES: $85, $95, $110. Third person $20. MC, Visa. ♥ ☕ ⊞ ⚉ ✁

A LUMBER BARON built this shingled Colonial Revival house at the turn of the century. From the large windows he could see three-masted ships come into port. Light and airy, with a grand interior staircase and a foyer as wide as the house, it was restored in the 1960s and again in the early 1990s. After the Hamlins bought it in 1996, in two weeks (!) they decorated "from scratch," furnished with antiques and Oriental rugs, and opened for the season. In Hollywood, Larry, now the official B&B chef, made and managed special-effects makeup for film. Cindi, a graphic and fine artist (and gardener), taught fine arts at the high school level. They traveled coastal New England for five years before finding their dream house, where "the gardens and lawn are set against the sea, a backdrop of changing color and delight."

IN RESIDENCE: In hosts' quarters—one chow/shar pei dog and two Siamese cats.

BED AND BATH: Three second-floor oceanview rooms with sitting area and desk. All private baths. One 25-by-18-foot room with English pine four-poster king/twins option, shower bath, wood-burning fireplace. Two with queen bed (one with wood-burning fireplace); one with claw-foot tub/shower bath, one with shower bath.

BREAKFAST: 8–8:30. Juice. Fresh fruit with garden mint garnish. Apple-stuffed French toast topped with sautéed apples, cinnamon, and almonds; scrambled eggs with bacon or sausage. Muffin repertoire includes blueberry almond, cranberry cinnamon, pumpkin ginger. (Special diets accommodated.) Served at tables for two set with crystal, silver, antique bone china, and cloth napkins in second-floor sunroom overlooking the bay, lighthouses, and islands.

PLUS: Central air conditioning. Late-afternoon and evening tea and cookies. Hair dryers in rooms.

Remembrance Bed & Breakfast Home   508/746-5160

265 Sandwich Street, Plymouth, MA 02360-2182

HOST: Beverly Bainbridge

LOCATION: Residential. One mile from historic Plymouth, Plimoth Plantation, and Route 3; a little more to beach. Five-minute walk to ocean (walking area). Five-minute drive to commuter rail to Boston. Twenty-minute drive to Cape Cod, one hour to Boston.

OPEN: Year round. Two nights appreciated on major holidays.

RATES: $70 shared bath, $85 with guaranteed private bath. $60 single. Room with one twin bed ($15 child, $20 adult) in conjunction with another room.

♥ ☛ ⊞ ❖ ⚏ ⚲

From Connecticut, Oregon, North Carolina, Ohio, Georgia, Massachusetts, Nova Scotia, England, and Scotland: *"Aptly named. . . . Definitely a spread-the-good-word place. . . . Felt as if we were visiting an old friend. . . . Immaculate . . . well-stocked library . . . breakfasts enticing to the palate and eye . . . a treasure. . . . Met me at bus station, showed me around Plymouth. . . . Charmed as soon as we entered the kitchen . . . each room cozy and welcoming . . . each morning woken by sound of birds . . . took lemon bread recipe home . . . enjoyed homemade raspberry sauce with French toast. . . . If only I had known how nice it was, would have planned to stay more than one night. . . . Remembrance is a harbor in a tempest . . . a jewel. . . . Beverly is a warm, lovely, caring person. . . . The high-light of our vacation and the best thing in Plymouth!" . . . Shared painting tips with me. . . . Aptly named."* (All echoed by many more, year after year.)

BEVERLY HAS experience as mother to two, grandma, art teacher, department store display designer, herb lady and open hearth cook at Plimoth Plantation, picture framer, and now as a calligrapher working at home. Her handmade gifts have sold in museum gift shops. (Some are now available in the Corner Cupboard Gift Shop in the sitting room here.) A sense of display, color, and style—with wicker, antiques, original art, faux finishes, fabrics, plants, and flowers—is everywhere in the 1920s center chimney cedar-shingled Cape-style house. One Boston-based interior designer commented that it was the prettiest B&B he had ever seen. It is lovely.

IN RESIDENCE: Two friendly and gentle indoor cats, Pandora and Morgan.

BED AND BATH: Three second-floor rooms with sloping ceilings. When private bath not guaranteed with one room, all rooms share one full bath and a downstairs half bath. Two rooms have antique brass double bed, air conditioning. For a single traveling with others—an antique white iron twin bedstead.

BREAKFAST: At guests' convenience. Repertoire includes fresh fruit; apple crisp; home-made muffins, breads, and scones; French toast with a variety of toppings; feather-bed eggs; crepes; blintzes; cereal; teas and freshly ground gourmet coffee. Special diets accom-modated. Served at Victorian ice-cream table in greenhouse—"British guests call it a

continued . . .

conservatory"—overlooking gardens, squirrels and chipmunks, bird feeders, and bird-houses and birdbaths, all flanked by old drystone wall.

PLUS: Fireplaced living room. Ironed linens. Down comforters. VCR, films, music, books, magazines, newspaper. Beach towels. Tea with shortbread or cookies. Topiary collection.

≈ Perryville Inn

508/252-9239

157 Perryville Road,
Rehoboth, MA 02769

800/439–9239
FAX 508/252-9054
E-MAIL pvinn@hotmail.com
www.perryvilleinn.com

HOSTS: Betsy and Tom Charnecki
LOCATION: Quiet. In rural community 7 miles east of Providence; 20 minutes to Wheaton College in Norton or Brown University and Rhode Island School of Design in Providence, R.I. Within an hour of Boston, Plymouth, Newport (R.I.) and Mystic (Conn.). Across from an eighteen-hole golf course open to the public. Near antiques shops.
OPEN: Year round. Minimum two-night stay on summer and fall weekends. "Reservations not required, but please call first."
RATES: $75–$105 private bath. $10 third person. Amex, Discover, MC, Visa.
♥ ♦ ⌗ ❖ ♠ ♣ ♫

≈ From Massachusetts: *"Perfect everything.... Lovely people and place ... good food beautifully presented ... peaceful ambiance.... Would love this as a getaway about once a month!"*

BRASS, OAK, and canopied beds. (Locally) refinished and reupholstered antiques. Locally handmade quilts. A huge, wonderful kitchen complete with potbellied stove. Immaculate housekeeping combined with comfortable country charm and family hospitality. All in a farmhouse—now on the National Register of Historic Places—that was built (two floors) in the 1820s and in 1897 (the bottom floor!). It was restored by the Charneckis in 1984, when they moved from Colorado for the small-community lifestyle here in Tom's child-hood hometown. Now the children are grown and gone. Wedding guests appreciate this B&B. So do lots of first-time B&B travelers, visitors to area colleges, businesspeople, and my neighbors. For their impressions (and fascinating reading), check out the Secret Drawer Society diaries in the night tables.

IN RESIDENCE: One cat named Junior (outside cat).
BED AND BATH: Four air-conditioned rooms, all with private baths, on two floors. King/twins option, queen, or double bed. One room has both a queen and a double bed. Cot and crib available.

BREAKFAST: Usually 8–10. Freshly squeezed orange juice, seasonal fruit, croissants, home-made bread, muffins and sticky buns. Special diets accommodated. Served in dining room or, weather permitting, on screened porch.

PLUS: Central air conditioning. First-floor sitting room with piano. Second-floor sitting/game room. Six acres of wooded grounds with trout stream. Access to additional 30 acres with ponds and old mill site. Within minutes, clambakes, hay and sleigh rides, and even champagne (after landing) hot-air balloon rides; all by arrangement.

⚓ The Allen House

781/545-8221

18 Allen Place,
Scituate, MA 02066-1302

FAX 781/545-8221
E-MAIL allenhousebnb@worldnet.att.net
www.allenhousebnb.com

HOSTS: Tom Fiske (resident innkeeper) and Meredith Emmons

LOCATION: On a hill overlooking harbor of this "wonderful, quiet, very New England town." Two-minute walk to everything—shops, restaurants, commuter bus to Boston (30 miles). Ten miles to Hingham for commuter boat to Boston; 35 to Cape Cod Canal.

OPEN: Year round.

RATES: May–October (plus holidays and vacation periods year round): Sunday–Thursday $109, $129, $139. Suite $159. $30–$40 more per night for two-night (Friday and Saturday) weekends. Single Friday of Saturday night $159, $179, $199, $219. November–April: Sunday–Thursday $69, $89, $99. Suite $119. Two-night weekends $10 more per night, suite $139. Single weekend night $99, $119, $129, suiter $159. Amex, Discover, MC, Visa.
♥ ⊞ ❖ ⚄ ⚒ 桃

NANTUCKET GETS the credit for inspiring Tom to open a B&B. Shortly after returning to the mainland, he saw an ad for the well-established Allen House, a welcoming 1905 Colonial Revival home. "After all my years as a director in a local gallery, and all Meredith's years of traveling the world over, we agreed (instantly) that this was 'it'—in an oceanside community with great restaurants, a movie theater, and plenty of antiques shops. By the time your book is published, we'll have completed the redecoration—with soothing light green, violet, yellow, and blue, for a summery feeling." The gas fireplaces give instant ambiance. All the furnishings are new Arts and Crafts reproductions, including lots of comfortable overstuffed seating. Tom's art collection is throughout. There are water views. The ocean breezes blow. Beaches are nearby. It's a haven for getaways, for tourists, and for many wedding guests too.

BED AND BATH: Six rooms, all private en-suite shower baths. Four second-floor rooms (two with ocean view) with queen or double bed. Garden suite with private exterior

continued . . .

entrance—queen bed, gas fireplace, whirlpool bath for two, solarium, air conditioning. Handicapped-accessible air-conditioned room with king/twins option, double shower bath, ocean view.

BREAKFAST: 8–10. Expanded continental with homemade muffins and breads; hot entrées such as French toast and pancakes on weekends. In fireplaced dining room or on screened porch.

PLUS: Tea at 5 P.M. Turndown service. Guest refrigerator.

⌁ *Salt Marsh Farm Bed & Breakfast*   508/992-0980

322 Smith Neck Road,   **E-MAIL** saltmarshf@aol.com
South Dartmouth, MA 02748-1441

    HOSTS: Sally and Larry Brownell
  LOCATION: Serene. Just over a mile to beach. Three miles from scenic Padanaram harbor; fifteen minutes from I-195; New Bedford's National Park, Whaling Museum, and working waterfront; and Martha's Vineyard and Cuttyhunk ferries. Great biking area.
     OPEN: Year round. Two-night minimum on holidays and May–October weekends.
   RATES: Tax included. $85–$99 per room. Varies according to season. MC, Visa.

   ♥ ☞ ⌂ ⌇ ⚮

WHATEVER YOUR definition of "real New England" or your fantasy of a simple country lifestyle may be, it fits this B&B. A wonderful 200-year-old weathered-shingled Federal house on 90 acres. Rhode Island Red hens, an old-fashioned flower garden, fruits, vegetables, and trails through a nature preserve with woods, wetlands, salt meadows, and tidal marshes. Cozy bedrooms. "Hardly a straight line in the house." Wood-burning fireplace in the living room. Enough family antiques to arouse your curiosity for hours. Spectacular bouquets in every room (bathrooms, too). And much more—including an apron-wearing hostess who greeted us with clothes basket in hand. "I love to listen to the gulls while hanging out the sheets." And an enthusiastic, knowledgeable, sharing host, the organic gardener, a town meeting member who is active in local land conservation efforts. When not outdoors, Larry is apt to be found caning or rushing an antique chair.

Before the Brownells, descendants of Plymouth colonist John Smith and parents of four grown children, returned to the family homestead in 1987, they lived in the Philadelphia area. There Larry was a banker and fund-raiser; Sally, a librarian. "We hosted so many out-of-town visitors that B&B here just seems natural." Although Salt Marsh Farm has but two guest rooms, it has appeared along with well-known upscale places in the *New York Times* and other major media's "recommended accommodations" lists.

IN RESIDENCE: Two cats. Lady Jane is long-haired; George's hair is short.

BED AND BATH: Two rooms, each with private bath, hall, and stairway. One room has two twin four-poster beds, bath with large old-fashioned tub. Second room—choice of one double bed or two twin four-poster beds; full bath.

BREAKFAST: Full 8–9, continental after 9. Earlier by request. Freshly squeezed juice. Prizewinning muffins and scones. Organic homegrown seasonal fruits and berries. Entrée repertoire includes French toast with special sauce; waffles (heart-shaped for honeymooners) that were pictured (Sally was, too) in a *Country Living Country Cooking* feature; pancakes; homemade granola; farm-fresh eggs prepared in a variety of ways. Special diets accommodated.

PLUS: Afternoon beverages. Beach towels and chairs. Three-speed and tandem bikes. Back-roads map with custom-highlighted "must-see" places. Forgotten necessities. Books everywhere.

✈ From New York, New Jersey, Connecticut, Oklahoma, California, Massachusetts: *"[Hosts] are veritable history books about the area. . . . For first time, could imagine myself, a city mouse, converting to country for good. . . . The most hospitable, relaxing, and just plain wonderful B&B. . . . Breakfast is a feast . . . delightful details . . . perfect blend of charm and comfort . . . impressive four-star B&B . . . a piece of heaven and history . . . . We've traveled the world over and have put the Salt Marsh, the Brownells, and this area on our 'must return' list."*

B ED AND BREAKFAST GIVES A SENSE OF PLACE.

☞ *Mulberry Bed and Breakfast*　　　　508/295-0684

257 High Street, Wareham, MA 02571-1407　　　　FAX 508/291-2909

HOST: Frances A. Murphy

LOCATION: Residential. On one-third acre. Next door to church. Across from house with orchard and illuminated fountain. Ten-minute walk to village. Five miles to local public beaches. Six miles to bridge over Cape Cod Canal. Fifty miles from Boston; 18 west of Plymouth.

OPEN: Year round.

RATES: June–September $60 double bed or twins, $70 king; singles $55. October–May $55 double or twins, $65 king; singles $50. Third person in room $10. Amex, Discover, MC, Visa. 👬 ♟ ❖ ✄

"THIS CAPE COD–style house was built for a blacksmith in 1847. My grandfather used it as a store before my parents made it their home when I was ten years old. All the furnishings have family-related stories. I make all my own jams—some with fruit from the unusual seven-trunk mulberry tree, which has had as much care as the house. . . . I started B&B in the traditional home-away-from-home style in the 1980s, when I was still teaching. My guests include tourists, Elderhostelers, international travelers, families, and people coming for events. Sometimes breakfast can last for hours!"

IN RESIDENCE: "Two guest-loving cats. Tinsel is gray with tinsel-colored fur tips and double paws. Smoky has beautiful green eyes."

BED AND BATH: Three rooms on two floors. First floor—room with double bed, fireplace with electric log, and phone shares shower bath with owner. Second-floor rooms, each with TV—one with king/twins option, other with double bed—share a bath with small tub (and a first-floor shower).

BREAKFAST: 7-9. Casseroles, French toast, pancakes. Homemade breads. Homemade jams—mulberry, strawberry, blackberry, grape, beach plum, crabapple—and pumpkin butter. Served at kitchen table or on deck that overlooks the mulberry tree "and a quiet churchyard!"

PLUS: Gas fireplace in living room. Spinet piano in music room. Pillow treats in local seashells.

Aᴸᴸ ᴛʜᴇ B&Bs with this ♟ symbol want you to know that they are a private home set up for paying guests (rather than an inn). Although definitions vary, these private home B&Bs tend to have one to three guest rooms. For the owners—people who enjoy meeting people—B&B is usually a part-time occupation.

☞ A Bed & Breakfast Agency of Boston (and Boston Harbor B&B)

47 Commercial Wharf, Boston, MA 02110-3801

PHONE: 617/720-3540 or (U.S. and Canada) 800/CITYBND (248-9262), 9 A.M.–9 P.M. daily. Free from United Kingdom: 0800-89-5128.
FAX: 617/523-5761
E-MAIL: bosbnb@aol
URL: www.boston-bnbagency.com
LISTINGS: One hundred forty-five. Most are located in downtown Boston—on the historic waterfront (a few on boats, many with harbor views from 1840 lofts as well as new buildings); in Faneuil Hall/North End areas of the Freedom Trail; in Back Bay, Beacon Hill, Copley Square, and the South End. All are private air-conditioned residences near public rapid transportation. Most are hosted B&Bs, but in addition there are a wide variety of unhosted studios and one- and two-bedroom condominiums (nightly, weekly, monthly).
RESERVATIONS: Last-minute callers accommodated. Two-night minimum preferred.
RATES: $65–$90 single, $70–$140 double. Weekly rates available. "Winter special," November 15–February, three nights for the price of two (based on availability). Booking fee: $10 per reservation. Nonrefundable deposit of 30 percent of entire cost of booking required. For cancellations made less than ten days before expected arrival, entire deposit forfeited. Amex, MC, Visa. ❖

FERNE MINTZ, an experienced host (whose lively beagle, Ferney, is on many guests' Christmas card lists), features placements with "hosts who put you in close touch with the city." Before starting the reservation service, Ferne did public relations, advertising, and special events. Her offerings include some 40-foot cabin cruisers with sundeck, TV, air conditioning, and galley kitchens. "And one architecturally designed houseboat is very popular."

PLUS: Tours arranged. Short-term (one week to six months) hosted and unhosted downtown housing available.

↝ Bed and Breakfast Associates Bay Colony, Ltd.

P.O. Box 57166, Babson Park, Boston, MA 02457-0166

> **PHONE:** 781/449–5302 or (U.S. and Canada) 800/347-5088. Monday–Friday, 9:30–5. Answering machine at other times. Closed Christmas week.
> **FAX:** 781/449–5958
> **E-MAIL:** info@bnbboston.com
> **URL:** www.bnbboston.com
> **LISTINGS:** One hundred fifty. Mostly historic properties—hosted private residences, guest apartments, and some small inns. Many are in downtown Boston—in Back Bay, Beacon Hill, South End, waterfront, and Copley Square areas—and Charlestown. A large number of private residences are in adjacent Cambridge and Brookline. Others are in a total of thirty-five eastern Massachusetts communities, extending to coastal towns on the north and south shores and including many on Cape Cod, Martha's Vineyard, and Nantucket. Descriptive listings on Web site or (free) by mail.
> **RESERVATIONS:** Most hosts require a two-night minimum stay, May–October. "We try to accommodate last-minute callers but prefer at least a week's notice." Available through travel agents, but service prefers direct contact with guests.
> **RATES:** $65–$125 single, $75–$175 double. (Suburbs tend to be less expensive than Boston.) Family and weekly rates available. Some homes offer the seventh night free and reduced winter rates. $20 agency service fee per booking. Thirty percent of total is required as a deposit. Full advance payment required on one-night stays and on special event weekends. Deposit minus $35 processing fee refunded on cancellations received at least fourteen days prior to arrival. Amex, MC, Visa. ❖

ARLINE KARDASIS and Marilyn Mitchell focus on minute details that even the experienced traveler may not think of. While maintaining high standards, they offer wide variety—"unforgettable luxury as well as basic comfort and convenience at a modest rate." Hosts, including those who have been with Bay Colony since it started in 1981, often speak of the professional, personal, and efficient service that the agency performs. Guests make note of "friendly, helpful, above-and-beyond service . . . treated as a real individual rather than just another statistic."

This reservation service is one of the founding members of Bed & Breakfast—The National Network (B&Bs throughout the United States, Canada, and United Kingdom).

PLUS: For short-term stays (one week to several months), there are house-sharing opportunities as well as unhosted apartments.

⚶ *Bed & Breakfast Reservations*
North Shore/Greater Boston/Cape Cod

P.O. Box 600035, Greater Boston Branch, Newtonville, MA 02460-0035

PHONE: 617/964-1606. Outside Massachusetts—800/832-2632 (in U.S. and
Canada). Monday–Friday 9–5 year round. Voice mail at other times.

FAX: 617/332-8572

E-MAIL: info@bbreserve.com

URL: www.bbreserve.com

LISTINGS: Eighty-eight. Many are within fifteen minutes of Boston and Logan
Airport—in oceanside towns and historic homes, convenient to colleges,
universities, and business areas.

Boston: Back Bay, Beacon Hill, Copley Square, Fenway, South End, and
waterfront—on a boat too. Just outside of Boston: in Arlington,
Brookline, Cambridge, Chestnut Hill, Newton, and farther west in
Concord, Sturbridge, and Woburn.

Cape Cod: Barnstable, Dennis, South Dennis, Dennis Port, Eastham,
Falmouth, Harwichport, West Harwich, Hyannis Port, Sandwich,
Yarmouth, Yarmouth Port.

North shore (Massachusetts): Cape Ann, including Gloucester,
Rockport, Essex; Beverly and Beverly Farms, Boxford, Hamilton,
Ipswich, Marblehead, Middleton, Newburyport, Salem.

Maine: Boothbay Harbor and Portland.

New Hampshire: East Andover in Sunapee Lake region; Londonderry.

Vermont: St. Johnsbury.

RESERVATIONS: Advance notice preferred; last-minute bookings are possible. Two-night
minimum May through October; three nights on holidays.

RATES: $65–$200 single. $75–$250 double. Family, weekly, and long-term rates
available. Deposit of 25 percent required. (For holidays, special events,
and fall bookings, nonrefundable deposit required at time of booking.)
Reservations are guaranteed for the number of nights reserved with deposit plus $15 agency fee charged to a credit card. On arrival, balance is
due to B&B in cash or travelers' checks unless stated otherwise at time
reservation is made. For balances processed through the agency on a
credit card, a 5 percent service fee is charged. A $35 fee is charged for all
cancellations. If cancellation is received at least fourteen days before expected arrival, balance is refunded. If cancellation received with less than
fourteen days' notice, the entire deposit is nonrefundable. No refunds
are given for portion of reservation that is not used. Amex, MC, Visa.

ACCOMMODATIONS are in private host homes and in small inns. They are all inspected annually by Suzanne Ross and Sheryl Felleman, two highly regarded professionals—appreciated by travelers and hosts—who have always had people-oriented careers. (They have

continued . . .

participated in two 250-mile Boston-to-New York bicycling fund-raisers to benefit AIDS patients.) Since 1991, when they took over this established agency, they have specialized in travel itineraries throughout New England. "We accommodate tourists (including families), business travelers, and groups (up to sixteen people). We know our hosts and their wonderful and unique homes and inns. We make appropriate matches, providing a memorable stay for guests that is a highlight for hosts too. If we cannot place a guest, we try to give a referral to another source."

This agency is a member of Bed & Breakfast Reservations World Wide, a trade association.

PLUS: Weekly vacation rentals on Cape Cod and the north shore. Discount coupons to Boston area attractions, museums, shops. Many B&Bs are accessible by commuter rail and bus from Boston. Many hosts provide complimentary transportation to and from train or bus stations; to/from Logan Airport for a fee. Some offer private tours. And they acknowledge special occasions.

☙ Host Homes of Boston

P.O. Box 117, Waban Branch, Boston, MA 02468-0001

PHONE: 617/244-1308 or 800/600-1308. Monday–Friday 9 A.M.–noon and 1:30–4:30 P.M.; reduced live hours November–March. Answering machine at other times. (Prompt response.) Closed major holidays.

FAX: 617/244-5156

LISTINGS: Fifty. Located in Boston area and west suburban communities plus some in coastal and country locations. They are in Boston (Beacon Hill, Back Bay, South End, and waterfront); in Brookline, Cambridge, Newton, and Wellesley; and in Medfield. Mostly hosted private residences. A few inns and one city club. Free booklet directory.

RESERVATIONS: At least two weeks' advance notice advised. Two- or three-night minimum stay (longer for apartments) required, except for reservations made within two days of arrival; $15 one-night surcharge for those last-minute bookings.

RATES: $75–$135 single, $80–$225 double. $15–$25 extra adult or child—infants excepted. $10 (minimum) service fee. (Winter weekly rates available.) Deposit of one night's lodging required; half of total required for short-term housing. Balance of payment (or cancellation) is due at the office at least seventy-two hours before date of arrival, or seven days before arrival if stay is five or more nights. For cancellations received within that time, all monies, less $40 service fee per room, refunded. Amex, MC, Visa.

MARCIA WHITTINGTON has carefully selected hosts who live in city brownstones or in close-to-Boston (older Victorian and Colonial) homes where guests can leave their car and use public transportation. Some "country-feeling" homes are within a half hour's drive of downtown Boston. Marcia is a longtime Boston area resident who knows the territory. Since 1982 she has managed all B&B inspections and reservations, giving personalized attention to both hosts and guests. It's a spirit and style that is appreciated by visitors from all over the world.

PLUS: Highlighted road and subway maps with reservation confirmations.

≈ University Bed & Breakfast, Ltd.

P.O. Box 1524, Brookline, MA 02446

PHONE: 617/738-1424
FAX: 617/738-1424
E-MAIL: llbb@juno.com
LISTINGS: Fifty private residences located in the metropolitan Boston area—in downtown Boston and in nearby Brookline, Cambridge, Jamaica Plain, Medford, Newton, and Somerville. They offer the ambiance of the countryside and convenience to the city, and are accessible to public transportation or within walking distance of universities, the medical complex, and other meeting places.
RESERVATIONS: A minimum of two days' stay is preferred.
RATES: $60–$125 single, $70–$150 double. $10 one-night surcharge. Prepayment required. If cancellation is received at least fourteen days before expected arrival date, refund less $20 processing fee is made. Some weekly (two weeks minimum) rates available. MC, Visa.

RUTH SHAPIRO and Sarah Yules accommodate visiting professionals and accompanying spouses and/or traveling companions who come to the Boston area for academic or other reasons. They also accommodate relatives and friends of area students.

Is A B&B LIKE A HOTEL? HOW MANY TIMES HAVE YOU HUGGED THE DOORMAN?

B&Bs ARE IN ALL DOWNTOWN BOSTON NEIGHBORHOODS—including Back Bay, Beacon Hill, the South End, and the waterfront—in brownstones, brick row houses, high-rise buildings, and converted warehouses.

For many travelers, the convenience of being in the city is primary. The Greater Boston area, however, is compact; several hosts in "outlying" (mostly suburban) areas are actually closer to downtown Boston than many who live in the city. If you have time to commute, many of these B&Bs are less expensive than in-town locations. Traffic and parking in the city can be time-consuming and frustrating, especially with major construction known as the "big dig" for the depression of the central artery. The public transportation system, relatively simple and color-coded, has convenient routes. Its schedules are not as dependable as those Europeans are used to; even so, the "T" is recommended for all city travels.

🦢 Bed and Breakfast Associates Bay Colony Host #M228

Boston, MA

> **LOCATION:** In Back Bay. Walk to Boston Public Garden, Newbury Street shops and cafés, and Symphony Hall. Four blocks to Prudential/Hynes Convention Center and Green Line of public transportation.
> **RESERVATIONS:** Year round through Bed and Breakfast Associates Bay Colony (page 230), 781/449-5302 or 800/347-5088.
> **RATES:** Vary according to season. $120–$150. Parking $12 per night.
> ♥ ⬛ ❖ ⚄ ⚕

IT'S PERFECT. A private retreat. A contemporary architect-designed garden apartment. It's in an 1869 five-story townhouse that was completely restored inside and out in time to have the garden open for a Back Bay garden tour in the spring of 1995. Previously, the college administrator and his wife, a former social worker and jewelry designer, lived in Chicago. "We're delighted to share our home and its walk-to-everything location in a city that everyone loves."

FOREIGN LANGUAGES SPOKEN: French and Spanish.
BED AND BATH: Private entrance to air-conditioned studio apartment with queen bed along library wall, full bath, private phone line, TV, wood-burning fireplace, French doors to brick garden patio. Kitchenette has two-burner stove, refrigerator, microwave,

coffeepot, dishwasher; convection oven available.

BREAKFAST: Serve yourself from kitchen stocked with fresh juice, rolls, bagels, muffins, coffee.

PLUS: On-premises parking "worth more than the house in Back Bay!"

> From Canada, Oklahoma, California: *"Everything we expected and more. . . . We'd like to take the courtyard back to Vancouver. . . . After years of traveling through the world, we can honestly say that this is one of the finest accommodations in which we have stayed . . . had a real cozy feel to it . . . loved browsing through the books . . . feel lucky to have experienced [the hosts'] warmth and hospitality."*

Beacon Hill Bed & Breakfast   617/523-7376

27 Brimmer Street, Boston, MA 02108   **E-MAIL** bhillbb@aol.com

HOST: Susan Butterworth

LOCATION: Overlooking Charles River. On quiet street in historic downtown residential neighborhood. Walk to everything, including Boston Public Garden, shopping, restaurants, Hynes Convention Center, Freedom Trail, subway system.

OPEN: Year round. Two-night minimum stay (one-night bookings at last minute only). Three-night minimum on holiday weekends.

RATES: Single or double occupancy $200–$225 spring through fall, $175 winter. $25 third person on rollaway or sofa bed. Ten percent less for seven or more nights. ✏ ▦ ❖ ⚔ ⚒

> From Ohio: *"An elegant, well-appointed six-story home . . . superb creative breakfasts."* From Alabama: *"Delightful. Personable, knowledgeable, talented, and interesting hostess."* From Massachusetts (via Louisiana): *"Even acted as liaison to realty companies."* From Japan: *"We enjoyed Charles Street in the morning and evening, the beautiful public garden, Institute of Contemporary Art . . . especially enjoyed good experience in American home. Can't remember having enjoyed ourselves so thoroughly anywhere."*

BUILT IN 1869 with elegant details, this very large brick row house has marble fireplaces, high ceilings, deep moldings, and common areas with handsome wallcoverings and fine antiques. (Large and comfortable guest rooms are simpler.) French touches reflect this San Francisco–born hostess's many years of living in France. Susan, a recently retired professional caterer, trained at La Varenne in Paris and has taught French in several New England schools.

FOREIGN LANGUAGE SPOKEN: French.

BED AND BATH: Two rooms and one apartment; all private baths. Second floor—queen-bedded room, shower bath, nonworking fireplace; double-bedded room with shower

continued . . .

bath and nonworking fireplace. Garden-level studio apartment (elevator to first floor for breakfast) with private entrance has queen bed; double sofa bed; new marble bath; phone; private use of garden; and, for bookings of one week or longer, a full kitchen.
BREAKFAST: 8:30–9 weekdays, 9–9:30 weekends and holidays. Extremely popular home-made granola. Muffins or coffee cake. Eggs or French toast or waffles, fruit, and "good, strong" coffee. Under crystal chandelier from Loire château. In large dining room over-looking the Charles River.
PLUS: Central air conditioning. Elevator for luggage. Nearby guarded parking lot, $18 for twenty-four hours; $5 per weekend day.

↜ Bed and Breakfast Associates Bay Colony Host #M129

Boston, MA

> **LOCATION:** On historic Beacon Hill. Walk to restaurants, theater, subway stop, shopping, historic sites.
> **RESERVATIONS:** Year round through Bed and Breakfast Associates Bay Colony (page 230), 781/449-5302 or 800/347-5088.
> **RATES:** $150–$175. ♥ ☞ ❖ ⅍

COMPLETE PRIVACY. With concierge assistance. Even the loan of an umbrella. And lots of brochures and printed information. The hosts, an attorney-turned-at-home-mom and her husband, an ardent sports fan who is in banking, are delighted to share their historic townhouse (new to them) with travelers from all over the world.

IN RESIDENCE: In hosts' quarters—one young daughter and one golden retriever.
FOREIGN LANGUAGES SPOKEN: Some French and Spanish.
BED AND BATH: Garden-level one-bedroom apartment (private entrance) with a double bed and exquisite toile-print bedcovering, large living room with nonworking black marble fireplace, full kitchenette, new tub/shower bath, air conditioning.
BREAKFAST: Self-serve continental.

↜ From Germany: *"Darling apartment . . . the perfect Beacon Hill oasis!"* From Texas: *"Wonderful hospitality. Fresh flowers. Great location. Fascinating city!"* From England: *"Fantastic! . . . So restful to return to after a hectic day."*

THINK OF BED AND BREAKFAST AS A PEOPLE-TO-PEOPLE CONCEPT.

☞ *Coach House*

Boston, MA

> **LOCATION:** Marvelous. Quiet, secluded gaslit street in (Beacon Hill) historic district. Two blocks to Boston Common on Freedom Trail. Walk to Quincy Market, fine shops and dining, theaters, convention hotels. One minute to Esplanade on Charles River for jogging or concerts. Red (twenty minutes to Harvard Square) and Green subway lines.
>
> **RESERVATIONS:** Available year round through Host Homes of Boston (page 232), 617/244-1308 or 800/600-1308. Two-night minimum.
>
> **RATES:** April–October $135 single, $175–$200 double. November–March $125 single, $175–$200 double. ☛ ⌀ ⌁

FOR A TRUE Boston experience, travelers from all over the world stay in this 1870s coach house, which in 1911 was converted by prominent Boston socialites into "The Toy Theatre." Plays by Oscar Wilde and George Bernard Shaw were performed in this avant-garde playhouse, intended to be "liberal in its selections from the drama." In the 1930s the building became a family home. Today its living room, one of the largest on Beacon Hill and complete with a raised area (the former stage), remains a gathering place for occasional concerts, political meetings, and social events. It's a townhouse decorated with antiques and with an eye for color and detail.

IN RESIDENCE: Two cats.

FOREIGN LANGUAGES SPOKEN: Fluent French, some Spanish.

BED AND BATH: Three air-conditioned rooms; phone and TV in each. Captain's Room on second floor has one twin bed, private en-suite shower bath. Toile Room on third floor has queen bed, private en-suite full bath. Two twin beds, en-suite full bath on third floor.

BREAKFAST: 8–9. Earlier by request. Fresh fruit, cereals, juice, baked goods with jams and jellies. Freshly ground coffee. Tea. Served in dining room.

PLUS: Central air conditioning. Use of formal living room with grand piano. Clock radios.

> ☞ Guests wrote: *"Elegant home . . . highlight of our vacation . . . congenial hosts . . . convenient to everything."*

I F YOU'VE BEEN TO ONE B&B, YOU HAVEN'T BEEN TO THEM ALL.

Bed and Breakfast Associates Bay Colony Host #M466

Charlestown, MA

LOCATION: On gaslit residential street with examples of Federal, Greek Revival, Italianate, and Queen Anne architecture. In next-door courtyard is a cottage where Mother Goose lived and wrote. We're at what we call the beginning of the Freedom Trail. Bunker Hill Monument is at the top of our street. Walk everywhere—to USS *Constitution* in Charlestown Navy Yard, where there are museums and a ferry (ten-minute ride) to downtown Boston; to bus and subway stop to downtown Boston; to a wide variety of restaurants, a shopping center, pharmacy, supermarket . . . our neighborhood." Half-hour walk to Boston.

RESERVATIONS: Year round through Bed and Breakfast Associates Bay Colony (page 230), 781/449-5302 or 800/347-5088.

RATES: $110–$140. 🚻 ☕ ❖ 🚭 ✂

From Nova Scotia, Virginia, Australia, Washington, Louisiana, Minnesota, and California: *"Hidden, charming retreat. . . . Enchanted with Charlestown. Wished we could have stayed several weeks instead of a few days. . . . Martha Stewart could take a lesson [from the hosts]. . . . Made our trek through the college circuit a little easier. . . . Convenient location. . . . Private, spacious accommodations. . . . After a hard day playing tourist, it was great to have a lovely place to return to."*

THIS "LOVELY PLACE," a restored 1870 Italianate three-story brick townhouse, has been home to the hosts since the late 1970s. Both are Boston natives and attorneys; he practices, she is at home. They offer a city orientation, hospitality, and plenty of privacy.

IN RESIDENCE: In hosts' quarters—two teenagers.

FOREIGN LANGUAGES SPOKEN: "None, really, but with lots of smiles and body language—and sometimes with the help of students whose parents are visiting from afar—we have hosted many who speak no English."

BED AND BATH: Private entrance to ground-level apartment. Antique double bed in one room. Tub/shower bath. Living room (with windows that look out onto rear yard) has double sleep sofa and TV. Pullman kitchen. Private phone line.

BREAKFAST: Delivered to your door—juice, fresh fruit, home-baked muffins and bread, cereal, milk, hot beverages.

PLUS: Snacks. Maps. Suggestions—including "Do not drive in Boston. If you plan to go north or south, rent your car at the end of your stay with us. Easy access from here north or south without going into the city."

➴ *Ailanthus House*

Boston, MA

> **LOCATION:** Historic South End neighborhood of Victorian brick bowfront houses. Walk to Hynes Convention Center, Copley Place, Back Bay Amtrak station, Symphony Hall, Prudential Center, museums, theater, fine restaurants.
> **RESERVATIONS:** Year round through Host Homes of Boston (page 232), 617/244-1308 or 800/600-1308. Two-night minimum; three nights for holidays and special events.
> **RATES:** $125–$135 per room. $50 third guest. ☛ ⊗ ⌇

A GUEST, a stained glass artist, won second prize in a 1999 national contest for stained glass for the front-door panel designed with ailanthus leaves (as seen on the tree in the front yard here). Inside, the tall-ceilinged rooms—with original moldings, heavy walnut doors, and ornate brass hardware—are furnished with Victorian antiques. "My grandfather bought the house for me—hoping it would make me settle down—in 1965. It worked!" Fresh painting, some kitchen renovations, and new baths were among changes in the late 1990s. The host, a Boston native, is a former manager of several businesses, including a light opera company and a symphony orchestra.

IN RESIDENCE: "Two intuitive cats, Hillary and Rex, receive mail from many guests."
FOREIGN LANGUAGES SPOKEN: "I've forgotten my French, and my Italian too!"
BED AND BATH: Three second-floor rooms. Two air-conditioned large rooms (can be a suite with connecting hall), each with queen bed, all-new en-suite tub/shower bath, decorative marble fireplace, phone, TV. Smaller double-bedded room for third party sharing a bath with a queen room.
BREAKFAST: Flexible timing. Hearty menu. Fresh fruits. Cereals. Baked goods. Muffins. Organic milk and butter. Jams and jellies. Hot beverages. Special diets accommodated. Served in dining room.
PLUS: Use of living room. Clock radios. Bottled water. Cookies. Fruit. Off-street parking, $10 per day.

> ➴ From New York, Ohio, New Mexico: *"Great place. . . . Outstanding host. . . . Wonderful conversationalist."*

IF YOU HAVE MET ONE B&B HOST, YOU HAVEN'T MET THEM ALL.

⇗ Bed and Breakfast Associates Bay Colony Host #M224

Boston, MA

LOCATION: On a quiet, tree-lined street with other Victorian brownstones. Walk to Copley Place, theater district, shops and cafés of Newbury Street, Boston's newest "restaurant row" on Tremont Street, Back Bay/Amtrak station (4 blocks).
RESERVATIONS: Year round through Bed and Breakfast Associates Bay Colony (page 230), 781/449-5302 or 800/347-5088.
RATES: Larger queen room $110 (winter)–$145; double room $95 (winter)–$115.
♯♯ ▬ ⊞ ⚔ ⚒

HOSPITALITY. Privacy. Location. Fine antiques. Art. Panache. Elegance. Comfort. Fresh flowers. A well-traveled host. A sense of place. It's all here in this restored six-storied Victorian that has gone through several changes—most recently from condominiums back to a private home with a separate B&B entrance, two guest floors, on-site off-street parking, and access to the garden. Delighted guests come from far (many countries) and near. Neighbors cheered when a bride from suburbia descended the steps for her limousine ride to nearby historic Trinity Church. The Texas-born host, a "star of the [tourism] industry" nominee for the Massachusetts Lodging Association, is a mediator and facilitator for a Massachusetts state agency.

BED AND BATH: On first two floors—two air-conditioned rooms, each with a phone and private bath. Room with queen bed, en-suite full bath, cable TV. Smaller room, also quite beautiful, has antique double bed, detached (lower-level) "designer" bath with glassed-in tile shower and brass fixtures.
BREAKFAST: Presented 7:30–9. Fresh fruit. Fresh orange juice. Breads, pastries, muffins, or scones. Dry cereals. Hot beverages. Served in formal dining room.
PLUS: Guests' sitting room with TV. Kitchenette with microwave, refrigerator (with juices), burners for tea or coffee. Private garden. Use of laundry. Parking $15/night.

⇗ Guests wrote: *"Better than a five-star hotel. . . . Memorable breakfast . . . fabulously presented . . . fresh flowers for a finishing touch . . . lovely home and neighborhood. . . . Beautiful surroundings. . . . Everything for one's comfort and relaxation . . . sensitive hosting . . . first-rate ambassador for Boston."*

HOSPITALITY IS THE KEYNOTE OF B&B.

⇗ *Bed and Breakfast Associates Bay Colony Host #M304*

Boston, MA

LOCATION: In South End, home to the country's largest collection of Victorian brownstones. Ten minutes on foot to Copley Place, the Hynes Convention Center, Symphony Hall, Newbury Street shopping and galleries, and public transportation.

RESERVATIONS: Year round through Bed and Breakfast Associates Bay Colony (page 230), 781/449-5302 or 800/347-5088.

RATES: $130–$185. ♥ ▆ ⊞ ❖ ⚥ ⅄

⇗ From Texas: *"Elegant decor . . . great touring advice."* From Florida: *"Two gracious hosts who added so much to our Boston experience."* From Montreal: *"Genuine warmth and hospitality . . . home a real comfort at the end of the day. . . . They need a Tucker [the dog] for every room. . . . A really lovely place—tasteful and homey."* From Montreal: *"A luxury bed and breakfast."*

OTHERS SAY this restored 1868 Victorian brick townhouse, furnished with many Victorian antiques, is "fabulous" or "gracious" or "just plain wonderful." It is home to two longtime Bostonians. One is an attorney; the other, a full-time host. Both enjoy the city's rich cultural resources and the many area restaurants.

IN RESIDENCE: One golden retriever—"the perfect B&B dog, our official greeter, who is mellow, relaxed, and, if you'd like, happy to accompany guests to neighborhood parks."

BED AND BATH: Three air-conditioned rooms with king (one is a four-poster) or queen bed; each with en-suite full bath, private phone, TV and VCR, hair dryer.

BREAKFAST: 8:30–10. Fresh fruit. Juices. Yogurts. Cereals. Hot beverages. On weekends— freshly baked homemade bread, muffins, scones. In large kitchen or garden patio.

⇗ *Bed and Breakfast Associates Bay Colony Host #M323*

Boston, MA

LOCATION: On a tree-lined street in Boston's South End. Walk to theater, restaurants, concerts. "Nine minutes to base of convention center escalator," according to one eighty-year-old guest.

RESERVATIONS: Year round through Bed and Breakfast Associates Bay Colony (page 230), 781/449-5302 or 800/347-5088.

RATES: $99–$115. ▆ ❖ ⚥ ⅄

⇗ Guests wrote: *"An oasis of warmth and beauty. Hot muffins, comfortable bed, big towels, books, friendly welcomes . . . lovely people with a lovely home. . . . I can't imagine a better place to stay in Boston. . . . On vacation and found ourselves saying 'we have to be home*

continued . . .

in time to . . .'—not the hotel, not the inn, but home. . . . All the comforts of home without the
family angst . . . marvelous kitchen aromas . . . wonderful neighborhood . . . fresh air, street
sounds at night, beautiful piano music. . . . A peaceful haven in a big adventurous city."

THIS HAVEN has a strong feeling of family. The fathers of both hosts grew up in the neighborhood. The hosts—an internationally recognized high-tech photographer and an avocational pianist—brought up their two children in this 1869 Victorian bowfront townhouse. Now renovated, it is furnished with many family pieces. "The armoire we recently acquired has lived in two different houses on our street."

BED AND BATH: Two large second-floor rooms—each with queen bed, air conditioning, and (nonworking) fireplace—share hall bath that has original soaking tub (with shower). **BREAKFAST:** At mutually agreed-upon time. Juice, fresh fruit, muffins or scones, coffee, brewed tea—"especially appreciated by our many English guests." **PLUS:** Off-street parking, $12.

☞ *The Bertram Inn*

617/566-2234

92 Sewall Avenue,
Brookline, MA 02146

800/295-3822
FAX 617/277-1887
E-MAIL BertramInn@msn.com
www.bertraminn.com

HOST: Bryan Austin
LOCATION: On a corner in a lovely residential neighborhood (private homes and some condominiums) with tree-lined streets, just one block from fine shops, restaurants, and trolley service (ten-minute, 85-cent ride on subway system) to downtown Boston. Within walking distance of Boston's Longwood medical area and the Museum of Fine Arts.
OPEN: Year round.
RATES: May–November $124–$159 double bed or two twins; $144–$199 queen; $164–$239 king. December–April $10–$30 less. Cot $20. Amex, MC, Visa.
♥ ⊞ ❖ ⚕ ❤○

THIS ATTRACTIVE 1907 Victorian/Tudor-style house is, as Bryan surmised in 1986 it would be, "perfect for B&B." (It was, too, for my own "overflow relatives.") Today the house has all new systems, new baths, fresh decor, and a wonderful collection—it grows and changes—of antiques and period furnishings. You almost have the feeling that Bryan updated Grandmother's solidly built residence with its leaded windows, stone fireplaces, and grand staircase complete with landing. This B&B is appreciated by international as well as domestic travelers. And by pet lovers who are delighted to know about the pet-friendly policy here.

Bryan learned about antiques and restoration from his mother, an antiques dealer. An English major in his undergraduate years, he is an award-winning historic preservationist who maintains the inn, teaches a how-to B&B course, and runs a 140-acre working farm in a nearby community.

IN RESIDENCE: A full-time manager.

FOREIGN LANGUAGES SPOKEN: Italian, Spanish, some Portuguese; varies according to staff.

BED AND BATH: Fourteen air-conditioned rooms with private baths, cable TV, and phones with data ports. (And inquire about expansion/annex in neighboring house.) First floor—king and queen sofa bed, wood-burning fireplace, private full bath; king and twin sofa bed, wood-burning fireplace, private full bath. Second floor—one room with king four-poster, five with queen (one four-poster), and one with double bed; private baths (some shower without tub). Third floor (steeply sloped ceilings; ceiling fans in two rooms)—king, one or two double beds, twin beds, and and one very large room with a king bed, twin sofa bed, and refrigerator.

BREAKFAST: Usually 8–9. Fresh fruit, juice, breads and jams, coffee cakes, yogurt, home-made muffins and pastries, bagels and cream cheese, cold cereals, and (hard-boiled) eggs from Bryan's farm. Buffet style in large room with wood-burning fireplace or, weather permitting, on the porch overlooking the garden.

PLUS: Great front porch (glassed in winter). Daily papers and flower arrangements. Snacks. Off-street parking (no charge). Turndown service with poetry and tomorrow's weather report.

➚ From California: *"Such a friendly and helpful staff, and a comfortable, refined atmosphere."* From Israel: *"The atmosphere of this inn and the attention paid to the little amenities of life is unique."* From Australia: *"Wonderful service, beautiful accommodations, delicious breakfasts."*

➚ *A Cambridge House Bed & Breakfast*   617/491-6300

2218 Massachusetts Avenue,   800/232-9989
Cambridge, MA 02140   TOLL-FREE FROM U.K. 800-96-2079
                                                    FAX 617/868-2848
                                          E-MAIL InnACH@aol.com
                                          www.acambridgehouse.com

HOSTS: Ellen Riley and Tony Femmino

LOCATION: On a main street with a smorgasbord of residences and businesses and restaurants. From front door, short bus ride to Harvard Square. Five-minute walk to subway stop that is two stops from Harvard Square; from there, a ten-minute subway ride to downtown Boston.

continued . . .

OPEN: Year round. April–December, two-night weekend minimum.
RATES: May–November $155–$209 single, $189–$275 double. Rest of the year
$109–$189 single, $139–$209 double. Vary according to size and amenities
in room. Amex, Diners, Discover, MC, Visa. ♥ ⊞ ❖ ⊗ ⊱

⫙ From England: *"Perfectly lovely. . . . An ideal base and oasis to and from
Europe."* From Washington, D.C.: *"A haven . . . every detail attended to . . . amazingly creative and beautiful inn."*

THIS 1892 HARTWELL and Richardson–designed house, a backdrop for Oprah Winfrey's
"Best Vacations in the World," has been featured on the BBC in Europe and on Boston's
WBZ-TV. It has hundreds of yards of designer fabrics—on windows, on walls, in entry-
ways. There are Oriental rugs and fine antiques. Of the six fireplaces, the tall intricately
carved one in the den is the most outstanding. And then there's the carriage house the
hosts created from a shell in the 1980s and completely redid (now, all rooms have private
baths) in 1999.

Ellen, former membership director of the Boston Chamber of Commerce, and Tony, a
former investment property broker, are Realtors who continue to make changes in the
decor, the gardens, and the rooms, too.

FOREIGN LANGUAGES SPOKEN: Italian and Portuguese.
BED AND BATH: Fifteen air-conditioned, carpeted rooms (vary in size) described in detail
on phone. On four floors in main house; on two floors in carriage house. All with private
bath, private phone and voice mail, and cable TV with remote control. Some rooms with
gas fireplace. Beds—several are canopied—include queen, double, and twins.
BREAKFAST: 7:15–9 weekdays, 8–10 weekends. Buffet with egg dishes, pastries, juices,
fresh fruit. Eat at separate tables in living room where classical music plays all day.
PLUS: Evening beverages and hors d'oeuvres with jazz. Afternoon coffee, tea, or mulled
cider with homemade cookies and brownies. Free parking.

*A*CCORDING TO GUESTS *(many are preservationists and/or house
restorers), there ought to be a medal for the meticulous work—
everything from research to labor—done by B&B owners. Indeed, many hosts have won
preservation awards.*

⨠ *Prospect Place*

112 Prospect Street,
Cambridge, MA 02139

617/864-7500

800/769–5303
FAX 617/576-1159
E-MAIL resv@prospectpl.com
www.prospectpl.com

HOSTS: Eric and Judy Huenneke
LOCATION: Urban. On well-lit main through street in Central Square. Fifteen-minute walk to Harvard Square or to MIT. Next door to art gallery. Five-minute walk to subway (or bus); one stop to Harvard Square, ten-minute ride to downtown Boston.
OPEN: Year round. Two-night minimum April–November.
RATES: April–November $105 shared bath, $120 private bath. Less in winter. MC, Visa. ♥ ⊞ ⌀ ⅄

⨠ From Vermont: *"Lovely room, great breakfast and music, and terrific hosts!"* From California: *"Comfortable accommodations . . . hospitality, impeccable. Within walking distance of both MIT and Harvard Square is a plus. Great location."*

LOCATION: THAT was Eric's interest, too, when, in 1994, the Huennekes bought this 1866 Italianate Victorian, which had been owned by one family for more than a hundred years. Restoration work includes the reproduction (can-hardly-tell) wood fence, twenty varieties of roses, updated baths, and the cut glass in the double front door—a copy of the original. Eric, a musician (and primary host), has done considerable faux painting, including some graining and marbling "Yes, I have done commissions in the past, but not anymore. Many guests ask about the history or architecture of this wonderful old house. It is appreciated by lots of foreign travelers, who feel very much at home here." Turn-of-the-century wallpaper is in the dining room. Furnishings are eclectic. Two grand pianos are in the living room. (You are welcome to play them.) Judy is a historian.

IN RESIDENCE: In hosts' quarters—three children, ages seven to sixteen.
BED AND BATH: Three air-conditioned second-floor rooms. Rear (quieter) room has double bed, view of yard, large private en-suite bath with new marble double shower. Two rooms with connecting door can be a suite: One has antique brass double bed; other has king/twins option. Shared updated tub/shower bath is down the hall.
BREAKFAST: Usually 8–9. Orange juice. Variety of specialty baked goods and breads from nearby Icelandic bakery. Fruit salad. Eggs "any way you'd like them." Natural cereals. Hot beverages. Served in Victorian dining room at table set with china and linens. With recorded classical music.
PLUS: Central air conditioning. "Directions to all those places guests have on their agenda." Visitors' pass for street parking. "We encourage walking and public transportation."

Just a Little West Reservation Services

JUST A LITTLE WEST B&Bs

🐦 Hawthorne Inn

462 Lexington Road,
Concord, MA 01742

978/369-5610

FAX 978/287-4949
E-MAIL inn@conordmass.com/
www.concordmass.com

HOSTS: Gregory Burch and Marilyn Mudry
LOCATION: In historic district of must-see picture-perfect historic New England town.
Next door to Alcott's Orchard House and Grapevine Cottage (where
Concord grape was developed). Across from Nathaniel Hawthorne's
"Wayside." On grounds with marvelous old trees, a small pond, fruit trees,
berry bushes, flowers. "Four museums—all the staffers are walking li-
braries—in the eight-tenths of a mile between here and town center."
Twenty-minute walk to Old North Bridge; ten-minute drive to bicycle
rentals; 2 miles to Walden Pond; twenty minutes to Harvard Square
(Cambridge); thirty-five to Boston (forty-five-minute train ride).
OPEN: Year round. Two-day minimum during fall foliage.
RATES: $150–$250 double, $125–$195 single ($25 more for queen). January–March,
reduced rates. Amex, Discover, MC, Visa. ♥ 👫 ⊞ ❖ 🐾 ⚬

A SENSE OF history (Gregory's ancestors settled in Concord in 1637), peace and relaxation,
family, privacy, and community too. It's all here in the eighteen-room altered Colonial
(1920s stucco exterior over 1870 clapboard) that the innkeepers restored in 1976 after
searching for an old house that would provide studio space. Gregory is a sculptor and
painter. Marilyn is a volunteer with hospice (and, in 1991, with an orphanage in Romania),
a quilter, and a Realtor. Their haven, on land once owned by Emerson, the Alcotts, and
Hawthorne, is furnished with a blend of antiques, eighteenth- and nineteenth-
century Ukiyoye (Japanese) prints, and Gregory's works. Business travelers return as
tourists. Many appreciate the fact that for every night's booking, a donation is made to
Habitat for Humanity International. Scholars and historians love it here. (Gregory and
Marilyn wrote and produced a one-hour video history of Concord.) And families are
warmly welcomed too.

IN RESIDENCE: In hosts' quarters, three teenagers. Three cats. One friendly German shepherd and a Queensland heeler.
BED AND BATH: Seven air-conditioned rooms with in-room phones and data ports. All
private baths (some tub and shower, others shower only). First floor (with skylights)—
two double-bedded rooms and one queen. Four rooms on second floor—two with

continued...

queen, one with double, and one with one double, one single, and a fold-out bed. Rollaway and crib available.

BREAKFAST: 8:30–10. Expanded continental with homemade honey molasses or Portuguese sweet bread, pound cake with yogurt topping, fresh fruit, cereal, homemade jams, French roasted/ground coffee.

PLUS: No TV. Books and poetry collections in each room. Fireplaced living room. Beverages. Fine toiletries. Games. Yard. Treehouse. Sandbox. "Recommendations for best bookstores and antiques shops; places to canoe, fish, walk in the woods; a great deli; a fine, reasonably priced restaurant; ice-cream stands."

⤳ *Timothy Jones House*

781/275-8579

231 Concord Road,
Bedford, MA 01730

FAX 781/276-1749
E-MAIL timjonesin@aol.com
http://members.aol.com/timjonesin/info.htm

> **HOSTS:** Ann and Sid Seamans
> **LOCATION:** Residential. On an acre of lawn, trees, gardens. On main road between Bedford (1 mile to center) and Concord (3 miles to center, "excellent restaurants," and trains to Boston). Three-mile walk through Great Meadows National Wildlife Refuge to Concord Bridge. Near bike path to Lexington and Cambridge.
> **OPEN:** Year round.
> **RATES:** $105–$120; $15 less November–March. Suites $190; $170 off-season. Weekly rates available. MC, Visa. ♥ ☛ ⊞ ⚗ ⤧ ❤

ARCHITECTURE AND history buffs have a particular appreciation for this 1775 Georgian Colonial, purchased by Ann and Sid in the 1980s. It was built by a Revolutionary War soldier—an artisan whose work was, in part, unearthed during the restoration work done by the hosts, both history majors. There are eight fireplaces, including a 9-foot-long kitchen hearth; two beehive ovens; original raised paneling and hardware; wide pine floors; and a new cedar roof. Furnishings include family pieces and some from England, where Sid did consulting in the 1990s. Earlier, Sid worked in publishing; Ann was a freelance indexer. After their daughter grew up and left, they opened the B&B in 1997.

FOREIGN LANGUAGE SPOKEN: French—*"un peu."*
BED AND BATH: Four large second-floor rooms (can be two two-room suites) that share connecting baths (one is tub/shower, other is shower without tub). Two rooms have private phone line and computer access. One room with queen pencil-post bed, two rooms with double bed, one room with twin beds. Rollaway and TV available.
BREAKFAST: 7:30–9; until 9:30 on weekends. Juices, fresh fruit, yogurt, homemade muffins, breads, English scones, bagels, toast. Muesli, cereals. Waffles, pancakes, or French toast.

PLUS: Screened porch with antique family rockers. Hammock. Living room with 1930s spinet piano and wood-burning fireplace. Afternoon tea.

⨎ Guests wrote: *"Beautiful inn . . . warm hospitality . . . a marvelous reliving of Revolutionary era . . . tranquil . . . yummy breakfast."*

⨎ *Amerscot House*

978/897-0666

P.O. Box 351, 61 West Acton Road,
Stow, MA 01775

FAX 978/897-6914
E-MAIL doreen@amerscot.com
www.amerscot.com

HOSTS:	Doreen and Jerry Gibson
LOCATION:	Quiet rural setting bordered by stone wall, wagon wheel by sign, lovely grounds. Next door to a farm; across from apple orchard. "Minutes to winery, excellent restaurants, three top golf courses, canoeing." Fifteen minutes to Concord or Sudbury, forty-five to Boston or Sturbridge. Five miles from Routes 495 and 2.
OPEN:	Year round.
RATES:	$100; suite $125. Single $5 less. Amex, MC, Visa. ♥ ⊞ ⚏ ⚺

"YOU'RE MISSING a great place!" said our well-traveled neighbors, who have joined the Gibsons for Scottish country dancing in their cathedral-ceilinged barn room (a newer structure) used for business meetings. They were right: This is a great place, a 1734 center chimney farmhouse that has been the Gibsons' home, "and our research and restoration project," for three decades. (Doreen gives a fascinating tour.) The keeping room Rumford fireplace glows on winter nights. Floors slope this way and that. Plants bloom in the greenhouse. (What a setting for breakfast or a cup of tea.) There's a blend of antiquity and modern comfort, with wide-board floors, Dutch ovens, beds with handmade quilts and electric mattress pads, private phone lines, and, in armoires, cable TV. Maybe you'll meet business travelers who return again and again. Or grandparents visiting local families, tourists, or getaway guests. Or anniversary celebrants who held their wedding here.

Scottish-born Doreen is a registered nurse who has experience as a midwife and airline stewardess. She also worked with Jerry, a financial planner, in his consulting business. The Gibsons, parents of four grown children, opened Amerscot as a B&B in 1990 on Robert Burns's birthday.

BED AND BATH: Three large air-conditioned rooms with nonworking fireplaces; all private baths. First-floor room has king/twins option. Second floor—queen four-poster and adjacent loft with two twin beds. Suite has canopied queen bed; sitting room; and bath with Jacuzzi, stall shower, marble walls, nonworking fireplace.
BREAKFAST: 7–9. Orange juice, fruit, granola. Pancakes, eggs Benedict, orange French

continued . . .

toast, Dutch babies, scrambled eggs with cream cheese and vermouth. In fireplaced dining room or in greenhouse.

PLUS: Croquet court. Individual thermostats. Beverages. Turndown service. Guest refrigerator. Fresh flowers.

From Germany: *"Despite some luxury hotels . . . Amerscot House was the best
overnight stay—and most friendly hostess and host—in all our five-week visit in the U.S.A."*
From California: *"We arrived as guests, and left as friends."* From North Carolina: *"Travel
every week. . . . Amerscot is a place to call 'home.'"* From England: *"Great conversations
around the breakfast table."*

Brock's Bed & Breakfast   781/444-6573

60 Stevens Road, Needham, MA 02492-3314

HOST: Anne Brock
LOCATION: In a quiet residential neighborhood, half a mile from Route 128, two miles
from the Massachusetts Turnpike (1-90). To Boston, 9 driving miles, ½ mile
to commuter train, or 3 miles to subway station with parking. Four miles to
Wellesley College; fifteen minutes to Boston College, thirty-five to
Cambridge.
OPEN: Year round.
RATES: $70 single, $75 double. ♥ ☞ ⊞ ✗ ✂

From Wisconsin: *"They don't charge enough!"* From Texas: *"A soothing back-
drop to the fast pace of Boston . . . breakfasts made to order with healthy doses of friendliness."*
From New York: *"My husband stayed there rather than the upscale hotel his expense account
would have covered."* From New Jersey: *"Your books have guided our way to many wonderful B&Bs, but our favorite is Brock's."* From Connecticut: *"The feeling of coming home."*

THOSE ARE just a few excerpts from a huge stack of letters written to me. What started
with area colleges in 1984 has become "a wonderful people business" here. The house, the
first by Royal Barry Wills, was built in 1922 when Wills was an architecture student at
MIT. It was built Cape style, with nooks and crannies, lots of built-ins, and high ceilings.
The flagstone walk, landscaping, and Williamsburg decor (renewed in 1996) have all been
done by the Brocks, second owners of the house as of 1966. Guests have much privacy;
the host's quarters are on a different level.

BED AND BATH: Three rooms share a full bath and a half bath. All rooms have air conditioner, ceiling fan, cross-ventilation. One on first floor with double four-poster. On second floor, one with two twin beds; one with queen bed.
BREAKFAST: 6–9 at time requested by guests the night before. Juices, fresh fruit cup, cereals, homemade muffins. Eggs with bacon or sausage; twenty-four-hour French toast

(marinated in eggs, cream, orange juice, vanilla, and sugar); blueberry pancakes; or Brocks' crepes.

PLUS: Rear sundeck. Good neighborhood for walking and jogging. Guest den with books and TV. Restaurants and gift shops nearby. Off-street parking.

≈ *Park Lane Bed and Breakfast*

11 Park Lane,
Newton Centre, MA 02459–1749

617/964-1666
800/PRANSKY
FAX 617/964-8588
E-MAIL pranpran@juno.com
www.bostonbandb.com

HOSTS: Patti and Jim Pransky
LOCATION: On quiet residential suburban street in neighborhood of Victorian and other older homes. Ten-minute walk to shops, boutiques, restaurants, lake (swimming) and trolley/subway (twenty-minute ride to downtown Boston). Within 2-mile radius of major highways—I-90, and Route 128/95. Two miles to Boston College.
OPEN: Year round. Two-night minimum mid-May through October.
RATES: May–October private bath with whirlpool $95. Shared bath $80 double bed, $70 king/twins. Less off-season. Singles $5 less. $10 extra bed. $10 one-night surcharge. Amex, Discover, MC, VISA. ♦♦ ▬ ⊞ ❖ ⚕ ⚲

≈ Hardly a day goes by without a Park Lane guest's comment card in my mailbox. From about 35 states and several countries, the message is clear: *"Well kept . . . safe and warm and neat as a pin . . . full of nooks and crannies and places to explore . . . B&B par excellence . . . very friendly and welcoming . . . terrific . . . comfortable . . . elegant . . . sparkling clean . . . delicious and plentiful breakfast. . . . I stay at B&Bs all over the country. This place is a gem, a wonderful find . . . beautifully decorated . . . super-duper hosts . . . great price . . . felt like we were staying with old friends . . . furnished nicely . . . very convenient . . . hosts thought about every detail . . . made us feel like family . . . made my Boston stay perfect . . . wonderful shopping, eating, parking, directions, sightseeing suggestions. . . . More than a place to stay: a place to come home to . . . a wealth of local information, directions, where to park, where to eat. . . . Our four-year-old son was 'king of the house'—with a firm touch, of course. . . . Top-notch."*

PATTI IS A former social worker. Jim, an ardent cyclist, is a real estate developer. Their 1910 Victorian/Colonial house was completely remodeled in 1988.

IN RESIDENCE: One son, age nine. One teen-aged daughter.
FOREIGN LANGUAGES SPOKEN: "A little French and Spanish."
BED AND BATH: Three air-conditioned rooms, each with cross-ventilation, individual thermostat, color TV with cable, private phone, and air filter available. Third floor—two

continued . . .

rooms, both with slanted ceilings and dormers; one with a double bed, other with king/twins option; shared tub/shower bath. Second floor—queen bed, dressing closet, bath with whirlpool tub, shower with filtered water and hand-held option.

BREAKFAST: 8:30–9:30. Homemade breads and jams, juices, fruit, muffins and bagels, cold cereal. Hot beverages. Served in many-windowed breakfast nook. "To-go" breakfasts provided, by request. Special diets accommodated.

PLUS: Central air conditioning on first two floors. Drinking and bath water is filtered. First-floor sitting room. Front porch. Exercise room. Basement playroom for children. Swing set and toys. Pass for lake. Bicycle storage. Trolley/subway passes for sale. Special occasions acknowledged.

⤞ Rockledge

Newton, MA

> **LOCATION:** One block from twenty-minute trolley ride to downtown Boston, Hynes Convention Center, Copley Square. On a quiet residential street. Walk to lake (swimming), village shops, restaurants.
>
> **RESERVATIONS:** Year round through Host Homes of Boston (page 232), 617/244-1308 or 800/600-1308. Two-night minimum.
>
> **RATES:** $81 shared bath. $95 private bath. ♥ ⊞ ⚡ ❤○

HERE IN THE same friendly neighborhood where our own children were brought up are two popular hosts who came to Boston for college and stayed—with the exception of periods when they lived in France and other countries. The hostess, a community activist/house restorer and "longtime piano student," and her husband share their knowledge of the area. They are familiar with art galleries, concerts, and out-of-the-way antiques shops; and "the Isabella Stewart Gardner Museum, unknown to many of our guests, is a big hit."

Their lovely large Victorian house is filled with books, Oriental rugs, and antiques. The unusual front hall mural was painted by a friend who, in all likelihood, inspired one of the hosts' daughters to study art.

IN RESIDENCE: Two affectionate cats, Chloe and Clementine.

FOREIGN LANGUAGES SPOKEN: French and German.

BED AND BATH: Three second-floor rooms. One with queen bed, private en-suite new (but with an old look) shower bath. Room with queen bed and one with two twins share hall shower bath.

BREAKFAST: Usually 7:30–9. Specialty breads and jams. Cereal. Cheese. Yogurt. Juice. Fresh fruit. Freshly ground or decaf coffee. Tea. In breakfast area of worth-a-magazine-feature kitchen overlooking garden, or in dining room. Hosts often join guests.

PLUS: Bedroom ceiling fans. Clock radios. Second-floor guest sitting room with TV. Wicker-furnished covered front porch. Off-street parking.

🐾 Guests wrote: *"Marvelous . . . with a real angel! . . . warm, welcoming, convenient to public transportation . . . filled with original artworks. . . . Chloe adopted us and made us feel one of the family."*

🐾 *The Arabian Horse Inn*

978/443-7400

277 Old Sudbury Road,
Sudbury, MA 01776-1842

800/272-2426 (800/ARABIAN)
FAX 978/443-0234
E-MAIL joanbeers@aol.com
www.arabianhorseinn.com

HOSTS: Joan and Rick Beers

LOCATION: "Hidden." A 9–acre horse farm in Sudbury center. Set back from road. With huge old trees, flowering bushes, woods, pastures, pond, stream, stone walls, and cross-country ski trail. Ten minutes to Concord's historic sites, apple orchards, and canoe rentals; five to natural wildflower preserve and to Great Meadows National Wildlife Refuge (3,000 acres) with nature/hiking trail; twenty to Boston Marathon starting (Hopkinton) and finishing (Boston) points. Ten minutes to top golf courses.

OPEN: Year round.

RATES: $219 king room; $299 three-room suite with wine, chocolates, and flowers; $269 (for two) in two-room suite with private bath; $40 more for four in suite. MC, Visa. ♥ ⊞ ⚷ 🐾

🐾 From England, Ireland, Massachusetts, New York, Florida, Arizona, Washington, D.C.: *"A wonderful retreat . . . ideal base to tour from . . . main suite would be suitable for royalty . . . warm welcome . . . first class. . . . Engaging, interesting, and cordial hosts . . . beautiful grounds . . . a stay we'll remember and likely repeat. . . . Our wedding party loved it. . . . I would move in permanently if I could. . . . Breakfast fit for royalty . . . attention to detail extraordinary. . . . A magical place!"*

IT's MAGICAL for country weddings too. And for many proposals. "To date, no one has said no! We bought this farm in 1984 and have never stopped working on it. . . . After our children graduated from college, we started B&B, expecting the farm to appeal to families. Not so! We host parents here for a getaway! They enjoy the surroundings—the pond with ducks and geese, the Arabian horses that we raise, the double swing suspended from the 200-year-old ash tree. And yes, we do give tours of the four-storied barn. I'm English. Rick, who has just retired from the auto repair business, is Canadian. We met in California. We love sharing this rambling, eclectically furnished seventeen-room 1880 Victorian house."

IN RESIDENCE: All outdoors—three cats, two dogs, two geese, two ducks, several chickens, and five ("foals due, maybe more next year") beautiful Arabian horses.

continued . . .

BED AND BATH: On second floor—one three-room suite, one two-room suite, and one room. All with private bath, Jacuzzi tub, phone, and voice mail. Larger suite has bedroom with canopied king bed and wood-burning fireplace; large dressing room with double sinks and a walk-in closet; huge bath with step-up two-person Jacuzzi and, on other side of room, a brass/glass shower. Room with antique four-poster king bed has sitting area with large bay window, two-person Jacuzzi tub, separate shower. Two-room suite has draped king four-poster and French doors that connect with 14-foot-square living room, Victorian claw-foot soaking tub, separate shower. French doors lead to huge private balcony overlooking pond and pastures.

BREAKFAST: Flexible timing. Traditional full English breakfast. Fresh bread made with homegrown rosemary and lavender. Homemade blueberry, banana nut, lemon, or poppy-seed muffins; croissants; or English muffins. Pancakes. Fresh fruit. Cereal. Yogurt. In kitchen, in dining room, on your own balcony, or under pergola.

PLUS: Central air conditioning. Living room with fireplace (Lopi stove) and grand piano. Cookies, chocolates, flowers. Porches. Carrots for horses. (Warning: You may be mesmerized and delayed for your day-trip plans.) Babysitting arranged. Pens and doghouses for two dogs. Overnight stabling for horses.

*C*AN'T FIND A LISTING *for the community you are going to? Check with a reservation service described at the beginning of this chapter. Through the service you may be placed (matched) with a welcoming B&B that is near your destination.*

NORTH OF BOSTON RESERVATION SERVICES

THE FOLLOWING RESERVATION SERVICES REPRESENT SOME B&Bs NORTH OF BOSTON:
Bed and Breakfast Associates Bay Colony, Ltd., page 230
Bed & Breakfast Reservations North Shore/Greater Boston/Cape Cod, page 231

ᗘ *Vine & Ivy Inn*

212 Hart Street,
Beverly Farms, MA 01915-2153

978/927-2917
800/975-5516
FAX 978/927-4610
E-MAIL antoniou@compuserve.com
www.vineandivy.com

HOST: James (Jim) C. Glesener
LOCATION: Residential (turn-of-century estate and farm) area. About 1 mile to ocean and to Beverly Farms center and train station. Half mile to Gordon College; 2 miles to Endicott College and Landmark School. Twenty miles north of Boston.
OPEN: Year round.
RATES: Main house: April 2–January 1 $135 single, $150 for two, $225 suite (sleeps three). Off-season $110 single, $120 for two, $180 suite. Barn: year round, $200 king, $225 suite. All major credit cards accepted. ♥ ⚅ ⚘ ❥

QUINTESSENTIAL country/New England—just four-tenths of a mile from Route 128! Charming. Cozy. Traditional. "Exquisitely restored and opulently decorated" (*Boston Globe* feature). The horseshoe-shaped fifteen-room Greek Revival Cape with attached barn and carriage house was built in 1920 for staffers of an equestrian estate. Now, in the courtyard formed by the horseshoe, there is a 32-by-16-foot pool. Perennial and vegetable gardens flourish on the grounds. Woods provide a backdrop.

Jim is a professional interior designer who, sorry, "can no longer do it for others." The breakfast room walls are covered with a richly textured Victorian-like pattern. Some guest rooms have an Early American feel. Fresh flower arrangements are everywhere. As Jim says, "It's Martha Washington, not Martha Stewart style!" He and Nick bought the property as a private home in 1997. They redid "everything" within four months, in time to host friends who suggested B&B. It was so well received that in 1999 they added two barn rooms—acclaimed by the hundreds who attended the grand opening. Sources are shared for antiques (gazillion shops in nearby Essex), for treasures of all kinds (a consignment shop in Manchester-by-the-Sea), and for fabrics too. And then there's the breakfast prepared by host Jim, who has a degree in hotel/restaurant management.

IN RESIDENCE: Nicholas Antoniou, a high tech marketing manager "who knows, from experience, the needs of a traveler." Two cats: "Max is mostly Siamese; Mommy, a tabby."
FOREIGN LANGUAGES SPOKEN: "French, Greek, and beginner's Japanese."
BED AND BATH: Four rooms and two suites; all very private. All with air conditioning, cross-ventilation, phone, TV, VCR, robes. All private baths. *Main house*—first floor has

one room with queen bed, claw-foot tub/shower. On second floor, one dormered room with queen bed, shower bath. Dormered corner suite has queen bed in one room, twin bed in other, tub/shower bath. *Converted barn*—king bed, tub/shower bath. Suite with double bed, living room with queen sofa bed, tub/shower bath. Crib available.

BREAKFAST: 7–8:30 weekdays. 8–9:30 weekends; served at hour requested by guests the night before. (Continental for early or late risers.) Freshly squeezed orange juice. Choice of French toast (house specialty); eggs any way; waffle with maple syrup or whipped cream; bagel with cream cheese and smoked salmon; eggs Florentine; eggs Benedict; or oatmeal. In breakfast room or in courtyard overlooking pool and grounds. At "romantic tête-à-tête table by window" or at table for six.

PLUS: Central air conditioning. Guest refrigerator with complimentary bottled water and sodas. Spacious living room with wood-burning fireplace. Pool towels. Fresh fruit. Sweets. Transportation provided to/from local train station and Gordon College. By advance arrangement, picnic baskets and dinner.

~ *Miles River Country Inn*   978/468-7206

823 Bay Road, P.O. Box 149,   FAX 978/468-3999
Hamilton, MA 01936   E-MAIL milesriver@mediaone.net
    www.milesriver. com

HOSTS: Gretel and Peter Clark

LOCATION: In estate and horse country. Down a long driveway, past fields, apple orchard, caretaker's house. On 30 acres of lawn, gardens, mature trees, outbuildings, two ponds, meadows, and marshes. Twenty minutes to Newburyport, Manchester-by-the-Sea, Salem, Gloucester, Rockport; ten minutes to Essex and its antiques shops; five to Ipswich and 6-mile-long Crane's Beach; five to Hamilton train station; forty minutes from Logan Airport and Boston.

OPEN: Year round. Minimum stay required on holidays and weekends during high season.

RATES: June–October and on holidays second floor $150, $160, $175, suite $225; third floor $120, $140. Rest of year $20 less. Singles $85–$95. Extra bed or crib $20. Housekeeping apartment, June–October, $160 for master bedroom only, $285 for four people, $345 for six. Amex, MC, Visa.

♥ ♦♦ ⬛ ⊞ ⤢ ♨ ☷ ♥○

~ From Massachusetts: *"Strolled down rolling lawn past gigantic evergreens . . . attempted to catch mist rising over the water, which may or may not show up on film . . . discovered path that led through woods, over bridges, up through pine forest, ending at a large field . . . silence broken by a bird call here and there . . . incredible sense of peace retained inside as well as out with soft antique colors . . . big beams . . . large open spaces. Bookcases*

continued . . .

enhance every room . . . unbelievable how totally relaxed I felt." From Maryland: *"Absolutely beautiful property . . . warm company . . . helpful hints of touring . . . marvelously prepared breakfasts. . . . Fantastic."*

THERE ARE meadows, woodlands, and marshes—beauty discovered by wedding planners and garden clubs too. The extensive perennial gardens, intentionally informal (natural-looking), are the pride of Gretel, a beekeeper who is a retired bilingual specialist. The rambling 200-year-old Colonial, home to the Clarks for thirty years, has twenty-four rooms (each quite different—one has walls covered with nineteenth-century bedsteads from Brittany) and twelve wood-burning fireplaces. Family heirlooms are among the eclectic furnishings. B&B guests are welcome to bird right here on the Atlantic flyway, hike, cross-country ski, enter the gate of the secret garden with its statued fountain. Sometimes in view nearby: carriage-driving competitions, pre-Olympic horse trials, world-class polo, and horse jumping.

Now Peter is a major energy developer in Latin America. Through their earlier careers, the Clarks lived in France, Germany, Norway, Chile, and Nigeria.

IN RESIDENCE: Lady, "spitting image of dog from *Lady and the Tramp*." Milana, a blue calico cat. A flock of chickens and guinea hens; forty beehives.
FOREIGN LANGUAGES SPOKEN: Spanish, French, and some German.
BED AND BATH: Eight rooms (room size and decor vary), four with working fireplace. On second floor: six rooms; two that share a bath can be a suite. Third floor: two (with slanted ceilings) share a bath. Queen, double, or twin beds. Rollaways and crib available. Also: housekeeping apartment.
BREAKFAST: 8–9 or 8:30–9:30. Homemade breads, muffins, scones. Fresh "home-laid" eggs/cheese casserole, pancakes, or waffles. Homemade fruit preserves and honey (from Gretel's bees). On terrace, in glassed-in alcove with expansive view of lawns, or in fire-placed dining room with original Colonial paneled walls.
PLUS: Fireplaced living rooms. Baby grand piano. Garden terraces. Trail maps. Bike routes.

*U*NLESS OTHERWISE STATED, *rates in this book are for two and in-clude breakfast in addition to all the amenities in "Plus."*

ᾱ *Town Hill B&B*   978/356-8000

16 North Main Street,   800/457-7799
Ipswich, MA 01938   FAX 978/356-8000
                                                          www.townhill.com

HOSTS: Chere (pronounced Sherrie) and Robert Statho
LOCATION: Overlooking town green, library, and two churches in historic district. On wide street, four doors from main thoroughfare. Walk to shops, fine restaurants, train station (for Rockport or Boston). Five-minute drive to Crane's Beach, two minutes to canoeing on Ipswich River. About a mile to ocean kayaking. Photographers' delight: "Just down the street from one of the oldest stone arched bridges in the country." Fifteen-minute drive to Newburyport, Salem, Gloucester; thirty-five minutes north of Boston.
OPEN: Year round except some time in January and February. Two-night minimum on holiday weekends.
RATES: Shared bath $75. Private bath: $85 double bed, $100 twin beds; queen $100, $125, $135 with futon bed, $150 with TV and sitting room. Amex, MC, Visa.
♥ ⊱

GUARANTEED: A good night's sleep. Once guests realize that Bob is a former mattress manufacturer who now owns a retail mattress shop, they often ask for a mini-seminar on bedding differences. When he and Chere, a former hairdresser, bought the twenty-three-room 1850 Greek Revival house "in a quiet area that is not too touristy," it had most recently been a home for elderly residents. The restoration work included the refinishing of all floors. More than 100 gallons of paint freshened the inside. Baths were added. New brass-and-iron beds are in the simply furnished guest rooms. Wicker seating is on the four-season sunporch. The U.S equestrian team are among the many guests who have enjoyed the hospitality here since the Stathos opened in 1995.

IN RESIDENCE: Two dogs, in hosts' building only.
BED AND BATH: Eleven air-conditioned rooms on first and second floors. Most have private baths; three baths with tub and shower, others shower only. King, queen, double, or twin beds. Five rooms with nonworking (decorative) fireplace. One suite with TV.
BREAKFAST: 8–9. Eggs-any-style and sausage, French toast, or cereal. Juice. Hot beverage. Served at antique pine dining room table.

   ᾱ Guests wrote: *"Rooms are large and sunny and very comfortable. . . . Exceptionally clean. . . . Breakfast was delicious, classic, substantial . . . cooked to order. . . . Chere and Bob were very informative about the town's history. . . . Enjoyed the nearby beach and the wonderful 1920s mansion of Richard Crane, the plumbing magnate. . . . Ipswich itself is inviting to explore. . . . Hospitable hosts."*

☞ Diamond District Breakfast Inn   781/599-4470

142 Ocean Street,   800/666-3076
Lynn, MA 01902-2007   FAX 781/599-5122
                                    E-MAIL diamonddistric@msn.com
                                         www.diamonddistrictinn.com

HOSTS: Sandra and Jerry Caron
LOCATION: In historic urban neighborhood—7 miles north of Logan Airport—with
            large Victorian homes and turn-of-the-century brick apartments. One short
            block to 3.5-mile-long ocean beach with jogging/cycling/walking path and
            restaurants. One block to bus service to Boston (thirty-minute ride). Ten-
            minute drive to Salem or Marblehead.
OPEN: Year round. Two-night minimum on holiday weekends and May–October.
RATES: $145 or $175 private bath; suites $185, $275. Rollaway $20. Amex, Diners,
            Discover, MC, Visa. ♥ ✄

☞ From England: *"We found this the most beautiful B&B in New England.* From
Connecticut: *"Parlor overlooking the ocean was exquisitely decorated with antique musical instruments."* From New Jersey: *"We were in Lynn for a funeral. Our stay at this lovely, well-run
B&B gave us both comfort and, indeed, pleasure."* From California: *"Referred by an area hotel
that was full. Turned out to be the hospitality highlight of our entire two-week New England
visit. . . . Even the veranda has comfortable chairs . . . immaculate. . . . Fresh flowers everywhere. . . . Breakfasts an epicurean delight, fruit artfully arranged."* From Maine: *"Engaging
hosts."* From Canada: *"One of the most beautiful places we have ever been to."*

THE CARONS HAVE put Lynn on the tourism map. Media attention includes *Country Inns*
magazine. Even Boston area residents who are familiar with the nearby ocean drive are
surprised to discover this Georgian-style National Register mansion, built in 1911 for a
local shoe manufacturer's family—and for entertaining. It has the feeling of a well-cared-
for ancestral home. The gracious foyer is complete with winding staircase. An 1895 Knabe
piano is in the enormous living room, which has a Mexican mahogany fireplace and a wall
of French doors leading to a 36-foot-wide veranda with ocean view beyond. There are
Oriental rugs, period furnishings, and paintings—acquired at auctions and area estate
sales when the Carons, who lived across the street, purchased the landmark property in
1986. The latest addition: a heated outdoor hot tub spa.
    Sandra, the official floral designer, a Texan whose smile exudes hospitality, has experi-
ence in airline sales. Her co-gardener, Jerry, is a certified public accountant whose interests
encompass aircraft, politics, and history.

BED AND BATH: Ten air-conditioned rooms; most with ceiling fan. All with private bath,
TV, and mechanical card locks. First floor—one room with antique four-poster canopied
queen bed, private full bath; another with two extra-long twin beds, private shower bath.
Studio with queen bed; private tub bath; separate entrance; private porch; remote-control
gas fireplace; kitchen area with microwave, refrigerator, and sink. Second floor—two

queen-bedded rooms, each with private full bath. Two-room suite with canopied king bed, whirlpool and two-person shower, log fireplace, deck with ocean views. Third floor—four rooms with queen or king beds, private baths.

BREAKFAST: 8–9:30 (earlier on request). Low-fat recipes for quiche, French toast omelet, Belgian waffles, blueberry pancakes. Homegrown tomatoes and herbs. Homemade muffins, bread, biscuits, scones, baked doughnuts. Fresh fruit. Vegetarian menu available.
PLUS: Sophisticated telephone system—individual room voice mail, wake-up and conference calls, speaker phone. Electric mattress warmers. Down comforters and pillows. Ironed sheets.

⋙ *The Bishop's Bed & Breakfast*   781/631-4954

10 Harding Lane,   FAX 781/631-2102
Marblehead, MA 01945   E-MAIL jbishop@shore.net
www.bishopsbb.com

HOSTS: Hugh and Judy Bishop
LOCATION: Seaside and quiet. With panoramic views from all rooms. On ¾ acre with seawall, gardens, beach. Walk to island at low tide for swim. In historic district with Colonial homes. Ten-minute walk to the harbor, fine restaurants, antiques shops; five minutes to New England's oldest graveyard and to weekend model boat races on Redd's Pond.
OPEN: Year round. Two-night minimum on weekends May–October and national holidays.
RATES: May–October and national holidays $85 double bed; $95 queen; $135 suite. Extra person $15. Less off-season. One night free for seven-night stay. Year round, midweek corporate rates. MC, Visa. ♥ ☛ ⊞ ❖ ⚄ ⅍ ☙

A SENSE OF place is here in the 1800s cottage that has been the Bishop family homestead for three generations. Hugh, a raconteur appreciated by guests from all over the world, is a stockbroker turned (more than thirty years ago) commercial fisherman. (He's also a golfer who enjoys the sand trap on the property.) Judy—"I'm a beginning golfer"—has lived in Europe as well as Seattle, where she was in real estate and advertising. At her fortieth Marblehead High School reunion, she re-met classmate Hugh. They married in 1997, redid guest rooms, and fulfilled Judy's long-held dream of opening a B&B. Floors are wide-board pine. Furnishings include wicker, Oriental rugs, family heirlooms—and no clutter. Waves lap the shoreline. Seabirds call. The view soothes.

IN RESIDENCE: Two cats not allowed in guests' quarters.
BED AND BATH: Three oceanside rooms; each with cable TV, many books, portable fan. First floor—large corner room with queen bed, en-suite tub/shower bath, dressing room, cross-ventilation, private entrance through greenhouse, private door to oceanside lawn. Second floor—up narrow, steep stairs to two rooms that share a tub/shower bath. (All

continued . . .

private baths planned by the time you are reading this book, however.) One is a corner room tucked under the eaves with double bed. The other has queen bed and skylight.
BREAKFAST: 8–9. Seasonal fruit. Juices. Fresh muffins, bagels, pastries, coffee cake. Cereal; granola and yogurt. Fine teas and coffee. Served in family kitchen with ocean view, non-working fireplace, and walls of fascinating family, house, and sailing photos. Or eat in the yard, by the sea.
PLUS: Welcoming beverage and snack. Fresh fruit and flowers. Newspapers. Off-street parking for cars, trailers, boats. Beach towels. Croquet. Tree swing. Cable TV in guest sitting room.

> From California, Delaware, New Jersey, Connecticut: *"Delightful—on our trip to see fall foliage. Loved it so much we booked a spring weekend for my in-laws. They loved it too. . . . Charming conversations with friendly and helpful hosts. . . . Bedrooms quaint and cozy with a spectacular view. . . . Short walk to secluded beach. . . . Wonderfully prepared breakfasts. . . . Immaculately clean, with tasteful decor. . . . Highly recommended. . . . Real down-to-earth people. . . . I can't imagine a more perfect and beautiful location."*

Harborside House   781/631-1032

23 Gregory Street,   E-MAIL swliving@shore.net
Marblehead, MA 01945-3241   www.shore.net/~swliving/

HOST: Susan Livingston
LOCATION: On a quiet one-way street in historic district of this eighteenth-century seacoast village. Walk to fine dining, antiques shops, art galleries, historic sites. Thirty minutes north of Logan Airport, downtown Boston, I-95.
OPEN: Year round. Two- or three-night minimum stay required on holiday weekends.
RATES: April–January and holidays $85. Off-season $75. $5 one-night surcharge.

FROM THIS intimate and comfortable mid-nineteenth-century house, built by a ship's carpenter and now decorated with panache, there are views of hundreds of sailboats in the famous harbor. In 1985 Susan made her home into a B&B, a welcoming place that blends her interests—sewing (bridal dressmaker), baking (recipes shared), arranging homegrown flowers, and history (she's a former historic house guide). Rooms are furnished with antiques and period wallcoverings. Many guests follow her suggested walking (sometimes by moonlight), jogging, or bicycling route along winding streets, past old-fashioned doorways and interesting gardens, to historic sites, shops, restaurants, and the beach.

Susan's major avocational interest is competitive Masters swimming; the proud grandmom is among the country's top ten in her age group.

FOREIGN LANGUAGE SPOKEN: *"Un petit peu de français."*

BED AND BATH: Up steep stairs to two second-floor rooms—each with desk, clock radio, TV—that share a full bath. Large (14 by 20 feet) harborview room with two antique twin beds tucked under the eaves. One room with double bed, back garden view. Rollaway available.

BREAKFAST: Usually 7–9. Self-serve after 9. Juice. Fresh fruit in season. Homemade applesauce; warm home-baked raisin bran, blueberry, or cranberry muffins; banana, muesli, or cranberry bread. Low-fat options. Cereals. Yogurt. On covered porch or in dining room with harbor view.

PLUS: Terry robes. Third-story deck. Fireplaced beamed living room. Flagstone patio. Secluded yard with gardens. Afternoon tea and cookies. Mineral water. Specialty chocolates. Menus of local restaurants.

➤ From Michigan: *"A calm and lovely place."* From Oklahoma: *"Just as we imagined New England would be."* From California: *"A most charming, helpful, and friendly hostess."*

➤ *Seagull Inn B&B*

106 Harbor Avenue,
Marblehead, MA 01945

781/631-1893

FAX 781/631-3535
E-MAIL host@seagullinn.com
www.seagullinn.com

HOSTS: Skip and Ruth Sigler
LOCATION: Residential setting among other beautiful old homes on island (Marblehead Neck) connected to mainland by long causeway. Minutes to lighthouse overlooking harbor. One mile to town, restaurants, shops. Two miles to Salem; 18 north of Boston.
OPEN: Year round. Two-night minimum on weekends May 1–November 1.
RATES: $100 first-floor suite. $150 second-floor suite. $200 apartment suite. $25 third person. MC, Visa. ♥ ♛ ⚷

OCEAN VIEWS. Sunsets. Sunrises if you're really an early bird. And a host dubbed by *Boston* magazine's "Best of Boston" as "best host with the most." The long blue house with flagstone walk lined with old-fashioned flowers began in the 1890s as a summer hotel. Home to the Siglers since 1969, it became their B&B in 1994. Light and airy, comfortable and inviting, this popular B&B has wonderful Shaker-syle furniture—all made from old pine by Skip. There are cherry floors, original artwork (Skip is a watercolorist), antiques, extensive gardens, great decks—and lots of red cedar Adirondack chairs. An "authors' corner" features books written by former guests.

In 1997, during the USS *Constitution*'s 200th anniversary sailing, two admirals stayed here. International guests, too, enjoy meeting Skip, a former construction company sales manager who is now president of the Marblehead Chamber of Commerce, and Ruth, a

continued . . .

computer analyst who gives Sunday morning yoga sessions—guests invited—on nearby Castle Rock, overlooking the ocean. Pure joy.

BED AND BATH: Three oceanview suites, all with private bath, air conditioning, TV/VCR, refrigerator, coffee maker, hair dryer, phone. First-floor book-lined room with cross-ventilation has queen four-poster, en-suite half bath, shower bath off private hall. Second-floor suite has queen four-poster, single daybed in sitting room, tub/shower bath (with barnboard walls) across the private hall; additional room with two twin beds. Apartment suite (accommodates five) with private entrance via multilevel decks has queen four-poster, rollaway, double sofa bed in living room, fully equipped kitchen, rooftop deck with incredible views.
BREAKFAST: Fresh fruit cup. Homemade granola. Homemade muffins, breads, biscotti. Juice and hot beverages. Self-service buffet at kitchen island or in dining room.
PLUS: Fireplaced living room. Upright piano in dining room. Sherry, candy, and nuts at bedside. Guest refrigerator stocked with water, soda, and ice. Video library.

     ✍ From Canada: *"Extremely warm welcome was the start of a fabulous week with Skip and Ruth . . . beautifully appointed rooms with fresh flowers . . . delicious homemade muffins . . . highly recommended."*

✍ *Spray Cliff on the Ocean*   781/631-6789

25 Spray Avenue,   800/626-1530
Marblehead, MA 01945   FAX 781/639–4563
                                              E-MAIL spraycliff@aol.com
                                                        www.spraycliff.com

    HOSTS: Roger and Sally Plauché
  LOCATION: Dramatic. Atop a seawall, with mesmerizing views of the Atlantic Ocean. In a residential neighborhood. Minutes' drive to historic district (Old Town). Steps to sandy beach, walking and cycling trails. Thirteen miles—half-hour drive—to Logan Airport.
     OPEN: Year round. Two-night minimum most weekends; three nights on major holiday weekends.
    RATES: May–October $180–$225. November–April $145–$185. Third person $25. Amex, MC, Visa. ♥ ⊞ ❖ ⚄ ⚘ ⚓

STILL THE PHONE rings from a *New York Times* "splash"—a recommendation together with a spectacular waterside photo by a guest. This light-filled oceanfront Victorian Tudor, also featured in *Country Inns* magazine and as a *Yankee* "Editor's Pick," has a feeling of space, simplicity, and elegance. Built in 1910 as a summer home and a B&B since the 1980s, it was once the scene of fashionable weddings. When Sally, an interior designer, and Roger, a former corporate executive, bought Spray Cliff in 1994, they decorated "everything but the view"—with fine fabrics, modern and comfortable seating, and wicker and sisal, and with checks, plaids, and lots of whites (even the carpeting). The Plauchés have lived in Ohio, New York, Arkansas, Pennsylvania, Illinois, and, from 1978 to 1985, in Marblehead. Here they have created a perfect place for business guests. And, for sure, a romantic getaway.

IN RESIDENCE: Zoe and Annabelle, "our miniature schnauzers, who love attention."
BED AND BATH: Seven rooms; five with ocean views. All with private baths and ceiling fans. First floor—queen bed, wood-burning fireplace, full bath, private oceanfront patio. Garden room has one king, one double bed, wood-burning fireplace, beamed ceiling, shower bath. Second floor—king bed, working fireplace, full bath; two queen-bedded rooms, one with shower bath, one with tub/shower bath. Third floor—two king-bedded rooms, shower baths.
BREAKFAST: 8–10. (Coffee and juice available before and after.) Strata or quiche. Homemade breads, muffins, croissants, scones, coffee cake. Fresh fruit, yogurt, juices, cereal. Buffet style in oceanfront gathering room that has fireplace and beamed ceiling.
PLUS: No TV. Complimentary beverages. Bottled water. Fresh flowers. Scented candles.

🐦 From Michigan: *"Exquisitely furnished . . . places everywhere to curl up and read or just listen to the ocean . . . fresh flowers . . . immaculately clean . . . plenty of privacy. . . . Roger and Sally are what make it special. . . . Publicity often stretches a place's strengths. In this case, it doesn't do it justice . . . a marvelous experience."* From California: *"A beautiful sunrise over the ocean."* From New York: *"Classy . . . five-star all the way."*

🐦 Clark Currier Inn　　　978/465-8363

45 Green Street, Newburyport, MA 01950-2626　　　800/360-6582

HOSTS: Mary, Bob, and Melissa Nolan
LOCATION: Urban historic downtown area. Three blocks to waterfront park and boardwalk. Walk to restaurants, museums, performing arts center, galleries, whalewatching excursions, commuter rail service to Boston. Minutes to Maudslay State Park (former estate) on Merrimack River (great cycling route) and Lowell's Boat Shop, where wooden boats are still made. Short drive to Parker River National Wildlife Refuge (birding and beachcombing).
OPEN: Year round. Two-night weekend minimum in summer and fall; three nights on holiday weekends.
RATES: Mid-January–mid-April $95–$105 double bed, $115–$125 queen. Mid-April–mid-January $115–$125 double, $135–$155 queen. $20 third person. Corporate rates and birding weekend packages available. Amex, Discover, MC, Visa. ⊗ ⅄ ♥♡

continued . . .

WINDOW SEATS, magnificent dentil moldings, Indian shutters, wide pumpkin pine floors, and period furnishings are inside this classic Federal (1803) shipbuilder's house. Outside—in back—there's a marvelous refuge (seen on garden tours) with gazebo, pergola, water garden, and walks made of brick from the dismantled YMCA.

History, small-city living, and a sense of community were just what the Nolans were looking for. In 1990 they moved here from New Jersey. Bob was a New York bank vice president and foreign exchange trader. Mary, an AT&T manager, was a political science lecturer at Rutgers University.

IN RESIDENCE: Daughter Melissa is thirteen. "Missy is our cat."
FOREIGN LANGUAGE SPOKEN: Some Spanish.
BED AND BATH: Eight air-conditioned rooms; each with phone and private en-suite shower bath. First floor—large room with canopied queen bed. Two adjoining rooms, each with double bed; one also has a single sofa bed. Second floor—one room with queen four-poster, enclosed porch. One with canopied queen bed, tub/shower bath, private sundeck. Third floor—double and two twins. Double and a twin bed. One room with canopied queen bed.
BREAKFAST: Usually 7:30–9. Low-fat/cholesterol granola cereal, breads, muffins, fruits, coffee, tea. In formal dining room or in garden room. (Or take tray to gazebo or your room.)
PLUS: Fireplaced living room. Cable TV in garden room. Second-floor library. Tea, 3–5 P.M. Evening sherry. Mints. Fruit. Babysitting arranged.

> ≈ From New Jersey: *"Nicely decorated, very clean, peaceful. . . . Mary and Bob are like old friends . . . share interesting stories about local history. . . . When on business, I bring coworkers and customers to experience a change of pace."* From Canada: *"Wonderful stay . . . beautiful inn . . . delicious and healthy breakfast . . . close to super restaurants . . . very helpful hosts."*

≈ The Windsor House

978/462-3778

38 Federal Street,
Newburyport, MA 01950

888/TRELAWNY (875-5296)
FAX 978/465-3443
E-MAIL tintagel@greennet.net
www.bbhost.com/windsorhouse

HOSTS: Judith and John Harris
LOCATION: Within walking distance of the harbor, shops, performance center. Across from historic Old South Church. Five-minute drive to ocean, Parker River National Wildlife Refuge, and Maudslay State Park (magnificent grounds on the Merrimack River).
OPEN: Year round. Two-day minimum on weekends; three on bank holidays.

RATES: Tax and service charge included. $145; singles $99. Less November–April. Additional guest $35. Corporate rates and winter packages. Amex, Discover, MC, Visa. ♥ ⚔

GUESTS FEEL as if they have come home to an English country house with a courtyard and garden, traditional Cornish breakfast, afternoon tea, a portrait of HM Queen Elizabeth II, British publications and John, a retired Royal Navy senior communications officer. He lived in a lovely cottage not far from King Arthur's castle when Judith met him (at a B&B in Tintagel, Cornwall, England) while she was studying Megalithic Britain. "We courted on the high cliffs of North Cornwall, married in 1990, and returned to this inn that I established in 1979. Now we visit England several times a year—to see grandchildren and to lead tours through King Arthur country and to ancient sacred sites." Here they work together with a Massachusetts Audubon sanctuary featuring field trips—birding on Wednesday mornings as well as special three-day trips during the year.

The former 1786 mansion/chandlery, refurbished in the mid-1990s, is a three-storied brick building that combines Colonial, Georgian, and Federal styles of architecture.

IN RESIDENCE: Trelawny, the cat.
FOREIGN LANGUAGES SPOKEN: A little French, less German.
BED AND BATH: Four large air-conditioned rooms; some with sleigh or four-poster beds. All with tea and coffee facilities. All private baths. First floor—double and queen bed, shower bath, private street entrance. Second floor—queen, full bath. Third floor—two rooms, each with king bed, shower bath.
BREAKFAST: 8–9. Traditional English menu—fresh fruit, eggs, turkey ham, tomatoes, mushrooms, beans. Sometimes pancakes or waffles. Bread and muffins. Their own brew of coffee. Watch preparations and chat with innkeepers (occasionally in Cornish dress) in huge brick-walled kitchen that has 14-foot ceiling.
PLUS: Gracious common room with TV and VCR. Meeting room accommodates ten people.

⤳ From New York: *"A soothing, charming, and historical stop . . . gracious hosts were entertaining and attentive—experts on local sights and history, as well as fascinating storytellers of life in merry England. And the breakfast! The Best! Dare I say—even better than Mom makes. Definitely, try their special blend of coffee."* From Massachusetts: *"A lovely experience. Plan to return with friends."*

*I*N THIS BOOK *a "full bath" includes a shower and a tub. "Shower bath" indicates a bath that has all the essentials except a tub.*

ᔆ *Addison Choate Inn*

49 Broadway, Rockport, MA 01966-1527

978/546-7543
800/245-7543
FAX 978/546-7638
www.cape-ann.com/addison-choate

HOST: Knox Johnson

LOCATION: Residential. On street that leads in/out of town. Five-minute walk to village center and harbor, ten to commuter rail service to Boston.

OPEN: Year round. Two-night minimum, weekends mid-June–October and holidays. Three-night minimum on July 4 weekend.

RATES: Mid-June–October $115–$150; Stable House, $800 weekly. November–mid-June, reduced rates. Singles $25 less. Amex, Discover, MC, Visa. ♥ ❖ ⚄ ⚞

ᔆ From a stack of detailed letters from Massachusetts, California, Ohio, Connecticut, Louisiana, New York, Washington, and Canada: *"Although it is 20 miles from my business contact, I always stay here. . . . Nice and quiet . . . so much within walking distance . . . plus an in-ground pool . . . friendly and helpful without being overbearing. . . . Knox produced books on local history . . . found family association. . . . Wonderful ideas for activities . . . great conversations about birds, architecture, design, cooking, gardening . . . rear cottage in a bucolic setting. . . . Meet other guests who also feel it is a home away from home . . . . Captain's Room is our favorite . . . modern baths . . . excellent beds . . . charming inn . . . impeccable . . . grounds show loving care . . . in town but doesn't give feeling of being 'in the midst.' . . . The perfect New England visit."*

MANY INTERNATIONAL travelers, too, agree with the local Realtor who in 1993 suggested that the Johnsons would make great innkeepers. Knox, an architectural designer and landscape architect, and his late wife Shirley, an interior designer who redirected the character of the mid-nineteenth-century Greek Revival style of the building, incorporated their hands-on experience in previous house restorations. Guest rooms are typically uncluttered, bright, and airy, with a wonderful summery touch and with imaginative combinations of color and fabrics, antiques and reproductions, Oriental and braided rugs, and original art.

BED AND BATH: Five large rooms and one suite—all air conditioned and all with private baths—on three floors accessed by three stairways. Plus two one-bedroom apartments (with TV) in the Stable House, which "accommodate two persons, or up to four who are good traveling companions." First floor—room with canopied queen bed. Second-floor Chimney Room also has canopied queen bed. Other rooms have antique twins, queen, or king beds. Oceanview third-floor suite (with view across townscape to ocean several blocks away) has canopied queen bed, TV, tub/shower bath, daybed in sitting room, private entrance.

BREAKFAST: 8–10 (earlier by arrangement). Juices. Yogurts. Homemade breads, muffins, coffee cakes, house-recipe granola. Fruit in season. Freshly ground house-blend coffee, teas (ready at 7:30). Special diets accommodated. Buffet style in dining room with beehive oven or on porch.

PLUS: Fireplaced living room. Well-stocked library. Intimate TV room. Refreshments, 4-6 P.M. Day-trip planning. Transportation from train. Special occasions acknowledged.

Inn on Cove Hill

978/546-2701

37 Mount Pleasant Street,
Rockport, MA 01966-1727

888/546-2701
www.cape-ann.com/covehill

HOSTS: Marjorie and John Pratt
LOCATION: One block from village, harbor, and shops. Close to beaches, golf; 1 mile to train to Boston. Bus servicing Cape Ann goes by the inn.
OPEN: April–October. Three-night minimum on summer and fall weekends and on holidays.
RATES: April–early June (excluding Memorial Day) $54 shared bath, $70–$110 private bath. Late June–October $54 shared bath; $74, $89, $115, or $128 private bath. ♥ ⚅ ⚒

THEY TOOK a trip around the world and stayed in many B&Bs. John, a civil (geotechnical) engineer, and Marjorie, a registered nurse, found that the idea of "being together, sharing a business in a lovely location" had strong appeal. Since their 1978 career change, the Pratts, who now live in a nearby residence, have completely and meticulously restored this classic square, three-story 1791 Federal home, the very inn where Marjorie and John spent their own honeymoon. What they offer all guests is a friendly atmosphere and the option of privacy.

Their attention to architectural detail can be seen in the wood-shingled roof, pumpkin pine floorboards, H and L hinges, dentil molding, and a spiral staircase with thirteen steps symbolizing the original thirteen colonies. Furnishings include fine family antiques, reproductions, and paintings—some done by artist guests. In a two-page spread, *Country Living* magazine called this inn "a New England treasure." English travelers wrote, "Beautifully decorated room . . . a lovely restful atmosphere. Heaven on earth, what more can I say?"

BED AND BATH: Eleven air-conditioned rooms (vary in size) on three floors. Nine with private bath. One first-floor room has private entrance. Third floor reached via a steep narrow stairway or outside metal spiral staircase. Rooms have queen bed (some canopied), queen and trundle, a double bed, or a double and a twin; some are four-posters or cannonball.
BREAKFAST: 8–9:30. (Coffee at 7.) Continental with one of seven varieties of muffins. Served around the pump garden (weather permitting), in living room, or on individual trays in guest rooms.
PLUS: Three porches, including one on third floor with harbor and ocean view. Hot spiced cider in fall, lemonade in summer, tea and cookies in spring. Will meet guests at train station. Off-street parking.

continued . . .

➤ From Pennsylvania: *"Spent our honeymoon here seven years ago. Everything is still beautiful. Rockport has got to be one of the most captivating and tranquil towns. The Inn on Cove Hill enhances it completely."*

➤ The Sally Webster Inn

978/546-9251

34 Mount Pleasant Street,
Rockport, MA 01966

(TOLL FREE) 877/546-9251
E-MAIL sallywebsterinn@hotmail.com
www.rockportusa.com/sallywebster

HOSTS: Rick and Carolyn Steere
LOCATION: Residential historic district. At the top of a hill (benches await at park halfway up) that is 4 blocks from Bearskin Neck area with its art galleries, shops, restaurants, and ocean. Short drive to (spectacular) Halibut Point State Park.
OPEN: February 14 through December. Two-night weekend minimum, mid-June through mid-October and holidays.
RATES: Vary according to bed size. $80–$95 mid-June through mid-October. $65–$79 off-season. MC, Visa. ♥ ⊞ ⚄ ⚄ ♥♡

EUROPEAN GUESTS often comment that this B&B is just what they imagined as a traditional New England home in a coastal town. Built in 1832, it has six fireplaces and wide-plank floors. Today it is fronted by a picket fence. All guest rooms have private baths. Since the Steeres, sailors who wished to relocate near the ocean, bought the property in 1998, they have renovated, decorated (traditionally), and gardened. Comfortable sofas are by the fireplace in the formal living room. Windsor chairs are in the Colonial dining room.

In Longmeadow, Massachusetts, Carolyn was a pediatric nurse before she was office manager for pediatricians. Rick was a greeting card company vice president. Now their youngest (of four) is in college. Here they offer a calm, peaceful environment, a romantic getaway, and concierge service.

BED AND BATH: Seven air-conditioned and carpeted rooms on three floors (sloped ceiling on third floor). All private en-suite baths—some tub/shower, others with shower only. King, queen (one is canopied), double (two canopied and two with additional single bed in room), or twin beds.
BREAKFAST: 8:30–10. Homemade bread, granola, and pastry. Yogurts. Cereals. Juice. Fresh fruit. Hot beverages. Plus, on Sunday, hot entrée. Buffet style in dining room. Eat at one table set for six, at another for four, or outside on the terrace.
PLUS: No TV. Wood-burning fireplace and piano in living room. Second-floor deck (accessible from yard too). Terrace, lawn, and arbor (for wedding ceremonies too). In summer, iced tea or lemonade with cookies at 4 P.M.

➤ From Georgia: *"We are B&Bers and found this place to be at the top rung."*
From England: *"Set a high standard for food and accommodations for the rest of our visit."*

☞ *Seacrest Manor*   978/546-2211

99 Marmion Way,   **www.rockportusa.com/seacrestmanor/**
Rockport, MA 01966-1988

HOSTS: Leighton T. Saville and Dwight B. MacCormack, Jr.
LOCATION: About 300 yards from the ocean, overlooking spectacular rocky coastline.
Across from the John Kiernan Nature Preserve, with short maintained trails
through woods to a dirt road that leads to the ocean. On 2 acres of gardens
and woodland. Along scenic shore route. One mile from center of
Rockport, off Route 127A.
OPEN: April through November. Three-day minimum on holidays, two-day on
weekends and most of the high season. Reservations required.
RATES: $104–$152 depending on bath arrangement. Singles $10 less. ♥ ✗ ✗ ♨

☞ From Virginia: *"The best of everything."* From Scotland: *"As close to Scottish*
hospitality as you can get." From Florida: *"Beautiful. Classic. Warm and memorable."*

LEIGHTON AND Dwight host in an English style intended as "concierge-type guest assistance." Hence the attention to turned-down beds, tea at four, shined gentlemen's shoes (a
few guests do leave them outside at night), and peace and quiet in a beautiful setting. As one
English couple wrote, "Seacrest Manor must be heaven—came for one, stayed for seven!"

The part Georgian, part Federal-style house, built in 1911 and an inn since the 1940s,
was for many years the summer home of Arthur Park of Boston's Durgin-Park restaurant
family. It's more than a quarter century since the two current hosts took it over. Dwight,
an ordained Congregational minister, was looking for an alternative career. (He had lived
in England for a few months and was on the faculty of three area colleges.) Leighton's
family home is three doors away. (He retired from his NBC executive position in 1985.)
They are assisted by Kay Henderson, another NBC retiree, as manager, and in 1994 they
hosted NBC-TV newsman Roger Mudd when he was keynote speaker at the dedication
of Rockport's new library.

The common areas feature classic wallcoverings, art from family collections, and a dramatic gold-leaf-framed floor-to-ceiling living room mirror that came from the old
Philadelphia Opera House. A hammock awaits on the grounds with their prizewinning
(tour) gardens. And then there's that endless ocean view from the big second-story deck.

IN RESIDENCE: Bailey, "a black Lab/beagle who greets guests."
FOREIGN LANGUAGE SPOKEN: Some French.
BED AND BATH: Eight carpeted rooms; two on first floor, rest on second (two are seaside
with picture windows and deck). Six with private full bath; one two-room suite with
shared full bath. Queen bed or king/twins option.
BREAKFAST: 7:30–9:30. A different specialty each day. Fresh fruit cup, juices, spiced Irish
oatmeal with chopped dates, dry cereals, bacon and eggs, toast and sometimes muffins.
Coffee, English tea, chocolate. At tables set with fine china and linens.

continued . . .

PLUS: Cable TV and radio in rooms. Mints on pillow with quote from Shakespeare. Huge living room with books, magazines, English publications. Library. Bedroom oscillating fans. Hammock between trees. Terrace. Complimentary newspapers Monday–Saturday. Beach towels. Bicycles ($7 for half day).

🐾 The Tuck Inn B&B

17 High Street, Rockport, MA 01966

978/546-7260

800/789-7260

E-MAIL tuckinn@shore.net

www.rockportusa.com/tuckinn/

HOSTS: Liz and Scott Wood
LOCATION: On a quiet street. One block from town center, 2 to beach and Bearskin Neck. Ten-minute walk to train station.
OPEN: Year round. Three-night minimum on holiday weekends; two nights June–October weekends.
RATES: Mid-June–late October $79–$99; suite (four people) $129. Late October–Mid-June $59–$79; suite $109. Third person $15. MC, Visa.
♥ ♦♦♦ ⚉ ⚰

🐾 From Idaho, California, and England: *"Clean, comfortable, reasonably priced . . . excellent and plentiful breakfast . . . friendly hosts."*

THIS IS A family-run place that welcomes families—and the many foreign travelers who like the idea of staying with a family. (Two of the offspring are in college now.) The Woods bought the 1790 Colonial house in 1991. They furnished simply and have since also purchased the next-door house. Scott has happily exchanged his days as an accountant for his role here as official baker. Boston-born Liz agrees that Rockport is a marvelous place to live. The whole family takes walks. And they can give restaurant recommendations too.

IN RESIDENCE: One teenager—Catherine.
BED AND BATH: Eleven air-conditioned rooms with twin beds, double, queen, or king; all private baths (some are shower only, others have tub and shower). Suite has queen bed in one room, two twin beds in other, large deck overlooking pool. Some rooms have private exterior entrance and/or outside deck. All have TV.
BREAKFAST: 8–9:30. Fresh fruit. Yogurt. Scott's specialties—homemade granola, muffins, bread, scones, biscuits. Cereal, juice, and hot beverages. Buffet style.
PLUS: Living room with fireplace and piano. Guest refrigerator. In-ground pool. Beach towels. Off-street parking.

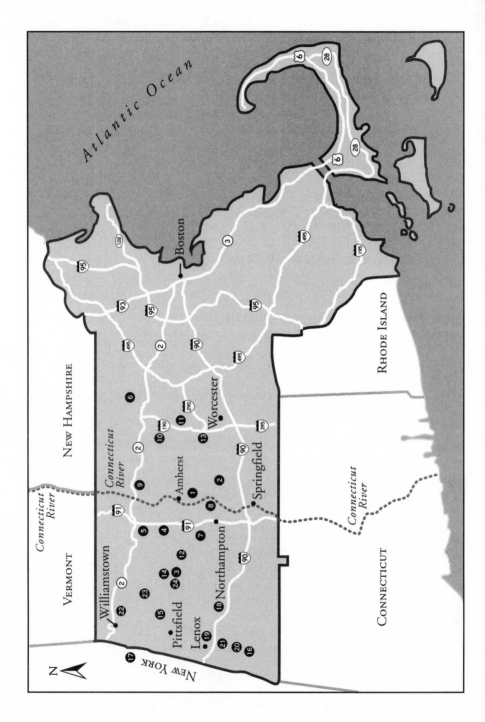

The numbers on this map indicate the locations of Central Massachusetts, Pioneer Valley, and Berkshires B&Bs described in detail in this chapter.

CENTRAL MASSACHUSETTS, PIONEER VALLEY, AND BERKSHIRES

Please see page 141 for Cape Cod, Martha's Vineyard, and Nantucket; Southeastern Massachusetts; Boston Area; Just a Little West; North of Boston.

Can't find the community you wish to visit? Check with a reservation service described at the beginning of this chapter.

Central Massachusetts and Pioneer Valley Reservation Services

ᔋ *The Hampshire Hills Bed & Breakfast Association*

P.O. Box 553, Worthington, MA 01098

> **PHONE:** 888/414-7664. Leave name and address for free brochure. And/or listen for telephone number of the "on duty" member host who is aware of available openings that fit your needs.
>
> **FAX:** 413/296-4599
>
> **E-MAIL:** info@hamphillsbandb.com
>
> **URL:** www.hamphillsbandb.com
>
> **LISTINGS:** Sixteen in the hills between the Berkshires and the Pioneer Valley. Most are open year round. Number of guest rooms range from one (the smallest B&B) to five. Amenities vary and include hot tubs, swimming pools, and hiking trails on the premises. Individual descriptions are in a free brochure.
>
> **RESERVATIONS:** All bookings are made directly with each B&B. Most B&Bs require two-night minimum on summer and holiday weekends.
>
> **RATES:** $40–$70 single. $50–$90 double. Most B&Bs require deposits. A few members accept credit cards.

IN AN EFFORT to promote tourism and to maintain the area's rural character, families were encouraged to offer bed and breakfast in the early 1980s. Five of the charter association members are still hosting in this low-key region, a true treasure. Hampshire Hills encompasses the "in between" towns of Becket, Blandford, Chesterfield, Cummington, Florence, Haydenville, Middlefield, Westhampton, Williamsburg, Windsor, Woronoco, and Worthington. Within the picturesque pocket are New England villages, farms, crafts studios, and restaurants. Visitors enjoy marvelous bicycling routes, cross-country skiing areas, antiquing, auctions, sugarhouses, agricultural fairs, natural beauty, waterfalls, and much peace and quiet. Nearby there are twelve colleges plus Berkshires attractions—among them Tanglewood, Jacob's Pillow, the Williamstown Theater, and museums. These include the recently opened MASS MoCA, a (huge) center for visual, performing, and media arts that is itself a work in progress.

A RESERVATION SERVICE WITH B&Bs IN CENTRAL MASSACHUSETTS AND THE PIONEER VALLEY:

Berkshire Bed & Breakfast Homes (page 292), 413/268-7244 or 800/762-2751, books many B&Bs in this area.

CENTRAL MASSACHUSETTS AND PIONEER VALLEY B&Bs

Allen House Victorian Inn

413/253-5000

599 Main Street, Amherst, MA 01002-2409

E-MAIL allenhouse@webtv.net
www.allenhouse.com

HOSTS: Alan and Ann Zieminski
LOCATION: In town, on 3 acres. Across the street from the Emily Dickinson House. Within walking distance of Amherst College; Hampshire College; University of Massachusetts; galleries, museums, shops, restaurants. Ten miles to Deerfield Village. On five-college (free) bus route. One-quarter mile to fabulous 8.5-mile paved bike trail, formerly an old rail trail.
OPEN: Year round. Two-night minimum on college and foliage weekends.
RATES: Vary according to season, number of people in room, and length of stay. Single $45–$125. Double $75–$150 May–October; $55–$115 off-season.
♥ ⚅ ⅄

A SUCCESS STORY. Historically accurate. "Like stepping back in time," say many guests, who appreciate this painted lady, an Amherst Historic Commission Preservation Award winner. The hand-carved cherry mantels of the Queen Anne Stick–style house are pictured in the Metropolitan Museum of Art catalog. Some of the wallpapers were designed by William Morris and Walter Crane. Built in 1886, the house still has original woodwork. The antiques have been collected through the years by Alan; he "has a perfect eye for spotting Aesthetic Period (1880s) pieces," according to his brother, Jonas, assistant innkeeper and retired teacher, who has helped to research the "Oscar Wilde period." Ann (a former dental hygienist and an artist at heart—and hand), other family members, museum staffers, and guests have also exchanged information with Alan, a biochemist turned full-time innkeeper. He lived in the house as a student before buying it "with the desire to make an eighteen-room Victorian into other than student housing." It is—and very up-to-date, complete with private phones and modems in every guest room.

For an encore, the Zieminskis, self-taught restoration experts, have just completed converting one of the outbuildings to a bicycle barn, a painted lady too, that is surely one of a kind. Now it's a small cottage with gingerbread fashioned by Alan, with porch and rockers and, inside, a good place for guests' bicycles and equipment. There's one more highlight at this B&B: A two-page *Bon Appétit* feature on the breakfasts attracted travelers from all over the world.

BED AND BATH: On first and second floors—seven rooms, all private baths, with a queen, a double or a double and one twin bed. Rollaway available.

continued...

BREAKFAST: At guests' convenience. Perhaps eggs Benedict, Swedish pancakes (Ann's family recipe), stuffed French toast, or Southwestern-style eggs.

PLUS: Central air conditioning. Bedroom ceiling fans. Beverages. Goose-down comforters and pillows. Afternoon and evening refreshments. Verandas. Off-street parking. For guests, two-for-one rentals at nearby bike shop.

⁗ From Connecticut: *"Beautiful . . . hearty and healthy breakfasts. . . . Warm hospitality."* From Massachusetts: *"Impeccable restoration."*

⁗ Carriage Towne Bed and Breakfast on the Common

413/323-0289

E-MAIL jskstoia@juno.com

17 Main Street,
Belchertown, MA 01007-0671

www.bbonline.com/ma/carriagetowne/

HOSTS: Steve and Joan Stoia and daughter Kindreth

LOCATION: In center of small New England town "without a shopping mall, but down the road from Quabbin Reservoir for hiking, picnicking, or just marveling at!" Across from common (trees, grass, benches, bandstand with summer concerts) and steepled churches. On the main road from the Massachusetts Turnpike to the University of Massachusetts. Ten-minute drive to Amherst or South Hadley; twenty minutes to Northampton.

OPEN: Year round. Two-night minimum for second and third weekends in May.

RATES: $80, $85 ($10 extra person), $90 with whirlpool. No charge for crib. Discover, MC, Visa. ⊞ ⠇ ⌫

THE FOUR-SQUARE National Register Colonial, long known as the Loving Cup Antiques Store, was a private residence when the Stoias found it and realized their thirty-year dream. "At ages twenty and twenty-one, we were University of Massachusetts residence hall parents in charge of 350 souls. We talked then of someday having an inn. Later, on a trip to England, we fell in love with the B&B concept." In the 1990s they searched for a historic property that could be a family business. Decor is "not Martha Stewartized"—without dried flowers and such—according to one guest. Wide-board floors are painted slate blue. Colors—bayberry green, tavern red, and putty, were selected by previous owners who consulted with Old Deerfield staff.

Steve works in the Amherst leisure services department with community theater and all the youth programs. Joan is on the staff of the University of Massachusetts career services department. They are weekend hosts who are permanent residents here. Kindreth, who lives with her husband and family in Amherst, is weekday hostess.

FOREIGN LANGUAGE SPOKEN: "A very little bit of Spanish."

BED AND BATH: Three large rooms, each with private bath, small refrigerator, TV/VCR. First floor—king bed, en-suite shower bath. Second floor—one air-conditioned room

with queen bed and a single daybed, en-suite tub/shower bath. One with queen four-poster, air conditioning, large bath with two-person Jacuzzi and separate shower.
BREAKFAST: 7-8 weekdays; 8-9 weekends. (Other times arranged with advance notice.) "Abundant." Freshly squeezed juice. Bagels, toast, and freshly baked goods. Cereals. Hot beverages. Served in one of two dining rooms by the 1770s open hearth.
PLUS: Upright piano in parlor. Fresh fruit. Complimentary beverages.

    Guests wrote: *"A wonderful introduction to B&Bs.... Beautiful accommodations ... interesting conversations ... incredibly comfortable beds ... immaculate facilities ... helpful hearts ... delicious breakfast ... first time traveling alone; certainly chose the right place."*

The Seven Hearths

412 Main Road, Route 143,
Chesterfield, MA 01012-9708

413/296-4312
FAX 413/296-4599
E-MAIL D7Hearths@aol.com
www.hamphillsbandb.com/sevenhearths

HOSTS: Doc and Denise LeDuc
LOCATION: Quiet, rural setting. Next door to library and museum. Across the street from town tennis courts. On a designated bicycle route. (In hiking country too.) Eighteen minutes west of Northampton, almost on the Berkshire County line.
OPEN: Year round. Two-night minimum on weekends.
RATES: $65–$90 shared bath. $105 private bath, fireplace. Singles $5 less. Reduced rates for stays of three nights or more. Cots available, $15. Discover, MC, Visa. ♥ ⊞ ❖ ✄ ✁

"WHERE IS THE center of Chesterfield?" asked the guest from Manhattan. "You're here!" responded Doc, a native of the area who enjoys explaining that the general store is the extent of the town center. When Doc and Denise, both in their forties, looked at this 1891 Dutch gambrel (renovated and "updated" many times over), they knew that their idea of "owning a B&B in semiretirement" would be speeded up. Opened in 1990, it's formal here and "country" there—with antiques and plants, with swags and sheer curtains, with old and some new characteristics.

Doc, a former social worker, has considerable experience as a stage lighting designer and contractor. Denise, a gardener/stained glass artist/cook/photographer, worked as fiscal director for a human service agency. Now she is operations manager for a computer networking firm.

IN RESIDENCE: In hosts' quarters—Jessie, a chocolate Lab, or Matt, the cat, may "visit guests upon request."
BED AND BATH: Four second-floor rooms. One large room with queen bed, daybed with trundle, wood-burning fireplace, sitting area, private tub/shower bath. One room with

continued ...

double bed and wood-burning fireplace and one with king/twins option and fireplace share full hall bath that is also shared by a fourth room (with double bed) booked by small groups or family parties.

BREAKFAST: 8-10. Juices. Fresh fruit. Denise's blue-ribbon (agricultural fairs) jams, breads, and muffins. Cereals. Freshly ground coffee. Teas. Entrée possibilities include baked stuffed (peach/raspberry) French toast, baked oven vegetable omelet, baked apple pancake, zucchini frittata. Sometimes, honey-glazed salmon as a side dish. Meats served by request. Special diets accommodated. Served in fireplaced dining room.

PLUS: Wood-burning fireplace and TV in living room. Hot tub. Guest refrigerator stocked with water, soda, yogurts.

      ⋙ From Virginia: *"I was a banker in western Massachusetts . . . often drove by this lovely old house that is now Seven Hearths. . . . Stayed there recently. . . . What they have done is truly wonderful—and magic. . . . Among the best facilities (including the Ritz at Laguna Niguel, California) we have stayed in. Doc and Denise are superior hosts."*

⋙ Sunnyside Farm   413/665-3113

21 River Road, Whately, MA 01093

HOSTS:	Mary Lou and Dick Green
LOCATION:	In a farming community, next door to Nourse Strawberry Farms; in area with good hiking possibilities. Along a wonderful cycling route that is flat, very rural, very much old New England. Five miles south of Deerfield, fifteen minutes from Northampton (restaurants) and Amherst; near many colleges and private schools.
OPEN:	Year round. Reservations required. All answering machine messages returned promptly.
RATES:	$95 king or twin beds, $85 double bed. $55 single. ♥ ☛ ⚔ ⚒

IF YOU'VE NEVER had grandparents who lived in a big yellow farmhouse with a red barn complete with big letters that spell out its name, here's the place; and it's well maintained and loved by family and B&B guests. The fourteen-room home was previously owned by Mary Lou's grandparents.

"This is one of the reasons I want to stay here and hand it down to our children and (eleven) grandchildren. I spent summers here as a child and have wonderful memories. . . . We have been living here since 1972, when we moved up from Northampton with our four children. (Two have been married on the grounds.) Except for extensive redecorating and recent redoing of the kitchen, the house is basically the same as when my grandparents remodeled it in 1920.

"My husband, a former comptroller at Amherst College, visits with guests in the evening when I am working as head nurse in the emergency department of Northampton's Cooley Dickinson Hospital. Breakfasts are a fun time for me. In season, not only do guests wake up to the aroma from one of the largest strawberry (and raspberry) farms in the Northeast, but some join me in picking before breakfast."

BED AND BATH: Three rooms, all with cross-ventilation (and window fans), share two baths (one full, one shower only). One large room with king bed, another with twin beds. One room with a double bed.
BREAKFAST: 8:15–9:30. Seasonal fruits, homemade muffins and jams, eggs, bacon or sausage, or a cheese strata. Please indicate special diets in advance. Served in country kitchen or at dining room table crafted by former guest.
PLUS: In-ground pool. Porches. Yard.

↬ From Massachusetts: *"Stay while on business . . . makes me feel as though I am on vacation. . . . Wonderful period home. Lovely people. Rooms are spacious, homey, well lit, clean, beautifully furnished. . . . Gourmet breakfasts 'from scratch.' And the views are great!"*

↬ *Brandt House Country Inn*

413/774-3329

29 Highland Avenue,
Greenfield, MA 01301

800/235-3329
FAX 413/772-2908
E-MAIL info@brandthouse.com
www.brandthouse.com

HOSTS: Ellen Villani and Kathy Reipold
LOCATION: Quiet. High on a hill, surrounded by 3½ acres of lawns and century-old evergreens. Hiking trails from here lead to panoramic views and town park—"great, too, for guests traveling with dogs." Five-minute walk to town and lighted skating pond. Five-minute drive to Historic Deerfield; within fifteen minutes of cross-country ski center in Northfield, many private schools, fly-fishing; twenty to Amherst and Northampton. Within 2 miles of I-91 and Route 2.
OPEN: Year round. Two-night minimum on May and October weekends.
RATES: May–September weekends $135 shared bath, $140–$195 private; weekdays $110 shared, $130–$195 private. November–April weekends $110 shared, $130–$150 private; weekdays $100 shared, $120–$140 private. Daily October $135 shared, $165–$195 private. $20 additional person. Corporate and long-term rates available. Amex, Discover, MC, Visa. ♥ ⊞ ❖ ❤♡

↬ From New Mexico: *"Beautiful home, wonderful breakfasts, and a most gracious staff make this B&B hard to leave."*

THIS ESTATELIKE turn-of-the-century sixteen-room Colonial Revival is made for entertaining; for B&B; for business meetings, weddings, and honeymooners. It fits owner Phoebe Compton's style—as did her Boston area brownstone, where she hosted before she moved here in 1986. An interior designer, she decorated the spacious, light-filled tall-

continued . . .

ceilinged rooms with a fascinating blend of contemporary and antique pieces, Oriental rugs, and works by local artists. The beamed living room has a fireplace, bay windows, and wonderful valley views. Another wood-burning fireplace and a regulation pool table are in the library. Wicker furniture and a swing are on the huge, inviting covered porch.

From the beginning, Ellen, a Greenfield native, has been on staff. She and her sister Kathy, who coordinates many special events (including lots of weddings), are star hosts. Phoebe, now a professional gardener, coordinates meetings here.

BED AND BATH: On second and third floors—eight large air-conditioned rooms (two with working fireplace); all with private phone and remote-control TV. Six have private full baths. Two with skylights. Two rooms that can be a suite share a large full bath. King, queen, double, twin, and extra twin beds available; all with feather beds and down comforters.

BREAKFAST: Usually 7:15–9. Juice, fresh fruit, homemade granola, homemade baked goods, freshly ground coffee. Plus, on weekends, eggs Benedict, cheese blintzes, Moravian frittata with cheese sauce, or French toast, all with bacon. At large oak dining room table overlooking terrace, in living room at table for two overlooking valley, or on covered porch.

PLUS: Upright piano. Guest refrigerators and microwave. Fresh fruit and flowers. Wraparound porches. (New) clay tennis court. "And, yes, we accept dogs! Children are welcome too."

🦅 *Wrangling Brook Farm*   978/448-8253

P.O. Box 138, 18 Kemp Street,   978/448-5427
West Groton, MA 01472-0138   FAX 978/448-8253 OR 448-3777
                                              E-MAIL wrangling@aol.com

      HOSTS: David and Lynne Gleason
   LOCATION: Rural and peaceful; just an hour from Boston. On a 30-acre working farm.
              Bordering 1,000 acres of conservation land with hiking, biking, and cross-
              country trails. Ten miles from Routes 495 and 2. Five minutes to Groton
              School and Lawrence Academy; thirty to Concord and Lowell. Near an-
              tiques shops, canoeing, and skiing (Wachusett Mountain and Nashoba
              Valley).
       OPEN: Year round.
      RATES: $115 queen with fireplace, $110 king with balcony, $100 double bed. Singles
              $5 less. Third person $20. Corporate rates available. Amex, Discover, MC,
              Visa. ♥ ⊞ ⌁ ⅙ 🐾 ❤️⟲

      🦅 From Vermont, California, Virginia, Massachusetts, Australia, France,
England: "*We'll never stay in a hotel again! . . . a delightful experience. . . . Highlight of our visit to New England . . . a beautiful home. . . . I wish all business travel would be as great. . . .*

The children loved the loft, cows, and dog . . . culinary delights . . . luxurious comfort . . . delightful animal sounds . . . much-needed serenity and most gracious hosts."

OTHER GUESTS write about being "spoiled" or "pampered" at this handsome Colonial-style homestead, built by the Gleasons in 1985. A reproduction of the house that burned on this wonderful site, it has six Rumford fireplaces, wide-board floors, hand-hewn beams, and "all the comforts associated with modern homes." Furnishings include antiques, Oriental rugs, and lots of comfortable seating. There's an in-ground pool. The "real New England" scene is complete with barns, gardens, stone walls, a brook—and, in the meadow, a herd of Belted Galloway cattle. The well-traveled hosts are avid pilots and bicyclists. Lynne is an attorney. David is a semiretired physician who is a part-time farmer. They opened their home as a B&B in 1995.

IN RESIDENCE: Shaka, a Bernese mountain dog, and Rum-Tum Tugger, a cat.
FOREIGN LANGUAGE SPOKEN: A little French.
BED AND BATH: Three large second-floor rooms; all with private en-suite bath, phone, cable TV. Antique queen four-poster, wood-burning fireplace, sitting area, shower bath. Room with king/twins option has shower bath, ceiling fan, skylights, French doors to private balcony (for continental breakfast, if you'd like) overlooking meadow. One room has double bed and a loft with two twin beds, skylight, full bath.
BREAKFAST: 7:30–9. Stuffed French toast, scrambled eggs with smoked salmon and chives, baked eggs or strata. Sausage pudding. Home-baked muffins, scones, and breads. Fruit. Juice. Homegrown sausage, bacon, vegetables, and herbs. Served in dining room by fireplace, or on screened porch overlooking brook and waterfall.
PLUS: Air-conditioned first floor. Whole-house fan. In-ground swimming pool. Afternoon refreshments. Many books and magazines. Local restaurant menus.

B&Bs OFFER THE OPPORTUNITY TO GET AWAY WITHOUT GOING AWAY.

⇗ The Knoll

413/584-8164

230 North Main Street, Florence,
Northampton, MA 01062-1221

FAX 603/308-0357
E-MAIL theknoll@crocker.com
www.crocker.com/~theknoll

HOSTS: Lee and Ed Lesko
LOCATION: In the Florence section of Northampton. Set far back from the road, on a knoll (an acre of lawn) overlooking 17 acres of farmland and forest. Three miles west of Smith College, 9 to Amherst, 15 to Mount Holyoke, 12 to Deerfield. Five-minute walk to beautiful public park.
OPEN: Year round. Minimum stay required for graduation and holiday weekends. Reservations preferred.
RATES: $55 single, $60 double, $65 twins. ☛ ⚅ 🍴

THE LESKOS talk of their four-year guests—those who bring their freshman children to school and stay here for every visit through graduation. We stayed during a spring cycling trip when the magnificent two-story-high Michigan redbud blossoms were peeking into our room. For the evening activity, we had our choice of contra dancing or a concert.

Now Ed, a Northampton native and former air force pilot, is retired from his window and door sales. Lee is originally from Biloxi, Mississippi. They live in a homey twelve-room English Tudor. In the corner of their large living room is a striking (in every sense of the word) 7-foot-tall grandfather clock made in Germany around 1900. Housekeeping is impeccable.

BED AND BATH: Three second-floor bedrooms share two baths (one has tub only—a deep "original" soaking tub; other has tub/shower). One room with twin beds, the others with double beds.
BREAKFAST: 8–8:30. Lee will usually join you for coffee after you have had your cereal, fresh fruit, their homegrown raspberries, strawberries, fresh farm eggs any style, bacon, homemade bread, muffins or coffee cake, and jam.
PLUS: Large screened porch. Tour grounds, if you'd like. Paths for jogging or walking. Walk to Look Park for its beautifully landscaped grounds, plenty of running and roaming space, playground, picnic grounds, and tennis courts.

⇗ Guests wrote: *"Sun-dried sheets smelled so wonderful! . . . Enjoyable stay."*

*C*AN'T FIND A LISTING *for the community you are going to? Check with a reservation service described at the beginning of this chapter. Through the service you may be placed (matched) with a welcoming B&B that is near your destination.*

⤖ *Clark Tavern Inn B&B*   413/586-1900

98 Bay Road,   FAX 413/587-9788
Hadley, MA 01035-9718   E-MAIL ruth@clarktaverninn.com
www.clarktaverninn.com

HOSTS: Mike and Ruth Callahan
LOCATION: Tranquil. On more than an acre of landscaped grounds. Surrounded by farmlands and private homes. Near town center on Route 47. Near extensive hiking and designated bicycling trails. Five-minute drive to Northampton and Amherst.
OPEN: Year round.
RATES: Summer $115–$135 with fireplace; $105–$125 with garden view. Winter $125–$145 fireplace; $100–$120 garden view. Higher rates for some college events and holidays. Amex, Discover, MC, Visa. ♥ ✄

⤖ From Connecticut: *"Feeling of complete relaxation and seclusion . . . decorated in antiques and quilts . . . makes you feel at home, not as if you shouldn't touch anything! . . . quiet, warm, welcoming."* From Massachusetts: *"Romantic . . . spent our honeymoon there . . . delivered wonderful breakfast to our room . . .spotless. . . . I'm British. One of the most delightful inns I've ever stayed in . . . breakfast artistically presented. . . . Mike and Ruth have thought of everything . . . renovations and decor respect the integrity of the beautiful old building . . . dining room with view of bird feeders and garden area beyond. . . . Ruth and Mike are unpretentious, friendly, and attentive. They have created a setting and an experience that you would definitely want to repeat."*

As GUESTS ATTEST, this historic haven, a 1742 Georgian Colonial, is picture-perfect inside and out. Saved from demolition (to make room for I-91) and moved to its present site in 1961, it has wide-plank floors, twelve-over-twelve windows, wing chairs by the fireplace, vintage puzzles and games in one of the two large common rooms, spacious and air-conditioned guest rooms, an in-ground pool, and lovely grounds. All the antiques were collected by Ruth, a registered nurse, and Mike, a physician's assistant, for their "someday" bed and breakfast. The Callahans, members of the Sierra Club and Greenpeace, purchased the property in 1993, opened in 1995, and have since been recommended by the *New York Times* in a Pioneer Valley feature.

IN RESIDENCE: Three cats—"two love being petted; one is shy." The Beatties, Ruth's parents: "Dad [Ed] is a great groundskeeper; Mom [Ruth], an invaluable help with housekeeping."
FOREIGN LANGUAGE SPOKEN: Some Spanish.
BED AND BATH: Three second-floor rooms, each with queen bed, private tub/shower bath, TV/VCR (in Colonial-style cabinet), private phone with modem access. Two rooms have canopied bed and wood-burning fireplace; one with cathedral ceiling overlooks gardens.
BREAKFAST: Usually 8–9:30. (Coffee earlier.) Choose from extensive menu the night before. Juices. Fruit course. Homemade muffins. Strawberry waffles, blueberry pancakes, or

continued . . .

French toast à l'orange. Breakfast meats and potatoes. Cereal. Yogurt. Served on poolside screened patio or by candlelight in dining room or guests' room.
PLUS: Wood-burning fireplace in living room. Guest refrigerator with complimentary bottled water, soda, champagne, or wine. Extensive gardens, benches in private sitting areas, oversized hammock, goldfish pond. Pets welcome with prior approval.

≈ *Bullard Farm B&B and Conference Center* 978/544-6959

89 Elm Street,   FAX 978/544-6959
North New Salem, MA 01364   E-MAIL bullard@shaysnet.com

HOST: Janet Kraft
LOCATION: Peaceful and beautiful. On 300 acres with open fields, woods, rhododen-
           dron gardens, hiking and cross-country ski trails, old mill sites. In a town
           with fifty residents—and 1794 Meetinghouse performing arts center. Three
           miles to Route 2. One mile to Route 202, Lake Mattawa, and Quabbin
           Reservoir; 13 miles to Northfield Mountain (cross-country skiing); 25 to
           Historic Deerfield and Northampton; 18 miles east of Amherst.
OPEN: Year round.
RATES: $70 single, $80 double. $20 third person on three-quarter bed or rollaway.
        Corporate rates. MC, Visa. 🏃 ⊞ ⚡ 🏃

"THE BULLARD family were lumbermen and have been in this 200-year-old Federal house for 130 years. My mother and her three sisters were born and married here. For my third career, I restored the farmhouse, which has been filled with vibrant people for as long as I can remember. It has family treasures including ancestral portraits (everyone asks) and antiques. After opening as a B&B in 1991, I converted the barn into a modern conference center that can accommodate 150 people. One field here leads to the river, another to a wooded ridge with scenic waterfall and gorge. Guests pick blueberries (a hundred cultivated bushes), find the old swimming hole, explore Quabbin Reservoir. They hike, cross-country ski, fish, and bike (annotated maps provided for 4- to 60-mile loops). It's just ninety minutes from Boston—and into another world!"

Bostonians feel like discoverers. Foreigners also love this place. Area colleges book meetings here. When I visited with West Virginians, they too felt very much at home at this hidden secret. When I returned with my husband, Janet shared restaurant suggestions and cycling routes. A church organist, she is a former piano teacher and retired human services counselor.

BED AND BATH: Four large second-floor rooms. One with twin beds (and a phone) shares bath with room that has double bed, working fireplace. Room with a double and a three-quarter bed, working fireplace, and phone shares a full bath with air-conditioned queen-bedded room. Rollaway and crib available.
BREAKFAST: Usually 8–10. Cheese strata or blueberry pancakes. Apple coffee cake,

muffins, cran/applesauce, homemade breads and pastries. In dining room (with organ) overlooking field, or in fireplaced breakfast room with exposed beams.
PLUS: Fireplaced living room. Robes provided. Badminton. Croquet. Horseshoe and volleyball courts. TV. "I can usually borrow playmates for children over three."

➳ From Utah: *"A very special place."* From Virginia: *"Charming house . . . delicious food."* From Washington, D.C.: *"It's terrific—and so is Janet."*

➳ *Fernside Bed & Breakfast*

978/464-2741

162 Mountain Road,
Princeton, MA 01541

(**OUTSIDE MASSACHUSETTS**) 800/545-2741
FAX 978/464-2065
E-MAIL fernside@msn.com
www.fernsideinn.com

HOSTS: Richard and Jocelyn Morrison
LOCATION: On a ridge "looking at Boston 55 miles away." Just down the road from Wachusett Mountain hiking trails. Three miles to Wachusett Mountain ski area. Fifteen miles north of Worcester. About ten minutes from Route 2 or I-190; forty-five minutes northeast of Sturbridge, thirty to Lexington and Concord. "Within five miles of several excellent restaurants."
OPEN: Year round. Two-night minimum on some holiday weekends and during peak foliage.
RATES: Vary according to view and size of bath. Sunday–Thursday $115–$145 queen with fireplace, $145 suite. Friday and Saturday $135–$165 queen with fireplace, $165 suite. $40 additional person. Amex, Diners, Discover, MC, Visa.
♥ ❖ ♨ ⅍

WITH THAT BIG wraparound porch and the antiques, reproductions, and Oriental rugs, the Federal mansion may feel like an old inn—but the yellow cedar clapboards are all new. The plastered-to-look-old walls are insulated. The wide pine, birch, and fir floors are refinished. From 1994 (when they bought the property) until the fall of 1996 (when they opened), Richard, formerly a high-tech CEO, and Jocelyn, a former preschool director, did most of the restoration—including all that woodwork around 102 windows. "Our previous experience was with a small Cape-style house that we added on to three times." Because the Morrisons, parents of three grown children, have lived in Princeton for almost two decades, they had long admired this Federal house, which was a private home; a boardinghouse for Harvard College professors and students; a tavern; and, for a hundred years (until 1989), a vacation club for Boston working women. Now it is on the National Register. Local residents are sharing anecdotes. Travelers are sharing rave reviews.

IN RESIDENCE: One dog, Gus, a golden retriever; one cat, Darth Vader.
BED AND BATH: Four rooms and two suites, each with private tiled bath and air conditioning.

continued . . .

First-floor suite, handicapped accessible, has two twin beds, separate sitting room with view and porch access. Second-floor suite has queen bed, separate sitting room, Boston views. Four rooms, each with canopied queen bed, fireplace, tub/shower (one has shower only) bath.

BREAKFAST: 8–9:30. Fresh fruit, homemade pastry or baked goods. Pancakes, Belgian waffles, crepes, or eggs with ham, sausage, or bacon. Granola, cereals. Served in large dining room with views of Wachusett Mountain and Boston.

PLUS: Upright piano in reading room. 4 P.M. refreshments. Fresh fruit and flowers. Fireplace in private dining room used for small groups. Turndown service. Croquet. Telescope (can be brought to porch). Album of Fernside photos dating back to 1919. Picnic baskets prepared; charge varies.

🐚 From California: *"Beautifully restored . . . impeccably clean . . . felt like a treasured guest in their home."* From New Hampshire: *"We often stay at B&Bs . . . one of the nicest . . . options at breakfast . . . a home away from home."* From Massachusetts: *"A spectacular spread at breakfast . . . friendly innkeepers . . . lovely room, well planned, two comfortable chairs in front of fireplace . . . soft drinks in our room. . . . We loved it!"*

🐚 *The Rose Cottage*   508/835-4034

24 Worcester Street, Routes 12 and 140,
West Boylston, MA 01583-1413

HOSTS: Michael and Loretta Kittredge
LOCATION: Country setting on landscaped grounds overlooking Wachusett Reservoir in area with good hiking, bird-watching. Forty-five minutes west of Boston. Ten minutes to Worcester, Wachusett Mountain ski area (snowmaking), or winery (tours and picnic area); 40 to Sturbridge Village.
OPEN: Year round. Two-night minimum on holiday, college graduation, and college parents' weekends. Reservations required.
RATES: $80 per room. $15 third person. ♥ ♦♦ ⊞ ⚒ ⚓

HOME TO THE Kittredges since 1984, this antiques-filled classic Gothic Victorian cottage has lots of gingerbread, tall windows, wide-board floors, white marble fireplaces, electrified gas fixtures, and lavender Sandwich glass doorknobs. Many of the "comfortable kind of Victorian furnishings" are family pieces or came from the barn antiques shop Loretta had right here. Loretta, a West Boylston native—and community activist—changes the seasonal decor and makes the wreaths and silk flower baskets. (She also provides lunch and/or dinner for weddings or business groups.) Cohost Mike, a semiretired engineer who sells storage units, is water commissioner for the town. The well-traveled Kittredges—"Mike has 1,000 cousins!"—often exchange travel stories with guests from all over the world.

BED AND BATH: Five rooms, each with ceiling fan. Private full bath for first-floor room with iron-and-brass double bed. Upstairs, three double-bedded rooms and one room with twin beds share two baths. (Crib available.) Two executive apartments for longer stays.
BREAKFAST: Usually 7:30–10. Everything is garnished. Always fresh fruit and juice. Imported and other special teas (served from extensive teapot collection) and coffees. Perhaps cheddar-bacon quiche with homegrown herbs, hot muffins. Or French toast and homemade pastry. With bacon or sausage. Cereals "with cholesterol- and diet-conscious guests in mind." Served by candlelight in air-conditioned dining room.
PLUS: Welcoming beverage. Cable TV in common room along with guest refrigerator. Always, fresh flowers. Fruit bowl. Larger dining room for meetings. Three porches. Large yard with umbrella tables and swings. Maps, sightseeing information, menus from local restaurants, cordless phone, iron, and magazines.

From California: *"Helped rejuvenate me . . . in the middle of a business trip."* From North Carolina: *"What a pleasure to return every few years to find the Kittredges still doing B&B in the way that we remembered."*

Twin Maples

413/268-7925

106 South Street,
Williamsburg, MA 01096

www.hamphillsbandb.com/twinmaples

HOSTS: Eleanor and Martin Hebert
LOCATION: Idyllic. Surrounded by fields (facing one with picture-perfect barn and oxen), gardens, stone walls—and mountain view. Two miles from village. Seven miles to Northampton; 9 to I-91 interchange; 25 to Springfield.
OPEN: Year round. Two-night minimum on holidays and for college commencements.
RATES: $60 single, $65 double. Large room $70 single, $75 double.

THE RESTORED—inside and out—200-year-old farmhouse has exposed beams in the dining room, a kitchen with large fireplace and Dutch oven, and antique as well as Colonial reproduction furnishings. To complete the scene, the Heberts, parents of five grown children, have renewed their interest in farming with a recently built sugarhouse and with haying, extensive gardens, Hereford cows, and, yes, a farm dog.

What started out to be a sometime/maybe activity has almost become the headquarters of B&B in the area. Eleanor, a former Williamsburg librarian, is very involved with B&Bs in the Hampshire Hills as well as in the Berkshires. Martin, a design engineer, now has his own company. We are returnees who agree with the New York guests who wrote, "Like the candy on the pillow . . . 'mint'!"

continued . . .

BED AND BATH: Three air-conditioned rooms in a guest wing share a full updated bath. One room has restored iron-and-brass double bed, nonworking fireplace. Another has iron-and-brass twin beds, nonworking fireplace. Third room has restored double brass bed.

BREAKFAST: 7:30–9 on weekdays, until 10 on weekends. "We cater to vegetarians." Juice, fresh fruit; omelets, French toast, buttermilk pancakes (with or without blueberries), sausage, homemade sweet breads; coffee, tea, and milk; homemade maple syrup. Served on table set with flowers, linens, and handcrafted pottery, in dining room or on screened porch.

PLUS: Candy treats from daughter's shop in Northampton, "Sweet Expectations." Cozy quilts in winter. Guests' sitting room with gas-fired fireplace, TV, and games. Woodstove in huge country kitchen. Screened porch. Picnic table. Violets in spring; cosmos in fall.

    ⚞ Guests wrote: *"My room was charming. . . . The greatest hostess who ever was! . . . beautiful view . . . antiques . . . bountiful and delicious breakfast prepared with a full heart . . . a truly wonderful vacation experience."*

⚞ Pine Hill Bed and Breakfast   508/791-1762

11 Pond Street, Paxton, MA 01612   FAX 508/791-0602

    HOSTS: Sally and Bud Fay
  LOCATION: Rural and tranquil. At end of a winding country road through 28 acres of woods and past stone walls, meadows, three old mill foundations, and a brook. Near reservoir "where one finds tranquil beauty interrupted only by the cry of the loon." Three miles north of Paxton center. Fifteen minutes west of Worcester. Twenty minutes to Old Sturbridge Village or Wachusett Mountain ski area; forty-five minutes to Brimfield flea market.
     OPEN: February–December.
    RATES: Double $70; single $60. Extra person $10. Suite $115–$130. ♥ ⚐ ⚑ ⚒

    ⚞ Excerpts from dozens of cards received from all over the country and Europe too: *"Enjoyed it so much that we made another trip from the Midwest to experience it again! . . . Very homey. Warm welcoming feeling. . . . Two of the nicest people we have ever met. . . . Wonderful experience with our three children in this gorgeous home. . . . Great hosts who adapted to fussy elderly guests! . . . Scrumptious breakfast. . . . Every detail attended to. . . . A home-away-from-home experience, even greeted with refreshments. . . . A wonderful feeling of history. Beautiful grounds, birdsong, great hospitality. . . . Peaceful . . . idyllic . . . Easy, laid-back style . . . interesting conversations. . . . Beautiful old home with lilacs. . . . A delightful place to snuggle down in bed on a cold windy pre-Halloween night. . . . A very comfortable and interesting home in a beautiful setting. . . . What a find!"*

IN A PICTURE-PERFECT setting guests find this restored 1750 farmhouse with its wide-plank floors, Oriental rugs, quilts, and flea market finds; and in the fall there's a crafts fair/house tour right here. When the five Fay children grew up, the Fays began B&B in 1986. Sally, official gardener, loves to hike to a cliff with mountain view. Bud, former selectman and engineer, now sells real estate.

BED AND BATH: Three stenciled rooms. Two large second-floor rooms—one with double bed and a single sofa bed and another with two antique three-quarter beds ("not for real tall folk") and air conditioner—share (robes provided) a bath with tub and hand-held shower. Up steep staircase to large third-floor air-conditioned room with high Victorian-style double bed in a nook separate from sitting area, skylight, shower bath, room with two twin beds and one youth bed.

BREAKFAST: 8:30. Fresh grapefruit/raspberry/cranberry compote in stemware. Eggs goldenrod, orange French toast, or banana nut pancakes. Homemade breads, poppy-seed or blueberry muffins. Served in dining room, in glassed/screened porch, or sometimes by woodstove in keeping room.

PLUS: Welcoming refreshments. Fresh fruit. Mints. Transportation to/from Worcester airport. For sale—jelly made with homegrown grapes and herbs; family cookbook with recipes spanning years from 1855 to 1994.

*I*NNKEEPING MAY BE *America's most envied profession. As one host mused, "Where else can you get a job where, every day, someone tells you how wonderful you are?"*

⁂ *Berkshire Bed & Breakfast Homes*

P.O. Box 211, Williamsburg, MA 01096

PHONE: 413/268-7244 or 800/762-2751. Monday–Friday, 9 a.m.–6 p.m., year round.

FAX: 413/268-7243

E-MAIL: berkbb33@Javanet.com

URL: www.berkshirebnbhomes.com

LISTINGS: Seventy-five "choice B&Bs" in central and western Massachusetts—from the Berkshires east to Sturbridge and Worcester. North and South County Berkshires (many near Tanglewood and Williams College), Pioneer Valley and Hampshire Hills (close to the five-college area), Greater Springfield (some near Civic Center and Big E), Sturbridge, and Worcester County. Also eastern New York State. Mostly hosted private residences; some unhosted private residences plus inns. Free (partial) list includes rates.

RESERVATIONS: Two weeks' advance notice is recommended. In the Berkshires, two- or three-night minimum stays are often required on weekends or holidays and during the Tanglewood season. Occasionally, last-minute one-night openings available.

RATES: $45–$125 single, $50–$295 double, $8 booking fee. For some locations, $5, $10, or $15 surcharge for one-night stays. One night's rate required as deposit. Deposit minus $25 processing fee refunded if cancellation is received at least two weeks prior to arrival date. "For less than two week's notice, no refund unless our office or your host can rebook your reserved room; full refund if room is rebooked." Amex, MC, Visa. ❖

ATTENTION TO detail is a hallmark of this highly regarded service. Since 1986 it has been owned and run by Eleanor Hebert, an experienced B&B host who was, for many years, a professional librarian. She is aware of the importance of meeting the needs and expectations of hosts and guests. "In addition to the Berkshires, travelers have discovered the Pioneer Valley, especially Northampton, which has become a year-round mecca for performances, shopping, dining, and recreational activities." Eleanor knows what needs to be done and does it—well.

PLUS: Short-term (several weeks) hosted and unhosted housing also available.

AN ASSOCIATION WITH SOME B&BS IN THE BERKSHIRES:
The Hampshire Hills Bed & Breakfast Association, page 276.

⤳ Cumworth Farm

413/634-5529

472 West Cummington Road,
Cummington, MA 01026

FAX 413/634-5411
E-MAIL farmered@mediaone.net

HOST: Ed McColgan
LOCATION: On a scenic rural road with mountain views, 3.4 miles from town center. Hiking trails nearby; 45 minutes to Tanglewood, Williamstown, Amherst; 30 to Northampton.
OPEN: May through October. Reservations required. Two-night minimum.
RATES: $85 double. $75 single. Midweek $70, $60. Cot $10/night.

⤳ From New Hampshire: *"Lost ourselves in rows upon rows of raspberries . . . walked 2 miles on the property."* From Maryland: *"On the college tour circuit with our oldest daughter . . . turned to your guide. . . . We prefer to stay where we feel part of the family . . . accommodations were comfortable . . . breakfasts were delicious . . . fed the sheep, discussed the merits of Ed's mower and preventing the sag in a clothesline, compared selling blueberries in Maryland versus Massachusetts, reviewed merits of various colleges . . . found it difficult to leave. . . . It is truly a magic place."*

WE TOO HAVE experienced this homey European-like B&B. You'll also get tips about restaurants, a great cycling route, and a fun Tuesday night auction. You can enjoy the hot tub or patio with views of fields, rolling hills, and gardens. Read by the parlor stove. Have tea by the kitchen stove. And get to know why this B&B has a lengthy roster of fans.

As a youngster Ed worked on potato, dairy, and tobacco farms. As an adult he has experience as college history professor, Massachusetts Bicentennial director, state legislator, Northampton city councilor, and Department of Public Health executive. He and his wife, a congregate housing coordinator until her death in 1995, bought this 200-year-old farmhouse in 1979. Through the years the parents of seven grown children had many animals and held a barn roofing (complete in one weekend). There are thousands of blueberry and raspberry bushes that produce plenty of fruit for jam and jelly. And the maple sugaring operation continues to use wood to boil sap that is collected from 2,500 taps.

BED AND BATH: Six second-floor rooms with either a double bed or two twins. Four rooms share a full bath. Two share a tub bath. Four have ceiling fans.
BREAKFAST: 8:30–9:30. Pancakes with homegrown berries and homemade syrup; French toast and bacon. Also cereal, fruit, and muffins. Served around the claw-footed oak table in kitchen with restaurant stove and dozens of hanging baskets.

⚡ The Dalton House

413/684-3854

955 Main Street,
Dalton, MA 01226-2100

FAX 413/684-0203
E-MAIL innkeeper@thedaltonhouse.com
www.thedaltonhouse.com

HOSTS: Gary and Bernice Turetsky
LOCATION: On the main street of a small town that is the home of the company that makes all the paper for U.S. currency. Close to Tanglewood and to cross-country and downhill skiing at Jiminy Peak and Brodie Mountain.
OPEN: Year round. Two-night minimum in July, August, and October and on holidays.
RATES: Vary according to room size. $108–$135 summer, $88–$115 fall, $68–$95 winter, $78–$105 spring. Suites $95–$125. Extra person $15. Amex, MC, Visa. ♥ ⊞ ⊁

"WE WERE DOING B&B—with a relaxed peaceful atmosphere at moderate rates—before we knew what a B&B was. We have made so many changes that we have torn down walls that we put up!" In-room phones with computer/fax jacks, the 20-by-40-foot in-ground swimming pool, a deck with colorful awning, a pool house, extensive gardens, and a large breakfast room with skylights are among the additions to this B&B, a main house connected to the converted carriage house by a walk-through greenhouse. Furnishings combine Shaker style with contemporary pieces and folk art.

The Turetskys moved from Freehold, New Jersey, in 1971 to be in the florist business in "this quaint town." Innkeeper friends in Vermont provided the inspiration for converting this property to a B&B. Now the three daughters are grown and gone. The flower shop was sold and moved in 1990. Guests, including campers' parents and skiers, speak of visiting with Bernice and Gary at "my place in the Berkshires."

BED AND BATH: Nine rooms—five in main house, four on first floor of carriage house—with two twin beds or a double bed. Plus two second-floor suites—one with two double beds, the other with a twin and a double—with exposed beams and very large sitting areas. All with private shower baths, cable TV, phone, individual heat control, air conditioning.
BREAKFAST: 7:30–9:30. Continental buffet. Summer menu: Fresh fruit and yogurt, pancakes or French toast on Sunday. Rest of year: Hot and cold cereals. Fruit and yogurt. Blueberry, cranberry nut, and banana muffins. Toast-your-own English muffins and bagels. Juice, coffee, hot chocolate, teas.
PLUS: Large sitting room with stone fireplace, old beams, piano. Patio and gardens. Stone walkways to secluded gazebo and quiet sitting places. Secluded picnic area. Discount tickets for Jiminy Peak ski area.

⚡ From England: *"Recommend it for amenities, comfort, homey atmosphere, friendly hosts."* From California: *"Shared lots of interesting facts about the area and Crane Company."* From New York: *"Very, very pleasant rooms."*

﹌ *The Turning Point Inn*   413/528-4777

3 Lake Buel Road,   **EMAIL** ordeno@aol.com
Great Barrington, MA 01230-9808   **www.greatbarrington.org**

HOSTS: Rachel, Dennis, and (daughter) Teva O'Rourke
LOCATION: On 2½ acres. Next door to Butternut ski resort. Walk to Appalachian Trail
and Monument Mountain. Five miles from New Marlborough (and popu-
lar wedding site). Fifteen minutes to Tanglewood.
OPEN: Year round. Two-day weekend minimum in summer and fall and on
holidays.
RATES: $90 queen or twins with semiprivate bath. $110 queen, private bath. $130
king with trundle bed, private bath ($150 for four). Cottage $230 (for up to
five people). $20 less off-season (November–April). Weekly rates available.
Inquire about Saturday night dinners. 🏃 ⊞ ✂ ❦

ONCE THE O'ROURKES decided to leave the metropolitan New York City area, Rachel, a
trained chef, taught culinary classes at the famed Canyon Ranch in Lenox. Because so
many enrollees requested that she become their personal cook "back home," she and
Dennis, a psychologist turned caterer, developed such a business—filling the freezers of
fabulous home kitchens with a supply of prepared dinners. One of their Berkshires catering jobs was the seventy-fifth birthday party of The Turning Point Inn's then-owner/cre-
ator. (In the early 1980s he had come here from New Jersey with the idea of opening a
small restaurant.) Since buying this intimate inn in 1998, the O'Rourkes have installed
their own dream commercial kitchen (still with original fireplace) where the doors are always open—especially for early risers, including children. All baking is done by Teva, a
professional pastry chef. Now the 200-year-old Federal building, originally known as the
Old Brick Tavern, has walls painted in soft muted colors. Sailcloth curtains hang from
loops. Beds are reproductions. Most rooms are closetless, with pegs in the Shaker style. It's
historic, contemporary-with-old-features, intentionally simple, informal, and friendly.

BED AND BATH: Six cozy second-floor rooms. Four with private baths—most with shower
only. Two share one full bath. Beds are king, queen, or twins; one room with king bed is
air conditioned and also has a trundle bed. Cots available. Cottage (breakfast provided in
the inn) has two bedrooms, living room, kitchen, heated sunporch.
BREAKFAST: 8–10. Homemade granola. Fresh fruit. Teva's muffins, scones, or bread.
Homemade preserves. By fire at long table—with old church bench on one side, chairs
on other.
PLUS: No TV. Two common rooms, one with fireplace. Lawn chairs. Tea available. Dogs
allowed in cottage only.

⋙ *Windflower Inn*

413/528-2720

684 South Egremont Road,
Great Barrington, MA 01230-1932

800/992-1993
FAX 413/528-5147
E-MAIL wndflowr@windflowerinn.com
www.windflowerinn.com

HOSTS: Claudia and John Ryan, Barbara and Gerry Liebert
LOCATION: On 10 acres with gardens and a pond. Across from country club with eighteen-hole golf course and tennis courts (available to public). Three miles from downtown Great Barrington, half mile to South Egremont.
OPEN: Year round. Two-night weekend minimum; three nights on weekends in July and August and on holidays.
RATES: Vary according to fireplace (or not) in room, day of week, and season. Weekends $110, $120, $140, $160, $180, $200. Weekdays $100–$180. Third person $25. Amex. ♥ ⁂ ⊞ ⚐ ♥○

LEGENDARY. Family run. Known for food, comfort and hospitality. Recipient of *Boston* magazine's New England Travel Guide's "coziest inn" designation. And to think it all started two decades ago when Barbara, a medical secretary known for her dinner parties, and Gerry, who had a plumbing and heating supply business on Long Island, created the acclaimed Tulip Tree Inn in Vermont. Five years later they asked daughter Claudia, a chef with experience at Vermont's Woodstock Inn and Boston's Ritz-Carlton Hotel, and John, a multifaceted gardener/painter/wallpaperer who has a degree in arboriculture, to become co-innkeepers in the Berkshires. After seventeen years of offering nightly dinners—to the public too—their Windflower Inn became a B&B in 1997. Some guests are returnees who first came with their own parents. The at-home feeling is enhanced with overstuffed sofas facing the living room fireplace. Designer linens are on the beds. There's a wraparound porch. An in-ground pool bordered with perennial gardens. And an up-and-coming third generation of innkeepers that prompts many guests to ask the secret to the success of this family magic.

IN RESIDENCE: In Ryans' home on the property—Jessica, age fourteen; Michael, age ten. Anna, an Airedale, and Cody, a mixed breed who looks like a black Newfoundland; both love to play.
FOREIGN LANGUAGES SPOKEN: "Very limited high school French and Spanish."
BED AND BATH: Thirteen air-conditioned rooms; six with fireplace. (Large rooms can accommodate one or two rollaways.) All rooms have TV and private bath—some with claw-foot tub/shower, some with modern tub/shower or stall shower (some extra large). First floor—three carpeted rooms (all open onto porch) with queen bed; one has large stone wood-burning fireplace, one has small fireplace (Duraflame logs). Ten second-floor rooms; four with queen bed (one has a queen and a single) have small Duraflame fireplace. King/twins option also available.
BREAKFAST: Monday–Saturday 8:30–9:30; Sunday 9–10 (earlier for skiers). Homemade challah French toast or wild blueberry or cottage cheese soufflé pancakes served with fried

egg and bacon. Homemade breads and pastries. Juice, muffins, fruit, cold cereal, hot beverages. In fireplaced dining room.

PLUS: Wood-burning fireplace in two living rooms; upright piano, library, and games in one. Afternoon tea and homemade cookies, pie, or cake. In-room massages booked. Fly-fishing lessons arranged.

➳ *Berkshire Mountain House*   518/733-6923

150 Berkshire Way,   800/497-0176
Stephentown, NY 12168-2602   FAX 518/733-6997
www.berkshirebb.com

HOSTS: Mona and Lee Berg
LOCATION: With panoramic mountain views. On 50 acres of meadows and forest, with walking trails and spring-fed pond. Thirty miles southeast of Albany. Close to Berkshires attractions in Massachusetts—10 minutes to Hancock Shaker Village and Jiminy Peak; 20 to Tanglewood; 25 to Williamstown.
OPEN: Year round. Two-night minimum July and August; three nights on weekends and holidays. Cottage and apartment three-night minimum July and August.
RATES: Private bath $107 double bed, $129 queen, $145 king. Shared bath $85–$99. Cottage (with breakfast) $269 per night for four people. Apartment $169 for two people. Extra person $15. Twenty percent less for one-week stay. Discover, MC, Visa. ♥ 👫 田 ⚔ 👪

THE VIEWS are so spectacular that this long, spacious contemporary house, built in the 1960s, was designed with walls of glass—even in the kitchen—and with sizable decks. Originally a private home and then a retreat in the 1970s, it was opened as a B&B in 1992. The Bergs bought it in 1996 when IBM's downsizing allowed Mona, a financial analyst who often entertained at home, to make her retirement dream come true earlier than planned. Co-innkeeper Lee is a pension planner and consultant. Furnishings include antiques, the upright piano Mona practiced on as a child, contemporary pieces, and collectibles including blue willow. Cousins clubs gather here. Honeymooners and others celebrating special occasions come. They relax in the ample common rooms. They explore the trails. And return.

BED AND BATH: On two levels in *main house*—eight rooms with king, queen, double, or twin beds. Three rooms have private bath (two with shower only, one with shower/tub); shared baths (maximum of two rooms per bath) for other five rooms. Plus apartment (sleeps two to four) with living room, dining room, air-conditioned bedroom, full kitchen. Air-conditioned *cottage* has queen bed in one room, private tub/shower bath, double with high-riser that opens to a queen in another room, queen pull-out sofa in living room,

continued . . .

TV/VCR, sliding glass doors to deck, a second bath (shower, no tub) and dressing room, fully equipped kitchen with microwave and dishwasher.

BREAKFAST: 8:30–10. Elaborate buffet—fresh fruit, juices, cereals, homemade granola, cakes, cookies, muffins, fruit compote, bagels, English muffins, breads from Zabar's in Manhattan, omelet, frittatas. "New recipes created all the time." Served in dining room with view from picture window. In warm weather, everyone eats on the deck.

PLUS: Saturday social hour at 5. Guest refrigerator. Hair dryers. Makeup mirrors. Robes in rooms. Designer linens. Upper-level room with fireplace and piano. Lower-level living room with fireplace, TV/VCR, and games.

℥ *Devonfield*

85 Stockbridge Road,
Lee, MA 01238

413/243-3298

800/664-0880
FAX 413/243-1360
E-MAIL innkeeper@devonfield.com
www.devonfield.com

HOSTS: Ben and Sally Schenck
LOCATION: Rural. On 40 acres of lawn and meadows with mountain views. Ten minutes to Tanglewood, 5 to Norman Rockwell Museum. Within half hour of six ski areas. Diagonally across from a nine-hole public golf course.
OPEN: Year round. Weekend minimum three nights July and August, two in October; two on holidays that are between Thursday and Monday.
RATES: July and August, Thursday–Sunday $165–$200 queen, $165–$275 king; Monday–Wednesday $110–$155 queen, $110–$200 king. September and October, Friday and Saturday $165–$200 queen, $165–$275 king; Sunday–Thursday $110–$155 queen, $110–$200 king. Winter and spring, Friday and Saturday $110–$150 queen, $110–$200 king; Sunday–Thursday $80–$110 queen, $80–$160 king. Weekend rates for some holidays. Third person $20. Amex, Discover, MC, Visa. ♥ ♦♦♦ ⊞ ❖ ♥♡

℥ From New York: *"A cut above the rest: Home and grounds . . . made us feel like one of the family . . . omelets made to order along with* New York Times *on the patio. . . . We loved it!!"* From Michigan: *"In twenty-seven years of B&B stays in England, Ireland, and North America we have found Devonfield to be, in every respect, the absolute best . . . better than a five-star hotel."* From New York: *"Outstanding . . . Suite #5 is perfect for families."* From Massachusetts: *"Friendly but not 'hovering' hosts . . . incredibly gracious . . . living room window overlooking vast Berkshire acres, fireplace flanked by bookshelves . . . arranged for privacy of small conversational groups as well as for sociability with other guests . . . breakfast was a high point . . . took a memorable walk on nearby country roads."* From Illinois: *"It had not been our first choice, but now we would return without even considering anyplace else."*

IT'S A GRACIOUS Colonial mansion that was the residence of Queen Wilhelmina of the Netherlands in 1942. "I just went looking at B&Bs for sale 'for fun'—and a year later (in 1994) we bought this traditionally furnished inn, which had been established by a chef and his wife," says Sally. A former social worker, she took lessons to learn how to cook (with aplomb) in front of guests. She and Ben, who was an insurance executive in central Massachusetts, have hosted several weddings. Among other memorable guests: an arborist who presented them with a report on the property's trees "and then roared off on his motorcycle," chauffeured guests, and people who met here and then rebooked for the same time next year.

BED AND BATH: Ten air-conditioned rooms; some with pastoral views, four with wood-burning fireplace. Queen (one is canopied), king, or king/twins option. All with en-suite full bath. Eight second-floor rooms or suites with interesting architectural details; one third-floor suite with skylight, bed under eaves, "spectacular" double Jacuzzi bath; and one recently built cottage that has cathedral-ceilinged living room with fireplace and ceiling fan, kitchenette, Jacuzzi bath, decks.
BREAKFAST: 8–10. Fresh juices. Fresh fruit dish. Granola. Eggs, French toast, or frittata. Homemade muffins and breads. A combination of buffet and service at dining room tables (large plus individual) set with family silver and fine china.
PLUS: In-ground pool in summer. TV in some rooms. Guest pantry. Tennis court. Croquet. Umbrella tables on patio. Loan of bicycles.

Amadeus House

15 Cliffwood Street,
Lenox, MA 01240

413/637-4770
800/205-4770
FAX 413/637-4484
www.amadeushouse.com

HOSTS: John Felton and (wife) Marty Gottron
LOCATION: On a residential street, minutes' walk to fine shops and restaurants; 1.5 miles to Tanglewood and to wildlife sanctuary; 13 miles to Hancock Shaker Village (Marty's passion).
OPEN: Year round. Two-night minimum on most weekends; three or four nights July and August weekends and some foliage weekends.
RATES: Vary according to room size. July and August weekends $165, $140, $125, $95; weekdays $115, $100, $90, $75; suite $235 weekends, $170 weekdays, $1,350 for the week. Late May–late June and after Labor Day through October weekends $140, $115, $105, $90; weekdays $105, $95, $85, $70; suite $200 weekends, $150 weekdays. November–mid-May weekends $125, $115, $100, $85; weekdays $95, $85, $75, $70; suite $155 weekends, $110 weekdays. Inquire about "Spa Indulgence" and other special packages. Third person $25. Amex, Discover, MC, Visa. ⊞ ⚥ ⌦

continued . . .

⋟ From New York, New Hampshire, Oregon, Massachusetts, New Jersey (all long, enthusiastic, detailed letters): *"Marty and John are genuinely interested in helping each guest tailor a stay that will be remembered for some time to come . . . great breakfast, beautifully presented—as was the afternoon tea. . . . We intend to return again and again. . . . Plenty of good books to read. . . . Classical music in living room . . . immaculate accommodations . . . easy access to the town. . . . Drove me to bus stop . . . atmosphere is more of a country home than an inn."*

THIS *Country Inns* magazine cover B&B is, just as John says, "not a palace, not overly decorated. It's Nirvana really, to be so close to so much. And recently many Bostonians have discovered our winter arrangements with one of the country's most renowned spas." The hosts rejuvenated this Colonial-turned-Victorian in 1993. John is a former National Public Radio deputy foreign editor who credits his passion for classical music to his high school band leader. (John played trumpet.) Marty is a former Washington, D.C., journalist who grew up in a small Ohio town. Now their freelance credits include *Congressional Quarterly* and *Symphony* magazine. Their B&B has walls painted in soft colors, country antiques and quilts, a huge collection of compact discs, and rooms named after composers.

IN RESIDENCE: "Bravo is a friendly black Lab."
BED AND BATH: Eight rooms (including one two-bedroom suite) in summer and fall; five rooms November–April. First floor—queen bed, full bath, woodstove, private porch. Second floor—four rooms with queen bed, private full bath. One room with queen bed shares (robes provided) full bath with room that has two twin beds. Third-floor air-conditioned suite—room with king bed, room with two twin beds, full kitchen, small bath with two-person shower.
BREAKFAST: 8–9:30. Omelets, orange waffles, pancakes, French toast, or quiche. Fresh fruit. Homemade muffins. Served at three large dining room tables.
PLUS: No TV. Afternoon tea by living room fire or on wraparound porch. (Passersby have been known to book a room so they can partake!) Guest refrigerator. Custom-made chocolate violins. Guest phone.

☜ *The Birchwood Inn*   413/637-2600

7 Hubbard Street, P.O. Box 2020,   800/524-1646
Lenox, MA 01240-2330   FAX 413/637-4604
      E-MAIL innkeeper@birchwood-inn.com
      www.birchwood-inn.com

HOST: Ellen Gutman Chenaux
LOCATION: High on a hill (at Main Street) overlooking the village. Steps to shops, restaurants, hiking and cross-country ski trails. Two miles to Tanglewood.
OPEN: Year round. Three-night weekend minimum in July and August.
RATES: July and August $90–$100 shared bath; $135–$225 private bath and air conditioning. Autumn $75–$95 shared bath; $115–$150 private bath; $140–$195 with fireplace. Other months $60–$75 shared bath; $85–$115 private bath; $125–$165 with fireplace. Additional person in room $20. Amex, Discover, MC, Visa. ♥ ⊞ ⚅ ⅟ ❦

"I WENT FROM the boardroom to the kitchen, instead of the other way around," declares the happy and energetic hostess, a New Jersey native who has lived in Chicago, Seattle, New York, Switzerland, and Toronto. Ellen has had careers as an English teacher, magazine editor and feature writer, and corporate communicator. She attributes her innkeeper's hat to extensive inn travel experiences, a love of history, and a knack for baking learned from her grandmother. Since 1999, when she bought the established B&B, a 233-year-old mansion, she has done considerable redecorating. "It will always be a work in progress!" Furnishings include Swiss, Canadian, and American antiques, Oriental carpets, and art.

     ☜ Guests from New York, Massachusetts, Maryland, Virginia, Florida, and New Jersey attest: *"Exquisite inn . . . delectable food. . . . Great ambiance. . . . Loved the charm, the extra touches (M&Ms and freshly baked chocolate chip cookies), great coffee, and thoughtfulness of the proprietor . . . memorable hospitality. . . . Cozy and elegant. . . . For the first time since I moved to New York City, my pulse relaxed."*

IN RESIDENCE: Assistant innkeeper Jeff Steinberg, Culinary of Institute of America graduate.
FOREIGN LANGUAGES SPOKEN: French and some Spanish.
BED AND BATH: Twelve rooms, including two in adjacent carriage house. *Main house:* Second-floor air-conditioned rooms have king (one with fireplace and TV), queen (two with canopy and fireplace), or twin beds. All private baths; four are shower only. Third floor—private bath for air-conditioned room with queen or king/twins option. Two double-bedded rooms share hall bath (robes provided). *Carriage house:* Two air-conditioned rooms, each with queen bed, gas fireplace. Rollaways available.
BREAKFAST: 8:30–10. (Coffee earlier.) Ellen's international repertoire includes Birchwood's Rise-and-Shine Soufflé and blueberry buttermilk pancakes. Egg beaters

continued . . .

available as an option. Homemade muffins, breads, fruit crisps, coffee cakes. Fruit, juice, cereal, Irish oatmeal, hot beverages. In fireplaced dining room.

PLUS: Homemade pies, tarts, squares, and cookies with hot mulled cider, English tea, lemonade, or iced tea—varies with season—5–6 daily. Fireplaced library and parlor. Ceiling fans in most main-house rooms. Wicker-furnished front porch. Gardens. In summer, loan of picnic baskets and blankets.

☞ Brook Farm Inn

413/637-3013

15 Hawthorne Street,
Lenox, MA 01240

800/285-7638
FAX 413/637-4751
E-MAIL innkeeper@brookfarm.com
www.brookfarm.com

HOSTS: Joe and Anne Miller

LOCATION: In a quiet wooded glen. Five-minute walk to village center. One mile to Tanglewood.

OPEN: Year round. Three-night weekend minimum July–Labor Day and some holiday weekends. Two nights on other weekends.

RATES: Vary according to room size, fireplace, floor location. Tanglewood season: $120–$150 Monday–Wednesday, $130–$205 Thursday–Sunday. Foliage: $90–$130 Monday–Thursday, $120–$160 Friday–Sunday. Early September, November–June: $90–$130 Monday-Thursday, $100–$140 Friday-Sunday. Discover, MC, Visa. ♥ ⊞ ⚔ ⅍

DURING TANGLEWOOD season you can hear practice sessions from the grounds of this attractive century-old home, which is complete with an in-ground pool and gardens. Right here chamber recitals are given during Sunday morning breakfast. Poetry readings are offered on Saturday afternoons. Every day a personal favorite poem of the day (from a collection of hundreds of books) is placed on a podium. The inn is furnished with traditional pieces, antiques, framed old posters, turn-of-the-century programs, and a collection of hand-carved shorebirds. Tanglewood performers, honeymooners, and wedding parties are among the many guests who appreciate the atmosphere of "total relaxation," the Millers' fulfilled dream. In New Jersey, Joe, a golfer, was in commercial construction; Anne, a tennis player, was a real estate paralegal.

IN RESIDENCE: Agnes, a yellow Labrador. Blanche, a black Labrador. "Bob is our mascot cat."

BED AND BATH: Twelve rooms, each with air conditioning, ceiling fan, phone, private bath (some shower only). Six with working fireplace. King/twins option or queen bed (some canopied). One room is on two levels. Some have 12-foot ceilings. Third floor rooms—one has a cathedral ceiling, skylights, and fireplace—are all tucked under the eaves. Rollaway available.

BREAKFAST: 8:30–10. Freshly squeezed orange juice. Homemade granola. Bread pudding (recipe shared), quiche, egg casserole, or French toast. Special diets accommodated. Served in breakfast room overlooking woods.

PLUS: Sherry. Fireplaced library with upright piano. No TV. (Very sociable) afternoon tea with homemade scones and jam. Guest refrigerator. Champagne for birthdays or anniversaries. Valentine's Day roses. Guest office/pantry with phone, fax, sink, ice maker, coffee, tea.

> ⤜ From Massachusetts: *"It is lovely. And the innkeepers have just the right touch."*

⤜ The Gables Inn   413/637-3416

81 Walker Street (Route 183), Lenox, MA 01240   800/382-9401

HOSTS: Mary and Frank Newton
LOCATION: In the village center, 1 mile from Tanglewood.
OPEN: Year round. Three-night minimum in July and August; two nights in October and on holiday weekends.
RATES: Vary according to room size, amenities, time of year, weekday or weekend. $80–$225. Suite (summer only) $225. Additional person $20. Discover, MC, Visa. ▦ ⌀

"YOUNG MAN, I see you have kept the Whartons' red damask wallpaper," said the eighty-two-year-old Lenox resident while visiting with Frank Newton in this former home of famed novelist Edith Wharton (author of *The Age of Innocence*).

For their eighth house restoration (six were Manhattan brownstones done while they lived in them), the Newtons, both former bankers, took on this elegant Queen Anne Berkshire Cottage built in the Gilded Age of 1885. In addition to hanging fresh red damask wallpaper, they restored the eight-sided library (which had become a restaurant with bar) and added a tennis court (racquets available), a greenhouse with solar-heated 50-foot pool (I loved the prebreakfast swim), and a Jacuzzi. And now there are two 500-square-foot suites. The Teddy Wharton Suite, with high-headboard bed and leather furniture, is a favorite with guests. The more feminine Edith Wharton Suite features Gibson Girl prints, a four-poster bed, and a bath with his-and-hers sinks. The Presidents' Room is complete with a collection that delights history buffs. The Show Business room has signed photos (plenty of nostalgia) and an extensive library. Throughout, there are period furnishings and examples of Mary Newton's painting, pierced lampshades, and quilting.

Depending on the season or year, Frank—the official baker, who has given/produced cooking demonstrations in Lenox and New York—finds time to write and produce shows and recordings; play piano; lecture on restoration and period style; and create even more area cultural events.

IN RESIDENCE: "Cat" is shy.

continued . . .

FOREIGN LANGUAGE SPOKEN: Spanish.

BED AND BATH: Seventeen air-conditioned rooms—including four suites—on three floors; nine have working fireplaces. All queen beds; some are canopied. All private baths.

BREAKFAST: 8–10. Waffles, pancakes, or French toast. Fruit, juice, homemade bread and pastry, coffee, tea. Cereal in the summer. Tables for two or four, or one for twenty. Note to summer guests: "We love the *Times* too! Please read it in the library rather than in the dining room."

PLUS: Afternoon or evening wine. Lounge chairs in quiet garden.

Garden Gables Inn

413/637-0193

135 Main Street, P.O. Box 52,
Lenox, MA 01240

FAX 413/637-4554
E-MAIL gardeninn@aol.com
www.lenoxinn.com

HOSTS: Mario and Lynn Mekinda

LOCATION: In historic district of village. Set back from the main road on 5 wooded acres with gardens, fruit trees, and huge old pines and maples. One mile from Tanglewood.

OPEN: Year round. Three-night minimum weekends July–August and on holiday weekends; two-night minimum weekends June and September–October.

RATES: Late June–Labor Day and late September–October: weekends $135 (double bed, smaller room) to $250 (king four-poster, whirlpool bath, porch), most rooms $150–$180; weekdays $110–$210. Mid-September, winter, and spring: weekends $110–$210, weekdays $95–$195. Third person $30. Amex, Discover, MC, Visa. ♥ ⊞ ⌀

IT'S HOME. It has white clapboards and green shutters. The gabled part with low ceilings was built in 1780. Subsequent additions were made to the private estate, which was an inn for thirty-five years before the Mekindas bought it in 1988. Now the B&B is centrally air conditioned and each room has a private phone with modem capability. Now the Mekindas' daughter, a "Teach for America" participant, is in law school, and their son is a doctoral student in the history of architecture.

"A tinkerer," Mario says he is. Every old-house owner would appreciate a Mario-in-residence. The results of his efforts include fresh, inviting rooms, tile baths, a homelike atmosphere. There are books, fireplaces, comfortable sofas, a baby grand piano, English antiques, Dutch and English eighteenth-century watercolors, and, in the guest rooms, early American furniture. On the spacious grounds there are gardens, a 72-foot-long in-ground pool with umbrella tables on the deck, and many trees.

In Canada Mario was a professional engineer who specialized in wind tunnel design. Lynn worked in public relations. Here Lynn writes and is active with the historical society. Mario is active with several arts organizations.

FOREIGN LANGUAGES SPOKEN: French and German.

BED AND BATH: Eighteen air-conditioned rooms (some with individual thermostat) on first and second floors in the inn; all with private bath (some with whirlpool tub). Four rooms in garden cottages. Rooms vary from small to large (new suites) with sitting area, cathedral ceiling, wood-burning fireplace, TV/VCR, and/or private balcony or deck. Beds (some are canopied) include king, queen, double, or two twins.

BREAKFAST: 8–10. Buffet. Homemade bran and blueberry muffins, cantaloupe and native berries, farm-fresh eggs, healthy cereals, cheese-filled crumb cakes, yogurts, croissants. In dining room overlooking gardens and pool.

PLUS: Late-afternoon wine or tea. Refrigerator. Down comforters. Beach towels. Games. TV and VCR.

➳ *Walker House*   413/637-1271

64 Walker Street,   800/235-3098
Lenox, MA 01240-2735   FAX 413/637-2387
                                                E-MAIL phoudek@vgernet.net
                                                      www.walkerhouse.com

HOSTS: Peggy and Richard Houdek
LOCATION: On a main street, set on 3 gorgeous acres. Within walking distance of shops, restaurants, and cross-country skiing. Within twenty-five minutes of Brodie, Jiminy Peak, and Butternut mountains. Buses from New York and Boston stop a block away.
OPEN: Year round. Three-night minimum in July and August and on all holiday weekends.
RATES: Late June–Labor Day: $125–$210 Thursday–Sunday, $90–$150 Monday–Wednesday. Early September: $90–$140 Friday, Saturday, Sunday; $80–$100 Monday–Thursday. Late September–October: $110–$160 Friday, Saturday, Sunday; $90–$120 Monday–Thursday. November–late June: $110–$140 Friday, Saturday, Sunday; $80–$100 Monday–Thursday. Winter theme packages available. ♥ ⊞ ✄ ❤◡

THEY WERE A successful arts-oriented couple living in a Spanish-style house on a southern California hill and looking for adventure. Once the Houdeks decided on the Berkshires, they set out to establish a B&B that would give them the feeling of having some friends visit for a few days. And it has been that way since 1980. (Family reunions and weddings take place here, too.) In California, Peggy was managing editor of *Performing Arts* magazine. Dick was director of public affairs at the California Institute of the Arts, a *Los Angeles Times* contributing critic, and a Long Beach Opera consultant. Now he's an arts consultant, a feature writer whose observations appear in a daily Berkshires newspaper, editor of the inn's very informative newsletter, and involved with the Lenox Town Hall

continued . . .

restoration as a performing arts center. (January–April, Dick makes frequent trips south.)

The art- and antiques-furnished 1804 house, once the house of the headmaster of the private Lenox School, is one of the last remaining examples of Federal architecture in Lenox. Each spacious guest room is named and decorated for a composer. "Whenever we have a request, we feature good films, operas, plays, concerts, and TV shows on a 12-foot-wide screen with surround sound in the Walker House Cinema (right here)."

IN RESIDENCE: "Six friendly but unobtrusive cats."
FOREIGN LANGUAGES SPOKEN: French and Spanish.
BED AND BATH: Eight air-conditioned rooms, five with working fireplace; one also has private veranda. All with private baths (two are shower only) and radios. Queen bed (six rooms), two double beds, or two twins.
BREAKFAST: 8–10. Juice, fresh fruit, several kinds of muffins and croissants, cold cereals, freshly ground coffee, many teas. Served around large oak tables (displacing huge seated stuffed animals) in dining room, or on wide plant-filled veranda overlooking acreage.
PLUS: Tea at 4. Parlor grand piano for professional performances or impromptu ones by guests or, occasionally, for accompanying Peggy, a trained singer. Old-time radio cassette library. Guest refrigerator. Large lawn for picnics. Tennis reservations (no charge) at Lenox Tennis Club across the street. "We welcome well-behaved pets by arrangement only." Pet-sitters available.

➳ From Australia: *"We loved the many antiques and collectibles and the sheer character of this house . . . delicious breakfasts with great classical and opera music . . . a clean, friendly gem."*

➳ The Inn at Stockbridge

413/298-3337

P.O. Box 618, Route 7,   888/466-7865
Stockbridge, MA 01262   FAX 413/298-3406
                                        E-MAIL innkeeprs@stockbridgeinn.com
                                                www.stockbridgeinn.com

HOSTS: Alice and Len Schiller
LOCATION: Quiet. Set back from main road. With long tree-lined driveway. On 12 acres with old trees, expansive lawn, perennial gardens, and panoramic mountain views. One mile to downtown Stockbridge. Three miles to Tanglewood and Norman Rockwell Museum.
OPEN: Year round.
RATES: July–October weekends, holidays, and special events $130 smaller queen-bedded room with hall bath, $205–$270 queen or king; weekdays $115 smaller room, $185–$225 queen or king. January–June and November–December weekends $115, $170–$215; weekdays $115, $150–$180. Extra person $30. Packages January–April. Amex, Discover, MC, Visa. ⊞ ✂

THIS GRACIOUS pillared Georgian-style mansion, a B&B since 1982, is the kind of place where guests—including concert pianists—play the baby grand piano in the 30-foot-long beamed living room. Or relax by the fire in the equally large and gracious library. Sometimes theater administrators are at the breakfast table. The pool and wraparound porch are summer attractions. In winter, borrow snowshoes "when we have snow!" for the short wooded trail.

The Schillers, too, enjoy the cultural activities that drew them to the Berkshires area in the first place. Alice, a home economics teacher, had coordinated special education programs with the New York City Restaurant School. Len, the former owner of a New Jersey–based office-cleaning business, took cooking classes "for fun." For this career change he brought memories of his mother's upstate New York summer boardinghouse—and the knowledge that his grandmother was an innkeeper in eastern Europe. Since buying the antiques-filled inn in 1994, the Schillers have painted, papered, reupholstered—and added a new building with four junior suites.

    ↄ Notes from guests to me sum it up: *"Comfortable and elegant. . . . Understated and elegant . . . casual but luxurious . . . beautifully decorated, relaxing, well kept. . . . Treated as if we were the only guests . . . helpful with dinner reservations and recommendations (always good!) . . . soft classical music always playing . . . grounds are pretty for strolling. . . . Len and Alice know the art of hospitality."*

IN RESIDENCE: "Our Shebe, an aging standard poodle, still makes an appearance during wine-and-cheese hour."

BED AND BATH: Twelve air-conditioned rooms (one is handicapped accessible); all with phone. All private baths; some with two-person Jacuzzi. Beds are king, king/twins, or queen (some are canopied); rollaway available. One room with private entrance and deck. In new (1998) cottage, all four large rooms have canopied king bed, gas fireplace, TV/VCR, individual thermostat, ceiling fan; two rooms have 6-foot whirlpool tub and separate shower.

BREAKFAST: 8:30-9:30. Juice. fruit. Caramel apple French toast, cottage cheese pancakes, or portobello mushroom and cheese strata. Cereals. Orange cranberry bread, cinnamon ring, muffins, sweet breads. Served in candlelit dining room that seats sixteen and in sitting room with option of tables for two.

PLUS: Wood-burning fireplace in living room and library. TV/game room. In-ground 20-by-40-foot pool. In-room complimentary sherry. Afternoon wine/juice/apple cider, locally prepared chèvre, and locally made flatbread (lavash). Guests' pantry.

To TIP OR NOT? (PLEASE TURN TO PAGE IX.)

☜ *Historic Merrell Inn*   413/243-1794

1565 Pleasant Street,   800/243-1794
South Lee, MA 01260-0318   FAX 413/243-2669
                                    E-MAIL info@merrell-inn.com
                                         www.Merrell-Inn.com

HOSTS: Charles and Faith Reynolds
LOCATION: On a main street in small village. Walk to two recommended restaurants—
one across the street and one next door. A little over 1 mile to the village of
Stockbridge; 5 miles to Tanglewood; 3 from I-90, Lee exit. Ten minutes to
ski areas (with snowmaking).
OPEN: Year round. Two-night weekend minimum year round; three nights on July,
August, and holiday weekends.
RATES: July–October weekdays $95–$115; $135 Riverview Suite. July–October week-
ends and holiday weekends $155–$175; $225 Riverview Suite.
November–June weekdays $85–$105, $125 suite; weekends $85–$125, $145
suite. MC, Visa. ♥ ♦♦ ⊞ ❖ ⚅ ⊱

AUTHENTICITY, CHARM (even a screened gazebo by the river), and old-fashioned hospitality are evident from the moment you sign in at the only surviving circular Colonial bar in
America. The grandfather clock in the central hallway dates from the late 1700s, when the
building was constructed. Authentic colors, researched by Faith and Charles, are a background for their period Hepplewhite and Sheraton furniture. The 200-year-old inn, once
a stagecoach stop, is on the National Register of Historic Places and is under historic
covenant with the Society for the Preservation of New England Antiquities. One guest
room was a ballroom. One parlor was the Tavern Room with 1817 birdcage bar. Now the
original keeping room with cooking fireplace and beehive oven is the dining room. The
work of the innkeepers, two former Rochester, New York, teachers, was recognized with a
1981 Massachusetts Historical Society Preservation Award, a Berkshire Visitors Bureau
Beautification Award, and coverage in the *Philadelphia Inquirer, Travel Holiday, USA
Today* (romantic Valentine's Day recommendation), and the *Jerusalem Post.*

BED AND BATH: Ten air-conditioned rooms on three floors; all with private tiled bath,
phone, and cable TV. Three with fireplace. King, queen, or twin beds (most are
canopied) with wing chairs or Chippendale sofas. New suite—king bed, fireplace, private
porch—in private wing overlooking the river. Cots available.
BREAKFAST: 8:30–10. From an open menu cooked to order. Cereal; omelets; sausage with
blueberry pancakes or French toast. Juice. Hot beverage. Served on handmade Bennington Pottery in keeping room at tables for two.
PLUS: Guest refrigerator. Grounds with old stone walls, English garden, 2 acres of lawns
to banks of Housatonic River. Two gazebos.

☜ From Argentina: *"Slept in eight cozy inns, and this is the best. . . . Not a dream.
It's true and it's great."* From Massachusetts: *"Like the Berkshire Hills . . . soothing, peaceful,*

inviting, and refreshing . . . a great place to escape to." From Connecticut: *"Captures the feeling of the nineteenth century while more than satisfying the expectations of twentieth-century travelers by anticipating all of their needs."*

☙ *Steep Acres Farm B&B*   413/458-3774

520 White Oaks Road, Williamstown, MA 01267-2227

HOSTS: Mary and Marvin Gangemi
LOCATION: High on a hill with panoramic views of New York, Vermont, and Massachusetts. Two miles from Clark Art Museum and Williamstown Theatre Festival. Adjacent to Appalachian and Long Trails. Forty minutes to Tanglewood. Many downhill ski areas within 20-mile radius.
OPEN: Year round.
RATES: Main house $50 single, $85 double. The Birches $85 shared bath, $150 king.
♥ ☎ ⊞ ⚵ ⚵ ♨ 林

"OUR GUESTS love the pond. They explore the 50 wonderful acres. The apple, cherry, peach, pear, and nut trees are flourishing. We no longer have cows, sheep, chickens, ducks, or pigs, but there are plenty of wild turkeys. We feed a herd of deer that appear regularly. Occasionally, there is a moose. One memorable day an otter showed up in the pond! Bird-watchers have a field day here. Our gardens get a boost from the greenhouse. And yes, B&B is a grand fit, because we have the room and have found that every guest has been wonderful."

The Gangemis bought this great site with house and three barns after they sold the summer camp where their six kids were first campers and then staff. Son Daniel, a professional landscaper, has his nursery on this property—as well as a modern (built in 1992) Colonial house with accommodations for B&B guests, located in a birch grove. Marvin, a golfer and a beekeeper "when the bears leave the hives alone," was a fifth-grade teacher. Mary, the creative chef, has also retired—from her nursing career.

IN RESIDENCE: Two dogs plus. (They breed Labrador retrievers.)
BED AND BATH: *Main house:* four rooms with antique beds share two full baths and a half bath. Two double-bedded rooms, one room with single bed, one with two twins. In Daniel's house. *The Birches*—one room with king bed, fireplace, TV, Jacuzzi, private bath, deck. One room with a queen bed shares a bath with room that has two twin beds.
BREAKFAST: Full. Varies. In main house, "today's menu started with a half pineapple (per person), sliced bananas, and strawberry garnish. Oatmeal blackberry pancakes are a hit. Sometimes I make a Mexican egg dish or breakfast puffs." Plus homemade muffins and breads. Eat by dining room fireplace in winter or on the glassed porch with its tri-state view in summer. Breakfast at The Birches includes fresh fruit and a specialty such as baked French toast with the Gangemis' own maple syrup.

continued . . .

PLUS: Ceiling fans on porch and in upstairs hall. Canoe, rowboat, and raft with diving board. Trout-filled pond. Three miles of hiking and cross-country ski trails. Spontaneous afternoon tea "when several UK guests are here!"

⟫⟫ *The Williamstown Bed and Breakfast*   413/458-9202

30 Cold Spring Road,   **E-MAIL** innkeeper@williamstownbandb.com
Williamstown, MA 01267-2751   **www.williamstownbandb.com**

HOSTS: Kim Rozell and Lucinda Edmonds
LOCATION: In a neighborhood of 1800s homes on the main road. Just off village green. With gardens, shade trees, red barn. Minutes' walk to college campus, theater, museums, village center.
OPEN: Year round. Two-night minimum on summer, holiday, and foliage season weekends.
RATES: April–November $85–$90 single, $100–$110 double. December–March $80–$85 single, $95–$100 double. ✹ ⚹ ⚹

⟫⟫ From Michigan: *"Really first class. . . . Kim and Lucinda, delightful young ladies, have done great things with the house."* From Massachusetts: *"Carefully chosen antiques. So far, they have refused offers on the Hoosier cabinet or the hand-carved pineapple beds, but I'll keep asking."* From Pennsylvania: *"Sparkling clean . . . special old photographs, lovely wallpaper. . . . Beds are among the most comfortable in which we've slept . . . breakfasts, excellent. . . . All the New England charm one would expect. But more importantly, greeting is warm and friendly . . . delightfully appointed rooms with bottled water on nightstands . . . more than sufficient light to read or work by anywhere in the room . . . electric eye night-lights. . . . Nothing is left to chance . . . comfortable living room with telephone programmed for fine dining spots . . . uniformly top-notch."*

STAYS AT IRISH B&Bs inspired these innkeepers "to change careers and pace. We looked at Massachusetts college towns and fell in love with Williamstown, a terrific community with a rich history and wonderful cultural and recreational opportunities." In 1989 they restored this Victorian—"not the ornate kind." Area antiques dealers (hints shared) helped to add to their furnishings.

Kim is a former meeting planner. Lucinda held an environmental services executive position.

IN RESIDENCE: Two cats in hosts' quarters.
FOREIGN LANGUAGES SPOKEN: "None fluently, but we have had numerous foreign guests . . . wonderful time exploring sign language and language dictionaries."
BED AND BATH: Four second-floor rooms; all private baths. Queen bed with tub/shower bath. Queen with shower bath. Double four-poster with shower bath. Room with two twin beds has shower bath down the hall.

BREAKFAST: Usually begins at 8. Hot dishes 8:30–9:30. Oven-puffed pancakes with fresh fruit, cheese blintzes, baked eggs with hot salsa sauce, French toast, or blueberry pancakes. Freshly baked muffins, bread (oatmeal is a favorite), scones. Cereals. Juices, freshly ground coffee, teas. Family style in dining room.
PLUS: Hot or cold afternoon beverages. Springwater in rooms. Large front porch.

⁂ *Windfields Farm* 413/684-3786

154 Windsor Bush Road, Windsor
Mailing address: 154 Windsor Bush Road, Cummington, MA 01026

HOSTS: Carolyn and Arnold Westwood
LOCATION: On 200 acres along a quiet dirt road. From West Cummington off Route 9, 2 miles uphill (winter guests should come prepared!). Twenty miles west to Pittsfield, 25 east to Northampton. Five miles to Notchview Reservation, 8 to Stump Sprouts and Hickory Hill for cross-country skiing. Forty minutes to Tanglewood, Hancock Shaker Village, and Williamstown; 30 to (new) Museum of Contemporary Art (MoCA) in North Adams.
OPEN: May–March 1. Two-night minimum on most weekends. Reservations required.
RATES: $60 single, $80 double. Suite—"not appropriate for children"—with private bath, $120. Midweek, 10 percent less. ♥ ☕ ⊞ ⚹ ⚴ ⚵

JUST THINKING about this B&B makes me feel good all over. The interesting house is a haven, way up and away, with scenic surroundings; but, in true B&B style, the hosts make the difference.

Arnold, retired as a Unitarian Universalist minister, now edits the town (pop. 800) newsletter and founded the town land trust. He built much of the solar addition, the Westwoods' part of the residence. Vegetables from Carolyn's organic garden win prizes at regional fairs, as do her flowers—"I love arranging them"—and her bread, pies, maple syrup ("five-time first prize winner"), and jams. Their 200-acre homestead borders Audubon's West Mountain Wildlife Sanctuary (hiking and cross-country skiing along the ridge), part of which was donated by the Westwoods. These hosts, who celebrated their fiftieth anniversary at an Elderhostel in 1995, are concerned with conservation, building community spirit, and "a better world for all."

Carolyn refers to "living in a sculpture," a summer retreat—a "mess" purchased in 1961—that became, after ten years of family work, a year-round "joyous house." The active/passive solar addition retains the pressed tin ceiling, paneled doors, and hand-hewn beams of the original c. 1815 cottage. The connecting (c. 1830) farmhouse is—since 1983— for guests, who have their own private entrance and living and dining rooms. Furnishings include many family antiques, carved pieces done by both Arnold's and Carolyn's mothers, and paintings done by artists the Westwoods know. There's a list of one hundred sighted

continued . . .

bird species. Among wildlife visitors: deer, fox, raccoons, porcupine, wild turkeys, and, yes, bear. We want to return. So do our neighbors and many readers of this book.

BED AND BATH: Two spacious corner bedrooms, "your castle as long as you're here." One with 1818 canopied double bed that belonged to Carolyn's great-great-grandmother. Queen walnut bed in other. Semiprivate full bath with old-time barber's sink and claw-foot tub with shower.
BREAKFAST: 7:30–9. Announced to strains of Mozart and Bach. Homegrown organic pro-duce, berries, eggs. Arnold's incredible pancakes, yogurt, maybe Irish oatmeal topped with granola, natural grain homemade muffins or popovers, Windfields' low-sugar jams. "Equal Exchange" organic coffee. Served in guests' dining room.
PLUS: Huge living room fireplace with plenty of wood. Bedroom fans. Blueberries along hiking trails. Spring-fed swimming pond with sandy beach. A short walk to waterfall in the state forest. Beverages. Guest refrigerator. Piano, hi-fi, extensive library including books for sale. Sun-dried towels. A place on newsletter mailing list, worth the stay in it-self. Occasional farm work-party weekends.

    From Massachusetts: "Even enjoyed a nighttime jog over the meadow and through the woods under a starlit sky." From Missouri: "The gardens, the pond, the hike to the waterfalls . . . and the proprietors made us feel relaxed and rejuvenated." From Virginia: "It is now our primary destination . . . peaceful and aesthetic surroundings, comfort, nourish-ment, intellectual stimulation, and flexibility. Carolyn and Arnold have the gift of embracing without smothering." From New York: "The world's most effective therapy for urban stress." From Philadelphia: "After being there only one hour, I arranged to extend our stay from three nights to four. If you like to be in quiet country surroundings, with the 'bestest' hosts and super breakfasts, this is the place. So far it's our favorite, and we look forward to returning." From New York: "Have stayed in a couple hundred B&Bs over the past twenty years. This is among the four or five best. . . . Hosts are unusually gracious and friendly; the setting is beautiful and the breakfast excellent." From Ohio: "Memorable and an inspiration."

GUESTS ARRIVE AS STRANGERS, LEAVE AS FRIENDS.

🐦 *The Hill Gallery Bed & Breakfast*   413/238-5914

137 East Windsor Road,
Worthington, MA 01098-9710

E-MAIL korzec@javanet.com
www.hamphillsbandb.com/hillgallery/

HOSTS: Walter Korzec
LOCATION: With wonderful views. On 23 acres (one acre is open) with lawns and trees and no visible neighbors. Set back from road at the top of a hill. Just off Route 9, midway between Northampton and Pittsfield (each 20 to 25 miles away). Forty minutes to Tanglewood. "Hiking, biking, and peace and quiet much closer!"
OPEN: Year round. Two-night weekend minimum in summer and on holidays.
RATES: Suite or king-bedded room $90 double, $65 single. Suite with four adults $130. Queen-bedded room with semiprivate bath $70 double, $50 single.
♥ ♦♦ ☜ ⊞ ⚱ ⅍ 🎎

THIS MULTILEVEL owner-designed and -built (with help) contemporary home has always been a haven for overnight guests—with the "extra room" for B&B guests since 1982. Now the house has been refurbished. Guests are welcome to tour—most do—and look at the antiques and artwork. Collections include duck decoys acquired at auctions or carved by Walter, a printmaker and painter who teaches at a nearby college. Guests also admire the pegged floors, the abundance of windows and views, and the floor-to-ceiling fieldstone fireplace in the cathedral-ceilinged living/dining room. There's a deck, two ponds, stone walls (built by Walter), and an art/antiques gallery.

BED AND BATH: Three rooms. Main level—room with king bed, wide-board floor, shower bath, phone, Palladian window overlooking two ponds and woods beyond. Smaller room with queen bed, semiprivate tub/shower bath shared with host. Private entrance to ground-floor suite—through recreation room (included in suite) and up a few steps to room with double bed, wide-board floor, full-length mirrors on four closet doors, windows too high for view, shower bath.
BREAKFAST: 8:30–9. Homemade pancakes, waffles, French toast, baked eggs and cheese. Fresh fruit. Homemade baked goods. Cereals. Served in dining room at maple table with captain's chairs. "CDs for all musical tastes."
PLUS: Individual thermostats. Room fans. Recreation room—not available when suite is booked—with pool table, library, phone, games, exercise bike, TV, working fireplace. Two porches. The "spectacle" of seeing resident bass in larger pond being fed. A long what-to-do list including back roads and woodland paths to explore.

     🐦 From Massachusetts and California: *"Made our graduation weekend a memorable event. . . . A convivial innkeeper!"*

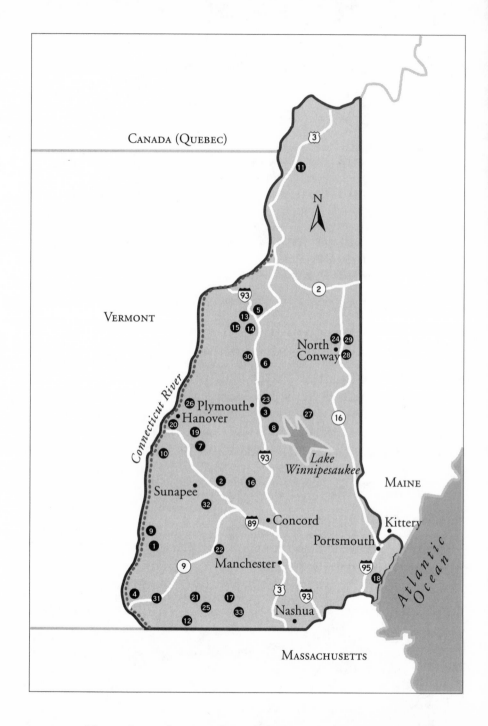

The numbers on this map indicate the locations of B&Bs described in detail in this chapter.

NEW HAMPSHIRE

➤ *Darby Brook Farm* 603/835-6624

Hill Road, Alstead, NH 03602

> **HOST:** Howard C. Weeks
> **LOCATION:** Rural. On a town road, 2 miles from the village. Six miles east of Connecticut River Valley, 15 north of Keene.
> **OPEN:** May–October.
> **RATES:** $30 per person. 👫 ☕ 👫

AUTHENTIC. A classic eighteenth-century Georgian house. Discovered by relatives and friends of area residents, who sometimes say that it is a bit like being in a museum. Every room except the kitchen has raised paneling. Moldings are beveled. There's stenciling. And beams. Other than plumbing and electricity and one kitchen window, everything is original. Where the wide floorboards (mostly painted) have been scuffed by boots, knots are exposed. The nineteenth-century furnishings were put in place when Howard's parents bought this house in 1929. A few newer pieces were made by Howard, who was a furniture designer in New York. Since 1980 he has become a farmer, with sheep and chickens, a vegetable garden, apple orchard, berry bushes, and some maple trees (for syrup). He directs guests to antiques shops, scenic roads, and the local lake. In the winter he is a cabinetmaker and lives in the house next door.

IN RESIDENCE: Darby, the dog.
BED AND BATH: Three rooms share one large full bath. One with two twin four-poster beds, working fireplace. One with double half-canopied bed, working fireplace. One room with a twin four-poster. Rollaway and crib available.
BREAKFAST: "Anything you wish." Cereal, fruit juice, bacon and eggs, muffins, toast, coffee. Howard joins guests.
PLUS: Fireplaced living and dining rooms, a treat in the fall. Tea or soft drinks. Beverages. Down comforters. Fresh flowers. Produce sold at farm.

B ED AND BREAKFAST IS THE HOTTEST TREND IN AMERICAN TRAVEL.

☞ Highland Lake Inn

603/735-6426

P.O. Box 164,
Maple Street,
East Andover, NH 03231

FAX 603/735-5355
www.highlandlakeinn.com

HOSTS: Mary and Peter G. Petras
LOCATION: On a quiet tree-lined street with "New England" view of spired church and private homes. Overlooks Highland Lake (fishing, swimming, and ice skating). On 12 acres with mountain views; abuts 21-acre nature conservancy area. One-room schoolhouse "just up the road." Within 15 minutes of Ragged Mountain and Gunstock ski areas and Loudon Raceway; 30 minutes to championship golf courses. Minutes to fine dining.
OPEN: Year round. Two-night minimum during foliage and on special Proctor Academy, Colby Sawyer College, and raceway weeks.
RATES: $85–$125. Extra person $30. Amex, Discover, MC, Visa. ♥ ⊞ ⚥ ⅄ ≋ ❤

MARY WAS IN banking; her husband, Peter, an engineer who built enormous bridges. At retirement time they sought "country life"; fell in love with this three-storied 1767 Colonial farmhouse and its location; moved out of New York City; and, together, renovated and insulated completely. Since opening the inn in 1994, they have added an air-conditioned dining room with panoramic view. Guests continue to write to me about "a find."

IN RESIDENCE: One caged rabbit in owners' quarters.
FOREIGN LANGUAGE SPOKEN: Greek.
BED AND BATH: Ten 14-foot-square soundproofed rooms, all private en-suite glass-stall shower baths. First floor has rooms with queen four-poster brass bed, gas fireplace, shower bath. Second and third floors have king, queen (some canopied or with additional twin bed), or twin beds, ceiling fans.
BREAKFAST: 7:30–9. Fresh seasonal fruit. Danish, coffee cake, homemade breads, biscuits, hot entrée, egg dish, waffles, pancakes; menu varies during guests' stay.
PLUS: Extensive Delft collection. Living room fireplace, TV, VCR. Welcoming refreshments. Fresh fruit. Beach towels. Fresh flowers.

☞ From Texas, Ohio, Connecticut, England, France: *"Staying at the inn was like living a fairy tale. Whole house filled with antiques . . . felt like we were visiting favorite relatives. . . . On the drive to the airport we were already making plans for another visit. . . . A sense of relaxation and comfort . . . can't consume all the food, but Grandma Petras sure works at getting you to do so. . . . From the country quilts on four-poster beds to beautiful hardwood floors, every inch sparkles with cleanliness . . . thick fluffy towels . . . quiet . . . romantic. . . . Peace and warmth. . . . Helped us store our bicycles, unloaded our car, made dinner reservations . . . hard to leave."*

≈ Glynn House "Victorian" Inn   603/968-3775

43 Highland Street,   800/637-9599
P.O. Box 719,   FAX 603/968-3129
Ashland, NH 03217-0719   E-MAIL glynnhse@lr.net
          http://new-hampshire-lodging.com

HOSTS: Betsy and Karol Paterman
LOCATION: Residential; two-minute walk from the village. In the Golden Pond/ White Mountains area; two-minute drive to Squam Lake swimming; within thirty minutes of Waterville, Loon, and Tenney mountains. One mile from I-93. Ten minutes to Plymouth State College and Holderness School.
OPEN: Year round.
RATES: $99 private bath. $135 bridal suite. $20 third person. Special foliage season rates. MC, Visa. ♥ ⚹

FROM THE TURRET to the oak foyer to carved oak woodwork to ornately patterned wallpaper, Victoriana is the theme at this B&B restored and opened in 1989. The hosts, former restaurateurs, are auction buffs and know which auctioneer specializes in furniture, Depression glass, or porcelain. They have this week's auction schedule (and a story about last week's find)—as well as books and magazines about antiques. They'll direct you to fine restaurants and the rolling waters of the Basin, their favorite scenic spot. Since retiring as sales manager for a food company, Betsy has become full-time co-innkeeper with Karol, the chef/plumber/electrician/gardener.

IN RESIDENCE: In hosts' quarters, teenagers Gracie and Chrissy; Christopher is ten.
FOREIGN LANGUAGES SPOKEN: Polish and Russian.
BED AND BATH: Four rooms and five suites (two in carriage house); each with air conditioner, new private bath, individual thermostat, TV/VCR; CD player in suites. Queen beds (most are canopied), one double bed, one room with queen and a single. Amenities vary; include double whirlpool tub and fireplace (gas or wood-burning).
BREAKFAST: Usually at 8:30 (coffee and tea an hour earlier). Whim-of-chef menu. Belgian waffles, thick French toast, or eggs Benedict. Maybe muffins or apple strudel.
PLUS: Beverage. Fruit basket. Fresh flowers. Mints on pillow.

≈ From New York, Massachusetts, New Jersey, New Hampshire, Vermont, Florida, Missouri, South Carolina, Illinois, Iowa, Connecticut, Pennsylvania: *"Every detail enhanced the romance and comfort of the beautiful inn . . . done to the nines in Victoriana . . . hummingbirds at flowers. . . . Treated us like relatives . . . spectacular breakfasts. . . . Top of list of our favorite B&Bs. . . . The place just gleams! . . . This place has it all. . . . Enjoyed it so much we stayed an extra day. . . . Charming. . . . Turret room with whirlpool tub was wonderful. . . . Picked Glynn House from your book. Everything was top-notch—perfect!"*

⋙ *Crestwood Chapel and Pavilion*   603/239-6393

400 Scofield Mountain Road,   FAX 603/239-7342
Ashuelot, NH 03441   www.crestwd.com

HOST: Gary O'Neal
LOCATION: Secluded. On 200 hilltop acres with expansive lawn, gardens, fountains, three-state views, country walks through woodlands and fields. Three miles from historic Ashuelot covered bridge. Eighteen miles from Keene, New Hampshire; 16 from Brattleboro, Vermont.
OPEN: Year round. Three-night minimum mid-September–late October and all major holidays.
RATES: $250–$350. Extra person $25. Dinner from $50 per person by advance reservation. Amex, Discover, MC, Visa. ♥ ♦♦ ⊞ ❖ ☀ ♙♙ ❤○

INTENTIONALLY an experience. With pampering. And complete privacy. (No hosting in the traditional B&B style.) Crestwood was built at the turn of the century as a home and religious retreat. During World War II it was a summer camp for European children. When Gary attended high school 3 miles from here, the property with "its commanding location" was unused. A photojournalist who now manufactures 100 percent postconsumer recycled paper, Gary bought Crestwood in 1978. He integrated his sense of design with his experiences from France, where he studied cooking, evaluated wines, and wrote for the *France Wine Journal*. Here he transformed a cluster of three structures—by restoring, expanding, and creating multitask buildings that accommodate elegant weddings and business meetings. Receptions are held in the Grand Salon, part of the original house, which has a dramatic vaulted ceiling.

FOREIGN LANGUAGES SPOKEN: By staff —French and Spanish.
BED AND BATH: Three spacious suites with TV/VCR, individual thermostats, robes. The *Pavilion*, a separate building, has one bedroom with king bed, TV, phone; other with two trundle beds. Plus a living room with TV/VCR, two fireplaces, marble bath with whirlpool tub, oversized shower, kitchen,laundry. In main house, the *Rectory*, one suite has handicapped-accessible room with double bed, shower bath, living room, kitchen. Upper suite has a room with queen bed and a loft with queen bed, fireplaced sitting room, two baths (one with double Jacuzzi), skylights, computer port, balcony.
BREAKFAST: 6:30–11. Hot croissants and *pain au chocolat* always available. Mini fruit sculptures. Pancakes, French toast, or waffles with locally produced maple syrup. Breads and pastries. Special diets accommodated. Delivered to suites on trays.
PLUS: Central air conditioning. Afternoon tea, wine, and hors d'oeuvres. Evening treats. Daily newspaper. Hot tub and sauna in gym near summit of mountain. Arrangements made for sleigh and carriage rides.

⋙ Guests wrote: *"Exquisite. Every creature comfort imaginable. Sunset view over Vermont from teahouse is breathtaking. . . . First-rate accommodations. . . . A little piece of heaven."*

㋛ Adair Country Inn

80 Guider Lane,
Bethlehem, NH 03574

603/444-2600
888/444-2600
FAX 603/444-4823
E-MAIL adair@connriver.net
www.adairinn.com

HOSTS: Judy and Bill Whitman

LOCATION: On a 200-acre estate with gardens, mountain views, and nearby woods. Ten miles to White Mountain National Forest. Ten minutes to Cannon Mountain, 20 to Bretton Woods, 40 to Loon Mountain. Adjacent to another estate (open to the public) on 1,200 acres with 2 miles of hiking/cross-country trails.

OPEN: Year round. Two-night minimum on weekends and during foliage. Three-night minimum on holiday weekends.

RATES: $145. $170 with fireplace; $195 with fireplace and two-person soaking tub; $210 suite with fireplace; $245 suite with fireplace, whirlpool, balcony; $295 cottage. Restaurant (thirty-three seats) open Wednesday–Sunday, eight months of year. Amex, MC, Visa. ♥ ⊞ ❖ ⚄ ⅍ ❤❍

IT'S A SLICE of paradise for romantics, and for business travelers too. With spectacular views from every room. With grounds that were originally designed by the Olmsted brothers of Boston's Emerald Necklace and Manhattan's Central Park fame. Built in 1927 for Dorothy Adair when she married a lawyer in her father's firm, the Georgian Colonial Revival, with two very large gathering rooms in addition to the dining room, is furnished with antiques and traditional pieces. Among the many books "that have always been here," guests sometimes find inscriptions from the 1920s or '30s.

As executive vice president for the Leo Burnett advertising agency, Bill traveled extensively for twenty-five years. Judy was a North Shore (Chicago) caterer who summered in New England. In 1998, after a yearlong search for a quiet, beautiful setting "with enough outdoor activities to appeal to our visiting grown children," they together transferred their joie de vivre to innkeeping. Now Bill, who grew up in a gardening family, is restoring more of the perennial gardens. Judy specializes in spectacular breakfasts. Guests speak of luxury and expectations that are surpassed.

IN RESIDENCE: Gilligan, fluffy cat, lives in hosts' quarters, greets guests outside.

BED AND BATH: *Main house* has nine rooms—two are suites (one with double Jacuzzi)—on second and third floors. King or queen beds. All with private bath, individual thermostat; most with gas fireplace; some with computer port. *Private cottage* has room with king bed, another with two twins, tub/shower bath, fireplaced living room, den with TV, kitchen, deck.

BREAKFAST: 8:30–9:15 (earlier with prior arrangement). Coffee and tea by 8. Sideboard includes granola, vanilla yogurt, bananas, juices. Fresh fruit, hot popovers with hand-whipped butter and preserves. Entrée may be lemon chiffon or pumpkin pancakes with

Vermont smoked bacon, waffles with seasonal fruit and maple-flavored sausage, scrambled eggs with mushrooms and cream cheese, or spinach and artichoke frittata. Served in fireplaced dining room.

PLUS: Tea and snacks, 4–5 P.M. Tap Room has granite foundation walls, massive fireplace, slate floors, vintage pool table, large-screen TV, video library, upright piano, puzzles and checkerboard. Small bar with set-ups, refrigerator, cheese and crackers. Tennis court for guests.

⚞ From New Hampshire, Illinois, Massachusetts, Vermont, Germany: *"One of the most romantic and beautiful inns on our New England trip. . . . perfect hosts. . . . Wish we could live there permanently . . . beautiful spacious rooms . . . immaculate and well-run. . . . Food is divine. . . . Personal touches are fantastic."*

⚞ *Mountain Fare Inn* 603/726-4283

Mad River Road, P.O. Box 553,
Campton, NH 03223

E-MAIL mtnfareinn@cyberportal.net
www.mountainfareinn.com

HOSTS: Susan and Nick Preston
LOCATION: At the edge of a small village in White Mountain National Forest. Surrounded by 6 acres. Ten miles west of Waterville Valley, 15 north of Squam Lake, 20 miles south of Loon and Cannon Mountains and Franconia Notch. Near golf, hiking, rock-climbing schools, bicycle rentals.
OPEN: Year round. Two-night minimum during ski season, foliage season, holiday weekends, and vacation weeks.
RATES: $40–$75 single, $85–$125 double. $105–$125 family of four. $5–$8 less midweek and off-season. Weekly summer family rates available.
♥ ⫟⫠ ⊞ ✦ ⚔ ⚒ ❤

THE PRESTONS coach competitive skiers including U.S. Ski Team members. They grow their own vegetables, herbs, and flowers. And they meet many outdoors-oriented guests who envy the "simple, down-home lifestyle" that provides privacy for couples and flexibility for families. The lifestyle has evolved since 1982, when Susan and Nick were boarders here and found an old brochure; it made them realize the potential of this 1830s heritage country farmhouse, which has lodged paying visitors since the 1880s. Teenaged sons Wes and Tim have grown up in the inn.

In 1992 the barn was renovated (new construction) with ski-tuning room, game room with Ping-Pong and billiards, and three large guest rooms. Furnishings in both buildings are country style with family treasures and printed fabrics. A welcoming red enamel woodstove stands in the entry room. Guests remember moose sightings; being snowed in; "better than home" hospitality; recommendations for back roads, hiking trails, waterfalls, and antiques dealers. And relaxation.

IN RESIDENCE: One cat—mostly outdoors.

continued . . .

FOREIGN LANGUAGE SPOKEN: Some French.

BED AND BATH: Ten rooms. *Main inn*—seven rooms, varying in size and decor; two with air conditioning. Six with private en-suite baths; one bath down the hall. Three family-sized rooms with three or four beds; one has a sitting room also, another has a bunk alcove. First-floor room has a queen and a twin bed, private bath. Cribs available. *Barn/carriage house*—three recently constructed rooms, private en-suite full baths. One with two double beds and one bunk bed. Third-floor air-conditioned honeymoon suite has queen bed, full bath, two twin beds in alcove.

BREAKFAST: 7:30–9 (ski season 6:30–9). "Hearty, wholesome natural foods for outdoors people." Eggs any style, herb and cheese omelet, blueberry muffins, French toast, pancakes and famous waffles. "We try to accommodate all dietary needs." In dining room that has an upright piano.

PLUS: Fireplaced living room with TV. Guest refrigerator. Après-ski refreshments. Window fans. Sauna. Babysitting. Soccer and volleyball fields. Game room with billiards. Swing set. Laundry service; $5 per load. Dinner for family reunions and ski, hiking, or biking groups. "A porch for 'settin'." Local day camp programs—soccer, hiking, biking, rock climbing—for kids; call ahead for family vacation ideas, camp registrations, and vacation packages.

From Massachusetts: *"Comfortable. Reasonably priced. Our family loved it."*

⋙ The "Inn" on Canaan Street   603/523-7310

92 Canaan Street,   FAX 603/523-9011
Canaan, NH 03741-9761   E-MAIL ltk@endor.com

> **HOSTS:** Lee and Louise Kremzner
> **LOCATION:** By lake. At the foot of Mount Cardigan on 14 acres. Two and a half miles up hill. Around corner from Cardigan Mountain School. Five minutes off Route 4; 25 minutes from Dartmouth College.
> **OPEN:** Year round. Two-night minimum for special school weekends. Reservations required.
> **RATES:** $85–$100 private baths. $20 cot. ♥ ♦♦ ⊞ ❖ ✗ ✗ ⚶ ♥♡

GUESTS ARE always asking, "How did you ever find this lovely place?" Located on a 1788 street that is in the National Register, it's the home of a Columbia professor (now a Canaan selectman) and his wife, a former nutritionist/consumer publicist (now on several community boards). Guests have a strong sense of place here in the restored "Federal but country-style house" that became the Kremzner's home in the early 1980s. "Once, when we thought of selling the inn (retiring) and moving away, we realized we 'have it all' right here!" The Kremzners share it all with Cardigan Mountain School parents, folks from Dartmouth, travelers on their way to Maine or somewhere else, many notables—and lots of people who come to catch their breath and to enjoy the views and the lake. "We love pampering them, sharing this area, laughing at ourselves, solving the world's problems, and relaxing over a fun breakfast." It's all true. My husband and I loved our stay.

IN RESIDENCE: Labrador Ginger, our "lovable aging wigglebottom."
FOREIGN LANGUAGE SPOKEN: A little French.
BED AND BATH: Four second-floor rooms, all with desk and comfortable chairs. Private baths—three are tub/shower, one is shower only. One canopied queen, working fireplace. Two king/twins options. One with two twins. Two rooms can be a suite. Cot available.
BREAKFAST: 8–9:30. (Earlier for meetings; brown bag breakfast for very early risers.) Buffet style, "all you'd like. Constantly changing menu with fruits, grains, and goodies." Juice, fruit, toast. Homemade sweet breads, muffins, scones, or popovers. Blueberry pancakes, egg dishes and herbs, yogurt, granola. Prepared by Louise, who has a collection of eight hundred cookbooks. Served in cozy Garden Room that opens onto porch.
PLUS: Books everywhere. Screened porch. Swimming. Cross-country skiing right here. Tea. Fruit. Library, games, movies. Badminton. Dinner during inclement weather and with theme weekends (antiques, auction, gardening, reading series). Barn antiques shop in warm weather. Inquire about Louise's cooking school sessions.

☞ *Watch Hill Bed and Breakfast*   603/253-4334

Old Meredith Road, P.O. Box 1605,   FAX 603/253-8560
Center Harbor, NH 03226   E-MAIL whbandb@worldpath.net

HOST: Barbara Lauterbach
LOCATION: Five-minute walk to Keepsake Quilting (quilt supply shop), village, and beach. Just off Route 25, on the northernmost end of Lake Winnipesaukee, near MS *Mount Washington* excursions, dogsled competitions, and ice fishing derby. On same road as post office and a farm. (Ask about the night the cows came.)
OPEN: Year round. Two-day minimum weekends June–Columbus Day.
RATES: $70 includes state meals and room tax. Single $5 less. Rollaway $15. Three nights or more, $5 less per night. Pets, by arrangement, $5/night. ☛ ⊞ ✂

SOME GUESTS place orders for a case of Barbara's tomato jam before the tomatoes are even planted. Barbara, too, is enthusiastic—about the view of the MS *Mount Washington* "precisely at 9:40 A.M.," about "the ancient locust trees of mammoth proportions," and about how her interests dovetailed into her 1989 B&B opening. A 1772 Cape with Victorian additions, the house is furnished with many English and American antiques, dog prints, and Staffordshires. (Barbara was a breeder of champion bullmastiffs.) She is a world-trained chef and food consultant; a former Ohio cooking school director who now teaches right here as well as at the New England Culinary Institute and appears on New Hampshire

continued . . .

television; a spokesperson for King Arthur flour; and a board member of the local planning board.

IN RESIDENCE: Martin, an Amazon parrot, "imitates female guests' laughter." Two cats: "super friendly" Frank, and Moxie, an orange Morris.

FOREIGN LANGUAGES SPOKEN: Fluent French. "Some Italian" (in 1996 Barbara attended total immersion language school in Italy). Some German too.

BED AND BATH: Four second-floor rooms; two have slanted ceilings. Two shared hall baths—one full, one shower only. King, queen, or two twin beds. Rollaway available.

BREAKFAST: Usually 7:30–8:30. Belgian waffles, maple French toast, sausage, "muffin du jour," eggs, home fries, mulled cider applesauce; homemade breads, jams, and jellies. In paneled room with fresh flowers, sterling silver, and linens or on screened porch with that lake view.

PLUS: Guest refrigerator. Beach towels. Horseshoes. Boccie balls. Quilting parties in dining and living rooms. Off-season cooking weekends.

     🐎 From Georgia, New Jersey, Vermont, Massachusetts: *"Of course the syrup was from New Hampshire, but how many B&Bs make their own sausage? . . . Quiet and relaxing. Great selection of books. . . . Bright, cheerful, cozy . . . A real home . . . terrific view of the lake and mountains beyond. . . . Lovely rooms and surroundings . . . Splendid breakfast elegantly served. . . . charming hospitality . . . Host, a world traveler, has great sense of humor. . . . Very good rates!"*

🐎 MapleHedge

355 Main Street, P.O. Box 638,
Charlestown, NH 03603-0638

603/826-5237
800/9MAPLE9 (962-7539)
FAX 603/826-5237
E-MAIL debrine@fmis.net
www.maplehedge.com

HOSTS: Joan and Dick DeBrine

LOCATION: Rural setting on Route 12 in New Hampshire's longest National Historic District—with occasional nostalgic sound from passing train. Surrounded by acres of grass, gardens, and 200-year-old maple trees. Thirty-five miles north to Dartmouth; 10 to world's longest two-span covered bridge; 12 to Saint-Gaudens National Historic Site.

OPEN: April–December. Two-night minimum on foliage and some holiday weekends.

RATES: $90, $95, or $105 for two. $125 for three in suite. Singles $5 less. Ten percent midweek corporate discount. MC, Visa. ♥ ⊞ ❖ ⚌ ⚍ 👫

⤷ From New Jersey, California, Pennsylvania, Georgia, Massachusetts, Illinois: *"Deserves acclaim. . . . Enjoyed being in an old but truly modern facility. . . . Elegant, tranquil, interestingly furnished . . . gourmet brunch for breakfast at a table set for a queen . . . ironed sheets . . . hand-picked homegrown flowers beautifully arranged . . . appropriate music, history of the area; an ambiance of total rest, relaxation, and pampering . . . jogged and found a lot of history in the cemetery behind the inn . . . the rooms are fun . . . exquisite antiques [but] not overbearing. . . . The best social hour. . . . Great location for day trips. . . . My parents had never stayed in an inn. . . . It was all they talked about . . . hosts are the soul of hospitality . . . most of all, felt comfortable and at home."*

ALL BY DESIGN. All a New England retirement dream come true. Now the transformed 1800s Federal Colonial, opened by Joan as a summer/fall B&B in 1990 and praised by *Country Living* magazine in 1991, has become a destination in itself. (Request a brochure and you'll also receive enticing detailed day-trip suggestions—and maybe a notice about the July Charlestown Yard Sale Day, initiated by Joan.) Until 1995 Dick was an air-conditioning contractor in California. Then he earned an MBA degree. Now he's involved in the community—and in golf (sand trap right here).

BED AND BATH: Five rooms; all private baths. Second floor—suite has large room with queen bed, sitting area, room with single bed; attached bath with double sink, claw-foot tub, hand-held shower, bidet. Queen bed, en-suite shower bath. Twin high four-posters, hall bath with double sink, and stall shower. Third floor—two queen-bedded rooms, each with shower bath; one is en-suite, other bath is across the hall.
BREAKFAST: Guests choose time; at 8:30 for three or more guests. (Granola and coffee available earlier.) Juice and granola. Fresh fruit and muffins or scones. Dutch babies, oatmeal pancakes, breakfast bread pudding. In dining room at large table set with linen and fine china.
PLUS: Central air conditioning. Double parlor with wood-burning fireplace. Sprinkler system. Hand-decorated pillow cases and sheets. Oversized towels. Turndown service. Locally made cheese. Croquet. Large porch.

☜ The Chase House B&B Inn   603/675-5391

RR 2, Box 909,   800/401-9455
Cornish, NH 03745   FAX 603/675-5010
                                          www.chasehouse.com

HOSTS: Barbara Lewis and (husband) Ted Doyle
LOCATION: On 160 acres along Route 12A. Runs parallel to Connecticut River (canoeing and fishing). With acres of lawn. Woods and meadows (hiking and snowshoeing). Across from Windsor, Vermont (Mount Ascutney Amtrak stop, car rentals available). Three miles south of Saint-Gaudens National Historic Site, 20 miles south of Dartmouth College. Within 40 minutes of Killington, Okemo, and Sunapee ski areas; 7 miles west to Ascutney.
OPEN: By reservation only, December 1 through end of October. (Closed Christmas. New Year's Eve dinner and dancing for overnight guests only; reservations by September 30.) Two-night minimum in September and October and on weekends year round. Restaurants within 5 to 30 minutes.
RATES: $105–$150. MC, Visa. ♥ ⊞ ⚔ ⅙ ♥♡

MORE ACCOLADES come from the National Trust for Historic Preservation and *Yankee* magazine for this restored inn, a combination of two eighteenth-century houses. Bill and Barbara Lewis bought the property in 1991; Later they built a 7,800-square-foot addition with a huge 1810 great room, moved from Vermont, with original exposed hand-hewn posts and beams, a raised-hearth fieldstone fireplace—and air conditioning. After Bill died in 1995, Barbara ran the inn solo until 1996. Then she was joined by Ted Doyle, "our longtime friend, who was involved in small technology-based businesses." In 1998 Barbara and Ted, hosts to many honeymooners, were married by the great room hearth.

BED AND BATH: Eight rooms (three suites); one room on first floor, all others on second. Each with individual thermostat, air conditioner, private tub and shower or shower-only bath. Four with queen bed (three are canopied), one with double bed. (Several rooms have additional four-poster twin or pull-out sofa bed—or both.) Three queen-bedded suites; one has TV, French doors onto deck, and private entrance.
BREAKFAST: At agreed-upon time (8:30 during foliage). Full country breakfast including home-baked goods, juice, granola, vanilla yogurt, seasonal fresh or cooked fruit. Meat dish and Amish friendship bread starter buttermilk pancakes, baked French toast, cheese-and-egg strata, scrambled eggs, eggs Benedict, or corned beef hash with poached eggs and mild salsa. With advance notice, special diets accommodated.
PLUS: Wood-burning fireplaces in common rooms and dining rooms. Guest refrigerator. Hot and cold beverages always available. Ironed sheets—really! Exercise room with Ping-Pong table. Chase House signature chocolates. Reception, meeting, and seminar facilities.

☜ From South Dakota: *"Truly wonderful."* From New Hampshire: *"Friendliest, warmest innkeepers."* From California: *"We loved it . . . Looking forward to our wedding rehearsal dinner in July."*

ᕦ *Rooms with a View*   603/237-5106

RR 1, Box 215, Forbes Road,   (N.H. ONLY) 800/499-5106, EXT. 1
Colebrook, NH 03576-9718

HOSTS: Sonja and Charles Sheldon
LOCATION: Very much off the beaten path. On a hillside of a former dairy farm. On a
snowmobile trail system. Six miles east of Colebrook center, shops, restaurants. Ten miles to skiing at The Balsams in Dixville Notch. Near fishing,
canoeing, hiking, golf, hunting. Two and a half hours from Montreal; 4½
from Boston.
OPEN: Year round.
RATES: Tax included, $65 shared bath, $70 private. Singles $15 less. MC, Visa.
♥ ⊞ ⚶ ⚶ ⚶ ◖

ᕦ From New Hampshire: *"Hospitality, food, and view are unsurpassed!"* From
Michigan: *"Walked in wildflower garden before scrumptious breakfast."* From Arkansas:
"Felt like visiting family." From Maine: *"Worth finding."*

"PEOPLE WONDER at the quiet and solitude and beautiful views that abound. Some stay
on the wraparound porch with a book. Artists paint the countryside. One Viennese opera
singer came on her honeymoon. A couple who came alone later booked the entire place
for themselves and friends. Snowmobilers leave from our door. Sometimes hot-air balloon
rides do too. And, year round, our guests enjoy the outdoor hot tub.

"After we fell in love with this area while vacationing one winter at The Balsams, we
built this farmhouse B&B in 1991. A Russian fireplace (which heats about half of the
house) is in the living room. Everyone gathers in the kitchen, especially when I'm cooking
at the three-ton soapstone stove that also heats the house. And they all want to know how
we ever found this location—and each other! I was working at a nursing home in Concord, Massachusetts, where Charlie, twenty years younger than I am, was a handyman.
We married in 1987. Here, Charlie is a porter at a nearby nursing home. I am fulfilling a
ten-year dream."

BED AND BATH: Seven rooms, each with a different view; all with Sonja's handmade
quilts. Second floor—three rooms with king/twins option and two double-bedded rooms
share two full baths. Third floor—two rooms, each with a double and two twin beds, one
with private full, other with private shower bath.
BREAKFAST: 6–10. Homemade muffins, bread, waffles, pancakes. Eggs any style, hot or
cold cereal, coffee, tea, milk, juice. Homemade jellies and honey. In dining room with
more views.
PLUS: Den with entertainment center that includes nature videos; satellite system. Down
comforters. Flannel sheets. Drying room for wet clothes. Croquet. Volleyball. Horseshoes. Boccie. Dart area.

☞ *Hannah Davis House* 603/585-3344

106 NH Route 119W, Fitzwilliam, NH 03447-9625

HOSTS: Kaye and Mike Terpstra

LOCATION: A few steps from common of this small New England town. In historic district. On a scenic route (119), with beaver pond and flyway "out back." Less than 2 hours from Boston or Hartford; 12 miles south of Keene; 28 east of Brattleboro, Vermont. "Within forty-five minutes of enough antiques shops to keep dealers busy for three days."

OPEN: Year round. Two-night minimum for some summer and fall weekends.

RATES: Per room. $60 double bed, $75 queen bed. With fireplace $85 queen bed, $105 suite or carriage loft, $115 extra-large suite. Additional person $20. Singles $10 less. Discover, MC, Visa. ♥ ♥♥ ⚫ ⊞ ❖ ⚕ ⅄ 🐾

EVERYTHING. It's all here. This c. 1820 Federal house with its original kitchen/hearth room, added baths with brass and porcelain fixtures, demolished and restored you-name-it, all embellished with antique furnishings and linens, country quilts, braided rugs, and fresh paint was enjoyed by the *Good Morning America* staff when they were broadcasting from Fitzwilliam. It's a favorite getaway, as noted in *Yankee* magazine, for Bev Davis of The Captain Lord Mansion, (page 104). And it is the home—a B&B since 1990—of an engineer and a social worker who owned and operated a small Brookline, New Hampshire, grocery store until they began work on this house in 1988. Kaye and Mike, who vary their personal touches, are the recipients of an "undoubtedly the best New England B&B" award from Scottish guests who exchanged holiday traditions. One couple who got engaged here returned a year later to be married in the poinsettia-filled kitchen. The Terpstras are sharers—of cooking and gardening tips, local history, bird identification, a secluded waterfall, a covered bridge.

IN RESIDENCE: "Bill, a Maine coon cat. Toby, a gregarious collie/shepherd mix. Tabatha, a happy, fluffy sheltie."

BED AND BATH: Six rooms. All private full baths. First-floor suite has private entrance, extra-long twins/king option, sitting room with double-size sleep sofa, two wood-burning fireplaces. On second floor, one canopied queen four-poster; one queen plus a twin bed, wood-burning fireplace; one "snug" double-bedded room. Private-entrance carriage barn has air-conditioned cathedral-ceilinged loft with queen bed in one room, sitting room with two wing-back chairs by wood-burning fireplace "inspired by our Santa Fe trip." "Popovers"—named for its private deck and elevated walkway that "pops over" backyard and bog—has extra-large room with high ceiling, queen bed; wood-burning fireplace and queen sofa bed in sitting room.

BREAKFAST: "The main event." (Even the menu is beautiful to look at.) Usually 8–9:30; tea and coffee earlier. Fresh fruit. Juices. Homemade granola, chunky applesauce, sour cream/poppy-seed or blueberry bread. Elaborate entrées—"new recipes all the time" — such as stir-fry chicken wrapped in crepes or stuffed French toast with cheesy Dijon sauce. Special diets accommodated with advance notice.

PLUS: Sitting room with stereo and piano, "but everyone ends up in the kitchen or on its long screened porch." A cupboard store with treasures for sale.

🕊 From New Jersey: *"A five-star stay. . . . Attention to utmost details in recreating Colonial atmosphere . . . feeling of being pampered and welcomed . . . lively conversation . . . individualized gourmet breakfasts . . . a little gem."* From Texas: *"Have stayed in several B&Bs in your New England book . . . this is by far the best B&B we've ever stayed in."* From New York: *"Warmth personified."*

🕊 *The Inn at Forest Hills*   603/823-9550

P.O. Box 783, Route 142,
Franconia, NH 03580-0783

RESERVATIONS 800/280-9550
FAX 603/823-8701
E-MAIL bbnebook@innfhills.com
www.innatforesthills.com

HOSTS: Gordon and Joanne Haym
LOCATION: On 5 wooded acres with two ponds, hiking, and ungroomed cross-country trails. Along a little-traveled road—with gorgeous mountain views—between Franconia and Bethlehem. Half mile from I-93. Five minutes to Cannon Mountain; 10 to fine dining in Franconia, Sugar Hill, Bethlehem, or Littleton.
OPEN: Year round. Two-night minimum on peak season weekends, during foliage, and on holidays.
RATES: Private bath $110 king, $95–$125 queen, $125 two-room suite. Foliage $40 more. Extra person $35–$45. MC, Visa. ♥ ⊞ ⚥ ⅍ ●♡

🕊 From England: *"As we were passing the inn, a voice spoke, saying 'come and visit' the type of silent voice heard by those who are fortunate enough to hear the words of Burns, Blake, and Wordsworth. This invitation and the overall ambiance and hospitality induced us not only to stay but to embark upon matrimony while resident in this beautiful place."*

THE SPACIOUS English Tudor, built in 1890 as a lodge for a grand summer hotel, was the residence for Franconia College's president in the 1960s and '70s. Now everything is redone with a neat, warm, and welcoming uncluttered look. Furnishings are a blend of country casual, modern, turn-of-the-century pieces, and locally made crafts.

In New Jersey Joanne, originally a home economics major, was a corporate officer in finance. Gordon, a small-business specialist who has consulted worldwide, was a chemical corporation executive. Now they are both justices of the peace, performing small weddings as well as renewal of vows. "With our children grown, we chose this wonderful lifestyle, a lifestyle that seems to be the dream of many guests, our extended family."

IN RESIDENCE: "Tiffany, our fat cat, in owners' quarters except to eat!"
BED AND BATH: Seven rooms, all private baths. First-floor room has queen, en-suite full

continued . . .

bath. Four large second-floor rooms. Two are extremely large and have en-suite full bath—one with king bed and sitting area, one with queen bed. Queen bed with shower bath. Queen bed, full bath (robes provided) across the hall. Third floor—one room with queen bed, en-suite shower bath. Suite has queen bed, sitting room with TV, full bath. **BREAKFAST:** 8:30; coffee at 7:30. Orange juice. Homemade granola with milk or yogurt, fresh fruit in season. Poached bananas, spiced pear compote, chilled pineapple with warm maple caramel sauce. Homemade bread or muffins with honey, strawberry butter, or vanilla cream cheese. Entrée possibilities—Belgian waffles; blueberry pancakes with a warm blueberry maple syrup; curried cream eggs in puff pastry; cinnamon, orange, raspberry, or other specialty French toast. By fireplace in winter. Next to open French doors and bird feeders (finches and hummingbirds) in warmer months.
PLUS: Large living room. Oversized fireplace in beamed Alpine Room. Solarium and Alpine Room have VCR, TV, games, library of recent books and movies on tape. Forty-five-foot-long covered porch overlooking mountains. Individual thermostats on all radiators. Guest pantry with refrigerator, microwave, coffees, teas, cocoa. Afternoon homemade cookies or cake. Inquire about option of dinner for skiers and cyclists.

৯ৈ *Bungay Jar*

Easton Valley Road, Easton, NH
Mailing address: P.O. Box 15, Franconia, NH 03580

603/823-7775
800/421-0701
FAX 603/444-0100
E-MAIL info@bungayjar.com
www.bungayjar.com
www.gardenswild.com

HOSTS:	Kate Kerivan and (husband) Lee Strimbeck
LOCATION:	Gorgeous. Franconia range of White Mountains. Tucked back from the road on 12 wooded acres with a lily pond, horse barn, pastures, and paths to a stream. Six miles south of Franconia. Ten minutes to I-93, Sugar Hill, Cannon Mountain, Lost River; 30 to Loon, Bretton Woods. Robert Frost Museum "just down the street." Near Echo Lake (swimming), golf courses, skiing, Appalachian Mountain Trail.
OPEN:	Year round. Two-night minimum during foliage season, holidays, and most weekends.
RATES:	Foliage season $120–$170; $225 suite or cottage ($170 off-season). Rest of year $110–$195. Third person $25. Amex, Discover, MC, Visa.

♥ ⊞ ⚿ ⚭ 柊

A TREAT. A feature in *Country Accents, Yankee,* and *Country Gardens* magazines. Built from an eighteenth-century post-and-beam barn, it is filled with antiques and collectibles, stained glass windows, quilts, English pub panels, Benny Goodman's 6-foot-long soaking tub, glass-topped lightning rods that hold up one railing . . . all arranged by Kate Kerivan, an award-winning landscape architect. In the early 1980s Kate and Lee, a patent attorney (recently retired), made this weekend getaway into a B&B complete with a two-storied fireplaced living room; a sauna; a small library; and multiple decks that offer mesmerizing mountain, garden, and meadow views. Kate's spectacular herb and perennial gardens—featured in many major national magazines—have led to the realization of another dream, the opening of "Gardens Wild," a garden shop (with workshops) located next to the B&B and horse pasture.

IN RESIDENCE: Son, Kyle, age fourteen. Two dogs, two cats, horses, and llamas.
BED AND BATH: Six rooms, most with mountain views; all with private baths. Garden suite with king bed; kitchen; fireplace; two-person raspberry-colored (!) whirlpool; minifridge with juice, coffee, and split of champagne; private porch and entrance. First floor—room with queen bed, attached private shower bath. Second floor—Victorian queen bed with private balcony, bath with 6-foot tub; canopied king bed, shower bath, interior reading balcony overlooking fireplaced two-storied common area. Third floor—suite with four skylights, king bed, gas fireplace, tub bath; another skylit room with antique double sleigh bed, shower bath, French doors to private balcony. Also private cottage in village—queen bed, fireplace, whirlpool, loft, atrium dining room, kitchen.
BREAKFAST: 8:30–9:30. Full buffet-style country meal. Popovers, garden produce and edible flowers in season, oatmeal pancakes with sautéed local apples, vegetable quiches, fresh herb-flavored breads. In dining room or on porch overlooking gardens and mountains.
PLUS: No TV. Tea or cider with homemade snacks 3–5 P.M. Coffee or tea anytime. CD player. Games. Croquet. Hammock. Summer afternoons: English-style cream teas in the gardens, $10 per person by reservation.

🐦 Guests wrote: *"Surpassed your glowing recommendation . . . picturesque. . . . Could look around for days and not see everything."*

ACCORDING TO MANY HOSTS: "GUESTS COME WITH PLANS AND DISCOVER THE JOYS OF HAMMOCK SITTING."

⤜ The Hilltop Inn

Sugar Hill, NH 03585

603/823-5695

800/770-5695
FAX 603/823-5518
E-MAIL bc@hilltopinn.com
www.hilltopinn.com

HOSTS: Mike and Meri Hern
LOCATION: In this tiny village with cheese store, post office (open three hours a day), and a historical museum. Ten minutes from Franconia Notch hiking and downhill skiing.
OPEN: Year round. Two-night minimum on summer and fall weekends and daily in foliage season.
RATES: January–late September and October 15–December $90 double, $100 queen; suites $110 queen, $120 king. Foliage season $25–$50 more. Additional guest $35. Cottage $195/couple; $225 during foliage; additional guest $35. Singles $10 less. Pets $10 per evening. Discover, MC, Visa.
♥ ⊞ ♥☌

"NEARBY THERE's a lovers lane—really!—with benches placed for sunset views."

"Well, it looks like a lovely place that you have booked for the wedding," said the English mother of the bride when she saw the BBC New England segment that was shot with the inn as a backdrop. *Outside, Yankee, Flower Garden, Country Almanac,* and *Country Decorating* have featured this inn, which is owned by two hikers and cross-country skiers who have 20 acres of cross-country ski trails right from the door. "Guests (and their pets—one even came with a llama) comment on the homey Victoriana, woodstove with nearby rocking chairs, handmade quilts, stenciling, local artists' work on display—and, outside, the gardens with perennials, thirty kinds of edible flowers, raspberries, vegetables, and hummingbirds, too. Many guests come for one night and stay several. We love them, the inn, the quiet country lanes to spectacular views, the town."

Meri discovered Sugar Hill when she visited a college friend in the 1960s. ("I never left.") She and Mike, a fly-fisherman and former electrical engineer, are now caterers. They make "ongoing changes" to the 1895 inn.

IN RESIDENCE: Beemer and Bogie, golden retriever/maremma (Italian sheepdog) mix sisters.
BED AND BATH: Six second-floor rooms, private full baths. Double or queen beds in smaller rooms; kings in others. Suites have king or queen with twin bed also. Crib available. Two-bedroom cottage with full kitchen, fireplaced living room, full bath.
BREAKFAST: 8:30–9:30 (coffee, tea, "cookies too" available 7:30 A.M.–10 P.M.). Hearty buffet. Cinnamon French toast, farm eggs, raspberry and wild blueberry pancakes, local berries and maple syrup. Locally smoked ham and bacon. Homemade jams and muffins. (Special diets accommodated with advance notice.) By dining room woodstove or on deck or porches.

PLUS: Guests' pets welcomed. Large deck with sunset views. Porch rockers. Ceiling fans. TV with VCR (more than 400 movies) in fireplaced sitting room. Library. Huge world map with pins indicating guests' home places. Teas or local cider with snacks. Transportation to/from Franconia bus stop.

⚶ From Massachusetts: *"Completely relaxing. We only left the inn for three hours all weekend!"* From England: *"Excellent stop on our honeymoon."*

⚶ *The Atwood Inn*

603/934-3666

71 Hill Road, Route 3A,
Franklin, NH 03235-9361

E-MAIL **info@atwoodinn.com**
www.atwoodinn.com

HOSTS: Fred and Sandi Hoffmeister
LOCATION: In lakes region, on wooded acreage with river. Ten minutes to Tilton School, 20 to Proctor Academy or to five lakes including Winnipesaukee; just 5 minutes to Webster Lake for swimming. Six miles to outlet shopping.
OPEN: Year round. Two-night minimum in October and on holiday weekends.
RATES: $65 single, $80–$90 double. Extra adult $25. Ages twelve to seventeen, $15 each, under twelve free. Amex, Discover, MC, Visa. ♥ ♦♦ ⊞ ⚶ ✕ ❤

⚶ Dozens of guests wrote: *Hospitality superb . . . historic ambiance delightful . . . attractive inside and out . . . full of charm . . . worth going for the breakfasts alone! . . . great hosts—who are happy! . . . romantic . . . suggested wonderful local places for antiques, an auction, wilderness walks, science center, ponds for canoeing . . . had two rooms connected by a comfortable room for our children to read and play . . . loved our room and the fireplace they would have blazing when we arrived 'home' every night. . . . Stayed during Laconia Bike Races. Breakfasts always different with plenty for all of us . . . linen cloths . . . late-night snacks . . . clean . . . quiet even though it's on a main road . . . never stayed in B&B before. It was great. Their dog is terrific too. . . . Have traveled in many countries; stayed in five-star hotels and elegant places. Sandi and Fred bring the best of these places to one beautiful Colonial bed and breakfast . . . gorgeous, with antiques. . . Make you feel right at home—or wishing it was your permanent home!"*

OBVIOUSLY, the Hoffmeisters are sharing their love of the lakes and the mountains, "the quiet, the peace, and the pace." On Cape Cod Fred had an insurance agency; Sandi, a New Hampshire native, was a nurse. In 1997, for their midlife career change, they bought this established B&B. Now Fred dovetails innkeeping with furniture making and farm work.

BED AND BATH: Seven rooms—some are air-conditioned—on three floors. All private shower baths. First floor has room with double and twin bed and fireplace. Second floor has three rooms with double bed and fireplace, and one with double and twin bed and tub bath. Third floor has two family rooms, each with a queen and two twin beds.

continued . . .

BREAKFAST: 8–10. (Earlier for business travelers.) Baked fruit pancake, ham and cheese strata, or breakfast pudding. Fruit, juice, baked breads, breakfast meats. Special diets accommodated with advance notice. In candlelit dining room or in gardens.
PLUS: Snacks and beverages always available. Refrigerator and microwave. Cable TV. Bicycle and ski storage. Umbrella table on deck and in gardens.

⟫ The Englewood Bed and Breakfast

603/934-1017

69 Cheney Street, Franklin, NH 03235-1102

888/207-2545

E-MAIL info@englewoodbnb.com
www.englewoodbnb.com

HOSTS: Laurie Nelson and Carla Diffenderfer
LOCATION: In lakes region. In quiet residential area. On a hill overlooking the city—and, in winter, the river. Five-minute walk to downtown and "a very good restaurant." Five miles from I-93. Within 15 minutes of private schools and outlet mall. Less than one hour to White Mountains, coastal destinations, or Manchester airport.
OPEN: Year round.
RATES: $75 queen bed. $65 double bed. Singles $10 less. Extra person $10. Amex, MC, Visa. ♥ ⊞ ✄

HAVE YOU EVER looked at a real estate guide while visiting an area? That did it for Carla, a paralegal, and Laurie, a software engineer, Maryland residents when they were here on a ski trip in 1994. Now the Queen Anne they fell in love with is totally restored. Floors are refinished. Painting and papering, too, is the work of the hosts, who were mentored by Laurie's helpful brothers, both carpenters. Many of the antiques and eclectic furnishings were purchased in the area. The perennials are beginning to mature. In summer guests sit on the private (can't be seen from the street) wraparound porch and listen to concerts from the downtown park where festivals are held. Since opening in 1998, the two early-thirtyish hosts have dovetailed innkeeping with their other jobs. And they have seen other fine old houses in this turn-of-the-century mill town "discovered" and revitalized. Guests express appreciation for the renovation (and wistfully wonder aloud about the time it took). They comment on the hospitality and on "all the extra touches in your comfortable home."

IN RESIDENCE: Tisch, a German shepherd/Lab mix. Butterscotch, a Calico cat.
BED AND BATH: Four second-floor rooms—three with queen bed (one with single sleeper chair also) and one with a double bed—share two full baths. (One bath has a Jacuzzi tub.) Robes provided.
BREAKFAST: Flexible hours. Baked blueberry French toast with maple sausage. Fresh fruit, breads, muffins, juice, coffee/teas. Served on lace-covered table in paneled dining room or on porch.

PLUS: TV/VCR in living room. Homemade baked goods in afternoon and/or evening. Local maple sugar candy. Guest refrigerator with complimentary beverages.

🐾 *Greenfield Bed & Breakfast Inn* 603/547-6327

Village Center, Forest Road, Routes 136 and 31 North,	800/678-4144
P.O. Box 400,	FAX 603/547-2418
Greenfield, NH 03047-0400	E-MAIL innkeeper@greenfieldinn.com
	www.greenfieldinn.com

HOSTS: Barbara and Vic Mangini
LOCATION: On 3 acres of lawn (or snow!) with view of Mount Monadnock. Adjacent to 3-acre meadow. On main road in small village. Three minutes from 400-acre Greenfield State Park; 15 from Peterborough and from Crotched and Temple Mountains; 90 from Boston airport; 45 from Manchester airport.
OPEN: Year round. Two-day minimum on three-day holidays, May–December. (No phone calls after 9:30 P.M.)
RATES: $69 or $79 private bath, $49–$59 shared (with one other room); $129 hayloft suite with kitchenette. Hideaway suite $149; $119 without spa room. Carriage house—private bath $69; studio $59. Entire carriage house with kitchen and living room—$139 for two, $159 for up to six people. Weekly rates available. MC, Visa. ♥ ♦♦ ⊞ ❖ ⚲ ♙ ❦♡

🐾 Guests wrote: *"Felt spoiled. . . . Fabulous breakfast. . . . Friendly host. . . . Great getaway."*

TWENTY MINUTES after the Manginis' B&B sign went up in 1986, the first guests—honeymooners—arrived. That couple and many others celebrating anniversaries return annually. "Bob and Dolores Hope, our friends for more than thirty years, also visited several times."

The FOR SALE sign on the big, beautiful white 1817 house was too much to resist just about the time the parents of six grown children were ready to retire to their nearby farm. Barbara decorated the original six guest rooms—now there are twelve, plus a separate cottage—with Victorian flair, white wicker, Laura Ashley linens, antiques, dolls, Victorian wallpapers, crystal, laces, and plants too. Enthusiastic Vic, who has been in advertising and marketing for decades, has found that corporate executives have a special appreciation for "the corporate rocking-chair meetings in the glass-walled deck house with mountain views." And then there's the new hot-tub spa room, booked just for the two of you.

BED AND BATH: Thirteen rooms, all with phones and air conditioning. Large street-level room has king/twins option, TV, private full bath with Jacuzzi. On second floor—king, double, or twin beds; most have private shower baths. One is a Jacuzzi bath. Two rooms share a full bath. One twin-bedded and one double-bedded room form a suite with private hallway. Hideaway Suite has option of private spa room. Rustic beamed Hayloft

continued . . .

Suite with private entrance and TV sleeps six. Carriage house has full kitchen, living room, TV, phones, and three rooms (king, double, or twin beds) with private baths. (Infants must have own portable crib.)

BREAKFAST: 7:30–9:30. "A party." Egg casseroles, strata (meatless or with sausage, ham, chicken). Barbara's home-baked muffins, one kind known as "miracle muffin." Her own cranberry/raisin/oat granola. Bagels. Cereals. Fresh fruit. Served with "crystal, china, and Mozart."

PLUS: In winter, Vic scrapes ice off windshields and warms your car in the morning. Bedroom ceiling fans. Fireplaced living room with TV. Access to fax, copier, video player, movie screen. Huge deck—wrapped around a maple tree—with mountain view.

⇶ D. W.'s Oceanside Inn

603/926-3542

365 Ocean Boulevard,
Hampton Beach, NH 03842

FAX 603/926-3549
E-MAIL oceansid@nh.ultranet.com
www.nh.ultranet.com/~oceansid

HOSTS: Duane (Skip) and Debbie Windemiller
LOCATION: Directly across the street from a wide, sandy beach. Five blocks north of tourist shops, arcades, restaurants, and outdoor stage with free summer nightly entertainment. Twelve miles south of Portsmouth (historic seaport with fabulous restaurants). Fifteen minutes north of Newburyport, Massachusetts. Fifty miles north of Boston and south of Portland, Maine.
OPEN: May–mid-October. Three-night minimum; shorter stays based on availability.
RATES: $130–$150. Less May–mid-June and mid-September–mid-October. Amex, Discover, MC, Visa. ⊘ ⅍ ☀

SURPRISE! The exterior of this added-on-to beach house is fairly plain. That impression does a flip-flop once you enter into the designer style of this home away from home. Victorian in feeling—with the "wow" effect—it has some antiques, hand-screened wall-coverings, paintings, curved walls, and some built-in beds. Floors have Oriental or braided rugs or wall-to-wall carpeting. Since buying the property in the late 1970s, the Windemillers have transformed it, and still, there are annual changes. The hosts have combined rooms, installed raised wood wainscoting, and, as this book was going to press, added interior columns to one guest room. Skip, a former (Killington, Vermont) freestyle skiing coach, had an earlier career in interior design. He and Debbie, a South Dakota native, also work together in their real estate business.

FOREIGN LANGUAGES SPOKEN: "Minimal French and German."
BED AND BATH: Nine rooms (two with ocean view); each with private bath, and in-room phone and safe. First floor—one room with queen bed, oversized shower. One room with

extra-long antique double bed, custom pull-down twin Murphy bed, dressing room, tub/shower bath. Second floor—rooms have king, two double beds, queen (with Murphy bed also), canopied double, or twin beds.

BREAKFAST: 8–9:15 (coffee available earlier). Select from menu the night before. French toast or egg dishes. Homemade toast, muffins, or bagels. Juice or fruit. Served in breakfast room (with gas fireplace) at individual tables set with long-stemmed glasses, silver, lace placemats.

PLUS: Central air conditioning. Wood-burning fireplace, upright piano, and TV/VCR in living room. No TVs in rooms. Parking. Guest refrigerator. Locker-room area for beach-goers; towels and chairs provided.

Moose Mountain Lodge

603/643-3529

P.O. Box 272,
Etna, NH 03750-0272

FAX 603/643-4119
E-MAIL meeze@aol.com
www.moosemountainlodge.com

HOSTS: Kay and Peter Shumway

LOCATION: With 100-mile panoramic view from huge porch. One mile up a winding dirt road (winter shuttle provided) to 350 acres with a "soothing view" of Connecticut River Valley below, Green Mountains beyond. Eight miles from the Dartmouth College campus and Connecticut River in Hanover. The Appalachian Trail crosses lodge property and continues over Moose Mountain.

OPEN: June 15–mid-October and December 26–early March. Two-day (Friday and Saturday) weekend reservations required.

RATES: Per person. B&B $75 single, $65 double, $48 age fourteen and under. $85–$95 ($48 fourteen and under) includes breakfast and dinner. B&B usually not offered in winter, when $75–$95 per person includes three meals here "on the top of the world." Ten percent discount for three or more nights. MC, Visa. ♥ 👫 ⊞ ❖ ⚅ 🗡 🎿

From Florida: *"This is one of those rare places that is better than what it says in the promotional literature. Kay and Peter deliver the unique kind of hospitality that can come only from people who are living their dream. It is this kind of love and special attention that keeps us coming back."*

IT'S ALL TRUE, and it's been so for a quarter century. The almost-legendary hosts were a hit for the very first England REI (sporting goods store) ski trip. They have also been hailed by *Condé Nast Traveler*. As they say, "We love to share this tranquil place, to introduce people to the beauty of our trails and the Beaver Pond with its wonderful animal and bird life. A person who gains the blessing of one mountain day is rich forever."

continued . . .

Their rustic building, built as a ski lodge in 1938, has a massive stone fireplace, pine walls, and couches and four-poster beds made of logs. Peter, the vegetable gardener/song leader/former wholesale lumber businessman, took tap dancing lessons to celebrate his sixtieth birthday; more recently he skied in the Swiss Alps and northern Quebec. Kay, a skier too, is the good cook who wrote the *Moose Mountain Lodge Cookbook*. Before breakfast she spins her goats' mohair and, in the new weaving room, creates rugs from the coarser fleece. The Shumways' guests come looking for peace and quiet and relaxation—and find it.

IN RESIDENCE: Tulla, a gray weimaraner, the perfect guide for walks. Four angora goats: Billy, Lenny, Eddie, and Barry. One pig named Sylvia Pigioli.
FOREIGN LANGUAGES SPOKEN: French; some Spanish.
BED AND BATH: Twelve rooms, all with views, share five full baths. Queen, double, double and twin, or two twins; one room has a double and two bunks.
BREAKFAST: 8–9. Huge. Could include homemade granola, fresh farm eggs, turkey sausage, black bean hash, hot cereals, or pancakes with Shumways' own maple syrup— "we made 20 gallons this year!"
PLUS: No TV. Player piano. Filled cookie jar. Hiking, cross-country skiing, and snowshoeing trails start at the front door. Three fireplaces used almost year round, even in summer on cool evenings. "Increasing numbers of moose and coyotes."

⇗ *Stonecrest Farm Bed & Breakfast*

119 Christian Street, Wilder, VT
Mailing address: P.O. Box B1163,
Hanover, NH 03755-1163

802/296-2425
800/730-2425
FAX 802/295-1135
E-MAIL Gail.Sanderson@Valley.net

HOST: Gail Sanderson
LOCATION: On 2 country acres with classic red barns. Near I-91 and I-89; 3.7 miles south of Dartmouth College, 13.6 east of Woodstock, Vermont.
OPEN: Year round. Closed December 24–January 1. Two-night minimum on Dartmouth's parents' weekends, September 15 through November 15, and holiday weekends.
RATES: April 15–November 15 $129–$144. November 16–April 14 $119–$135. Third person $30. Singles $20 less. Ten percent less for one-week stay. Corporate rates. Amex, MC, Visa. ♥ ☎ ⊞ ❖ ⚄ ✂

⇗ From New York, Colorado, New Jersey: *"Felt as though we had been invited to someone's country home. Only this was better because I didn't have to do the dishes!... helpful hostess... Breakfast a real treat... beautifully prepared... Antiques... fresh flowers... comfortable elegance.... Atmosphere is friendly, the decor especially charming.... Setting is lovely."*

FOLLOWING YEARS of world travel and academic administration, the Sandersons moved to this stately 1810 house. It has much stonework, a curved oak staircase, and a 34-foot-long beamed living room with French doors that lead to a terrace. Paintings, Oriental rugs, and antiques add to the ambiance.

Since Gail redecorated and opened as a B&B, she has also become a practicing attorney. And she teaches at Dartmouth's Institute for Lifelong Education. She sings in a regional opera company, enjoys hiking, and often suggests visiting the Saint-Gaudens National Historic Site with its lovely gardens; the tour of the sculptor's studio includes the showing of a film produced by Gail's son, Paul.

IN RESIDENCE: Tessa and Tosca, tricolor collies.
FOREIGN LANGUAGES SPOKEN: "Very limited German and French."
BED AND BATH: Six rooms, all private en-suite baths. First floor—queen bed, full bath. Second floor—two queen-bedded rooms, each with cedar shower bath. Room with grandparents' mahogany canopied double bed, shower bath. One with twin beds, full bath. Honeymooners' favorite—queen bed, skylights, shower bath, private entrance.
BREAKFAST: 8–9:30. Could be baked frittata with peppers, garlic, and parmesan with maple sausage and heart-shaped cornbread muffins; or apple-cinnamon buttermilk pancakes and bacon. Fresh strawberries with rhubarb sauce, cranberry scones, lemon-ginger muffins. Yogurt and granola. In fireplaced dining room with individual bouquet at each place, or served on flower-filled terrace.
PLUS: Living room fireplace/woodstove. Baby grand piano. Bedroom ceiling or floor fans.

🐦 *The Harrisville Squires' Inn Bed & Breakfast*

(VOICE OR TDD) 603/827-3925

FAX 603/827-3622

797 Chesham Road, Box 19,
Harrisville, NH 03450-0019

E-MAIL squiresinnBB@top.monad.net
www.harrisvillesquiresinn.com

HOSTS: Doug and Pat McCarthy
LOCATION: Tranquil. On 50 acres with 4–6 miles of trails. One-half mile from idyllic nineteenth-century textile village, a National Historic Landmark, with nine lakes and, in center, a mill over canal, a weaving center, and a supply shop. Five miles to Mount Monadnock, 12 to Crotched and Temple Mountains.
OPEN: Year round. Minimum stay required during fall foliage.
RATES: $80–$85 private bath, $90 room with private Jacuzzi bath. Third person $35. Tour planning and packages, $50–$145, include custom-planned itinerary, reservations, T-shirt. MC, Visa. ♥ ⊞ ❖ ⚶ 🐾 ❤🐾

GUESTS COME FOR romance and relaxation; for Doug's custom-designed Monadnock Bicycle Touring day or overnight routes (on- and off-road, through covered bridges and small villages); for hiking and cross-country skiing right here; for reunions; and for

continued ...

(many) weddings. Pat, who is a justice of the peace, "takes care of food, lodging, and flowers. The bride and groom only have to show up!"

Located in one of the most photographed towns in New England, this 1842 house was once the caretaker's residence on a working farm and is decorated in country style. A recent addition and big hit: a hot tub in the Meditation Garden. Before hosting, Pat was an interpreter for the deaf and a Hilton Hotel restaurant manager. Now she dovetails innkeeping with the barn gallery/studio where she works on commissioned stained glass pieces. Doug teaches eighth-grade special needs students. Both know American Sign Language.

IN RESIDENCE: "In hosts' area—four lovable cats and one malamute husky."
BED AND BATH: Five large rooms; all private baths. First-floor wheelchair-accessible room has queen bed, full bath, large sitting area. Second floor: Room with canopied queen bed, full hall bath next door. Queen bed, Jacuzzi tub, plus shower. King/twins option, double shower bath. Queen bed and single bed, TV, full bath.
BREAKFAST: 8–9. Juices. Fruit. Homemade breads, muffins. Entrée changes daily; hosts' own maple syrup. Cereals. Hot fruit dessert. Special diets accommodated. In dining room or in garden area.
PLUS: Fireplaced living room. Tea with cakes, breads, and cookies. Grounds with gardens, small fish pools, lawn chairs. Swimming in nearby pond. On-site gallery with local artwork and jewelry.

> Guests wrote: *"Comfortable, charmingly decorated—Fabulous breakfast. . . . Followed Pat's maps to vistas to paint. . . . A warm, friendly couple who go 'the extra mile' to make your stay a memorable one."*

The Inn at Maplewood Farm

603/464-4242
800/644-6695
FAX 603/464-5401
E-MAIL j_simoes@conknet.com
www.conknet.com/maplewoodfarm/

447 Center Road,
Hillsborough, NH 03244-1478

HOSTS: Jayme Simoes
LOCATION: Rural. "Cows [with cowbells] are our nearest neighbors." In a town of 4,300 people. On 14 acres with historic barns, gardens, small apple orchard. Close to the village, restaurants, golf, tennis, lake, auctions, Franklin Pierce Homestead, antiquing, trout fishing, hiking, stone-arched bridges, fields of wildflowers, maybe a beaver dam. Hillsborough Balloon Festival in July.
OPEN: May–November. Two-night minimum on most holiday and special weekends; three nights on Columbus Day (October) weekend.
RATES: $75 weekdays, $85 weekends and foliage; $20 third person. Large suite $125–$135. Ten percent less, five nights or more. Amex, Diners, Discover, MC, Visa. ♥ ❖ ⌀ ⅄ 桥

A SUCCESS STORY. An experience. A treat for the eyes and ears. A farmhouse in this time-less spot. The *New York Times, Yankee* magazine, and the *Boston Globe* are among the publications that have featured Jayme's collection of antique radios and tapes of old programs. Thanks to a transmitter that broadcasts to the B&B only, you can lie in bed and listen to *Jack Armstrong, Fibber McGee and Molly, Lights Out,* Fred Allen, and big band music too.

Jayme and his wife, Laura, were in their early twenties when they left their Boston jobs in public relations and marketing in 1993. They restored the farmhouse (from apartments), became active in the community, and created the B&B as a getaway destination. In 1998 Laura became publicity director for New Hampshire's Office of Travel and Tourism.

IN RESIDENCE: Two Boston terriers not allowed in guest areas.

FOREIGN LANGUAGES SPOKEN: Portuguese and Spanish.

BED AND BATH: Four spacious suites (two are air-conditioned); all private baths. First floor—king bed, bath with extra-large shower, gas fireplace, private exterior entrance. Second floor (private entrance from parking area)—queen bed in one room, double bed in other, cathedral beamed ceiling with skylight, tub/shower bath, gas fireplace, private deck. Queen bed in one skylit room, twin bed in adjoining room, large shower bath. Queen four-poster, wood-burning fireplace, tub/shower bath, wicker-furnished sitting room, two skylights.

BREAKFAST: 8:30–9:30. (Picnic breakfasts for early departures.) Fresh fruit course. Granola, muffins, scones, bread, and jams. "Always full" cup of coffee. Served in dining room or on porch.

PLUS: "Kettle always on in guest kitchen." Sitting room with TV and wood-burning fire-place. Turndown service. Guest refrigerator. Beach towels. Croquet. Horseshoes.

⤜ From New York: *"This B&B restored our faith in the concept. A true bucolic experience, from the great drive up to the inn, to the cowbells ringing, to the forest next door. . . . Antiques-filled rooms without any sacrifice of comfort or modernity. . . . Great mountain biking right from the inn."*

KEY TO SYMBOLS

♥   Lots of honeymooners come here.

⭢⭠   Families with children are very welcome.

🐖   This B&B is a private home, not an inn.

⊞   Groups can reserve this entire B&B.

❖   Travel agents' commissions paid.

🐾   Sorry, no guests' pets allowed.

⚡   No smoking inside *or* no smoking at all.

⚟   Waterfront location.

🚶   Off the beaten path.

❤⊃   Weddings booked here. For details, please inquire.

❧ *The Inn on Golden Pond*   603/968-7269

P.O. Box 680,   FAX 603/968-9226
Holderness, NH 03245-0680   E-MAIL innongp@lr.net
www.newhampshirebandb.com

HOSTS: Bill and Bonnie Webb
LOCATION: On 50 wooded acres with trails. Across the street from Squam Lake, setting for the film *On Golden Pond.* Twenty minutes to White Mountain National Forest. Four miles from I-93. Near many maple sugaring shacks and great 45-minute (gradual) hike to mountaintop for "unsurpassed view of fifty to sixty islands."
OPEN: Year round. Two-night minimum on holiday weekends and on weekends between May 15 and October 30.
RATES: Double $125. Suite $150. Third person $30. Some ski, honeymoon, anniversary, birthday, or winter dinner package rates. Amex, MC, Visa. ♥ ❖ ✍ ✄

IF YOU HAVE seen the film, your expectations of a fairly undeveloped area will be fulfilled. And if you're looking for a family-run inn where you get to know the innkeepers and other guests (and still there's a respect for privacy), this is the place—immaculate and comfortable (not lavish) in a location that appeals to outdoor-oriented and international travelers, including many honeymooners and some well-known names too.

"Because it's fifteen years since we came from California—where we worked in guidebook publishing and data processing—we feel very close to New Hampshire and this community." (Bill is a selectman and Bonnie works with hospice.) It's thirteen years since Becky and her brother Ricky arrived from Korea. They have grown up in this 1879 country home which is surrounded by stone walls, antique split rail fences, flowers, bushes, and shade trees.

IN RESIDENCE: Ricky and Becky are teenagers.
BED AND BATH: Eight air-conditioned rooms (one is a suite); each with private bath (some full, some tub or shower only) and individual thermostat. King or queen beds; two rooms with a queen and a twin bed.
BREAKFAST: 8:30–9:30. Cooked by Bonnie. Entrées such as apple pancakes or eggs and bacon. Homemade bread and muffins. Fresh fruit. At individual tables. Usually a very social time. Innkeeper/waiter Bill joins guests for coffee.
PLUS: Turndown service. Fireplaced living room. Hair dryers. Picnic tables. Lawn games. A 60-foot screened porch. Ice and glasses. Swimming (small fee) at town beach just around the corner. Their own cookbook.

From Connecticut: *"Spotless. . . . Good food. . . . Wonderful hosts."*

St. Peter's-on-the-Mount   603/968-7984

St. Peter's-on-the-Mount, Shepard Hill Road,   E-MAIL claremowbray@hotmail.com
Box 196, Holderness, NH 03245-0196   www.eagle1st.com/stpeters1.htm

HOSTS: Clare and Larry Mowbray
LOCATION: Quiet. Rural setting atop a landscaped hill with gardens and tall pine wood-
land. Five-minute walk to fine dining in village center. Eight minutes from
I-93. Half mile to Squam Lake ("Golden Pond") tours and kayak/canoe
rentals. Half hour to three ski areas. Five minutes to Science Center, 15 to
Lake Winnipesaukee. Near hiking trails.
OPEN: May–December. Two-night weekend minimum, June–mid-October.
RATE: $120 per night. ♥ ❖ ⚅ ⚔

From New Hampshire, Florida, Scotland, New York: *"A perfect honeymoon. . . .
Even had our music selection playing when we entered the marvelous room. . . . Besides the
architecture and fabulous stained glass windows, fabulous owners who made us feel special.
Personal, friendly attention. . . . Many tips for dining, shopping, fishing, hiking, sightseeing,
and for hidden treasures we would have missed. . . . We enjoyed ourselves so much that we
forgot to pay our bill! (Clare forgot also.)"*

ABSOLUTELY ONE of a kind. A large and lovely 1888 stone church (converted to a residence
by previous owners) with huge sloping roof. There are stained glass windows (in guest
bath too) and mirror framed by moldings from the church altar. Woodwork is ash.
Paneling is chestnut. The skylit Caribbean Room, a sunroom with heated tile floor, has a
hot tub and French doors opening onto a deck. Hospitality is memorable.
  This has been the Mowbrays' residence since 1997. Multifaceted Clare, a recently
retired school counselor, also has experience as a photographer, as an artist (her current interest is painting on silk), and as an innkeeper on Virgin Gorda. Larry, a bicyclist, is the
beloved (he is!) local postmaster.

IN RESIDENCE: "Kiko, our quiet, friendly golden Lab/greyhound—a gem from British
Virgin Islands."
FOREIGN LANGUAGES SPOKEN: "Some Spanish and French."
BED AND BATH: Very private suite has queen bed in large room with three double sets of
opening windows, tub/shower bath, stereo with CD library, phone, individual thermo-
stat, private exterior entrance.
BREAKFAST: Guests' choice of hour, 7–10. Clare's waffles or Larry's pancakes with hot
New Hampshire maple syrup. Fresh fruit compote, homemade muffins or coffee cake,
juices, coffee. Served on china with crystal in Caribbean Room or in formal dining room.
PLUS: Wood-burning stove in formal living room. Brick patio with mountain views.
Clear well water.

⋙ *Carter Notch Inn*   603/383-9630

P.O. Box 269, Carter Notch Road,   800/794-9434
Jackson, NH 03846-0269   FAX 603/383-9642
                        www.journeysnorth.com/carternotch.html

HOSTS: Jim and Lynda Dunwell
LOCATION: Quiet. On a country road overlooking Eagle Mountain golf course and
Wildcat River Valley. "Walk 250 yards and dangle your feet in spectacular
Jackson Falls. Or turn left, get on the Appalachian Mountain Trail, and walk
to Maine or Georgia." Cross-country trails at doorstep. Ten-minute walk to
village and fine restaurants; 15 minutes to outlets.
OPEN: December–March and May–October. Two-night minimum on weekends
and foliage season.
RATES: December and May $59–$89. Rest of year $79–$109, except holidays and
foliage season $99–$129 (plus 10 percent gratuity). Treehouse rooms $119–
$179 (plus 10 percent gratuity). Additional person $15. Amex, Discover,
MC, Visa. ♥ ⊞ ❖ ⚡ ♥♡

IT'S COTTAGE STYLE—inside and out. With wallcoverings, quilts, dried flowers, oak, and
wicker. With a spectacular wraparound porch. And a year-round outdoor hot tub. Once
the residence of the neighboring Eagle Mountain House (resort hotel) owner, it was converted to a B&B in 1994 by the Dunwells, who have lived in the area—as innkeepers and
in retailing—for nearly three decades. Jim, a former navy pilot, a lover of old fixer-uppers,
and Kiwanis Club president, is a graduate of Michigan State University's hotel program.
In this, the Dunwells' fourth inn, he and Lynda host many skiers, hikers, wedding guests,
unwinders, New England sightseers (suggestions offered), and innkeeper wannabes too.

IN RESIDENCE: "Tucker, a chocolate Lab seen in L.L. Bean's Christmas catalog, loves to
cuddle. Sadie is a lovable lap cat."
BED AND BATH: Seven rooms (four with fireplace, two with Jacuzzi). Some have an in-
room sink; four rooms have slanted ceilings. All with private bath. Second floor—queen,
queen and twin bed, or double and twin bed. Third floor—two "treehouse" rooms; each
has spectacular views, private deck, fireplace, Jacuzzi tub for two, tile shower; one has
king bed, the other has queen. Futon and crib available.
BREAKFAST: 7:30–9 (continental after 9:30). Grand Marnier French toast, apricot/cheese
French toast, apple/blueberry whole wheat or pumpkin pancakes, or egg puff cheese dish.
Fresh fruit. Juices. Cereals. Hot breads, muffins, or sour cream coffee cake.
PLUS: Central air conditioning. Living room with upright piano and wood-burning
fireplace. Afternoon refreshments. Guest refrigerator. Year-round hot tub on outside
deck. Beach towels. Use of neighboring resort hotel's outdoor pool, tennis courts, and
golf course.

    ⋙ Guests wrote: *"We loved it. Jim is the ultimate innkeeper. Perfect place
to vacation."*

☞ *Benjamin Prescott Inn*   603/532-6637

Route 124 East, Jaffrey, NH 03452-1810   FAX 603/532-6637

HOSTS: Janice and Barry Miller
LOCATION: Overlooking a working dairy farm on Route 124, 2.3 miles east of town center. Near Cathedral of the Pines, Mount Monadnock, Sharon Art Center.
OPEN: Year round. Two-night minimum on summer and fall weekends.
RATES: $75–$90 single. For two $75–$90; suites $95 second floor, $140 third floor. $15 extra person. Ten percent senior citizen discount. Weekly/monthly rates available. Amex, MC, Visa. ♥ ⊞ ❖ ✄

TLC IN THE FORM of nightly homemade chocolate truffles in a basket. Fresh berries in the fruit breads. All appreciated by guests who come for a getaway, mountain views, antiquing, hiking, or local colleges.

After Barry, an avocational wood-carver, had spent twenty-six years in the corporate hotel world, the Millers moved in 1988 from Michigan to this 1853 Greek Revival house, once owned by Vannevar Bush, an engineer whose work gave birth to the computer. They created a warm, inviting ambiance with country antiques and decorated some rooms with Jan's stenciling and needlepoint. Here, each spring they tap the 300-year-old maple trees.

BED AND BATH: Ten rooms; all private baths. First floor—queen, double, or twin beds. Second floor—king, queen, double. Suite has double brass bed, small sitting room. Rollaway available. Third-floor suite has room with canopied king four-poster bed and, in alcoves, two double beds; across-hall sitting room with queen bed, cathedral ceiling, skylight, wet bar, minirefrigerator, private balcony with fantastic countryside views.
BREAKFAST: 8–9:30 (7:30 available for business travelers). Juices. Fruit breads. Jan's creations include cinnamon sourdough French toast, Dutch apple pancakes, and Prescott Rarebits (cheese dish).
PLUS: Air conditioning and TV in suites. Ceiling fans. Phone jacks in rooms. Transportation to and from Jaffrey airport and to restaurants (for cyclists, too). Executive conference room available.

    ☞ From Rhode Island: *"Clean, cozy, and comfortable."* From New Hampshire: *"Attractive grounds . . . very nice common area . . . good food."*

IF YOU HAVE MET ONE B&B HOST, YOU HAVEN'T MET THEM ALL.

IF YOU'VE BEEN TO ONE B&B, YOU HAVEN'T BEEN TO THEM ALL.

⇜ Loch Lyme Lodge

603/795-2141

70 Orford Road, Route 10,
Lyme, NH 03768

800/423-2141
FAX 603/795-2141
E-MAIL lochlymelodge@valley.net

HOSTS: Paul and Judy Barker
LOCATION: On a spring-fed lake surrounded by hills. On Route 10 (which must be crossed to reach the waterfront). One mile north of the village. Eleven miles from Dartmouth College, 4 miles from Dartmouth Skiway.
OPEN: Year round. Closed Thanksgiving and Christmas days. Three-night minimum on Columbus Day weekend.
RATES: $44 single, $58 double. $8 age seven and under, $16 ages eight through fifteen. One-time charge of $6 for crib. ⋔ ✗ ✄ ☵

"IMMEDIATELY AFTER Labor Day we close the cabins (some are booked into the year 2010!) and move from the barn (the location of our summer apartment) into the main Lodge. We move all the tables and chairs out of the dining rooms (which become our living room and piano room) and reopen as a bed and breakfast. This is a rustic vacation spot with a private waterfront and 125 acres of fields and woodlands. We offer very simple furnishings, fresh air, clean water, and stars in a clear sky. There are no televisions, telephones, or credit cards accepted." *Redbook* magazine concurred in 1998, describing a "low-key . . . lovely spot."

By 1923 the 1784 farmhouse had become part of a boys' camp and a lodging place for campers' parents and tourists too. Eventually Judy's parents ran it as a resort. When Judy and Paul left their teaching careers in 1977, they took over and added "homey B&B, not 1990s designer style" in their home.

IN RESIDENCE: Jon Paul, eighteen, and Josh, twelve. Three cats—"various ages."
FOREIGN LANGUAGES SPOKEN: Paul speaks Spanish, Judy a little French.
BED AND BATH: Three second-floor rooms with king, double, or two twin beds share (with hosts and guests) two full baths, one upstairs, one downstairs. Cot and crib available.
BREAKFAST: Usually 8–9; flexible. Full country breakfast served family style on the sunporch. Busy bird feeder in view.
PLUS: Fireplaced living room. Beverages. Canoe on the lake during fall foliage. Babysitting possible. No smoking inside, fall, winter, and spring; discouraged in summer cabins.

⇜ From Massachusetts, New Jersey, Connecticut: *"On a warm early spring weekend, we loved all that space in the great outdoors; a canoe; the welcoming family environment; a beautifully served, substantial breakfast; and a great suggestion—the Dartmouth Powwow. Marvelous. . . . Accommodations with a relaxed, old-fashioned flair. . . . Enjoyed sledding—and, on the frozen lake, cross-country skiing. . . . Entered the ambiance of a Grandma Moses farmhouse after a brisk fall walk. . . . A real home away from home."*

☇ *Olde Orchard Inn*   603/476-5004

RR Box 256,   800/598-5845
Moultonborough, NH 03254   FAX 603/476-5419
                E-MAIL innkeep@oldeorchardinn.com
                www.oldeorchardinn.com

HOSTS: Mary and Jim Senner

LOCATION: Along a country road, on 12 acres with meadows, orchards (600 fruit trees and still more being planted), pond, and brook (for fishing). One mile from Route 25 and from 200-year-old country store and the town's one blinking light. Five-minute walk through orchard across the street to "a very good restaurant"; 15 to Audubon Society's 200-acre Loon Center with nature trails, picnicking, lake frontage, gift shop; 20-minute walk to quiet Lake Winnipesaukee beach. Ten-minute drive to country's largest quilt supply shop.

OPEN: Year round. Two-day minimum during foliage season and some weekends.

RATES: Double bed $75. Queen $85; $110 with fireplace, $140 with fireplace and whirlpool. Third person $25. Crib $5. ♥ ♦♦ ⊞ ❖ ⚔ ⚜ ♨ ♥○

AFTER LOOKING "all over," the Senners bought this restored late-eighteenth-century Cape in 1992. They painted inside and out, planted an English garden, and furnished—without clutter—with Oriental rugs and Colonial and "foreign service eclectic we gathered over a twenty-five-year period while living in Afghanistan, India, Nepal, Sudan, and Finland." (Jim retired in 1994.) Mary, a quilter and former first-grade teacher, did all the stenciling. The wooden part of this house was built in 1790. In 1812 an addition was built with bricks fired from clay on the property. The screened gazebo, large deck, more wood-burning fireplaces, and whirlpool baths are among additions made in 1996.

IN RESIDENCE: Rosie, Jim's mother, an inspiration for Mary's genealogical work. Daughter Laura, during college vacations. One Labrador retriever.

FOREIGN LANGUAGES SPOKEN: Jim speaks Farsi and some Arabic and Finnish.

BED AND BATH: Nine rooms (all with TV and air conditioning, some with wood-burning fireplace) in private wing with private entrance. Queen or double beds. All with en-suite full tile baths; some with whirlpool tub. Cot and crib available.

BREAKFAST: 8–9. Juice, fruit; sticky buns or other baked goods. Pancakes, omelets, or eggs.

PLUS: Guest sitting room with fireplace, TV. Sauna. Meeting and game room. The fragrance and sight of spring orchard blossoms.

      ☇ From Pennsylvania: *"Appreciated up-to-date tiled bathroom . . . gourmet breakfast with cherry berry coffee cake—my favorite."* From Texas: *"A charming, charming inn. We hated to leave."* From England: *"They made our trip something we will always remember."*

⟫ The Buttonwood Inn on Mt. Surprise   603/356-2625

P.O. Box 1817, Mount Surprise Road,   800/258-2625
North Conway, NH 03860-1817   FAX 603/356-3140
                                  E-MAIL button_w@moose.ncia.net
                                  www.buttonwoodinn.com

HOSTS: Peter and Claudia Needham
LOCATION: Secluded. At top of hill on dead end road on side of Mount Surprise. On 17
          acres of woods, spacious lawns, gardens, cross-country/hiking trails. Two
          miles from Route 16, village, shopping, dining; 1 mile to downhill skiing.
OPEN: Year round (except April). Two-night weekend minimum year round.
RATES: May–late June (holidays excepted) and November–Christmas $90–$120,
          $150 with fireplace. Late June–mid-September, late October–November,
          and January–March $105–$140, $175 with fireplace. Mid-September–mid-
          October $125–$160, $195 with fireplace, $10 one-night surcharge. Third per-
          son $25, $15 ages four through eleven. Reunion and corporate retreat rates
          available. Amex, Discover, MC, Visa. ♥ ♦♦♦ ⊞ ❖ ⚔ ⚕ ♟ ●○

⟫ From Maine, New Hampshire, Massachusetts, New Jersey, Vermont,
Florida, Rhode Island, England: *"Fabulous meals . . . charming . . . so very clean . . . warm,
cozy country atmosphere . . . quaint . . . serene . . . wonderfully quiet convenient location . . .
If we didn't live in London, we would go every weekend. . . . Easygoing, friendly, helpful hosts
. . . a great living room for laughing and making plans to right the world. . . . Have stayed in
B&Bs from coast to coast. Claudia and Peter were, by far, the most wonderful hosts. . . . Great
stargazing by the pool. . . . It's heaven!"*

GUESTS AND the media concur. The added-on-to 1820s farmhouse and its innkeepers are
loved! Inviting Shaker-style decor, all recently done, includes country antiques, quilts,
stenciling, print wallpapers, and Waverly fabrics. There are wide-board pine floors. Plenty
of common space on two levels with fireplaces. Grounds include Peter's award-winning
gardens and the 40-foot-long pool with an old barn foundation as a backdrop. Custom
itinerary planning—for hikes, waterfalls, covered bridges, picnic lunch places, shopping,
you name it—is a feature.

Before the Needhams bought this B&B in 1993, Peter, who converted a barn to his first
home, had experience in manufacturing and innkeeping (in Stowe, Vermont). Claudia, a
former teacher who had experience in sales for a children's book publisher, is the founder
of North Conway's sell-out Polar Express event, an early December recreation of the children's book by Chris Van Allsburg.

IN RESIDENCE: Daughters Amanda, age fifteen, and Katherine, twelve. "Emily, our black
Lab, is aging gracefully."
BED AND BATH: Ten second-floor guest rooms; some are dormered. One king/twins op-
tion; the rest are queens, some with additional twin day or Murphy bed. All private baths

(most en-suite) with tub/shower or shower only. Amenities vary—gas fireplace, ceiling fan, air conditioning, two-person Jacuzzi, family arrangements.

BREAKFAST: 8–9:30. (Coffee and tea from 7. Brown bag meal for before-7 departures. 7–8 menu—eggs, cold cereals, muffins, juice, hot beverage.) Daily special or eggs any style. Blueberry Crumble French Toast, ham-and-cheese strata with fruit salad, pancakes, multigrain baked cereal, yogurt, fruit. Coffee cakes—many low fat. Egg Beaters available. Special diets accommodated with advance notice.

PLUS: Afternoon refreshments. Custom packages. Guest refrigerator. Horseshoes, sand-box, swings. Upright piano, VCR, movies. Backpacks with first-aid kits, fanny packs, even bottled water.

⚞ The Farm By the River

603/356-2694

2555 West Side Road,
North Conway, NH 03860-5925

888/414-8353
FAX 603/356-3938
E-MAIL info@farmbytheriver.com
www.farmbytheriver.com

HOSTS: Rick and Charlene Davis

LOCATION: Pastoral. On 65 acres of forest and pastures (still hayed) with barns; hand-cut granite fence posts in upper fields; Saco River (sandy beach, swimming, fly-fishing) bordering lower fields; old family graveyards; gardens; cross-country skiing, snowshoeing, panoramic mountain views. Half mile to Echo Lake State Park; 1 mile to village; 3 to outlets.

OPEN: Year round. Two- or three-night minimum on holiday weekends and during fall foliage.

RATES: Late September–late October and some holidays $80–$115 semiprivate bath; private bath $105–$135, with Jacuzzi $140–$160, Jacuzzi and fireplace $140–$189. April–late June and November–mid-December $60–$75 semi-private bath; private bath $70–$80, with Jacuzzi $110–$130; Jacuzzi and fire-place $120–$140. Late June–late September, last week in October, and mid-December–March $70–$80 shared bath; private bath $80–$95, with Jacuzzi $120–$135; Jacuzzi and fireplace $130–$160. Singles $15–$20 less. Additional person $25. Ages five through eleven, $10; under five free. MC, Visa. ♥ ♦♦ ▦ ❖ ⚐ ⚒ ☘ ♥♡

THIS REALLY IS Grandmother's house Rick's grandmother's boardinghouse from 1950 to 1979. Rick, a former soil scientist who is the seventh generation to live on this land granted in 1771 by King George III of England, married Charlene, a landscape architect/ graphic designer and artist, in 1992. They reopened the farmhouse in 1993; named rooms after Grandmother's "regulars"; and, in 1994, received an award for sensitivity to historic

continued . . .

preservation. Baths, Jacuzzis, and fireplaces have been added. Eclectic furnishings span 125 years and include many agricultural artifacts. Year-round horseback riding and winter sleigh rides are now offered. And weddings take place here. Tradition continues.

IN RESIDENCE: Lucy, a weimaraner, often accompanies guests on mile-long walk through fields to the river. Nineteen horses; two Belgians pull a sleigh.
FOREIGN LANGUAGE SPOKEN: Spanish.
BED AND BATH: Ten air-conditioned rooms; all private baths. King, queen, or double bed; some with a single bed too. Amenities vary and include feather beds, two-person Jacuzzi and/or fireplace, mountain views. Two suites, perfect for families. Second-floor front wing has four rooms. Separate stairs to two-room suite and two other rooms in back wing.
BREAKFAST: 7:45–9:15. Fresh fruit platter. French toast almondine, Belgian waffles with strawberries, blueberry pancakes (a favorite), or vegetable omelet. Homemade muffins. Served by fire or on deck with garden and mountain views.
PLUS: Wood-burning fireplaces in living and dining rooms. 1907 McPhail piano. Porch rockers. Winter Saturday evening refreshments. Fly fishing and art workshops.

⟐ From Vermont, Virginia, Philadelphia, New York: *"Enchanting. Came for one night, stayed for three. . . . Traveled alone. Lovely visit. Charming, helpful hosts. Delicious breakfasts. . . . Enjoyed sitting in the garden and watching the horses. . . . Southern Hospitality in New Hampshire! . . . It's what New England is all about. Could never be duplicated in a new home or hotel."*

⟐ Nereledge Inn Bed & Breakfast   603/356-2831

River Road, P.O. Box 547,   FAX 603/356-7085
North Conway, NH 03860-0547   E-MAIL info@nereledgeinn.com
                                          www.nereledgeinn.com

HOSTS: Valerie and Dave Halpin
LOCATION: Just off (main road) Route 16, on the road to Echo Lake State Park and Cathedral Ledge; 100 yards from Saco River. Within walking distance of dining, shopping, fishing, swimming, climbing, movie theater, "almost everything!"
OPEN: Year round. Two- or three-night minimum on some weekends.
RATES: Vary according to season. Shared bath—twins or double bed $59–$89; queen $64–$94. Private bath—queen and twin bed, shower bath $69–$119; queen bed, half bath $69–$99; queen bed, private hall shower bath $64–$119; queen bed, en-suite shower bath $74–$119; full en-suite bath and queen bed with single futon or adjoining room with twin bed $79–$129. Extra adult $20. Children $1 each year of age up to twelve. Amex, Discover, MC, Visa. ♔ ⊘ ✄

🦅 From Canada, California, Pennsylvania, Connecticut, Massachusetts, Indiana, New Hampshire, Texas, Arizona, Washington: *"Not the fanciest but by far the most hospitable B&B we ever stayed in. Casual, still allows privacy. . . . Outstanding, imaginative, diverse breakfasts. . . . Firm beds. . . . Peaceful. . . . Dry sense of humor. . . . Led us on the best biking trail we have ever experienced . . . Not only recommended a local horse show but secured a show poster for our daughter. . . . After a day of ice climbing, it's really nice to go to a cozy, warm (both in temperature and atmosphere), neat, sparkling clean, old-style B&B."*

CONTINUALLY, from far and wide, letters extol this old-fashioned inn built in 1787. In 1981 Valerie, a beginning skier and classical music lover, established the B&B style she knew from her native England—where she was a teacher before becoming a commodities broker in Florida. Here she met Dave, expert skier, mountain bike rider, runner (with Pinga), professional landscaper, and former Hawaii resort manager. (Now he is deputy fire chief and a home beer brewer.) In 1994, the year Nereledge was featured in *Outside* magazine, the Halpins built an addition. The letters go on: "Walls lined with photos of climbers. . . . We lived and hiked in Switzerland, but the Nereledge, 1,100 miles from our home [Indiana], makes the White Mountains our first choice."

IN RESIDENCE: Pinga, "a large photogenic dog."
BED AND BATH: Eleven rooms (ten with air conditioning) on second and third floors. Twin, double, or queen beds; some with extra bed and/or adjoining room. Private baths are en-suite, in hall, or half bath. (See "rates" above.) Shared baths for two or three rooms that also have access to full first-floor bath. Crib and rollaway available.
BREAKFAST: 7:30–9:30. (Continental after 9:30.) Juices. Eggs, French toast, pancakes, omelet (a meal in itself); bacon, sausage, or ham. Hot or cold cereal. Homemade muffin or toast. Apple crumble and vanilla ice cream. In room with woodstove, sunny exposure.
PLUS: Three sitting rooms; one with wood-burning fireplace, darts, and backgammon. Guest refrigerator and microwave. Baby grand piano. Sprinkler system. Equipment room for skis, boots, climbing gear. Ski-waxing area. Bicycle shed. Gardens. Maps and day-trip suggestions. Babysitting arranged. Option of packed lunch.

IS A B&B LIKE A HOTEL? HOW MANY TIMES HAVE YOU HUGGED
THE DOORMAN?

⤳ *Wyatt House Country Inn*   603/356-7977

P.O. Box 777, Route 16,   800/527-7978
North Conway, NH 03860   E-MAIL wyatthouse@!webtv.net
                                                        www.wyatthouse.com

HOSTS: Bill and Arlene Strickland
LOCATION: In the villlage. Along Route 16, with backdrop of woods (path to river for fishing or swimming) and mountains. Short walk to many activities, restaurants, Saco River, outlet shopping. Minutes to four major ski areas.
OPEN: Year round.
RATES: $55 single. $65 double bed. $75–$189 suites with private decks. $20 additional person. Special rates April 1–June 15. Valentine's packages with flowers and chocolates. Amex, Discover, MC, Visa. ♥ ⊞ ❖ ⚔ ⅄ ⛏

LACE. FRINGE. Ruffles. Antique photographs. Victoriana *everywhere*. A breakfast that is intentionally memorable. Almost-famous chocolate chip cookies in a bottomless cookie jar. Bedtime sherry. Always, plenty of pampering. All offered in this 1870s home, which has been the Stricklands' B&B since 1992. That was the year Bill and Arlene decided to stop the twenty-three-year two-hour (each way) commute to their Manhattan jobs as an American Express Company director and a paralegal. In New York Arlene also served as president of the Babylon Historical and Preservation Society.

IN RESIDENCE: Spats, a popular, declawed cat, greets guests.
BED AND BATH: Seven rooms; five with private baths, air conditioning, color cable TV. First floor—queen-bedded room, shower bath, private exterior entrance and porch; two-person Jacuzzi suite has queen bed, TV, private deck. Second floor—suite has canopied queen four-poster bed, shower bath, TV, deck. Another two-room suite has queen bed, queen sofa bed in adjoining room, shower bath, TV, deck. Two double-bedded rooms share full hall bath. Third-floor suite has double bed, sitting area, cable TV, private bath with claw-foot tub, hand-held shower.
BREAKFAST: (Option of breakfast in bed.) Seatings for eight at 8 and 9:30. (Coffee and muffins available at 6.) Spinach and cheese quiche, shirred eggs with sausage, soufflé, or fresh blueberry pancakes. Homemade granola, muffins, bread, and jams. Juice. Fresh fruit. Freshly brewed coffee. Served on English Wedgwood by candlelight with chamber music. In dining room or on porch.
PLUS: Fireplaced living room. Welcoming study. Beach towels. Guest refrigerator. Fresh fruit. Candy. Box lunches. Restaurant menus and discounts. Porch rockers. Hammock. Picnic tables, bikes. Adirondack chairs. Champagne for honeymooners. English tea and crumpets, 3–7 P.M.

⤳ From Canada: *"A little bit of heaven."* From New York: *"Five-star breakfast."*

ᕲ The Forest, A Country Inn

P.O. Box 37, Route 16A at the Intervale,
Intervale, NH 03845-0037

603/356-9772

800/448-3534
FAX 603/356-5652
E-MAIL forest@moose.ncia.net
www.forest-inn.com

HOSTS: Bill and Lisa Guppy
LOCATION: On 25 wooded acres on a quiet country road. With 40 miles of groomed cross-country trails at the door. Between—2 miles from—Jackson and North Conway village.
OPEN: Year round (except April). Two-night minimum on most weekends; three nights on holiday weekends.
RATES: Mid-December–March $95; $130 with fireplace, $140 cottage rooms. May–June $85, $90, $110. July–September 20 $95, $120 cottage rooms. September 20–October 20 $115, $140, $160. Late October–mid-December $80, $90, $110. Singles, $10 less. Additional adult in room $20. Spring, winter midweek, and bike packages. May and November, two-night specials. Amex, Discover, MC, Visa. ♥ ⊞ ❖ ⚲ ⚹ ⚚

"WE BOUGHT this well-kept century-old inn in 1995 after staying at B&Bs for many years and after one innkeeper told us that her inn was for sale. That planted the seed!"

In Vermont Bill was an engineer and a contractor; Lisa, a medical technologist. Their white clapboard mansard-roofed inn is furnished with Victorian (wallpapers) and country (quilts) flair. Gas fireplaces have period mantels. On the grounds there's a gardenside pool, a picnic area with lawn chairs and gas grills, and a 25-acre forest blazed with walking and skiing trails.

BED AND BATH: Eight inn rooms on second and third floors (four are air-conditioned; ceiling fans in third-floor rooms) plus three cottage rooms; all private baths. Inn rooms have king/twins option or queen; three with gas fireplace. Stone cottage has two separate rooms (one has screened porch), each with own entrance, queen bed, wood-burning fireplace or gas fireplace. Other cottage has queen bed, gas fireplace, Jacuzzi tub.
BREAKFAST: 8–9:30. All homemade breads. Eggs or specialty of the day—cinnamon French toast topped with homemade jam, spiced Belgian waffles, apple or blueberry pancakes. Cereals. Served in dining room at tables for two; soft music in background.
PLUS: Afternoon refreshments. Guest refrigerator. Wood-burning fireplace and piano in living room. TV room. Glass/screened porch with woodstove. Gas grills and picnic tables. "Bike the Whites" bicycle tour arrangements.

ᕲ From New Jersey: *"A beautiful inn with warm friendly hosts who make you feel at home. Spent our honeymoon here. We will definitely return!"*

☞ The Wilderness Inn   603/745-3890

Routes 3 and 112, RFD 1, Box 69,   800/200-WILD
North Woodstock, NH 03262-9709   FAX 603/745-6367
                                          E-MAIL wildernessinn@juno.com
                                          www.musar.com/wildernessinn

HOSTS: Michael and Rosanna Yarnell
LOCATION: Residential, with river in backyard. Just south of intersection, facing a spired church and surrounding mountains. Three miles to Loon Mountain, 8 to Cannon, 20 to Bretton Woods and Waterville Valley. About a mile from I-93.
OPEN: Year round. Two-night minimum during foliage and on holidays.
RATES: $60–$105. $70–$115 suites and $80–$125 cottage. $10 additional person. Winter and spring midweek discount. ♥ ♛ ⊞ ❖ ⚥ ✄ ◖◗

☞ From Massachusetts: *"An aura of warmth radiates from both the sitting room hearth and the Yarnells' quiet loving care. . . . Gourmet meals . . . a little piece of paradise."*

OR, AS ONE returnee said in the morning, "I've been dreaming about this breakfast for a whole year!" In addition, there's a sense of life in "a solid, small New England community" in this shingled cottage-style house, which was built by a lumber baron in 1912. It has mahogany-trimmed living and dining rooms, examples of the Yarnells' stained glass work and stenciling in guest rooms, and eclectic furnishings throughout. The newest conversation piece is the photo album of the family's 1999 winter round-the-world sabbatical. The children were home-schooled through Hawaii, Fiji, Australia, New Zealand, Bali, Malaysia, Thailand, and India (where they visited Rosanna's mother, a Peace Corps member). Michael is a Cornell-trained hotelier. Rosanna, a French teacher of Italian and Indian parentage, was born and raised in Ethiopia.

IN RESIDENCE: In 1994-built Cape house on the property—Charles Orion, age eleven; Pia Camille, age nine.
FOREIGN LANGUAGES SPOKEN: French, Italian, Bengali, Amharic.
BED AND BATH: Seven rooms, all with private bath, on two floors. Two queen-bedded rooms, private shower baths. One room with two double beds, private shower bath. Two family suites, each with a queen bed, two twin beds, and private full bath. Two small double-bedded rooms; one with tub bath, other with shower bath. Also, queen-bedded cottage with gas fireplace and beamed ceiling, built by Michael, overlooking river. Crib available.
BREAKFAST: 7:30–10. A major draw. Fresh fruit salad, juice, homemade muffins, teas, freshly ground coffee. Entrées include many varieties of pancakes, crêpes with sour cream and hot applesauce, omelets, French toast topped with maple syrup or homemade apple and cranberry syrups. In warm weather, served on long enclosed porch. Option of continental breakfast in bed.
PLUS: Tea or mulled cider with snacks. Stenciling and comforters. Backyard (river) swimming hole. Babysitting arranged. New on-site travel agency.

☞ *The Post and Beam Bed & Breakfast*   603/847-3330

HCR 33, Box 380, Centre Street,   888/376-6262

Sullivan, NH 03445-9703   FAX 603/847-3306

E-MAIL postandbeam@monad.net

www.postandbeambb.com

HOSTS: Darcy Bacall and Priscilla Hardy

LOCATION: Rural. Just off Route 9 on 2.5 acres with two barns. Adjacent to old town hall and pottery shop. Bordered by creek that "babbles in spring and fall." Ten minutes northeast of Keene and good restaurants; 2 miles to Apple Hill Chamber Players and Otter Brook State Park; 15 minutes to Harris Center for Conservation Education; 20 to Mount Monadnock and covered bridges.

OPEN: Year round. Two-night minimum on holiday and October weekends.

RATES: May–October weekends $99 private bath, $85 private half bath, $75 shared bath; Sunday–Thursday $10 less. November–April $10 less. Amex, Discover, MC, Visa. ♥ ⊞ ⚷

☞ Guests wrote: *"Delightful oasis . . . what a find . . . comfy, cozy, charming . . . treated like friends . . . great food . . . exceeded expectations."*

AGAIN, BRITISH hospitality inspired a lifestyle change. Upon returning from their 1995 trip to England, Priscilla and Darcy decided that they would look for a rural location and open their own B&B, a relaxed place with a casual atmosphere. Here it is, opened in 1996—their renovated 200-year-old farmhouse with wide pine floors, latches on room doors, beehive oven in the living room fireplace, hand-hewn beams, braided rugs, quilts, antiques purchased locally, fresh country decor—and a recently added gazebo with year-round hot tub.

Both hosts are registered nurses. Darcy dovetails innkeeping with her work for the Department of Public Health in Boston. Priscilla is health officer for the town of Sullivan.

IN RESIDENCE: In house, but not allowed in guests' rooms, two dogs—one dalmatian and one Shetland sheepdog—announce your arrival. Five cats.

FOREIGN LANGUAGE SPOKEN: "Some French."

BED AND BATH: Seven rooms. First floor—handicapped accessible room with queen bed, gas-stove fireplace, private hand-held shower bath. Second floor—king- or queen-bedded rooms have private shower bath or private half bath with shared (with one other room) tub/shower bath. Third floor (slanted ceilings with original beams)—two air-conditioned rooms, one with a queen and a double bed, the other with king bed, share shower bath. Rollaways available.

BREAKFAST: 8–9:30. (Continental available at 7.) Fresh juice and fruit. Homemade granola. Homemade bread and blueberry or apple muffins . Pancakes, omelets, Belgian waffles, or Dutch babies with maple or blueberry/strawberry syrup. Bacon or sausage. (Vegetarian and lactose-free diets accommodated with advance notice.) In candlelit dining room with music or on deck.

PLUS: Gas-stove fireplace and TV/VCR in living room. Afternoon snacks. Patio with swing. New sprinkler system. Suggestions for "secluded romantic ponds."

⌦ *The Rosewood Country Inn*   603/938-5253

67 Pleasant View Road,   800/938-5273
Bradford, NH 03221-3113   FAX 603/938-5253 (CALL FIRST)
                                              E-MAIL rosewood@conknet.com
                                              www.bbonline.com/nh/rosewood/

HOSTS: Lesley and Dick Marquis
LOCATION: A quiet country road; about 1½ miles west from town. Ten minutes to
          Mount Sunapee and Lake Sunapee. Forty minutes to Hanover.
OPEN: Year round. Two- or three-night minimum on holiday or special weekends.
RATES: Per room for one or two—$85–$175. Two-bedroom suite (sleeps four, can be
       two separate rooms) $150. Extra person $25. Packages for mother-and-daughter
       and Dickens (December) weekends. Amex, MC, Visa. ♥ ⊞ ❖ ⚉ ⅍ ❤♡

⌦ From Connecticut, Massachusetts, New Hampshire: *"Romantic. . . . Serene.
Watched doe in the field. Basked in warmth of fireplaces. Superb food beautifully presented
with fine china and crystal. . . . Enjoyed camaraderie during Dickens Weekend and quiet time
in a beautiful setting. . . . Elegant but homey. Everyone inspired to redecorate their own home!
Without Lesley and Dick, it would be just a 'pretty place to stay.'"*

A HIT! For unwinding. For mother-and-daughter weekends. For weddings. And once a
Victorian summer resort, where Hollywood stars including Mary Pickford and Douglas
Fairbanks stayed. The "elegant but unpretentious English country house feeling" is a hallmark of Dick and Lesley, former Rhode Island hospital administrators. In 1991 they
bought the building which had been gutted and vacant for fifteen years. Now it has rose-
colored shutters, refinished floors, stenciled walls, traditional furnishings, comfortable antiques, and Laura Ashley fabrics.

IN RESIDENCE: Two daughters, Sarah and Becky, in family's ten-room wing.
BED AND BATH: Eleven rooms—some are suites with fireplace—on second and third
floors. All private baths: tub/shower, double-headed shower for two, or double Jacuzzi
and separate shower. King, queen, double, or twin beds (some are canopied). Air conditioning in eight rooms; window fans in others.
BREAKFAST: 8–9:30. Three courses. Homemade muffins or Danish pastry. Warm fruit
compote, peaches with vanilla yogurt and raspberry sauce, or chilled fruit soup. Oven
apple pancakes with cider sauce, broccoli quiche with corn or date-bread pudding, or
blueberry stuffed French toast. (Vegetarian option with advance notice.) Served with candlelight in fireplaced dining room or on sunlit porches.
PLUS: Fireplaced living room. Woodstove and (concealed) TV in tavern room. Wicker-
furnished porch. Perennial gardens. Horse-drawn carriage and hay rides arranged.

⇒ *Stepping Stones*

603/654-9048

RFD 1, Box 6, Bennington Battle Trail,
Wilton Center, NH 03086-9751

888/654-9048
FAX 603/654-6821

HOST: Ann Carlsmith

LOCATION: Quiet country setting in Monadnock hills. Facing a reservoir. Near historic Frye Mill, Monadnock Music concert series, Wapack (hiking) Trail. Two minutes from a picturebook village; 13 to Peterborough. Six miles to Temple Mountain, 20 west of Nashua, 64 north of Boston.

OPEN: Year round. Reservations recommended.

RATES: $60–$65 double, $40 single. All private baths. Seventh night free.

♥ ♦♦♦ ☎ ⊞ ❖ ⅍ ♖

⇒ From Maine, New York, Massachusetts, Michigan, New Hampshire, Pennsylvania, Indiana, Rhode Island, California, Connecticut, Vermont: *"A home that is a masterpiece of Ann's work. . . . Every detail—inside and out—is truly inspiring. . . . Art, flowers, and handweaving everywhere. . . . Winding paths and terraces among spectacular perennial gardens . . . . Her gardens are magical. Warm and snug in winter. . . . Breakfasts are to die for—truly! . . . Imaginative, healthy, filling, delicious. . . Comfort, elegance, a warm welcome. . . . Ann was there when we needed her, gone when we didn't. . . .Helpful in locating hiking spots, church suppers . . . classical CDs in living room. . . . My fantasy B&B. . . . This place is really a 'found treasure.'"*

GUESTS' GLOWING letters praise the art history major who became a landscape designer and garden consultant in the mid-1980s. She spends winters weaving (rugs, throws, pillows) on the many looms in her nineteenth-century house, the nurturing project that has followed her child-rearing years. Perhaps you have come for concerts, weaving lessons, antiquing, or theater—or for rejuvenation. When you tear yourself away, Ann can direct you to a 30-foot waterfall or to a back road lined with farms. A haven indeed.

IN RESIDENCE: Thumbelina and Largo, the cats. Stanza (named after Mozart's wife) and Sheba, the dogs. "All kept out of bedrooms." Bantams in the yard.

BED AND BATH: Three second-floor rooms; all private baths. Twin beds, hall tub bath. Double bed, hall full bath. Queen bed, en-suite shower bath.

BREAKFAST: By 10. Belgian waffles or French toast with maple syrup or homemade preserves, sausages, omelets, croissants, quiches, fruit and nut granola with yogurt, homemade muffins and sweet breads, seasonal fruit and orange juice. In solar breakfast room that has plants, pottery, a woodstove, and a view of garden.

PLUS: Beverages and ginger cookies. An opportunity to visit gardens and to observe weaving. Extensive garden library. Down comforters and pure cotton bedding. Window fans. Guest refrigerator. Wood-burning fireplace, color TV, stereo, books and magazines in living room. Wreaths and handweaving for sale.

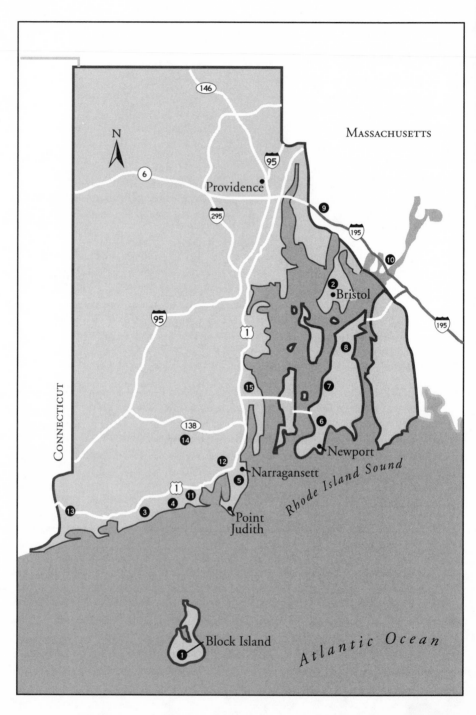

The numbers on this map indicate the locations of B&Bs described in detail in this chapter.

RHODE ISLAND

Can't find the community you wish to visit? Check with a reservation service
described at the beginning of this chapter.

❧ *Anna's Victorian Connection*

5 Fowler Avenue, Newport, RI 02840

> **PHONE:** 401/849-2489 or 800/884-4288. Reservations made daily in May, June, September, and October, 9 A.M.–6:30 P.M.; July and August 8 A.M.–6:30 P.M.; November–April 9 A.M.–5 P.M. Answering machine takes messages at other hours.
>
> **FAX:** 401/847-7309
>
> **E-MAIL:** annas@aiconnect.com
>
> **URL:** www.hotcotsreservations.com
>
> **LISTINGS:** Two hundred. Some inns; mostly private residences within fifteen minutes of downtown Newport. Some are in unhosted, self-catered houses and apartments. A few are in other Rhode Island communities—Block Island, Bristol, Charlestown, East Greenwich, Middletown, North Kingstown, Portsmouth, Providence, and Wickford—and in the southeastern Massachusetts border communities of Fall River, Rehoboth, Seekonk, Somerset, and Swansea.
>
> **RESERVATIONS:** Advance notice preferred. Some available through travel agents. Two-night summer weekend minimum. "Most of our accommodations require a three-night minimum for holiday weekends and special events such as the Newport Folk and Jazz Festivals."
>
> **RATES:** $25–$150 single. $50–$325 double. One half of total bill required as a deposit. Balance due upon arrival. Refunds of 90 percent for cancellations made at least two weeks before scheduled arrival date. Amex, CB, Diners, Discover, EnRoute, MC, Visa.

A WIDE VARIETY of annually inspected properties (using standards of Bed & Breakfast, The National Network of Reservation Services)—a place on the harbor, a Cape Cod–style home, an antebellum Ocean Drive mansion, neighborhood Victorian houses, and historic inns—are represented by Susan White, creator of this seventeen-year-old service. Susan hosts in her own Victorian home and teaches a how-to-run-a-B&B course. In addition, following her recent retirement as a school guidance counselor, Susan and another host have opened an educational counseling service. The Anna's Victorian Connection staff prides itself on "careful matches" for lodgings as well as restaurant reservations and activity arrangements.

⇗ Bed & Breakfast Referrals of South Coast Rhode Island

P.O. Box 562, Charlestown, RI 02813-0562

>PHONE: 800/853-7479, 9:30 A.M.–9 P.M. Out-of-hours calls answered next morning.
>
>LISTINGS: Twenty-four. All are B&Bs located near the south coastline of Rhode Island—between Wickford on Narragansett Bay and Westerly near the Connecticut border. Some are close to I-95 or the University of Rhode Island; all are near or a short drive from beaches. Communities represented include Carolina, Charlestown, Green Hill, Matunuck, Narragansett, North Kingstown, Richmond, South Kingstown, Wakefield, Westerly, West Kingston, Wickford Village, and Wyoming. Free brochure briefly describes each B&B: its size (although most have two, three, or four guest rooms, a few have more; one has eleven); and its price category (up to $59, $60–$89, or $90 and up during summer season).
>
>RESERVATIONS: Travelers make their own reservations directly with a B&B. (Please see description below.)
>
>RATES: $50–$110 singles. $50–$195 doubles. Many of the B&Bs take credit cards. Inquire about off-season weekend package rates. Some B&Bs pay travel agents' commission.

WELCOME! This free-to-the-public referral service, established in 1995, covers an area that's a popular destination for vacationers, out-of-season "must get away" travelers, University of Rhode Island visitors, and people on business stopovers. All calls to the toll-free number are answered by a helpful and knowledgeable B&B owner who is aware of vacancies or last-minute cancellations in all the properties represented. You are given up to three appropriate suggestions and an invitation to call back if unsuccessful in booking.

ANOTHER RESERVATION SERVICE WITH SOME B&Bs IN RHODE ISLAND:
Covered Bridge, page 2

⁂ *The Barrington Inn*

401/466-5510

P.O. Box 397,

FAX 401/466-5880

Beach and Ocean Avenue,

E-MAIL barrington@ids.net

Block Island, RI 02807

www.blockisland.com/barrington

HOSTS: Joan and Howard Ballard

LOCATION: On a knoll overlooking Great Salt Pond. Three quarters of a mile from ferry (departs from Point Judith, thirty-minute drive from Newport); one-half mile from island airport. Five-minute walk to beach.

OPEN: May through October. Advance reservations necessary for summer weekends. Two-night minimum June, July, August, and weekends; three and/or four nights on holiday weekends, spring through fall.

RATES: Weekends mid-June–Labor Day $120, $135, $168; May 1–mid-June, September, October $65–$125. Monday–Thursday $10–$20 less. Third person in room $20. Discover, MC, Visa. ♥ ⊞ ⚥ ⚕

⁂ From New Hampshire: *"We found a home . . . comfortable, spotless, and the views superb . . . delicious breakfast . . . recommended for those who like a personal greeting, privacy, and a firm bed."*

I CONCUR. All in a great location for a before-breakfast beach walk. With a host, a former shipyard manager, whose family has vacationed on the island since the turn of the century. When the Ballards lived in Michigan, Joan was mother to four (now grown) and a secretary. It's a long story, but it ends (or begins, really) with the purchase of what was a family summer home.

Furnishings include wicker and antiques—all in keeping with a big old farmhouse—"but we're constantly making changes and redecorating." Old photographs include one of the original 1886 house. Other photographs—of tall ships, sunsets, and island scenes—are Howard's work. On the grounds there's an old apple orchard favored by many colorful birds.

BED AND BATH: Six carpeted rooms of various sizes on three levels. All with private shower baths and ceiling fans. On second floor, double or queen bed, sliding glass doors to private deck, water views. Third floor—two rooms with sitting areas; one has queen bed, the other a queen and a twin; both with wonderful water views. Plus two apartments.

BREAKFAST: 8–9:30. (At 7:30 for some racing periods. With advance notice, continental available for early departures.) Fresh fruit cup, juices, cereal; homemade muffins, breads, and jams. Sometimes blackberry cobbler or apple Betty. Hot and cold beverages. Served by Joan and Howard in dining room and/or on deck.

PLUS: Rental kayaks (for use in two ponds) and bicycles. Good map of island. Beverages. Well water. Two living rooms, one with color TV, VCR, games. Guest refrigerator. Ice. Deck with water view and sunsets. Outside shower and changing room. Bike rack. Off-street parking. Off-season, will meet guests at ferry or airport.

➤ From New York: *"Fabulous room . . . serenity but five minutes to 'the action.' Biked the entire island, kayaked all of (nearby) Great Salt Pond, taking time to picnic on our own 'private' beach . . . heaven."*

➤ *The Sea Breeze*

401/466-2275
800/786-2276
www.blockisland.com/seabreeze

Spring Street, P.O. Box 141,
Block Island, RI 02807-0141

HOSTS: The Newhouse family
LOCATION: On the crest of a hill overlooking a 2-acre meadow and pond, with broad view of the ocean and coastline. Five-minute walk to restaurants, shops, and ferry landing.
OPEN: Year round. Two-night minimum; three nights on holiday weekends Memorial Day–Columbus Day.
RATES: $80–$130 shared bath. $150–$190 private bath. Less off-season. MC, Visa.
♥⊞⚹☀❤

"THE GARDENS are always evolving with several hundred varieties of perennials, roses, and flowering shrubs. They make the perfect spot for small weddings. And the five original cottages are now four, completely renovated with the feel of seaside cottages."

Mary Newhouse, a Manhattan artist, and her physician husband—gardeners who adore this island—listened when one of their daughters suggested B&B for the compound of five very tired houses purchased in 1979. Together the family planned and redid. Rooms were enlarged and filled, without clutter but with flair—with English chintzes, country antiques, and contemporary art. Honeymooners, too, love this spectacular natural setting.

FOREIGN LANGUAGES SPOKEN: German, some Spanish and Italian, depending on family members in residence.
BED AND BATH: Ten rooms—some with cathedral ceilings—with double or twin beds, on first and second floors. All shower baths; five are private. Six rooms have ocean views; four have private porches.
BREAKFAST: 8:30–9:30. Viennese coffee, English tea. Freshly baked croissants or muffins, homemade preserves, fruit, juice. Served on trays in sitting room (may be taken to rooms or onto porch or lawns), or in baskets brought to rooms with private baths.
PLUS: Kayak for use on the pond. Library. Sitting room. Guest refrigerator, sink, and glasses.

⋙ *Rockwell House Inn*   401/253-0040

610 Hope Street,   800/815-0040
Bristol, RI 02809-1945   FAX 401/253-1811
                                          E-MAIL rockwellinn@ids.net

HOSTS: Debra and Steve Krohn
LOCATION: On a half acre with the state's largest tulip tree. On a main street block of large historic homes. Walking distance to Narragansett Bay; antiques shops (focus of a 1997 *Yankee* magazine story); restaurants; 14-mile bike path (along water to Providence); and five museums, including America's Cup International Hall of Fame. Two miles to Blithewold mansion and arboretum and to Roger Williams University. Twenty minutes to Providence, Newport, winery tour.
OPEN: Year round. Two-night weekend minimum; three nights on holidays and special events.
RATES: $100–$150 April–October; $85–$140 November–March. $40 extra person. Corporate discounts. Amex, Discover, MC, Visa. ♥ ⊞ ❖ ⚥ ⅄

THIS **WEDDING CAKE** house—with some Georgian, Greek Revival, Italianate, and Victorian features—has been featured in *Smithsonian* magazine. Corporate travelers, romantics, wedding planners, the governor, musicians, architects, an astronaut—all are happy that the house was saved by the family who restored it in 1973. Everyone asks about the spectacular stencils throughout. As Debra says, "The designs were researched, cut by hand, and done by the 1984 buyer, who spent seven years on a ladder!"

In California Steve worked for Gallo wines. Debra was a speech pathologist. When Steve delved into the New England wine scene, then in its infancy, Debra became an assistant innkeeper in Newport. "In 1991 we bought this wonderful pink house. It has 8-foot pocket doors, high ceilings, intricate parquet and inlaid floors, a fireplaced courting corner, and eclectic furnishings." And it has Debra—a runner, rug-hooking-bee participant, and active resident of this fascinating small community.

IN RESIDENCE: "Many guests want to take Misha, our oft-photographed bichon frise, home!" Seventeen-year-old family bird, Princess, an umbrella cockatoo.
FOREIGN LANGUAGE SPOKEN: Spanish.
BED AND BATH: Four large rooms, each with ceiling fan; all private baths (with hair dryer). On first floor—king/twins option, full bath, gas fireplace. On second floor—room with king/twins option, shower. King/twins option, gas fireplace, sink in room, shower bath. Queen bed, sink in room, full bath.
BREAKFAST: 7–10. Dutch puffed pancakes, stuffed breakfast pudding, or elaborate French toast. Homemade granola, bread, muffins, preserves, lemon poppy-seed cake. Yogurt. Fresh fruit cup. Freshly ground and brewed gourmet coffees. Served on 30-foot-long terrazzo-tiled porch or in candlelit dining room.

PLUS: Two parlors—one with TV and video collection. Secret garden with pond and waterfall. Terrace. Afternoon tea or sherry. His and hers robes. Terrace. Wine tasting and tour weekends.

> ➵ *Guests wrote: "Inn and town are picture perfect. . . . Excellent hospitality . . . relaxing, comfortable. . . . Debra should be on Rhode Island's list of natural wonders!"*

➵ *William's Grant Inn*

401/253-4222

154 High Street,   800/596-4222
Bristol, RI 02809   FAX 401/254-0987

HOSTS: Diane and Warren Poehler; son Matthew and Janet, his wife.
LOCATION: On the July 4 parade (seen by 250,000 people) route. In quiet old neighborhood with many restored homes. Five-minute walk to Bristol harbor, restaurants, antiques shops, town common with gazebo. Five blocks to $2.50 movie theater. Short drive to 33-acre Blithewold Gardens; museums; and a park with incredible water views, beaches, and bike path.
OPEN: Year round. Two-night minimum on weekends and holidays.
RATES: Per room. May–October $95 shared bath, $105 private bath. November–April $85 shared bath, $95 private bath. Amex, Discover, MC, Visa. ♥ ⊞ ❖ ✄ ✁

EXUBERANCE HERE art thou—especially on the part of Diane and daughter-in-law Janet, primary innkeepers. Their dream come true of "true New England" is this 1808 Federal/Colonial house with picket fence, a B&B that they purchased in 1998. Furnishings are traditional. Decorative accessories include Thai masks and African and European artworks—collections from the years when Warren, an engineer (now a teacher), was an army officer and later in the oil business. (Diane was a teacher "all over.") Janet has lived most of her life in New Zealand. Matthew, a Desert Storm veteran who works in computers, is an active member of a medieval reenactment group.

IN RESIDENCE: Kodi, "our official inn dog." Rusty, seventeen year-old cat from New Zealand.
BED AND BATH: Five queen-bedded rooms with ceiling fans and nonworking fireplaces. Three first-floor rooms; two have shower baths. Room with private hallway has bath with tub and shower. Two second-floor rooms (can be a suite) share a tub bath.
BREAKFAST: 8–9:30. Fresh fruit. Freshly baked muffins or cranberry orange scones. Repertoire includes Portuguese French toast; blueberry and apple-cinnamon pancakes; fresh vegetable strata; and a New Zealand favorite, bacon-and-egg pie. Served in kitchen or on patio.
PLUS: Second-floor air-conditioned guest parlor with TV. Beverages.

One Willow by the Sea   401/364-0802

1 Willow Road, Charlestown, RI 02813-4162   E-MAIL josyrealty@ids.net

HOSTS: Denise Dillon Fuge

LOCATION: Rural setting, residential neighborhood. On major flyway. Very close to beaches, theater, fine dining. Within half hour of Block Island ferry, country's second oldest synagogue (in Newport), Providence's Riverwalk, Mystic (Connecticut).

OPEN: Year round. Two-day minimum on summer weekends, national holidays, and University of Rhode Island and Brown University graduations.

RATES: April 15–October 31, $80 queen bed, two-room suite. $70 queen bed. $50 single. Off-season, $10 less. Discount for weekday reservations for four or more days. ♥ ⁙ ⊯ ⊞ ⚔ ⚒ ⚖ ❤

A FLEXIBLE HOSTESS. A comfortable kick-off-your-shoes-and-relax split-level house furnished with "good" antiques and comfortable sofas and lots of books and flowers. A sundeck and gardens where you can "hear the sea and sniff the sea breezes, listen to songbirds and enjoy starlit skies. Romantics love the outdoor shower on moonlit nights!"

Denise spent thirty-one years in Manhattan. As a youngster in London, she met and was inspired by the suffragists. In the 1980s she was president of the New York City NOW chapter during the equal rights campaign. Denise has experience in publishing, speaking (the women's movement and B&B are among her current topics) and lobbying. In fall and winter, she "borrows a friendly dog" for beach walks.

IN RESIDENCE: Two busy Siamese cats. Minou "takes role of discreet morning greeter seriously, while Joe keeps an eye out for possible feline invaders onto the property."

FOREIGN LANGUAGES SPOKEN: "Slightly fractured French; some understanding of Danish, Norwegian, Swedish."

BED AND BATH: Three rooms. Main floor: Two queen-bedded rooms share a full bath. Lower level: A two-room suite has sitting room, TV, VCR, queen-bedded room, private bath. Rollaway available.

BREAKFAST: Usually 8:30–10. Cantaloupe with ginger, vanilla yogurt, fresh fruit, bagels, blueberry muffins, and "my son's killer croissants from the best deli in town." Juices. French crepes; Irish oatmeal; English scrambled eggs with ham, cheese, and asparagus tips. On sundeck at umbrella tables or indoors. "Special diet needs respected."

PLUS: Sun-dried sheets and towels. Ceiling fans. Bedside radio. Champagne and flowers for special occasions. Freezer and refrigerator available. Garage for canoes, kayaks, surfboards, bicycles, beach equipment. Room for boat trailers.

From Florida, Connecticut, New York: *"Warm, caring hostess . . . bright, clean rooms . . . out-of-this-world breakfasts . . . shared recipes as well as plantings (that she was thinning). . . . Stayed during our son's graduation weekend . . . all details meticulously attended to!"*

🐾 Green Shadows   401/783–9752

803 Green Hill Beach Road, Green Hill, RI   E-MAIL dckratz@home.com
Mailing address: 803 Green Hill Beach Road,
Wakefield, RI 02879-6228

HOSTS: Don and Mercedes Kratz
LOCATION: Quiet and rural. Fronted by a stone wall, on a wooded acre with sound of surf and view of pond. Ten-minute walk to ocean beach (and view of Block Island). Five-minute bike ride to wildlife preserve. Fifteen minutes to Narragansett and Watch Hill. Three miles to Theatre-By-The-Sea, 10 to University of Rhode Island, 25 east of Mystic. Near art galleries, shops, restaurants.
OPEN: Year round. Two-night minimum on summer weekends; three nights on holiday weekends.
RATES: May–October $95 detached bath; $105 attached bath. Off-season $75–$85.
  ▪ ⚰ ⅍

WELL, IT WAS a little old house with a great location when the Kratzes bought it in 1983 as a summer residence. Now it's a big (triple the size) architect-designed country house with a private B&B area—all sited on that great location. "The big winner? The large screened porch, with ocean breeze coming across Green Hill Pond and views of goldfinches at bird feeders and our local red fox, who puts in an appearance, sometimes on cue." Until their retirement in 1993 (the year before rebuilding), Don and Mercedes traveled on several continents while they were with IBM Corporation. As hosts since 1995, "we've hosted schoolmates of thirty years ago, tourists from Europe, a few celebrities, many returnees . . . great people!" "Wonderful" is how guests describe Green Shadows.

IN RESIDENCE: Two eighteen-year-old brother and sister cats, not allowed in guest rooms.
BED AND BATH: Two spacious rooms, each with king bed, on the guest (first) floor with large closets, private tile baths. One has shower bath across the hall; the other has attached full bath, views of pond and secluded backyard.
BREAKFAST: 8:30. Fresh fruit, eggs, muffins, coffee cakes, waffles, chocolate chip French bread. On screened porch overlooking Zen garden and bird feeders or in adjacent breakfast area.
PLUS: Cable TV and VCR in guests' common room. Beverages and snacks. Window fans. Guest refrigerator. Outside hot/cold shower. Transportation from Kingston train or Wakefield bus station.

B ED AND BREAKFAST GIVES A SENSE OF PLACE.

❧ Four Gables   401/789-6948

12 South Pier Road, Narragansett, RI 02882-3760

HOSTS: Terry and Barbara Higgins
LOCATION: Residential. One block off Route IA, a major scenic route. On a main town road. Walk to ocean beach (half block), dock (for fishing), shops, restaurants. Nearby hiking trails, bicycle routes, kayaking. Ten-minute drive to Block Island ferry; fifteen to Newport.
OPEN: Year round. Two-night weekend minimum, late May through early September.
RATES: $80 queen. $90 king/twins. $60–$70 November–April and weekdays in May and October. Midweek (year round) 15 percent less, three-night minimum. MC, Visa. ♥ ☞ ⊞ ❖ ☄

THIS IS THE same place that became almost famous (often referred to by journalists) when in an earlier edition I noted that a guest was introduced to her husband by the then hosts (previous owners). "The best *we* can report is several engagements and many wedding parties," say Barbara, a landscape designer, and Terry, an attorney. In 1993 the Higginses were living in another Narragansett house and planning on doing B&B there, until they fell in love with this 1898 Shingle Style cottage. The Arts and Crafts interior has wonderful woodwork, four fireplaces, interesting nooks and crannies, a massive cross-gambrel roof, and a verandah enjoyed by a well-known fiddler who provided a private mini–Cajun fiddler festival right here. Barbara and Terry have furnished with antiques and handcrafted items. And their maturing (labeled) perennial and herb gardens are a joy.

IN RESIDENCE: "Lucy, our very friendly Bernese mountain dog [who accompanied the Higginses on a cross-country auto trip]; Max and Roxie, our Maine coon cats."
FOREIGN LANGUAGE SPOKEN: Spanish.
BED AND BATH: Two second-floor rooms with antique four-posters—one king, one queen—share bath (robes provided) that has claw-foot tub/shower. Plus half bath on first floor.
BREAKFAST: Usually 8–9. Apple pancakes with local maple syrup or cheese crepes with blueberry ginger sauce. (Or low-fat, vegetarian menu.) Fresh fruit, home-baked breads (strawberry nut a specialty) and muffins. Homemade preserves. Served in oceanview dining room or on veranda.
PLUS: Bedroom ceiling fans. Discount beach passes and bridge tokens. Living room fireplace. Tea. TV by request. Turndown service. Guest refrigerator. Patio grill. Picnic table. Antiques sources. "A special Block Island beach suggestion." Transportation provided from Providence airport or Kingston train station. Off-street parking.

❧ From Maine, Massachusetts, New York, New Jersey, Connecticut, Pennsylvania, Texas, Illinois: *"Terrific. . . . Incredible breakfasts—huge, varied, freshly made. . . . Hosts are reliable area guides. . . . Breathtaking view of Narragansett Bay from cozy porch . . . a beautifully decorated house that transports guests back to a time hinting of an Edith*

Wharton novel. . . . Hosts are friendly; animals are lovable as well . . . simple but with character! . . . Elegant bedroom. Luxurious bath. Many amenities . . . Sweaters in progress; a quilt in the making. . . . From dining room—peaceful view of ocean. . . . Embraced by the atmosphere and caring. . . . Lucy takes away any homesickness for your own dog."

The 1900 House
401/789-7971

59 Kingstown Road, Narragansett, RI 02882-3309

HOSTS: Bill and Sandra Panzeri
LOCATION: On a side street (Victorian homes) that leads to ocean wall. Five-minute walk to shops, fine dining, historic Towers, ocean beach, movie theater.
OPEN: Year round. Two-night minimum May 15–October 15 weekends.
RATES: $85 shared bath. $95 private bath. Singles $10 less. Off-season, $65. Additional futon $10 per person. "In season, stay six nights, be our guest for seventh." ♥ ⬛ ⊞ ⚔ ⚏ ❤○

"THROUGH OUR own travels we became addicted to the B&B concept, and started our own in 1989. We restored this Victorian house, installed exterior gingerbread and window boxes, decorated (and redecorated), and furnished with Oriental rugs and memories of the past. Now there's an enamel woodstove in the collectibles-filled kitchen. Guests enjoy our quilt collection, a feast of fabric and design. They look at 3-D images with the stereoscope, thumb through hundreds of antique postcards, and discover treasures throughout the house."

Bill has established marvelous flower and vegetable gardens. Sandy, a counselor and watercolorist, is a board member of several civic organizations.

IN RESIDENCE: Chris and Fred, two cats restricted from guest rooms.
BED AND BATH: Three second-floor rooms. One room with canopied double bed, TV, private bath with claw-foot tub and hand-held shower. Two rooms, each with TV and antique double bed, share shower bath.
BREAKFAST: 8:30–9:30. Unlimited refills. Juices. Strawberries (from Bill's garden) and cream, or baked stuffed apple. Homemade muffins. Belgian waffles, baked croissants framboise, or tarragon eggs and bacon. In dining room with woodstove and view of bird feeder.
PLUS: A book swap in each bedroom. Screened wraparound porch. Guest refrigerator. Outside hot/cold shower. Bike and surfboard storage. Special occasions acknowledged.

From California, New York, Wisconsin: *"Felt like home. Amazing breakfasts, to boot . . . layout provided privacy and space . . . wonderful morning kitchen smells. . . . Appreciated "touchability" of antiques . . . Filled with family treasures . . . tea and cookies at night. . . . So wonderful I returned to stay another three nights."*

⨋ *The Old Clerk House*   401/783-8008

49 Narragansett Avenue, Narragansett, RI 02882-3386   FAX 401/783-8008
          E-MAIL plwat@aol.com

HOST: Patricia Watkins
LOCATION: One block from Narragansett Beach and mile-long seawall walk. In residential pier section. Six miles to Block Island ferry. Fine restaurants, shops, and cinema within 4-block radius.
OPEN: Year round. Two-day minimum on weekends May 1–October 15.
RATES: May 1–October 30 king $125 for two, $100 for one; queen $95 for two, $85 for one. Off-season $15–$30 less. ♥ ☕ ❖ ⌀ ⅃

⨋ From Massachusetts, New York, New Jersey, Pennsylvania, Connecticut, Rhode Island, Washington, D.C.: *"A wonderful B&B. . . . Perfect hostess. . . . Many thoughtful extras . . . relaxing . . . full of charm. . . . Had mixup with travel agent's booking. Sent to Old Clerk House. What could have been a disaster was a stroke of luck . . . absolutely gorgeous garden . . . especially memorable and substantial breakfast beautifully served . . . good music. . . . Enjoyed Pat's pets, as we sorely missed our own. . . . A lovely find. . . . Thank you, Bernice!"*

PROFESSIONAL PHOTOGRAPHERS and artists, too, have discovered this house with its white picket fence and thriving rosebushes. The "warm glow" c. 1890 house, formerly owned by a succession of town clerks, was completely redone by Pat, a computer consultant who worked as a technical reference specialist with an international development organization. Guests ask about the clocks. They admire the "very English" yard and the ornamental pond with koi and goldfish. And they request recipes. For someplace different, Pat will suggest "a delightful nearby village huddled around a cove, a historic house nestled in a woody hollow with millstream, or a short drive to a restored carousel, a work of art and a ride not to be missed!"

IN RESIDENCE: Four cats "never allowed in guest areas. Max is the car inspector. Persian Miss Moppet is chief inspector of guests and their luggage, if given the opportunity. Pansy, her daughter, was born on April Fool's Day. Tigger is a flame-point Himalayan. Billy and Jessie are friendly, quiet collie dogs."
FOREIGN LANGUAGES SPOKEN: French and "rusty" German.
BED AND BATH: Two air-conditioned second-floor rooms, each with private full bath, color cable TV, and VCR. Front room has queen cannonball bed and a twin bed. Large "romantic" suite with dormer windows, king bed, sitting room with view.
BREAKFAST: 7:30–9:30. All "from scratch, no mixes." Menu includes cranberry or orange juice. Fruit. Cereal. Blueberry, apricot almond, or walnut cream cheese muffins. Toast with butter, homemade jams. Crepes with strawberry sauce, portobello mushroom and cheddar cheese omelet, French toast, Belgian waffle, or wild Maine blueberry pancakes.
PLUS: Refreshment tray. Acknowledgment of celebrations. Video library. Record and CD player; classical to pop music. Games. Transportation from bus (3 blocks away) or from Kingston train station. Half-price beach passes.

☞ The Richards   401/789-7746

144 Gibson Avenue, Narragansett, RI 02882

HOSTS: Steven and Nancy Richards
LOCATION: On a quiet, private, dead-end road. One mile from center of town. One-quarter mile from ocean; one mile to beach.
OPEN: Year round. Two-night weekend minimum; three nights on holiday weekends; four on August weekends. "Please indicate expected arrival time."
RATES: Queen $85. King $100. Suites with queen $125. Two bedroom suite $135 for two, $175 for four people. ♥ ☏ ⚶ ⚸

☞ From Tennessee: *"Stately . . . fantastic breakfasts . . . they obviously enjoy sharing their lovely home and gardens."* From New York: *"A visit to the Richardses is truly a special occasion. Private . . . a perfect honeymoon retreat."*

THIS SHOWPLACE, a gabled 1884 stone house noted in the *New York Times* and *Rhode Island Monthly,* has become a destination for (nonsmoking) travelers from all over the world. A circular gravel driveway leads to a copper cupola–topped entrance of what was a 20-acre estate. Inside there's a grand 40-foot-long entrance hall (with elevator, no longer used, such as you have never seen); eleven fireplaces; deep windowsills; spectacular kitchen (now); Oriental rugs and antiques; and, every year, more draperies sewn by Nancy, more self-custom-mixed paints, and more gorgeous gardens too.

The Richardses purchased the house (that process is part of the interesting history) in 1988, after hosting in a Narragansett Cape-style house for ten years. Steven, weekend co-chef and former director of a state legislature program, is an international financial consultant for commercial real estate.

IN RESIDENCE: Two cats, not allowed in guest areas.
BED AND BATH: Two large second-floor rooms with fireplaces, plus two suites. One room with king, private tub bath, and one with canopied queen bed share hall shower bath. Suite with canopied queen bed, private hand-held shower/tub bath. In private wing—suite with two rooms (one with king bed, one with queen) that do not share a wall; sitting area with wood-burning fireplace, shower bath.
BREAKFAST: 8:45. (Please give advance notice for special diets or for continental, available until 9:45.) Fresh fruit. Repertoire (never repeated, even for two-week stays) includes zucchini frittata, orange French toast with hot orange syrup and whipped cream, gingerbread pancakes with lemon sauce, or Steven's johnnycakes. Pumpkin or chocolate macaroon muffins. Blended gourmet coffee. In formal dining room.
PLUS: Fireplaces everywhere; most use Duraflame logs. Guest refrigerator. Library. Patio. Badminton. Sherry. Bench in shade garden—and, sometimes, deer too.

⤳ Anna's Victorian Connection Host #196

Newport, RI

LOCATION: Residential neighborhod. Ten-minute walk to Cliff Walk and First Beach. One mile to harbor.

OPEN: Year round through Anna's Victorian Connection (page 360) 401/849-2489 or 800/884-4288. E-mail annas@aiconnect.com. Two-night minimum in summer and on holiday weekends.

RATES: April 15–October 15 $175–$240 weekends, $125–$175 midweek. Less off-season. ⊞ ⚲ ⚴

FINE WOODWORK—moldings and paneling—serves as a backdrop for the family heirlooms and reproductions in this 1882 Victorian which the hosts redecorated in 1996 when they moved from Manhattan. "Often the craftsmen would comment on what a beautiful B&B this house, once the home of Rear Admiral William S. Sims, U.S.N., would be," say the hosts, a history buff (and former financial analyst) and his wife, a nurse. And in 1998 it happened—with guest rooms named for former U.S. presidents, with memorabilia and books, with paintings and photographs hung throughout the house. Romantics, too, appreciate the ambiance.

Breakfasts are memorable. And according to a Washington, D.C. guest (one of many): "This is the best White House I've ever stayed in."

IN RESIDENCE: In hosts' quarters (only)—three children, two dogs, one cat.

BED AND BATH: Four second-floor air-conditioned and carpeted rooms with private en-suite baths—two with tub/shower, two with shower only. King or queen beds with fine linens. Cable TV "that can be hidden."

BREAKFAST: 8–10. Brought to your room. Entrée possibilities include pancakes, French toast, eggs Benedict, omelets. Option of continental menu. Served with fine china.

PLUS: Afternoon tea in the "Diplomatic Reception Room." Rose garden.

*T*HE TRADITION *of paying to stay in a private home—with breakfast included in the overnight lodging rate—was revived in time to save wonderful old houses, schools, churches, and barns all over the country from the wrecking ball or commercial development.*

⁊ Anna's Victorian Connection Lighthouse

Newport, RI

LOCATION:	On a small Narragansett Bay island "with the best views of the bay, a wind generator, and some edible plants." A mile from Newport and Jamestown; just south of Newport Bridge.
RESERVATIONS:	Year round (April–June the island belongs mostly to birds during their nesting season) through Anna's Victorian Connection (page 360), 401/849-2489 or 800/884-4288. E-mail annas@aiconnect.com. (If the weather is too rough, Anna's Victorian Connection will arrange for mainland accommodations.) Note that weekends are booked long in advance.
RATES:	May–September weekends $140 double, $115 single; weekdays (excluding holidays) $115 double, $90 single. Rest of year $25 less. Foundation members ($15 individual, $30 families) $20 less. Apartment booked by the week ($600) in summer; monthly, rest of year. Transportation (extra charge) via scheduled launch. Mainland parking fee charged in season.

♥ ⊞ ⚮ ⚗

FALL ASLEEP to the sound of waves, foghorn, and bell buoy. Wake up in your high brass bed to a fantastic view of the boat-filled bay. It's "an upscale camping experience"—there's limited running water and you bring your own ice and food. Since 1992 these cozy overnight accommodations complete with turn-of-the-century ambiance have been discovered by romantics, historians, and adventurers.

Here, away from it all, is this two-storied 1869 mansard-roofed house topped by a light tower that was deactivated in 1971. Thanks to the nonprofit Rose Island Lighthouse Foundation, the property has been restored as a public site and self-sufficient environmental center. (Some summer day-trippers come for a picnic, bird-watching, and a tour of the working lighthouse and the grounds.) Now there are new double-hung windows. The first floor has an in-floor radiant heating system. The small museum area has natural history exhibits in addition to photographs and memorabilia that have been provided by grandsons of two long-term lighthouse keepers.

BED AND BATH: Two first-floor waterview rooms, each with an extra-long double bed, share a WC that has an "ecologically sound pump-your-own toilet." Second-floor keeper's apartment (inquire about responsibilities such as checking weather report and raising the flag) has a room with queen bed; one large kitchen/living/dining room with sofa bed, microwave, woodstove for heat, gas cooking stove, refrigerator, and player piano; hot and cold running water, tiled full bath.

BREAKFAST: Bring your own provisions. Use of gas hot plate or outdoor grill, old-fashioned icebox.

PLUS: Summer outdoor solar shower. Down comforters. Gas barbecue. Accessible catwalk. Reminders: Bring fishing poles. Wear sneakers. Inquire about use of rowboat and kayak.

⤳ *Clark Spooner House*   401/849-6261

One Elm Street,   FAX 401/847-1943
Newport, RI 02840-2511   E-MAIL cclark@jftr.com
www.clarkspoonerhouse.com

HOSTS: David and Carole Clark
LOCATION: Quiet. In The Point, a historic residential district, just 2½ blocks from hustle-bustle waterfront with shops and restaurants.
OPEN: Year round. Two-night minimum June–September.
RATES: $150 May–October; $125 November–April. ■ ⊞ ⚔ ⚒

JUST RIGHT—for travelers and for the Clarks, sailors who often came to Newport when they lived in an oceanfront condo in Plymouth, Massachusetts. After buying this 1740 house, listed on the National Register, they gutted and rebuilt most of it over a year's time before opening as a B&B in 1998. All six fireplaces are revitalized. "But I haven't yet tried the beehive oven," says Carole, the bread baker—and seamstress. Keeping room floorboards came from the attic. Many antiques were bought locally. The wing chairs and beds are new. Chimney bricks are exposed on the third floor. Together, Carole and David did all the papering and painting (Colonial colors). They built a stone wall and created a secret garden. Now the couple, who met when they worked at the same company (she in marketing, he as a chemist), dovetail their jobs as Newport Chamber of Commerce membership director and analytical instrumentation sales manager with hosting delighted travelers. And the travelers, in turn, write to me:

⤳ From New York: "*Instantly, their home was our home . . . quiet, intimate, and extremely welcoming. Carole and David are beautiful, inside and out. Being with them at breakfast was our favorite part of the day!*" From California: "*Charming, comfortable, immaculate accommodations. . . . Fine hospitality. . . . Breakfast was special—varied, delicious, presented with elegance. . . . Outstanding.*"

IN RESIDENCE: In hosts' quarters—an elderly American Eskimo dog and two cats.
BED AND BATH: Three air-conditioned rooms; all private baths. Large second-floor room—canopied queen bed, shower bath. Third floor—two rooms, each with queen four-poster, bath with shower and single Jacuzzi.
BREAKFAST: 8:30–9:30 (coffee available earlier). Waffles, pancakes, omelets, French toast, or eggs Benedict. Fresh fruit appetizer. Death-by-chocolate cake, carrot cake, crème brûlé. "Life is short. We eat dessert first." Served with sterling silver and china in dining room or on the patio.
PLUS: TV/VCR in sitting room. Fresh fruit and flowers. Custom map with directions that avoid in-town traffic.

☜ *Cliffside Inn*

401/847-1811

2 Seaview Avenue,
Newport, RI 02840

800/845-1811
FAX 401/848-5850
E-MAIL cliff@wsii.com
www.cliffsideinn.com

HOST: Stephan Nicolas
LOCATION: In a quiet residential area, a half block from Cliff Walk. Six blocks to Bellevue Avenue mansions; 15 minutes' walk to waterfront, 5 to First Beach.
OPEN: Year round. Two-night minimum on weekends.
RATES: $185–$325. Fireplaced rooms start at $205; with fireplace and Jacuzzi, at $235. Suites $295–$450. Inquire about November–April package rates. Amex, Discover, MC, Visa. ♥ ❖ ✄ ⊱ ☙

WHAT BECAME known as one of Newport's best-kept secrets, thanks to a reader of this book, is a haven—sort of a small hotel—for romantics and art lovers too. The house is filled with period furnishings and decorated with wonderful wallcoverings and fabrics. The *New York Times* and *Philadelphia* magazine have featured the works of Beatrice Turner, who lived and painted here for the first half of this century. Reproductions of her self-portraits are throughout the high-ceilinged, bay-windowed summer "cottage," which was built in 1880 by the governor of Maryland.

Win Baker, Cliffside's owner, is responsible for extensive research on the few remaining Turner works, including one that was found in Pennsylvania and now hangs in the inn's parlor. Stephan Nicolas, a Johnson & Wales graduate who has been innkeeper since 1993, was born into a culinary family; his grandfather headed L'Ecole Hôtelière in Paris.

BED AND BATH: On three floors in main house plus two-suite cottage—a total of fifteen rooms, each with fireplace, air conditioning, telephone, ceiling or window fan, private tub/shower bath; most have double Jacuzzi (one has a "media center" within). Eight are suites with VCR and movies. King, queen (one canopied). Attic Room has cathedral ceiling, four skylights. Governor's Suite has king bed, French doors to bath with fireplace, 1994 whirlpool bath and restored 1890 birdcage shower. Two-storied Tower Suite in re-created wing has "everything." Seascape Suite has ocean views.
BREAKFAST: 8–10. (Juice-and-coffee room service 7–9.) Homemade granola, muffins, and coffee cakes. Fruit. Yogurt. French toast, eggs Benedict, walnut pancakes or waffles. Freshly squeezed orange juice. Freshly ground coffee. Special diets accommodated.
PLUS: Individual thermostats. Elaborate afternoon tea. Porch rockers. Beach towels. Bicycle storage. Fresh flowers in baths. Off-street parking.

☜ From New York, Rhode Island, New Jersey, England: *"Spectacular . . . heaven in Newport. . . . Everything was perfect. . . . Wonderful. The full Monty."*

⤳ 1855 Marshall Slocum House

401/841-5120

29 Kay Street,
Newport, RI 02840-2735

FAX 401/846-3787
800/372-5120
E-MAIL marshallslocuminn@edgenet.net
www.marshallslocuminn.com

HOST: Joan and (daughter) Julie Wilson
LOCATION: Canopied by a copper beech, on a street of Victorian homes. Five-minute walk to waterfront, shops, and harbor. Fifteen-minute walk to beach.
OPEN: Year round. Reservations preferred. Two-night minimum on summer weekends, three nights on holidays and special event weekends.
RATES: (Include Wednesday night lobster dinner with three-day midweek stay.) Memorial Day–Columbus Day $115–$165. Off-season $90–$135. Amex, MC, Visa. ▦ ⚔

"YES, MY HOME has turned out to be home away from home for sailors, students, writers, croquet players, musicians, international visitors . . . every one with an interesting tale to tell, and many return every year. . . . I've tried to take breakfast to state of the art. Guests have shared their expertise, and I share my recipes, some of which are painted on the kitchen wall tiles."

Before buying this restored Victorian in 1985, Joan managed an orange grove in Florida. And then there was a short interlude as a travel agent. Now she is a craftswoman who makes jam, reads, fishes in the Florida keys, and visits children and grandchildren in California and Europe. Her friendly house is furnished with family heirlooms, antiques, and collectibles.

IN RESIDENCE: Buttons, "our tailless cat, graciously accepts pats from kitty lovers."
BED AND BATH: Five large rooms, one skylit, on two floors; all with private tub/shower or shower-only bath. Queen, king, or twin beds; air conditioning or ceiling fan in each room.
BREAKFAST: 8–10. (Coffee earlier.) Perhaps Belgian waffles with fresh strawberries or peach French toast. Plus homemade bread, fruit, juice, cereal. Served in dining room or on back deck overlooking large shaded backyard.
PLUS: Afternoon refreshments. Front porch rockers. Yard with garden and koi pond. Parlor with wood-burning fireplace, TV, VCR, movies (including *The Great Gatsby*, made in Newport). Dinner and picnics (extra charge) by request. Off-street parking.

⤳ From England: *"Joan Wilson is a joy to stay with."* From South Africa: *"An ideal base during my visit, which was in connection with a book I was writing. . . . [Located] in an attractive and quiet part of town . . . tastefully furbished and well run. . . . Joan Wilson is a most friendly and knowledgeable person . . . breakfast a full and tasty meal."*

▰ The Elliott Boss House

20 Second Street,
Newport, RI 02840-2415

401/849-9425
FAX 401/848-9832
E-MAIL elliottboss@edgenet.net
www.elliottboss.com

HOSTS: Loretta and Tom Goldrick
LOCATION: On a quiet street with brick sidewalks in historic (Colonial) and residential "Point" section. One block from the water; two blocks to Visitors' Center; 10 minutes' walk to harbor, shops, restaurants.
OPEN: Year round. Two-night minimum July–September. Three-night minimum on July 4, Jazz Festival, and Labor Day weekends.
RATES: May 16–October $150 weekends and holidays, $125 weekdays. November–March $105 weekends and holidays, $85 weekdays. April–May 15 $125, $105. ♥ ☎ ⊞ ❖ ⚡

THIS "FAVORITE" of English travel professionals who were in Newport for their annual conference (held on a different continent every year) is a restored 1820 Federal-style clapboard house filled with marvelous treasures from around the world. It has been part of Wine-Tasting, Christmas Candlelight, and Secret Garden tours. After writers for the *New York Times* and *International Herald Tribune* were guests in 1996, they wrote about this B&B "in a quiet backwater overlooked by many tourists . . . simple . . . wide polished floorboards . . . windows overlooking gardens . . . followed their suggestion for museum . . . became so absorbed in displays [in house], almost forgot our tour of North America's oldest synagogue." Home to the Goldricks, former Newport booksellers, the former boatbuilder's house has been their B&B since 1986, when local innkeepers requested they lodge overflow guests. "We gulped, said 'yes,' and began a wonderful way of life—discussing politics, food, fashion, music, careers—and learning about different points of view from people all over the world."

Tom was chief financial officer at colleges in Geneva, New York and in the Boston area. Now he takes courses at the Newport Art Museum, is active in a local church, and pursues his interests in model railroading and sailing. As a writer Loretta focused on travel; now she is studying French at a local university.

BED AND BATH: Two second-floor air-conditioned rooms with individual thermostats and TV. One with canopied queen bed, en-suite full bath. Other has king/twins option, private full bath "8 steps down the hall." (Robes provided.)
BREAKFAST: Flexible. Usually 9–10 weekends; 8:30–9:30 weekdays. (Departures for early flights accommodated.) Juice, muffins, and coffee available before serving time. Full menu—juices, fresh fruit, homemade muffins, and granola. Waffles and sausage, peach or plum clafouti; blueberry pancakes and bacon; or rhubarb cobbler and ham. Served on fine china at table for four or on awninged terrace.
PLUS: Books galore—including local history. Living room has air conditioning and wood-burning fireplace. Fresh fruit and flowers. Before-and-after albums for house and gorgeous secret garden.

▰ From Oklahoma travel agent: "*Highly recommended. . . . Delightful hosts. Excellent location. Superb accommodations.*"

≈ Elm Tree Cottage

336 Gibbs Avenue,
Newport, RI 02840

401/849-1610
888/ELM-TREE
FAX 401/849-2084
E-MAIL info@elm-tree.com
www.elm-tree.com

HOSTS: Thomas and Priscilla Malone

LOCATION: On a lovely acre of land in estate neighborhood, 1½ blocks from the ocean and Cliff Walk. Within 15-minute walk of restaurants. One mile to America's Cup Avenue.

OPEN: February–December. Two-night weekend minimum; three nights June–October and on holiday and special event weekends.

RATES: Vary according to season (highest rate May–October). $155–$225 queen bed. $185–$275 first-floor junior suite or king bed. $295–$425 Windsor Room.
田 ⊗ ⊁

A TRUE STORY that sounds a bit like fantasy. Two personable Long Island stained glass artists/designers (for religious, commercial, and residential buildings) fell in love with Newport and innkeeping. In 1989, when they were substitute innkeepers for one week, they took time for a bicycle ride and found this 1882 Shingle Style summer "cottage" surrounded by weeds and in need of everything. A year later, having used their talents, skills, and advanced degrees in interior design, fine arts, and woodworking, they furnished with fine antiques from auctions and estate sales. Soon after its opening, the elegant B&B, with a marvelous open-style floor plan, was discovered by the staff of *Mirabella* magazine. It's been on *Country Inns* magazine's "top twelve," and Star Service named it one of the world's most outstanding properties. The spacious (enormous) and gracious (welcoming) living room—with grand piano and Oriental rugs—overlooks Easton Pond and First Beach. The hosts' eye for color, design, and texture is everywhere—in linens and fabrics in English and French country styling, in window treatments and Louis XV French beds. To this day the rooms keep getting more lavish. More guests commission stained glass works by the hosts. Here the cuisine, too, is a fine art.

IN RESIDENCE: In hosts' quarters, three daughters and lop-eared bunnies.

BED AND BATH: Six air-conditioned rooms, each with private en-suite bath; five with Duraflame log fireplaces. First floor—English hunt theme with queen bed, shower bath. Five second-floor rooms—with more stained glass windows each year. Windsor Room, 39 by 20 feet, with king bed, two living room seating arrangements, winter water views, crystal-chandeliered full bath with two-person whirlpool. Queen bed, bath with soaking tub, separate shower. Queen canopied bed, full bath. King bed, shower bath with two seats. King bed, marble bath with two-person soaking tub, separate shower.

BREAKFAST: Hot beverages available at 7:30. Buffet 8:30–10; entrée served 8:30–9:30. Intentionally special. Homemade granola, fruit, French vanilla yogurt, breads, muffins, cobblers, bread puddings. Entrée may be French toast soufflé with whipped maple cream, château potatoes topped with poached egg and Parmesan cheese sauce, quiche Lorraine

in crepe cups with broiled tomato. At tables set for two with flowers, candles, fine linens and china.
PLUS: Turndown service. Coffee always available. BYOB bar. Sometimes, a tour of hosts' workshop. Off-street parking.

↬ Guests wrote: *"It's what you envision when you think of Newport grandeur. . . . Romantic and exquisitely done rooms. . . . Tom and Priscilla made our vacation perfect."*

↬ Hydrangea House Inn

401/846-4435

16 Bellevue Avenue,
Newport, RI 02840-3206

800/945-4667
FAX 401/846-6602
E-MAIL hydrangeahouse@home.com
www.hydrangeahouse.com

HOSTS: Grant Edmondson and Dennis Blair
LOCATION: On top of Newport's historic hill (in center of walking district), with brick sidewalks, gas lighting, old trees, and shops. Across from Viking Hotel. Five-minute walk to harbor, 10 to first mansion on Bellevue Avenue and to the beach.
OPEN: Year round. Two-night minimum on weekends, three nights on holidays and event weekends.
RATES: May through October $125 double bed, $165 queen, $210 king, $250–$280 suite. Off-season $125 double, $150 queen, $165 king, $185–$195 suite. 2-4-1: November through April: with Sunday–Wednesday check-in, second night is free. Deposit required. MC, Visa. ♥ ⊞ ❖ ⚔ ⚒

A TRANSFORMATION by Newport antiques dealers. Here in an 1876 building that was, in 1988, shops, apartments, and offices, is a gracious B&B—"not a mansion"—created by Dennis, a former customer service administrator, and Grant, a former construction company owner.

Now the first floor is a contemporary fine arts gallery, the breakfast room for overnight guests. Antiques, sculpture, paintings, fine fabrics, and attention to detail are throughout. In the rear, a 500-square-foot verandah overlooks hydrangea gardens. It's the "special place with a welcome mat out for new friends" that Grant and Dennis imagined during their long property search.

IN RESIDENCE: Two cats. "Miss Kitty is suave and sophisticated. Chester is fat and lazy."
BED AND BATH: Seven air-conditioned and carpeted second- and third-floor rooms. All private baths; some full, some shower only. Queen or double beds. Air-conditioned "suite," a very large paneled, dramatically decorated room, has canopied king bed, whirlpool, gas fireplace, Oriental rug in sitting area, TV/VCR.
BREAKFAST: 8:30–9:30. Homemade everything. Freshly squeezed juice. Fruit salad. Granola. Raspberry pancakes or seasoned egg entrée. English muffins and breads. "Our own blend of coffee." In gallery or on verandah.

continued . . .

PLUS: Gas fireplace in parlor. Afternoon refreshments. Crystal water glasses. Fresh flowers. Afternoon tea. Bedtime chocolate chip cookies and milk. Guest refrigerator. Spontaneous "turn-of-the-century gossip." Off-street parking. Tour bus, city bus, and airport shuttle leave from the door.

↞ From New York: *"Our first and very impressive bed and breakfast."* From France: *"Un charmant petit nid."*

↞ The Melville House

401/847-0640

39 Clarke Street,
Newport, RI 02840-3023

800/711-7184
FAX 401/847-0956
E-MAIL innkeeper@ids.net
www.melvillehouse.com

HOSTS: Vincent DeRico and Christine Leone
LOCATION: Terrific. On a quiet one-block-long gaslit street (where part of Steven Spielberg's *Amistad* was shot) among other restored Colonial houses. One block from harbor. Around corner from shops and restaurants. Short walk to Touro Synagogue and Trinity Church.
OPEN: Year round. Two-night minimum on weekends, three nights on holidays and events.
RATES: May 1–October 31, $125–$165. November 1–April 30, $85–$125. Fireplace suite (in winter only) $165. Amex, Discover, MC, Visa. ⊞ ❖ ⚯ ⚰

↞ Guests wrote: *"A jewel. . . . We came for one night and stayed for three. . . . A romantic place for a thirtieth anniversary. . . . Expert advice on eateries and places to see. . . . A mini-museum that's really a home. . . . Blueberry ginger waffles a wonderful memory."*

ATTRACTIVE AND WELCOMING. Featured in *Good Housekeeping* magazine's "Weekend Getaways." It's an unpretentious restored 1750 (low-ceilinged) house with oak pieces, braided rugs, lace curtains, and collectibles—and smallish rooms. Vince, a former park ranger and restaurant manager, bought this historic urban B&B in 1993. He subsequently hired Chris as a temporary innsitter and guests' accolades convinced him to bring her on full time.

BED AND BATH: Seven rooms. A first-floor double-bedded room has private shower bath. On second floor, four rooms, each with a double bed, have private shower baths. Winter suite (champagne upon arrival and option of breakfast in bed) has queen bed, Franklin stove insert in fireplace, and a large shower bath; converted in summer to two rooms (one with two twin beds) with shared bath.
BREAKFAST: Summer, 8–10; continental available earlier or later. Winter, 8:30–9:30. Homemade granola, muffins, breads, buttermilk biscuits, scones, Yankee corn bread. Stuffed French toast, fresh fruit sourdough pancakes, Rhode Island johnnycakes.

PLUS: Central air conditioning. Wood-burning fireplace in cozy and comfortable living room. Complimentary 4–6 P.M. tea, sherry, homemade out-of-this-world biscotti and raspberry/white chocolate cheesecake; in winter, homemade soup. Use of gas grill. Sometimes, hosted barbecues here. Off-street parking.

⚞ *Old Beach Inn*

401/849-3479

19 Old Beach Road,
Newport, RI 02840

888/303-5033
FAX 401/847-1236
E-MAIL info@oldbeachinn.com
http://oldbeachinn.com

HOSTS: Luke and Cyndi Murray
LOCATION: In a lovely residential neighborhood just around the corner from Newport Art Museum. Seven-minute walk to harbor, shops, restaurants; 10 minutes to mansions or beach.
OPEN: Year round. Two-night weekend minimum April–June, September, October; three nights on July, August, and special event and holiday weekends.
RATES: Per room. $135–$185 May–October. $100–$155 April and November. $85–$135 December–March. Third person $20. Amex, Discover, MC, Visa.
♥ ⊞ ⌀ ⌁

FLAIR EVERYWHERE. And an obvious love of design, flowers (and floral prints), antiques, whimsy, hand-painted furniture—and people. The 1879 Gothic Victorian was just what the Murrays were looking for shortly after they were married in 1989. Since, they've redecorated several times, added a pond and gazebo to the yard, and done a fabulous remodeling job to the carriage house. And they've been hailed in a gorgeous Japanese magazine spread as well as in *Yankee* and *Boston*.

In addition to innkeeping, Cyndi gardens and is full-time manager at the University of Rhode Island oceanography information center. Her mother created the curtains and duvets, the dolls and cloth rabbits. Multifaceted Luke is bar manager at the Black Pearl Restaurant.

IN RESIDENCE: In carriage house, Callan, age eight; Jake, age six.
BED AND BATH: Seven air-conditioned rooms, all private baths, all with deep wall-to-wall carpeting. Five rooms with working fireplace or stove. *Main house*—first-floor room with queen bed, TV, private full bath. On second floor: queen or double bed; one full bath, three shower baths. In *carriage house*—private exterior entrance for each of two queen-bedded rooms, each with shower bath, individual thermostat, TV. Rollaway available.
BREAKFAST: 8:30–10. Freshly squeezed juice, fresh fruit and yogurt, granola, locally made baked goods, toast-your-own bread and bagels, coffee, tea. Cooked entrée on Sundays. At individual tables in elegant dining room; French doors lead onto flower-filled back porch overlooking grounds.

continued . . .

PLUS: Living, sitting, and dining rooms with fireplaces. Guest pantry; tea and coffee makings provided. Chocolates. Patio. Transportation to/from bus. Off-street parking.

>> From E-mail: *"Wonderful! The innkeepers were exceptional . . . inn tastefully decorated . . . room warm and inviting, as were the two sitting rooms. Highly recommended!"*

>> *Polly's Place*   401/847-2160

349 Valley Road, Route 214, Newport, RI 02842

HOST: Polly Canning

LOCATION: On the Newport–Middletown line, a mile from Newport harbor and beach. On Route 214. Fronted by split rail fence and rosebushes.

OPEN: February–November. Two-night weekend minimum Memorial Day–Labor Day and on holidays.

RATES: Memorial Day–October 30, $90–$135. Off-season, $75–$100.

♥ ᵢ⫪ᵢ ☛ ⊞ ❖ ⚲ ⚝ ❤♡

AS A NEWPORT realtor and B&B hostess, Polly has met film crews and many sailing crew members, as well as croquet players who participated in championship games. Her own travels have taken her to Australia and Africa, where she visited some guests who have stayed in her comfortably furnished extended Cape house.

"The newest addition is a hot tub under the stars! Guests enjoy the large backyard with Adirondack chairs, gazebo, gardens, and weeping willow by the brook. Sometimes they linger in the kitchen or on the deck. I love to bake and often cook dinners for groups at the end of their sailing or filming day. It's a good feeling to see people who arrive as strangers leave as friends."

BED AND BATH: Four rooms. (Egg-crate foam on all beds.) Two first-floor rooms, one with a double, one with king/twins option, share a shower bath. On second floor, two large rooms, each with king-sized bed, private full bath. Plus one-bedroom suite (by the week or month) with kitchen and private entrance.

BREAKFAST: 8–9:30. Strawberry waffles, stuffed French toast, garden quiche, or frittatas. Juices, fruit salad, yogurt, cereal, breads, homemade muffins and jams, coffee, tea. Special diets accommodated. In dining room or on trellised deck overlooking yard with gardens, brook, birds, and sometimes foxes.

PLUS: Living room with brick fireplace and grandfather clock. Bedroom ceiling fans. Fresh flowers. Sometimes, in season, take-home veggies from the garden.

>> From New York, Missouri, Philadelphia: *"Clean and comfortable . . . not fancy . . . cozy and homelike . . . quiet and relaxing . . . gracious hostess . . . knew all the fun things to do."*

⫘ *Rhode Island House*

77 Rhode Island Avenue, Newport, RI 02840-2761

401/848-7787

FAX 401/849-3104
E-MAIL RIH77@wsii.com
www.RhodeIslandHouse.com

HOST: Michael Dupré

LOCATION: Quiet Victorian estate neighborhood. Ten-minute walk to beaches, Cliff Walk, mansions; 15 to shops and waterfront.

OPEN: Year round. Two-night minimum on weekends, three nights on holidays and event weekends.

RATES: May–October weekdays $165–$225, weekends $185–$240. Off-season weekdays $125–$175, weekends $165–$195. Vary according to amenities. ♥ ❖ ⅄

TIMING. A big, beautiful, light-filled private Victorian house with extraordinary multi-paned wide bay windows, many fireplaces, paneled French doors to large common rooms, and arched hallways. All done over in the 1980s with new wiring et al. All for sale in 1993 when Michael, a classical French and contemporary chef (trained at La Varenne in Paris) with experience at Hammersmith Farm and other Newport estates, was interested in opening a B&B.

Furnishings include family antiques and auction finds—rattan, Chippendale, and Americana, with paintings and some bronze sculptures. Windows have sheers and lace; some have "treatments." Press features include a *Country Inns* spread and a glorious *Providence Journal* "food" feature. Off-season, Michael offers memorable weekend cooking classes.

IN RESIDENCE: One singing canary.

FOREIGN LANGUAGE SPOKEN: French.

BED AND BATH: Five carpeted and air-conditioned second-floor rooms with queen beds (two are four-posters). Some with separate dressing area. All private baths; two are shower only, some with separate marble and mirrored Jacuzzi room. Four rooms have working fireplaces.

BREAKFAST: 8:30-10. (Coffee at 7:30.) Buffet sideboard with fresh fruit, granola, juice, homemade breads, muffins. Individually prepared hot entrées such as eggs Florentine, blueberry/lemon French toast, cheese soufflé. Vegetarian option offered. In fireplaced color-filled dining room. (With advance notice, special diets accommodated.)

PLUS: Fireplaced living room, library, morning room. Late-afternoon tea available. Fresh fruit. Mints. Cookie jar. Turndown service. Beach towels. Picnic baskets arranged. Offstreet parking. Video tour of Hammersmith Farm showing Michael preparing a formal dinner there.

⫘ From Pennsylvania: *"Wonderful! . . . refreshments after jaunts in town or on the beach . . . atmosphere so relaxing . . . room was airy, peaceful, and very comfortable . . . special breakfast."*

✍ The Inn at Shadow Lawn
401/847-0902

120 Miantonomi Avenue,
800/352-3750

Middletown, RI 02842
FAX 401/848-6529

E-MAIL randy@shadowlawn.com
www.shadowlawn.com

HOSTS: Selma and Randy Fabricant

LOCATION: Five-minute drive to center of Newport; on Newport–Middletown line. Fronted by a huge lawn in a neighborhood of Cape homes. (Sister house is one block away.)

OPEN: Year round. Two-night minimum on summer weekends, three during special events.

RATES: Spring–fall $125 weekdays, $185–$190 weekends. Plus $35 with kitchen. Off-season $99–$125. Package rates for romantic or antiques weekends and for yacht sails. Amex, CB, Diners, MC, Visa ♥ 🕴 🐖 ⊞ ❖ ⚔ ⚖ 🐾

GRAND. (And, yes, kids are very welcome.) Designed by Richard Upjohn, the architect for Trinity Church in New York and Kingscote in Newport, it's a cross between Italianate and Stick Style. Now on the National Register, the 1856 house is being meticulously restored—the Grand Ballroom was recently completed—by Randy, formerly a lawyer. With the help of friends, Randy refinished the magnificent mahogany woodwork in the breathtaking 18-foot-tall entrance hall. Doorways are arched. The floor is parquet. There are stained glass windows, crystal chandeliers, restored friezes (discovered under wallpaper), and—Randy's latest passion—gardens.

In true B&B style, guests remember the conversations at least as much as the surrounding elegance and antiques. Selma, Randy's mother, was a teacher for thirty-five years in New Jersey. (Her mother was a pioneer in the field of remedial reading.) As the wife of an agent with a major shoe corporation, Selma did a lot of traveling and entertaining in Europe. The Fabricants' treasure, "found" by them in 1994 and noted in two *Victorian Homes* features, is a large-scale restoration that is truly a labor of love.

IN RESIDENCE: In innkeepers' quarters—three labs, Miranda, Katherine, and Lady Cordielia; one cat, Cassiopeia.

BED AND BATH: Eight air-conditioned spacious rooms (mixture of furnishings—at the moment) with king or queen bed, on second and third floors. Seven rooms have working fireplaces. All rooms have private full bath, sitting area, TV, refrigerator, with complimentary Italian mineral water, telephone. Four third-floor rooms have option of kitchen.

BREAKFAST: Usually 8–10. Apple- or blueberry-filled pancakes; Belgian waffles; French toast or egg soufflé. Juices. Cereals. Croissants. Danish pastry. Served at one large table and at another that seats eight, in dining room with a fireplace and yards of damask and lace fashioned into historically accurate window treatments.

PLUS: Port or sherry in library. Verandah overlooking the front lawn.

➳ *Anna's Victorian Connection Host #195*

Portsmouth, RI

LOCATION: Pastoral. No sound of cars. On 2½ acres with large old trees, paddock, and stables (boarded horses) surrounded by 400 acres (for bird-watchers and walkers) of a former nursery. Five and a half miles from downtown Newport; 1½ to Sakonnet River; 2 to 4 miles to beaches.

RESERVATIONS: Year round through Anna's Victorian Connection (page 360), 401/849-2489 or 800/884-4288. E-mail annas@aiconnect.com. Two-night minimum on Jazz and Folk Festival weekends and on holidays.

RATES: $120–$150. $150–$185 with Jacuzzi. Weekdays about $15 less.

♥ ♦♦ ⊞ ❖ ⚄ ⚘ ♜

"Now WE KNOW that the nineteen-room Federal house, built on land deeded by King George III of England, dates back to 1770. When we bought it twenty-seven years ago, just weeks after we were married, it was a fixer-upper. We've done all that—and decided, in 1995, that it was time to share it."

Among their first guests was a couple who planned to move to their preferred location in Newport after the weekend. They entered the gates, drove the quarter mile to the white clapboard Federal house with black shutters, saw the porch rockers, the idyllic setting, and "the most beautiful room we've ever stayed in"—and arranged to stay right here for the week. The front foyer has a marble floor and graceful curving staircase. Wood-burning fireplaces are in the dining and living rooms. Furnishings are Victorian. Curtains are lace. The host is an electrical engineer. His wife is a college English instructor and technical writer and editor.

BED AND BATH: Two large air-conditioned rooms, each with queen bed, TV, private en-suite bath. Room with wood-burning fireplace has bath with shower, no tub. Room with arch divider has shower and Jacuzzi.

BREAKFAST: 8–10:30. Juices. Fruit with cream and yogurt dressings. Bagels, muffins, jams, cereals, hot beverages. Served from reproduction Victorian bar constructed with oak, marble, stained glass, and mirror. Eat in dining room, on the patio, or in your room.

*A*DDITIONAL NEWPORT *B&Bs are available through Anna's Victorian Connection, page 360.*

☙ Historic Jacob Hill Farm
Bed and Breakfast Inn

508/336-9165

888/336-9165

120 Jacob Street, Seekonk, MA 02771-1602

FAX 508/336-0951

E-MAIL Jacob-hill-farm@juno.com

www.Inn-Providence-RI.com

HOSTS: Bill and Eleonora Rezek

LOCATION: A quiet rural hilltop. "Incredible sunsets." Overlooking 50 acres with barn, paddocks, hay fields, woods, oft-photographed antique carriage on front lawn. Among other large properties bordered by stone walls. Minutes to many antiques shops on Route 44. Ten minutes to Brown University in Providence, Rhode Island; 45 to Newport, Plymouth, Mystic, or Cape Cod; 60 to Boston.

OPEN: Year round. Two-night weekend minimum, three on holiday weekends.

RATES: $120; $165–$250 with whirlpool bath. Two-bedroom suite $150–$180. Extra person $25. Some multinight packages and corporate rates for singles. Cottage rates $140–$265. Amex, Discover, MC, Visa. ♥ ⊞ ❖ ⚸ ⅟ ❤◐

☙ From Nova Scotia: *"Exceptional . . . immaculate . . . exquisite collections . . . friendly and warm."* From Ohio: *"Have stayed in many B&Bs. . . . Jacob Hill Farm was our best and most memorable . . . make you feel welcome."* From Texas: *"Helped our long-distance work seem less like work and more like a vacation! . . . Accommodated our unique requirements, including entertaining spouses while some team members had to work late. . . . Recommendations for weekend adventures and best calamari takeout . . . five-star service!"*

WHERE VANDERBILTS participated in horse shows, in the 1920s when this then 200-year-old farmhouse was a hunt club, we now have a B&B that was featured on Home and Garden TV in 1999. The eight-year restoration, completed by the Rezeks in 1998, "replaces our Long Island home, which our friends dubbed 'Bill and El's B&B' even before we had decided to open one." Light colors, traditional wallcoverings and furnishings, and fresh everything give an inviting feeling. A gazebo on the grounds is sometimes the site of a small wedding. Business travelers love the location (and the hospitality). There's a tennis court, an in-ground pool, and a hammock suspended from an old oak tree. And, fun-loving Bill's concierge sevice including suggestions for area tours.

In New York, Bill, a collector of antique toys and glass, worked in his family's plumbing business; El sold AT&T computer systems. Here, close to El's hometown, the enthusiastic (and successful) innkeepers are immersed in the history of the farm and the area.

FOREIGN LANGUAGE SPOKEN: Polish.

BED AND BATH: One cottage, plus, in main house, seven rooms (five are air conditioned and have TV and phone) on three floors; some become suites when rooms are combined. All private baths. Beds—some are canopied—are king, king/twin option, or queen. Amenities vary and include wood-burning stove or fireplace, French doors to full bath with two-person Jacuzzi, bath with two sinks, sliding glass doors to small private porch. Cottage sleeps up to

six; has two bedrooms, shower bath, kitchen, living room with sleep sofa, TV, fireplace.
BREAKFAST: At time arranged with guests the night before. Blueberry pancakes, award-winning stuffed French toast, or omelets. Fruit, muffins, bagels, cereals. In dining room with woodstove or on the deck.

🦅 *Touisset Waterfront*   508/676-9560
845 Pearse Road, Swansea, MA 02777

HOST: Martha Smith
LOCATION: In a quiet neighborhood that's "great for walking." With a large lawn between the house and saltwater Coles River. Two miles and two turns from Route 195. Two miles to Warren, R.I., and bicycle path along the water to Bristol. Eight miles to Bristol, R.I.; 11 to Providence; 22 to Newport.
OPEN: April–November, for sure. Call for other times. Two-night minimum on weekends; three nights on holiday weekends.
RATES: $110 shared bath. Suite $135 two guests; $175 for four guests. ⊞ 🏃 ❤️○

A REAL SEASIDE cottage. Originally part of an early-1900s summer colony for nearby Fall River textile mill owners, this was Martha's grandfather's house, the place where she spent many summers. "It's so quiet that guests often sleep later than intended!" The entire first floor is paneled. White wicker and bamboo furnishings "that have always been here" are freshened with chintzes in what some guests call "Martha Stewart style." The porch ceiling, a conversation piece, is embedded with shells, beach glass, and some coins. Before she opened the property as a B&B, Martham now a first-grade teacher, was marketing director for the Tennis Hall of Fame in Newport.

BED AND BATH: On second floor—two rooms and one suite, all with designer comforters and linens, ceiling fan, cross-ventilation, water view. One room with queen four-poster and one with king/twins option share a hall tub/shower bath and a half bath. Suite has one room with queen bed, another with seven windows and king/twins option with attached tub/shower bath.
BREAKFAST: Flexible hours. Overnight soufflé (house specialty), buttermilk pancakes, omelets, or eggs Benedict. Fruit muffins. Juice and hot beverages. Served in dining room overlooking bay.
PLUS: Popular awninged porch overlooking water. Wood-burning fireplace and TV in living room. Fishing poles for use right here. Swimming (rocky beach).

🦅 From Vermont: *"Consider myself a 'super sleuth' of good places to stay . . . a charming, rustic, comfortable seaside cottage where I felt totally at home and happy."* From New York: *"Decor is lovely, food fantastic, location excellent; and, most of all, Martha is a natural and gracious host."* From England: *"Freshly cut flowers, smart linen, an abundance of plump towels. My stay at this little gem was made all the more memorable by the warm and accommodating hostess."*

⌘ *Admiral Dewey Inn*   401/783-2090

668 Matunuck Beach Road,   800/457-2090
South Kingstown, RI 02879-7021   www.AdmiralDeweyInn.com

HOST: Joan LeBel
LOCATION: In a small village, 1 straight mile from Route 1, 75 yards to the surf and great beach with boardwalk. Across from farm stand. Fifteen-minute walk to wildlife refuge. Ten miles to University of Rhode Island; half mile to Theatre-By-The-Sea; 20 miles to Mystic, Connecticut, and Newport; 4 to Block Island ferry.
OPEN: Year round. Two-night minimum on weekends May–November.
RATES: $90–$140. Single 15 percent less. $20 rollaway. MC, Visa.
♥ ⊞ ❖ ⅍ ⛰ 𝄞 ❤

THIS MIRACLE, Joan's salvation of this Victorian showplace with wraparound porch, is an award-winning inn that has been called "one of five great inns down by the seashore" by *Rhode Island Monthly*. The former beach boardinghouse, a 137-ton plumbingless wreck in 1987, was moved onto a new foundation (see pictorial history album). Now on the National Historic Register, it has indoor baths, claw-footed tables, brass and tall-headboard beds, overstuffed living room chairs, Victorian wallpaper, and lace curtains. Joan, a former antiques dealer and Realtor who has taught in Hawaii, Japan, and Europe, furnished the inn with fine old pieces.

IN RESIDENCE: "Brat and Cat, twin black fluffy litter mates."
FOREIGN LANGUAGES SPOKEN: Polish and French.
BED AND BATH: Ten rooms, each furnished in a different period; most with ocean view. Eight with private shower bath. Two share a full bath. Queen, double, or twin beds. Rollaway available.
BREAKFAST: 8:30–11. Buffet on 1840s table. Fresh fruit, juices, homemade breads and muffins, English muffins or bagels, coffee and tea.
PLUS: Fruit, beverages, munchies always available. Outside shower. Beach towels. Down comforters. Special occasions acknowledged. Pickup at Amtrak station or Westerly airport. Porch rockers. Off-street parking.

⌘ Guests wrote: *"Ten plus . . . great haven near a spectacular beach . . . spacious, clean, comfortable . . . absolutely delightful innkeeper . . . like your favorite aunt . . . informal, friendly atmosphere. . . . Joan LeBel is just plain fun. . . . After an emotional [wedding] day, it was perfect to have the peace and quiet of this lovely Victorian B&B . . . Would not have missed the breakfast—even to catch a ferry! Joan made us feel special."*

H OSPITALITY IS THE KEYNOTE OF B&B.

➤ *Sugar Loaf Hill B&B*   401/789-8715

607 Main Street, Wakefield, RI 02879

HOSTS: David and Stephanie Osborn
LOCATION: Rural setting with big barn and yard in back. Along a main road. Across from 80-acre farm with extensive stone wall and meadow. Ten minutes to beaches or Block Island ferry; 8 to University of Rhode Island or Theatre-By-The-Sea; 20 to Newport; 30 to casinos. Five-minute walk downhill to town and restaurants.
OPEN: Year round.
RATES: $120 suite. $80–$95 queen. $75–$85 twins, shared bath. 👫 📷 ⊞ ❖ 🐾 🍴

A TRUE B&B experience awaits in this 1840 Greek Revival house with 1700s ell that the Osborns bought after signing an agreement penned by the owners on a kitchen table napkin. The lovable llamas came with the purchase. So did much revitalization work in preparation for the B&B opening in 1998. If the weather is "right," you may have a ride along the Narragansett waterfront in the Osborns' 1949 or 1951 MG convertibles. (David, a salesman, restores them as a hobby.) Or you may hear about some neighborhood tales. (Stephanie grew up a mile down the road.) Or about travels; Stephanie, a hairdresser for thirty years, is now a travel agent specializing in cruises—which she and David take several times a year. One English couple came for two days and stayed for nine. Guests from Michigan wrote about the gracious hospitality, "the topic of conversation all the way back to Kalamazoo."

IN RESIDENCE: Two llamas, Deli and Annie. Two "mostly outdoor" cats.
FOREIGN LANGUAGES SPOKEN: Little Spanish and Greek.
BED AND BATH: One suite and two rooms on second floor. Suite includes low-ceilinged room with queen bed, private full bath, skylight, sitting room. Sliding glass doors to private upper deck overlooking woods. Room with queen bed has wood-burning fireplace, private shower bath. Room with king/twins option shares tub/shower bath.
BREAKFAST: 7:15. (Juice and muffins available 6:30–9.) Fresh fruit, bananas or raspberries and cream, or baked apples. German apple or johnnycakes; eggs with bacon, or sausage; pancakes; thick French toast. Served in fireplaced dining room or outside.
PLUS: Wood-burning fireplaces in den (with TV/VCR) and living room. Afternoon snacks. Guest refrigerator. Beverages. Front porch rockers with farm view.

B&Bs OFFER THE ULTIMATE CONCIERGE SERVICE.

﹋ *Grandview Bed & Breakfast*

212 Shore Road, Westerly, RI 02891

401/596-6384

800/447-6384

FAX: CALL TO ACTIVATE

E-MAIL: info@GrandviewBandB.com

www.GrandviewBandB.com

HOST: Patricia Grande

LOCATION: High on a hill, set back from Route 1A, overlooking Block Island Sound and Winnapaug Pond. Walk to golf courses and tennis courts; short drive to beaches, restaurants, Newport, Watch Hill, Mystic Seaport, Foxwoods/Mohegan Sun casinos.

OPEN: Year round. Advance reservations required. Two-night minimum on weekends Memorial Day–Columbus Day.

RATES: $85–$105 Memorial Day–Columbus Day. $70–$90 off-season. Senior citizens' discount. $15 extra person. Amex, MC, Visa. ♥ ♦♦ ☎ ⊞ ❖ ⚡ ⚘ ❤☽

﹋ Guests wrote to me about *"the quintessential hostess . . . A-plus for warmth, friendliness, cleanliness, food . . . unpretentious . . . welcomed our seven-year-old daughter with open arms . . . brilliant choice for our family reunion . . . for our wedding. . . . Customers who attend our company conference love to stay at Grandview. . . . The 'at home' place to book our actors and theater guests. . . . A base for our birding group . . . a 4:30 a.m. coffeepot for my fisherman husband. . . . Retreat groups break into song before each discussion or art session. . . . Serene, tranquil setting. . . . Our 16-year-old son came—reluctantly—with us. Pat won him over . . . cookies upon arrival, catered to his vegetarian taste, invited him to investigate TV and video in adjoining wing. . . . He characterized Pat's hospitality: 'She's just like a mom without the nagging.' As for us, we enjoyed a wonderful ocean view from our room as we caught up on our sleep and reading. . . . A lovely experience."*

AND AN AWARD to boot—for "impeccable surroundings, warmth and hospitality to guests, and caring for the community." The big turn-of-the-century house with wraparound stone porch and ocean view was the inspiration for Pat's third career, another perfect match. A former chamber of commerce president, Pat was a teacher and later worked in broadcasting.

BED AND BATH: Nine rooms with a king, a double, or two twin beds. Some with porch and/or water view. Family room (cot available) with small refrigerator, large sink, cable TV. Private shower baths (one has antique tub also) for four rooms (with ceiling and oscillating fans) in wing attached to main house by family room. Some shared baths with shower and/or tub.

BREAKFAST: 8–9:30. Strawberry shortcake, blueberry cobbler, hot cranberry apple crisp with whipped cream, "or today's new recipe." Freshly baked muffins. For toaster, bagels, English muffins, raisin bread. Fruit; yogurt; cereals; juices, coffee, tea. Buffet on sunporch or on open wraparound porch.

PLUS: Welcoming beverage. Fruit. Fieldstone living room fireplace. Family room in wing with cable TV, VCR, video library, games. Adirondack chairs on spacious grounds. Outside shower. Babysitting with notice.

⤳ *Woody Hill B&B*   401/322-0452

149 South Woody Hill Road,   E-MAIL **woodyhill@riconnect.com**
Westerly, RI 02891-5901   **www.woodyhill.com**

HOST: Ellen L. Madison
LOCATION: Just off busy Route 1, but really in the country, on top of hill surrounded by acres of woods and fields. Two miles from ocean beaches. Minutes from Mystic Seaport, Newport, Foxwoods Resort Casino.
OPEN: Year round. Two nights preferred for summer and holiday weekends.
RATES: $70–$98. $125 room with French doors to garden and pool; $159 suite with library. $10 additional person (floor mattress for children) in room. Off-season $10–$35 less. ♥ ♦♦♦ ▰ ⊞ ❖ ⚔ ⅛ ♥☌

ROCKING CHAIRS overlook the flower and herb gardens, a 40-foot in-ground pool and a 10-acre field with deer (frequently) and woods beyond. This rambling Colonial you-can-hardly-tell reproduction is a welcoming country place "without manicured lawns" that has been discovered by romantics on a getaway, small reunions, and wedding planners too. "So far, nary a drop of rain has fallen on a wedding guest or bride!" Fireplaces are made with old bricks. There are wide floorboards, nooks and crannies, antiques, and a library with walls of books, shuttered windows, and window seats.

My husband and I loved our stay during a cycling/swimming vacation. Another time I met Virginians on a genealogical mission, who were here because they had read (in this book) that Ellen's family has lived within a 2-mile radius of her house since 1636. This multifaceted hostess, a high school English teacher with a Ph.D., hosts winter fireplace cooking weekends where you do as little or as much as you wish.

IN RESIDENCE: Two cats—Bailie, "a tiny black-and-white dynamo, and Opie, her bigger, more sedate brother."
BED AND BATH: Four rooms. First floor—large room with curtained queen bed, one three-quarter bed, cable TV/VCR, French doors to gardens and pool, hall double shower, private entrance; can be a suite if combined with library, which has queen sofa bed. Garden (entrance) room with double bed, en-suite shower bath. Second floor—large room with one double bed and one curtained queen bed, en-suite shower bath. Another large room with canopied queen bed, private next-to-door hall full bath.
BREAKFAST: 8–9:30. A huge repertoire. Maybe strawberry nut or blueberry ginger muffins, seasonal fruit with interesting sauces, pear sauce and waffles or apple crisp. Served in keeping room with walk-in fireplace and bake-oven.
PLUS: Grill and refrigerator at pool for guests' use.

⤳ From New Hampshire, New York, Massachusetts, Connecticut: *". . . hard to find such a memorable place in these days of rush, rush, rush. . . . Perfect setting for my daughter's summer wedding . . . Antiques-filled rooms with just the right blend of simplicity and elegance . . . suggestions for restaurants and sightseeing were 'right on'. . . . Breakfast pleases the eye and palate. . . . Genuine exuberance and hospitality."*

➷ The Metcalfs   401/783-3448

3682 Kingstown Road, West Kingston, RI 02892-1410

HOSTS: Barbara and Brian Metcalf
LOCATION: In a residential area along Route 138, main road from I-95 (8 miles from
   B&B) to Newport (18 miles). Two miles to historic Kingston Village and
   University of Rhode Island; 27 miles to Mystic, Connecticut.
OPEN: Year round. Two-night weekend minimum June–Labor Day.
RATES: $75 May–November 15. $65 November 15–April. Single, 10-percent less.
   Third-night discount. Amex, MC, Visa. ♥♥ ⅙

A REAL COTTAGE. Not a gilded age mansion! A 1920s cottage that the Metcalfs, inspired by
a B&B trip to the British Isles, completely renovated before opening in 1997. Decor is
fresh and crisp, comfortable and immaculate. Now the hosts, Rhode Island natives who
are parents of five grown sons, meet appreciative travelers from all over the world. Some
are overflow guests of area residents, who are very pleased with the changes made to this
visible (main road) property.
   Brian's job as project supervisor for a construction company took the Metcalfs to
Tennessee and to North Carolina, where they built their own new home. Barbara has uti-
lized her business management degree as a personal banker.

IN RESIDENCE: In hosts' quarters—two black Labs.
BED AND BATH: On second (guests') floor—two air-conditioned rooms. One with queen
bed, private tub/shower bath. King/twins option with private shower bath.
BREAKFAST: 7–9:30. (After 9:30—fruit, rolls, coffee.) Fresh fruit. Homemade fruit
muffins and breads. Pancakes, waffles, or quiche. Juice. Hot beverages. Served in breakfast room or on deck. Special diets accommodated with advance notice.
PLUS: Ceiling fans in every room but the dining room. TV/VCR in living room. Wicker-
furnished front porch. "Hidden" deck and backyard with picket fence and gardens.
Lots of where-to-go and what-to-do suggestions.

   ➷ From Pennsylvania: "What makes this B&B so special are the two people who
run it. Barbara and Brian are gracious, friendly, and caring. Their home is spotless and inviting . . . breakfasts beautiful and delicious . . . provided transportation to and from train station . . . like a visit with family."

> U NLESS OTHERWISE STATED, rates in this book are per room for two
>   and include breakfast in addition to all the amenities in "Plus." As for
> taxes and gratuities, please see page IX.

☞ *The Haddie Pierce House*   401/294-7674

146 Boston Neck Road, North Kingstown, RI 02852-5758   FAX 401/294-7674
E-MAIL haddie@bigplanet.com
www.haddiepierce.com

HOSTS: Darya and John Prassl
LOCATION: Residential. Surrounded by expansive lawn, mature trees, and flowers. Set
back from street—with other restored homes—that leads (5-minute walk)
to beach on Narragansett Bay. Five-minute walk to village shops. Fifteen-
minute drive to Newport, 30 to Block Island ferry or to Providence. Ten
minutes from 1-95.
OPEN: Year round.
RATES: May–October $97 queen with fireplace, private bath; $87 queen, twin or
double with shared bath. November–April $10 less. Singles $10 less.
Kayaking packages. Amex, Discover, MC, Visa. ☞ ⊞ ⚬ ⚬

THIS VICTORIAN National Register house with widow's walk and wraparound porch is
home to John, a mathematics teacher at the Naval Academy Preparatory School, and
Darya, a technology company representative. From their three years (1984–1987) of living
in Germany, they brought back memories of extensive travels and B&B stays. After purchasing this house in 1994, they restored it (and the carriage house too) and decorated
with pastels, lace curtains, and Victorian furnishings. Now they garden. They are walkers
and skiers. And they are active in the local historical society. As hosts they greet guests
who "are pleasantly surprised by the charm and quietness of Wickford—its proximity
both to well-known attractions and to a wonderful lesser-known place for hiking, biking,
or a picnic lunch."

IN RESIDENCE: One golden retriever, Chelsea. Miss B, a calico cat.
BED AND BATH: Four air-conditioned second-floor rooms. Queen room with fireplace
(and a Victorian doll collection) has private shower bath; can become a suite with another queen-bedded room. That second queen-bedded room, one with a double bed, and
one with two twins share two baths (one tub, one shower).
BREAKFAST: 8–9:30. Fresh fruit; bread or muffins. Apple-stuffed French toast, crepes,
pannekoekan (a Dutch pancake), or fiesta egg casserole. Served in dining room furnished
with French antiques.
PLUS: Double parlor with wood-burning fireplace in each room. Late-afternoon refreshments. Fresh fruit. Front porch with wicker and Adirondack chairs. Brick patio.

☞ From Vermont, Massachusetts, Texas: *"Ambiance, graciousness, Victoriana—a
delight!. . . One of the nicest places I've ever stayed. . . . Apple pancakes to die for."* From
Spain: *"Made me feel like I was at home."*

✈ *The John Updike House*   401/294-4905

19 Pleasant Street, Wickford Village,   E-MAIL **updikebnb@cyberzone.net**
North Kingstown, RI 02852-5019

HOSTS: Mary Anne and Bill Sabo
LOCATION: Overlooking Wickford Harbor and Narragansett Bay, with view of fishing
boats, yachts, and Wickford's famous morning and sunset light, an artist's
delight. On tree-lined street in historic village that "guests fall in love with."
Five-minute walk—past interesting doorways and well-tended gardens of
eighteenth- and nineteenth-century clapboard houses—to shops, galleries,
Old Narragansett Church (antique organ, no electricity). Within ten minutes of Newport and beaches; 25 minutes to Providence.
OPEN: Year round.
RATES: $90 per room. $180 two-room suite. $195 suite with kitchen. $10 one-night
surcharge. 🏃 ⚑ 🎁 🐾 🍴 🎿

✈ From Australia: *"After traveling for two months in Spain and France, in small
inns, this B&B was a revelation. Scrupulously clean, carefully selected furnishings, up-to-date
bathroom, comfortable bed, private balcony overlooking cove . . . plus ongoing travel information from the hosts."* From Florida, New York, Massachusetts, Texas, Colorado: *"The most
mystical, enchanting experience. . . . Happiness abides. . . . Breakfast is exceptional. (I'm an
extremely health-conscious and fussy eater!) . . . Ate lunch on deck with magnificent view overlooking gardens and bay. . . . Loved being close to town and not needing a car . . . town itself is
made for walking and gawking at well-kept historic buildings and gardens. . . . Everything
was 'just right' or exceeded our expectations."*

WHAT MORE is there to say? Pictured in the state's film-location brochure, this handsome
250-year-old center chimney Georgian house, named for its Colonial builder (no relation
to author John Updike), has been the Sabo's home since 1980. On the National Register
and a B&B since 1985, it is filled with period furnishings—all featured in a *Country
Traditional Decorating Ideas* article. Bill was a senior chief in the U.S. Navy and then a research administrator. Mary Anne, formerly an interior designer, is also retired.

FOREIGN LANGUAGES SPOKEN: "Some rusty and fractured French and Spanish."
BED AND BATH: Private exterior entrance to guest (second) floor that has two large front
rooms (good cross-ventilation), one with a double spool bed, other with two four-poster
twin beds; shared tub/bath shower; a large guest living room with TV and phone; and a
large deck with that mesmerizing view. Full kitchen available.
BREAKFAST: 6–9. Waffles, crepes (Hungarian *palacsinta*), puffed oven pancakes, Scotch
scones, homemade jellies and jams, syrup from homegrown or locally harvested fruit.
Fresh fruit, juice, hot beverages. Served in sunroom overlooking water.
PLUS: Private entrance. Access to private saltwater beach. Beach towels. Window fans.
Fresh fruit. Tea and coffee always available. Off-street parking.

KEY TO SYMBOLS

♥ Lots of honeymooners come here.

†ⁱ† Families with children are very welcome.

📺 This B&B is a private home, not an inn.

⊞ Groups can reserve this entire B&B.

❖ Travel agents' commissions paid.

🐾 Sorry, no guests' pets allowed.

🚭 No smoking inside *or* no smoking at all.

🌊 Waterfront location.

👥 Off the beaten path.

❤️ Weddings booked here. For details, please inquire.

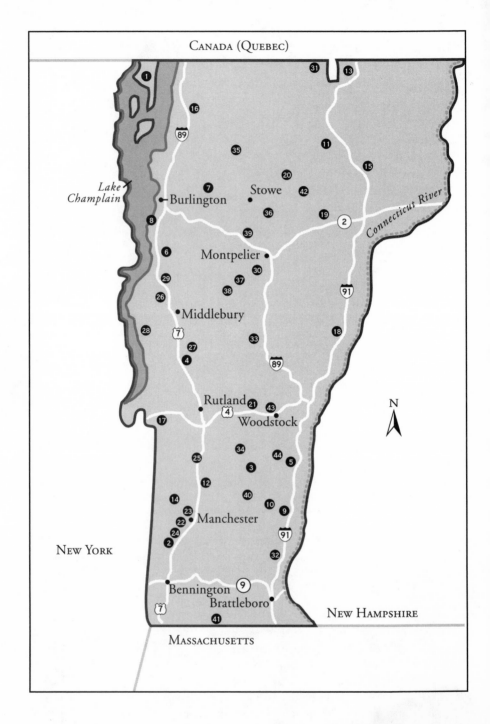

CANADA (QUEBEC)

Lake
Champlain

Burlington

Stowe

Montpelier

Middlebury

Rutland
Woodstock

Manchester

NEW YORK

Bennington
Brattleboro

NEW HAMPSHIRE

MASSACHUSETTS

Connecticut River

N

*The numbers on this map indicate the locations of B&Bs described in
detail in this chapter.*

VERMONT

*Can't find the community you wish to visit? Check with a reservation service
described at the beginning of this chapter.*

VERMONT RESERVATION SERVICE

≫ *American Country Collection*

1353 Union Street, Schenectady, NY 12308

PHONE: 518/370-4948 or 800/810-4948 (for reservations) Monday–Friday 10–5. Other times by chance. Closed holidays.

FAX: 518/393-1634

E-MAIL: Carolbnbres@MSN.com

URL: www.BandBReservations.com

LISTINGS: One hundred. Mostly hosted private residences. Some are inns. Many are on the National Register of Historic Places. Vermont listings include Bennington, Burlington, Hartland, Jacksonville, Middletown Springs, Wallingford, Waterbury, and Wolcott. In the Berkshires of western Massachusetts: Great Barrington, Lee, Lenox, Pittsfield. In New York State, most are in the Albany/Saratoga, middle and lower Hudson Valley, Catskills, Central Leatherstocking, Lake George, Lake Champlain, and eastern Adirondack regions. Complimentary directory available.

RESERVATIONS: Two weeks in advance preferred. Last-minute accepted when possible. Two- to three-day minimum stay at some locations in season.

RATES: $60–$75 single, $75–$175 double. Some weekly rates. Senior citizen discounts midweek (excluding foliage season, holidays, and Saratoga in August). $5–$10 one-night administrative fee. Deposit required is equal to one night's lodging. If cancellation made no less than fourteen days (thirty days in season) before scheduled arrival, deposit refunded less $10 service fee; same refund policy for less than fourteen days (thirty days in season) if room is rebooked. Amex, Discover, MC, Visa.

SINCE 1986 this reservation service has selected hosts who enjoy people and who are involved in their communities. "And they are creative cooks!" Owner/director Carol Matos, a tax consultant and former training manager, is a B&B hostess in her own home. Because she personally visits and inspects each B&B, she is knowledgeable about the unique qualities of each accommodation and its hosts.

PLUS: Romance and dinner packages available. Pickup at transportation points provided by some hosts. Short- and long-term stays booked for relocation and business purposes.

~ *Thomas Mott Homestead Bed & Breakfast* 802/796-3736

63 Blue Rock Road,
Alburg, VT 05440-4002

RESERVATIONS 800/348-0843
FAX 802/796-373
E-MAIL tmott@together.net
www.thomas-mott-bb.com

HOST: Patrick J. Schallert
LOCATION: All by itself on Lake Champlain, with wonderful mountain views, sunrises, sunsets. An hour to Montreal Island, Burlington, Adirondack Mountains; fifteen minutes to rural Isle La Motte—perfect for cycling; 1.5 miles east of Highway 2.
OPEN: Year round.
RATES: $75–$95. $10 for extra person. Amex, CB, Diners, Discover, MC, Visa.
♥ ⬛ ⊞ ❖ ⚰ ⚷ ♨ 林 🐾

~ From dozens of guests notes written to me: *"Treated like king and queen . . . full moon glistening on the lake . . . .Felt pampered and comfortable. . . . Sensitive about allowing private time yet available. . . . Funny and warm. . . . The place has a special spirit. . . . Pat knew just where to send us for dinner . . . spotless . . . lots of windows . . . tranquil . . . Cette maison est chaleureuse et l'accueil est unique. On se sent chez soi!!"*

EXUBERANT PAT loves making guests happy. Ben & Jerry's delivery truck comes every Thursday to refill the help-yourself ice-cream freezer. The 1838 farmhouse was totally renovated (beams still show) in 1987 after Pat retired from his travels to French châteaux and German estates, where he purchased premium and rare wines to distribute through his Los Angeles–based company. (A former Jesuit, he is also a ham radio buff—K6KAG/1—and has master's degrees in criminology and liberal arts.) Here he cooks, takes pictures of every guest (for you and the album), provides canoes, and greets many international and business travelers—as well as those who come to do everything and then just stay here. It was a perfect stop for us during a drive/cycle trip through northern Vermont.

BED AND BATH: Five lakeview rooms with handmade quilts, private bath, individual thermostat. First-floor corner room with a queen and a twin bed, full bath. Second-floor rooms (each with ceiling fan) have queen (one is extra long, one has fireplace and private balcony) or king "that Kareem could get lost in"; private entrance.
BREAKFAST: Usually 6:30–9. "Like a Chinese meal, with everyone trying something different." Berry pancakes; decadent French toast with five kinds of nuts, cream cheese, pure vanilla from Mexico, home-ground nutmeg; omelets with fresh crab or shrimp. Homemade jams.

PLUS: Boat dock. Fireplaced living room. Upright piano. Lawn games. Three porches. Fresh fruit. Flowers for honeymooners. Gazebo. Cross-country skiing and snowmobiling

⚓ Hill Farm Inn

458 Hill Farm Road,
Arlington, VT 05250-9311

802/375-2269
800/882-2545
FAX 802/375-9918
E-MAIL hillfarm@vermontel.com
www.hillfarminn.com

HOSTS: Craig and Kathleen Yanez
LOCATION: Peaceful setting on 50 acres (6 are Federal conservation lands). With mile-long nature trail from inn along Battenkill River (fishing) and back. One-half mile off Route 7A. At the foot of Mount Equinox. Four miles south of Manchester.
OPEN: Year round. Two-night minimum for foliage season weekends and some holiday weekends.
RATES: $65–$75 shared bath; $95–$125 private bath; suites: $125–$150; Cabins (open May–October) $75–$145. Additional guests $20 per adult; children's rates vary. Packages include Thanksgiving weekend with dinner, Christmas cut-your-own-tree, maple sugaring (March), antiquing (April).
♥ 🚶 ⊞ 🎿 🍴

THERE AREN'T many New England B&Bs with a large red barn and silo. This genuinely old-fashioned inn, with appeal for families as well as romantics, has been welcoming guests since 1920. The main (Federal) building was built in 1830, while the Cape guest house dates back to 1790. Surrounded by 50 acres of lawns, gardens, and farmlands, the inn has a real-farm atmosphere complete with sheep, goats, chickens, rabbits, two cats, and one dog. There's an upright piano in the homey living room and a wraparound porch with rockers. As Kathleen says, "It's grandmother's country house!"

Kathleen is the daughter of the innkeepers at the (nearby) Inn on Covered Bridge, Norman Rockwell's former home. Before taking over the Hill Farm Inn in 1998, Kathleen and Craig had eight years' experience at a smaller Vermont B&B. Here, where refurnishing and redecorating "will always be ongoing," they have combined some rooms into suites. And they prepare dinners for family reunions.

IN RESIDENCE: In hosts' quarters—three children.
BED AND BATH: Eleven rooms on first and second floors of main inn and guest house. Private or semiprivate baths. King, queen, double, or twin beds available. Plus two suites (each with gas fireplace, TV, private porch and entrance)—one with sitting room, skylight, ceiling fan, and air conditioning; one with small living room and kitchenette. Four cabins (two with kitchenettes) are available May–October.

continued . . .

BREAKFAST: 7:30–9:30. Cooked to order from menu. Buttermilk blueberry pancakes, French toast, eggs (almost) any style. Country sausage and bacon. Homemade toast, muffins, and granola. Oatmeal and cold cereal. Juices. Hot beverages. In fireplaced dining room with classical music.

PLUS: Fireplace and TV in two parlors. Table fans. Indoor and outdoor games, swing set. Snowshoes, cross-country skis, and ice skates for use on premises. Wine or beer available.

ᔥ *The Leslie Place*   802/259-2903

Box 62, Belmont, VT 05730

HOST:	Mary K. Gorman
LOCATION:	Quiet! On undeveloped (west) side of Okemo Mountain. On dirt road, minutes from a paved one, with meadows, mountain views, and, in summer, cows. Near Long Trail, horseback riding, swimming, museums, canoeing—lots! Fifteen minutes to Weston Priory and Playhouse; 25 miles from Route 91.
OPEN:	May 1–November 1. Two-night minimum on foliage weekends. Advance reservations recommended.
RATES:	Vary according to season. $65–$75 double bed. $70–$85 larger rooms. $20 each additional person. Singles $10 less. ⊞ ⚔ ⚒ ⚘

ᔥ Guests wrote to me: *"Made to feel like extended family . . . where guests set the pace . . . magnificent Vermont vistas . . . a place of natural beauty and harmony . . . slept soundly far from the madding crowd . . . privacy . . . extensive old-fashioned flower gardens . . . charming, spacious, uncluttered yet old-world style; real Vermont . . . and Mary's French toast is simply the best."*

IT WAS DIFFERENT when Mary moved in in 1975. "The house had been empty for sixteen years. No bathrooms, water, heat, or electricity! I was young and determined, I guess. Although my family had doubts, I didn't, as I milked cows next door and restored this house. Everything was done by the Gorman Method, mixed with tears, laughter, frustration, and pleasure. I furnished with a rescued schoolhouse piano, hooked rugs, some of my own oil paintings, and a Kalamazoo cookstove. Now I sell firewood in the fall, make maple sugar in the spring, and share my home with wonderful guests."

BED AND BATH: Three rooms; all private shower baths. First floor—smaller room with double bed. Second floor—two large rooms, both with sloping ceilings; one with queen bed; the other with queen bed and one twin bed.

BREAKFAST: Until 9:30. Menu varies daily. French toast, egg dishes, pancakes, or apple crisp. Homemade muffins or breads, maple syrup, and granola. Cereals. Juice. Coffee. Served in guests' dining room. Special diets accommodated with advance notice.

PLUS: Guests' common room. Guest kitchenette (separate small room). Living room with gas-burning cast iron stove. Library with extensive Vermont collection. Games. TV. Picnic table. Lawn lounge furniture. Gazebo.

🐦 The Lilac Inn

53 Park Street,
Brandon, VT 05733-1121

802/247-5463
800/221-0720
FAX 802/247-5499
E-MAIL lilacinn@sover.net
www.lilacinn.com

HOST: Michael Shane
LOCATION: On historic, tree-lined street. Minutes' walk to village center with Brandon Artists' Guild, antiques shops, town hall (being restored), museums. Close to Warren Kimble (folk artist) Studio, mountain biking, golf. Fifteen minutes north to cross-country skiing, thirty north to Middlebury College, thirty minutes south to Killington downhill slopes.
OPEN: Year round. Two-night minimum on holidays and mid-September–mid-October.
RATES: $120–$190. Holidays and foliage season $185–$260. Package rates for theme weekends including yoga, journal writing, couples' retreats. Amex, Discover, MC, Visa. ♥ ⊞ ❖ ⚔ ⚒ ❦

"JUST WHAT I imagined a country inn to be," say many first-time guests. The grand-scale National Historic Register property, a Greek Revival mansion fronted by five arches, was a two-year restoration project in the early 1990s. In California, Michael was a contractor fulfilling clients' dreams of a home, studio, or restaurant. Here, together with a designer, he created a luxury inn for getaways, for weddings, and for chamber or family concerts too —"all in a marvelous small town that is being rediscovered in the best of ways."

Inside there's an intimate library with wood-burning fireplace. An informal dining room with Windsor chairs. And a glassed-in ballroom with crystal chandeliers and an 1860s square grand piano. Grounds—made for strolling or stargazing—have gardens, a small pond, a gazebo, a patio, and a putting green.

IN RESIDENCE: Two dogs (pugs). Two cats: one Himalayan and one alley cat.
BED AND BATH: Nine air-conditioned second-floor rooms vary in size and amenities. Eight have queen beds; three with wood-burning fireplace. One room has two canopied twin beds. All en-suite private tiled baths; bridal suite has whirlpool tub.
BREAKFAST: 8–9; 10 on Sundays. Fresh herb omelets, stuffed French toast, hot/cold cereals, yogurts. Homemade breads and muffins. Juices. Fresh fruit. Served (buffet style on weekends) in breakfast conservatory.
PLUS: Dinners, by reservation, for overnight guests, Wednesday–Saturday. Inquire about special events.

🐦 Old Mill Inn

79 Stone Mill Dam Road,
Brandon, VT 05733-9522

802/247-8002

800/599-0341
E-MAIL oldmill@together.net
www.oldmillbb.com

HOSTS: Cindy and Ed Thomas
LOCATION: Quiet. One mile from Brandon green. On 5 acres of woods, meadows, farmland, and "rushing stream with swimming hole." Forty minutes south to Killington or north to Shelburne Museum. Near miles of hiking and biking trails. Eighteen-hole public golf course (cross-country ski, snowshoe, and hike in winter) borders property.
OPEN: Year round. Two-night minimum September 15–October 31.
RATES: $75 weekdays, $85 weekends. September 1–November 1 and holidays $85 weekdays, $95 weekends. Singles $20 less. Extra adult in room $30; child $20. ♥ 🛇 🛏 🎏 🐕 🐾 🎿

"FOR OUR move to Vermont, after Ed's 1995 retirement as an electronics engineer, we searched for a country place with a stream, mountain views, barns and outbuildings for a studio and woodworking shop, a historic farmhouse with a coziness to it. Our first stay—in the late 1980s—at this former dairy farm, a restored 1786 Colonial, was because of your book, Bernice. Even then it felt like home, decorated with country antiques—much like our restored 1684 New Jersey residence, where we kept a few pleasure horses for foxhunting. And it just happened to be a B&B. Happily, we decided to dovetail innkeeping with our woodworking (Ed) and folk art painting (Cindy) projects." Guests, too, appreciate this style of hosting:

🐦 From Massachusetts and Minnesota: *"Unique . . . hospitality is 'homespun'. . . friendly and fun . . . felt like a guest of the family enjoying their charming living room, TV room, library, and cozy kitchen . . . farm atmosphere with all the animals. . . . Loved it!"*

IN RESIDENCE: Daisy, a golden retriever. Maggie, a cock-a-poo. Barn cats, chickens, and miniature horses—Bess and Punkin.
BED AND BATH: Four second-floor rooms, each with handmade quilts, sitting area, private bath, individual thermostat, hair dryer. Queen bed, ceiling fan, hall tub/shower bath. Double bed, en-suite shower bath, air conditioning. A double and a twin bed, en-suite tub/shower bath, air conditioning. Another with a double and a twin, en-suite shower bath, deck overlooking golf course. Rollaway and crib available.
BREAKFAST: 7:30–9:30. French toast, eggs, pancakes, quiche, waffles. Ed's specialty—omelets with farm-fresh eggs, sausage or bacon, and home fries. Homemade breads and muffins. Juice, fresh fruit, and hot beverage. Served in breakfast room that has mural done by Cindy.
PLUS: Complimentary wine and cheese hour. Two living rooms (one with satellite TV) with gas-fired woodstoves. Library with computer hookup. Wicker-furnished porch. Campfire pit for "s'mores." Special occasions acknowledged. Antiques shop and folk art gallery on site.

ᕗᕗ *Rosebelle's Victorian Inn*   802/247-0098

P.O. Box 370, Route 7,   888/767-3235
Brandon, VT 05733-0370   E-MAIL rosebel@together.net
                                                      www.rosebelles.com

HOSTS: Ginette and Norm Milot
LOCATION: On main road. Minutes' walk to historic town center and fine restaurants.
Close to Killington, Pico, Sugarbush downhill and Blueberry Hill and
Mountain Top cross-country skiing. Fourteen miles north of Rutland, 13
south of Middlebury, 10 to Long Trail entrance. Great snowshoeing, hiking,
biking. One mile to eighteen-hole Neshobe Golf Course.
OPEN: Year round. Two-night minimum on holiday weekends.
RATES: Weekends $75–$85 shared bath, $85–$95 private. Singles $10 less. Package
rates. Senior discounts. Amex, MC, Visa. ♥ ☎ ⊞ ❖ ⚔ ⅍

THIS 1839 Second French Empire telltale mansard, now listed on the National Register,
was once part of the Underground Railway. The fireplaced living room is furnished with
Victorian pieces. Etched glass is in the front door. The gardens, matured since the Milots
bought the inn in 1990, attract butterflies and hummingbirds. And then there's the lawn
swing that "everyone tries. It's a conversation piece!"

Norm, a state college food service director, has been in the food service industry since
the early 1960s. He and Ginette, self-appointed official inn painter (of gingerbread too),
have lived in Canada, New York, New Jersey, and Massachusetts.

IN RESIDENCE: One dog—Heidi, a black female pug. Rosie, a tiger cat. And Sebastian, a
bluepoint Himalayan. Two ducks.
FOREIGN LANGUAGE SPOKEN: *Ici on parle Français.*
BED AND BATH: Five spacious rooms with individual thermostats. Second floor—three
rooms with queen or double beds share two baths (two could be private); one bath has
shower, the other a claw-foot tub. Third floor—private shower baths for room with extra-
long twin beds and room with queen bed; intricate custom-made tin ceilings with fans.
BREAKFAST: 7:30–9. Seasonal fresh fruit, juices, gourmet flavored coffee, homemade pastries. Cooked-to-order omelet or Ginette's orange French toast with pure Vermont maple
syrup. "No one leaves hungry!" Served in dining room or on porch.
PLUS: Porch rockers. Fireplaced living room. Afternoon tea. Fresh fruit. Croquet.
Information on bicycle routes, hiking trails, covered bridges. Gift shop on premises.

ᕗᕗ Guests wrote: *"Delightful accommodations, service, and company . . . delicious
food . . . very friendly innkeepers."*

⤳ *Mill Brook B&B*   802/484-7283

Route 44, P.O. Box 410,   E-MAIL millbrook@outboundconnection.com
Brownsville, VT 05037-0410   www.outboundconnection.com/millbrook.htm

HOST: Kay Carriere
LOCATION: Across from Mount Ascutney, in a rural village "with famous summer baked
bean suppers; back roads for walking or mountain cycling; and, next to
property, a brook." Ten miles from I-91, 16 south of Woodstock, 30 to
Dartmouth College. Walk to covered bridge.
OPEN: Year round. Two-night minimum on weekends; three nights Christmas
week and Columbus Day (October) and February Presidents' weekends.
RATES: Vary according to room size. $67–$97, suites $107–$137. Foliage and
Presidents' weekends and Christmas holiday week $77–$107, suites
$117–$147. Singles $10 less. Extra person $25; children under twelve free.
$20 short-stay surcharge on weekends, holidays, and foliage season. Fourth
night free. Extended weekend discounts. Whole house rate (14 guests).
Amex, MC, Visa. ♥ 👫 ☞ ⊞ ❖ 🍴 ⚔ ♥○

"WE ARE A farmhouse—not a mansion—with a down-home feeling. We have antiques
and some more recent pieces, a wood-burning stove, board games, croquet and volleyball,
a hammock, picnic tables, a grill—and, on the deck, a hot tub. (Reminder: Bring swim
suits.) Sheets are line-dried and hand-ironed year round. Cloth napkins are used, even for
tea—served with cake year round; in ski season we add soup. You can go anywhere and
have a Sara Lee cake, but not here. Sit in the gazebo by the brook. There's a mountain to
climb and a brook to fish or swim in (or listen to). Need a thermos, backpack, ski jacket?
It's yours for the borrowing."

Kay, "Mom" or "Aunt Kay" according to guests, is a food writer/cookbook author, a New
Orleans native who was a college hospitality instructor and hotel salesperson in New Jersey.
She makes all her jellies, pies, and omelets with native apples, berries, and vegetables.

IN RESIDENCE: Son Mike, a chef, and his dog, a black Lab.
FOREIGN LANGUAGES SPOKEN: A very little Spanish, Italian, and French.
BED AND BATH: Two rooms and three family suites; all private shower baths. First floor—
room with king bed, one with a double and a single. Up narrow steep staircase to second
floor—suite with queen bed, one single bed/lounge, claw-foot tub bath. Suite with queen
bed, trundle daybed. Suite with double bed in sitting room, single and double in bedroom.
BREAKFAST: Usually 8–9 and "to go." Hot cereal, fruit, juice. Coffee cake, home-baked
bread, or fortune popovers. Entrée—meat dish, egg dish, or pancakes prepared to order.
PLUS: Four common rooms. Ceiling fans in most guest rooms. Playpen. Crib.
Babysitting. TV. Microwave and refrigerator in tea room. In-house bakery "when time allows." Gallery with local artists' work.

⤳ From Massachusetts, Florida, Rhode Island, New York, Connecticut, New
Jersey, Washington, D.C., South Africa: *"Gourmet cooking . . . quaint house . . . cozy rooms*

. . . relaxed atmosphere . . . felt pampered . . . even gave biscuits to our dog. [Author's note: Inquire about pet policy.] *Plentiful, delicious, varied food . . . charming setting . . . caring innkeeper. . . . A wizard at victuals. . . . Like coming home to Mom after a long absence. . . . Best B&B I have stayed at in the U.S., Ireland and England."*

The Pond House at Shattuck Hill Farm   802/484-0011

Shattuck Hill Road,   E-MAIL Gretel.Schuck@valley.net
P.O. Box 234, Brownsville, VT 05037   www.pondhouseinn.com

HOSTS: David Raymond and Gretel Schuck
LOCATION: On a 10-acre farm—along a back (dirt) road—with herb gardens, pastures, woods, "unlimited cross-country skiing outside the back door," secluded spring-fed pond (for swimming and skating), and miles of stone walls. Five minutes to skiing at Ascutney, 20 to Okemo, 35 to Killington. Minutes to Long and Appalachian Trails. Fifteen miles south of Woodstock. Ten miles to Saint-Gaudens museum (and summer lawn concerts) in New Hampshire; 30 minutes to Dartmouth College.
OPEN: Year round. Two-night minimum on weekends.
RATES: (Candlelit dinner with wine included.) $150 for two; $45 extra person. Spring ski packages available. ☞ 田 ⚹ 🐎 ❤○

TALK ABOUT recreating the Renaissance era: "Because so many of our guests focus on outdoor sports, especially skiing and mountain biking, they appreciate having dinner right here. And I like to cook! I am an Ohioan, a teacher who was a chemical engineer before I worked as a gold trader at the New York Stock Exchange. Skiing introduced me to Vermont, where I met David, a native Vermonter who works with—and travels for—a large computer company. When he is here, there may be discussions about the science of chopping and stacking wood. In 1995 we opened this 1830s Cape house—with new baths, some family antiques, Oriental rugs, and a touch of Laura Ashley. . . . Some guests come with a bunch of books and make us their spot to relax. . . . We're on the Green Mountain Horse Association trail, so if you come with your own horse, we can provide accommodations in our 200-year-old restored barn. . . . Polite dogs are welcome too!"

IN RESIDENCE: Jackson, "our handsome and perpetually happy Australian shepherd/greyhound. Guests have threatened to steal him!"
FOREIGN LANGUAGE SPOKEN: French.
BED AND BATH: Three queen-bedded rooms. All private baths. First-floor room has private tub/shower bath. Second floor—two rooms each with slanted ceilings and shower bath.
BREAKFAST: 7:30–9:30. Apple and cheddar omelets with sautéed sweet potatoes and bacon; or pumpkin waffles with homemade chicken, apple, and sage sausage. Yogurt with fresh strawberries. Muffins. Granola. In candlelit dining room by the fire.

continued . . .

PLUS: "Gobs of books." No TV. Afternoon tea and biscotti. Wine, cheese, fruit, olives, and crackers served in garden during summer. Skating on pond in winter; Saturday night bonfires. Bicycle rentals and mountain bike tours arranged. Babysitting. Transportation (for you and bicycle) to/from Windsor Amtrak station (6 miles) and West Lebanon, N.H. airport. Fresh fruit and flowers. Picnics ($10 for two people). Northern Italian dinner repertoire includes lobster risotto or chicken roasted with garlic, white wine, herbs, and cognac.

> ≫ From Texas, West Virginia, Washington, D.C., Connecticut: *"Very good food. . . . Scenic grounds and pond are beautiful . . . gracious and interesting hosts. . . . Quiet country elegance. . . . Soul restoring!"*

≫ By the Old Mill Stream— A Bed & Breakfast

802/482-3613

84 Richmond Road, Hinesburg, VT 05461

FAX 802/482-3613
E-MAIL stream@together.net

HOSTS: Michelle and Steven Fischer
LOCATION: Country setting. Fronted by a stone wall with embedded millstone. With barn, waterfall, and woods in back. Twenty minutes southeast of downtown Burlington; 10 minutes to Shelburne Museum. Thirty minutes to Bolton Valley ski area.
OPEN: Year round. Two-night weekend minimum May–Labor Day, on holidays, and in foliage season.
RATES: $90 queen bed, private bath. $65 double bed, shared bath. Singles $10 less. Third person/cot, $15. ♦♦ ☛ ⊗ ⊱

THE REAL THING: a waterfall in the backyard of a rambling landmark miller's house. The abode, built in 1867 on land above a (woolen) mill, still has six-over-six windows (some with original wavy glass), a tin-ceilinged dining room with wainscoting, wide-board floors, front and (hidden) back staircase, and nooks and crannies. Steve is a dentist and accomplished fly-fisherman. Michelle, who has a passion for gardening and cooking, worked in the corporate world. "We bought this property in 1994, decorated with wall-coverings and paint, and retained all the old wood trim. Our country pieces are touchable! New York relatives and friends who visited frequently encouraged us to do B&B for the rest of the world." And so it is that they now have an extended family—people who love to hike, ski, bike, canoe, and explore the area. Guests enjoy the waterfall view from a hammock or from patio Adirondack chairs. They follow the narrow path down into the ravine and discover the foundation of the mill. Skiers are greeted with hot chocolate. Welcome home.

IN RESIDENCE: Lukas, age seven. Two dogs. "Sprocket is a snow-loving Norwegian elkhound mix; Nicholas, a water-loving, stick-chasing golden retriever."

FOREIGN LANGUAGE SPOKEN: Steve is fluent in German.

BED AND BATH: Three rooms, each with a phone. First floor—large air-conditioned room with queen bed, window seat, large private tub bath with hand-held shower. Second floor—two rooms with individual (winter) thermostats. One has queen bed, adjoining sitting room, and private shower bath; other room under eaves has double bed, shared (robes provided) tub/shower bath.

BREAKFAST: 8–9. Prepared with homegrown and Vermont products. Entrée possibilities—lemon-blueberry pancakes or Belgian waffles topped with freshly picked strawberries. Served on back deck with waterfall view, in candlelit dining room, or at kitchen bar.

PLUS: Entire first floor is air conditioned. Double living room has TV and, in black marble fireplace, a glass-fronted woodstove. Board games. Pool table in one side of double living room. Fresh fruit. Fresh flowers. Perennial, herb, and vegetable gardens.

🐾 From New York, Massachusetts, Vermont, England: *"This the best place! Fantastic setting, beautiful home, great breakfasts, and warm and welcoming hosts. . . . THE place for traveling families. . . . Have stayed at many B&Bs throughout the United States . . . Highly recommended. . . . Enjoyed local flavour and fresh ingredients . . . friendly dogs . . . climbed to a lovely waterfall . . . excellent mattress. . . . Personal and away-from-it-all atmosphere."*

🐾 *Homeplace Bed and Breakfast*
P.O. Box 96, Jericho, VT 05465

802/899-4694

FAX 802/899-2986

HOST: Mariot Huessy

LOCATION: Down a half-mile-long driveway to a quiet spot in a 100-acre woodland with miles of cross-country and hiking trails. One and a half miles off Route 15; 15 miles to Burlington, half hour to Shelburne Museum, 45 minutes to Stowe and Mount Mansfield. Near University of Vermont, Ben & Jerry's ice-cream factory.

OPEN: Year round. Reservations appreciated. Two-night foliage minimum.

RATES: Shared bath $55 single, $65 double. Private bath $65 single, $75 double.

♥ 🕴 💺 ⊞ ❖ ⅄ 🦌 💕

MORE RECENT guests have a hard time outdoing the Ohio couple who wrote an eighty-two-line poem on everything from "appointments fit for bride and groom" to "A flock of sheep with bells and bleat. They seemed to say, 'We're glad to meet.'"

Spring is the season for sugaring and newborn lambs. In addition to the sheep, in the barn there are horses and donkeys, chickens, and ducks. The wonderful modern sprawling home, built by the Huessys with "more window than wall" in 1968, was home to eleven children, who grew up surrounded by Vermont craftwork, family European and American antiques, and books everywhere. Today the younger Huessys live as close as "down the road" and as far away as Montana (cowboy now in grain sales) and Poland (international

continued . . .

service work). One is a costume designer turned minister. One is a welder. One lived in a tepee in the 1960s. One daughter, married to a successful Vermont dairy farmer, is a lobbyist in Montpelier. Another is a family lawyer in North Carolina. . . . There's no lack of conversation at this loved B&B!

IN RESIDENCE: Two friendly dogs—a golden retriever and an Australian shepherd. Two cats.

BED AND BATH: In a separate wing, four ground-floor rooms (with ceiling fans) and two full baths. (Room can have private or shared bath.) One room has two antique twin beds; another has twin beds made by a local craftsperson. A third room has a double bed, a twin bed, and a crib. Fourth room has double bed. Crib and cot available.

BREAKFAST: Usually 7:30–9:30. Juice, fresh fruit, "homegrown" eggs, Vermont smoked bacon, pancakes, homemade muffins or breads, and freshly ground coffee. By woodstove or in dining room.

PLUS: Fireplaced living room with piano, games, puzzles, flagstone floor, Oriental rugs, floor-to-ceiling windows. Hundreds of books for all ages. Gorgeous perennial gardens. Maps for on-site trails. Pond for swimming (at your own risk). Their own wool, fleeces, and maple syrup for sale.

 From Vermont: *"Country living at its finest . . . three good nights' sleep . . . magnificent breakfasts."* From Texas: *"Grateful for all the information shared and above-and-beyond things . . . hospitality that made our stay special."*

Sinclair Inn Bed & Breakfast   802/899-2234

389 Vermont Route 15, Jericho, VT 05465   800/433-4658
                                                         FAX 802/899-2234
                                   E-MAIL sinclairinn@worldnet.att.net
                                   www.virtualcities.com/vt/sinclair.htm

HOSTS: Jeanne and Andy Buchanan
LOCATION: Four-minute walk to village green. Five miles to Underhill State Park (Mount Mansfield trails); 18 to Smugglers' Notch ski area (return via Ben & Jerry's ice-cream plant); 14 northeast of Burlington; 13 miles to Lake Champlain. "Seven miles to excellent restaurant."
OPEN: Year round. Two-night minimum April through November and holidays.
RATES: April–late October queen $90 (smaller room), $100 (larger room), $130 (with fireplace). King $110. Handicapped-accessible king/twins option $110. Extra person $20. Off-season $10 less. Discover, MC, Visa. ♥ ⊞ ❖ ⚡ ⅙ ♥♡

"I NEVER WANT to leave," said one guest upon entering this Queen Anne gem. It's Victorian outside painted in three shades of teal green with mauve and beige accents and with turrets and towers. Inside there's leaded and stained glass, a fretwork stairway valance, nine kinds of rich woodwork, and octagonal bedrooms. Since the Buchanans bought "this house that hugs you" in 1993, Jeannie has decorated with large-floral papers, lace curtains, and Oriental rugs. For this house restoration, the Buchanans' fifth, Andy, a civil engineer who oversaw Vermont bridge and road construction, has added an interior stairway, done some stained glass work, and turned hundreds of spindles. There's a gazebo veranda facing the rear panoramic view of wetlands and river against a backdrop of rolling hills. Almost everyone takes a walk from the octagonal deck to a stone path, through shrubs and gardens, past a pond with waterfall, and on to a forest wedding circle with lawn reception tent area. You can tell that these hosts, parents of eight grown children, are in their element with their "expanded family."

BED AND BATH: Six air-conditioned rooms, all private en-suite baths (four with shower, two with tub/shower). Handicapped-accessible first-floor room with king/twins option and wheelchair-accessible shower. Second-floor rooms have a king or queen bed; one queen-bedded room has a fireplace. One room has a queen and a single bed. **BREAKFAST:** 8:30. Blueberry pancakes, Belgian waffles, cinnamon-raisin French toast, or eggs Benedict. Vermont maple syrup and meats. Orange juice, fresh fruit, breads and homemade muffins. In chandeliered dining room. Special diets accommodated. **PLUS:** Fireplaced living room. Library. Guest refrigerator. Wicker-furnished porches. Gardens with bird feeders. Lift and rental discounts for Smugglers' Notch. Inquire about guided Nordic ski trips. (Andy knows the area trails well.) Barn exercise room.

Guests wrote: *"From the cookie jar to the knitted slippers, everything was wonderful. . . . beautiful grounds and gardens. . . . First class!"*

Heart of the Village Inn

5347 Shelburne Road,
Shelburne, VT 05482

802/985-2800
877/808-1834
FAX 802/985-2870
E-MAIL innkeeper@heartofthevillage.com
www.heartofthevillage.com

HOSTS: Bobbe Maynes, (Ms.) Stevie Spaulding, LouAnn Chaffee
LOCATION: In center of National Register village. Next to town green and library. Across from town hall. A block from 45-acre Shelburne Museum. Walk to antiques stores, country store, Vermont Teddy Bear factory. One mile to Shelburne Farms (trails, tours, Mozart Festival). On Route 7. Ten minutes south of Burlington; 6 miles to Burlington airport.
OPEN: Year round.
RATES: $95–$165 (vary according to size and location). $195 two-room suite with Jacuzzi. Amex, MC, Visa. ♥ 🕴 ⊞ 🚫 ✄ 🐾

continued . . .

THIS "OASIS of elegance and charm in a world of mayhem"—in the words of a New Hampshire guest—opened in 1997 after the 1880s Victorian house was restored and the barn rebuilt with new foundation and interior. There are overstuffed chairs in the living rooms. Original woodwork and wainscoting along main staircase. Historic elements in barn entryway. Some barn rooms have skylights, wood paneling, and wallpaper.

Need suggestions? You've come to the mecca. Bobbe was Vermont commissioner of tourism for five years. Stevie worked with a motor tour coach company. LouAnn was with the local chamber of commerce for almost two decades.

BED AND BATH: Five rooms in main house; four rooms (two are handicapped accessible), including one suite, in barn. All with private bath (most have tub/shower combinations), air conditioning, jacks for TV/VCRs, phones with jack for modem. King/twin options, queen, or double beds. Carpeted suite has bath with large shower plus two-person Jacuzzi in sitting room.

BREAKFAST: Usually 8–10:30. Buffet of fresh fruit, muffins, granola and toppings, yogurt, juices, hot beverages. Served French toast, baked puffed pancake, or eggs Benedict soufflé with fresh asparagus. Breakfast meats. At tables for two, three, or four. Summer Sunday mornings, picnic basket–style on lawn.

PLUS: Gas fireplace in living room. Rockers on wraparound porch. Guest pantry with beverages in refrigerator. Afternoon tea, November–April. Transportation to/from bus, train, or Burlington airport.

➢ Guests wrote: *"Rooms I would love to have in my own home. . . . Glorious colors. . . . Warm, welcoming service . . . helped me enjoy trip I was slightly hesitant to take alone. . . . Wonderful place to calm the mind. . . . Celebrated ten years of marriage in magical loft getaway, a cloud palace!"*

SOME EXECUTIVES who book a meeting at an inn return on a weekend for a getaway. Some on a getaway return with colleagues for a meeting.

⟱ *Inn Victoria*

On the Green, P.O. Box 788, Chester, VT 05143

802/875-4288

800/732-4288
FAX 802/875-3529
www.innvictoria.com

HOSTS: K.C. and Tom Lanagan
LOCATION: With the purple shutters at end of village green in a town that is a treasure for architecture buffs (walking tour) and offers theater, a bookstore with lecture series, art galleries, shops, and "three good restaurants" within walking distance.
OPEN: Year round. Depending on season or holiday, some two- or three-day minimums.
RATES: (High tea or après ski included.) $95 queen; $125 with Jacuzzi, soaking tub, or fireplace. $150 queen with fireplace and Jacuzzi or king with extra-large whirlpool. $325 loft suite. MC, Visa. ♥ ♥♥ ⊞ ⚡ ⚥ ♥♡

THE FIRST Lanagan magic-wand treatment gutting and redoing was applied to this Second Empire house in 1988. In 1999, after a three-year "sabbatical" in California, the Lanagans returned to this B&B and its interim additions—fireplaces, an outdoor hot tub, and new rooms in the carriage house. K.C.'s latest facelift ("Bernice, Californians will understand") has lots of Victorian touches with damasks, moiré, antique linens, china, silver, and crystal.

Tom, a communications consultant, was president of a computer company. Multi-faceted K.C. has experience as an antiques dealer, artist, teapot shop (next door) owner, and costume seamstress for the Chester Players.

IN RESIDENCE: Baby Face, Himalayan cat, "the inn's Queen Victoria."
BED AND BATH: Nine air-conditioned rooms with king, queen, double or twin beds. All private baths, some with Jacuzzi, one with large soaking tub and separate shower; one hall bath. *Main house* (second and third floors)—six rooms. Of three rooms in *carriage house,* one is handicapped accessible and has a working fireplace and, for an extra guest, a Murphy bed. Another is a loft suite that sleeps up to eight and has three baths, full kitchen, living room with fireplace and Palladian window, private deck. Rollaways and crib available.
BREAKFAST: 8–9. Cinnamon-raisin French toast with maple butter, whole wheat buttermilk pancakes, eggs Benedict, scones. Served in the formal dining room (with armchairs that invite lingering) under a huge antique chandelier. Special diets accommodated with advance notice.
PLUS: High tea served in 35-foot-square fireplaced living room. Huge two-level rear deck. Screened porch. TV. In renovated carriage house, cathedral-ceilinged great room (loft) for workshops.

∻ The Madrigal Inn

61 Williams River Road,
Chester, VT 05143-9304

800/854-2208
FAX 802/463-8169
E-MAIL Madrigal@sover.net
www.sover.net/~madrigal

HOSTS: Ray and Nancy Dressler
LOCATION: On 60 acres, a former farm, with mountain meadows, woods, wildlife, and, in every direction, marvelous views. Four miles west of I-91, exit 6; 20 minutes to Okemo Mountain.
OPEN: Year round. Three-night minimum on holiday weekends.
RATES: $95–$130, $140 suite. $20 additional person in room. Ten percent less for clergy, military, and seniors, excluding holiday weekends and foliage season.
♥ ⊞ ❖ ⚔ ⚻ ♨ ♟ ❧

To THINK the idea for this post-and-beam building was sketched on a drugstore napkin on the Dresslers' second date when they were in college in the 1950s! Almost four decades later they built, with huge Palladian windows, French doors, and a three-storied living room brick fireplace. It has deep green carpeting. It's without clutter or excessive décor; there are wing and Windsor chairs and a 7-foot antique Steinway grand piano. The Vermont dream became a reality after the family (four children) lived in twenty-two homes during the years when Ray was a pastor in the Midwest and then a navy chaplain. Now they host retreats and group seminars, crafts workshops, or even your own wedding on site.

IN RESIDENCE: Prince, a tricolored collie, "a wonderful greeter."
FOREIGN LANGUAGES SPOKEN: A little German, French, and Japanese.
BED AND BATH: Eleven rooms—two have terraces—on three levels; all private full baths. King/twins option with private exterior entrance. Queen-bedded handicapped-accessible room. Queen and twin beds plus room for rollaway. Four-poster and canopied queens. Twin beds. Extra-long king/twins option.
BREAKFAST: 8–9:30; ski season 7–8:30. (Year round, coffee at 6:30.) Blueberry pancakes or French toast with Vermont maple syrup. Or eggs and bacon or sausage. Homemade muffins. Juice, fruit, coffee, tea, cocoa. In fireplaced dining room by candlelight.
PLUS: Fireplaced library. Individual thermostats. Down comforters. Room fans. No TV. Refreshments. Fresh fruit. Light fare dinner by request. Use of sleds, toboggans. Three miles of hiking and cross-country ski trails and pond.

∻ From Massachusetts: *"A nurturing quality."* From New York: *"Made our Stellafane Star Party Convention experience more complete . . . a warm and sincere welcome . . . rooms are beautifully decorated in country style . . . great breakfast . . . quintessential innkeepers."*

➣ *The Inn at High View*

802/875-2724

753 East Hill Road,
Andover, VT 05143

FAX 802/875-4021
E-MAIL HIVIEW@aol.com
www.innathighview.com

HOSTS: Greg Bohan and Sal Massaro
LOCATION: On a quiet country road with panoramic mountain views. Just outside small
village; 6 miles northwest of Chester. On 72 acres with hiking and cross-
country ski trails that connect to 9-mile network. Fifteen minutes to
Okemo Mountain, half hour to Bromley and Stratton, 45 minutes to
Killington. Near golf, antiquing, Weston Playhouse (10 minutes).
OPEN: Year round except for two weeks in April and November. Two-night mini-
mum most winter weekends; three nights on some holiday weekends.
RATES: $95–$135. Suite $155. Extra person $20. Packages available. Weekend dinner
option, $30 per person. MC, Visa. ♥ ♦♦ ⊞ ❖ ✄ ♨ ♥○

THE POST-AND-BEAM farmhouse—the original part was built in 1789—is comfortable,
with Oriental rugs, a large curved modern living room sofa where some guests curl up
with a good book by the fire, some antiques, and Queen Anne dining room furnishings.

Greg, a former partner in a New York accounting firm that specialized in the hospitality industry, "had B&B in the back of my mind even when I attended the Cornell School
of Hotel Administration." Now he conducts innkeeping-as-a-career sessions here, and
consults with hospitality industry clients. Greg and Sal, a native of Luzzano, Italy, offer
acclaimed hospitality and food. As one guest from Virginia wrote, "On any scale, top
billing. . . . Our stay was just too short."

IN RESIDENCE: One cocker spaniel.
FOREIGN LANGUAGES SPOKEN: Italian and Spanish.
BED AND BATH: Eight rooms, some with slanted ceilings, on first and second floors. All
private baths (some shower without tub), most en suite (robes provided for two hall
baths). Double (some canopied), queen (private entrance and pool view), or king/twin
beds (with treehouse feel). Two two-room suites, each with private entrance and an antique rocking horse. One has two queens and a double daybed; other suite has two double beds and a single daybed.
BREAKFAST: 8–9. French toast, pancakes, or waffles with fruit; stuffed French toast with
cream cheese and apricots and raspberries; bacon and eggs with homemade biscuits.
PLUS: Lawns, gardens, rock garden pool, and gazebo that are studied in Vermont Off
Beat "Backyard Land Management" seminars held here. Hot cider. Coffee and tea always
available. Upright piano. Transportation to/from Rutland (new station with rental cars
available) and Bellows Falls Amtrak.

≫ Craftsbury Bed & Breakfast   802/586-2206
on Wylie Hill

Craftsbury Common, VT 05827

HOST: Margaret Ramsdell
LOCATION: High. Rural. Peaceful. About a mile from Craftsbury Common, 2 from
Craftsbury Outdoor Center (whose groomed and tracked cross-country ski
trails pass through fields of this B&B). Near miles of back roads (good for
mountain bikes) and lakes. Thirty miles from Stowe.
OPEN: Year round. Reservations preferred.
RATES: $55 single room. Double $60 smaller room; $75 larger room. Crib or roll-
away $5–$20. ♥ ⁂ ☕ ⊞ ⚸ ⚻ ⚴

≫ From Idaho, Vermont, Massachusetts: *"Setting looks out over gentle roll of
hills, valleys, and forests . . . skied from front door, over a frozen lake, and onto local trail system. . . . Best of all is Margie's warm and generous hospitality. . . . Her house is a home."*

THE HOSTESS, too, enjoys her 1860s farmhouse. "I feel so peacefully in tune with my surroundings; the views, sunrises, sunsets, rainbows, and startlingly beautiful moonrise seen
through slats of our barn. It is a joy to share this with guests. . . . When the family was
young, we had a summer residential riding camp here. Since converting to a traditional-
style B&B in 1984, I've met an octogenarian who came for one week and stayed for six,
honeymooners, and many cross-country skiers, cyclists, hikers, walkers—all looking for
R&R in a wonderful setting."

FOREIGN LANGUAGE SPOKEN: French.
BED AND BATH: In separate wing—four ground-floor rooms with individual thermostats
and queen, double, or twin beds share two shower baths. Main house—second-floor
queen-bedded room and room with extra-long double bed share full bath with hostess.
Rollaway and crib available.
BREAKFAST: 8–9:30. Juice, fruit. Raspberry waffles, cinnamon apple pancakes, or French
toast with hot applesauce. Or cinnamon apple coffee cake and omelets with Vermont cheddar. Homemade corn bread. In dining room (off country kitchen with woodstove) at table
set with hand-thrown pottery, silver, fresh flowers; view of bird feeder outside window.
PLUS: Area bicycling routes. Woodstove in guests' living room. No TV. Bedroom table
fans. Dinner arranged for cyclists or groups.

*A*LL THE B&Bs *with this* ☕ *symbol want you to know that they
are a private home set up for paying guests (rather than an inn).
Although definitions vary, these private home B&Bs tend to have one to three guest
rooms. For the owners—people who enjoy meeting people—B&B is usually a part-time
occupation.*

≈ The Quail's Nest Bed and Breakfast

P.O. Box 221, Main Street,
Danby, VT 05739-0221

802/293-5099
800/599-6444
FAX 802/293-6300
E-MAIL quailsnest@quailsnestbandb.com

HOSTS: Greg and Nancy Diaz
LOCATION: In center of quiet village, just off Route 7, with antiques shops, waterfall, farmlands, wonderful guided hiking tours. Thirteen miles north of Manchester; 2.6 miles to Appalachian Trail and a 2-mile hike to "a beautiful and peaceful lake."
OPEN: Year round. Two-night minimum on Presidents' Day (February), Memorial Day, July 4, Labor Day, and New Year's weekends and during foliage season. Three-night minimum on Columbus Day weekend.
RATES: $85 per room. $70 single. $120 suite. $10 more on holidays and during foliage season. Additional person $10. Less midweek off-season. Ten percent discount for five or more days. Package rates for murder mystery, quilt sampler, holiday shop-and-wrap, and cookie party weekends. Amex, Discover, MC, Visa. ♥ ♦♦ ⊞ ✗ ✄

≈ From New York, New Jersey, Pennsylvania, Massachusetts, Vermont: "We needed a quiet-alone twenty-four hours. . . . Exceptional attention to detail. . . . Homey . . . knowledgeable about the area. . . . Nice crafts, beautiful quilts, hearty breakfast . . . casual . . . very clean . . . warm and friendly hosts."

"OUR SEARCH for a perfect B&B in a perfect Vermont town brought us here in 1994—after we left the corporate world and after we loved managing a Vermont guest house together. Greg is a doctor of philosophy (yes, sometimes guests get very involved in discussions), computer programmer, and writer. When I was five, I began designing and sewing doll clothes. As a teenager, I learned much from my grandfather, a tailor, who lived with us. Now I design and make quilts and old-fashioned clothing. (I've always felt that I was born in the wrong era!) This 1835 house was a private residence, a ski lodge, and a post office before being converted to a B&B in 1985."

IN RESIDENCE: "Our reigning princess—Sara, a calico cat," in hosts' quarters or on lawn.
BED AND BATH: Six air-conditioned rooms. All private baths. First-floor room with a king-size bed, beamed ceiling, shower bath. Second floor—king or queen (one in slanted-ceilinged room) with shower bath. One queen-bedded room has tub/shower bath and two sinks.
BREAKFAST: 8 (usually 7:30 in winter)–9. (Tomorrow's menu posted at nightly tea.) Home-baked breads, muffins, scones. Hot cereal with warm maple syrup, oven-baked omelets, hot blueberry sauce on pancakes. Special dietary needs accommodated with advance notice. Nancy, in early American dress, serves family style.
PLUS: Living room fireplace. Baldwin spinet piano. Game area. Hammock. Backyard deck. Garden. Lemonade or hot mulled cider or tea with homemade goodies. Guest refrigerator.

⁂ The Birchwood Bed and Breakfast   802/873-9104

P.O. Box 550, 48 Main Street,   FAX 802/873-9121
Derby Line, VT 05830-0550   E-MAIL birchwd@together.net
                                             www.together.net/~birchwd

HOSTS: Betty and Dick Fletcher
LOCATION: In Northeast Kingdom. A pristine village setting with panoramic mountain
views. Five-minute walk to concerts in historic landmark opera house
(Canadian border runs down the middle of hall!), and to 14-acre village
park. Ninety minutes to Montreal.
OPEN: Year round. Two-night minimum on summer and fall weekends.
RATES: $75–$80 per room. $20 per extra person. ☞ ⊞ ⚿ ⚄

⁂ From New Hampshire, Maine, Montana, England, Florida: *"Everything was
just perfect . . . welcomed us into their home. Food, atmosphere, and hospitality unsurpassable! . . .
Recommendations on local eateries are a must. . . . Table settings are sure to be envied even by
Martha Stewart. . . . Great area advice. . . . Staying here is like being treated as queen for a day."*

THE 1920 Federal Colonial was restored by the Fletchers before they opened as a B&B in
1993 and after Dick, an avid golfer, retired as a Honeywell international manager. When
they lived in Boston, Betty, now active in an antiques cooperative, was a teacher. They
were inspired by their own extensive travels and stays in B&Bs and country inns.
Furnishings in this lovely home include Oriental rugs, antiques, porcelain, silver, and
paintings—a marvelous lifetime collection.

BED AND BATH: Three large antiques-filled second-floor rooms; all private shower baths.
Canopied maple queen, pineapple double, or twin beds; Waverly wallcoverings and fabrics.
BREAKFAST: 8–9. Fresh fruit, fruit-filled crepes, Belgian waffles with warm fruit compote,
homemade muesli, homemade muffins or croissants, gourmet coffee. Served in sunlit or
candlelit dining room with fresh flowers.
PLUS: Fireplaced living room. Woodstove in dining room. No TV. Afternoon beverages.
Porch with wicker and rockers. Designer linens and soaps. Recommendation for spectac-
ular 360-degree viewing area.

✿ *Cornucopia of Dorset*

P.O. Box 307, Dorset, VT 05251-0307

802/867-5751
800/566-5751
FAX 802/867-5753
E-MAIL innkeepers@cornucopiaofdorset.com
www.CORNUCOPIAofDORSET.com

HOSTS: John and Trish Reddoch
LOCATION: In National Historic District. With fieldstone walls, split-rail fence, deep yard. Walk to pubs, fine dining, Dorset Theatre. Ten minutes north of Manchester.
OPEN: Year round, except April and Christmas Eve/Day. Two-night minimum on weekends and during fall foliage; three-night minimum on holiday weekends.
RATES: $125–$145 king. With fireplace $150–$175 four-poster king/twins option or four-poster queen; $140–$175 canopied queen; $210–$255 cottage suite. Seasonal midweek specials. Amex, MC Visa. ♥ ⊞ ❖ ⚅ ⚲

ROMANCE IS thematic here! John had restaurant experience in Beverly Hills, California. Subsequently he managed a San Francisco restaurant, where he met Trish. They married, moved to a small California town for family living, and established a service business. Twenty years later, in the 1990s, they explored New England, decided to spend the rest of their lives in this part of Vermont, and fell in love with Dorset, "a pristine country village with wonderful dining, a professional theater, and a great artist community."

They also fell in love with Cornucopia, "one of Vermont's most appealing B&Bs" (*New York Post*). In the summer of 1999 they bought this distinctive and oh-so-livable nineteenth-century clapboard Colonial, complete with the dining room's huge (14-by-26) gorgeous "very old" Oriental rug as well as most of the furnishings that provide a luxurious *feeling*—comfortable but not pretentious. Reddoch touches include their own antiques and art collection. They have continued the style noted in the *New York Times*: "Every detail is programmed for tranquillity." Guests are greeted with a flute of champagne with floating fresh fruit. With just four rooms and one spectacular cathedral-ceilinged carriage house, the Reddochs are carrying on the Cornucopia tradition of personal attention, privacy, and amenities.

IN RESIDENCE: Molly, a golden retriever who loves people.
BED AND BATH: Four air-conditioned second-floor rooms with sitting areas, CD player, private full baths (one has shower only). King bed; canopied queen with wood-burning fireplace; four-poster queen with gas fireplace; four-poster king/twins option with gas fireplace. Sensational air-conditioned cottage has queen-bedded skylit loft overlooking fireplaced living room, a large full bath, fully equipped kitchen, private patio.
BREAKFAST: 8-9:00. (Optional wake-up tray with coffee or tea and fresh flowers for main-house guests.) Repertoire includes warmed spiced fruit compote with sour cream and almonds, baked croissant à l'orange with crème fraîche, baked raspberry puff pancakes with pecans, warm maple syrup, sausage links.

continued . . .

PLUS: The "champagne welcome" plus fruit, chocolates, and freshly baked cookies in room. Fireplaced library and living room. Plant-filled sunroom with cable TV/VCR. Classical music. Self-serve beverages and sweets. Robes. Wool mattress covers. Oversized towels. French doors lead from dining room to marble patio. Covered porch. Perennial gardens. Turndown service.

☜ *Marble West Inn*

Dorset West Road, P.O. Box 847,
Dorset, VT 05251-0847

802/867-4155
800/453-7629
FAX 802/867-5731
E-MAIL marwest@sover.net
www.marblewestinn.com

HOSTS: Bonnie and Paul Quinn
LOCATION: A quiet, rural (estatelike) historic district on scenic Dorset West Road—"please don't confuse with Manchester West Road." On 2 acres with meadows, two small ponds (with rainbow trout), and mountain stream. Between Manchester's outlets and restaurants (5 miles) and Dorset (2 miles). Great cycling area. Near hiking, skiing, canoeing. Two miles to swimming hole.
OPEN: Year round. Two-night minimum during foliage season; three nights on some holiday weekends.
RATES: $90–$100 double beds; $110–$145 queen or king (twins option available) with fireplace; $130–$175 suite with queen and fireplace. Amex, MC, Visa.
♥ ⊞ ⚡ ⅙ ❤

☜ Guests wrote: *"Bonnie and Paul outdo themselves.... Went beyond our expectations.... A beautiful inn ... peace and quiet ... great place to relax, to get away from it all."*

AWAY FROM it all, yet minutes from everything. With panoramic mountain views. And with innkeepers who love sharing their dream come true—"innkeeping in quintessential Vermont." In 1999 Bonnie and Paul bought this established inn, a marble-columned 1840 Greek Revival. They have added fireplaces and air conditioning, redone all the baths, and redecorated with Waverly fabrics. The entry hallways were done in the 1970s by Adele Bishop, a well-known stencilist. Furnishings are traditional.

In Massachusetts the Quinns were in the printing business. Earlier, Paul had restaurant experience.

IN RESIDENCE: Anne Mari Virtanen, "a big hockey fan from Finland" who assists in the inn and with the Quinns' two school-aged sons.
BED AND BATH: Eight air-conditioned rooms, four with fireplace; all private baths. First floor: king/twins option, shower bath, private exterior entrance; suite with queen bed, sitting room, fireplace. Six second-floor rooms (three with fireplace) reached by two separate stairways: rooms with queen bed (one is four-poster, one has canopy); king/twins

option (one with shower bath); one room with king four-poster, soaking tub and shower); one room with double bed, shower bath.

BREAKFAST: 8:30–9:30. Repertoire includes strawberry/kiwi pancakes; Belgian waffles in assorted flavors; spinach and cheese frittatas; French toast stuffed with bananas with warm maple syrup. Juice, muffins, hot beverages. With candlelight and classical and jazz music. "Please give advance notice for special diets."

PLUS: Fireplace in library and music rooms. No TV. Refreshments. Turndown service. Beer and wine license.

⤳ *Inn at Mountain View Creamery*   802/626-9924

Box 355, Darling Hill Road,   FAX 802/626-9924
East Burke, VT 05832   E-MAIL innmtnview@kingcon.com
                                                         www.innmtnview.com

HOSTS: Marilyn and John Pastore

LOCATION: Spectacular. On 440 acres with gorgeous huge red stable, carriage houses, barns—including the state's largest cow barn. Five minutes to Burke Mountain; 15 to Lake Willoughby.

OPEN: Year round. Two-night minimum during holiday weeks and foliage season.

RATES: Vary according to size of room. $135–$210. Ten percent less for three or more nights and for singles; 15 percent less for everyone March 20–June 1 and October 30–December 10. Midweek Burke Mountain ski packages. Amex, MC, Visa. ♥ 👫 ⊞ ❖ ⚒ 🎿 👪 💕

⤳ From Vermont Bicycle Touring: *"Lovingly and authentically . . . warm gracious welcome . . . one of the favorites on our list!"* From North Carolina: *"Setting captured our hearts."* From Massachusetts: *"Both quaint and elegant. Food exceptional. . . . Inspiring site for our company's retreat."* From Minnesota: *"View was awesome . . . acres delightful for walks."*

COUNT THE WAYS! Guests extol (at length) this 1890 red brick Georgian Colonial building opened as a B&B in 1990. Once part of Elmer Darling's gentleman's farm, which produced butter and cheese for his New York City Fifth Avenue hotel, the entire enormous property has been restored by the Pastores. Now the creamery is filled in country manor style with antiques, chintzes, quilts, and stenciled floors. There's plenty of privacy. Meeting space. Wedding space. And, from meadows here, access to a 124-mile network for hiking, mountain cycling, and cross-country skiing. All featured on Boston television and in *Ski* magazine, and photographed for *Country Living*.

Marilyn, a former teacher of Russian, remembers writing contracts for her immigrant grandmother/builder. John is a Boston cardiologist. They and Laurelie, an East Burke native Vermonter who is a former caterer and restaurateur, are thanked by guests for "peace, quiet, and beauty."

continued . . .

IN RESIDENCE: Laurelie Welch, manager. Roxie, a Scottish terrier. "Three shy Herefords and one outgoing holstein." And two Percherons for joyful narrated hay and sleigh rides (fee charged).

FOREIGN LANGUAGES SPOKEN: Russian. Some Japanese.

BED AND BATH: Ten second-floor rooms, all private shower baths. Queen, double, or twin beds. Rollaway and crib available. Also, a two-bedroom cottage with fireplace, kitchen and Jacuzzi.

BREAKFAST: 8–9. Home-baked breads, fresh fruit, yogurt, frittata with red pepper, cocoa granola, oatmeal pancakes with maple syrup. In brick-walled breakfast room with ceiling fans; classical music plays.

PLUS: Fireplaced living room. Vermont dairy farming video for children. Afternoon tea or hot cider. Two Ping-Pong tables. Vegetable and perennial gardens. Fifty-six-foot patio bordered by lightposts. Box stalls for equestrians who trailer their horses and wish to ride. On-premises restaurant open Friday–Sunday. Massage appointments on site. Meeting space.

≈ Tetreault's Hillside View Farm Bed and Breakfast

802/827-4480

Box 2860, South Road, Fairfield, VT 05455

HOSTS: Jacqueline and Albert Tetreault
LOCATION: On a 236-acre farm, with brook (for daydreaming) and distant mountain backdrop. In a village neighborhood. Two-minute walk to country store with florist and antiques. In hilly cycling country. Ten-minute drive to I-89, 40 to Burlington, 30 to Smugglers' Notch ski area. Ten miles east of St. Albans.
OPEN: Year round.
RATES: Larger room $55 for two. Smaller room $40 for one. Rollaway $10. ♥ ☞ ⚉

A RARE VERMONT B&B is this genuine 1850s farmhouse, restored by the Tetreaults, who have lived here for more than forty years. Jackie, the flower gardener, made all the braided rugs and quilts. Albert, a retired dairy farmer, received a "Vermont Barn Again" award for maintaining and preserving the wonderful red barn. He is happy to share a tale or two about farm life and about Fairfield, the birthplace of President Chester A. Arthur. "We meet skiers and cyclists and, of course, many who come for foliage. And we remember the young couple who became engaged during a walk they took in the middle of the night."

FOREIGN LANGUAGE SPOKEN: French.

BED AND BATH: Three second-floor double-bedded rooms—two are large, one is small—share a shower bath (sometimes booked as private bath with larger room).

BREAKFAST: Usually 8 or 9. Juice, fresh fruit cup, homemade blueberry muffins, sweet breads, toast, maple syrup, raspberry jam, hot beverages. "Can last up to two hours!"

PLUS: Fireplaced living room. Air-conditioned downstairs. TV room. Flannel sheets. Chocolates.

⤞ From Maryland, Oregon, Ontario, Ohio: *"The house is beautifully decorated, but more important is how delightful the Tetreaults are. . . . Delicious food. . . . Felt like family. . . . Shared home and good cheer. . . . Heaven!"*

⤞ *Maplewood Inn*

Route 22A South, RR 1, Box 4460,
Fair Haven, VT 05743-9721

802/265-8039
800/253-7729
FAX 802/265-8210
E-MAIL maplewd@sover.net
www.sover.net/~maplewd

HOSTS: Lisa Ne Jame Osborne and (husband) Don Osborne
LOCATION: Pastoral setting with mountain views. On a major road. From Route 4, exit 2, it's 1 mile south of historic village center. Minutes to Lakes Bomoseen and Saint Catherine. Forty minutes west of Killington and Pico ski areas.
OPEN: Year round. Two-night minimum on foliage weekends and some holidays.
RATES: $80 double bed. $95 queen. $130 suite. $220 expanded suite for four. Holidays and foliage season $90 double, $105 queen, $150 suite; $240 expanded suite. $20 third person. Pets, allowed in one room. $30 for one or two nights. Amex, Discover, MC, Visa. ♥ ⊞ ❖ ⊁

THE GREEK REVIVAL Maplewood Dairy homestead (1880–1979) was an established B&B when Lisa and Don bought this "cozy, inviting, friendly place" in 1999. They furnished with traditional pieces—"with many antiques but mostly reproductions that look like the 1850s only they are comfortable!" Both hosts are originally from upstate New York, just over the Vermont border. They met in Colorado, where Lisa, daughter of a restauranteur, was comptroller for a skiwear fabric supplier. Don is a natural gas engineer. "After almost twenty years, innkeeping brought us back east." Here they greet travelers who enjoy sunsets from the porch and quiet times by the fire. Guests write: "Welcoming hosts . . . a lovely place so very much like home . . . a beautiful home!"

IN RESIDENCE: "One sweet balck Labrador, not allowed in guest areas."
BED AND BATH: Five air-conditioned rooms (four with gel-fueled fireplaces), including two suites. All private baths (all en suite except one); shower/tub or shower (two with two nozzles) without tub. Double or queen beds. One suite has a queen and a double bed, full living room. Rollaways available.
BREAKFAST: Usually 8–10. Fruit cup, egg, pastries, homemade breads and muffins, cereals and granola. Juices. Hot beverages. In front breakfast room with mountain views.
PLUS: One in-room phone with private number. Evening refreshments served. Hot beverages and goodies always available. Wood-burning fireplace in guest parlor. Board games Sitting room with library.

⋙ Silver Maple Lodge & Cottages

802/333-4326

520 U.S. Route 5 South,
Fairlee, VT 05045

800/666-1946
E-MAIL scott@silvermaplelodge.com
www.silvermaplelodge.com

HOSTS: Sharon and Scott Wright
LOCATION: One mile south of town center; close to I-91. Close to Leda's Pizza
Restaurant (popular with local residents and tourists). Opposite open farmland with barn. Views of White Mountains to the east, Green Mountains to
the west; 17 miles from Dartmouth College.
OPEN: Year round.
RATES: In inn (no smoking)—shared bath $52 single, $56 double; private bath
$62–$72 single, $64–$74 double. Cottages (smoking and pets allowed) —
$69–$74 single, $72–$86 double. Ten-speed bicycles $10/day (includes
shuttle, if needed). Special packages offered. Amex, Discover, MC, Visa.
♥ ♦♦ ⊞ ❖

DECOR IS simple country in this expanded 1790s farmhouse, which became an inn in the
early 1900s. Pine-paneled cottages were added in the 1950s. (Another with two units in
the 1990s!) Since the Wrights bought the property in the mid-1980s, they have added
baths; a common room fireplace; and, in the cottages, air conditioning.

Scott, an award-winning pumpkin grower who grew up on a nearby farm, and Sharon
offer suggestions for do-it-yourself tours, for cycling, for canoeing, and for walking from
inn to inn or from Silver Maple as a base. They'll direct you to antiques auctions; suggest
a lobster, clam, wild game, or steak supper; or arrange for a champagne hot-air balloon
ride.

IN RESIDENCE: "Stephanie is eight; Stacie, six. Our cat, Albert Riley, has the life of Riley."
BED AND BATH: Eight second-floor rooms in the inn; four rooms with sinks. All private
baths (with tub or shower) except for two rooms that share a full bath. King, double, or
twin beds. Cottages (preferred by romantics) with private baths have king, two doubles, a
queen and a twin, or three twins. One cottage is handicapped accessible; two have kitchenettes and wood-burning fireplace. Cot available.
BREAKFAST: Usually 7–9. Very continental; self-serve. Juice, fruit, homemade breads or
rolls, coffee or tea.
PLUS: Ceiling fans in two guest rooms. Screened wraparound porch. Piano. Games.
Croquet, badminton, shuffleboard, volleyball. Picnic tables among the apple trees.
Babysitting arranged.

≋ Carolyn's Victorian Inn   802/472-6338

15 Church Street, P.O. Box 1087,   FAX 802/472-6338
Hardwick, VT 05843-1087   E-MAIL vctrninn@together.net
                                        www.pbpub.com/vermont/carolyns.htm

HOST: Carolyn Hunter Richter
LOCATION: In a small Vermont town, 20 miles northeast of Stowe, 5 miles to Caspian
Lake. Within 5 miles of three cross-country ski centers. Walk to free tennis
courts. Bike touring country.
OPEN: Year round. Two-night minimum in foliage season and on major holidays.
RATES: King $90 smaller room, $100 larger room. Suite (two rooms) $125. Singles
$15 less. MC, Visa. ♥ ♦♦ ✗ ⚮

≋ From Vermont: *"Pampered with every conceivable amenity . . . chocolates in
our room, huge selection of lush towels . . . everything you might want and had forgotten . . .
decor reflects Carolyn's gracious and fun-loving nature. . . . Gorgeous rooms . . . memorable
breakfasts . . . a real treasure."*

THE COTTAGE Victorian has original cherry woodwork, hardwood floors, cypress staircase,
and oak wall-to-wall bookcase. Many of the antiques acquired at area auctions came complete with a "story." Carolyn, an elementary school counselor, is a mountain biker, skier,
motorcycle rider, and children's therapist who enjoys cooking and baking.

IN RESIDENCE: One daughter during college breaks.
FOREIGN LANGUAGE SPOKEN: A little French.
BED AND BATH: Four second-floor rooms (accessible by two interior stairways)—all with
feather beds—share one second-floor full bath and one first-floor half bath. Three rooms
have king/twins option; one with half-crown canopy. One room has double four-poster,
gas fireplace, ceiling fan, and a sink. Rollaway and crib available.
BREAKFAST: 8–10; other times arranged. Maybe lemon poppy-seed French toast with
homemade strawberry jam, or banana walnut pancakes with Vermont maple syrup; or
soufflélike casserole with French bread, cheddar cheese, eggs, and smoked ham. Juices,
granola, cereals, seasonal fruits, rhubarb coffee cake, lemon/blueberry muffins, homemade breads and scones.
PLUS: Tea and sweets upon arrival. Evening sherry by fire or in library. Bedroom fans.
Porch rockers. Children's crib, toys, high chair. Guest refrigerator. Dinner ($12.50).
Victorian cream teas, $15.

*C*AN'T FIND A LISTING *for the community you are going to? Check
with a reservation service described at the beginning of this chapter.
Through the service you may be placed (matched) with a welcoming B&B that is near
your destination.*

❧ *Somerset House*   802/472-5484

130 Highland Avenue, P.O. Box 1098   800/838-8074
Hardwick, VT 05843-1098   E-MAIL gaillard@together.net

HOSTS: Ruth and David Gaillard
LOCATION: A quiet neighborhood of turn-of-the-century houses. "In a small (but not
small-minded!) untouristy town with friendly and helpful people, strollable
streets day and night." One block from river, main-street shops, restaurants,
and "a very good bookstore." Near hiking trails, lakes, cross-country ski
areas, covered railroad bridge. In Northeast Kingdom, 30 miles north of
Montpelier; 40 minutes to Stowe.
OPEN: Year round.
RATES: $79–$90. $59–$70 single. $20 rollaway. $15 cot for child. Up to age two, no
charge. MC, Visa. ♥ ♛ ⊞ ⚹ ⚸ ♒

❧ From New Jersey, California, Nevada, Massachusetts, Vermont, and
England: *"Seems to have gotten all the good things' together in a single facility. The house is
lovely, elegant, yet comfortable and extremely homelike. . . . Marvelous antiques . . . sculptures
. . . exquisite oil paintings. Impeccably clean. . . . Piles of fresh towels magically renewed
throughout the day. . . . Porches and gardens are lovely . . . reading materials appeal to many
interests, levels, and ages. . . . Our teenage children love the pristine feeling, the friendliness,
and hosts' accurate recollection of their favorite foods and drinks. . . . Hostess has knack for interesting conversation. . . . Outstanding breakfasts. . . . Fresh organic fruits with all the trim-
mings. . . . Well-done pot of coffee. . . . A remarkably generous low price."*

"AFTER HOMESTEADING (bees, goats, chickens, orchard, organic fruits and vegetables) in
northern Vermont for ten years and then living in England for two, we bought (in 1988)
this grand old 1894 Queen Anne home—and began an ongoing 'sympathetic renovation'
of every inch. We started with family heirlooms, added pieces we picked up and restored
. . . all tied together with color and luck! B&B was inspired by a stay in Somerset in my
native England."

Ruth's interests range from cooking to painting to gardening, from dancing to crewing
on David's Star boat. David, a piano tuner, plays bass and loves to sail. Recently the Gaillards,
who use nontoxic cleaners, energy-efficient lightbulbs, and organic foods, received an
award from the governor for becoming one of Vermont's first Green Hotels.

BED AND BATH: Four second-floor rooms, all private baths. Cozy rear queen-bedded
room with balcony, en-suite shower bath. Large round tower room with queen bed,
tub/shower bath "just two steps away." One smaller room with two twin beds, en-suite
tub/shower bath. Queen-bedded room with bay windows, balcony, hall shower bath.
BREAKFAST: Usually 7–9. Perhaps omelet (local free-range eggs) with fresh pesto, pine
nuts, garden tomatoes and herbs; egg/cheese tortilla with avocado and salsa; orange cinnamon challah French toast; waffles or pancakes with cinnamon apples. Always fresh
fruit. Herbal and English teas.

PLUS: Porch rockers. Fireplaced sitting room. Upright piano. Pump organ. No TV. Fans. Adult-sized swing hangs from two butternut trees. Fresh flowers and fruit. Hedged secret garden with goldfish pond.

✈ *Fitch Hill Inn*

258 Fitch Hill Road,
Hyde Park, VT 05655-9733

802/888-3834

800-639-2903
FAX 802/888-7789
E-MAIL fitchinn@aol.com
www.gostowe.com/saa/fitchhill

HOSTS: Richard A. Pugliese and Stanley E. Corklin
LOCATION: Rural. On 4 hilltop acres with hiking. Within 15 minutes' drive of Stowe and Smugglers' Notch downhill ski areas, 45 to Jay Peak. Ten major cross-country ski centers within 20-mile radius. Spectacular mountain views. Five-minute walk to historic Hyde Park (population 475) and (summer) opera house. Four miles from Long Trail and from a reservation with "no development and plenty of loons." One-third mile off Routes 100 and 15.
OPEN: Year round. Two- or three-day minimum December 25–January 3 and during peak seasons.
RATES: Double bed $85–$125. Queen $95–$135. Suite $145–$189. Apartment $145–$189. Less October 20–December 20 and April 15–June 15. Children under twelve, free. Extra adult $15. Skiing, canoeing, bike, and golf packages. Amex, Discover, MC, Visa. ♥ ♦♦♦ ⊞ ❖ ⚔ ⚒ ♨ ❤

✈ From Virginia, Canada, New Jersey, England, Vermont, California, Ohio, Illinois, Texas, Florida, Massachusetts, New York, New Hampshire, Scotland, Wisconsin: *"Splendid... remarkable attention to detail... a veritable sanctuary... a marvelous honeymoon.... Hosts with good sense of humor... made New England just as we'd imagined.... Delightful examples of quilting... deliciously different breakfasts.... Was attending a wedding by myself. Felt pampered, relaxed... lovely grounds... fabulous view... provided excellent hints, hidden secrets, cycling routes and maps.... Bravo!"*

RICHARD HAS "always had a summer camp in Vermont" and is now doing what he "always wanted to" (running an inn). Stanley is rector in Enosburg Falls. In Illinois they were both Episcopal clergymen. In 1991 they restored this c. 1797 Federal house and furnished with period antiques. The outdoor hot tub has a backdrop of mountains and woods. *Bon Appétit* and *Country Living* magazines have also discovered this inn.

IN RESIDENCE: In hosts' quarters, a Siamese cat.
FOREIGN LANGUAGES SPOKEN: Spanish and some French.
BED AND BATH: Four second-floor rooms (one with a double bed, three with a queen), all with private baths (three shower only, one has tub/shower). Cathedral-ceilinged suite has

continued...

queen bed and double pull-out sofa, full bath with two-person Jacuzzi, living room, fireplace, cable TV and VCR. Studio apartment has one queen and one double bed, woodburning fireplace, cable TV and VCR, full bath with Jacuzzi, deck and patio.

BREAKFAST: 8–10. Caramel French toast, blueberry pancakes with Vermont maple syrup, baked Brie en croute, spinach/feta cheese frittata, fresh orange juice, cereals, Green Mountain coffee. On decks in warmer months.

PLUS: Air conditioning and ceiling fans in all rooms. Wood-burning living room fireplace. Late-afternoon tea. Color cable TV; 250 videos. Picnic baskets ($15 for two). By reservation, "five-course gourmet dinners"; $60 for two. Sherry, robes, mints in room.

✍ *Fox & Pheasant Inn*   802/422-8770

1265 Bear Mountain Road, P.O. Box 305,   FAX 802/422-4242
Killington, VT 05751-0305   E-MAIL unwind@foxpheasantinn.com
      www.foxpheasantinn.com

     HOSTS: Charlie Brunell and Nina Tasi
   LOCATION: Quiet. On 3 acres at foot of Bear Mountain—with views of Killington's ski slopes a half mile away. Across from tennis courts. Eighteen miles east of Rutland, 17 west of Woodstock. Fifty minutes to Dartmouth College.
     OPEN: December–Mid-April and late June–mid-October. Two-night weekend minimum in fall and winter; three nights Christmas–New Years and Presidents' Day weekend.
     RATES: Winter $140–$155. Summer $90. Fall $140; $15 more with fireplace set-up. Holidays $170–$185. Additional person $20. MC, Visa. ♥ ⊞ ⚄ ⤙ 𣏕

    ✍ From Connecticut, New York, England: *"Location is magnificent . . . immaculate and charming. . . . Been there five times. The best B&B in the Green Mountains . . . hosts knowledgeable re: ski conditions, antiquing, new restaurants . . . respectful of guests' privacy. . . . Nina, a ski ambassador, taught our daughter trails back to the inn . . . spacious sunny rooms with great views . . . walking-distance health club with free use of equipment, pool, sauna . . . friendly, helpful, interesting hosts. . . . We love their dog, too . . . sitting rooms are so pleasant. . . . [has a] great spirit that soothes the soul."*

THOSE GUESTS say it all. The hosts, too, are mighty content. Before they opened in 1995, Nina, a chemist, was in sales and service for a Danish company in Connecticut that produces industrial enzymes. Charlie, also based in Connecticut, was in charge of the company's North American operations. By remodeling and expanding the former Sunrise Village reception center, they created an inn with lots of open space and many skylights. Furnishings include comfortable seating, Vermont-made mission- and Shaker-style beds, handmade quilts, Vermont-forged lamps, and the hosts' art collections.

IN RESIDENCE: In hosts' quarters, one friendly black Labrador.
FOREIGN LANGUAGE SPOKEN: French.

BED AND BATH: Six queen-bedded guest rooms. Four with fireplace. All with private bath; one on second floor has two-person whirlpool tub.
BREAKFAST: 7:30–9:30 in winter; 8–10 summer and fall. Buffet with homemade breads and muffins. Cereal, yogurt, fresh fruit. Juices, coffee, tea. In two dining areas with mountain views.
PLUS: Upright piano, wet bar, TV. Porch. Concierge service for golf, restaurant, skiing, canoeing arrangements. Homemade cookies, tea, coffee always available in afternoon.

⇗ The Peak Chalet

802/422-4278

P.O. Box 511, 184 South View Path,
Killington, VT 05751

FAX 802/422-4278 (CALL FIRST)
E-MAIL Home@ThePeakChalet.com
www.ThePeakChalet.com

HOSTS: Diane and Greg Becker
LOCATION: Wooded hill. With incredible mountain views. On a dirt road. Two tenths of a mile off Killington access road. Within 3 miles of ski lifts, mountain biking, hiking, golf, restaurants, entertainment, shops. Twenty miles west of Woodstock. Ten miles east of Rutland.
OPEN: Year round. Two-night minimum on winter weekends.
RATES: Spring $55–$85 double occupancy, $65–$105 three people in room. Summer $55 double, $65 triple. Fall $85 double, $110 triple. Winter $65–$110 double; $80–$135 triple. $145 double, $180 triple per room during Christmas week and Presidents' Day weekend. Amex, Diners, MC, Visa.
♥ ♦♦ ☛ ⊞ ❖ ⚔ ⅟

BAVARIA ALMOST. By design. Alpine chalet–like, with a panoramic backdrop of mountains, this B&B was well built in the late 1970s by a German couple who imported the hand-fashioned front door from Germany. It is minutes from everything, yet you arrive with the feeling that you are in the middle of nowhere. It is just what the Beckers were looking for in 1990—someplace with a homelike atmosphere—when they were engaged to be married and interested in relocating from Connecticut. Greg, an accountant, and Diane, a registered nurse, furnished with reproduction beds (each room is different); antique accents; and, in the put-your-feet-up kind of living room, comfortable seating.

FOREIGN LANGUAGE SPOKEN: German.
BED AND BATH: Four carpeted rooms; three on entry level, one (very private) on lower level. Each has queen bed (two rooms have a twin bed also), private shower bath, mountain or garden views.
BREAKFAST: 7–9. Buffet-style continental with freshly baked breads, muffins, or pastries; hot and cold cereals; fresh fruit; juice; hot beverages. In guests' living room at tables set with fine china and cloth napkins.

continued . . .

PLUS: Living room with stone fireplace, TV, VCR, stereo, guest mini-refrigerator. Perennial gardens.

≈ From New York: *"Have tried many Killington area B&Bs, inns, and private rentals . . . this B&B is the best solution . . . quality and value . . . inviting layout and décor . . . location is a bonus . . . on quiet street . . . one minute from any store or restaurant on the main strip . . . only five-minute ride to the base lodge. . . . In summer, found Greg's intimate knowledge of local hiking and mountain biking trails invaluable."*

≈ The Inn at Ormsby Hill   802/362-1163

Historic Route 7A, 1842 Main Street,   800/670-2841
Manchester Center, VT 05255   FAX 802/362-5176
                                                    E-MAIL ormsby@vermontel.com
                                                            www.ormsbyhill.com

HOSTS: Ted and Chris Sprague
LOCATION: On an estate ringed by mountain views. Two miles south of the village, shops, fine restaurants.
OPEN: Year round. Two-night minimum on weekends and some holidays.
RATES: Weekends $215, $230, $255. Midweek $50 less. Fall foliage, Christmas–New Year's week, and February holiday weekend $265, $280, $305. Friday supper for two, $35 including gratuities. Singles $20 less. Discover, MC, Visa.
♥ ❖ ⚮ ✁

THIS IS IT—the inn selected to be featured with Kellogg's new Country Inn Specialties cereal. And the inn selected to redecorate a room with Sanderson Wallcoverings and Fabrics. All those TV and print ads and cereal packages come to life as you drive through the handsome gates and onto the estate, a Historic Register property. For many guests, including me, the showstopper is the huge light-filled conservatory (breakfast room) built to resemble the stern cabin of a ship with sizable windows looking out on the gardens and mountains. "Even though we're in ski country, many of our guests come primarily for relaxation, romance, and renewal," say the Spragues, who had an acclaimed Maine inn and restaurant for eight years before buying and expanding Ormsby Hill. Earlier, Ted, a former New England soccer team player, taught chemistry for seventeen years on Cape Cod. Chris, the daughter of a gourmet food shop owner, was office manager of a Boston law firm.

IN RESIDENCE: Truffles, a Labrador retriever "who loves guests who love her."
BED AND BATH: Ten air-conditioned and fireplaced rooms (six with individual thermostat, several with beamed ceiling) with king (plus a daybed in one room) or queen beds—many canopied. All private baths; all with two-person Jacuzzi (and a signature rubber ducky), some with view of wood-burning or gas (some with remote control) fireplace.

One first-floor room is handicapped accessible; two have a private exterior entrance. Largest room has vaulted ceiling, sitting nook, oversized Jacuzzi, two-person shower. **BREAKFAST:** At 9. (Buffet style 8–10 on weekends with hot entrée served at 9 followed by dessert—cranberry, peach, or apple crisp or warm gingerbread, any and all with vanilla ice cream.) Main entrée may be baked pancakes; scrambled eggs in puff pastry; wild mushroom risotto; leek, bacon, and gorgonzola polenta; raisin bread pudding with seasonal topping. **PLUS:** Welcoming refreshments. Radio and hair dryer in each room. In-room phones. Fireplaces in conservatory and living room. TV room. Tea or sherry in late afternoon. Complimentary soft drinks in guest refrigerator. All with those expansive views from hammock, wicker-furnished porch, and patio.

⁂ *The Inn at Manchester*

802/362-1793

Historic Route 7A,
P.O. Box 41, Manchester, VT 05254

800/273-1793
FAX 802/362-3218
E-MAIL imanevermontel.com
www.innatmanchester.com

HOSTS: Harriet and Stan Rosenberg and daughter Amy Hill
LOCATION: In the village. Set back from road. On 4 acres of lawn, meadows, gardens, trees. About a mile to outlets. Eight miles to Bromley ski area, 17 to Stratton, 35 to Rutland.
OPEN: Year round. Two-night minimum on most weekends.
RATES: $104–$169 July through October, $20–$25 less off-season. Plus 15 percent gratuity. $25 extra person. Packages available. Amex, Discover, MC, Visa.
♥ ❖ ✗ ✂

⁂ From New York, New Jersey, Connecticut, Florida, Vermont, Colorado, Massachusetts, Pennsylvania: *"Our brief stay was wonderful and unforgettable . . .superb service . . . great breakfas. . . . Loved the simplicity of the place. . . . We're going back . . . relaxing. . . . Peaceful . . . fabulous staff. . . . Loved lounging in the hammock surrounded by majestic pine trees. . . . Owners took real care for our comfort. . . . Thomas Wolfe was wrong when he said you can't go home again. Our second stay was even better than the first."*

AND SO IT has been for twenty years, since Harriet, a former sixth-grade teacher, and Stan, a stockbroker, left Long Island for the Vermont they had enjoyed on many of their own vacations. Now most of the rooms in "our no-froufrou inn" have wood-burning fireplaces. All have private baths. The inn, featured in a National Trust for Historic Preservation calendar as well as on the cover of one National Trust directory, has expanded. *Gourmet* magazine has printed three recipes. Harriet still loves redecorating and

continued . . .

searching for antique finds. Tea and cakes are served every afternoon. And Saturday night's wine and cheese party is a big hit.

BED AND BATH: Fourteen air-conditioned antiques-furnished rooms (most have individual thermostat) plus four second-floor suites. King or queen beds plus daybed in most rooms; all private baths. Third-floor rooms (least expensive) are under eaves. Carriage house (great for families) has four rooms plus a common room.
BREAKFAST: 8–9:30. Fresh fruit, poached peaches with raspberry sauce, or melon with berries. Oatmeal in winter. Always, homemade granola and cereals. Cooked-to-order entrée—pancakes, cottage cakes, cinnamon French toast, omelets, Belgian waffles. "Everything made from scratch!"
PLUS: In-ground pool. Front porch with hanging plants. Upright piano in fireplaced living room. TV in rear common room. Guest refrigerator. Apples, candy, nuts. Annual Christmas Open House.

☞ *The Battenkill Inn*   802/362-4213

6342 Vermont Route 7A, Sunderland, VT   800/441-1628
P.O. Box 948,   FAX 802/362-0975
Manchester Village, VT 05254   E-MAIL innfo@Battenkillinn.com
                                                     www.Battenkillinn.com

HOSTS: Laine and Yoshi Akiyama
LOCATION: On 7 acres along Historic Route 7A, with pond (fly-fishing right here), lawns, and meadows bordering the Battenkill River. Four minutes south of Manchester Village.
OPEN: Year round. Two-night minimum on holiday weekends and in foliage season.
RATES: November–February and summer $105, $110, $120; $145 with fireplace. March–May: $100, $105, $115, $130. Foliage and holidays $125–$150. MC, Visa. ♥ ⊞ ⚔ ⚕ ❦

THIS COULD be known as the "follow your heart" inn. Yoshi, who has science degrees— "but I always loved art and design"—from universities in Japan and Michigan, was executive producer of Tokyo Disneyland. Laine, who was also a designer for Los Angeles–based Walt Disney Imagineering, had become a traveling consultant for the themed entertainment industry. When they decided to leave the corporate world for innkeeping, they "fell in love with Manchester" and with this 1840 Italianate Victorian. The inn had been done over by the previous owners, an architect/carpenter/artist and his wife, an interior designer/ seamstress. The personable Akiyamas, who may someday have their own studio here, took over in the fall of 1996. Now the world comes to their doorstep. And their guests write to me: "Exudes comfort and coziness . . . amazing breakfasts . . . fantastic hosts . . . delightful."

IN RESIDENCE: Two golden retrievers, Duncan and Linus, restricted to hosts' quarters—"but guests can say hi!"
FOREIGN LANGUAGE SPOKEN: Japanese.
BED AND BATH: Eleven air-conditioned and carpeted rooms on two floors, with king, queen (some canopied), or double beds. All private shower baths. One first-floor room has queen bed, gas fireplace. Another is handicapped accessible. Four rooms have wood-burning fireplaces; three have French doors leading to porch with spectacular mountain views.
BREAKFAST: 8–9:30. Special of the day could be almond French toast, eggs Benedict, or raspberry-stuffed French toast served with bacon, ham, or sausage with fresh fruit or vegetable garnish. Homemade muffins. Juice. Fresh fruit. Served in two dining rooms—a larger one, with striking red wallpaper is more formal; the more intimate country-style room seats eight.
PLUS: Ceiling fans in most rooms. Coffee, tea, and cookies always available. Evening wine and hors d'oeuvres. TV in sitting room. Picnic baskets ($15–$30). Guest refrigerator. Turndown service. An entire booklet of area activities in all seasons and weather.

I.B. Munson House B&B Inn

802/446-2860

37 South Main Street, P.O. Box 427,
Wallingford, VT 05773-0427

888/519-3771
FAX 802/446-3336
E-MAIL ibmunson@vermontel.com
www.ibmunsoninn.com

HOSTS: Jo Ann and Tom Brem
LOCATION: On two-lane Route 7 (30-mph speed limit) in a valley village with antiques shop (across the street), library, town hall, "two excellent restaurants," two country stores, a clock shop and a quilt shop, and an 1818 red schoolhouse once attended by the founder of Rotary International. The Appalachian Trail is 2.6 miles away. Twenty minutes to Killington, Pico, and Okemo ski resorts; Vermont marble exhibit; Manchester (shopping). Five minutes to lake swimming.
OPEN: Year round. Two-night minimum on holiday weekends.
RATES: $75–$110 double. $125–$150 queen. Fall foliage and some holidays $15 more. Singles $15 less. Additional person $25. AARP, AAA, and extended stay discounts. Amex, MC, Visa. ♥ ⊞ ❖ ⚔ ⅄

THE WOW FACTOR. It's what the Brems looked for during their in-depth inn search. And it's what guests comment on here. Crank the antique (original) ringer on the colored-glass front door. Enter the very Victorian hall, part of the art gallery, with its graceful curved staircase. The National Register Italianate Victorian was built in 1856 for I. B. Munson, a wealthy sheep farmer, who raised twelve children in this house. Restored in 1992, it has

continued . . .

Waverly wallcoverings, lace curtains, Oriental and hooked rugs, intricate (painted) wood-work, lots of windows, and antique furnishings. In 1999 the Brems, "ardent B&B goers for fifteen years," moved from Ohio, where Tom managed a galvanizing plant; Jo Ann had her own engineering consulting company. "We wanted to welcome travelers into a home at-mosphere. This house, our 'painted lady', is in a wonderful area to live in and visit."

IN RESIDENCE: In hosts' quarters—two indoor cats.
BED AND BATH: Seven rooms; two are air-conditioned suites with beds in two rooms. All vary in size, shape, amenities (fireplace and/or ceiling fan). All private baths (some shower only, others with tub/shower); five are en-suite, two in hall. Beds are queen-sized or double.
BREAKFAST: 8, 8:30, 9. (Coffee and tea earlier.) Tom's fresh fruit dishes. Yogurt and granola. Eggs, pancakes, or French toast with ham or sausage. Muffins and homemade bread. Juice. Hot beverages. Served by fire in chandeliered dining room at tables for two or four.
PLUS: Fireplaced dining room, living room, and library/TV/game room. Tea and home-made cookies at 3. Wicker-filled porch. Daily Internet weather printout.

᳓ From Connecticut, California, Canada: *"Great host and hostess. . . . Breakfast was a special treat. . . . A beautiful and restful place."*

᳓ Cornwall Orchards Bed & Breakfast   802/462-2272

1364 Route 30, Cornwall, VT 05753-9261   **E-MAIL** cornorch@together.net

HOSTS: Juliet and Bob Gerlin
LOCATION: Rural. On 14 acres—with barn—along a ridge with both Green and Adirondack mountain views. Next to one small orchard and across from two others. Two miles— "three minutes" —to Middlebury College (golf course open to the public). Near Long Trail for hiking. Minutes from cross-country ski trails. Forty-five minutes to Burlington or to Sugarbush or Mad River Glen; 25 to Middlebury College Snowbowl.
OPEN: Year round. Two-night minimum on holiday, summer, and foliage weekends.
RATES: $85 per room. $15 extra person. ♦♦ ⊞ ⊿ ⊱

᳓ From New York, Texas, Connecticut, Rhode Island, Massachusetts, Vermont, and New Jersey: *"A gem . . . newly renovated, modern farmhouse; homey, roaring fireplace every night . . . spotless . . . five stars! . . . Early-morning hike along a trail through the property followed by a skip-lunch breakfast is a great way to start the day . . . a wealth of area information. . . . Everything is homemade or Vermont grown. . . . Fun, warm, gracious hosts. . . . We would gladly move in permanently. . . . Stay when traveling on business. Setting, service, and ambiance unmatched in the area. . . . A special treat. . . . Intricate Yankee crafts-manship. . . . Wonderful views. . . . We love this place!"*

THE GERLINS love it too. When they restored the 1784 expanded Cape in 1994, they made it bright and sunny, with lots of pine and no clutter; with tab curtains on the windows; and with books, wing chairs, and a Moroccan rug by the fire. Here the hosts hike, ski, canoe, and sail—and share the mystique of Vermont, a place they had long wanted to live in. In Connecticut Juliet was an assistant to a musician and composer; Bob, a justice of the peace, was a lawyer.

BED AND BATH: Five rooms; all private baths. Four with queen beds, one with a twin and a three-quarter bed. Three first-floor rooms (one is handicapped accessible) with individual thermostats and tub/shower baths. Second-floor rooms have tiled shower baths.
BREAKFAST: 7–9. Whole-grain organic pancakes, French toast, or free-range eggs any style. Vermont sausage, bacon, or ham. Homemade applesauce and strawberry-rhubarb compote, in season. Local maple syrup. Fresh fruit. Fresh orange juice. Homemade granola.
PLUS: Late-afternoon refreshments. Down comforters. Fresh fruit and flowers.

～ Judith's Garden Bed & Breakfast   802/247-4707

The Goshen–Ripton Road,   E-MAIL gardenbb@together.net
Goshen, VT 05733-9209   www.virtualcities.com/vt/judithsgarden.htm

HOSTS: Judith Irven and (husband) Dick Conrad
LOCATION: Quiet. "Out in the country—with no other house in view." On 30 acres surrounded by Green Mountain National Forest's trails for hiking, cross-country skiing, snowshoeing. Eight miles to downhill skiing; 7 to Brandon, 15 to Middlebury.
OPEN: Year round. Two-night weekend minimum except April and November.
RATES: $75–$95. Singles $5 less. Rollaway $15. ♥ ⃰ ⊞ ❖ ✄ ⅍ ⅍

THE PERFECT weekend getaway for the hosts became their year-round residence in 1994 when Dick, a Middlebury College graduate, and English-born Judith left their positions in the telephone industry. Five truckload trips later, Judith's New Jersey gardens were transplanted here. Now a professional landscape and garden designer, she tends the inn's extensive perennial beds, display borders, herbs, and edible flowers. And now the 1840s wing—with wide-board floors on the first floor—is attached to a new back ell: a cathedral-ceilinged country kitchen/dining room that has garden and mountain views and French doors leading into a working greenhouse.

IN RESIDENCE: Bary, a black dog often "borrowed by guests for morning walks. 'Little Cat' is bigger since named."
BED AND BATH: Three rooms in 1840s wing with individual thermostats, en-suite baths. First floor—double bed, shower bath. Second floor—queen bed, tub/shower bath; room with twin beds, shower bath.

continued . . .

BREAKFAST: 8:30–9:30. Fruit dish, cereal, low-fat homemade granola, and different homemade breads and muffins baked daily. Special diets accommodated with advance notice. Served in spacious country kitchen.

PLUS: Plenty of lawn. Stone fireplaces with woodstoves in living room and country kitchen. Upright piano in living room. Tea or lemonade and cookies. Evening meal by prior arrangement—$15 per person.

       🐦 From New York, New Jersey, Florida, Massachusetts, Vermont, Texas: *"An oasis. . . . Bedazzling gardens . . . warblers, hummingbirds, butterflies. . . . A piece of paradise . . . intimate. Not too big. Not stuffy. . . Clean and comfortable . . . country charm . . . personable hosts offer genuine hospitality. . . . Peaceful ambiance . . . easy drive to Middlebury . . . divine, generous, healthy, homemade breakfasts . . . hiking trails just outside the door . . . reasonably priced. . . . Great!"*

🐦 *Shoreham Inn & Country Store*   802/897-5081

51 Inn Road, P.O. Box 182,   800/255-5081
Shoreham, VT 05770   **E-MAIL** shoreinn@together.net

HOSTS:	Jim and Julie Ortuno
LOCATION:	In a small village setting with hiking/cross-country trail. Surrounded by apple orchards and farms. Twelve miles to Middlebury or to Mount Independence. Five miles from ferry crossing to Fort Ticonderoga.
OPEN:	Year round.
RATES:	$85–$95. Singles $20–$30 less. Extra person $15. MC, Visa. 🛆 🎲 ❖ 🚭 ⚕

"THIS IS FUN—and especially great for men who think staying at a B&B is like putting on a tie!" That guest's comment just about sums up the decor and hosting style of the Ortunos. Since moving from California in 1997, they have made many changes to this rambling added-on-to frame hotel. They decorated guest rooms with wallpaper, photos, fabrics, quilts, and collectibles that fit into themes including Lake Champlain, Carousel, Black Bear, Fly-Fishing, Baseball, and Farm. In Julie's signature "no white" style, the living room has apricot/peach walls with deep teal trim. The balustrade was originally in a local church. Eclectic and antique furnishings include two (named) carousel horses, both restored by co-innkeeper/storekeeper Jim, who is also an upholsterer (in great demand) of vintage cars, boats, and furniture. Julie has experience in the travel industry followed by several years as a kindergarten teacher. Shoreham Inn fans include both tour-company and independent cyclists as well as hikers, sightseers, and parents of college students.

IN RESIDENCE: Marcus, age eleven; and Chelsea, age nine.

BED AND BATH: Ten rooms on three floors with queen or extra-long twins/king option. First floor—room with en-suite bath. Second floor—seven rooms; all private baths (some attached, some in hall). Two third-floor rooms share a bath.

BREAKFAST: 8:30. French toast, pancakes, or eggs. Sausage, cereal, muffins. Juice. Coffee and tea. In large beamed dining room by fire.
PLUS: Two sitting rooms with wood-burning fireplace. No TV. Guest refrigerator. Deck. Wine and beer license. Next-door country store for groceries, Vermont crafts, take-out sandwiches, salads, pizza.

⌃ *Strong House Inn*   802/877-3337

94 West Main Street,
Vergennes, VT 05491

FAX 802/877-2599
E-MAIL innkeeper@stronghouseinn.com
www.stronghouseinn.com

HOSTS: Mary and Hugh Bargiel
LOCATION: Rural. On Route 22A between two working farms. One mile south of Vergennes center. Twenty-two miles south of Burlington; 15 to Shelburne Museum or Middlebury; 7 to Lake Champlain, 30 to Sugarbush resort. Ten-minute drive to New York state ferry.
OPEN: Year round.
RATES: ($20 more, mid-September–October.) King bed $95. Queen $85; $120 with fireplace and canopied bed. Suites $120–$175. Additional person $30. Rabbit Ridge $115, $125, $165; $250 Adirondack Room. Package rates for quilting weekends. Amex, MC, Visa. ♥ ⊞ ❖ ⚔ ⤫ ❦

THE "PERFECT B&B for pampering"—a National Historic Register Greek Revival furnished with antiques and traditional pieces—"grows" through every edition of this book. A recently opened annex on the ridge across from the parking area, another Greek Revival, includes some beamed cathedral-ceilinged rooms, one with English period furniture, and an Adirondack Room with floor-to-ceiling stone fireplace and a double Jacuzzi tub. Since the Bargiels purchased the meadow and forest behind the inn, guests enjoy walking trails in warm months, sledding in winter. An arbor leads to vegetable and formal herb gardens with an English cottage as a backdrop. For sunsets, gourmet basket dinners, or renewal of wedding vows, there's an Amish-built gazebo. Mary had experience in catering (and real estate) in Florida. Here, she has been named "Person of the Year" by the Small Business Administration and "Innkeeper of the Year" by the Vermont Restaurant and Lodging Association. November through May, noon to 4 p.m., she serves a "totally civilized" tea to the public. And she hosts winter quilting seminars that attract guests from all over the country.

IN RESIDENCE: Pandy, a black house cat.
BED AND BATH: Fourteen rooms with king or queen bed. All private baths. *Main house* (centrally air conditioned)—eight rooms (one has canopied bed and fireplace). One has queen four-poster, shower bath, living room with double sofa bed, cable TV. *Rabbit Ridge*

continued . . .

Country House—six air-conditioned rooms (one has a trundle bed also), cable TV, telephone, coffee niche, breakfast area; amenities vary and include French doors to private balcony, mountain or countryside views, fireplace, double Jacuzzi.
BREAKFAST: 8–9. Quiche, omelets, crepes, eggs Benedict, French toast, fresh-baked muffins, fresh fruit, bacon or sausage. On fine china and pewter in formal dining room in main house. Rabbit Ridge guests have option of a continental breakfast delivered to their room.
PLUS: Central air conditioning. Fireplaced living room and library. Upright piano. Individual thermostats. Evening tea, appetizers, or desserts. Turndown service for suites. Guest refrigerator. Wine/beer-licensed guest beverage center. Picnic baskets, $15 per person. Dinner baskets with china, silver, and linen, $22.50 per person. Dinner option (winter months), $25 per person. Coming: a new conference center on site.

> From Massachusetts: *"'Country elegance' is perhaps an overused term, but in this case it is a perfect description . . . warm and cozy atmosphere . . . unsurpassed hospitality."*

Whitford House Inn

Addison, VT
Mailing address: 912 Grandey Road,
Vergennes, VT 05491-8851

802/758-2704
800/746-2704
FAX 802/758-2089
E-MAIL whitford@together.net
www.whitfordhouseinn.com

HOSTS: Barbara and Bruce Carson
LOCATION: Tranquil. On a scenic "undiscovered" lane off the beaten track. With 180-degree view of Adirondack Mountains. Adjacent to protected wildlife area. Twelve miles to Middlebury and Vergennes, 20 to Fort Ticonderoga, 25 to Shelburne Museum, 2 to Lake Champlain.
OPEN: Year round.
RATES: Main house $110–$150. Guest house $150–$175. Additional guest $25.
♥ ♦ ⚹ ⚹ ♥

> From Illinois, Colorado, New Jersey, California, Ohio, England:
"Epitomizes Vermont's best. Our favorite B&B on a bike tour . . . immaculate . . . eclectically decorated without clutter . . . terrific views from verandah. . . . Felt nurtured by more than the lovely breakfast on beautiful china. It was hard to leave. . . . Lots of good conversation; rest; food my husband is still talking about . . . a gem."

THIS IDYLLIC RETREAT, a c. 1790s country home, is complete with hosts who, happily for travelers, thought it a natural for an inn. In California Barbara taught English; Bruce was an electromechanical engineer. In 1988, after their daughter graduated from Middlebury College, the Carsons "found" and restored this 200-year-old added-on-to farmhouse. The inn with its wraparound front porch has been featured in *Yankee, Builder/Architect,* and *Vermont* magazines and on *Home and Garden TV.* The welcoming interior has wide-board floors, Morris chairs by the fire, and a blend of antiques and modern art.

IN RESIDENCE: Two beagles. One cat.

BED AND BATH: Three rooms with views of meadow and mountains. All have private full baths. Main house—first-floor double-bedded room; two second floor bedrooms with king/twins option. Adjacent guest house—king/twins option, private full bath with radiant heated floor, separate sitting area with double sofa bed, wet bar.

BREAKFAST: At hour requested by guests. Scalloped apples and fresh fruit. Frittatas, Belgian waffles, or French pancakes with fresh berries. Homemade breads, muffins, jams. Special diets accommodated.

PLUS: Refreshments with hors d'oeuvres or homemade cookies. Wood-burning fireplaces in beamed-ceilinged living room and in (extensive) library. Baby grand piano. Window fans. Turndown service. Down pillows and comforters. No TV. Picnic baskets arranged. Dinners by prior reservation. Use of canoe and bicycles.

⚞ *Northfield Inn*   802/485-8558

228 Highland Avenue, Northfield, VT 05663-1448

HOST: Aglaia Stalb

LOCATION: In historic district. Overlooks village and Norwich University. Five miles west of I-89; 9 miles south of Montpelier; 23 miles south of Stowe; 16 miles to Sugarbush. Near restaurants and New England Culinary Institute (for dinner).

OPEN: Year round. Two-night minimum September 15–October 25 and during special events.

RATES: Queen bed $95 private bath, $85 shared. Single bed $75. Two-room suite (for four) $190. Three-room suite (for six) $285. Getaway packages. MC, Visa. ♥ ⊞ ⌖ ⌿ ❦

Condé Nast Traveler included this inn among its top 100 1996 readers choice awards. *GQ* featured it in a 1997 Taiwanese issue. From the porches there are panoramic views of gardens, mountains, and sunsets. A welcoming fireplace blazes in the winter. Restored in 1990, this twenty-five-room Victorian, once the home of a Borneo princess (who died in Northfield in 1997), has Palladian windows in four gables and lots of natural woodwork. Decor features floral wallcoverings, Oriental rugs, antiques, and period lighting fixtures. Recent additions include a fitness room, and beyond the meadow, a woodland pond.

Aglaia, formerly a section head of computer resources with Grumman Aerospace Corporation, has also worked as an interior designer. She owned and managed a construction company and has experience in real estate sales and investments. "Here we meet an intellectually stimulating and culturally fascinating group of dignitaries, tourists, corporate executives, and many who come for beautiful (small) weddings."

FOREIGN LANGUAGE SPOKEN: Greek.

BED AND BATH: Six large rooms, each with ceiling fan and private bath, plus a two-room

continued . . .

suite (sleeps four; can be two separate rooms that share a tub-and-shower bath) and a three-room suite (can be three private rooms that share a shower bath). Most rooms have a queen bed with feather bedding. Private baths have glass-enclosed showers; one also has claw-footed tub.

BREAKFAST: Full 7–10. Continental thereafter. Crepes, stuffed French toast, German apple pancakes, eggs Benedict, soufflé, or stuffed omelets. Fresh fruit and homemade jams. Special ethnic menus prepared. Table is set with bone china, crystal, linen, fine lace.
PLUS: Afternoon tea. In winter, soup at noon. Butler's pantry with refrigerator, fresh fruit, home-baked goods, snacks; "Make yourself at home." Down comforters and pillows. Two parlors. Skiers' lounge. TV/video lounge with extensive video library. Conference room. Croquet. Horseshoes. Dinners for groups.

> ≫ Guests wrote: "Beautiful . . . congenial . . . peaceful."

≫ Rose Apple Acres Farm

802/988-4300

721 East Hill,
North Troy, VT 05859-9376

877/879-9135
FAX 802/988-2309

HOSTS: Jay, Cam, and (son) Courtney Mead
LOCATION: Rural and quiet Northeast Kingdom, with spectacular views of Canadian Sutton Range. "To Canada, one mile as the crow flies; two hours' drive to Montreal." Five miles to end of Long Trail. Ten miles to Jay Peak ski area. Less than a mile from Route 105. Near antiquing, covered bridges, Big Falls on Missisquoi River. "Great chefs at many restaurants within 10 miles."
OPEN: Year round. "Advance reservations a must!"
RATES: Per room. $50 shared bath. $60 private bath. Three-day doll-making package rates include dinners and doll(s). Discover, MC, Visa. ♥ ☛ ❖ ⚄ ⅄ 鴙

> ≫ From Canada: "*Unspoiled charm, magnificent setting, reasonable rates, comfortable living arrangements, great food, myriad of activities—even sleigh rides . . . very relaxing, beyond our expectations . . . feel like you're staying with friends.*"

"NO, YOU DON'T have to dress for dinner," laughs Cam when she gets a call from someone who hasn't been to "a real B&B" before. Here you can pick apples or berries, swim in a farm pond, learn to milk a goat, or cross-country ski. Enjoy the farmers' porch in a rocker. Or, for a very special opportunity, come for three days and make your own porcelain doll. Before Cam became an expert at this craft, she was a music and choir director on Cape Cod. During our stay, Jay, a former building materials buyer, suggested a cycling stop at a hidden—we never would have found it on our own—swimming hole with waterfall where we spent all day. They hardly make B&Bs like this anymore.

IN RESIDENCE: Son Courtney is a farrier (and an ironwork craftsman) who tends a flock of thirty-plus sheep. Ten horses; two are Belgians that pull antique sleighs, plow, and harrows. Three collies—(mother) Mollie and her offspring Lady and Pippin. S.S. is a barn cat.
BED AND BATH: Three second-floor rooms. One with king bed and private full bath. Two rooms, each with one double bed and one twin, share a full bath.
BREAKFAST: 8–9. "Homemade granola and maple muffins are favorites." Maybe mapled apples or blueberry buckle. Served in tin-ceilinged kitchen.
PLUS: Living room with Franklin fireplace for guests. Transportation provided to/from end of Long Trail; small fee charged.

﹏ Hickory Ridge House Bed & Breakfast

802/387-5709

53 Hickory Ridge Road South,
Putney, VT 05346

800/380-9218
FAX 802/387-4328
E-MAIL MAIL@hickoryridgehouse.com
www.HickoryRidgeHouse.com

HOSTS: Linda and Jack Bisbee
LOCATION: On 8 acres with perennial gardens, woods for hiking, views of rolling meadows and hills. Near theater, music festivals, artists' studios, canoeing and kayaking (on Connecticut River). Two miles from Putney village, 10 north of Brattleboro.
OPEN: Year round. Two-night minimum on holiday and foliage season weekends.
RATES: $125–$165 per room. Cottage suite $170–$220. Rollaway $18. Single and corporate rates available Sunday-Thursday. Amex, MC, Visa.
♥ ⊞ ⚼ ⅄ ⚛ ♥♡

A DREAM MATCH! Jack was a designer/builder and Linda was in banking before they had a smaller B&B (for three years) a few miles away. In 1998 they acquired this 1808 Federal brick country manor, an established B&B. Once a college president's residence, this architectural gem, listed in the National Register of Historic Places, features spacious rooms and halls, a grand stairway, and Palladian window. The Bisbees have repainted and wallpapered, furnished with antiques and traditional furnishings, and expanded the gardens. Itinerary planning is a specialty. So are Linda's "to die for" breakfasts.

BED AND BATH: Seven large rooms and one suite; all with private bath, air conditioning, TV/VCR, phone, king or queen bed. *Main house*—six rooms. First-floor room is handicapped accessible. On second floor, three rooms have working fireplace; one other room has ceiling fan and gas fireplace-stove. *Cottage*—room with king bed has deck, private entrance; suite has queen bed, large fireplaced living room, full kitchen.
BREAKFAST: 8–9:30. Freshly squeezed orange juice. Croissant, French toast, cheese stratas, ginger and banana pancakes. Breakfast meats. Homemade breads and coffee cakes.

continued . . .

Served in stenciled dining room (with woodstove) or on deck overlooking gardens and meadow.

PLUS: Wood-burning fireplace in living room. Upright piano in the morning room. Tea and cookies. Guest refrigerator.

⋙ *Placidia Farm Bed and Breakfast*   802/728–9883

1470 Bent Hill Road,   **www.obs-us.com**
Randolph, VT 05060-9413   **www.bedandbreakfast.com**

HOSTS: Viola Frost-Laitinen and Don Laitinen
LOCATION: Six miles north of Randolph, 1.5 miles up a dirt road. On 81 quiet acres with mountain views, pond, brook, Christmas tree farm. Near alpine and cross-country skiing areas.
OPEN: Year round. Two-night minimum on holiday weekends and in foliage season.
RATES: $90–$115. $40 each additional guest. $12 per child ages two through ten.
♥ ☕ ⚄ ⊱

⋙ From Connecticut, New Jersey, New York, California, Massachusetts: *"Super place and hosts. Spacious, comfortable, and simple—no Jacuzzi—accommodations ... breathtaking views ... welcoming goodies ... exquisite flower beds, a manicured lawn ... breakfast in room with windows on three sides ... hummingbirds sipping nectar just ten feet away.... Makes you want to move to Vermont.... A best-kept secret ... a wonderful place to feel at peace.... First class."*

JUST THE ONE suite. All for you. As Vi notes, "Many guests want to buy this place—'paradise', they say—and do just what we do! For everyone, there's peace and quiet and plenty of privacy." Once a weekend retreat, the hand-hewn log house, completely remodeled in 1996, is home to Vi, a former federal government tax adjuster, and Don, a skilled woodworker who is a retired occupational health engineer.

IN RESIDENCE: Two cats—Fawn and BD.
FOREIGN LANGUAGE SPOKEN: A little German.
BED AND BATH: Suite/apartment—large bedroom with double bed and rollaway, queen sofa bed in living room. Fully equipped kitchen with microwave. Full bath. Private entrance and deck.
BREAKFAST: Usually 8–9. Omelets, German apple pancakes, fresh eggs, or waffles. Popovers or homemade muffins. Fresh fruit and juices. On plant-filled sunporch with linen and fine china.
PLUS: Living room with TV, radio, books, cards, games. Fans. Aquatic garden. Cedar deck. Hiking. Make-your-own cross-country trails on property.

⚖ *High Pastures*

802/773-2087

Cold River Road,
Shrewsbury, VT 05738

877/819-9500
FAX 802/775-2110

HOSTS: Taffy and Hull Maynard
LOCATION: Rural. On the Long and Appalachian Trails. On 125 acres with mountain biking, hiking and cross-country ski trails. Eight miles from Route 7 or Rutland; 2 miles to village of North Shrewsbury. Fifteen miles to Okemo Mountain, 20 to Killington.
OPEN: Year round. Two-night minimum on major holiday weekends.
RATES: $75 shared bath. $85 private bath. $15 extra bed. $10 extra bed under age five. Cabin $90 for two; $100 with breakfast. ♥♥ ⊞ ✄ ⩜ ♥○

"YOU ENRICHED our lives," wrote guests about their stay at this 200-year-old farmhouse. Once an inn, it was restored by the Maynards, who have lived here since the 1960s. Now that their four children are grown, they share High Pastures with guests who swim in the pool, play tennis, and explore trails. Some guests have been introduced to cross-country skiing right here. All in peace. Without crowds. March is lambing month. June is sheep-shearing month. Just about everyone walks (five minutes) up to the log cabin for the spectacular view and, sometimes, a cider party. What a setting for really getting away from it all—with the option of breakfast in the main house.

Taffy, a native Vermonter, teaches physical education. Hull is an insurance agent who, in 1996, became a state senator by two votes!

IN RESIDENCE: Winston, an English springer spaniel, "our people lover." On the farm—sheep, chicken, turkeys, pigs.
BED AND BATH: Five rooms with queen, double, or twin beds. First floor—one room has private exterior entrance, a queen bed, fireplace, sitting area, shower bath. Narrow stairs to second floor—room with a queen bed, a twin bed, sitting area, private bath with clawfoot tub, separate shower. Two rooms, each with two twin beds, and one small room with a double bed share a full bath. "Primitive" log cabin that sleeps eight has a chemical toilet, a gas stove for cooking, gas refrigerator, no heat; "running water planned for publication date of this book."
BREAKFAST: Until 10. Fresh fruit. Pancakes, baked French toast, omelets, or quiche. Homemade bread. Served in country kitchen.
PLUS: Wood-burning fireplace and grand piano in living room. Picnic baskets ($6). Babysitting. Perennial and vegetable gardens. Suggestions for activities, shopping, antiquing.

♨ *Maple Crest Farm*   802/492-3367

Shrewsbury, VT
Mailing address: Box 120, Cuttingsville, VT 05738

HOSTS: William and Donna Smith
LOCATION: High, with great views and Long Trail hiking (and cross-country ski) trails right here. Ten miles south of Rutland, 10 north of Ludlow. Near Killington and Okemo ski areas.
OPEN: Year round. Two-night minimum during holidays and foliage season.
RATES: Include tax. $32.50 single. $54 double with shared bath; $59.50 with private half bath. Apartments (extra charged for breakfast if farmhouse seating available) $75 for two adults, $10/additional adult. $5 per child. One night's deposit required . ♥ ⊞ ⚅ ⌇

THIS LEGENDARY B&B has been discovered by *Country Living* and *Yankee* magazines. And by artists, quilters (who come for workshops), retreat planners, and photographers. They all comment about "true Vermont hospitality" where farming and sugar making are carried on by a fifth and a sixth generation. The antiques and personal treasures reflect Smith activities through the years.

Except for the first twenty years, when it was run as a tavern, this twenty-seven-room landmark built in 1808 has been a private home, each generation welcoming guests on a small scale. Robert Frost and past governors slept here. In 1969 Donna started B&B here as it is today: "noncommercial—a real home away from home."

Donna, a bank director who has served on the board of directors for the Fletcher Farm School of Arts and Crafts, teaches theorem painting; she is also accomplished in Bauernmaleri German folk art painting.

IN RESIDENCE: Star, a Yorkshire terrier. About forty-five cattle in the meadows.
BED AND BATH: Six large rooms (two are suites with private half baths), each with a double and a single bed; woodstove in some rooms. One first-floor room with half bath shares full bath with second-floor rooms. Two apartments; each sleeps five. Cot and crib available.
BREAKFAST: 8:15–9:30. Full country meal with bacon and eggs, buttermilk pancakes with Smiths' award-winning maple syrup, homemade muffins and jams.
PLUS: Seasonal flowers. Beverage. Tour of farm and maple sugaring operation.

♨ From Washington, Rhode Island, California: *"The most memorable part of the trip. . . . I had to arrive late at night and leave early in the morning, yet was met with great warmth. In that short time I knew it was a place that I wanted to return to with my family. . . . Snowed in during a blizzard and loved it."*

⚞ Smugglers' Notch Inn

802/644-2412

Church Street, Jeffersonville, VT

800/845-3101

Mailing address: P.O. Box 280,

FAX 802/644-2881

Jeffersonville, VT 05464

E-MAIL info@smugglers-notch-inn.com

www.smugglers-notch-inn.com

HOSTS: Cynthia Barber and (husband) Jon Day

LOCATION: In a rural village on the National Register of Historic Places. Next door to old town hall, now a post office. On Route 108, one-quarter mile south of Route 15. Five miles to Smugglers' Notch ski area. Forty minutes to Jay Peak ski area. To Stowe, in summer, 25 minutes via Smugglers' Notch Scenic Highway; in winter (when mountain pass is closed), 40 minutes.

OPEN: Year round. Two-night minimum February and Christmas holiday weeks, during fall foliage, and holidays.

RATES: Gratuities included. $75–$125. April–late May and late October–mid-December $60–$85. (Rates vary according to room size and location.) $15 extra person over age twelve. $10 ages two through twelve. Singles $10 less. Multiple-night-stay discounts. Group rates. Amex, MC, Visa.

♥ ⛨ ⊞ ⚅ ⚘ ♥♡

⚞ From Massachusetts, New York, and biking tours: *"In ten years of traveling, especially in the Northeast . . . the first time I felt more than comfortable at a place that is not home. . . . Cool with our three-year-old. . . . All recommendations were right on . . . clean, well-kept . . . treated like family . . . excellent breakfasts . . . imaginative dishes . . . . celebrated our engagement here. . . . Go the extra mile. . . . Awesome, awesome, awesome."*

THE QUILTS are locally made. The towels are fluffy and the soaps are glycerine. The 1791 farmhouse property has an in-ground pool, and on the rear deck, a year-round hot tub. Yet, overall, this is an old-fashioned New England inn with simple decor and good food. Old-fashioned hospitality, too, is a feature offered by white-bearded Jon, a former naval architect now famous for his breads and muffins, and Cynthia, who managed a research project at Children's Hospital in Boston. They had much experience (and fun) leading cycling and cross-country ski trips for New England's largest cycling organization and for the Appalachian Mountain Club. A conversation at one Vermont inn inspired them to choose innkeeping as their career change in 1995.

BED AND BATH: Eleven second-floor rooms. Each with private full bath (one with Jacuzzi; one with gas fireplace). King, queen, double, or twin beds.

BREAKFAST: 8–9. Fresh fruit, juices, low-fat granola, homemade baked goods. Cinnamon oatmeal pancakes or egg dishes and locally made sausage. Served in converted ballroom with woodstove and hardwood floors.

PLUS: Gas fireplace and TV in tin-ceilinged living room. Restaurant on premises seats about fifty. Bar has five stools and copper foot rail. Detailed instructions and maps for more than twenty cycling routes that begin at the front door.

➳ Brass Lantern Inn

717 Maple Street,
Stowe, VT 05672-4250

802/253-2229

u.s./CANADA 800/729-2980
UK 0 800 9623 32
FAX 802/253-7425
E-MAIL brasslntrn@aol.com
www.brasslanterninn.com

HOST: Andy Aldrich

LOCATION: Half a mile from village center. Within ten minutes of "everything," including restaurants, downhill and cross-country skiing, tennis, golf, hot-air ballooning, concerts, theater, sleigh and surrey rides, antiquing.

OPEN: Year round. Two-night minimum during foliage and on holiday and ski season weekends. Four-day minimum Christmas–New Year's week.

RATES: (For stays of two or more nights, health club privileges included.) Late June–mid-September and January–March $90–$110 twin or double bed; queen bed $110–$145 with whirlpool, $135–$165 with fireplace. Mid-September–late October and Christmas week $100–$175 double, $125–$195 whirlpool, $150–$220 fireplace and whirlpool. April–late June and late October–Christmas $80–$100 double, $110–$125 whirlpool, $130–$150 fireplace and whirlpool. Singles $10 less. Packages include skiing, golf, honeymoon/anniversary, fly/drive, spa, outdoor adventure, romance, attractions, history. Amex, MC, Visa. ♥ ❖ ⚔ ⚒ ❤

MANY EUROPEANS have discovered this intimate inn. Honeymooners and other romantics are among those who appreciate the fireplaces, whirlpool tubs, and antiques (but no clutter). An active farm from 1800 until 1965, this was a lodge and then a restaurant before the Aldriches made it into an inn, an award-winning restoration with wainscoting, wide-planked floors, and a beamed living room that has a view of Mount Mansfield. There's stenciling, small-print wallpapers, and handmade quilts. And food that the Gourmet Diners Society of North America acknowledged with a "Restaurant [inn category] of Distinction" designation. Andy, a 251 Club member—that means he has visited every Vermont city and town—dovetails innkeeping with his Stowe-based construction business.

BED AND BATH: Nine air-conditioned antiques-furnished rooms (most with Mount Mansfield view); all private baths. Larger rooms, some with fireplace and whirlpool, in farmhouse and attached renovated barn, have queen bed (some canopied), full bath (some with whirlpool). Cozy farmhouse double-bedded gable rooms have shower baths.

BREAKFAST: 8–9:30. All homemade. Entrée made with Vermont produce and products might be French toast, apple crepes, blueberry pancakes, or egg casserole. Fruit, juice, hot beverages. Special diets accommodated.

PLUS: Central air conditioning. Patio. Tea and dessert. Maps for self-guided walking, driving, hiking, and biking tours. Bath with shower for after checkout. Transportation arranged to/from airport, train, or bus. Recommendations for everything "from spa to sleigh rides to candlelit restaurants."

🐦 Ski Inn

802/253-4050

Route 108, Stowe, VT 05672-4822

E-MAIL harriet@ski-inn.com
www.ski-inn.com/bc

HOST: Harriet Heyer, assisted by daughter Lyndall and her husband, Scott Dorwart
LOCATION: Set back from the highway on 27 wooded acres, 5.2 miles to Stowe village. Five-minute drive to Stowe ski area.
OPEN: Year round. May–November as a B&B; dinners served in winter.
RATES: Per person, double occupancy. $22.50 shared bath, $25–$30 private bath. In winter (includes breakfast and dinner) $55 shared bath, $65 private bath.

🕅 ⊞ ❖ 🛇 🍴

A LEGEND. An old-fashioned inn with a big fieldstone fireplace, knotty pine walls, and a Ping-Pong table. It was built by Larry Heyer in 1941 when Stowe was primarily a summer resort, when some folks weren't quite sure that skiing would be more than a fad. Fifty years later Larry and Harriet, parents of Lyndall, a former U.S. ski team member, were still saying, "We started the trend of intimate country inns and have refused to expand."

In the 1940s, Harriet had public relations experience in Manhattan. Now, between seasons, she bicycles in the United States and Europe. In the winter she cross-country skis occasionally and downhill skis almost every day. "My daughter has successfully talked me out of trying snowboarding." And sometimes she hosts returnees who represent three generations.

BED AND BATH: Ten large rooms on two floors, each with a double and a single bed. Some rooms have private full baths.
BREAKFAST: In B&B season, continental (until noon) with homemade jellies and preserves from wild elderberry, chokecherry, blueberry, or rhubarb. In winter, breakfast 8–9, dinner at 6:30 with homemade everything.
PLUS: Flat hiking road on property. More than 30 miles of cross-country ski trails outside the back door. Outdoor fireplace and patio. Trout stream. Game room with "in tune" upright piano. Loan of a ski jacket "sometimes needed by guests from as far away as South America."

🐦 From New York: *"Into the driveway, over a wooden bridge, and you're into another world. . . . Roomy, charming, comfortable, spotless. . . . Has intimacy of being at Mother's big, roomy house, without the responsibilities . . . sound of babbling brook . . . soothing classical music . . . excellent plentiful food, not gourmet but touched up with homemade and homegrown goodies."* From Maryland: *"Thirty-three years ago I spent one summer night on way to Canada. . . . Had a chance to return this summer with my 32-year-old daughter. . . . Made a three-day reservation. . . . Thoroughly enchanted, we stayed a week, making Ski Inn our home-away-from-home while touring the whole region."*

✒ Stone Hill Inn   802/253-6282

89 Houston Farm Road,   FAX 802/253-7415
Stowe, VT 05672-4225   E-MAIL stay@stonehillinn.com
                                                       www.stonehillinn.com

HOSTS: Hap and Amy Jordan
LOCATION: Set back from road in a secluded wooded hilltop area along Route
108/Mountain Road. Three miles north of Stowe village; 4.7 miles south of
Stowe's ski area's main base lodge. Next to antiques shop. Across road from
dairy farm and Stowe Recreation Path.
OPEN: Year round. Two-night minimum on weekends (exception: last-minute
availability) and during fall foliage. Three-night minimum on some holiday
weekends. Four nights for Christmas/New Year's week.
RATES: Early April–mid-June, $250. Mid-June–mid-September and mid-
October–mid-December, $295. Early January–late March, $385. Late
December through holiday week and mid-September–mid-October, $425.
Packages available. Amex, Diners, MC, Visa. ♥ ⊞ ❖ ⚸ ⅍ ♥♡

THIS FRIENDLY nine-room inn has everything from two-person Jacuzzis facing a fireplace
to private golf club access, from soundproof rooms to use of toboggan and snowshoes
right here. And plenty of privacy. "Let's just build it!" said the Jordans when they couldn't
find such a place. Indeed, they have. They fulfilled their dream and opened in 1998. The
young—"now about thirty"—couple met when Hap was a chef at Amy's family-run
restaurant in Virginia.

      ✒ Guests from Florida, Connecticut, and Massachusetts—including many
nonskiing winter guests—snail-mailed and emailed to me: *"Incredible inn. They left nothing out!. . . . Amy and Hap knew just when to offer assistance. . . . Like having your own personal assistant. . . . Memorable gourmet breakfasts . . . a wonderful romantic getaway . . .
perfect setting for my proposal. . . . We will be back!"*

IN RESIDENCE: Two cats in hosts' quarters.
BED AND BATH: All on one level—nine rooms (one handicapped accessible), each with
king bed, sitting area, TV/VCR, individually controlled heat and air conditioning, CD
player, two-sided fireplace visible from bedroom and from two-person Jacuzzi in bath,
double sink vanity, shower stall with built-in seat, hair dryer.
BREAKFAST: 7–9:30 winter; 7:30–10 rest of year. (Coffee and tea available at 6:30.) Fruit
course. Homemade baked goods. Choice of three entrées such as smoked salmon quiche,
apple and Brie omelets, huevos rancheros, oatmeal griddle cakes with apple cider sauce.
Home fries, sausage, or bacon. In fireplaced breakfast room at tables for two.
PLUS: Year-round outdoor hot tub. Large stone fireplaces in living room and game room
(billiard table, games, cards). Movie library. Soft drinks and snacks in guest pantry. Hors
d'oeuvres daily at 5 p.m. Hammock. Guest laundry room. Boot-drying room. Ski/snow-
board lockers.

🐦 *The Inn at Round Barn Farm*

1661 East Warren Road,
Waitsfield, VT 05673-0247

802/496-2276 (B-A-R-N)

FAX 802/496-8832
E-MAIL roundbarn@madriver.com
www.innattheroundbarn.com

HOST: AnneMarie Simko-DeFreest

LOCATION: Dramatic. Less than 2 miles from Route 100, through the covered bridge and over a hill to 245 acres of gardens, ponds, meadows, and woods. Fifteen minutes from Sugarbush (North and South) and Mad River ski areas.

OPEN: Year round. Two-night minimum preferred on weekends.

RATES: Double bed $135. Queen bed $150; $165 canopied with Jacuzzi; $185 with fireplace, steam shower, cathedral ceiling. King/twins $185 with fireplace and steam shower. King with oversized Jacuzzi, steam shower, fireplace $220; king suite (separate living room) $250. Singles $10 less. Amex, MC, Visa. ♥ ❖ ⚄ ⚄ ⚄ ❤

IT'S ALL HERE: Cows in the meadows. A 19-mile cross-country ski center. A nineteenth-century farmhouse rebuilt with superb craftsmanship by the Simkos to a style it had never known. It's furnished with a marvelous blend of textures and colors, with country antiques, whimsy, and contemporary crafts. There's a 60-foot-long lap pool in the huge twelve-sided tri-level former dairy barn, which is now booked for concerts, lots of weddings, business conferences, and art shows and for cooking, photography, and watercolor workshops. (Climb to the cupola for an incredible view.) Extensive press coverage has included *Colonial Homes, Country Inns,* and the *New York Times.*

Since AnneMarie's parents, Jack and Doreen Simko, established the inn, they have seen AnneMarie become primary innkeeper, wedding planner, wife of a dairy farmer, mother of two, and cookbook coauthor. Jack, who was in the floral business in New Jersey, grows papyrus, water lilies, and the inn's edible flowers. The family has created what many guests—including romantics—consider the ultimate inn.

BED AND BATH: Eleven rooms, some with gas fireplace. All private baths; some with Jacuzzi or steam shower. Some canopied, antique, or custom-made beds. Luxury rooms have original beamed cathedral ceilings, gas fireplaces, air conditioning, floor-to-ceiling windows, paddle fans, phones.

BREAKFAST: 8:15–9:30. Maybe cottage cheese pancakes with raspberry sauce, blueberry Belgian waffles, or French toast with Grand Marnier. Homemade muffins. Baked fruit in winter. Colombian coffee.

PLUS: Late-afternoon hors d'oeuvres. Individual thermostats. Pool table. Classical music in fireplaced library. Homemade cookies. Snowshoe and cross-country ski rentals. Learn-to-ski packages and valleywide cross-country ski passes available.

⇗ Lareau Farm Country Inn

802/496-4949
800/833-0766
FAX 802/496-7979

Box 563, Route 100,
Waitsfield, VT 05673-0563

HOST: Susan Easley

LOCATION: Rural setting. In a large open meadow (with horses and, in back, a dramatic rock face), 1 mile south of Waitsfield. Along "crystal-clear Mad River" for swimming, canoeing, fishing. Near soaring, horseback riding, antiquing. Five miles to Mad River Glen and Sugarbush ski areas.

OPEN: Year round except two weeks in April and in November. Two-day minimum on weekends, three days on holidays and peak periods.

RATES: Jacuzzi suite $95/$110/$135 (weekday/weekend/holiday). Private baths $80/$90/$110. Shared bath $70/$80/$90. Discount on five-night (Sunday–Thursday) stays. Singles $10 less during nonholiday periods. Package rates for women-only weekends and for Wannabe Weekends (for those who would like to live in Vermont). MC, Visa.

♥ ⭐⭐ ⊞ ❖ ⚔ ⚮ ⚌ ⚒ 🐾

ON 60 ACRES of undeveloped land, with river and towering rock face, is this inn with a comfortable country look. Susan makes the hand-tied quilts and designs the menus with Vermont products. The many-windowed dining room has a gazebo-styled porch with hanging flower baskets that attract hummingbirds in the summer. A permanent pavilion is the site of many weddings. Many guests hike and cross-country ski through the "enchanted forest." And many write to me about loving "the relaxed atmosphere" at this "home away from home."

IN RESIDENCE: "Our zoo— three dogs, four cats, and two horses."

BED AND BATH: Thirteen rooms of various sizes with king, queen, double—plus one or two singles—or twin beds. Eleven with private baths (with tub or shower); one suite with double Jacuzzi, high Victorian queen bed, ceiling fan. Two double-bedded rooms share a shower bath.

BREAKFAST: Generally 8–9. Fresh fruits or hot compote. Homemade muffins—sometimes made from the garden pumpkins. Egg soufflés or "light-as-a-feather" blueberry pancakes. Farm-fresh eggs. Green Mountain coffee.

PLUS: In winter, afternoon hors d'oeuvres; cross-country skiing and sleigh rides right here. Room fans. Boccie. Horseshoes. Walking path. By arrangement, dinners for groups. Weekends, American Flatbread (restaurant) open in barn on premises. Susan's shibori scarves for sale.

☞ *Beaver Pond Farm Inn*

802/583-2861

1225 Golf Course Road,
Warren, VT 05674-9761

FAX 802/583-2860
E-MAIL beaverpond@madriver.com
www.beaverpondfarminn.com

HOSTS: Bob and Betty Hansen

LOCATION: On a scenic back road 200 yards from the first tee of Club Sugarbush Golf Course (open to the public), designed by Robert Trent Jones. Minutes to restaurants and shops. On 15 miles of groomed cross-country ski trails. One mile to Sugarbush downhill ski area.

OPEN: Year round except mid-April to mid-May. Reservations required. Two-day weekend minimum during fall and winter and on holidays.

RATES: Per person, double occupancy. $108–$118 king/twins option; $98–$108 queen. Thanksgiving, golf, fly-fishing, and summer concert packages available. MC, Visa. ♥ ⊞ ❖ ⚄ ⚮ ❤◌

☞ From England: *"Full of atmosphere and magic, but also very comfortable . . . picturesque surroundings."* From New York: *"Betty is an incredible cook—energetic and creative . . . interesting, witty, and intelligent hosts."*

OTHER MANHATTANITES still talk about the B&B cooking demonstration Betty, a cooking school instructor, gave in New York City. A *Newsday* feature referred to the "kind of charm that many visitors go to Vermont for . . . affordably priced accommodations . . . innkeepers who spoil you." Many Europeans, too, appreciate the hospitality in this comfortable antiques-furnished vacation home, a B&B that the well-traveled Hansens created from a vacant farmhouse in 1977. Since, they have made many changes. And they have become matchmakers for a guest and a longtime friend.

In New Jersey Betty was a caterer, Bob a banker for twenty-seven years. Betty is active in the United States Golf Association. Bob, an ardent fisherman, will guide you.

IN RESIDENCE: One gray cat named Jasper.

FOREIGN LANGUAGE SPOKEN: French. (Betty attended the Sorbonne.)

BED AND BATH: Five carpeted rooms; all private tub/shower baths (with hair dryers). One on first floor has French doors, private deck. King, queen, or twin beds. Cot available.

BREAKFAST: 8–9:30. Three choices offered each morning! Maybe smoked salmon "caught and smoked by Bob" and scrambled eggs. Or amaretto French toast, orange-yogurt pancakes, or apple-raisin-walnut pancakes. Homemade Danish pastries. Vermont sausage. Served on antique china with sterling silver in dining room or on large deck.

PLUS: Beverages. Setups and hors d'oeuvres. Classical music. Perennial gardens. Suggested bicycle routes (15–70 miles).

✎ *The Sugartree Inn*

2440 Sugarbush Access Road,
Warren, VT 05674

802/583-3211
800/666-8907
FAX 802/583-3203
E-MAIL sugartree@madriver.com
www.sugartree.com

HOSTS: Frank and Kathy Partsch
LOCATION: Wooded. With panoramic mountain views. Three miles west of Waitsfield, one-quarter mile to Sugarbush resort area. Near championship golf course.
OPEN: Year round. Two-night minimum during foliage and on holidays and winter weekends.
RATES: Per person, double occupancy. $40–$50 summer, $45–$63 winter, $55–$68 foliage and holiday periods. Singles $65–$90. Triple $35–$52. Midweek, three- to five-day stay, 10 percent less. Amex, Discover, MC, Visa.
♥ ⊞ ❖ ⚔ ⚒

✎ From Illinois, England, Massachusetts, Connecticut: *"Outstanding. Warm and charming hosts. . . . Clean and beautifully decorated rooms. . . . It was a bit of a shock finding, in Frank, an American with whom you could talk cricket . . . peaceful place to stay. . . . Breakfasts unmatched. . . . We work in the hotel industry, and we know a good place when we see it. This is it."*

"HERE CHIPMUNKS eat out of your hand in summer, and hummingbirds can be seen at the flower-filled window boxes." There are quilts and needlepoint pieces, some made by Frank's grandmother, and a tall clock made by Frank. Antiques include a 1900s Estey pump organ. Frank is a banker turned innkeeper, house renovator, and folk art wood-carver. Kathy, who worked in insurance, is co-innkeeper/chef. The two skiers came here from Boston in 1992. This property was once a lodge and has a gingerbread gazebo (the site of at least one elopement) on landscaped grounds.

BED AND BATH: Nine carpeted rooms; two with air conditioning. All with individual thermostats, phones, private (full or shower) baths. Antique beds are canopied, four-poster, or brass. First-floor suite has queen bed, gas fireplace, large full bath. Second-floor rooms have a double and a single, a queen, or a double. Rollaway available.
BREAKFAST: 8–9:15; 8–9 in ski season. Waffles, three-cheese egg casserole, Dutch apple puff pancake, or pancakes with Vermont maple syrup. Homemade fruit sauces and butters. Homemade breads.
PLUS: Fireplaced living room. Ski storage room with Frank's boot-drying system (dry and warm boots await in the morning). Hair dryers. Late-afternoon snacks. Guests' refrigerator. Wicker-furnished porch. Suggestions for waterfalls, swimming holes, day trips, beer trek (to breweries). Sauna, hot tub, pool, tennis (fee charged) at nearby sports center.

⋙ *Grünberg Haus Bed & Breakfast*

Route 100 South, 94 Pine Street,
Waterbury, VT 05676-9621

802/244-7726
800/800-7760
FAX 802/244-1283
E-MAIL grunhaus@aol.com
www.waterbury.org/grunberg

HOSTS: Christopher Sellers and Mark Frohman
LOCATION: In Ben & Jerry's hometown, on acres of meadows and woodlands. Twenty miles to Sugarbush, Stowe, Mad River Glen ski resorts.
OPEN: Year round. Two-night minimum during foliage season.
RATES: $59–$75 queen bed. $59–$80 two double beds. $35–$55 single. Extra person in room $10 "permanent" bed, $20 rollaway. Private baths $30–$40 more. Cabins $79–$115, carriage house $89–$145 (suite). Ten percent less for senior citizens, military personnel, and travel industry professionals. Discover, MC, Visa. ♥ ⚄ ⅄

A LONG LANE, a dramatic approach, leads up to this Tyrolean-style chalet built by hand in 1971 and bought by Chris and Mark in 1989. In the living room are a massive fieldstone fireplace, an 8-foot grand piano (a focal point for Chris's talents), an antique carved pump organ, and a huge picture window with bird feeders beyond. As Mark, a former school board president, says, "Full house turns into a party." Even their brochure is fun to read. The imaginative, popular, and well-traveled innkeepers are known for their concerts, crafts fairs, Octoberfests, and fund-raisers for various causes. Mark has experience with Westin Hotels and United Airlines. Chris, a professional musician and teacher who also worked with neighborhood revitalization groups in Chicago, is active with area community planning and cultural groups.

IN RESIDENCE: Two cats, Fritz and Mama. Chickens (Mark had chickens when he and Chris lived in the Midwest), doves, fancy pigeons.
BED AND BATH: Thirteen rooms. *Main inn*—one first-floor room with two double beds, private shower bath. Second floor has nine cozy rooms, each with access to balcony. Private baths for three rooms or one connecting bath between every two rooms. Rooms have queen bed (one canopied) or two double beds. Rollaways available. Plus, along wooded trails—*two secluded cabins* (available Memorial Day through October), each with queen-sized bed, and one *carriage house* with two queen beds, skylights, balconies, modern kitchen.
BREAKFAST: 8–10. Fresh eggs for sure. Entrée might be ricotta-stuffed French toast, maple pear and cheddar omelets, or egg-stuffed baked potatoes. Fresh fruit creations. Carrot-walnut muffins or peach yogurt bread. In dining room by a 21-foot-wide window.
PLUS: Beams everywhere. Hot soup or cider by woodstove in BYOB pub. Hot tub. Sauna. Guest refrigerator. Snowshoes. Window fans. Transportation to/from airport, bus, or train.

Inn at Blush Hill

802/244-7529

Blush Hill Road, Box 1266,   800/736-7522
Waterbury, VT 05676   FAX 802/244-7314
E-MAIL INNATBH@aol.com
www.blushhill.com

HOST: Pamela Gosselin
LOCATION: At the top of a country road, overlooking golf course and mountains. One mile from I-89, off Route 100. Within twenty minutes of Stowe and Sugarbush ski areas. Adjacent to Ben & Jerry's ice-cream plant; within 2 miles of "great shopping" and sampling of specialty food products—Cold Hollow Cider Mill, Green Mountain Chocolate Company, Green Mountain Coffee Roasters, Cabot Creamery (cheese).
OPEN: Year round.
RATES: Fireplace room $79–$89 summer, $85–$89 winter, $130 fall. Queen canopied bed and enormous window $89–$95 summer and winter, $130 fall; with Jacuzzi $89–$95 summer and winter, $130 fall. Other rooms $65–$89 summer and winter; $110–$120 fall. April and November, special offers. Rollaway or extra person $15. Golf and ski packages. Amex, Discover, MC, Visa. ♥ ⊞ ❖ ✄ ✁

"ONE OF THE state's most appealing B&Bs," according to the *New York Post*, has grounds and views that make this a perfect place for a wedding. Honeymooners, skiers, and canoeists have also discovered the 1790s Cape with four wood-burning fireplaces (one is a woodstove with glass) and wide-board floors—all decorated with warm colors, country prints, coordinated fabrics and some lace, and auction finds.

The Gosselins, skiers all, arrived here on a 20-degree-below-zero day in 1988. Since then the kids have become assistant innkeepers. Chris, who works at Ben & Jerry's, gives tips about tour times. Pam finds time for golf. ("Need a fourth?") And when she's at a Little League game, you might find a note on door in what some guests think of as "Vermont style."

IN RESIDENCE: Christopher is seventeen; Tyler is eleven.
BED AND BATH: Five rooms, all private baths. First floor—queen brass bed, original 1760 fireplace (Duraflame used), ceiling fan, shower bath. Upstairs—canopied queen bed (with view of sunrise from behind the mountain), 150-inch-wide window with mountain view, en-suite full bath. Room with queen bed, with antique love seat, en-suite Jacuzzi bath and shower. Antique oak queen bed, en-suite bath with claw-foot tub and shower. Room with a double and one twin bed, private hall (robes provided) full bath. Rollaway available.
BREAKFAST: 8–9. (Continental earlier or later.) French toast or apple pancakes topped with Ben & Jerry's ice cream, Vermont maple syrup, and fresh fruit. Homemade breads and muffins. Juice. Homemade granola. Special diets accommodated. Served at 10-foot-long farmhands' table in country kitchen overlooking mountains.

PLUS: Heated mattress pads. Porch rockers. Games. CD player. Piano. TV with VCR and movie selections. Afternoon and evening refreshments.

≈ *From Massachusetts:* *"An incredible setting, a charming home, and the host is terrific."* From New Jersey: *"The breakfast was so good, we decided to stay another night."*

≈ *The Darling Family Inn*

815 Route 100, Weston, VT 05161-5404

802/824-3223

FAX 802/824-3223

HOSTS: Chapin and Joan Darling
LOCATION: Half mile north of village (home of famous Vermont Country Store), with panoramic view of mountains and farmland. Near Bromley, Magic, Stratton, and Okemo Mountains; summer theater, antiques, crafts, art exhibits. Three miles from Weston Priory.
OPEN: Year round. Two-night minimum on weekends.
RATES: $80–$125 per room depending on size and location. Special rates for a stay of five or more nights. ♥ ⊞

THIS STYLE of country living, lauded by *Gourmet* magazine, attracts many returnees, including an annual reunion of guests who met here in the 1980s. American and English antiques are in a Colonial setting—no clutter!—created and re-created by Chapin, a skilled woodworker who was a Connecticut life insurance executive. To the 170-year-old farmhouse he has built an addition "that still allows us to stay small so that we can continue—as we have for twenty years—to provide surprises." Hardware is fashioned by son Jeff, a blacksmith. Another son, Eric, created detailed handcrafted wooden items. Dried flower wreaths, hand-painted wood and tin items, even thimbles and angels cut from 200-year-old wood are examples of Joan's artistry.

IN RESIDENCE: Mandy, the dog. Sometimes, visiting family members.
BED AND BATH: Five second-floor rooms, all private full baths. Canopied queen bed, twin beds, and double beds (one canopied) available. Two housekeeping cottages where children of any age and pets are welcome.
BREAKFAST: 8–10. Juices (freshly squeezed orange juice); bacon, ham, and sausage; any style eggs, omelets; home fries; French toast or berry pancakes. Cloth napkins. Chapin cooks. Joan serves by candlelight.
PLUS: In-ground 17-by-36-foot swimming pool. In season, hayrides and sleigh rides nearby (fee charged). Beverages. Fireplaced living room. Library with woodstove. Chapin's guitar accompaniment for impromptu sing-alongs.

≈ *From Texas:* *"I'm an artist and appreciated all the touches. . . . Lights in every window welcomed us at night. . . . Good conversation around the fire. . . . Can't wait to go back."*

⤳ *Whitingham Farm Bed & Breakfast*　　802/368-2620

742 Abbie Morse Road, Whitingham, VT 06361　　　　　800/310-2010

FAX: 802/368-2304

E-MAIL whitingbb@aol.com

www.whitinghamfarm.com

HOSTS: Newt and Gini Brosius

LOCATION: Secluded. On 50 acres with pasture, woods, streams, wildlife, trails, miles of stone walls. Within fifteen minutes of Wilmington (Mount Snow), lake (paddleboats, fishing, and swimming), Marlboro Music Festival, and Brattleboro in Vermont. Twenty minutes to Deerfield and Shelburne Falls in Massachusetts. Near many fine restaurants.

OPEN: Year round. Two-night minimum on weekends (except April 1–Memorial Day weekend).

RATES: Gratuity and carriage or sleigh ride included with three-night stay. $140 king/twins. Queen $120 garden view, $130 view of Mount Monadnock. Additional person $25. Barn and board available for horses. Packages— Valentine's Day, Ice Fishing Derby, July 4, Back-to-School (parents only), Cut-Your-Own Tree. ♥ ☙ ⊞ ⚡ 🐎 ❤○

A MIRAGE—ALMOST. A picturesque town road through the B&B property leads to a rise and your first view of the 140-year-old Greek Revival farmhouse with Mount Monadnock in the distance. "Built in the mid-1800s, it comes complete with a history that seems to have a safe-haven aura about it. After two years of searching, we saw this snow-covered farm, took a walk on snowshoes, and bought the property in a day!"

The college sweethearts—"we met when we were assigned neighboring chapel seats"— moved with their horses from a small farm outside of Philadelphia. They restored and up-dated before opening as a B&B in 1995. In Pennsylvania Newt knew the "meetings/ memos/mergers insurance world." Here he did most of the construction. Gini, a former software consultant, decorated with crisp country flair, with striped silk wallpaper in the fireplaced living room and antiques throughout. You are welcome to turn on the 1913 elec-tronic baby grand player piano. Borrow snowshoes or bring your own cross-country skis for their 2½ miles of groomed woodland trails. Take a 1-, 2- or 5-mile ride with Newt in the antique sleigh or reproduction open carriage. It's rural. And peaceful. And beautiful. With views that steal the show.

IN RESIDENCE: "Puddy Cat, an outside barn cat who thinks he's a horse. Max, our friendly, calm Lab/spaniel is 'groomsman' on our carriage rides, which are led by our three Morgan horses and our Morgan-Percheron pair."

FOREIGN LANGUAGE SPOKEN: "Some French."

BED AND BATH: Three rooms, each with ceiling fan and private bath. First-floor room with king/twins option, sitting area, tub/shower bath. Two second-floor rooms, each with queen bed; one has oversized shower with seat; larger room has high (step provided) four-poster bed, shower bath. Rollaway and crib available.

BREAKFAST: 8–9. (Freshly squeezed juice, fruit salad, homemade muffins and preserves, and granola until 9:30.) Entrée choices include morning crepes, pancakes, French toast, eggs, or baked oatmeal with apple-maple syrup. Served in formal dining room overlooking perennial gardens.
PLUS: Afternoon tea. Fruit basket in room. Hammock-for-two under pine trees. Croquet. Volleyball.

﷽ *Golden Maple Inn*

802/888-6614

Route 15, P.O. Box 35,
Wolcott Village, VT 05680-0035

800/639-5234
FAX 802/888-6614
E-MAIL GOLDNMAPLE@aol.com
www.goldenmaple.com

HOSTS: Dick and Jo Wall
LOCATION: On Route 15, in small village along the Lamoille River, "great for trout fishing; canoeing; and observing beaver, river otter, blue heron, and deer and fox in evening." Near country's last remaining covered railroad bridge, cross-country ski trails; twenty minutes to Stowe, Craftsbury, Cabot Creamery.
OPEN: Year round. Two-night minimum on holiday and foliage weekends.
RATES: $69 two twin beds. $64 double bed. $79 suite. Singles $15 less. $15 extra person. Amex, Discover, MC, Visa. ♥ ⊞ ⚔ ⚸ ♨

﷽ From New York, Vermont, Pennsylvania, Washington, D.C. , Indiana: *"Sumptuous yet healthy breakfast . . . warm elegant personal touches . . . knowledgeable hosts . . . . Felt thoroughly refreshed in their care! . . . We chose Golden Maple because they offered a great winter getaway package. Now we would choose it because of experiencing the BEST food, company, atmosphere, and personal attention that we have ever had. . . . Had car trouble. Dick arranged for it to be fixed, drove us from the garage (more than once), AND recommended alternative carless activities. All this on top of wonderful accommodations and fabulous food. . . . No one could make a stay in magical Vermont more wonderful . . . honeymoon as romantic as we hoped . . . comfortable antiques . . . great time canoeing—followed a majestic blue heron . . . much love and TLC here."*

WHY VERMONT? Dick is a retired competitive sailor and mountain climber who worked for many years in the ship- and yacht-building industry. He says, "I picked up an oar, put it on my shoulder, and walked inland until someone asked what it was. That's where I settled down in 1990." Guests have come from as far away as Australia and Russia. Some book for one night and stay for three. Fly-fishing devotees have come from as far away as England for Dick's hand-tied flies and advice on local streams. Canoeists appreciate shuttle service for the return (upstream) trip. Skiers often arrange for dinner right here. Cyclists have their choice of touring or mountain bikes. And day-trippers use a great

continued . . .

map—with Ben & Jerry's and Cabot Creamery tours included—another Golden Maple Inn production.

In Yarmouth, Maine, Jo managed computer operations for a national footwear company. She and Dick are world travelers who love innkeeping in the Northeast Kingdom.

IN RESIDENCE: In carriage house—Missy, "our bashful calico."
BED AND BATH: Three spacious rooms with nautical decor; all private baths. Ground-floor honeymoon suite has double bed, fireplace, bath with Victorian tub and hand-held shower. Second floor—room with double four-poster bed, hall shower bath; room with two four-poster twin beds, en-suite shower bath. Rollaways available.
BREAKFAST: 7–10. (Continental before or after.) Freshly baked bread. Fresh fruit, home-made granola, oven-baked French toast with blueberries and local maple syrup. Spicy baked farm-fresh eggs. Filled croissants. Bacon-mushroom quiche and scones. Juice. Hot beverages. Served in dining room with sterling silver, china, and crystal.
PLUS: Library. Parlor. Riverside flagstone terrace with Adirondack chairs. Afternoon tea and homemade sweets. Ceiling fans. Turndown service. Flowers and vegetables from Jo's river gardens. Optional dinner by reservation. Rentals—bicycles $25/day; canoes $25. Ask about their "rain dance" saga.

⤚ *The Ardmore Inn*

802/457-3887

23 Pleasant Street,
Woodstock, VT 05091-0466

800/497-9652
FAX 802/457-9006
E-MAIL ArdmoreInn@aol.com
www.ArdmoreInn.com

HOSTS: Giorgio Ortiz
LOCATION: In the historic district on Route 4. Minutes' walk to covered bridge, shops, restaurants, and galleries. Twenty-minute drive to Killington.
OPEN: Year round.
RATES: $110 double, $135 queen, $175 king. Amex, MC, Visa. ♥ ⊞ ⚉ ⚭ ❤

GIORGIO IS A native of Peru who has lived on three continents. While running his Florida-based transportation company, which brought speedboats to New England, he stayed in many B&Bs. And he dreamed of "living in a big old house surrounded by elegant things." When he helped Bill Gallagher, a native Vermonter who hosted a Woodstock homestay, he learned that the family that owned the town's oldest general store was selling this handsome red slate–roofed 1850 Victorian Greek Revival house. With some help from contractors, Giorgio was very involved in the restoration. Now all baths have Vermont marble floors. Walls are painted in soft pastels. Throughout there are Oriental rugs and, from Bill's family, antique furnishings. Since opening in 1994, Giorgio has become known for his warm personality, for his cooking, and for his suggestions: "From great restaurants to places to get lost to a secret path along the river to water holes . . . you name it, I have been there! Relax and let me plan for you!" (He does.)

FOREIGN LANGUAGES SPOKEN: Spanish. Some French.

BED AND BATH: Six rooms; all but king bed are antiques. All private baths. First floor—queen bed, large private bath with two-person (extra-large) Jacuzzi, Roman-style (open) marble shower. Five second-floor rooms, all with shower baths. Three with queen bed (one is a four-poster) and sitting area. Smaller room has double bed, exposed beams. Larger room has king bed, gas fireplace, slanted ceilings, dormer windows.

BREAKFAST: 8:30–9:30. Fresh fruit. Juice. Homemade baked goods. Teas and espresso bar. Main course might be a "Woodstock Sunrise": Vermont flatbread filled with fresh eggs sautéed with oyster mushrooms, green and red peppers, fresh basil, and Vermont cheddar, baked and served with breakfast meat. In formal dining room with silver service and French flatware.

PLUS: Gas fireplace in living room. Chocolates. Wicker-furnished verandah. Lawn chairs. Carriage and sleigh rides arranged.

    From Tennessee, Massachusetts, New York, Switzerland, Northern Ireland: *"Marvelous inn . . . tastefully furnished. . . . I loved the cozy atmosphere and personal attention . . . perfect romantic getaway with a great in-town location. . . . An elegantly comfortable retreat . . . scrumptious meals beautifully presented . . . hearty and fresh. . . . A very agreeable and funny host. . . . Giorgio provided much information—both practical and historical—about the area and attractions. He artfully struck a balance of being available and attentive yet also cognizant of when privacy was appreciated. A welcome respite from our 'other' life. . . . Felt fortunate to find it."*

Deer Brook Inn

802/672-3713

5354 U.S. Route 4, Woodstock, VT 05091-9772

HOSTS: Brian and Rosemary McGinty

LOCATION: Rural. On 5 acres by the Ottauquechee River. Five miles west of the village. Thirty minutes to Dartmouth College, twenty to I-89 and I-91; 9 miles to Killington ski area.

OPEN: Year round. Two-night minimum most weekends, in foliage season, and Christmas week.

RATES: Sunday–Thursday $75 ($50 single), $95 suite. Friday and Saturday $95 ($70 single), $115 suite. Foliage season and Christmas $105 ($80 single), $125 suite. Extra person over two years old $15. Amex, MC, Visa. ♥ ♦♦ ⊞ ⋇ ⋇

    From many guests: *"The essence of New England. . . . Exposed beams, beautiful stenciling, handmade quilts, wide-pine floors. . . . Homey, comfortable, clean, bright, cheerful . . . What a wonderful way to start a life together—staring up at the stars, making*

continued . . .

plans . . . peaceful . . . stupendous breakfasts. . . . Our 16-month old loved Deer Brook, Nutmeg (the dog), and the McGinty children. . . . Like Thoreau's Walden, it is a place about how to live and what to live for . . . charming hostess . . . bright and cheerful home . . . Fell asleep to the sound of the brook across the road. . . . What more could you ask for?"

ALL THANKS to Rosemary, a nurse, and Brian, who were on the ski patrol in Breckenridge, Colorado. Before they opened here in 1988, they spent a year restoring the 1820s Colonial farmhouse. "And still, always, there are new quilts, fresh paint, new decor." And still, always, first-time guests enjoy the hosts as much as the place.

IN RESIDENCE: James is twelve years old; Kelly is ten. One golden retriever, Nutmeg.
BED AND BATH: Four rooms (two with skylight) and one suite. All with river view, private full bath, air conditioning. First-floor suite has queen bed, separate room with queen sofa bed, TV. Second floor—one room with king bed and three queen-bedded rooms (two have additional twin bed). Rollaway and crib available.
BREAKFAST: 7–9. Hot entrée may be feather-bed eggs or baked apple pancake (most-requested recipes). Cold cereal. Fresh fruit. Juice. Homemade muffins, breads, or coffee cake.
PLUS: Air-conditioned living and dining rooms. Individual thermostats. Complimentary champagne for honeymooners. Front porch.

The Woodstocker Bed & Breakfast   802/457-3896

61 River Street (Route 4),
Woodstock, VT 05091

FAX 802/457-3897
E-MAIL woodstocker@valley.net
www.scenesofvermont.com/woodstocker/index.html

HOSTS: Thomas and Nancy Blackford
LOCATION: On Route 4 "in this picture-perfect village." Five-minute walk to town green, shops, restaurants, galleries. Across from a swimming pool. Around corner from hiking trail up Mount Tom.
OPEN: Year round.
RATES: $85–$105 queen, $95–$115 two doubles, $115–$135 suite. High season (foliage, Christmas, Presidents' week, some holidays) $135 queen, $145 two doubles, $155 suite. MC, Visa. ♥ ♦ ⊞ ❖ ⚉ ⚑

From Rhode Island, New York, Ohio: "Restful and relaxing ambiance . . . delightful young hosts . . . casual, individual, quaint rooms. . . . . Among the places we absolutely love—due to the hospitality and friendliness of Nancy and Tom and their dog, the excellent accommodations, and a superb breakfast. . . . With two small children, found kitchenette very convenient. . . . Common room (and checkers) made us feel at home."

MAYBE YOU, too, will want to take Chelsea for a walk (or even suggest that she accompany you home). Almost equal in the popularity category: the hosts from Cleveland, Ohio—a certified public accountant (Tom) and a high school English teacher (Nancy) —who decided to change careers so that they could work together. In 1996 they bought this well-established B&B, a two-storied 1830 Cape-style house. They remodeled here, installed carpeting there. Leather furnishings are in the common room. Some accent pieces are antiques. Intentionally, this is a casual, comfortable (and happy) inn.

IN RESIDENCE: Daughter Rebecca Christine, born July 21, 1999. Chelsea is a Lab mix.
BED AND BATH: Nine rooms (rear rooms are quietest) with queen (one is canopied) or two double beds, on first and second floors. Two are suites—one with a double and a twin bed, living room, TV, kitchen, dining area; the other a queen and a twin bed, living room, kitchen, dining area, deck. Seven rooms do not share a wall with another room. All rooms have tub/shower bath and individual thermostats. Most have air conditioning. Crib and rollaway available.
BREAKFAST: 8:30–9:30. Fresh fruit. Juice. Homemade granola, bagels, muffins. Hot dish such as puffed pancakes, apple/berry crisp, or cheese/egg bake. Buffet style.
PLUS: Afternoon tea and baked goods. Guest refrigerator. Cedar room with hot tub (sign-up arrangement). Laundry available. Transportation provided to/from bus stop in Woodstock or Amtrak station in White River Junction.

ᴁ *Bailey's Mills Bed and Breakfast*

1347 Bailey's Mills Road,
Reading, VT 05062-9708

802/484-7809
800/639-3437
FAX 802/484-0014
E-MAIL goodfarm@vermontel.com
www.scenesofvermont.com
www.bbonline.com/vt/baileysmills

HOSTS: Barbara Thaeder and (husband) Donald Whitaker
LOCATION: Quiet. Along a winding country lane, overlooking an 1805 rural cemetery. On 50 acres with stone walls, bridge over brook to meadows, woods, cross-country and hiking paths, stream, picnic tables, horse trails, tiny pond (for swimming) with float. Adjacent to farms with horses, cows, and llamas. Five-minute drive to 1815 House Restaurant; 10 miles north to Woodstock for pub food and fine dining; antiquing; stables offering trail, wagon, and sleigh rides.
OPEN: Year round. Two-night minimum on weekends; three nights on some holiday and foliage weekends.
RATES: Late May–September $85 rooms, $100 suite; December–March $100; $10 less midweek. Less in November and April–late May. $25 more during foliage season. Singles $10 less. Five-night discount. ♥ ☕ ⊞ ❖ ⚔ 🐾 💗

continued . . .

Ecstatic European and American guests from Massachusetts, New York, California, Vermont, Germany, England: "The most wonderful B&B on our round-the-world honeymoon. . . . Left renewed in spirit, filled with fresh air, fabulous food, laughter, and the stillness that comes from being in a place that is in such harmony with its natural surroundings. . . . They know where to find ripe blackberries; sample the best Vermont restaurants (and how to get there on a scenic back road); view the night sky to find the current celestial phenomena; and bike, hike, run, loll, or amble. . . . In an atmosphere steeped in vintage Vermont, this charming B&B is filled with beautiful antiques. . . . Greeted us with tea and cookies and an unspoken come-into-the-kitchen whenever kind of attitude . . . gave an interesting house tour. . . . Watched hummingbirds from flower-bedecked front porch . . . well maintained . . . allows guests their privacy . . . provided child-size cutlery and dishes for our eleven-month-old. . . . When I played a few old dance numbers on the piano on the third floor (former ballroom/meeting room) I could imagine couples socializing . . . at night could hear rushing water as the spring thaw resulted in an active stream. . . . There was something about this place that was very calming for both of us. . . . We're going back."

"MY PARENTS were avid auctiongoers for more than twenty years after they bought this beautiful and fascinating seventeen-room brick house in 1970. It's actually a combined country store, worker housing, and mill owner's quarters—decorated with traditional wallcoverings and fabrics. When my mother, now widowed, wanted to sell, the house pulled me in. We bought it in 1993."

FOREIGN LANGUAGES SPOKEN: Limited French, Spanish, Italian.
BED AND BATH: Up good-morning staircase to three second-floor rooms, each with private full bath. Two queen-bedded rooms have sitting area and (Duraflame) fireplace. Honeymoon suite has one large room with king bed, one many-windowed garden room overlooking brook.
BREAKFAST: 8–9:30. Juices, fresh fruit, cereals, granola, homemade pies and muffins, yogurt, Vermont cheeses, hazelnut coffee, teas, hot chocolate. Sundays—waffles topped with maple syrup and homemade berry sauce. Buffet style by candlelight in room with large hearth and brick beehive oven or on front porch.
PLUS: No TV. Fireplaced library with more than two thousand books. Sunporch. Drinks, fruit, and cookies available all day. Lawn games. Porch swings and rockers. Hammock. Horseback riding: two stables offer trail rides, wagon rides and sleigh rides.

IF YOU HAVE MET ONE B&B HOST, YOU HAVEN'T MET THEM ALL.
IF YOU'VE BEEN TO ONE B&B, YOU HAVEN'T BEEN TO THEM ALL.

GEOGRAPHICAL INDEX

ALPHABETICAL INDEX